THE OXFORD AUTHORS

General Editor: Frank Kermode

BEN JONSON was born probably in June 1572, probably in Westminster, where he died also in August 1637. His contemporary literary reputation rivalled, and perhaps surpassed, that of Shakespeare. Amongst his completed surviving works are seventeen plays, more than thirty court masques and entertainments, an English grammar, a commonplace book (*Discoveries*), and a large and varied corpus of poetry.

IAN DONALDSON is Professor of English and Director of the Humanities Research Centre at the Australian National University, Canberra. His publications include *The World Upside-Down: Comedy From Jonson to Fielding* (1970), *The Rapes of Lucretia: A Myth and its Transformations* (1982), and an Oxford edition of *Ben Jonson: Poems* (1975).

THE OXFORD AUTHORS

BEN JONSON

EDITED BY

IAN DONALDSON

Oxford   New York

OXFORD UNIVERSITY PRESS

1985

Oxford University Press, Walton Street, Oxford OX2 6DP

London New York Toronto
Delhi Bombay Calcutta Madras Karachi
Kuala Lumpur Singapore Hong Kong Tokyo
Nairobi Dar es Salaam Cape Town
Melbourne Auckland

and associated companies in
Beirut Berlin Ibadan Mexico City Nicosia

Oxford is a trade mark of Oxford University Press

British Library Cataloguing in Publication Data
Jonson, Ben
Ben Jonson.—(Oxford authors)
I. Title   II. Donaldson, Ian
822'.3   PR2602
ISBN 0-19-254178-1
ISBN 0-19-281339-0 Pbk

Library of Congress Cataloging in Publication Data
Jonson, Ben. 1573?–1637.
Ben Jonson.
(The Oxford authors)
Bibliography: p. Includes index.
I. Donaldson, Ian. II. Title. III. Series.
PR2602.D66 1985 822'.3 85-3012
ISBN 0-19-254178-1
ISBN 0-19-281339-0 (pbk.)

Set by Wyvern Typesetting Ltd.
Printed in Great Britain by
M & A Thomson Litho Ltd.
East Kilbride, Scotland

CONTENTS

INTRODUCTION

A TRUE understanding of the achievement of Ben Jonson, T. S. Eliot remarked many years ago, can be gained only from 'intelligent saturation in his work as a whole'.[1] It is admirable advice, though also perhaps a little daunting. Jonson's 'work as a whole' runs to eleven large volumes (including commentaries, introductions, and notes) in the magisterial Oxford edition prepared by C. H. Herford and Percy and Evelyn Simpson in the course of half a century's labours. The present edition, which draws upon and seeks modestly to supplement its great Oxford predecessor, can offer, on the other hand, no more than a generous selection of Jonson's writing and opinion. Taken together, its contents will nevertheless give some sense of the breadth and variousness of Jonson's powers.

The basic facts about Jonson's life are briefly summarized in the Chronology to be found on pages xix–xx of this edition; they are more spaciously surveyed in the first volume of Herford and Simpson's edition.[2] It is natural to think that our knowledge of Jonson the man is further enlarged by a reading of his work; for Jonson seems to be an author who reveals himself freely and readily within his own writing. The ninth poem of *The Underwood*, for example, offers, as Jonson himself put it (*Conversations with Drummond*, 585), 'a picture of himself'. What is 'pictured' in the poem is not merely the poet's emotional state, but also— in a literal, painterly sense—his physical appearance:

> Oh, but my conscious fears
> That fly my thoughts between,
> Tell me that she hath seen
> My hundred of grey hairs,
> Told seven-and-forty years,
> Read so much waste, as she cannot embrace
> My mountain belly, and my rocky face;
> And all these through her eyes have stopped her ears.
>
> (*The Underwood*, 9. 11–18)

In other poems, likewise, Jonson himself seems solidly present; so

---

[1] 'Ben Jonson', in *Selected Essays* (London, 1934), p. 148; first published *TLS* 13 November 1919.

[2] Herford and Simpson's account should be supplemented by two articles by Mark Eccles, *RES* xii (1936), 257–72, and *RES* xiii (1937), 385–97. See also J. B. Bamborough, *TLS* 8 April 1960, and Wayne H. Phelps, *NQ* NS 27 (1980), 146–9.

solidly, indeed, that it also seems only natural that on more than one occasion he should refer with some precision to his bodily weight, as though humorously offering such information as evidence and authentication of an inner plight:

> . . . being a tardy, cold
> Unprofitable chattel, fat and old,
> Laden with belly, and doth hardly approach
> His friends, but to break chairs or crack a coach.
> His weight is twenty stone, within two pound,
> And that's made up as doth the purse abound.
> (*The Underwood*, 56. 7–12)

In other ways, too, Jonson enforces the sense of his poetic presence. His very name returns repeatedly in his verse, a reminder of his authorial aims, achievements, and personality: 'Ben Jonson his best piece of poetry' (*Epigrams*, 45. 10); 'Ben | Jonson, who sung this of him, ere he went | Himself to rest' (*The Underwood*, 70. 84–6); 'Sir, you are sealèd of the tribe of Ben' (*The Underwood*, 47. 78).

With the dramatic work, Jonson's presence is felt in another way. Like Bernard Shaw, Jonson enjoys interposing himself between his plays and his readers, appraising and interpreting on our behalf. Through his prologues and epilogues, his dedications and epistles and addresses to the reader, Jonson gives his considered verdict of the value of his work, and seems impatiently to await our response. Like Shaw, he seems to have been a disconcertingly opinionated spectator of his own work in performance, being readily critical of the conduct of both actors and audience. Dekker in *Satiromastix* pictures Jonson (alias 'Horace') making 'vile and bad faces at every line'.[3] 'I am looking lest the poet should hear me, or his man, Master Brome, behind the arras', says the Stage Keeper apprehensively in the Induction to *Bartholomew Fair*, as though expecting an entrance by the author himself. Such an event would not have been unprecedented. When *Poetaster* proved unpopular in 1601, Jonson wrote an Apologetical Dialogue to be performed at the end of the play, permitting the irate figure of 'The Author'—probably represented on stage by Jonson himself—to come out from behind the arras and remonstrate with his ungrateful audience. One may (again) be reminded of Bernard Shaw's assertive style of self-presentation; of, say, the puppet play *Shakes versus Shav*, in which Shav is depicted in successful disputation with Shakes, engaging the latter (in a very Jonsonian manner) in a fist-fight, and felling him for the count of ten.

---

[3] Thomas Dekker, *Satiromastix*, v. ii. 342–3: ed. Josiah H. Penniman (Boston and London, 1913).

Such self-presentations are, of course, both smaller and larger than life itself. Although Jonson, like Shaw, seems to show himself openly in his work, the relationship between authorial persona and authorial life is in fact at all times highly problematical. Older scholars such as F. G. Fleay were prepared to regard much of Jonson's writing as thinly veiled autobiography. 'A Celebration of Charis', for example (*The Underwood*, 2), seemingly told of the fifty-year-old poet's infatuation with a lady of the court circle: the scholar's primary task was to sleuth out her identity. Fleay thought that Charis was Lady Elizabeth Hatton, who was 'manifestly' also the subject of *The Underwood*, 19, and 'probably' the Venus of Jonson's *The Haddington Masque*. Herford and Simpson, though more cautious about this equation, agreed that Charis 'was probably the lady who played Venus' in this masque. Later they changed their minds: that role, they acknowledged, would have been played by a boy actor.[4] But if it is to be argued that the 'Charis' sequence is in some sense autobiographical, other facts need to be recognized. The sequence incorporates lyrical material that Jonson had written over a ten-year period, including a song—'Do but look on her eyes'—that had previously been heard in quite another context in Jonson's comedy *The Devil is an Ass*. 'O so white! O so soft! O so sweet is she!': 'she' may perhaps be a woman whom Jonson loved, but 'she' is also the dramatic character Mrs Fitzdottrel, wooed by Wittipol in the presence of her own husband. The highly wrought, playfully dramatic narrative of the sequence as a whole determinedly defies, even as it seemingly invites, biographical exegesis.

Jonson's ode beginning 'Helen, did Homer never see' (*The Underwood*, 27) presents the biographically minded scholar with similar problems. The poet apparently wishes to commemorate an actual love, an actual woman:

> And shall not I my Celia bring
> Where men may see whom I do sing?   (31–2)

Yet the ode could also be interpreted as saying that it is obligatory for poets to express wishes of this sort, whatever their actual circumstances may be. 'My Celia' is also the recipient of the lyrical proposal offered in *The Forest*, 5:

> Come, my Celia, let us prove,
> While we may, the sports of love . . .   (1–2)

[4] See Herford and Simpson, i. 53, iii. 605; and notes to *The Underwood*, 19, in this edition.

Yet this song, too, has an earlier dramatic context, for it is sung in the third act of *Volpone* by Volpone himself to Corvino's wife, Celia, whom he is bent upon seducing. The song is a translation of Catullus' famous invitation to the woman he chose to call 'Lesbia', whom scholars reckon to be Clodia, wife of Quintus Metellus Celer.[5] If the woman referred to in *The Underwood*, 27, as 'my Celia' has a real identity, it is tantalizingly overlaid by the identities, real and fictitious, of other women.

> And shall not I my Celia bring
> Where men may see whom I do sing?

The question is silently resolved in the negative. Jonson does not bring 'Celia' where men may see whom he does sing. The nature of her identity and of Jonson's professions of love remains entirely a matter for speculation.

Jonson's classical borrowings have sometimes bewildered readers, especially those who expect the first-person pronoun to mean precisely what it says. In 1788 the dramatist Richard Cumberland revealed with a piously scandalized flourish that Jonson's celebrated lyric 'Drink to me only with thine eyes' (*The Forest*, 9) was not in fact original:

> I was surprised the other day to find our learned poet Ben Jonson had been poaching in an obscure collection of love-letters, written by the sophist Philostratus in a very rhapsodical stile merely for the purpose of stringing together a parcel of unnatural, far-fetched conceits, more calculated to disgust a man of Jonson's classic taste, than to put him upon the humble task of copying them, and fathering the translation.[6]

Cumberland may have been especially sensitive on the question of literary imitation, having been pilloried by Sheridan in *The Critic* a few years earlier (as Sir Fretful Plagiary) for his own dramatic thefts. A closer examination might have shown Cumberland that more than 'the humble task of copying' had been involved in the creation of Jonson's delicate lyric.[7] But the shock which Cumberland apparently felt at discovering this classical source may perhaps be attributable in part to the fact that the lyric, once revealed as an imitation, can no longer seemingly be regarded as a spontaneous expression of actual passion. The 'me' of the lyric no longer seems to be, in any simple sense, Ben Jonson himself; it seems in part Philostratus, or Jonson-playing-Philostratus. If originality,

[5] Gordon Williams, *Tradition and Originality in Roman Poetry* (Oxford, 1968), p. 528.

[6] Richard Cumberland, *The Observer*, vol. ix, no. cix (1788), p. 136.

[7] See A. D. Fitton-Brown, *MLR* liv (1959), 554–7; but also Gordon Braden, *The Classics and English Renaissance Poetry* (New Haven and London, 1978), pp. 166–70.

sincerity, and spontaneity are regarded as necessary, and necessarily related, components in poetry, such a confusion of authorial voice will naturally seem radically confusing.

Jonson's habit of 'playing' Philostratus, Catullus, Horace, Martial, and other figures from the classical past does not, however, necessarily rob his work of personal feeling, nor is it to be dismissed as idle plagiarism. Jonson is both passionate and serious. His writing repeatedly turns upon observed correspondences between his own acts, opinions, sentiments, and dilemmas and those of great writers of former ages. In the margin of his own copy of Scriverius' Martial, beside Martial's epigram on a jealous rival who attempts to discredit him with the emperor Domitian, Jonson wrote the single word, 'Inigo'. Martial's relationship to Domitian is seen at this moment to correspond with Jonson's relationship to his monarch; Martial's rival, to correspond with Jonson's old ally and enemy, Inigo Jones. The perception was to prompt in turn a petitionary poem by Jonson to King Charles, a poem which (as so often) implicitly compares past and present times.[8] The fact that Jonson's poem has a Roman model does not mean that it is without personal force or personal application; on the contrary, the model gives his emphatically personal request a classical authority and strength. A similar appeal to the past can be seen in this episode reported in the *Conversations with Drummond* (264–7):

> Being at the end of my Lord Salisbury's table with Inigo Jones, and demanded by my Lord why he was not glad, 'My Lord', said he, 'You promised I should dine with you, but I do not', for he had none of his meat. He esteemed only th[a]t his meat which was of his own dish.

Jonson's quip is taken from an epigram of Martial's to which we know he was much attached:[9]

> Since I am asked to dinner, no longer, as before, a purchased guest, why is not the same dinner served to me as to you? . . . why do I dine without you, although, Ponticus, I am dining with you?

Jonson's experience at Robert Cecil's table satisfyingly corresponds with Martial's experience at the table of Ponticus; poets (it is implied) have ever suffered such indignities at the hands of great men. By 'playing' Martial, Jonson also strategically protects himself, speaking as he does in a voice not uniquely and offensively his own. The poem comes to his

---

[8] *The Underwood*, 76; cf. Martial, IV. xxvii.
[9] Martial, III. lx; cf. *Conversations with Drummond*, 371–2, 548–9.

mind again when he praises Robert Sidney's hospitality in 'To Penshurst':

> Where the same beer and bread and self-same wine
> That is his lordship's shall be also mine;
> And I not fain to sit, as some this day
> At great men's tables, and yet dine away.
>
> *(The Forest,* 2. 63–6)

'This day' is just like Martial's day. The same insults, the same pretensions, the same hollow hospitality recur—but so too, redeemingly, does the rare true host, and the rare true poet, who notices such things.

History as Jonson perceives it is not a changing and evolving process, producing an infinite series of unique moments. Instead, it is a repetitive and in part predictable affair, whose individual moments may be seen to resemble other moments that have occurred in the past or may occur in the future. To echo the poets of the past is not therefore a servile or insignificant act; it is rather a salute to their authority, a telling (and in turn authoritative) location of the present relevance and application of what they, in their age, have observed and written. Oscar Wilde's comment on Ben Jonson was apt: 'He made the poets of Greece and Rome terribly modern.'[10]

The pronoun 'I' in Jonson's writing has thus at times an oddly plural or impersonal force. Even when he seems most vigorously and unquestionably himself, Jonson may be gathering to himself the attributes, or voicing the sentiments, of other writers from other ages:

> Let me be what I am: as Virgil cold,
> As Horace fat, or as Anacreon old;
> No poet's verses yet did ever move,
> Whose readers did not think he was in love.
>
> *(The Underwood,* 42. 1–4)

'What I am' is inevitably compounded in part of what other writers have been: even Jonson's fatness has classical precedent. Jonson further admits that poetical and historical truth do not always coincide. For the poet's readers to be moved by his verses, they must '*think* he was in love', whatever the facts of the matter may have been. As Jonson wrote elsewhere, 'poet never credit gained | By writing truths, but things like truths, well feigned'.[11]

---

[10] *The Artist as Critic: Critical Writings of Oscar Wilde,* ed. Richard Ellmann (New York, 1969), pp. 34–5.

[11] *Epicoene,* second prologue, ll. 9–10.

Perhaps the most perplexing of all Jonson's writings from a biographical viewpoint is his commonplace book, *Discoveries*. A. C. Swinburne in his *Study of Ben Jonson* (1889) read the *Discoveries* as spiritual autobiography; throughout the collection he confidently detected the stamp of Jonson's own character, and rejoiced 'in the presence and the influence of one of the noblest, manliest, most honest and most helpful natures that ever dignified and glorified a powerful intelligence and an admirable genius'.[12] Swinburne may well have been justified in attributing these qualities to Jonson, but the interpretative problems involved in any reading of the *Discoveries* are more complex than he realized. Many of the sentiments that Jonson records in *Discoveries* appear—it is true—to derive in a quite unmediated way from personal experience and observation. Jonson's syntax repeatedly claims such sentiments as his own: 'I have known . . .', 'I have ever observed . . .', 'I have seen . . .', 'I have considered . . .', 'I have discovered . . .', 'I have marked . . .'. But on closer examination it becomes apparent that what Jonson has known, observed, seen, considered, discovered, and marked are the writings of other scholars, whose first-person statements he often simply transcribes.[13]

I have known a man vehement on both sides, that knew no mean, either to intermit his studies or call upon them again. When he hath set himself to wri[t]ing, he would join night to day, press upon himself without release, not minding it, till he fainted; and when he left off, resolve himself into all sports, and looseness again, that it was almost a despair to draw him to his book; but once got to it, he grew stronger and more earnest by the ease. (835–43)

Swinburne took this note to be 'another fragment of autobiography', assuming that the man referred to here was none other than Jonson himself.[14] Perhaps he was right. But it needs also to be noticed that the passage is borrowed from the elder Seneca, describing the habits of his friend the rhetorician Porcius Latro. Possibly Jonson saw a resemblance between his own working habits and those of Porcius Latro; possibly he had an actual acquaintance in mind; possibly he was just following Seneca. We simply cannot tell.

Swinburne similarly hailed the famous passage on memory (487 ff.) as 'mental autobiography', and lamented the fact that Shakespeare had not written with similar frankness about himself.[15] This time the personal

---

[12] A. C. Swinburne, *A Study of Ben Jonson* (London, 1889), p. 130.
[13] *Discoveries*, ll. 872, 934, 1081, 1105, 1122, 1140: see the annotation in this edition.
[14] Swinburne, op. cit., p. 147.
[15] Ibid., p. 137.

touch is indeed more evident, but again it is important to observe that Jonson is here following Seneca the elder; that what the passage *remembers* are not simply Jonson's own notable powers of remembrance, but those even more prodigious powers of Seneca himself. 'My conceit of his person was never increased toward him by his place or honours', writes Jonson with sturdy independence at the outset of a paragraph about Lord Bacon (948 ff.). The entire paragraph turns out to be a transcription of a letter from Fr. Fulgenzio Micanza to the first Earl of Devonshire. Jonson's act of transcription may perhaps be presumed to imply endorsement of its sentiments, but the statement is not quite so self-revealing or so sturdily independent as it at first appears.

After working for many years on an edition of Jonson's *Discoveries*, the French scholar Maurice Castelain became increasingly disenchanted with the work he was attempting to annotate. The *Discoveries*, it appeared, were not in any substantial sense original; they did not directly and unambiguously reveal what Jonson himself thought and felt; they did not seem, in the fullest sense of the word, to be truly *his*. Castelain's introduction to his edition of *Discoveries* in 1906 thus opens paradoxically and despondently:

> There is a kind of contradiction underlying the present work, its main purport being to prove that the *Discoveries* might be, without any serious objection, left out of the Jonsonian canon; that, practically, the book is not his; or, at least, that the merit and interest of it are for the most attributable to other men.[16]

Castelain failed to perceive the full significance of Jonson's selection, variation, and domestication of his many classical and Renaissance sources.[17] Nor did Castelain notice that throughout these writings Jonson returns to the very problem that Castelain himself was attempting to describe: the problem of distinguishing between literary imitation and literary plagiarism; of locating a writer's individual voice in passages inherited from others. What Jonson discusses, in short, might be called the ethical problem of literary *discoveries*. How can a writer legitimately appropriate, and pass off as his own, thoughts and phrases he has picked up in other people's books?

In addressing these questions, Jonson condemns 'all the essayists, even their master Montaigne', for the vice of indiscriminate copying.

---

[16] Ben Jonson, *Discoveries*, ed. Maurice Castelain (Paris and London, n.d. [1906]), p. vii.

[17] See, however, Castelain's survey of these matters on pp. xv ff. of his introduction. The relatively slight reworking of certain passages in *Discoveries* is to be explained in part by the status of the collection: see headnote, pp. 735–6.

'These, in all they write, confess still what books they have read last, and therein their own folly, so much that they bring it to the stake raw and undigested' (737–9). He condemns with equal force those who invent authorities for what they have written, feigning 'whole books and authors' (744), and those who pretend that they read no books or authors whatever, hoping thus

to divert the sagacity of their readers from themselves, and cool the scent of their own fox-like thefts; when yet they are so rank, as a man may find whole pages together usurped from one author . . . (748–52)

Jonson's movements here may themselves seem fox-like, for throughout this section of the *Discoveries* he is in fact borrowing freely from Quintilian. We may remember the comment made by Dryden's Crites about Jonson's use of the ancients, in the *Essay of Dramatic Poesy*: 'he was not only a professed imitator of Horace, but a learned plagiary of all the others; you track him everywhere in their snow'.[18] But not all borrowing is surreptitious, as Dryden's Neander in the same debate is quick to reply: Jonson 'has done his robberies so openly that one may see he fears not to be taxed by any law'.[19] It may be a greater temerity for a writer to believe that he is totally self-sufficient. Jonson's sternest criticism is indeed reserved for those

obstinate contemners of all helps and arts; such as presuming on their own naturals (which perhaps are excellent) dare deride all diligence, and seem to mock at the terms when they understand not the things, thinking that way to get off wittily with their ignorance. (757–62)

The 'helps and arts' referred to here are not merely stylistic but also intellectual. No writer, in Jonson's view, is wholly original; no writer exists in a literary vacuum; those who reckon to depend 'on their own naturals' do so at their own cost.

Jonson's understanding of the concept of literary personality is therefore significantly different from that which has prevailed since Romantic times. For Jonson, the authorial 'I' who speaks in any writer's work may be in part fictitious, in part compounded from the personae of other writers; biographical deduction from work to life is therefore more than ordinarily hazardous. Yet literary imitation for Jonson is more than a matter of passive and impersonal agglomeration of writings of the past. 'For to all the observations of the ancients, we have our own experience;

[18] John Dryden, *Of Dramatic Poesy and Other Critical Essays*, ed. George Watson, 2 vols. (London and New York, 1962), i. 31.
[19] Ibid. i. 69.

which, if we will use and apply, we have better means to pronounce.' The ancients therefore are 'guides, not commanders' (*Discoveries*, 136–41). A writer appropriates what he needs from his sources, and remains, in an ultimate sense, 'himself'. Jonson discusses this process of absorption and resistance in an important passage in *Discoveries* (which—characteristically—itself derives from other sources):

> The third requisite in our poet or maker is imitation, to be able to convert the substance or riches of another poet to his own use. To make choice of one excellent man above the rest, and so to follow him till he grow very he, or so like him as the copy may be mistaken for the principal. Not as a creature that swallows what it takes in crude, raw, or indigested, but that feeds with an appetite, and hath a stomach to concoct, divide, and turn all into nourishment. Not to imitate servilely (as Horace saith) and catch at vices for virtue, but to draw forth out of the best and choicest flowers, with the bee, and turn all into honey: work it into one relish and savour, make our imitation sweet . . . (2890–902)

'So to follow him *till he grow very he*': this notion is central to Jonson's art.

A similar notion is central also to the art of Volpone, Mosca, Face, and Subtle, each of whom is a master of impersonation. Volpone attracts the attention of Celia while impersonating the mountebank Scoto of Mantua —impersonating him with such success, Mosca assures him, that 'Scoto himself could hardly have distinguished' (II. iv. 36). Later in the play Mosca dresses in the clothes of his master, while Volpone dons the garb of the drunken Commendatore; together, they admire their skill in simulation:

> *Volpone.* Am I then like him?
>   *Mosca.*   Oh, sir, you are he:
> No man can sever you.
>   *Volpone.*   Good.
>   *Mosca.*   But, what am I?
>   *Volpone.* 'Fore heav'n, a brave *clarissimo*, thou becom'st it!
> Pity thou wert not born one. (V. v. 1–4)

Volpone and Mosca purloin the identities of other people as coolly as they purloin their property. 'But, what am I?' Mosca's question has a deeper significance than Volpone recognizes; for Mosca, who at this moment is beginning to assume the authority and life of his master, is less trustworthy and less knowable than he seems. An older generation of critics thought Jonson's dramatic characters to be fixed and simple. In fact his major characters are quite giddyingly complex; their 'real' identity—what remains when they have stopped play-acting—is always

in doubt. It is significant that *The Alchemist* should open with an
argument about the nature of identity:

> *Face.*   Why, who
> Am I, my mongrel? who am I?
> *Subtle.*   I'll tell you,
> Since you know not yourself——   (I. i. 12–14)

Despite Subtle's explicitness on the matter, the question of Face's
identity remains teasingly unanswered right to the end ('Speak for
thyself, knave': v. v. 157). As his very name suggests, he seemingly
consists entirely of externals, of 'face', of boldness, of that which he
chooses to imitate.

The impersonations of Volpone, Mosca, Face, and Subtle are both
like and unlike those more serious impersonations which Jonson himself
practises throughout his work. They are parodies of a higher art, 'fox-
like thefts' whose ultimate aim is further theft. At a deeper level, perhaps,
there may be a partial affinity between Jonson's own practices and those
of the illusionists and confidence men whom he creates. The central aim
and activity of the theatre is, after all, impersonation; and if William
Drummond is to be believed (*Conversations*, 254–8), Jonson was
prepared on at least one occasion to practise this art outside the confines
of the theatre: dressing as an old astrologer with a white beard and a long
gown, and inviting a lady to a solemn consultation in the suburbs, by 'the
light of [a] dim-burning candle, up in a little cabinet reached unto by a
ladder'. The high-minded severity of the Epistle Dedicatory to *Volpone*
and the address 'To the Reader' of *The Alchemist* may have been in part
occasioned by Jonson's wish publicly to dissociate himself from the
mischievous energies of the major characters of the plays, to which in
part he was also attracted. But like much else that we may wish to say
about Ben Jonson, this must remain at the level of guesswork.

The text of this edition is a modernized version of that established by
Herford and Simpson. Obsolete spellings have been retained here and
there in order to preserve a rhyme ('wull', not 'will', in *Epigrams*, 90. 17)
or a syllable ('babion', not 'baboon', *Epigrams*, 129. 12); a significant
reminder of etymology ('holy-day', not 'holiday', *The Underwood*,
84. ix. 63), or a play upon words or letters ('lanthorn', not 'lantern',
The Underwood, 43. 10; 'Marie', not 'Mary', *Ungathered Verse*, 41). The
flexibility of contemporary spelling allowed Jonson to play upon
homonyms in a way in which modern spelling does not permit: 'travel'/
'travail', 'waste'/'waist', 'lose'/'loose', 'mode'/'mood', etc.; in such cases

a note normally alerts the reader to the existence of a secondary sense. Jonson's punctuation, which to modern eyes and ears may seem intolerably heavy, has been lightened in order to allow both prose and verse to move more freely, though still in relation to the relative speed, hesitation, and deliberation of the original. Special problems are involved in modernizing the at times ambiguous texts of the *Conversations with Drummond*; these problems are touched on in the headnote to that section. Jonson's elaborate system of marking elisions, partial elisions, and syllabications in his verse lines has not been exactly reproduced; a line such as 'As if they'ador'd the Head, whereon th'are fixt', for example, is rendered 'As if they adored the head whereon they're fixed' (*Ungathered Verse*, 41. 28). Verbal contractions have been spelled out and placed within square brackets; editorial stage directions are also enclosed within square brackets. Textual variants of interest or significance are indicated in the notes, as are occasional departures from the readings of Herford and Simpson. For full textual apparatus, as for much else, the reader is referred to their edition.

The significance of Jonson's literary borrowings will be evident from the foregoing argument of this Introduction. The notes of this edition attempt to indicate these wherever possible, and—in the case of the poems in particular—to make Jonson's source materials accessible to readers who may have little or no knowledge of Greek or Latin. Translations are taken where possible from Loeb editions, sometimes with minor emendments. Where there is a familiar alternative English title, this is cited in preference to the Greek or Latin title (e.g. *To Marcia, on Consolation*, not *De Consolatione ad Marciam*); in other cases (e.g. *Tristia*) the classical title remains.

The annotation to Jonson's poems in this edition is an extensively revised and supplemented version of the annotation to be found in my 1975 Oxford Standard Authors/Oxford Paperbacks *Ben Jonson: Poems*. I have taken the opportunity also to revise and amend in a number of minor ways the text presented in that edition, and have been much assisted in this task by the watchfulness of Steven L. Bates, co-compiler of *A Concordance to the Poems of Ben Jonson* (Athens, Ohio, 1978).

I am grateful also to the General Editor, Professor Kermode, and to my colleagues Professor Graeme Clarke and Dr J. C. Eade for much kindness and advice extended during my preparation of this edition.

C.I.E.D.

Humanities Research Centre
The Australian National University
Canberra

CHRONOLOGY*

?1572   Jonson born (?11 June), one month after death of his father, 'a grave minister of the gospel'; his mother remarries, to bricklayer, not long after; family lives near Charing Cross; Jonson attends private school in St Martin's Church, and later Westminster School: taught by William Camden.

?1588   Leaves Westminster School.

early 1590s   Works as bricklayer; military service in Flanders: 'In his service in the Low Countries he had, in the face of both the camps, killed an enemy and taken *opima spolia* from him' (*Conv. Dr.* 199–200).

1594   Marries Anne Lewis (14 Nov.): 'a shrew yet honest' (*Conv. Dr.* 208). Children of this marriage include: Benjamin (?1596–1603: commemorated in *Epig.* 45); Mary (probably b. soon after 1598, d. aged six months: commemorated in *Epig.* 22); Joseph (b. Dec. 1599); Benjamin (Feb. 1608–18 Nov. 1611). Jonson probably had other children, legitimate and illegitimate.

1597   Mentioned in Henslowe's diary as an actor; likely to have begun this career before this date.
Imprisoned for his share in lost play, *The Isle of Dogs* (Aug.–Oct.).

1598   Indicted (22 Sept.) for killing a fellow actor, Gabriel Spencer, in a duel; pleads self-defence, given benefit of clergy, branded on thumb, goods confiscated. Converted to Catholicism while in prison: 'thereafter he was twelve years a papist' (*Conv. Dr.* 205). Listed by Francis Meres in *Palladis Tamia* amongst English playwrights 'best for tragedy'.

1600–1   'War of the Theatres', with Dekker and Marston.

1601, 1602   Paid for 'additions' to *The Spanish Tragedy* (25 Sept.; 22 June).

1602   'Ben Jonson the poet now lives upon one Townshend, and scorns the world' (i.e. Sir Robert Townshend; Manningham's diary, Feb.). Jonson later lives five years with Esmé Stewart, Lord Aubigny; separated during this period from his wife.

1603   Death of Queen Elizabeth (24 Mar.); accession of King James I.

1605   Jonson and co-authors imprisoned for libellous references in *Eastward Ho!*
Gunpowder plot (5 Nov.): Jonson assists Privy Council with inquiries.

1606   Jonson and wife before Consistory Court on charges of recusancy.

1612–13   In France as tutor to Sir Walter Raleigh's son, Walter.

* For dates of individual works by Jonson, see pp. 614–15.

1616	Publication of Folio of Jonson's *Works*, containing (*inter alia*) *Epigrams* and *The Forest*.
	Granted royal pension of 100 marks p.a. (Feb.).
1618–19	Journey on foot to Scotland; guest of William Drummond of Hawthornden and others.
1619	Honorary degree from Oxford (17 July).
1619–	?Deputy Professorship of Rhetoric, Gresham College, London.
1623	Fire destroys Jonson's library and manuscripts (Nov.).
1625	Death of King James (27 Mar.); accession of King Charles I.
1628	Jonson suffers paralytic stroke.
	Made City Chronologer after death of Thomas Middleton (payment withheld 1631–4, because of Jonson's inactivity in office).
1630	Pension increased from 100 marks to 100 pounds p.a., plus annual tierce of royal sack.
1631	Culmination of feud with Inigo Jones.
1637	Dies; buried in Westminster Abbey (mid Aug.).
1638	Publication of *Jonsonus Virbius* (memorial tributes).
1640	Publication in Quarto by John Benson, from surreptitiously acquired manuscripts, of *An Execration Upon Vulcan* and 'divers epigrams'; reissued in same year in Duodecimo, with *Ars Poetica* and *The Gypsies Metamorphosed*.
1640–1	Publication of Jonson's 2nd Folio, in two volumes, containing (*inter alia*) *The Underwood*: collected by Sir Kenelm Digby from Jonson's papers.

VOLPONE

TO

THE MOST NOBLE AND MOST EQUAL SISTERS
THE TWO FAMOUS UNIVERSITIES
FOR THEIR LOVE AND ACCEPTANCE
SHOWN TO HIS POEM IN THE PRESENTATION
BEN JONSON
THE GRATEFUL ACKNOWLEDGER
DEDICATES
BOTH IT AND HIMSELF

Never (most equal sisters) had any man a wit so presently excellent, as
that it could raise itself; but there must come both matter, occasion,
commenders, and favourers to it. If this be true, and that the fortune of
all writers doth daily prove it, it behoves the careful to provide well
toward these accidents; and having acquired them, to preserve that part
of reputation most tenderly, wherein the benefit of a friend is also
defended. Hence is it that I now render myself grateful, and am studious
to justify the bounty of your act; to which, though your mere authority
were satisfying, yet, it being an age wherein poetry and the professors of
it hear so ill on all sides, there will a reason be looked for in the subject. It   10
is certain, nor can it with any forehead be opposed, that the too much
licence of poetasters in this time hath much deformed their mistress; that
every day, their manifold and manifest ignorance doth stick unnatural
reproaches upon her. But for their petulancy, it were an act of the
greatest injustice either to let the learned suffer, or so divine a skill
(which indeed should not be attempted with unclean hands) to fall under
the least contempt. For if men will impartially, and not asquint, look
toward the offices and function of a poet, they will easily conclude to
themselves the impossibility of any man's being the good poet, without
first being a good man. He that is said to be able to inform young men to   20
all good disciplines, inflame grown men to all great virtues, keep old men
in their best and supreme state, or, as they decline to childhood, recover
them to their first strength; that comes forth the interpreter and arbiter of
nature, a teacher of things divine no less than human, a master in

manners; and can alone (or with a few) effect the business of mankind: this, I take him, is no subject for pride and ignorance to exercise their railing rhetoric upon. But it will here be hastily answered that the writers of these days are other things: that not only their manners, but their natures are inverted; and nothing remaining with them of the dignity of poet but the abused name, which every scribe usurps; that now, especially in dramatic or (as they term it) stage-poetry, nothing but ribaldry, profanation, blasphemy, all licence of offence to God and man is practised. I dare not deny a great part of this (and am sorry, I dare not) because in some men's abortive features (and would they had never boasted the light) it is over-true; but that all are embarked in this bold adventure for hell, is a most uncharitable thought, and, uttered, a more malicious slander. For my particular, I can (and from a most clear conscience) affirm that I have ever trembled to think toward the least profaneness; have loathed the use of such foul and unwashed bawdry as is now made the food of the scene. And howsoever I cannot escape, from some, the imputation of sharpness, but that they will say I have taken a pride, or lust, to be bitter, and not my youngest infant but hath come into the world with all his teeth; I would ask of these supercilious politics, what nation, society, or general order, or state I have provoked? what public person? whether I have not (in all these) preserved their dignity, as mine own person, safe? My works are read, allowed (I speak of those that are entirely mine); look into them: what broad reproofs have I used? where have I been particular? where personal? except to a mimic, cheater, bawd, or buffoon, creatures (for their insolencies) worthy to be taxed? Yet, to which of these so pointingly as he might not either ingenuously have confessed, or wisely dissembled his disease? But it is not rumour can make men guilty, much less entitle me to other men's crimes. I know that nothing can be so innocently writ or carried, but may be made obnoxious to construction; marry, whilst I bear mine innocence about me, I fear it not. Application is now grown a trade with many; and there are that profess to have a key for the deciphering of everything: but let wise and noble persons take heed how they be too credulous, or give leave to these invading interpreters to be over-familiar with their fames, who cunningly and often utter their own virulent malice under other men's simplest meanings. As for those that will (by faults which charity hath raked up, or common honesty concealed) make themselves a name with the multitude, or (to draw their rude and beastly claps) care not whose living faces they entrench with their petulant styles: may they do it without a rival, for me; I choose rather to live graved in obscurity, than share with them in so preposterous a fame. Nor can I blame the wishes of those severe and wiser patriots, who providing the hurts these licentious spirits may do in a state, desire rather to see fools and devils, and those antique relics of barbarism retrieved, with all other ridiculous and exploded follies, than behold the wounds of private men, of princes, and nations. For, as Horace makes Trebatius speak, among these 70

——*Sibi quisque timet, quamquam est intactus, et odit.*

And men may justly impute such rages, if continued, to the writer, as his sports. The increase of which lust in liberty, together with the present trade of the stage, in all their misc'line interludes, what learned or liberal soul doth not already abhor? where nothing but the filth of the time is uttered, and that with such impropriety of phrase, such plenty of solecisms, such dearth of sense, so bold prolepses, so racked metaphors, with brothelry able to violate the ear of a pagan, and blasphemy to turn the blood of a Christian to water. I cannot but be serious in a cause of this nature, wherein my fame and the reputations of divers honest and 80 learned are the question; when a name, so full of authority, antiquity, and all great mark, is——through their insolence——become the lowest scorn of the age; and those men subject to the petulancy of every vernaculous orator, that were wont to be the care of kings and happiest monarchs. This it is that hath not only rapt me to present indignation, but made me studious heretofore; and by all my actions to stand off from them; which may most appear in this my latest work——which you, most learned arbitresses, have seen, judged, and to my crown, approved ——wherein I have laboured, for their instruction and amendment, to reduce not only the ancient forms, but manners of the scene: the 90 easiness, the propriety, the innocence, and last the doctrine, which is the principal end of poesy, to inform men in the best reason of living. And though my catastrophe may, in the strict rigour of comic law, meet with censure, as turning back to my promise, I desire the learned and charitable critic to have so much faith in me to think it was done of industry: for with what ease I could have varied it nearer his scale (but that I fear to boast my own faculty) I could here insert. But my special aim being to put the snaffle in their mouths, that cry out, we never punish vice in our interludes, etc. I took the more liberty; though not without some lines of example drawn even in the ancients themselves, the goings-out 100 of whose comedies are not always joyful, but oft-times the bawds, the servants, the rivals, yea, and the masters are mulcted: and fitly, it being the office of a comic poet to imitate justice, and instruct to life, as well as purity of language, or stir up gentle affections. To which I shall take the occasion elsewhere to speak. For the present (most reverenced sisters) as

I have cared to be thankful for your affections past, and here made the understanding acquainted with some ground of your favours, let me not despair their continuance, to the maturing of some worthier fruits: wherein, if my muses be true to me, I shall raise the despised head of
110 poetry again, and stripping her out of those rotten and base rags wherewith the times have adulterated her form, restore her to her primitive habit, feature, and majesty, and render her worthy to be embraced and kissed of all the great and master-spirits of our world. As for the vile and slothful, who never affected an act worthy of celebration, or are so inward with their own vicious natures, as they worthily fear her, and think it a high point of policy to keep her in contempt with their declamatory and windy invectives: she shall out of just rage incite her servants (who are *genus irritabile*) to spout ink in their faces, that shall eat farther than their marrow, into their fames; and not Cinnamus the
120 barber with his art shall be able to take out the brands, but they shall live, and be read, till the wretches die, as things worst deserving of themselves in chief, and then of all mankind.

The Persons of the Play

Volpone, *a Magnifico*
Mosca, *his Parasite*
Voltore, *an Advocate*
Corbaccio, *an old Gentleman*
Corvino, *a Merchant*
Avocatori, *four Magistrates*
Notario, *the Register*
Nano, *a Dwarf*
Castrone, *an Eunuch*
Grege [*the crowd*]
Politic Would-be, *a Knight*

Peregrine, *a Gent[leman]-traveller*
Bonario, *a young Gentleman*
Fine Madam Would-be, *the Knight's wife*
Celia, *the Merchant's wife*
Commendatori, *Officers*
Mercatori, *three Merchants*
Androgyno, *a Hermaphrodite*
Servitore, *a Servant*
Women

The Scene:

Venice

VOLPONE,

OR

THE FOX

THE ARGUMENT

V olpone, childless, rich, feigns sick, despairs,
O ffers his state to hopes of several heirs,
L ies languishing; his parasite receives
P resents of all, assures, deludes; then weaves
O ther cross-plots, which ope themselves, are told.
N ew tricks for safety are sought; they thrive; when, bold,
E ach tempts th' other again, and all are sold.

PROLOGUE

Now, luck yet send us, and a little wit
   Will serve, to make our play hit;
According to the palates of the season,
   Here is rhyme, not empty of reason.
This we were bid to credit, from our poet,
   Whose true scope, if you would know it,
In all his poems still hath been this measure,
   To mix profit with your pleasure;
And not as some (whose throats their envy failing)
   Cry hoarsely, 'All he writes is railing':   10
And when his plays come forth, think they can flout them,
   With saying, 'He was a year about them'.
To these there needs no lie but this his creature,
   Which was, two months since, no feature;
And though he dares give them five lives to mend it,
   'Tis known, five weeks fully penned it:
From his own hand, without a coadjutor,
   Novice, journeyman, or tutor.

Yet thus much I can give you as a token
   Of his play's worth, no eggs are broken,   20
Nor quaking custards with fierce teeth affrighted,
   Wherewith your rout are so delighted;
Nor hales he in a gull, old ends reciting,
   To stop gaps in his loose writing;
With such a deal of monstrous and forced action
   As might make Bedlam a faction;
Nor made he his play for jests stol'n from each table,
   But makes jests to fit his fable.
And so presents quick comedy, refined,
   As best critics have designed;   30
The laws of time, place, persons he observeth,
   From no needful rule he swerveth.
All gall and copperas from his ink he draineth,
   Only a little salt remaineth;
Wherewith he'll rub your cheeks, till red with laughter,
   They shall look fresh a week after.

Act I, Scene i

[Volpone's house]

[Enter Volpone and Mosca]

Volpone. Good morning to the day; and next, my gold!
Open the shrine, that I may see my saint.

[Mosca reveals the treasure]

Hail the world's soul, and mine! More glad than is
The teeming earth to see the longed-for sun
Peep through the horns of the celestial Ram,
Am I, to view thy splendour, darkening his;
That lying here, amongst my other hoards,
Show'st like a flame by night; or like the day
Struck out of chaos, when all darkness fled
Unto the centre. Oh, thou son of Sol   10
(But brighter than thy father) let me kiss
With adoration, thee, and every relic
Of sacred treasure in this blessèd room.
Well did wise poets by thy glorious name,
Title that age which they would have the best;

Thou being the best of things, and far transcending
All style of joy in children, parents, friends,
Or any other waking dream on earth.
Thy looks when they to Venus did ascribe,
They should have given her twenty thousand Cupids;   20
Such are thy beauties, and our loves! Dear saint,
Riches, the dumb god, that giv'st all men tongues;
That canst do naught, and yet mak'st men do all things;
The price of souls; even hell, with thee to boot,
Is made worth heaven! Thou art virtue, fame,
Honour, and all things else! Who can get thee,
He shall be noble, valiant, honest, wise——
    Mosca. And what he will, sir. Riches are in fortune
A greater good than wisdom is in nature.
    Volpone. True, my belovèd Mosca. Yet I glory   30
More in the cunning purchase of my wealth
Than in the glad possession, since I gain
No common way; I use no trade, no venture;
I wound no earth with ploughshares; fat no beasts
To feed the shambles; have no mills for iron,
Oil, corn, or men, to grind 'em into powder;
I blow no subtle glass; expose no ships
To threatenings of the furrow-facèd sea;
I turn no moneys in the public bank;
Nor usure private——
    Mosca.   No, sir, nor devour   40
Soft prodigals. You shall ha' some will swallow
A melting heir as glibly as your Dutch
Will pills of butter, and ne'er purge for't;
Tear forth the fathers of poor families
Out of their beds, and coffin them, alive,
In some kind, clasping prison, where their bones
May be forthcoming, when the flesh is rotten.
But your sweet nature doth abhor these courses;
You loathe the widow's, or the orphan's tears
Should wash your pavements, or their piteous cries   50
Ring in your roofs, and beat the air for vengeance.——
    Volpone. Right, Mosca, I do loathe it.
    Mosca.   And besides, sir,
You are not like the thresher that doth stand
With a huge flail, watching a heap of corn,

And, hungry, dares not taste the smallest grain,
But feeds on mallows and such bitter herbs;
Nor like the merchant, who hath filled his vaults
With Romagnía and rich Candian wines,
Yet drinks the lees of Lombard's vinegar:
You will not lie in straw, whilst moths and worms   60
Feed on your sumptuous hangings and soft beds.
You know the use of riches, and dare give, now,
From that bright heap, to me, your poor observer,
Or to your dwarf, or your hermaphrodite,
Your eunuch, or what other household trifle
Your pleasure allows maintenance.——

    Volpone.   Hold thee, Mosca,
                            [*Gives him money*]
Take, of my hand; thou strik'st on truth in all:
And they are envious, term thee parasite.
Call forth my dwarf, my eunuch, and my fool,
And let 'em make me sport. [*Exit Mosca*] What should I do,   70
But cocker up my genius and live free
To all delights my fortune calls me to?
I have no wife, no parent, child, ally,
To give my substance to; but whom I make,
Must be my heir: and this makes men observe me.
This draws new clients, daily, to my house,
Women and men of every sex and age,
That bring me presents, send me plate, coin, jewels
With hope that when I die (which they expect
Each greedy minute) it shall then return   80
Tenfold upon them; whilst some, covetous
Above the rest, seek to engross me, whole,
And counterwork the one unto the other,
Contend in gifts, as they would seem, in love.
All which I suffer, playing with their hopes,
And am content to coin 'em into profit,
And look upon their kindness, and take more,
And look on that; still bearing them in hand,
Letting the cherry knock against their lips,
And draw it by their mouths, and back again. How now!   90

Act I, Scene ii

[Enter Nano, Androgyno, Castrone, and Mosca]

Nano. Now, room for fresh gamesters, who do will you to know,
    They do bring you neither play, nor university show;
And therefore do entreat you, that whatsoever they rehearse,
    May not fare a whit the worse, for the false pace of the verse.
If you wonder at this, you will wonder more ere we pass,
    For know, here [*Pointing to Androgyno*] is enclosed the soul of
        Pythagoras,
That juggler divine, as hereafter shall follow;
    Which soul (fast and loose, sir) came first from Apollo,
And was breathed into Aethalides, Mercurius's son,
    Where it had the gift to remember all that ever was done.   10
From thence it fled forth, and made quick transmigration
    To goldy-locked Euphorbus, who was killed, in good fashion,
At the siege of old Troy, by the cuckold of Sparta.
    Hermotimus was next (I find it in my charta)
To whom it did pass, where no sooner it was missing,
    But with one Pyrrhus of Delos it learned to go a-fishing;
And thence did it enter the Sophist of Greece.
    From Pythagore, she went into a beautiful piece,
Hight Aspasia, the meretrix; and the next toss of her
    Was again of a whore: she became a philosopher,   20
Crates the Cynic (as itself doth relate it).
    Since, kings, knights, and beggars, knaves, lords and fools gat it,
Besides ox and ass, camel, mule, goat and brock,
    In all which it hath spoke, as in the cobbler's cock.
But I come not here to discourse of that matter,
    Or his one, two, or three, or his great oath 'By quater!',
His musics, his trigon, his golden thigh,
    Or his telling how elements shift; but I
Would ask how of late thou hast suffered translation,
    And shifted thy coat in these days of reformation?   30
Androgyno. Like one of the reformèd, a fool, as you see,
    Counting all old doctrine heresy.
Nano. But not on thine own forbid' meats hast thou ventured?
Androgyno. On fish, when first a Carthusian I entered.
Nano. Why, then thy dogmatical silence hath left thee?
Androgyno. Of that an obstreperous lawyer bereft me.

Nano. Oh wonderful change! When sir lawyer forsook thee,
    For Pythagore's sake, what body then took thee?
Androgyno. A good dull mule.
Nano.   And how! by that means,
    Thou wert brought to allow of the eating of beans?   40
Androgyno. Yes.
Nano.   But from the mule, into whom didst thou pass?
Androgyno. Into a very strange beast, by some writers called an ass;
By others, a precise, pure, illuminate brother,
    Of those devour flesh, and sometimes one another;
And will drop you forth a libel, or a sanctified lie,
    Betwixt every spoonful of a nativity pie.
Nano. Now quit thee, for heaven, of that profane nation,
    And gently report thy next transmigration.
Androgyno. To the same that I am.
Nano.   A creature of delight?
    And, what is more than a fool, an hermaphrodite?   50
Now 'pray thee, sweet soul, in all thy variation,
    Which body wouldst thou choose, to take up thy station?
Androgyno. Troth, this I am in, even here would I tarry.
Nano. 'Cause here, the delight of each sex thou canst vary?
Androgyno. Alas, those pleasures be stale and forsaken;
    No, 'tis your fool wherewith I am so taken,
The only one creature that I can call blessèd:
    For all other forms I have proved most distressèd.
Nano. Spoke true, as thou wert in Pythagoras still.
    This learnèd opinion we celebrate will,   60
Fellow eunuch (as behoves us) with all our wit and art,
    To dignify that whereof ourselves are so great and special a part.
Volpone. Now very, very pretty! Mosca, this
    Was thy invention?
Mosca.   If it please my patron,
    Not else.
Volpone.   It doth, good Mosca.
Mosca.   Then it was, sir.

Song

    Fools, they are the only nation
    Worth men's envy or admiration;
    Free from care, or sorrow-taking,
    Selves and others merry making:

All they speak or do is sterling.   70
Your fool, he is your great man's darling,
And your ladies' sport and pleasure;
Tongue and bauble are his treasure.
E'en his face begetteth laughter,
And he speaks truth free from slaughter;
He's the grace of every feast,
And sometimes the chiefest guest:
Hath his trencher and his stool,
When wit waits upon the fool.
         Oh, who would not be   80
               He, he, he?   (*One knocks without*)

Volpone. Who's that? Away! Look Mosca. [*Exeunt Nano, Castrone*]
Mosca.   Fool, be gone,
                                        [*Exit Androgyno*]
'Tis Signior Voltore, the advocate;
I know him by his knock.
    Volpone.   Fetch me my gown,
My furs, and night-caps; say my couch is changing,
And let him entertain himself awhile
Without i' the gallery. [*Exit Mosca*] Now, now, my clients
Begin their visitation! vulture, kite,
Raven, and gor-crow, all my birds of prey,
That think me turning carcass, now they come: 90
I am not for 'em yet.

                  [*Enter Mosca*]

            How now? the news?
    Mosca. A piece of plate, sir.
    Volpone.   Of what bigness?
    Mosca.   Huge,
Massy, and antique, with your name inscribed,
And arms engraven.
    Volpone.   Good! and not a fox
Stretched on the earth, with fine delusive sleights,
Mocking a gaping crow? ha, Mosca?
    Mosca.   Sharp, sir.
    Volpone. Give me my furs. Why dost thou laugh so, man?
    Mosca. I cannot choose, sir, when I apprehend
What thoughts he has, without, now, as he walks:
That this might be the last gift he should give;   100

That this would fetch you; if you died today,
And gave him all, what he should be tomorrow;
What large return would come of all his ventures;
How he should worshipped be, and reverenced;
Ride, with his furs, and foot-cloths; waited on
By herds of fools and clients; have clear way
Made for his mule, as lettered as himself;
Be called the great and learnèd advocate:
And then concludes, there's naught impossible.
   Volpone. Yes, to be learnèd, Mosca.
   Mosca.   Oh no: rich   110
Implies it. Hood an ass with reverend purple,
So you can hide his two ambitious ears,
And he shall pass for a cathedral doctor.
   Volpone. My caps, my caps, good Mosca! Fetch him in.
   Mosca. Stay, sir, your ointment for your eyes.
   Volpone.   That's true;
Dispatch, dispatch; I long to have possession
Of my new present.
   Mosca.   That, and thousands more,
I hope to see you lord of.
   Volpone.   Thanks, kind Mosca.
   Mosca. And that, when I am lost in blended dust,
And hundred such as I am, in succession——   120
   Volpone. Nay, that were too much, Mosca.
   Mosca.   You shall live,
Still, to delude these harpies.
   Volpone.   Loving Mosca!
'Tis well, my pillow now, and let him enter.   [*Exit Mosca*]
Now, my feigned cough, my phthisic, and my gout,
My apoplexy, palsy, and catarrhs,
Help, with your forced functions, this my posture,
Wherein, this three year, I have milked their hopes.
He comes, I hear him——uh, uh, uh, uh, oh!——

Act I, Scene iii

[*Enter Mosca, with Voltore, carrying plate*]

   Mosca. You still are what you were, sir. Only you,
Of all the rest, are he commands his love,

And you do wisely to preserve it thus
With early visitation, and kind notes
Of your good meaning to him, which, I know,
Cannot but come most grateful. Patron, sir.
Here's Signior Voltore is come——

Volpone.   What say you?

Mosca. Sir, Signior Voltore is come this morning,
To visit you.

Volpone.   I thank him.

Mosca.   And hath brought
A piece of antique plate, bought of St Mark,   10
With which he here presents you.

Volpone.   He is welcome.
Pray him to come more often.

Mosca.   Yes.

Voltore.   What says he?

Mosca. He thanks you, and desires you see him often.

Volpone. Mosca.

Mosca.   My patron?

Volpone.   Bring him near, where is he?
I long to feel his hand.

Mosca.   The plate is here, sir.

Voltore. How fare you, sir?

Volpone.   I thank you, Signior Voltore.
Where is the plate? Mine eyes are bad.

Voltore.   I'm sorry
To see you still thus weak.

Mosca. [*Aside*]   That he is not weaker.

Volpone. [*Grasping plate*] You are too munificent.

Voltore.   No, sir, would to heaven
I could as well give health to you, as that plate.   20

Volpone. You give, sir, what you can. I thank you. Your love
Hath taste in this, and shall not be unanswered.
I pray you see me often.

Voltore.   Yes, I shall, sir.

Volpone. Be not far from me.

Mosca. [*To Voltore*]   Do you observe that, sir?

Volpone. Hearken unto me still; it will concern you.

Mosca. [*To Voltore*] You are a happy man, sir, know your good.

Volpone. I cannot now last long——

Mosca. [*To Voltore*]   You are his heir, sir.

Voltore. Am I?
Volpone. I feel me going——uh, uh, uh, uh——
I am sailing to my port——uh, uh, uh, uh——
And I am glad, I am so near my haven.   30
  Mosca. Alas, kind gentleman, well, we must all go——
  Voltore. But, Mosca——
  Mosca.   Age will conquer.
  Voltore.   'Pray thee hear me.
Am I inscribed his heir for certain?
  Mosca.   Are you?
I do beseech you, sir, you will vouchsafe
To write me i' your family. All my hopes
Depend upon your worship. I am lost,
Except the rising sun do shine on me.
  Voltore. It shall both shine and warm thee, Mosca.
  Mosca.   Sir.
I am a man that have not done your love
All the worst offices: here I wear your keys,   40
See all your coffers and your caskets locked,
Keep the poor inventory of your jewels,
Your plate and moneys, am your steward, sir,
Husband your goods here.
  Voltore.   But am I sole heir?
  Mosca. Without a partner, sir, confirmed this morning;
The wax is warm yet, and the ink scarce dry
Upon the parchment.
  Voltore.   Happy, happy, me!
By what good chance, sweet Mosca?
  Mosca.   Your desert, sir;
I know no second cause.
  Voltore.   Thy modesty
Is loath to know it; well, we shall requite it.   50
  Mosca. He ever liked your course, sir, that first took him.
I oft have heard him say, how he admired
Men of your large profession, that could speak
To every cause, and things mere contraries,
Till they were hoarse again, yet all be law;
That, with most quick agility, could turn,
And re-turn; make knots, and undo them;
Give forkèd counsel; take provoking gold
On either hand, and put it up: these men,

He knew, would thrive, with their humility.   60
And, for his part, he thought, he should be blest
To have his heir of such a suffering spirit,
So wise, so grave, of so perplexed a tongue,
And loud withal, that would not wag, nor scarce
Lie still, without a fee; when every word
Your worship but lets fall, is a cecchine!   (*Another knocks*)
Who's that? one knocks, I would not have you seen, sir.
And yet——pretend you came and went in haste;
I'll fashion an excuse. And, gentle sir,
When you do come to swim in golden lard,   70
Up to the arms in honey, that your chin
Is borne up stiff with fatness of the flood,
Think on your vassal; but remember me:
I ha' not been your worst of clients.
   Voltore.   Mosca——
   Mosca. When will you have your inventory brought, sir?
Or see a copy of the will? (Anon!)
I'll bring 'em to you, sir. Away, be gone,
Put business i' your face.   [*Exit Voltore*]
   Volpone.   Excellent, Mosca!
Come hither, let me kiss thee.
   Mosca.   Keep you still, sir.
Here is Corbaccio.
   Volpone.   Set the plate away,   80
The vulture's gone, and the old raven's come.

Act I, Scene iv

   Mosca. Betake you to your silence and your sleep:
Stand there, and multiply. [*Puts plate aside*] Now, shall we see
A wretch who is indeed more impotent
Than this can feign to be, yet hopes to hop
Over his grave.
               [*Enter Corbaccio*]
         Signior Corbaccio!
You're very welcome, sir.
   Corbaccio.   How does your patron?
   Mosca. Troth, as he did, sir, no amends.

Corbaccio. What? mends he?
Mosca. No, sir: he is rather worse.
Corbaccio. That's well. Where is he?
Mosca. Upon his couch, sir, newly fallen asleep.
Corbaccio. Does he sleep well?
Mosca. No wink, sir, all this night, 10
Nor yesterday, but slumbers.
Corbaccio. Good! He should take
Some counsel of physicians; I have brought him
An opiate here, from mine own doctor——
Mosca. He will not hear of drugs.
Corbaccio. Why? I myself
Stood by while 'twas made, saw all the ingredients,
And know it cannot but most gently work.
My life for his, 'tis but to make him sleep.
Volpone. [*Aside*] Aye, his last sleep, if he would take it.
Mosca. Sir,
He has no faith in physic.
Corbaccio. Say you, say you?
Mosca. He has no faith in physic: he does think, 20
Most of your doctors are the greater danger,
And worse disease to escape. I often have
Heard him protest that your physician
Should never be his heir.
Corbaccio. Not I his heir?
Mosca. Not your physician, sir.
Corbaccio. Oh, no, no, no,
I do not mean it.
Mosca. No sir, nor their fees
He cannot brook; he says, they flay a man,
Before they kill him.
Corbaccio. Right, I do conceive you.
Mosca. And then, they do it by experiment,
For which the law not only doth absolve 'em 30
But gives them great reward; and he is loath
To hire his death, so.
Corbaccio. It is true, they kill
With as much licence as a judge.
Mosca. Nay, more:
For he but kills, sir, where the law condemns,
And these can kill him too.

Corbaccio.   Aye, or me,
Or any man. How does his apoplexy?
Is that strong on him still?
  Mosca.   Most violent.
His speech is broken, and his eyes are set,
His face drawn longer than 'twas wont——
  Corbaccio.   How? how?
Stronger than he was wont?
  Mosca.   No, sir; his face   40
Drawn longer than 'twas wont.
  Corbaccio.   Oh, good.
  Mosca.   His mouth
Is ever gaping, and his eyelids hang.
  Corbaccio.   Good.
  Mosca. A freezing numbness stiffens all his joints,
And makes the colour of his flesh like lead.
  Corbaccio.   'Tis good.
  Mosca. His pulse beats slow and dull.
  Corbaccio.   Good symptoms still.
  Mosca. And from his brain——
  Corbaccio.   Ha? how? not from his brain?
  Mosca. Yes, sir, and from his brain——
  Corbaccio.   I conceive you, good.
  Mosca. Flows a cold sweat, with a continual rheum,
Forth the resolvèd corners of his eyes.
  Corbaccio. Is't possible? Yet I am better, ha!   50
How does he with the swimming of his head?
  Mosca. Oh, sir, 'tis past the scotomy; he now
Hath lost his feeling, and hath left to snort;
You hardly can perceive him that he breathes.
  Corbaccio. Excellent, excellent, sure I shall outlast him!
This makes me young again, a score of years.
  Mosca. I was a-coming for you, sir.
  Corbaccio.   Has he made his will?
What has he given me?
  Mosca.   No, sir.
  Corbaccio.   Nothing? ha?
  Mosca. He has not made his will, sir.
  Corbaccio.   Oh, oh, oh.
What then did Voltore, the lawyer, here?   60
  Mosca. He smelt a carcass, sir, when he but heard

My master was about his testament——
As I did urge him to it, for your good——
    Corbaccio. He came unto him, did he? I thought so.
    Mosca. Yes, and presented him this piece of plate.
    Corbaccio. To be his heir?
    Mosca.   I do not know, sir.
    Corbaccio.   True,
I know it too.
    Mosca. [*Aside*] By your own scale, sir.
    Corbaccio.   Well,
I shall prevent him yet. See, Mosca, look
Here, I have brought a bag of bright cecchines,
Will quite weigh down his plate.
    Mosca.   Yea, marry, sir!   70
This is true physic, this your sacred medicine,
No talk of opiates, to this great elixir.
    Corbaccio. 'Tis *aurum palpabile*, if not *potabile*.
    Mosca. It shall be ministered to him in his bowl?
    Corbaccio. Aye, do, do, do.
    Mosca.   Most blessed cordial!
This will recover him.
    Corbaccio.   Yes, do, do, do.
    Mosca. I think it were not best, sir.
    Corbaccio.   What?
    Mosca.   To recover him.
    Corbaccio. Oh, no, no, no; by no means.
    Mosca.   Why, sir, this
Will work some strange effect if he but feel it.
    Corbaccio. 'Tis true, therefore forbear; I'll take my venture;   80
Give me it again.
    Mosca.   At no hand, pardon me;
You shall not do yourself that wrong, sir. I
Will so advise you, you shall have it all.
    Corbaccio. How?
    Mosca.   All, sir, 'tis your right, your own; no man
Can claim a part; 'tis yours, without a rival,
Decreed by destiny.
    Corbaccio.   How? how, good Mosca?
    Mosca. I'll tell you, sir. This fit he shall recover——
    Corbaccio. I do conceive you.
    Mosca.   And on first advantage

Of his 'gained sense, will I re-importune him
Unto the making of his testament: 90
And show him this.
    Corbaccio.   Good, good.
    Mosca.   'Tis better yet,
If you will hear, sir.
    Corbaccio.   Yes, with all my heart.
    Mosca. Now would I counsel you, make home with speed;
There, frame a will, whereto you shall inscribe
My master your sole heir.
    Corbaccio.   And disinherit
My son?
    Mosca. Oh, sir, the better: for that colour
Shall make it much more taking.
    Corbaccio.   Oh, but colour?
    Mosca. This will, sir, you shall send it unto me.
Now, when I come to enforce——as I will do——
Your cares, your watchings, and your many prayers,   100
Your more than many gifts, your this day's present,
And, last, produce your will; where——without thought
Or least regard unto your proper issue,
A son so brave, and highly meriting——
The stream of your diverted love hath thrown you
Upon my master, and made him your heir;
He cannot be so stupid or stone dead,
But out of conscience and mere gratitude——
    Corbaccio. He must pronounce me his?
    Mosca.   'Tis true.
    Corbaccio.   This plot
Did I think on before.
    Mosca.   I do believe it.   110
    Corbaccio. Do you not believe it?
    Mosca.   Yes, sir.
    Corbaccio.   Mine own project.
    Mosca. Which when he hath done, sir——
    Corbaccio.   Published me his heir?
    Mosca. And you so certain to survive him——
    Corbaccio.   Aye.
    Mosca. Being so lusty a man——
    Corbaccio.   'Tis true.
    Mosca.   Yes, sir——

Corbaccio. I thought on that too. See, how he should be
The very organ to express my thoughts!

Mosca. You have not only done yourself a good——

Corbaccio. But multiplied it on my son?

Mosca.   'Tis right, sir.

Corbaccio. Still, my invention.

Mosca.   'Las sir, heaven knows,
It hath been all my study, all my care,   120
(I e'en grow grey withal) how to work things——

Corbaccio. I do conceive, sweet Mosca.

Mosca.   You are he,
For whom I labour here.

Corbaccio.   Aye, do, do, do:
I'll straight about it.

Mosca. [*Aside*]   Rook go with you, raven.

Corbaccio. I know thee honest.

Mosca. [*Aside*]   You do lie, sir——

Corbaccio.   And——

Mosca. [*Aside*] Your knowledge is no better than your ears, sir.

Corbaccio. I do not doubt, to be a father to thee.

Mosca. [*Aside*] Nor, I, to gull my brother of his blessing.

Corbaccio. I may ha' my youth restored to me, why not?

Mosca. [*Aside*] Your worship is a precious ass——

Corbaccio.   What say'st thou?   130

Mosca. I do desire your worship to make haste, sir.

Corbaccio. 'Tis done, 'tis done, I go.   [*Exit*]

Volpone. [*Leaping up*]   Oh, I shall burst;
Let out my sides, let out my sides——

Mosca.   Contain
Your flux of laughter, sir; you know, this hope
Is such a bait, it covers any hook.

Volpone. Oh, but thy working, and thy placing it!
I cannot hold; good rascal, let me kiss thee:
I never knew thee in so rare a humour.

Mosca. Alas, sir, I but do as I am taught:
Follow your grave instructions, give 'em words,   140
Pour oil into their ears, and send them hence.

Volpone. 'Tis true, 'tis true. What a rare punishment
Is avarice to itself!

Mosca.   Aye, with our help, sir.

Volpone. So many cares, so many maladies,

So many fears attending on old age,
Yea, death so often called on, as no wish
Can be more frequent with 'em; their limbs faint,
Their senses dull, their seeing, hearing, going,
All dead before them; yea, their very teeth,
Their instruments of eating, failing them——   150
Yet this is reckoned life! Nay, here was one,
Is now gone home, that wishes to live longer!
Feels not his gout nor palsy, feigns himself
Younger by scores of years, flatters his age
With confident belying it, hopes he may
With charms, like Aeson, have his youth restored;
And with these thoughts so battens, as if fate
Would be as easily cheated on as he,
And all turns air! (*Another knocks*) Who's that there now? a third?
  Mosca. Close, to your couch again; I hear his voice.   160
It is Corvino, our spruce merchant.
  Volpone. [*Lying down*]   Dead.
  Mosca. Another bout, sir, with your eyes. [*Anoints them*] Who's there?

Act I, Scene v

[*Enter Corvino*]

  Mosca. Signior Corvino! come most wished for! Oh,
How happy were you, if you knew it, now!
  Corvino. Why? what? wherein?
  Mosca.   The tardy hour is come, sir.
  Corvino. He is not dead?
  Mosca.   Not dead, sir, but as good;
He knows no man.
  Corvino.   How shall I do then?
  Mosca.   Why, sir?
  Corvino. I have brought him, here, a pearl.
  Mosca.   Perhaps he has
So much remembrance left as to know you, sir;
He still calls on you: nothing but your name
Is in his mouth. Is your pearl orient, sir?
  Corvino. Venice was never owner of the like.   10
  Volpone. Signior Corvino.

Mosca.   Hark!

Volpone.   Signior Corvino.

Mosca. He calls you; step and give it him. He's here, sir,
And he has brought you a rich pearl.

Corvino.   How do you, sir?
Tell him, it doubles the twelfth carat.

Mosca.   Sir,
He cannot understand, his hearing's gone;
And yet it comforts him, to see you——

Corvino.   Say,
I have a diamond for him, too.

Mosca.   Best show it, sir,
Put it into his hand; 'tis only there
He apprehends: he has his feeling yet.
See, how he grasps it!

Corvino.   'Las, good gentleman!   20
How pitiful the sight is!

Mosca.   Tut, forget, sir.
The weeping of an heir should still be laughter,
Under a visor.

Corvino.   Why, am I his heir?

Mosca. Sir, I am sworn, I may not show the will
Till he be dead. But here has been Corbaccio,
Here has been Voltore, here were others too,
I cannot number 'em, they were so many,
All gaping here for legacies; but I,
Taking the vantage of his naming you,
——'Signior Corvino, Signior Corvino'—— took   30
Paper, and pen, and ink, and there I asked him
Whom he would have his heir? 'Corvino.' Who
Should be executor? 'Corvino.' And,
To any question he was silent to,
I still interpreted the nods he made,
Through weakness, for consent: and sent home the others,
Nothing bequeathed them, but to cry and curse.

Corvino. Oh, my dear Mosca. (*They embrace*) Does he not perceive us?

Mosca. No more than a blind harper. He knows no man,
No face of friend nor name of any servant,   40
Who 'twas that fed him last or gave him drink;
Not those he hath begotten or brought up
Can he remember.

Corvino.   Has he children?

Mosca.   Bastards,
Some dozen or more that he begot on beggars,
Gypsies and Jews and black-moors, when he was drunk.
Knew you not that, sir? 'Tis the common fable.
The dwarf, the fool, the eunuch are all his;
He's the true father of his family,
In all, save me: but he has given 'em nothing.

   Corvino. That's well, that's well. Art sure he does not hear us?   50

   Mosca. Sure, sir? why, look you, credit your own sense.

                           [*He shouts in Volpone's ear*]

The pox approach, and add to your diseases,
If it would send you hence the sooner, sir.
For your incontinence, it hath deserved it
Throughly, and throughly, and the plague to boot.
[*To Corvino*]—— You may come near, sir—— Would you would once
   close
Those filthy eyes of yours, that flow with slime,
Like two frog-pits; and those same hanging cheeks,
Covered with hide instead of skin——nay, help, sir——
That look like frozen dish-clouts, set on end.   60

   Corvino. Or like an old smoked wall, on which the rain
Ran down in streaks.

   Mosca.   Excellent, sir, speak out;
You may be louder yet: a culverin
Dischargèd in his ear would hardly bore it.

   Corvino. His nose is like a common sewer, still running.

   Mosca. 'Tis good! and what his mouth?

   Corvino.   A very draught.

   Mosca. Oh, stop it up——

   Corvino.   By no means.

   Mosca.   'Pray you let me.
'Faith, I could stifle him rarely with a pillow,
As well as any woman that should keep him.

   Corvino. Do as you will, but I'll be gone.

   Mosca.   Be so;   70
It is your presence makes him last so long.

   Corvino. I pray you, use no violence.

   Mosca.   No, sir? why?
Why should you be thus scrupulous? 'pray you, sir.

   Corvino. Nay, at your discretion.

Mosca.   Well, good sir, be gone.

Corvino. I will not trouble him now to take my pearl?

Mosca. Puh, nor your diamond. What a needless care
Is this afflicts you? Is not all here yours?
Am not I here? whom you have made? your creature?
That owe my being to you?

Corvino.   Grateful Mosca!
Thou art my friend, my fellow, my companion,   80
My partner, and shalt share in all my fortunes.

Mosca. Excepting one.

Corvino.   What's that?

Mosca.   Your gallant wife, sir.

                                  [*Exit Corvino*]

Now, is he gone; we had no other means
To shoot him hence, but this.

Volpone.   My divine Mosca!
Thou hast today outgone thyself. (*Another knocks*) Who's there?
I will be troubled with no more. Prepare
Me music, dances, banquets, all delights;
The Turk is not more sensual in his pleasures,
Than will Volpone. [*Exit Mosca*] Let me see, a pearl!
A diamond! plate! cecchines! Good morning's purchase;   90
Why, this is better than rob churches yet,
Or fat, by eating once a month a man.

                    [*Enter Mosca*]

Who is't?

Mosca. The beauteous Lady Would-be, sir,
Wife to the English knight, Sir Politic Would-be,
——This is the style, sir, is directed me——
Hath sent to know how you have slept tonight,
And if you would be visited.

Volpone.   Not now.
Some three hours hence——

Mosca.   I told the squire so much.

Volpone. When I am high with mirth and wine; then, then.
'Fore heaven, I wonder at the desperate valour   100
Of the bold English, that they dare let loose
Their wives to all encounters!

Mosca.   Sir, this knight
Had not his name for nothing; he is politic,

And knows, howe'er his wife affect strange airs,
She hath not yet the face to be dishonest.
But had she Signior Corvino's wife's face——
    Volpone. Has she so rare a face?
    Mosca.   Oh, sir, the wonder,
The blazing star of Italy! a wench
O' the first year! a beauty ripe as harvest!
Whose skin is whiter than a swan, all over!   110
Than silver, snow, or lilies! A soft lip,
Would tempt you to eternity of kissing!
And flesh that melteth in the touch to blood!
Bright as your gold! and lovely as your gold!
    Volpone. Why had not I known this before?
    Mosca.   Alas, sir.
Myself but yesterday discovered it.
    Volpone. How might I see her?
    Mosca.   Oh, not possible;
She's kept as warily as is your gold:
Never does come abroad, never takes air,
But at a window. All her looks are sweet   120
As the first grapes or cherries, and are watched
As near as they are.
    Volpone.   I must see her——
    Mosca.   Sir,
There is a guard of ten spies thick upon her,
All his whole household: each of which is set
Upon his fellow, and have all their charge,
When he goes out, when he comes in, examined.
    Volpone. I will go see her, though but at her window.
    Mosca. In some disguise, then.
    Volpone.   That is true. I must
Maintain mine own shape, still, the same: we'll think.   [*Exeunt*]

Act II, Scene i

[*A secluded corner of the Piazza, before Corvino's house*]
[*Enter Sir Politic Would-be and Peregrine*]

    Sir Politic. Sir, to a wise man, all the world's his soil.
It is not Italy, nor France, nor Europe,
That must bound me, if my fates call me forth.

Yet, I protest, it is no salt desire
Of seeing countries, shifting a religion,
Nor any disaffection to the state
Where I was bred, and unto which I owe
My dearest plots, hath brought me out; much less
That idle, antique, stale, grey-headed project
Of knowing men's minds and manners, with Ulysses;   10
But a peculiar humour of my wife's,
Laid for this height of Venice, to observe,
To quote, to learn the language, and so forth——
I hope you travel, sir, with licence?
    Peregrine.   Yes.
    Sir Politic. I dare the safelier converse—— How long, sir,
Since you left England?
    Peregrine.   Seven weeks.
    Sir Politic.   So lately!
You ha' not been with my lord ambassador?
    Peregrine. Not yet, sir.
    Sir Politic.   'Pray you, what news, sir, vents our climate?
I heard, last night, a most strange thing reported
By some of my lord's followers, and I long   20
To hear how 'twill be seconded.
    Peregrine.   What was't, sir?
    Sir Politic. Marry, sir, of a raven, that should build
In a ship royal of the King's.
    Peregrine. [*Aside*]   This fellow
Does he gull me, trow? or is gulled?—— Your name, sir?
    Sir Politic. My name is Politic Would-be.
    Peregrine. [*Aside*]   Oh, that speaks him——
A knight, sir?
    Sir Politic. A poor knight, sir.
    Peregrine.   Your lady
Lies here in Venice for intelligence
Of tires, and fashions, and behaviour
Among the courtesans? the fine Lady Would-be?
    Sir Politic. Yes, sir, the spider and the bee oft-times   30
Suck from one flower.
    Peregrine.   Good Sir Politic!
I cry you mercy; I have heard much of you.
'Tis true, sir, of your raven.
    Sir Politic.   On your knowledge?

Peregrine. Yes, and your lion's whelping in the Tower.
Sir Politic. Another whelp!
Peregrine.   Another, sir.
Sir Politic.   Now, heaven!
What prodigies be these? The fires at Berwick!
And the new star! These things concurring, strange!
And full of omen! Saw you those meteors?
    Peregrine. I did, sir.
Sir Politic.   Fearful! Pray you sir, confirm me,
Were there three porpoises seen above the bridge,   40
As they give out?
    Peregrine.   Six, and a sturgeon, sir.
Sir Politic. I am astonished!
Peregrine.   Nay, sir, be not so;
I'll tell you a greater prodigy than these——
    Sir Politic. What should these things portend?
Peregrine.   The very day
(Let me be sure) that I put forth from London,
There was a whale discovered in the river
As high as Woolwich, that had waited there,
Few know how many months, for the subversion
Of the Stode fleet.
    Sir Politic.   Is't possible? Believe it,
'Twas either sent from Spain, or the Archdukes!   50
Spinola's whale, upon my life, my credit!
Will they not leave these projects? Worthy sir,
Some other news.
    Peregrine.   Faith, Stone, the fool, is dead,
And they do lack a tavern fool extremely.
    Sir Politic. Is Mas' Stone dead?
Peregrine.   He's dead, sir——why, I hope
You thought him not immortal? [*Aside*] Oh, this knight,
Were he well-known, would be a precious thing
To fit our English stage; he that should write
But such a fellow, should be thought to feign
Extremely, if not maliciously.
    Sir Politic.   Stone dead!   60
    Peregrine. Dead. Lord! How deeply, sir, you apprehend it!
He was no kinsman to you?
    Sir Politic.   That I know of.
Well! that same fellow was an unknown fool.

Peregrine. And yet you knew him, it seems?

Sir Politic.   I did so. Sir,
I knew him one of the most dangerous heads
Living within the state, and so I held him.

Peregrine. Indeed, sir?

Sir Politic.   While he lived, in action.
He has received weekly intelligence,
Upon my knowledge, out of the Low Countries——
For all parts of the world——in cabbages;   70
And those dispensed again to ambassadors
In oranges, musk melons, apricots,
Lemons, pome-citrons, and such-like; sometimes,
In Colchester oysters, and your Selsey cockles.

Peregrine. You make me wonder!

Sir Politic.   Sir, upon my knowledge.
Nay, I have observed him, at your public ordinary,
Take his advertisement from a traveller
(A concealed statesman) in a trencher of meat;
And instantly, before the meal was done,
Convey an answer in a toothpick.

Peregrine.   Strange!   80
How could this be, sir?

Sir Politic.   Why, the meat was cut
So like his character, and so laid as he
Must easily read the cipher.

Peregrine.   I have heard
He could not read, sir.

Sir Politic.   So 'twas given out,
In polity by those that did employ him;
But he could read, and had your languages,
And to it, as sound a noddle——

Peregrine.   I have heard, sir,
That your baboons were spies; and that they were
A kind of subtle nation, near to China.

Sir Politic. Aye, aye, your Mamuluchi. Faith, they had   90
Their hand in a French plot or two; but they
Were so extremely given to women, as
They made discovery of all; yet I
Had my advices here, on Wednesday last,
From one of their own coat; they were returned,
Made their relations, as the fashion is,

And now stand fair for fresh employment.
    Peregrine. [*Aside*]   'Heart!
This Sir Pol will be ignorant of nothing.
It seems, sir, you know all?
    Sir Politic.   Not all, sir. But
I have some general notions; I do love   100
To note, and to observe: though I live out,
Free from the active torrent, yet I'd mark
The currents and the passages of things
For mine own private use; and know the ebbs
And flows of state.
    Peregrine.   Believe it, sir, I hold
Myself in no small tie unto my fortunes
For casting me thus luckily upon you;
Whose knowledge, if your bounty equal it,
May do me great assistance in instruction
For my behaviour and my bearing, which   110
Is yet so rude and raw——
    Sir Politic.   Why, came you forth
Empty of rules for travel?
    Peregrine.   Faith, I had
Some common ones from out that vulgar grammar
Which he that cried Italian to me taught me.
    Sir Politic. Why, this it is that spoils all our brave bloods;
Trusting our hopeful gentry unto pedants——
Fellows of outside, and mere bark. You seem
To be a gentleman, of ingenuous race——
I not profess it, but my fate hath been
To be where I have been consulted with,   120
In this high kind, touching some great men's sons,
Persons of blood and honour——
    Peregrine.   Who be these, sir?

Act II, Scene ii

[*Enter Mosca and Nano disguised as mountebank's attendants;
they proceed to erect a stage*]

    Mosca. Under that window, there it must be. The same.
    Sir Politic. Fellows, to mount a bank! Did your instructor
In the dear tongues never discourse to you

Of the Italian mountebanks?
   Peregrine.   Yes, sir.
   Sir Politic.   Why,
Here shall you see one.
   Peregrine.   They are quacksalvers,
Fellows that live by venting oils and drugs?
   Sir Politic. Was that the character he gave you of them?
   Peregrine. As I remember.
   Sir Politic.   Pity his ignorance.
They are the only knowing men of Europe!
Great general scholars, excellent physicians,   10
Most admired statesmen, professed favourites,
And cabinet counsellors to the greatest princes!
The only languaged men of all the world!
   Peregrine. And I have heard they are most lewd impostors;
Made all of terms and shreds; no less beliers
Of great men's favours than their own vile medicines,
Which they will utter upon monstrous oaths——
Selling that drug for twopence, ere they part,
Which they have valued at twelve crowns before.
   Sir Politic. Sir, calumnies are answered best with silence: 20
Yourself shall judge. Who is it mounts, my friends?
   Mosca. Scoto of Mantua, sir.
   Sir Politic.   Is't he? Nay, then
I'll proudly promise, sir, you shall behold
Another man than has been phant'sied to you.
I wonder, yet, that he should mount his bank
Here in this nook, that has been wont to appear
In face of the Piazza! Here he comes.

        [*Enter Volpone as a mountebank, followed by a crowd*]

   Volpone. [*To Nano*] Mount, zany.
   Grege.   Follow, follow, follow, follow, follow.
   Sir Politic. See how the people follow him! He's a man
May write ten thousand crowns in bank here. Note,   30
Mark but his gesture: I do use to observe
The state he keeps, in getting up!
   Peregrine.   'Tis worth it, sir.
   Volpone. Most noble gentlemen, and my worthy patrons, it may seem
strange, that I, your Scoto Mantuano, who was ever wont to fix my bank
in face of the public Piazza, near the shelter of the Portico to the

Procuratìa, should now, after eight months' absence from this illustrious
city of Venice, humbly retire myself into an obscure nook of the Piazza.

Sir Politic. Did not I, now, object the same?

Peregrine.   Peace, sir.

Volpone. Let me tell you. I am not, as your Lombard proverb saith, cold
on my feet, or content to part with my commodities at a cheaper rate than   40
I accustomed: look not for it. Nor that the calumnious reports of that
impudent detractor, and shame to our profession——Alessandro Buttone, I mean——who gave out, in public, I was condemned a *'sforzato* to
the galleys, for poisoning the Cardinal Bembo's . . . cook, hath at all
attached, much less dejected me. No, no, worthy gentlemen, to tell you
true, I cannot endure to see the rabble of these ground *ciarlitani*, that
spread their cloaks on the pavement as if they meant to do feats of
activity, and then come in lamely with their mouldy tales out of
Boccaccio, like stale Tabarine, the fabulist; some of them discoursing
their travels, and of their tedious captivity in the Turks' galleys, when   50
indeed (were the truth known) they were the Christians' galleys, where
very temperately they ate bread and drunk water, as a wholesome
penance, enjoined them by their confessors, for base pilferies.

Sir Politic. Note but his bearing, and contempt of these.

Volpone. These turdy-facy-nasty-paty-lousy-fartical rogues, with one
poor groatsworth of unprepared antimony, finely wrapped up in several
'scartoccios, are able very well to kill their twenty a week, and play; yet
these meagre starved spirits, who have half-stopped the organs of their
minds with earthy oppilations, want not their favourers among your
shrivelled, salad-eating artisans, who are overjoyed that they may have   60
their ha'p'orth of physic; though it purge 'em into another world, it
makes no matter.

Sir Politic. Excellent! Ha' you heard better language, sir?

Volpone. Well, let 'em go. And gentlemen, honourable gentlemen,
know that for this time our bank, being thus removed from the clamours
of the *canaglia*, shall be the scene of pleasure and delight; for, I have
nothing to sell, little, or nothing to sell.

Sir Politic. I told you, sir, his end.

Peregrine.   You did so, sir.

Volpone. I protest, I and my six servants are not able to make of this
precious liquor so fast as it is fetched away from my lodging by gentlemen   70
of your city, strangers of the Terra Firma, worshipful merchants, aye,
and senators too, who ever since my arrival have detained me to their
uses by their splendidous liberalities. And worthily. For what avails your
rich man to have his magazines stuffed with *moscadelli* or of the purest

grape, when his physicians prescribe him, on pain of death, to drink
nothing but water, cocted with aniseeds? Oh, health! health! the blessing
of the rich! the riches of the poor! Who can buy thee at too dear a rate,
since there is no enjoying this world without thee? Be not then so sparing
of your purses, honourable gentlemen, as to abridge the natural course of
life——   80

Peregrine. You see his end?

Sir Politic.   Aye, is it not good?

Volpone. For when a humid flux or catarrh, by the mutability of air, falls
from your head into an arm, or shoulder, or any other part, take you a
ducat, or your cecchine of gold, and apply to the place affected: see what
good effect it can work. No, no, 'tis this blessed *unguento*, this rare
extraction that hath only power to disperse all malignant humours, that
proceed either of hot, cold, moist, or windy causes——

Peregrine. I would he had put in dry too.

Sir Politic.   'Pray you, observe.

Volpone. To fortify the most indigest and crude stomach, aye, were it of
one that through extreme weakness vomited blood, applying only a warm   90
napkin to the place, after the unction and fricace; for the *vertigine* in the
head, putting but a drop into your nostrils, likewise, behind the ears, a
most sovereign and approved remedy; the *mal caduco*, cramps, convul-
sions, paralyses, epilepsies, *tremor cordia*, retired nerves, ill vapours of the
spleen, stoppings of the liver, the stone, the strangury, *hernia ventosa*,
iliaca passio; stops a *disenteria* immediately; easeth the torsion of the small
guts; and cures *melancolia hypocondriaca*, being taken and applied according to my printed receipt. (*Pointing to his bill and his glass*) For this is the
physician, this the medicine; this counsels, this cures; this gives the
direction, this works the effect; and——in sum——both together may   100
be termed an abstract of the theoric and practice in the Aesculapian art.
'Twill cost you eight crowns. And Zan Fritada, 'pray thee sing a verse,
extempore, in honour of it.

Sir Politic. How do you like him, sir?

Peregrine.   Most strangely, I!

Sir Politic. Is not his language rare?

Peregrine.   But alchemy,
I never heard the like; or Broughton's books.

[*Nano sings*]

Song

Had old Hippocrates, or Galen,
(That to their books put medicines all in)

But known this secret, they had never
(Of which they will be guilty ever)   110
Been murderers of so much paper,
Or wasted many a hurtless taper:
No Indian drug had e'er been famèd,
Tobacco, sassafras not namèd;
Ne yet, of guacum one small stick, sir,
Nor Raymond Lully's great elixir.
Ne had been known the Danish Gonswart,
Or Paracelsus, with his long sword.

Peregrine. All this yet will not do: eight crowns is high.

Volpone. No more. Gentlemen, if I had but time to discourse to you the   120
miraculous effects of this my oil, surnamed *oglio del Scoto*, with the
countless catalogue of those I have cured of the aforesaid, and many
more diseases; the patents and privileges of all the princes and com-
monwealths of Christendom; or but the depositions of those that
appeared on my part, before the signiory of the Sanità, and most learned
college of physicians; where I was authorized, upon notice taken of the
admirable virtues of my medicaments and mine own excellency in matter
of rare and unknown secrets, not only to disperse them publicly in this
famous city, but in all the territories that happily joy under the government of the most pious and magnificent states of Italy. But may some   130
other gallant fellow say, Oh, there be divers that make profession to have
as good, and as experimented receipts, as yours. Indeed, very many have
essayed, like apes in imitation of that, which is really and essentially in
me, to make of this oil; bestowed great cost in furnaces, stills, alembics,
continual fires, and preparation of the ingredients——as indeed there
goes to it six hundred several simples, besides some quantity of human
fat for the conglutination, which we buy of the anatomists——but when
these practitioners come to the last decoction: blow, blow, puff, puff, and
all flies in *fumo*. Ha, ha, ha! Poor wretches! I rather pity their folly and
indiscretion than their loss of time and money; for those may be   140
recovered by industry, but to be a fool born is a disease incurable. For
myself, I always from my youth have endeavoured to get the rarest
secrets, and book them, either in exchange, or for money; I spared nor
cost nor labour, where anything was worthy to be learned. And
gentlemen, honourable gentlemen, I will undertake, by virtue of chemical art, out of the honourable hat that covers your head, to extract the
four elements——that is to say, the fire, air, water, and earth——and
return you your felt without burn or stain. For whilst others have been at

the *balloo,* I have been at my book; and am now past the craggy paths of
study, and come to the flowery plains of honour and reputation.   150
Sir Politic. I do assure you, sir, that is his aim.
Volpone. But to our price.
Peregrine.   And that withal, Sir Pol.
Volpone. You all know, honourable gentlemen, I never valued this
ampulla, or vial, at less than eight crowns, but for this time I am content to
be deprived of it for six; six crowns is the price; and less in courtesy, I
know you cannot offer me: take it, or leave it, howsoever; both it and I am
at your service. I ask you not as the value of the thing, for then I should
demand of you a thousand crowns, so the Cardinals Montalto, Fernese,
the great duke of Tuscany, my gossip, with divers other princes have
given me; but I despise money. Only to show my affection to you,   160
honourable gentlemen, and your illustrious state here, I have neglected
the messages of these princes, mine own offices, framed my journey
hither only to present you with the fruits of my travels. Tune your voices
once more to the touch of your instruments, and give the honourable
assembly some delightful recreation.
Peregrine. What monstrous and most painful circumstance
Is here, to get some three or four gazets!
Some threepence, i' the whole, for that 'twill come to.

Song
You that would last long, list to my song,
Make no more coil, but buy of this oil.   170
Would you be ever fair? and young?
Stout of teeth? and strong of tongue?
Tart of palate? quick of ear?
Sharp of sight? of nostril clear?
Moist of hand? and light of foot?
(Or I will come nearer to't)
Would you live free from all diseases?
Do the act your mistress pleases;
Yet fright all aches from your bones?
Here's a medicine for the nones.   180

Volpone. Well, I am in a humour, at this time, to make a present of the
small quantity my coffer contains: to the rich, in courtesy, and to the
poor, for God's sake. Wherefore, now mark: I asked you six crowns; and
six crowns, at other times, you have paid me; you shall not give me six
crowns, nor five, nor four, nor three, nor two, nor one; nor half a ducat;

no, nor a *moccenigo*: six . . . pence it will cost you, or six hundred pound—
—expect no lower price, for by the banner of my front, I will not bate a
bagatine, that I will have only a pledge of your loves, to carry something
from amongst you, to show I am not contemned by you. Therefore now,
toss your handkerchiefs, cheerfully, cheerfully; and be advertised, that   190
the first heroic spirit that deigns to grace me with a handkerchief, I will
give it a little remembrance of something beside, shall please it better
than if I had presented it with a double pistolet.

    Peregrine. Will you be that heroic spark, Sir Pol?
                     (*Celia at the window throws down her handkerchief*)
Oh, see! The window has prevented you.

    Volpone. Lady, I kiss your bounty: and for this timely grace you have
done your poor Scoto of Mantua, I will return you, over and above my oil,
a secret of that high and inestimable nature, shall make you for ever
enamoured on that minute wherein your eye first descended on so mean,
yet not altogether to be despised, an object. Here is a powder concealed   200
in this paper, of which, if I should speak to the worth, nine thousand
volumes were but as one page, that page as a line, that line as a word: so
short is this pilgrimage of man (which some call life) to the expressing of
it. Would I reflect on the price? Why, the whole world were but as an
empire, that empire as a province, that province as a bank, that bank as a
private purse, to the purchase of it. I will only tell you: it is the powder
that made Venus a goddess——given her by Apollo——that kept her
perpetually young, cleared her wrinkles, firmed her gums, filled her skin,
coloured her hair; from her, derived to Helen, and at the sack of Troy,
unfortunately, lost; till now, in this our age, it was as happily recovered by   210
a studious antiquary out of some ruins of Asia, who sent a moiety of it to
the court of France——but much sophisticated——wherewith the
ladies there now colour their hair. The rest, at this present, remains with
me, extracted to a quintessence: so that wherever it but touches, in youth
it perpetually preserves, in age restores the complexion; seats your teeth,
did they dance like virginal jacks, firm as a wall; makes them white as
ivory, that were black as——

Act II, Scene iii

[*Enter Corvino*]

    Corvino. Spite o' the devil, and my shame! Come down here,
                  (*He beats away the mountebank, etc.*)
Come down! No house but mine to make your scene?

Signior Flaminio, will you down, sir? down?
What, is my wife your Franciscina, sir?
No windows on the whole Piazza here
To make your properties, but mine? but mine?
Heart! ere tomorrow I shall be new-christened,
And called the *Pantalone di besogniosi*
About the town.   [*Exit*]
  Peregrine.   What should this mean, Sir Pol?
  Sir Politic. Some trick of state, believe it. I will home.   10
  Peregrine. It may be some design on you.
  Sir Politic.   I know not.
I'll stand upon my guard.
  Peregrine.   It is your best, sir.
  Sir Politic. This three weeks, all my advices, all my letters,
They have been intercepted.
  Peregrine.   Indeed, sir?
Best have a care.
  Sir Politic.   Nay, so I will.
  Peregrine. [*Aside*]   This knight,
I may not lose him, for my mirth, till night.   [*Exeunt*]

Act II, Scene iv

[Enter Volpone and Mosca]

  Volpone. Oh, I am wounded!
  Mosca.   Where, sir?
  Volpone.   Not without;
Those blows were nothing, I could bear them ever.
But angry Cupid, bolting from her eyes,
Hath shot himself into me like a flame,
Where now he flings about his burning heat,
As in a furnace an ambitious fire,
Whose vent is stopped. The fight is all within me.
I cannot live, except thou help me, Mosca;
My liver melts, and I, without the hope
Of some soft air from her refreshing breath,   10
Am but a heap of cinders.
  Mosca.   'Las, good sir!
Would you had never seen her.

Volpone.   Nay, would thou
Hadst never told me of her.
   Mosca.   Sir, 'tis true;
I do confess, I was unfortunate,
And you unhappy; but I'm bound in conscience,
No less than duty, to effect my best
To your release of torment, and I will, sir.
   Volpone. Dear Mosca, shall I hope?
   Mosca.   Sir, more than dear,
I will not bid you to despair of aught
Within a human compass.
   Volpone.   Oh, there spoke   20
My better angel. Mosca, take my keys,
Gold, plate, and jewels, all's at thy devotion;
Employ them how thou wilt; nay, coin me, too,
So thou in this but crown my longings——Mosca?
   Mosca. Use but your patience.
   Volpone.   So I have.
   Mosca.   I doubt not
To bring success to your desires.
   Volpone.   Nay, then,
I not repent me of my late disguise.
   Mosca. If you can horn him, sir, you need not.
   Volpone.   True:
Besides, I never meant him for my heir.
Is not the colour o' my beard and eyebrows   30
To make me known?
   Mosca.   No jot.
   Volpone.   I did it well.
   Mosca. So well, would I could follow you in mine,
With half the happiness; and yet I would
Escape your epilogue.
   Volpone.   But, were they gulled
With a belief, that I was Scoto?
   Mosca.   Sir,
Scoto himself could hardly have distinguished!
I have not time to flatter you now, we'll part:
And, as I prosper, so applaud my art.   [*Exeunt*]

Act II, Scene v

[Corvino's house]

[Enter Corvino and Celia]

Corvino. Death of mine honour, with the city's fool?
A juggling, tooth-drawing, prating mountebank?
And at a public window? where, whilst he,
With his strained action and his dole of faces,
To his drug-lecture draws your itching ears,
A crew of old, unmarried, noted lechers
Stood leering up, like satyrs; and you smile,
Most graciously! and fan your favours forth
To give your hot spectators satisfaction!
What, was your mountebank their call? their whistle?   10
Or were you enamoured on his copper rings?
His saffron jewel with the toadstone in it?
Or his embroidered suit with the cope-stitch,
Made of a hearse-cloth? Or his old tilt-feather?
Or his starched beard? Well! you shall have him, yes.
He shall come home and minister unto you
The fricace for the mother. Or, let me see,
I think you'd rather mount? would you not mount?
Why, if you'll mount, you may; yes truly, you may:
And so you may be seen, down to the foot.   20
Get you a cithern, lady vanity,
And be a dealer with the virtuous man;
Make one——I'll but protest myself a cuckold,
And save your dowry. I am a Dutchman, I!
For if you thought me an Italian,
You would be damned ere you did this, you whore;
Thou'ldst tremble, to imagine that the murder
Of father, mother, brother, all thy race,
Should follow, as the subject of my justice!
    Celia. Good sir, have patience!
    Corvino.   What couldst thou propose   30
Less to thyself than in this heat of wrath,
And stung with my dishonour, I should strike *[Taking his sword]*
This steel into thee, with as many stabs
As thou wert gazed upon with goatish eyes?
    Celia. Alas, sir, be appeased! I could not think

My being at the window should more now
Move your impatience than at other times.
   Corvino. No? not to seek and entertain a parley
With a known knave? before a multitude?
You were an actor, with your handkerchief!   40
Which he, most sweetly, kissed in the receipt,
And might (no doubt) return it with a letter,
And point the place where you might meet: your sister's,
Your mother's, or your aunt's might serve the turn.
   Celia. Why, dear sir, when do I make these excuses?
Or ever stir abroad, but to the church?
And that so seldom——
   Corvino.   Well, it shall be less;
And thy restraint before was liberty
To what I now decree: and therefore, mark me.
First, I will have this bawdy light dammed up;   50
And till it be done, some two or three yards off
I'll chalk a line, o'er which, if thou but chance
To set thy desperate foot, more hell, more horror,
More wild, remorseless rage shall seize on thee
Than on a conjurer that had heedless left
His circle's safety ere his devil was laid.
Then, here's a lock which I will hang upon thee;
And now I think on't, I will keep thee backwards:
Thy lodging shall be backwards, thy walks backwards,
Thy prospect——all be backwards; and no pleasure,   60
That thou shalt know, but backwards. Nay, since you force
My honest nature, know it is your own
Being too open makes me use you thus.
Since you will not contain your subtle nostrils
In a sweet room, but they must snuff the air
Of rank and sweaty passengers——(*Knock within*) One knocks.
Away, and be not seen, pain of thy life;
Not look toward the window: if thou dost——
Nay stay, hear this——let me not prosper, whore,
But I will make thee an anatomy,   70
Dissect thee mine own self, and read a lecture
Upon thee to the city and in public.
Away! [*Exit Celia*] Who's there?
                [*Enter Servitore*]
   Servitore. 'Tis Signior Mosca, sir.

Act II, Scene vi

Corvino. Let him come in, his master's dead. There's yet
Some good to help the bad.

[*Enter Mosca*]

My Mosca, welcome!
I guess your news.
   Mosca.   I fear you cannot, sir.
   Corvino. Is't not his death?
   Mosca.   Rather the contrary.
   Corvino. Not his recovery?
   Mosca.   Yes, sir.
   Corvino.   I am cursed,
I am bewitched, my crosses meet to vex me.
How? how? how? how?
   Mosca.   Why, sir, with Scoto's oil!
Corbaccio and Voltore brought of it,
Whilst I was busy in an inner room——
   Corvino. Death! that damned mountebank! But for the law,   10
Now I could kill the rascal; it cannot be
His oil should have that virtue. Ha' not I
Known him a common rogue, come fiddling in
To the *osteria* with a tumbling whore,
And when he has done all his forced tricks, been glad
Of a poor spoonful of dead wine, with flies in it?
It cannot be. All his ingredients
Are a sheep's gall, a roasted bitch's marrow,
Some few sod earwigs, pounded caterpillars,
A little capon's grease, and fasting spittle: 20
I know 'em to a dram.
   Mosca.   I know not, sir.
But some on't, there, they poured into his ears,
Some in his nostrils, and recovered him;
Applying but the fricace.
   Corvino.   Pox o' that fricace!
   Mosca. And since, to seem the more officious,
And flattering of his health, there they have had,
At extreme fees, the college of physicians
Consulting on him, how they might restore him:

Where one would have a cataplasm of spices,
Another, a flayed ape clapped to his breast, 30
A third would ha' it a dog, a fourth an oil
With wild cat's skins; at last, they all resolved
That to preserve him was no other means
But some young woman must be straight sought out,
Lusty, and full of juice, to sleep by him;
And to this service (most unhappily,
And most unwillingly) am I now employed,
Which here I thought to pre-acquaint you with,
For your advice, since it concerns you most,
Because, I would not do that thing might cross 40
Your ends, on whom I have my whole dependence, sir;
Yet, if I do it not, they may delate
My slackness to my patron, work me out
Of his opinion; and there all your hopes,
Ventures, or whatsoever, are all frustrate.
I do but tell you, sir. Besides, they are all
Now striving, who shall first present him. Therefore——
I could entreat you, briefly, conclude somewhat:
Prevent 'em if you can.
    Corvino.   Death to my hopes!
This is my villainous fortune! Best to hire 50
Some common courtesan?
    Mosca.   Aye, I thought on that, sir.
But they are all so subtle, full of art,
And age again doting, and flexible,
So as——I cannot tell——we may perchance
Light on a quean, may cheat us all.
    Corvino.   'Tis true.
    Mosca. No, no; it must be one that has no tricks, sir,
Some simple thing, a creature, made unto it;
Some wench you may command. Ha' you no kinswoman?
God's so—— Think, think, think, think, think, think, think, sir.
One o' the doctors offered there his daughter. 60
    Corvino. How!
    Mosca.   Yes, Signior Lupo, the physician.
    Corvino. His daughter?
    Mosca.   And a virgin, sir. Why? Alas
He knows the state of's body, what it is;
That naught can warm his blood, sir, but a fever;

Nor any incantation raise his spirit;
A long forgetfulness hath seized that part.
Besides, sir, who shall know it? some one, or two——
    Corvino. I pray thee give me leave. [*He walks aside*] If any man
But I had had this luck—— The thing, in itself,
I know, is nothing—— Wherefore should not I   70
As well command my blood and my affections
As this dull doctor? In the point of honour,
The cases are all one of wife and daughter.
    Mosca. [*Aside*] I hear him coming.
    Corvino.   She shall do't; 'tis done.
Slight, if this doctor, who is not engaged,
Unless it be for his counsel (which is nothing)
Offer his daughter, what should I, that am
So deeply in? I will prevent him——wretch!
Covetous wretch! Mosca, I have determined.
    Mosca. How, sir?
    Corvino.   We'll make all sure. The party you wot of   80
Shall be mine own wife, Mosca.
    Mosca.   Sir, the thing
(But that I would not seem to counsel you)
I should have motioned to you at the first:
And, make your count, you have cut all their throats.
Why, 'tis directly taking a possession!
And in his next fit we may let him go.
'Tis but to pull the pillow from his head,
And he is throttled; it had been done before,
But for your scrupulous doubts.
    Corvino.   Aye, a plague on't,
My conscience fools my wit. Well, I'll be brief,   90
And so be thou, lest they should be before us;
Go home, prepare him, tell him with what zeal
And willingness I do it; swear it was
On the first hearing (as thou mayest do, truly)
Mine own free motion.
    Mosca.   Sir, I warrant you,
I'll so possess him with it, that the rest
Of his starved clients shall be banished, all;
And only you received. But come not, sir,
Until I send, for I have something else
To ripen, for your good——you must not know it.   100

Corvino. But do not you forget to send, now.
Mosca.   Fear not.   [*Exit*]

Act II, Scene vii

Corvino. Where are you, wife? My Celia? Wife?

[*Enter Celia*]

                                    What, blubbering?
Come, dry those tears. I think thou thought'st me in earnest?
Ha? By this light, I talked so but to try thee.
Methinks the lightness of the occasion
Should ha' confirmed thee. Come, I am not jealous.
    Celia. No?
    Corvino.   Faith, I am not, I, nor never was;
It is a poor, unprofitable humour.
Do not I know, if women have a will,
They'll do 'gainst all the watches o' the world?
And that the fiercest spies are tamed with gold?   10
Tut, I am confident in thee, thou shalt see it;
And see, I'll give thee cause too, to believe it.
Come, kiss me. Go, and make thee ready straight
In all thy best attire, thy choicest jewels,
Put 'em all on, and with 'em thy best looks;
We are invited to a solemn feast
At old Volpone's, where it shall appear
How far I am free from jealousy or fear.   [*Exeunt*]

Act III, Scene i

[*A street*]

[*Enter Mosca*]

    Mosca. I fear I shall begin to grow in love
With my dear self, and my most prosperous parts,
They do so spring and burgeon; I can feel
A whimsy i' my blood: I know not how,
Success hath made me wanton. I could skip
Out of my skin now, like a subtle snake,

I am so limber. Oh! your parasite
Is a most precious thing, dropped from above,
Not bred 'mongst clods and clot-poles here on earth.
I muse the mystery was not made a science,   10
It is so liberally professed! Almost
All the wise world is little else in nature
But parasites, or sub-parasites. And yet,
I mean not those that have your bare town-art,
To know who's fit to feed 'em; have no house,
No family, no care, and therefore mould
Tales for men's ears, to bait that sense; or get
Kitchen-invention, and some stale receipts
To please the belly and the groin; nor those,
With their court-dog-tricks, that can fawn and fleer, 20
Make their revénue out of legs and faces,
Echo my lord, and lick away a moth:
But your fine, elegant rascal, that can rise
And stoop, almost together, like an arrow;
Shoot through the air as nimbly as a star;
Turn short, as doth a swallow; and be here,
And there, and here, and yonder, all at once;
Present to any humour, all occasion;
And change a visor swifter than a thought!
This is the creature had the art born with him; 30
Toils not to learn it, but doth practise it
Out of most excellent nature; and such sparks
Are the true parasites, others but their zanies.

Act III, Scene ii

[*Enter Bonario*]

 Mosca. Who's this? Bonario? old Corbaccio's son?
The person I was bound to seek. Fair sir,
You are happ'ly met.
  Bonario.   That cannot be, by thee.
 Mosca. Why, sir?
  Bonario.   Nay, 'pray thee know thy way, and leave me:
I would be loath to interchange discourse
With such a mate as thou art.

Mosca.   Courteous sir,
Scorn not my poverty.
    Bonario.   Not I, by heaven;
But thou shalt give me leave to hate thy baseness.
    Mosca. Baseness?
    Bonario.   Aye, answer me, is not thy sloth
Sufficient argument? thy flattery?   10
Thy means of feeding?
    Mosca.   Heaven, be good to me!
These imputations are too common, sir,
And easily stuck on virtue when she's poor;
You are unequal to me, and howe'er
Your sentence may be righteous, yet you are not,
That ere you know me, thus proceed in censure;
St Mark bear witness 'gainst you, 'tis inhuman. [*Weeps*]
    Bonario. [*Aside*] What? does he weep? the sign is soft and good!
I do repent me that I was so harsh.
    Mosca. 'Tis true that, swayed by strong necessity,   20
I am enforced to eat my careful bread
With too much obsequy; 'tis true, beside,
That I am fain to spin mine own poor raiment,
Out of my mere observance, being not born
To a free fortune; but that I have done
Base offices, in rending friends asunder,
Dividing families, betraying counsels,
Whispering false lies, or mining men with praises,
Trained their credulity with perjuries,
Corrupted chastity, or am in love   30
With mine own tender ease, but would not rather
Prove the most rugged and laborious course,
That might redeem my present estimation——
Let me here perish, in all hope of goodness.
    Bonario. [*Aside*] This cannot be a personated passion!
I was to blame, so to mistake thy nature;
'Pray thee forgive me, and speak out thy business.
    Mosca. Sir, it concerns you; and though I may seem
At first to make a main offence in manners,
And in my gratitude unto my master,   40
Yet, for the pure love which I bear all right,
And hatred of the wrong, I must reveal it.
This very hour your father is in purpose

To disinherit you——
   Bonario.   How!
   Mosca.   And thrust you forth,
As a mere stranger to his blood; 'tis true, sir.
The work no way engageth me, but as
I claim an interest in the general state
Of goodness and true virtue, which I hear
To abound in you; and, for which mere respect,
Without a second aim, sir, I have done it.   50
   Bonario. This tale hath lost thee much of the late trust
Thou hadst with me; it is impossible.
I know not how to lend it any thought
My father should be so unnatural.
   Mosca. It is a confidence that well becomes
Your piety; and formed, no doubt, it is
From your own simple innocence, which makes
Your wrong more monstrous and abhorred. But sir,
I now will tell you more. This very minute,
It is, or will be doing; and, if you   60
Shall be but pleased to go with me, I'll bring you,
(I dare not say where you shall see, but) where
Your ear shall be a witness of the deed;
Hear yourself written bastard; and professed
The common issue of the earth.
   Bonario.   I'm 'mazed!
   Mosca. Sir, if I do it not, draw your just sword,
And score your vengeance on my front and face;
Mark me your villain. You have too much wrong,
And I do suffer for you, sir. My heart
Weeps blood, in anguish——
   Bonario.   Lead. I follow thee.   [*Exeunt*] 70

Act III, Scene iii

[*Volpone's house*]

[*Enter Volpone*]

   Volpone. Mosca stays long, methinks. Bring forth your sports
And help to make the wretched time more sweet.

      [*Enter Nano, Androgyno, Castrone*]

Nano. Dwarf, fool, and eunuch, well met here we be.
    A question it were now, whether of us three,
Being, all, the known delicates of a rich man,
    In pleasing him, claim the precedency can?
    Castrone. I claim for myself.
    Androgyno.   And so doth the fool.
    Nano. 'Tis foolish indeed; let me set you both to school.
First, for your dwarf, he's little, and witty,
    And everything, as it is little, is pretty;   10
Else, why do men say to a creature of my shape,
    So soon as they see him, it's a pretty little ape?
And why a pretty ape? But for pleasing imitation
    Of greater men's action, in a ridiculous fashion.
Beside, this feat body of mine doth not crave
    Half the meat, drink, and cloth, one of your bulks will have.
Admit, your fool's face be the mother of laughter,
    Yet, for his brain, it must always come after:
And though that do feed him, it's a pitiful case,
    His body is beholding to such a bad face.   (*One knocks*) 20
    Volpone. Who's there? My couch, away, look, Nano, see:
Give me my caps, first——go, enquire. [*Exeunt Nano, Androgyno,*
                        Castrone; Volpone lies down] Now, Cupid
Send it be Mosca, and with fair return.

                  [*Enter Nano*]

    Nano. It is the beauteous madam——
    Volpone.   Would-be——is it?
    Nano. The same.
    Volpone.   Now, torment on me; squire her in:
For she will enter, or dwell here for ever.
Nay, quickly, that my fit were past. [*Exit Nano*] I fear
A second hell too, that my loathing this
Will quite expel my appetite to the other;
Would she were taking, now, her tedious leave.   30
Lord, how it threats me, what I am to suffer!

Act III, Scene iv

[Enter Nano, Lady Politic Would-be]

Lady Would-be. I thank you, good sir. 'Pray you signify
Unto your patron I am here.——This band
Shows not my neck enough——I trouble you, sir,
Let me request you, bid one of my women
Come hither to me——in good faith, I am dressed
Most favourably today. It is no matter,
'Tis well enough.

[Enter 1st Woman]

           Look, see, these petulant things!
How they have done this!
    Volpone. [Aside]   I do feel the fever
Entering in at mine ears; oh, for a charm
To fright it hence.
    Lady Would-be.   Come nearer. Is this curl   10
In his right place? or this? why is this higher
Than all the rest? you ha' not washed your eyes yet?
Or do they not stand even i' your head?
Where's your fellow? call her.   *[Exit 1st Woman]*
    Nano. [Aside]   Now, St Mark
Deliver us! Anon, she'll beat her women
Because her nose is red.

[Enter 1st and 2nd Women]

    Lady Would-be.   I pray you, view
This tire, forsooth. Are all things apt, or no?
    Woman. One hair a little, here, sticks out, forsooth.
    Lady Would-be. Does't so forsooth? and where was your dear sight
When it did so, forsooth? what now? bird-eyed?   20
And you, too? 'pray you both approach, and mend it.
Now, by that light, I muse you're not ashamed!
I, that have preached these things so oft unto you,
Read you the principles, argued all the grounds,
Disputed every fitness, every grace,
Called you to counsel of so frequent dressings——
    Nano. [Aside] More carefully than of your fame or honour.
    Lady Would-be. Made you acquainted what an ample dowry
The knowledge of these things would be unto you,

Able, alone, to get you noble husbands   30
At your return: and you, thus, to neglect it?
Besides, you seeing what a curious nation
The Italians are, what will they say of me?
The English lady cannot dress herself;
Here's a fine imputation to our country!
Well, go your ways, and stay i' the next room.
This fucus was too coarse too, it's no matter.
Good sir, you'll give 'em entertainément?   [*Exeunt Nano, Women*]
    Volpone. [*Aside*] The storm comes toward me.
    Lady Would-be.   How does my Volp?
    Volpone. Troubled with noise, I cannot sleep; I dreamt   40
That a strange fury entered now my house,
And with the dreadful tempest of her breath,
Did cleave my roof asunder.
    Lady Would-be.   Believe me, and I
Had the most fearful dream, could I remember it——
    Volpone. [*Aside*] Out on my fate; I ha' given her the occasion
How to torment me: she will tell me hers.
    Lady Would-be. Methought, the golden mediocrity
Polite, and delicate——
    Volpone.   Oh, if you do love me,
No more; I sweat and suffer at the mention
Of any dream; feel, how I tremble yet.   50
    Lady Would-be. Alas, good soul! the passion of the heart.
Seed-pearl were good now, boiled with syrup of apples,
Tincture of gold, and coral, citron-pills,
Your elecampane root, myrobalans——
    Volpone. [*Aside*] Ay me, I have ta'en a grasshopper by the wing.
    Lady Would-be. Burnt silk, and amber, you have muscadel
Good i' the house——
    Volpone.   You will not drink, and part?
    Lady Would-be. No, fear not that. I doubt we shall not get
Some English saffron——half a dram would serve——
Your sixteen cloves, a little musk, dried mints,   60
Bugloss, and barley-meal——
    Volpone. [*Aside*]   She's in again,
Before I feigned diseases, now I have one.
    Lady Would-be. And these applied, with a right scarlet-cloth——
    Volpone. [*Aside*] Another flood of words! a very torrent!
    Lady Would-be. Shall I, sir, make you a poultice?

Volpone.   No, no, no;
I'm very well; you need prescribe no more.
    Lady Would-be. I have, a little, studied physic; but, now,
I'm all for music; save, i' the forenoons,
An hour or two for painting. I would have
A lady, indeed, to have all letters and arts,   70
Be able to discourse, to write, to paint,
But principal (as Plato holds) your music
(And so does wise Pythagoras, I take it)
Is your true rapture; when there is concent
In face, in voice, and clothes; and is, indeed,
Our sex's chiefest ornament.
    Volpone.   The poet,
As old in time as Plato, and as knowing,
Says that your highest female grace is silence.
    Lady Would-be. Which o' your poets? Petrarch? or Tasso? or Dante?
Guerrini? Ariosto? Aretine?   80
Cieco di Hadria? I have read them all.
    Volpone. [Aside] Is everything a cause to my destruction?
    Lady Would-be. I think I ha' two or three of 'em about me.
    Volpone. [Aside] The sun, the sea will sooner both stand still,
Than her eternal tongue! nothing can 'scape it.
    Lady Would-be. Here's *Pastor Fido*——
    Volpone. [Aside]   Profess obstinate silence,
That's now my safest.
    Lady Would-be.   All our English writers,
I mean such as are happy in the Italian,
Will deign to steal out of this author mainly;
Almost as much as from Montaignié;   90
He has so modern and facile a vein,
Fitting the time, and catching the court-ear.
Your Petrarch is more passionate, yet he,
In days of sonneting, trusted 'em with much.
Dante is hard, and few can understand him.
But for a desperate wit, there's Aretine!
Only, his pictures are a little obscene——
You mark me not?
    Volpone.   Alas, my mind's perturbed.
    Lady Would-be. Why, in such cases, we must cure ourselves,
Make use of our philosophy——
    Volpone.   O'y me.   100

Lady Would-be. And as we find our passions do rebel,
Encounter 'em with reason; or divert 'em,
By giving scope unto some other humour
Of lesser danger; as in politic bodies,
There's nothing more doth overwhelm the judgement,
And clouds the understanding, than too much
Settling and fixing, and (as 'twere) subsiding
Upon one object. For the incorporating
Of these same outward things into that part
Which we call mental, leaves some certain faeces   110
That stop the organs, and, as Plato says,
Assassinates our knowledge.
    Volpone. [*Aside*]   Now the spirit
Of patience help me!
    Lady Would-be.   Come, in faith, I must
Visit you more a-days, and make you well;
Laugh, and be lusty.
    Volpone. [*Aside*]   My good angel save me.
    Lady Would-be. There was but one sole man in all the world
With whom I ere could sympathize; and he
Would lie you often, three, four hours together,
To hear me speak and be, sometime, so rapt,
As he would answer me quite from the purpose,   120
Like you, and you are like him, just. I'll discourse
And't be but only, sir, to bring you asleep,
How we did spend our time and loves together
For some six years.
    Volpone.   Oh, oh, oh, oh, oh, oh.
    Lady Would-be. For we were *coaetanei*, and brought up——
    Volpone. [*Aside*] Some power, some fate, some fortune rescue me!

Act III, Scene v

[*Enter Mosca*]

    Mosca. God save you, madam.
    Lady Would-be.   Good sir.
    Volpone.   Mosca! Welcome,
[*Aside*] Welcome to my redemption!
    Mosca. [*Aside*]   Why, sir?

Volpone. [*Aside*]   Oh,
Rid me of this my torture, quickly, there;
My madam with the everlasting voice:
The bells in time of pestilence ne'er made
Like noise, or were in that perpetual motion;
The cockpit comes not near it. All my house,
But now, steamed like a bath with her thick breath.
A lawyer could not have been heard; nor scarce
Another woman, such a hail of words   10
She has let fall. For hell's sake, rid her hence.
  Mosca. [*Aside*] Has she presented?
  Volpone. [*Aside*]   Oh, I do not care,
I'll take her absence upon any price,
With any loss.
  Mosca.   Madam——
  Lady Would-be.   I ha' brought your patron
A toy, a cap here, of mine own work——
  Mosca.   'Tis well,
I had forgot to tell you, I saw your knight,
Where you'd little think it——
  Lady Would-be.   Where?
  Mosca.   Marry,
Where yet, if you make haste, you may apprehend him,
Rowing upon the water in a gondola,   20
With the most cunning courtesan of Venice.
  Lady Would-be. Is't true?
  Mosca.   Pursue 'em, and believe your eyes;
Leave me to make your gift. [*Exit Lady Would-be*] I knew 'twould take.
For lightly, they that use themselves most licence,
Are still most jealous.
  Volpone.   Mosca, hearty thanks,
For thy quick fiction, and delivery of me.
Now, to my hopes, what sayest thou?

                [*Enter Lady Would-be*]

  Lady Would-be.   But, do you hear, sir?——
  Volpone. [*Aside*] Again; I fear a paroxysm.
  Lady Would-be.   Which way
Rowed they together?
  Mosca.   Toward the Rialto.
  Lady Would-be. I pray you lend me your dwarf.

Mosca.   I pray you, take him.

                             [*Exit Lady Would-be*]

Your hopes, sir, are like happy blossoms, fair,   30
And promise timely fruit, if you will stay
But the maturing; keep you at your couch,
Corbaccio will arrive straight, with the will:
When he is gone, I'll tell you more.   [*Exit*]
    Volpone.   My blood,
My spirits are returned; I am alive:
And like your wanton gamester at primero,
Whose thought had whispered to him, not go less,
Methinks I lie, and draw——for an encounter.

Act III, Scene vi

[*Enter Mosca, leading Bonario to a hiding-place*]

   Mosca. Sir, here concealed, you may hear all. But 'pray you
Have patience, sir; (*One knocks*) the same's your father, knocks;
I am compelled to leave you.
    Bonario.   Do so.   [*Exit Mosca*]
                        Yet
Cannot my thought imagine this a truth.

Act III, Scene vii

[*Mosca opens door to Corvino and Celia*]

   Mosca. Death on me! you are come too soon, what meant you?
Did not I say I would send?
    Corvino.   Yes, but I feared
You might forget it, and then they prevent us.
    Mosca. [*Aside*] Prevent? did e'er man haste so for his horns?
A courtier would not ply it so, for a place.
Well, now there's no helping it, stay here;
I'll presently return.
    Corvino.   Where are you, Celia?
You know not wherefore I have brought you hither?
   Celia. Not well, except you told me.
    Corvino.   Now I will:

Hark hither.   *[They talk apart]*

    Mosca. (To Bonario) Sir, your father hath sent word,   10
It will be half an hour ere he come;
And therefore, if you please to walk the while
Into that gallery——at the upper end,
There are some books to entertain the time;
And I'll take care no man shall come unto you, sir.
    Bonario. Yes, I will stay there. *[Aside]* I do doubt this fellow.   *[Exit]*
    Mosca. There, he is far enough; he can hear nothing;
And for his father, I can keep him off.
    Corvino. Nay, now, there is no starting back; and therefore,
Resolve upon it: I have so decreed.   20
It must be done. Nor would I move it afore,
Because I would avoid all shifts and tricks,
That might deny me.
    Celia.   Sir, let me beseech you,
Affect not these strange trials; if you doubt
My chastity, why lock me up, for ever:
Make me the heir of darkness. Let me live
Where I may please your fears, if not your trust.
    Corvino. Believe it, I have no such humour, I.
All that I speak, I mean; yet I am not mad:
Not horn-mad, see you? Go to, show yourself   30
Obedient, and a wife.
    Celia.   O heaven!
    Corvino.   I say it,
Do so.
    Celia. Was this the train?
    Corvino.   I've told you reasons;
What the physicians have set down; how much
It may concern me; what my engagements are;
My means; and the necessity of those means,
For my recovery: wherefore, if you be
Loyal, and mine, be won, respect my venture.
    Celia. Before your honour?
    Corvino.   Honour? tut, a breath;
There's no such thing in nature: a mere term
Invented to awe fools. What is my gold   40
The worse for touching? clothes, for being looked on?
Why, this is no more. An old, decrepit wretch,
That has no sense, no sinew; takes his meat

With other's fingers; only knows to gape,
When you do scald his gums; a voice; a shadow;
And what can this man hurt you?
 Celia. [*Aside*]   Lord! what spirit
Is this hath entered him?
 Corvino.   And for your fame,
That's such a jig; as if I would go tell it,
Cry it on the Piazza! who shall know it,
But he that cannot speak it, and this fellow,   50
Whose lips are i' my pocket?——save yourself:
If you'll proclaim it, you may. I know no other
Should come to know it.
 Celia.   Are heaven and saints then nothing?
Will they be blind, or stupid?
 Corvino.   How?
 Celia.   Good sir,
Be jealous still, emulate them; and think
What hate they burn with, toward every sin.
 Corvino. I grant you: if I thought it were a sin,
I would not urge you. Should I offer this
To some young Frenchman, or hot Tuscan blood,
That had read Aretine, conned all his prints,   60
Knew every quirk within lust's labyrinth,
And were professed critic in lechery;
And I would look upon him, and applaud him,
This were a sin: but here, 'tis contrary,
A pious work, mere charity, for physic,
And honest polity, to assure mine own.
 Celia. O heaven! canst thou suffer such a change?
 Volpone. Thou art mine honour, Mosca, and my pride,
My joy, my tickling, my delight! go, bring 'em.
 Mosca. Please you draw near, sir.
 Corvino.   Come on, what——   70
You will not be rebellious? by that light——
 Mosca. Sir, Signior Corvino, here, is come to see you.
 Volpone. Oh.
 Mosca. And hearing of the consultation had,
So lately, for your health, is come to offer,
Or rather, sir, to prostitute——
 Corvino.   Thanks, sweet Mosca.
 Mosca. Freely, unasked, or unentreated——

Corvino.   Well.
Mosca. As the true, fervent instance of his love,
His own most fair and proper wife; the beauty
Only of price in Venice——
  Corvino.   'Tis well urged.
  Mosca. To be your comfortress, and to preserve you.   80
  Volpone. Alas, I'm past already! 'pray you, thank him
For his good care and promptness, but for that,
'Tis a vain labour, e'en to fight 'gainst heaven;
Applying fire to a stone——uh, uh, uh, uh——
Making a dead leaf grow again. I take
His wishes gently, though; and you may tell him,
What I've done for him; marry, my state is hopeless!
Will him to pray for me; and to use his fortune
With reverence when he comes to it.
  Mosca.   Do you hear, sir?
Go to him with your wife.
  Corvino.   Heart of my father!   90
Wilt thou persist thus? come, I pray thee, come.
Thou seest 'tis nothing. Celia! By this hand,
I shall grow violent. Come, do't, I say.
  Celia. Sir, kill me, rather: I will take down poison,
Eat burning coals, do anything——
  Corvino.   Be damned.
Heart, I will drag thee hence, home, by the hair;
Cry thee a strumpet through the streets; rip up
Thy mouth unto thine ears; and slit thy nose,
Like a raw rochet—— Do not tempt me, come.
Yield, I am loath—— Death! I will buy some slave,   100
Whom I will kill, and bind thee to him, alive;
And at my window hang you forth, devising
Some monstrous crime, which I, in capital letters,
Will eat into thy flesh with aquafortis
And burning corsives on this stubborn breast.
Now, by the blood thou hast incensed, I'll do it!
  Celia. Sir, what you please, you may, I am your martyr.
  Corvino. Be not thus obstinate, I ha' not deserved it:
Think who it is entreats you. 'Pray thee, sweet;
Good faith, thou shalt have jewels, gowns, attires,   110
What thou wilt think, and ask. Do but go kiss him.
Or touch him, but. For my sake. At my suit.

This once. No? not? I shall remember this.
Will you disgrace me, thus? do you thirst my undoing?
  Mosca. Nay, gentle lady, be advised.
  Corvino.   No, no.
She has watched her time. God's precious, this is scurvy;
'Tis very scurvy: and you are——
  Mosca.   Nay, good sir.
  Corvino. An errant locust, by heaven, a locust! Whore,
Crocodile, that hast thy tears prepared,
Expecting how thou'lt bid 'em flow.
  Mosca.   Nay, 'pray you, sir,   120
She will consider.
  Celia.   Would my life would serve
To satisfy.
  Corvino. 'Sdeath, if she would but speak to him
And save my reputation, 'twere somewhat;
But, spitefully to effect my utter ruin!
  Mosca. Aye, now you have put your fortune in her hands.
Why i' faith, it is her modesty, I must quit her;
If you were absent, she would be more coming;
I know it: and dare undertake for her.
What woman can, before her husband? 'Pray you,
Let us depart and leave her here.
  Corvino.   Sweet Celia,   130
Thou mayst redeem all yet; I'll say no more.
If not, esteem yourself as lost. [*Celia begins to leave*] Nay, stay there.
                         [*Exeunt Corvino, Mosca*]
  Celia. O God and his good angels! Whither, whither
Is shame fled human breasts? that with such ease
Men dare put off your honours and their own?
Is that which ever was a cause of life
Now placed beneath the basest circumstance?
And modesty an exile made, for money?
  Volpone. (*He leaps off from his couch*) Aye, in Corvino, and such earth-
    fed minds,
That never tasted the true heaven of love.   140
Assure thee, Celia, he that would sell thee
Only for hope of gain, and that uncertain,
He would have sold his part of paradise
For ready money, had he met a cope-man.
Why art thou 'mazed, to see me thus revived?

Rather applaud thy beauty's miracle;
'Tis thy great work: that hath, not now alone,
But sundry times, raised me, in several shapes,
And but this morning, like a mountebank,
To see thee at thy window. Aye, before   150
I would have left my practice, for thy love,
In varying figures, I would have contended
With the blue Proteus, or the hornèd flood.
Now, art thou welcome.
    Celia.   Sir!
    Volpone.   Nay, fly me not.
Nor let thy false imagination
That I was bed-rid, make thee think I am so;
Thou shalt not find it. I am now as fresh,
As hot, as high, and in as jovial plight,
As when, in that so celebrated scene,
As recitation of our comedy   160
For entertainment of the great Valois,
I acted young Antinous; and attracted
The eyes and ears of all the ladies present,
To admire each graceful gesture, note, and footing.

Song

    Come, my Celia, let us prove,
    While we can, the sports of love;
    Time will not be ours for ever,
    He, at length, our good will sever;
    Spend not then his gifts in vain.   170
    Suns that set may rise again:
    But if once we lose this light,
    'Tis with us perpetual night.
    Why should we defer our joys?
    Fame and rumour are but toys.
    Cannot we delude the eyes
    Of a few poor household spies?
    Or his easier ears beguile,
    Thus removèd by our wile?
    'Tis no sin love's fruits to steal;   180
    But the sweet thefts to reveal:
    To be taken, to be seen,
    These have crimes accounted been.

Celia. Some serene blast me, or dire lightning strike
This my offending face.
    Volpone.   Why droops my Celia?
Thou hast in place of a base husband found
A worthy lover; use thy fortune well,
With secrecy, and pleasure. See, behold,
What thou art queen of; not in expectation,
As I feed others, but possessed, and crowned.   190
See, here, a rope of pearl; and each, more orient
Than that the brave Egyptian queen caroused:
Dissolve, and drink 'em. See, a carbuncle,
May put out both the eyes of our St Mark;
A diamond would have bought Lollia Paulina,
When she came in, like star-light, hid with jewels
That were the spoils of provinces; take these,
And wear, and lose 'em: yet remains an ear-ring
To purchase them again, and this whole state.
A gem but worth a private patrimony   200
Is nothing: we will eat such at a meal.
The heads of parrots, tongues of nightingales,
The brains of peacocks and of ostriches
Shall be our food; and could we get the phoenix,
Though nature lost her kind, she were our dish.
    Celia. Good sir, these things might move a mind affected
With such delights; but I, whose innocence
Is all I can think wealthy, or worth the enjoying,
And which once lost, I have naught to lose beyond it,
Cannot bè taken with these sensual baits.   210
If you have conscience——
    Volpone.   'Tis the beggar's virtue;
If thou hast wisdom, hear me, Celia.
Thy baths shall be the juice of July-flowers,
Spirit of roses and of violets,
The milk of unicorns, and panther's breath
Gathered in bags, and mixed with Cretan wines.
Our drink shall be preparèd gold and amber;
Which we will take until my roof whirl round
With the vertigo; and my dwarf shall dance,
My eunuch sing, my fool make up the antic.   220
Whilst, we, in changèd shapes, act Ovid's tales,
Thou, like Europe now, and I like Jove,

Then I like Mars, and thou like Erycine,
So of the rest, till we have quite run through
And wearied all the fables of the gods.
Then will I have thee in more modern forms,
Attired like some sprightly dame of France,
Brave Tuscan lady, or proud Spanish beauty;
Sometimes, unto the Persian Sophy's wife;
Or the Grand Signior's mistress; and, for change,   230
To one of our most artful courtesans,
Or some quick Negro, or cold Russian;
And I will meet thee in as many shapes;
Where we may, so, transfuse our wandering souls   [*Kisses her*]
Out at our lips, and score up sums of pleasures,   [*Sings*]

    That the curious shall not know,
     How to tell them, as they flow;
    And the envious, when they find
     What their number is, be pined.

 Celia. If you have ears that will be pierced; or eyes   240
That can be opened; a heart, may be touched;
Or any part, that yet sounds man, about you:
If you have touch of holy saints, or heaven,
Do me the grace to let me 'scape. If not,
Be bountiful, and kill me. You do know
I am a creature hither ill betrayed
By one whose shame I would forget it were.
If you will deign me neither of these graces,
Yet feed your wrath, sir, rather than your lust;
It is a vice, comes nearer manliness,   250
And punish that unhappy crime of nature
Which you miscall my beauty. Flay my face,
Or poison it with ointments for seducing
Your blood to this rebellion. Rub these hands
With what may cause an eating leprosy,
E'en to my bones and marrow; anything,
That may disfavour me, save in my honour.
And I will kneel to you, pray for you, pay down
A thousand hourly vows, sir, for your health,
Report, and think you virtuous——
 Volpone.   Think me cold,   260
Frozen, and impotent, and so report me?

That I had Nestor's hernia, thou wouldst think.
I do degenerate and abuse my nation
To play with opportunity thus long:
I should have done the act, and then have parleyed.
Yield, or I'll force thee.
    Celia.   Oh! just God.
    Volpone.   In vain——
    Bonario. (*He leaps out from where Mosca had placed him*) Forbear, foul
    ravisher! libidinous swine!
Free the forced lady, or thou diest, impostor.
But that I am loath to snatch thy punishment
Out of the hand of justice, thou shouldst yet
Be made the timely sacrifice of vengeance,
Before this altar, and this dross, thy idol.
Lady, let's quit the place, it is the den
Of villainy; fear naught, you have a guard:
And he, ere long, shall meet his just reward.   [*Exeunt Bonario, Celia*]
    Volpone. Fall on me, roof, and bury me in ruin,
Become my grave, that wert my shelter. Oh!
I am unmasked, unspirited, undone,
Betrayed to beggary, to infamy——

Act III, Scene viii

[*Enter Mosca, bleeding*]

    Mosca. Where shall I run, most wretched shame of men,
To beat out my unlucky brains?
    Volpone.   Here, here.
What! Dost thou bleed?
    Mosca.   Oh, that his well-driven sword
Had been so courteous to have cleft me down
Unto the navel; ere I lived to see
My life, my hopes, my spirits, my patron, all
Thus desperately engagèd by my error.
    Volpone. Woe on thy fortune!
    Mosca.   And my follies, sir.
    Volpone. Thou'st made me miserable.
    Mosca.   And myself, sir.
Who would have thought he would have hearkened so?

27

10

Volpone. What shall we do?

Mosca.   I know not; if my heart
Could expiate the mischance, I'd pluck it out.
Will you be pleased to hang me? or cut my throat?
And I'll requite you, sir. Let's die like Romans,
Since we have lived like Grecians.   *(They knock without)*

Volpone.   Hark, who's there?
I hear some footing——officers, the Saffi,
Come to apprehend us! I do feel the brand
Hissing already at my forehead: now,
Mine ears are boring.

Mosca.   To your couch, sir; you
Make that place good, however. [*Volpone lies down*] Guilty men   20
Suspect what they deserve still. [*Opens door*]
                  Signior Corbaccio!

Act III, Scene ix

[*Enter Corbaccio*]

Corbaccio. Why! how now? Mosca!

[*Enter Voltore behind*]

Mosca.   Oh, undone, amazed, sir.
Your son——I know not by what accident——
Acquainted with your purpose to my patron
Touching your will, and making him your heir,
Entered our house with violence, his sword drawn,
Sought for you, called you wretch, unnatural,
Vowed he would kill you.

Corbaccio.   Me?

Mosca.   Yes, and my patron.

Corbaccio. This act shall disinherit him indeed;
Here is the will.

Mosca.   'Tis well, sir.

Corbaccio.   Right and well.
Be you as careful now for me.

Mosca.   My life, sir,   10
Is not more tendered; I am only yours.

Corbaccio. How does he? will he die shortly, thinkst thou?

Mosca.   I fear
He'll outlast May.
   Corbaccio.   Today?
   Mosca.   No, last out May, sir.
   Corbaccio. Couldst thou not gi' him a dram?
   Mosca.   Oh, by no means, sir.
   Corbaccio. Nay, I'll not bid you.
   Voltore. [*Comes forward*]   This is a knave, I see.
   Mosca. [*Aside*] How, Signior Voltore! Did he hear me?
   Voltore.   Parasite!
   Mosca. Who's that? Oh, sir, most timely welcome——

                                       [*Joins Voltore*]
   Voltore.   Scarce
To the discovery of your tricks, I fear.
You are his, only? and mine, also? are you not?
   Mosca. Who? I, sir!
   Voltore.   You, sir. What device is this   20
About a will?
   Mosca.   A plot for you, sir.
   Voltore.   Come,
Put not your foists upon me, I shall scent 'em.
   Mosca. Did you not hear it?
   Voltore.   Yes, I hear, Corbaccio
Hath made your patron, there, his heir.
   Mosca.   'Tis true,
By my device, drawn to it by my plot,
With hope——
   Voltore.   Your patron should reciprocate?
And you have promised?
   Mosca.   For your good, I did, sir.
Nay more, I told his son, brought, hid him here,
Where he might hear his father pass the deed;
Being persuaded to it, by this thought, sir,   30
That the unnaturalness, first, of the act,
And then his father's oft disclaiming in him,
(Which I did mean to help on) would sure enrage him
To do some violence upon his parent.
On which the law should take sufficient hold,
And you be stated in a double hope:
Truth be my comfort and my conscience,
My only aim was to dig you a fortune

Out of these two, old rotten sepulchres——
  Voltore. I cry thee mercy, Mosca.
  Mosca.   Worth your patience,   40
And your great merit, sir. And see the change!
  Voltore. Why? what success?
  Mosca.   Most hapless! you must help, sir.
Whilst we expected the old raven, in comes
Corvino's wife, sent hither by her husband——
  Voltore. What, with a present?
  Mosca.   No, sir, on visitation
(I'll tell you how, anon), and, staying long,
The youth he grows impatient, rushes forth,
Seizeth the lady, wounds me, makes her swear,
Or he would murder her (that was his vow)
To affirm my patron to have done her rape: 50
Which how unlike it is, you see! and hence
With that pretext he's gone to accuse his father,
Defame my patron, defeat you——
  Voltore.   Where's her husband?
Let him be sent for straight.
  Mosca.   Sir, I'll go fetch him.
  Voltore. Bring him to the Scrutineo.
  Mosca.   Sir, I will.
  Voltore. This must be stopped.
  Mosca.   Oh, you do nobly, sir.
Alas, 'twas laboured all, sir, for your good;
Nor was there want of counsel in the plot:
But fortune can, at any time, o'erthrow
The projects of a hundred learnèd clerks, sir.   60
  Corbaccio. [*Coming forward*] What's that?
  Voltore.   Wilt please you, sir, to go along?
                     [*Exeunt Voltore, Corbaccio*]
  Mosca. Patron, go in, and pray for our success.
  Voltore. Need makes devotion; heaven your labour bless.   [*Exeunt*]

Act IV, Scene i

[A street]

[Enter Politic and Peregrine]

   Sir Politic. I told you, sir, it was a plot; you see
What observation is. You mentioned me
For some instructions: I will tell you, sir,
Since we are met here in this height of Venice,
Some few particulars I have set down
Only for this meridian, fit to be known
Of your crude traveller, and they are these.
I will not touch, sir, at your phrase, or clothes,
For they are old.
   Peregrine.   Sir, I have better.
   Sir Politic.   Pardon,
I meant, as they are themes.
   Peregrine.   Oh, sir, proceed: 10
I'll slander you no more of wit, good sir.
   Sir Politic. First, for your garb, it must be grave and serious;
Very reserved and locked; not tell a secret,
On any terms, not to your father; scarce
A fable, but with caution; make sure choice
Both of your company and discourse; beware
You never speak a truth——
   Peregrine.   How!
   Sir Politic.   Not to strangers,
For those be they you must converse with most;
Others I would not know, sir, but at distance,
So as I still might be a saver in 'em;   20
You shall have tricks else, passed upon you hourly.
And then for your religion, profess none,
But wonder at the diversity of all;
And for your part protest, were there no other
But simply the laws o' the land, you could content you:
Nick Machiavel and Monsieur Bodin, both,
Were of this mind. Then must you learn the use
And handling of your silver fork at meals;
The metal of your glass——these are main matters,
With your Italian——and to know the hour   30
When you must eat your melons and your figs.

Peregrine. Is that a point of state too?
Sir Politic.   Here it is.
For your Venetian, if he see a man
Preposterous in the least, he has him straight;
He has: he strips him. I'll acquaint you, sir:
I now have lived here, 'tis some fourteen months;
Within the first week of my landing here,
All took me for a citizen of Venice,
I knew the forms, so well——
    Peregrine. [*Aside*]   And nothing else.
    Sir Politic. I had read Contarini, took me a house,   40
Dealt with my Jews, to furnish it with movables——
Well, if I could but find one man, one man,
To mine own heart, whom I durst trust, I would——
    Peregrine. What? what, sir?
    Sir Politic.   Make him rich; make him a fortune;
He should not think again. I would command it.
    Peregrine. As how?
    Sir Politic.   With certain projects that I have;
Which I may not discover.
    Peregrine. [*Aside*]   If I had
But one to wager with, I would lay odds now
He tells me instantly.
    Sir Politic.   One is (and that
I care not greatly who knows) to serve the state   50
Of Venice with red herrings for three years,
And at a certain rate, from Rotterdam,
Where I have correspondence. There's a letter
Sent me from one o' the States, and to that purpose;
He cannot write his name, but that's his mark.
    Peregrine. He is a chandler?
    Sir Politic.   No, a cheesemonger.
There are some other too with whom I treat
About the same negotiation,
And I will undertake it, for 'tis thus,
I'll do't with ease, I've cast it all. Your hoy   60
Carries but three men in her and a boy,
And she shall make me three returns a year:
So, if there come but one of three I save,
If two, I can defalk. But this is now
If my main project fail.

Peregrine.   Then you have others?
Sir Politic. I should be loath to draw the subtle air
Of such a place without my thousand aims.
I'll not dissemble, sir, where'er I come
I love to be considerative; and 'tis true,
I have at my free hours thought upon   70
Some certain goods unto the state of Venice,
Which I do call my cautions; and, sir, which
I mean (in hope of pension) to propound
To the Great Council, then unto the Forty,
So to the Ten. My means are made already——
   Peregrine. By whom?
   Sir Politic.   Sir, one, that though his place be obscure,
Yet he can sway, and they will hear him. He's
A *commendatore.*
   Peregrine.   What, a common sergeant?
   Sir Politic. Sir, such as they are, put it in their mouths,
What they should say, sometimes: as well as greater.   80
I think I have my notes to show you——
   Peregrine.   Good, sir.
   Sir Politic. But you shall swear unto me, on your gentry,
Not to anticipate——
   Peregrine.   I, sir?
   Sir Politic.   Nor reveal
A circumstance—— My paper is not with me.
   Peregrine. Oh, but you can remember, sir.
   Sir Politic.   My first is
Concerning tinder-boxes. You must know,
No family is here without its box.
Now sir, it being so portable a thing,
Put case, that you or I were ill affected
Unto the state; sir, with it in our pockets,   90
Might not I go into the Arsenale?
Or you? come out again? and none the wiser?
   Peregrine. Except yourself, sir.
   Sir Politic.   Go to, then. I, therefore,
Advértise to the state, how fit it were,
That none but such as were known patriots,
Sound lovers of their country, should be suffered
To enjoy them in their houses; and even those,
Sealed at some office, and at such a bigness,

As might not lurk in pockets.
    Peregrine.   Admirable!
    Sir Politic. My next is how to enquire and be resolved   100
By present demonstration, whether a ship,
Newly arrivèd from Soría, or from
Any suspected part of all the Levant,
Be guilty of the plague; and where they use,
To lie out forty, fifty days, sometimes,
About the Lazaretto, for their trial;
I'll save that charge and loss unto the merchant,
And in an hour clear the doubt.
    Peregrine.   Indeed, sir?
    Sir Politic. Or——I will lose my labour.
    Peregrine.   'My faith, that's much.
    Sir Politic. Nay, sir, conceive me. 'Twill cost me, in onions,   110
Some thirty livres——
    Peregrine.   Which is one pound sterling.
    Sir Politic. Beside my waterworks; for this I do, sir.
First, I bring in your ship 'twixt two brick walls——
But those the state shall venture——on the one
I strain me a fair tarpaulin, and in that
I stick my onions, cut in halves. The other
Is full of loopholes, out at which I thrust
The noses of my bellows; and those bellows
I keep, with waterworks, in perpetual motion,
Which is the easiest matter of a hundred.   120
Now, sir, your onion, which doth naturally
Attract the infection, and your bellows, blowing
The air upon him, will show instantly
By his changed colour, if there be contagion,
Or else remain as fair as at the first.
Now 'tis known, 'tis nothing.
    Peregrine.   You are right, sir.
    Sir Politic. I would I had my note.
    Peregrine.   'Faith, so would I:
But you ha' done well, for once, sir.
    Sir Politic.   Were I false,
Or would be made so, I could show you reasons,
How I could sell this state, now, to the Turk;   130
Spite of their galleys, or their——
    Peregrine.   Pray you, Sir Pol.

Sir Politic. I have 'em not about me.

Peregrine.   That I feared.
They're there, sir?

Sir Politic.   No, this is my diary,
Wherein I note my actions of the day.

Peregrine. 'Pray you, let's see, sir. What is here? '*Notandum,*
A rat had gnawn my spur-leathers; notwithstanding,
I put on new, and did go forth; but first
I threw three beans over the threshold. *Item,*
I went and bought two toothpicks, whereof one
I burst immediately in a discourse   140
With a Dutch merchant 'bout *ragion del stato.*
From him I went and paid a *moccenigo*
For piecing my silk stockings; by the way,
I cheapened sprats; and at St Mark's I urined.'
'Faith, these are politic notes!

Sir Politic.   Sir, I do slip
No action of my life, thus, but I quote it.

Peregrine. Believe me it is wise!

Sir Politic.   Nay, sir, read forth.

Act IV, Scene ii

[Enter Lady Politic Would-be, Nano, Women]

Lady Would-be. Where should this loose knight be, trow? sure, he's
    housed.

Nano. Why, then he's fast.

Lady Would-be.   Aye, he plays both with me:
I pray you, stay. This heat will do more harm
To my complexion than his heart is worth.
I do not care to hinder, but to take him.
How it comes off!   *[Rubbing her face]*

[1st] Woman.   My master's yonder.

Lady Would-be.   Where?

[2nd] Woman. With a young gentleman.

Lady Would-be.   That same's the party!
In man's apparel. 'Pray you, sir, jog my knight;
I will be tender to his reputation,
However he demerit.

Sir Politic.   My lady!
Peregrine.   Where?   10
Sir Politic. 'Tis she indeed, sir, you shall know her. She is,
Were she not mine, a lady of that merit
For fashion and behaviour, and for beauty
I durst compare——
   Peregrine.   It seems you are not jealous,
That dare commend her.
   Sir Politic.   Nay, and for discourse——
   Peregrine. Being your wife, she cannot miss that.
   Sir Politic. [*The groups meet*]   Madam,
Here is a gentleman, 'pray you, use him fairly;
He seems a youth, but he is——
   Lady Would-be.   None?
   Sir Politic.   Yes, one
Has put his face as soon into the world——
   Lady Would-be. You mean, as early? but today?
   Sir Politic.   How's this!   20
   Lady Would-be. Why in this habit, sir, you apprehend me.
Well, Master Would-be, this doth not become you;
I had thought the odour, sir, of your good name
Had been more precious to you; that you would not
Have done this dire masssácre on your honour;
One of your gravity and rank, besides!
But, knights, I see, care little for the oath
They make to ladies: chiefly their own ladies.
   Sir Politic. Now, by my spurs, the symbol of my knighthood——
   Peregrine. [*Aside*] Lord! How his brain is humbled, for an oath.   30
   Sir Politic. I reach you not.
   Lady Would-be.   Right, sir, your polity
May bear it through thus. [*To Peregrine*] Sir, a word with you.
I would be loath to contest publicly
With any gentlewoman; or to seem
Froward, or violent (as *The Courtier* says),
It comes too near rusticity in a lady,
Which I would shun, by all means; and however
I may deserve from Master Would-be, yet
To have one fair gentlewoman thus be made
The unkind instrument to wrong another,   40
And one she knows not——aye, and to perséver——
In my poor judgement is not warranted

From being a solecism in our sex,
If not in manners.
    Peregrine.   How is this!
    Sir Politic.   Sweet madam,
Come nearer to your aim.
    Lady Would-be.   Marry, and will, sir.
Since you provoke me with your impudence,
And laughter of your light land-siren here,
Your Sporus, your hermaphrodite——
    Peregrine. [*Aside*]   What's here?
Poetic fury and historic storms!
    Sir Politic. The gentleman, believe it, is of worth,   50
And of our nation.
    Lady Would-be. Aye, your Whitefriars nation!
Come, I blush for you, Master Would-be, aye;
And am ashamed you should ha' no more forehead
Than thus to be the patron or St George
To a lewd harlot, a base fricatrice,
A female devil in a male outside.
    Sir Politic.   Nay,
And you be such a one, I must bid adieu
To your delights. The case appears too liquid.
    Lady Would-be. Aye, you may carry it clear, with your state-face!
But for your carnival concupiscence,   60
Who here is fled for liberty of conscience,
From furious persecution of the marshal,
Her will I disple.   [*Seizing Peregrine by his clothing; exit Sir Politic*]
    Peregrine.   This is fine, i' faith!
And do you use this often? Is this part
Of your wit's exercise, 'gainst you have occasion?
Madam——
    Lady Would-be. Go to, sir.
    Peregrine.   Do you hear me, lady?
Why, if your knight have set you to beg shirts,
Or to invite me home, you might have done it
A nearer way by far.
    Lady Would-be.   This cannot work you
Out of my snare.
    Peregrine.   Why? Am I in it then?   70
Indeed, your husband told me you were fair,
And so you are; only your nose inclines——

That side that's next the sun——to the queen-apple.
   Lady Would-be. This cannot be endured by any patience.

Act IV, Scene iii

[Enter Mosca]

   Mosca. What's the matter, madam?
   Lady Would-be.   If the Senate
Right not my quest in this, I will protest 'em
To all the world no aristocracy.
   Mosca. What is the injury, lady?
   Lady Would-be.   Why, the callet
You told me of, here I have ta'en disguised.
   Mosca. Who? this? what means your ladyship? the creature
I mentioned to you is apprehended now,
Before the Senate, you shall see her——
   Lady Would-be.   Where?
   Mosca. I'll bring you to her. This young gentleman
I saw him land this morning at the port.   10
   Lady Would-be. [Releasing Peregrine] Is't possible! How has my judge-
     ment wandered!
Sir, I must, blushing, say to you, I have erred,
And plead your pardon.
   Peregrine.   What! more changes yet?
   Lady Would-be. I hope you ha' not the malice to remember
A gentlewoman's passion. If you stay
In Venice, here, please you to use me, sir——
   Mosca. Will you go, madam?
   Lady Would-be.   'Pray you, sir, use me. In faith,
The more you see me, the more I shall conceive,
You have forgot our quarrel.   *[Exeunt Lady, Mosca, etc.]*
   Peregrine.   This is rare!
Sir Politic Would-be? no, Sir Politic bawd!   20
To bring me thus acquainted with his wife!
Well, wise Sir Pol, since you have practised thus
Upon my freshmanship, I'll try your salt-head:
What proof it is against a counter-plot.   *[Exit]*

Act IV, Scene iv

[*The Scrutineo*]

[*Enter Voltore, Corbaccio, Corvino, Mosca*]

Voltore. Well, now you know the carriage of the business,
Your constancy is all that is required
Unto the safety of it.
    Mosca.   Is the lie
Safely conveyed amongst us? Is that sure?
Knows every man his burden?
    Corvino.   Yes.
    Mosca.   Then, shrink not.
    Corvino. But knows the advocate the truth?
    Mosca.   Oh, sir,
By no means. I devised a formal tale
That salved your reputation. But be valiant, sir.
    Corvino. I fear no one but him; that this his pleading
Should make him stand for a co-heir——
    Mosca.   Co-halter.   10
Hang him: we will but use his tongue, his noise,
As we do Croaker's, here.   [*Pointing to Corbaccio*]
    Corvino.   Aye, what shall he do?
    Mosca. When we ha' done, you mean?
    Corvino.   Yes.
    Mosca.   Why, we'll think,
Sell him for *mummia*, he's half dust already.
[*To Voltore*] Do not you smile to see this buffalo,   [*Pointing to Corvino*]
How he doth sport it with his head?—— [*Aside*] I should
If all were well and past. (*To Corbaccio*) Sir, only you
Are he, that shall enjoy the crop of all,
And these not know for whom they toil.
    Corbaccio.   Aye, peace.
    Mosca. (*To Corvino*) But you shall eat it. (*Then to Voltore again*) Much!
        Worshipful sir,   20
Mercury sit upon your thundering tongue,
Or the French Hercules, and make your language
As conquering as his club, to beat along,
As with a tempest, flat, our adversaries;
But, much more, yours, sir.
    Voltore.   Here they come, ha' done.

Mosca. I have another witness if you need, sir,
I can produce.
  Voltore.   Who is it?
  Mosca.   Sir, I have her.

Act IV, Scene v

[*Enter 4 Avocatori, Bonario, Celia, Notario, Commendatori*]

  1st Avocatore. The like of this the Senate never heard of.
  2nd Avocatore. 'Twill come most strange to them when we report it.
  4th Avocatore. The gentlewoman has been ever held
Of unreprovèd name.
  3rd Avocatore.   So the young man.
  4th Avocatore. The more unnatural part that of his father.
  2nd Avocatore. More of the husband.
  1st Avocatore.   I not know to give
His act a name, it is so monstrous!
  4th Avocatore. But the impostor, he is a thing created
To exceed example!
  1st Avocatore.   And all after-times!
  2nd Avocatore. I never heard a true voluptuary   10
Described, but him.
  3rd Avocatore.   Appear yet those were cited?
  Notario. All but the old magnifico, Volpone.
  1st Avocatore. Why is not he here?
  Mosca.   Please your fatherhoods,
Here is his advocate. Himself's so weak,
So feeble——
  4th Avocatore. What are you?
  Bonario.   His parasite,
His knave, his pandar; I beseech the court,
He may be forced to come, that your grave eyes
May bear strong witness of his strange impostures.
  Voltore. Upon my faith and credit, with your virtues,
He is not able to endure the air.   20
  2nd Avocatore. Bring him, however.
  3rd Avocatore.   We will see him.
  4th Avocatore.   Fetch him.
                                    [*Exeunt Officers*]

Voltore. Your fatherhoods' fit pleasures be obeyed,
But sure, the sight will rather move your pities
Than indignation; may it please the court,
In the meantime, he may be heard in me.
I know this place most void of prejudice,
And therefore crave it, since we have no reason
To fear our truth should hurt our cause.
    3rd Avocatore.   Speak free.
    Voltore. Then know, most honoured fathers, I must now
Discover to your strangely abusèd ears,   30
The most prodigious and most frontless piece
Of solid impudence and treachery,
That ever vicious nature yet brought forth
To shame the state of Venice. This lewd woman,
That wants no artificial looks or tears
To help the visor she has now put on,
Hath long been known a close adulteress
To that lascivious youth there; not suspected,
I say, but known; and taken in the act,
With him; and by this man, the easy husband,   40
Pardoned; whose timeless bounty makes him now
Stand here, the most unhappy, innocent person
That ever man's own goodness made accused.
For these, not knowing how to owe a gift
Of that dear grace, but with their shame, being placed
So above all powers of their gratitude,
Began to hate the benefit; and in place
Of thanks, devise to extirp the memory
Of such an act. Wherein, I pray your fatherhoods,
To observe the malice, yea, the rage of creatures   50
Discovered in their evils, and what heart
Such take, even from their crimes. But that, anon,
Will more appear. This gentleman, the father,
Hearing of this foul fact, with many others,
Which daily struck at his too-tender ears,
And grieved in nothing more than that he could not
Preserve himself a parent (his son's ills
Growing to that strange flood) at last decreed
To disinherit him.
    1st Avocatore.   These be strange turns!
    2nd Avocatore. The young man's fame was ever fair and honest.   60

Voltore. So much more full of danger is his vice,
That can beguile so, under shade of virtue.
But as I said, my honoured sires, his father
Having this settled purpose (by what means
To him betrayed, we know not) and this day
Appointed for the deed; that parricide,
(I cannot style him better) by confederacy
Preparing this his paramour to be there,
Entered Volpone's house (who was the man
Your fatherhoods must understand, designed   70
For the inheritance) there, sought his father:
But with what purpose sought he him, my lords?
I tremble to pronounce it, that a son
Unto a father, and to such a father
Should have so foul, felonious intent.
It was, to murder him. When, being prevented
By his more happy absence, what then did he?
Not check his wicked thoughts; no, now new deeds——
Mischief doth ever end, where it begins——
An act of horror, fathers! He dragged forth   80
The agèd gentleman that had there lain, bed-rid,
Three years and more, out off his innocent couch,
Naked, upon the floor, there left him; wounded
His servant in the face; and with this strumpet,
The stale to his forged practice——who was glad
To be so active (I shall here desire
Your fatherhoods to note but my collections,
As most remarkable)——thought at once to stop
His father's ends, discredit his free choice,
In the old gentleman, redeem themselves   90
By laying infamy upon this man,
To whom, with blushing, they should owe their lives.
    1st Avocatore. What proofs have you of this?
    Bonario.   Most honoured fathers,
I humbly crave there be no credit given
To this man's mercenary tongue.
    2nd Avocatore.   Forbear.
    Bonario. His soul moves in his fee.
    3rd Avocatore.   Oh, sir.
    Bonario.   This fellow,
For six sols more, would plead against his maker.

VOLPONE

IV. V

IV. V

1st Avocatore. You do forget yourself.

Voltore.   Nay, nay, grave fathers,
Let him have scope; can any man imagine
That he will spare his accuser, that would not   10
Have spared his parent?

1st Avocatore.   Well, produce your proofs.

Celia. I would I could forget I were a creature.

Voltore. Signior Corbaccio!

4th Avocatore.   What is he?

Voltore.   The father.

2nd Avocatore. Has he had an oath?

Notario.   Yes.

Corbaccio.   What must I do now?

Notario. Your testimony's craved.

Corbaccio.   Speak to the knave?
I'll ha' my mouth first stopped with earth; my heart
Abhors his knowledge; I disclaim in him.

1st Avocatore. But for what cause?

Corbaccio.   The mere portent of nature.
He is an utter stranger to my loins.

Bonario. Have they made you to this!

Corbaccio.   I will not hear thee: 110
Monster of men, swine, goat, wolf, parricide,
Speak not, thou viper.

Bonario.   Sir, I will sit down,
And rather wish my innocence should suffer
Than I resist the authority of a father.

Voltore. Signior Corvino!

2nd Avocatore.   This is strange!

1st Avocatore.   Who's this?

Notario. The husband.

4th Avocatore.   Is he sworn?

Notario.   He is.

3rd Avocatore.   Speak then.

Corvino. This woman (please your fatherhoods) is a whore
Of most hot exercise, more than a partridge,
Upon record——

1st Avocatore.   No more.

Corvino.   Neighs like a jennet.

Notario. Preserve the honour of the court.

Corvino.   I shall,   120

And modesty of your most reverend ears.
And yet I hope that I may say, these eyes
Have seen her glued unto that piece of cedar,
That fine well-timbered gallant; and that here [*Touching his forehead*]
The letters may be read, thorough the horn,
That make the story perfect.
 Mosca. [*Aside to Corvino*] Excellent! Sir.
 Corvino. [*To Mosca*] There is no shame in this, now, is there?
 Mosca.   None.
 Corvino. Or if I said, I hoped that she were onward
To her damnation, if there be a hell
Greater than whore and woman——a good Catholic   130
May make the doubt.
 3rd Avocatore. His grief hath made him frantic.
 1st Avocatore. Remove him hence.
 2nd Avocatore.   Look to the woman. (*She swoons*)
 Corvino.   Rare!
Prettily feigned! Again!
 4th Avocatore.   Stand from about her.
 1st Avocatore. Give her the air.
 3rd Avocatore.   What can you say?
 Mosca.   My wound,
May it please your wisdoms, speaks for me, received
In aid of my good patron, when he missed
His sought-for father, when that well-taught dame
Had her cue given her, to cry out a rape.
 Bonario. Oh, most laid impudence! Fathers——
 3rd Avocatore.   Sir, be silent,
You had your hearing free, so must they theirs.   140
 2nd Avocatore. I do begin to doubt the imposture here.
 4th Avocatore. This woman has too many moods.
 Voltore.   Grave fathers,
She is a creature of a most professed
And prostituted lewdness.
 Corvino.   Most impetuous!
Unsatisfied, grave fathers!
 Voltore.   May her feignings
Not take your wisdoms; but this day she baited
A stranger, a grave knight, with her loose eyes,
And more lascivious kisses. This man saw 'em
Together on the water in a gondola.

Mosca. Here is the lady herself, that saw 'em too,   15
Without; who then had in the open streets
Pursued them, but for saving her knight's honour.
  1st Avocatore. Produce that lady.
  2nd Avocatore.   Let her come.   *[Exit Mosca]*
  4th Avocatore.   These things,
They strike with wonder!
  3rd Avocatore.   I am turned a stone!

Act IV, Scene vi

[Enter Mosca with Lady Politic Would-be]

  Mosca. Be resolute, madam.
  Lady Would-be. *[Pointing to Celia]* Aye, this same is she.
Out, thou chameleon harlot; now thine eyes
Vie tears with the hyena: dar'st thou look
Upon my wrongèd face? I cry your pardons.
I fear I have, forgettingly, transgressed
Against the dignity of the court——
  2nd Avocatore.   No, madam.
  Lady Would-be. And been exorbitant——
  4th Avocatore.   You have not, lady.
These proofs are strong.
  Lady Would-be.   Surely I had no purpose
To scandalize your honours, or my sex's.
  3rd Avocatore. We do believe it.
  Lady Would-be.   Surely, you may believe it.   10
  2nd Avocatore. Madam, we do.
  Lady Would-be.   Indeed, you may; my breeding
Is not so coarse——
  4th Avocatore.   We know it.
  Lady Would-be.   To offend
With pertinacy——
  3rd Avocatore.   Lady.
  Lady Would-be.   Such a presence:
No, surely.
  1st Avocatore. We well think it.
  Lady Would-be.   You may think it.

1st Avocatore. Let her o'ercome. [*To Bonario and Celia*] What witnesses
    have you
To make good your report?
    Bonario.   Our consciences.
    Celia. And heaven, that never fails the innocent.
    4th Avocatore. These are no testimonies.
    Bonario.   Not in your courts,
Where multitude, and clamour overcomes.
    1st Avocatore. Nay, then you do wax insolent.
    Voltore.   Here, here,   20
The testimony comes that will convince
And put to utter dumbness their bold tongues.
                        (*Volpone is brought in, as impotent*)
See here, grave fathers, here's the ravisher,
The rider on men's wives, the great impostor,
The grand voluptuary! Do you not think,
These limbs should affect venery? or these eyes
Covet a concubine? 'Pray you, mark these hands:
Are they not fit to stroke a lady's breasts?
Perhaps he doth dissemble?
    Bonario.   So he does.
    Voltore. Would you ha' him tortured?
    Bonario.   I would have him proved.   30
    Voltore. Best try him then with goads, or burning irons;
Put him to the *strappado*. I have heard,
The rack hath cured the gout: faith, give it him,
And help him of a malady, be courteous.
I'll undertake, before these honoured fathers,
He shall have yet as many left diseases,
As she has known adulterers, or thou strumpets.
Oh, my most equal hearers, if these deeds,
Acts of this bold and most exorbitant strain,
May pass with sufferance, what one citizen   40
But owes the forfeit of his life, yea fame,
To him that dares traduce him? Which of you
Are safe, my honoured fathers? I would ask
(With leave of your grave fatherhoods) if their plot
Have any face or colour like to truth?
Or if unto the dullest nostril here,
It smell not rank and most abhorrèd slander?
I crave your care of this good gentleman,

Whose life is much endangered by their fable;
And as for them, I will conclude with this: 50
That vicious persons when they are hot and fleshed
In impious acts, their constancy abounds:
Damned deeds are done with greatest confidence.
   1st Avocatore. Take 'em to custody, and sever them.
   2nd Avocatore. 'Tis pity two such prodigies should live.
                          [Celia and Bonario are taken out]
   1st Avocatore. Let the old gentleman be returned with care;
I'm sorry our credulity wronged him.   *[Volpone is taken out]*
   4th Avocatore. These are two creatures!
   3rd Avocatore.   I have an earthquake in me!
   2nd Avocatore. Their shame, even in their cradles, fled their faces.
   4th Avocatore. You've done a worthy service to the state, sir,   60
In their discovery.
   1st Avocatore.   You shall hear ere night
What punishment the court decrees upon 'em.
   Voltore. We thank your fatherhoods.   *[Exeunt Avocatori, etc.]*
                    How like you it?
   Mosca.   Rare.
I'd ha' your tongue, sir, tipped with gold for this;
I'd ha' you be the heir to the whole city;
The earth I'd have want men, ere you want living:
They're bound to erect your statue in St Mark's.
Signior Corvino, I would have you go
And show yourself, that you have conquered.
   Corvino.   Yes.
   Mosca. It was much better that you should profess   70
Yourself a cuckold thus, than that the other
Should have been proved.
   Corvino.   Nay, I considered that;
Now it is her fault.
   Mosca.   Then, it had been yours.
   Corvino. True, I do doubt this advocate still.
   Mosca.   I' faith,
You need not, I dare ease you of that care.
   Corvino. I trust thee, Mosca.
   Mosca.   As your own soul, sir.
                        [Exit Corvino]
   Corbaccio.   Mosca.
   Mosca. Now for your business, sir.

Corbaccio.   How? ha' you business?
Mosca. Yes, yours, sir.
Corbaccio.   Oh, none else?
Mosca.   None else, not I.
Corbaccio. Be careful then.
Mosca.   Rest you, with both your eyes, sir.
Corbaccio. Dispatch it.
Mosca.   Instantly.
Corbaccio.   And look that all,   80
Whatever, be put in, jewels, plate, moneys,
Household-stuff, bedding, curtains.
Mosca.   Curtain-rings, sir——
Only, the advocate's fee must be deducted.
Corbaccio. I'll pay him now: you'll be too prodigal.
Mosca. Sir, I must tender it.
Corbaccio.   Two cecchines is well?
Mosca. No, six, sir.
Corbaccio.   'Tis too much.
Mosca.   He talked a great while,
You must consider that, sir.
Corbaccio.   Well, there's three——
Mosca. I'll give it him.
Corbaccio.   Do so, and there's for thee.   [*Exit*]
Mosca. Bountiful bones! What horrid strange offence
Did he commit 'gainst nature, in his youth,   90
Worthy this age? [*To Voltore*] You see, sir, how I work
Unto your ends; take you no notice.
Voltore.   No,
I'll leave you.   [*Exit*]
Mosca.   All is yours, the devil and all,
Good advocate. Madam, I'll bring you home.
Lady Would-be. No, I'll go see your patron.
Mosca.   That you shall not——
I'll tell you why. My purpose is to urge
My patron to reform his will; and for
The zeal you've shown today, whereas before
You were but third, or fourth, you shall be now
Put in the first; which would appear as begged,   100
If you were present. Therefore——
Lady Would-be.   You shall sway me.   [*Exeunt*]

Act V, Scene i

[Volpone's house]

[Enter Volpone]

Volpone. Well, I am here, and all this brunt is past;
I ne'er was in dislike with my disguise
Till this fled moment; here 'twas good, in private,
But in your public——*cavé*, whilst I breathe.
'Fore God, my left leg 'gan to have the cramp;
And I apprehended, straight, some power had struck me
With a dead palsy. Well, I must be merry,
And shake it off. A many of these fears
Would put me into some villainous disease,
Should they come thick upon me: I'll prevent 'em.   10
Give me a bowl of lusty wine, to fright
This humour from my heart. (*He drinks*) Hum, hum, hum!
'Tis almost gone, already; I shall conquer.
Any device now, of rare, ingenious knavery,
That would possess me with a violent laughter,
Would make me up again! (*Drinks again*) So, so, so, so.
This heat is life; 'tis blood, by this time. Mosca!

Act V, Scene ii

[Enter Mosca]

Mosca. How now, sir? does the day look clear again?
Are we recovered? and wrought out of error,
Into our way? to see our path before us?
Is our trade free, once more?
Volpone.   Exquisite Mosca!
Mosca. Was it not carried learnedly?
Volpone.   And stoutly.
Good wits are greatest in extremities.
Mosca. It were a folly beyond thought to trust
Any grand act unto a cowardly spirit.
You are not taken with it enough, methinks?
Volpone. Oh, more than if I had enjoyed the wench;   10
The pleasure of all womankind's not like it.

Mosca. Why, now you speak, sir. We must here be fixed;
Here we must rest; this is our masterpiece:
We cannot think to go beyond this.
   Volpone. True,
Thou'st played thy prize, my precious Mosca.
   Mosca. Nay, sir,
To gull the court——
   Volpone. And quite divert the torrent,
Upon the innocent.
   Mosca. Yes, and to make
So rare a music out of discords——
   Volpone. Right.
That yet to me's the strangest! How thou'st borne it!
That these, being so divided 'mongst themselves,
Should not scent somewhat, or in me or thee,
Or doubt their own side.
   Mosca. True, they will not see't.
Too much light blinds 'em, I think. Each of 'em
Is so possessed, and stuffed with his own hopes,
That anything unto the contrary,
Never so true, or never so apparent,
Never so palpable, they will resist it——
   Volpone. Like a temptation of the devil.
   Mosca. Right, sir.
Merchants may talk of trade, and your great signiors
Of land that yields well; but if Italy
Have any glebe more fruitful than these fellows,
I am deceived. Did not your advocate rare?
   Volpone. Oh——'My most honoured fathers, my grave fathers,
Under correction of your fatherhoods,
What face of truth, is here? If these strange deeds
May pass, most honoured fathers——' I had much ado
To forbear laughing.
   Mosca. It seemed to me, you sweat sir.
   Volpone. In troth, I did a little.
   Mosca. But confess, sir,
Were you not daunted?
   Volpone. In good faith, I was
A little in a mist, but not dejected;
Never but still myself.
   Mosca. I think it, sir.

Now (so truth help me) I must needs say this, sir,
And out of conscience for your advocate:
He's taken pains, in faith, sir, and deserved,
(In my poor judgement, I speak it, under favour,
Not to contrary you, sir) very richly——
Well——to be cozened.

Volpone.   'Troth, and I think so too,
By that I heard him, in the latter end.

Mosca. Oh, but before, sir; had you heard him first,
Draw it to certain heads, then aggravate,   50
Then use his vehement figures——I looked still,
When he would shift a shirt; and doing this
Out of pure love, no hope of gain——

Volpone.   'Tis right.
I cannot answer him, Mosca, as I would,
Not yet; but for thy sake, at thy entreaty,
I will begin e'en now to vex 'em all:
This very instant.

Mosca.   Good, sir.

Volpone.   Call the dwarf
And eunuch forth.

Mosca.   Castrone, Nano!   [*Enter Nano, Castrone*]

Nano.   Here.

Volpone. Shall we have a jig now?

Mosca.   What you please, sir.

Volpone.   Go,
Straight, give out about the streets, you two,   60
That I am dead; do it with constancy,
Sadly, do you hear? Impute it to the grief
Of this late slander.   [*Exeunt Nano, Castrone*]

Mosca.   What do you mean, sir?

Volpone.   Oh,
I shall have instantly my vulture, crow,
Raven, come flying hither on the news
To peck for carrion, my she-wolf and all,
Greedy, and full of expectation——

Mosca. And then to have it ravished from their mouths?

Volpone. 'Tis true. I will ha' thee put on a gown,
And take upon thee as thou wert mine heir;   70
Show 'em a will: open that chest, and reach
Forth one of those that has the blanks. I'll straight

Put in thy name.
    Mosca.   It will be rare, sir.
    Volpone.   Aye,
When they e'en gape, and find themselves deluded——
    Mosca. Yes.
    Volpone.   And thou use them scurvily. Dispatch,
Get on thy gown.
    Mosca.   But, what, sir, if they ask
After the body?
    Volpone.   Say, it was corrupted.
    Mosca. I'll say it stunk, sir; and was fain to have it
Coffined up instantly, and sent away.
    Volpone. Anything, what thou wilt. Hold, here's my will.   80
Get thee a cap, a count-book, pen and ink,
Papers afore thee; sit, as thou wert taking
An inventory of parcels. I'll get up
Behind the curtain, on a stool, and hearken,
Sometime peep over, see how they do look,
With what degrees their blood doth leave their faces!
Oh, 'twill afford me a rare meal of laughter.
    Mosca. Your advocate will turn stark dull upon it.
    Volpone. It will take off his oratory's edge.
    Mosca. But your *clarissimo*, old round-back, he   90
Will crump you, like a hog-louse, with the touch.
    Volpone. And what Corvino?
    Mosca.   Oh, sir, look for him,
Tomorrow morning, with a rope and a dagger,
To visit all the streets; he must run mad.
My lady too, that came into the court
To bear false witness for your worship——
    Volpone.   Yes,
And kissed me 'fore the fathers, when my face
Flowed all with oils.
    Mosca.   And sweat, sir. Why, your gold
Is such another medicine, it dries up
All those offensive savours! It transforms   100
The most deformèd, and restores 'em lovely,
As 'twere the strange poetical girdle. Jove
Could not invent to himself a shroud more subtle,
To pass Acrisius' guards. It is the thing
Makes all the world her grace, her youth, her beauty.

Volpone. I think she loves me.

  Mosca.   Who? The lady, sir?

She's jealous of you.

  Volpone.   Dost thou say so?

  Mosca.   Hark,

There's some already.

  Volpone.   Look.

  Mosca.   It is the vulture:

He has the quickest scent.

  Volpone.   I'll to my place,

Thou, to thy posture.

  Mosca.   I am set.

  Volpone.   But Mosca,   110

Play the artificer now, torture 'em, rarely.   [*He retires*]

Act V, Scene iii

[*Enter Voltore*]

Voltore. How now, my Mosca?

  Mosca.   Turkey carpets, nine——

Voltore. Taking an inventory? That is well.

Mosca. Two suits of bedding, tissue——

  Voltore.   Where's the will?

Let me read that the while.   [*Corbaccio is carried in*]

  Corbaccio.   So, set me down,

And get you home.   [*Exeunt porters*]

  Voltore.   Is he come now to trouble us?

Mosca. Of cloth of gold, two more——

  Corbaccio.   Is it done, Mosca?

Mosca. Of several velvets, eight——

  Voltore.   I like his care.

Corbaccio. Dost thou not hear?

[*Enter Corvino*]

  Corvino.   Ha! is the hour come, Mosca?

(*Volpone peeps from behind a traverse*)

Volpone. [*Aside*] Aye, now they muster.

  Corvino.   What does the advocate here?

Or this Corbaccio?

[*Enter Lady Would-be*]

Corbaccio.   What do these here?
Lady Would-be.   Mosca!   10
Is his thread spun?
Mosca.   Eight chests of linen——
Volpone. [*Aside*]   Oh,
My fine Dame Would-be too!
Corvino.   Mosca, the will,
That I may show it these, and rid 'em hence.
Mosca. Six chests of diaper, four of damask——There.
                                        [*Gives them the will*]

Corbaccio. Is that the will?
Mosca.   Down-beds, and bolsters——
Volpone. [*Aside*]   Rare!
Be busy still. Now they begin to flutter:
They never think of me. Look, see, see, see!
How their swift eyes run over the long deed,
Unto the name, and to the legacies,
What is bequeathed them there——
Mosca.   Ten suits of hangings——   20
Volpone. [*Aside*] Aye, i' their garters, Mosca. Now their hopes
Are at the gasp.
Voltore.   Mosca the heir!
Corbaccio.   What's that?   [*Takes the will*]
Volpone. [*Aside*] My advocate is dumb; look to my merchant:
He has heard of some strange storm, a ship is lost,
He faints. My lady will swoon. Old glazen-eyes
He hath not reached his despair yet.
Corbaccio.   All these
Are out of hope; I'm sure the man.
Corvino.   But Mosca——
Mosca. Two cabinets——
Corvino.   Is this in earnest?
Mosca.   One
Of ebony.——
Corvino.   Or do you but delude me?
Mosca. The other, mother of pearl——I am very busy.   30
Good faith, it is a fortune thrown upon me——
Item, one salt of agate——not my seeking.
Lady Would-be. Do you hear, sir?

Mosca.   A perfumed box——'pray you forbear,
You see I am troubled——made of an onyx——
Lady Would-be.   How!
    Mosca. Tomorrow, or next day, I shall be at leisure
To talk with you all.
    Corvino.   Is this my large hope's issue?
    Lady Would-be. Sir, I must have a fairer answer.
    Mosca.   Madam!
Marry, and shall: 'pray you, fairly quit my house.
Nay, raise no tempest with your looks, but hark you:
Remember what your ladyship offered me   40
To put you in an heir; go to, think on't.
And what you said e'en your best madams did
For maintenance, and why not you? Enough.
Go home, and use the poor Sir Pol, your knight, well,
For fear I tell some riddles: go, be melancholic.   [*Exit Lady Would-be*]
    Volpone. [*Aside*] Oh, my fine devil!
    Corvino.   Mosca, 'pray you a word.
    Mosca. Lord! will not you take your dispatch hence yet?
Methinks of all you should have been the example.
Why should you stay here? with what thought? what promise?
Hear you: do not you know I know you an ass?   50
And that you would most fain have been a wittol
If fortune would have let you? that you are
A declared cuckold, on good terms? This pearl,
You'll say, was yours? Right. This diamond?
I'll not deny it, but thank you. Much here, else?
It may be so. Why, think that these good works
May help to hide your bad; I'll not betray you,
Although you be but extraordinary,
And have it only in title, it sufficeth.
Go home, be melancholic too, or mad.   [*Exit Corvino*] 60
    Volpone. [*Aside*] Rare, Mosca! How his villainy becomes him!
    Voltore. Certain, he doth delude all these for me.
    Corbaccio. Mosca the heir?
    Volpone. [*Aside*]   Oh, his four eyes have found it!
    Corbaccio. I'm cozened, cheated, by a parasite-slave;
Harlot, thou'st gulled me!
    Mosca.   Yes, sir. Stop your mouth,
Or I shall draw the only tooth is left.
Are not you he, that filthy covetous wretch

With the three legs, that here, in hope of prey,
Have, any time this three year, snuffed about
With your most grovelling nose; and would have hired   70
Me to the poisoning of my patron? Sir?
Are not you he that have today in court
Professed the disinheriting of your son?
Perjured yourself? Go home, and die, and stink;
If you but croak a syllable, all comes out.
Away and call your porters; go, go, stink.   [*Exit Corbaccio*]
    Volpone. [*Aside*] Excellent varlet!
    Voltore.   Now, my faithful Mosca,
I find thy constancy.
    Mosca.   Sir?
    Voltore.   Sincere.
    Mosca.   A table
Of porphyry——I mar'l you'll be thus troublesome.
    Voltore. Nay, leave off now, they are gone.
    Mosca.   Why, who are you?   80
What, who did send for you? Oh, cry you mercy,
Reverend sir! Good faith, I am grieved for you,
That any chance of mine should thus defeat
Your (I must needs say) most deserving travails;
But I protest, sir, it was cast upon me,
And I could almost wish to be without it,
But that the will o' the dead must be observed.
Marry, my joy is that you need it not,
You have a gift, sir (thank your education),
Will never let you want while there are men   90
And malice to breed causes. Would I had
But half the like, for all my fortune, sir.
If I have any suits——as I do hope,
Things being so easy, and direct, I shall not——
I will make bold with your obstreperous aid,
Conceive me, for your fee, sir. In meantime,
You that have so much law, I know ha' the conscience
Not to be covetous of what is mine.
Good sir, I thank you for my plate: 'twill help
To set up a young man. Good faith, you look   100
As you were costive; best go home and purge, sir.   [*Exit Voltore*]
    Volpone. [*Emerging*] Bid him eat lettuce well. My witty mischief,
Let me embrace thee. Oh, that I could now

Transform thee to a Venus—— Mosca, go,
Straight, take my habit of *clarissimo*,
And walk the streets; be seen, torment 'em more:
We must pursue, as well as plot. Who would
Have lost this feast?
   Mosca.   I doubt it will lose them.
   Volpone. Oh, my recovery shall recover all.
That I could now but think on some disguise   110
To meet 'em in: and ask 'em questions.
How I would vex 'em still, at every turn!
   Mosca. Sir, I can fit you.
   Volpone.   Canst thou?
   Mosca.   Yes, I know
One o' the *commendatori*, sir, so like you;
Him will I straight make drunk, and bring you his habit.
   Volpone. A rare disguise, and answering thy brain!
Oh, I will be a sharp disease unto 'em.
   Mosca. Sir, you must look for curses——
   Volpone.   Till they burst;
The Fox fares ever best when he is cursed.   [*Exeunt*]

Act V, Scene iv

[*Sir Politic Would-be's house*]

[*Enter Peregrine disguised, and three Merchants*]

   Peregrine. Am I enough disguised?
   1st Merchant.   I warrant you.
   Peregrine. All my ambition is to fright him only.
   2nd Merchant. If you could ship him away, 'twere excellent.
   3rd Merchant. To Zant, or to Aleppo?
   Peregrine.   Yes, and ha' his
Adventures put i' the Book of Voyages,
And his gulled story registered, for truth?
Well, gentlemen, when I am in a while,
And that you think us warm in our discourse,
Know your approaches.
   1st Merchant.   Trust it to our care.   [*Exeunt Merchants*]
               [*Enter Woman*]
   Peregrine. Save you, fair lady. Is Sir Pol within?   10

Woman. I do not know, sir.
   Peregrine.   'Pray you, say unto him,
Here is a merchant, upon earnest business,
Desires to speak with him.
   Woman.   I will see, sir.   [*Exit*]
   Peregrine.   'Pray you.
I see the family is all female here.

[Enter Woman]

   Woman. He says, sir, he has weighty affairs of state
That now require him whole; some other time
You may possess him.
   Peregrine.   'Pray you, say again,
If those require him whole, these will exact him,
Whereof I bring him tidings. [*Exit Woman*] What might be
His grave affair of state now? how to make   20
Bolognian sausages here in Venice, sparing
One o' the ingredients?

[Enter Woman]

   Woman.   Sir, he says he knows
By your word 'tidings' that you are no statesman,
And therefore wills you stay.
   Peregrine.   Sweet, 'pray you return him,
I have not read so many proclamations
And studied them for words, as he has done,
But—— Here he deigns to come.   [*Exit Woman*]

[Enter Sir Politic Would-be]

   Sir Politic.   Sir, I must crave
Your courteous pardon. There hath chanced today
Unkind disaster 'twixt my lady and me;
And I was penning my apology   30
To give her satisfaction, as you came now.
   Peregrine. Sir, I am grieved I bring you worse disaster;
The gentleman you met at the port today,
That told you he was newly arrived——
   Sir Politic.   Aye, was
A fugitive punk?
   Peregrine.   No, sir, a spy set on you;
And he has made relation to the Senate,
That you professed to him to have a plot

To sell the state of Venice to the Turk.
   Sir Politic. Oh me!
   Peregrine.   For which, warrants are signed by this time,
To apprehend you, and to search your study,   40
For papers——
   Sir Politic.   Alas, sir. I have none but notes
Drawn out of play-books——
   Peregrine.   All the better, sir.
   Sir Politic. And some essays. What shall I do?
   Peregrine.   Sir, best
Convey yourself into a sugar-chest,
Or, if you could lie round, a frail were rare,
And I could send you aboard.
   Sir Politic.   Sir, I but talked so
For discourse' sake, merely.   (*They knock without*)
   Peregrine.   Hark, they are there.
   Sir Politic. I am a wretch, a wretch.
   Peregrine.   What will you do, sir?
Ha' you ne'er a currant-butt to leap into?
They'll put you to the rack, you must be sudden.   50
   Sir Politic. Sir, I have an engine——
   3rd Merchant. [*Within*]   Sir Politic Would-be?
   2nd Merchant. [*Within*] Where is he?
   Sir Politic.   ——that I have thought upon
     before time.
   Peregrine. What is it?
   Sir Politic.   ——I shall ne'er endure the torture!——
Marry, it is, sir, of a tortoise-shell,
Fitted for these extremities; 'pray you sir, help me.
Here, I've a place, sir, to put back my legs;
Please you to lay it on, sir, with this cap
And my black gloves; I'll lie, sir, like a tortoise,
Till they are gone.
   Peregrine. [*Helping him into the shell*] And call you this an engine?
   Sir Politic. Mine own device——good sir, bid my wife's women   60
To burn my papers.   [*Exit Peregrine*]
                        ([*The Merchants*] *rush in*)
   1st Merchant.   Where's he hid?
   3rd Merchant.   We must,
And will, sure, find him.
   2nd Merchant.   Which is his study?   [*Enter Peregrine*]

1st Merchant.   What
Are you, sir?
  Peregrine. I'm a merchant, that came here
To look upon this tortoise.
    3rd Merchant.   How?
    1st Merchant.   St Mark!
What beast is this?
  Peregrine.   It is a fish.
    2nd Merchant.   Come out here.
  Peregrine. Nay, you may strike him, sir, and tread upon him;
He'll bear a cart.
    1st Merchant. What, to run over him?
  Peregrine.   Yes.
    3rd Merchant. Let's jump upon him.
    2nd Merchant.   Can he not go?
  Peregrine.   He creeps, sir.
    1st Merchant. Let's see him creep. [*Prods him*]
  Peregrine.   No, good sir, you will hurt him.
    2nd Merchant. Heart, I'll see him creep; or prick his guts.   70
    3rd Merchant. Come out here.
  Peregrine.   'Pray you sir, creep a little.
    1st Merchant.   Forth!
    2nd Merchant. Yet further!
  Peregrine.   Good sir, creep.
    2nd Merchant.   We'll see his legs.
    3rd Merchant. God's so, he has garters!
    1st Merchant.   Aye, and gloves!
    2nd Merchant.   Is this
Your fearful tortoise?   (*They pull off the shell and discover him*)
  Peregrine. [*Removing his disguise*] Now, Sir Pol, we are even;
For your next project, I shall be prepared:
I am sorry, for the funeral of your notes, sir.
    1st Merchant. 'Twere a rare motion, to be seen in Fleet Street!
    2nd Merchant. Aye, i' the term.
    1st Merchant.   Or Smithfield, in the fair.
    3rd Merchant. Methinks, 'tis but a melancholic sight!
  Peregrine. Farewell, most politic tortoise.   [*Exit with Merchants*]
                    [*Enter Woman*]
  Sir Politic.   Where's my lady?   80
Knows she of this?
  Woman.   I know not, sir.

Sir Politic.   Enquire.   [*Exit Woman*]
Oh, I shall be the fable of all feasts,
The freight of the *gazetti*, ship-boys' tale,
And, which is worst, even talk for ordinaries.

[*Enter Woman*]

Woman. My lady's come most melancholic home,
And says, sir, she will straight to sea, for physic.
        Sir Politic. And I, to shun this place and clime for ever;
Creeping with house on back; and think it well
To shrink my poor head in my politic shell.   [*Exeunt*]

Act V, Scene v

[*Volpone's house*]

([*Enter*] *Volpone, Mosca, the first in the habit of a* Commendatore; *the other, of a* Clarissimo)

Volpone. Am I then like him?
        Mosca.   Oh, sir, you are he:
No man can sever you.
        Volpone.   Good.
        Mosca.   But, what am I?
        Volpone. 'Fore heav'n, a brave *clarissimo*, thou becom'st it!
Pity thou wert not born one.
        Mosca.   If I hold
My made one, 'twill be well.
        Volpone.   I'll go and see
What news, first, at the court.   [*Exit*]
        Mosca.   Do so. My Fox
Is out on his hole, and ere he shall re-enter
I'll make him languish in his borrowed case,
Except he come to composition with me.
Androgyno, Castrone, Nano!

[*They enter*]

All.   Here.   10
        Mosca. Go recreate yourselves abroad; go, sport.   [*Exeunt the three*]
So, now I have the keys, and am possessed.
Since he will needs be dead afore his time,
I'll bury him, or gain by him. I'm his heir;

And so will keep me, till he share at least.
To cozen him of all were but a cheat
Well placed; no man would construe it a sin:
Let his sport pay for't. This is called the Fox-trap.   [*Exit*]

Act V, Scene vi

[A street]

[Enter Corbaccio and Corvino]

Corbaccio. They say the court is set.
Corvino.   We must maintain
Our first tale good, for both our reputations.
Corbaccio. Why? mine's no tale; my son would there have killed me.
Corvino. That's true, I had forgot; mine is, I am sure.
But for your will, sir.
Corbaccio.   Aye, I'll come upon him
For that hereafter, now his patron's dead.

[Enter Volpone, disguised]

Volpone. Signior Corvino! and Corbaccio! sir,
Much joy unto you.
Corvino.   Of what?
Volpone.   The sudden good,
Dropped down upon you——
Corbaccio.   Where?
Volpone.   And, none knows how——
From old Volpone, sir.
Corbaccio.   Out, arrant knave.   10
Volpone. Let not your too much wealth, sir, make you furious.
Corbaccio. Away, thou varlet.
Volpone.   Why sir?
Corbaccio.   Dost thou mock me?
Volpone. You mock the world, sir; did you not change wills?
Corbaccio. Out, harlot.
Volpone.   Oh! belike you are the man,
Signior Corvino? 'Faith, you carry it well;
You grow not mad withal; I love your spirit.
You are not over-leavened with your fortune.
You should ha' some would swell now, like a wine-fat,
With such an autumn—— Did he gi' you all, sir?

Corvino. Avoid, you rascal.

Volpone.   Troth, your wife has shown   20
Herself a very woman; but you are well,
You need not care, you have a good estate
To bear it out, sir, better by this chance.
Except Corbaccio have a share?

Corbaccio.   Hence, varlet.

Volpone. You will not be a'known, sir; why, 'tis wise.
Thus do all gamesters, at all games, dissemble.
No man will seem to win.   [*Exeunt Corbaccio, Corvino*]
                    Here comes my vulture,
Heaving his beak up i' the air, and snuffing.

Act V, Scene vii

[Enter Voltore]

Voltore. Outstripped thus, by a parasite? a slave?
Would run on errands? and make legs, for crumbs?
Well, what I'll do——

Volpone.   The court stays for your worship.
I e'en rejoice, sir, at your worship's happiness,
And that it fell into so learnèd hands,
That understand the fingering——

Voltore.   What do you mean?

Volpone. I mean to be a suitor to your worship,
For the small tenement, out of reparations:
That at the end of your long row of houses,
By the Piscaria; it was, in Volpone's time,   10
Your predecessor, ere he grew diseased,
A handsome, pretty, customed, bawdy-house
As any was in Venice (none dispraised)
But fell with him; his body and that house
Decayed together.

Voltore.   Come, sir, leave your prating.

Volpone. Why, if your worship give me but your hand
That I may ha' the refusal, I have done.
'Tis a mere toy to you, sir, candle rents;
As your learn'd worship knows——

Voltore.   What do I know?

Volpone. Marry no end of your wealth, sir, God decrease it.   20
Voltore. Mistaking knave! What, mock'st thou my misfortune?
Volpone. His blessing on your heart, sir, would 'twere more.

[*Exit Voltore*]

Now to my first again, at the next corner.   [*Stands aside*]

Act V, Scene viii

[*Enter Corbaccio, Corvino (Mosca, passant)*]

Corbaccio. See, in our habit! see the impudent varlet!
Corvino. That I could shoot mine eyes at him, like gunstones!
Volpone. But is this true, sir, of the parasite?
Corbaccio. Again, to afflict us? monster!
Volpone.   In good faith, sir,
I'm heartily grieved a beard of your grave length
Should be so over-reached. I never brooked
That parasite's hair; methought his nose should cozen;
There still was somewhat in his look did promise
The bane of a *clarissimo*.
Corbaccio.   Knave——
Volpone.   Methinks,
Yet you, that are so traded i' the world,   10
A witty merchant, the fine bird, Corvino,
That have such moral emblems on your name,
Should not have sung your shame, and dropped your cheese,
To let the Fox laugh at your emptiness.
Corvino. Sirrah, you think the privilege of the place,
And your red saucy cap, that seems to me
Nailed to your jolt-head with those two cecchines,
Can warrant your abuses. Come you, hither;
You shall perceive, sir, I dare beat you. Approach.
Volpone. No haste, sir, I do know your valour well,   20
Since you durst publish what you are, sir.
Corvino.   Tarry,
I'd speak with you.
Volpone. [*Retreating*] Sir, sir, another time——
Corvino. Nay, now.
Volpone.   Oh God, sir! I were a wise man,
Would stand the fury of a distracted cuckold.

Corbaccio. What! Come again?   (*Mosca walks by 'em*)
Volpone.   Upon 'em, Mosca; save me.
Corbaccio. The air's infected, where he breathes.
Corvino.   Let's fly him.
                                                  [*Exeunt*]

Volpone. Excellent basilisk! turn upon the vulture.

Act V, Scene ix

[*Enter Voltore*]

Voltore. Well, flesh-fly, it is summer with you now;
Your winter will come on.
    Mosca.   Good advocate,
'Pray thee, not rail, nor threaten out of place thus;
Thou'lt make a solecism (as madam says).
Get you a biggin more; your brain breaks loose.
    Voltore. Well, sir.
    Volpone.   Would you ha' me beat the insolent slave?
Throw dirt upon his first good clothes?
    Voltore.   This same
Is doubtless some familiar!
    Volpone.   Sir, the court
In troth stays for you. I am mad, a mule,
That never read Justinian, should get up   10
And ride an advocate. Had you no quirk,
To avoid gullage, sir, by such a creature?
I hope you do but jest; he has not done it;
This's but confederacy, to blind the rest.
You are the heir?
    Voltore.   A strange, officious,
Troublesome knave! thou dost torment me.
    Volpone.   I know——
It cannot be, sir, that you should be cozened;
'Tis not within the wit of man to do it:
You are so wise, so prudent; and 'tis fit,
That wealth and wisdom still should go together.   [*Exeunt*] 20

Act V, Scene x

[*The Scrutineo*]

[*Enter 4 Avocatori, Notario, Commendatori, Bonario, Celia, Corbaccio, Corvino*]

1st Avocatore. Are all the parties here?
Notario.   All but the advocate.
2nd Avocatore. And here he comes.

[*Enter Voltore, Volpone*]

1st Avocatore.   Then bring 'em forth to sentence.
Voltore. Oh, my most honoured fathers, let your mercy
Once win upon your justice, to forgive——
I am distracted——
Volpone. [*Aside*]   What will he do now?
Voltore.   Oh,
I know not which to address myself to first,
Whether your fatherhoods, or these innocents——
Corvino. [*Aside*] Will he betray himself?
Voltore.   Whom, equally,
I have abused, out of most covetous ends——
Corvino. [*To Corbaccio*] The man is mad!
Corbaccio.   What's that?
Corvino.   He is possessed.   10
Voltore. For which, now struck in conscience, here I prostrate
Myself at your offended feet for pardon.   [*He kneels*]
1st and 2nd Avocatori. Arise.
Celia.   Oh heaven, how just thou art!
Volpone. [*Aside*]   I'm caught
I' mine own noose——
Corvino.   Be constant, sir, naught now
Can help but impudence.
1st Avocatore.   Speak forward.
Commendatore.   Silence!
Voltore. It is not passion in me, reverend fathers,
But only conscience, conscience, my good sires,
That makes me now tell truth. That parasite,
That knave hath been the instrument of all.
2nd Avocatore. Where is that knave? fetch him.
Volpone.   I go.   [*Exit*]

Corvino. Grave fathers, 20
This man's distracted; he confessed it now;
For, hoping to be old Volpone's heir,
Who now is dead——

   3rd Avocatore. How?

   2nd Avocatore. Is Volpone dead?

   Corvino. Dead since, grave fathers——

   Bonario. Oh, sure vengeance!

   1st Avocatore. Stay——
Then he was no deceiver?

   Voltore. Oh no, none;
The parasite, grave fathers.

   Corvino. He does speak
Out of mere envy, 'cause the servant's made
The thing he gaped for; please your fatherhoods,
This is the truth; though, I'll not justify
The other, but he may be somedeal faulty. 30

   Voltore. Aye, to your hopes, as well as mine, Corvino,
But I'll use modesty. Pleaseth your wisdoms
To view these certain notes, and but confer them;
As I hope favour, they shall speak clear truth.

   Corvino. The devil has entered him!

   Bonario. Or bides in you.

   4th Avocatore. We have done ill, by a public officer
To send for him, if he be heir.

   2nd Avocatore. For whom?

   4th Avocatore. Him that they call the parasite.

   3rd Avocatore. 'Tis true;
He is a man of great estate now left.

   4th Avocatore. Go you and learn his name, and say the court 40
Entreats his presence here, but to the clearing
Of some few doubts.   *[Exit Notario]*

   2nd Avocatore. This same's a labyrinth!

   1st Avocatore. Stand you unto your first report?

   Corvino. My state,
My life, my fame——

   Bonario. [Aside] Where is't?

   Corvino. Are at the stake.

   1st Avocatore. Is yours so too?

   Corbaccio. The advocate's a knave,
And has a forkèd tongue——

2nd Avocatore.   Speak to the point.
Corbaccio. So is the parasite, too.
1st Avocatore.   This is confusion.
Voltore. I do beseech your fatherhoods, read but those.
                                        [*Giving them papers*]
Corvino. And credit nothing, the false spirit hath writ;
It cannot be but he is possessed, grave fathers.   [*Exeunt*] 50

Act V, Scene xi

[*A street*]

[*Enter Volpone*]

Volpone. To make a snare for mine own neck! and run
My head into it, wilfully! with laughter!
When I had newly 'scaped, was free and clear!
Out of mere wantonness! Oh, the dull devil
Was in this brain of mine when I devised it,
And Mosca gave it second; he must now
Help to sear up this vein, or we bleed dead.

[*Enter Nano, Androgyno, Castrone*]

How now! who let you loose? whither go you now?
What? to buy gingerbread? or to drown kitlings?
Nano. Sir, Master Mosca called us out of doors,   10
And bids us all go play, and took the keys.
Androgyno.   Yes.
Volpone. Did Master Mosca take the keys? why so!
I am farther in. These are my fine conceits!
I must be merry, with a mischief to me!
What a vile wretch was I, that could not bear
My fortune soberly? I must ha' my crotchets,
And my conundrums! Well, go you, and seek him;
His meaning may be truer than my fear.
Bid him, he straight come to me, to the court;
Thither will I, and if't be possible,   20
Unscrew my advocate, upon new hopes:
When I provoked him, then I lost myself.   [*Exeunt*]

Act V, Scene xii

[*The Scrutineo*]

[*Enter 4 Avocatori, etc., as before*]

1st Avocatore. [*With Voltore's papers*] These things can ne'er be
   reconciled. He here
Professeth that the gentleman was wronged,
And that the gentlewoman was brought thither,
Forced by her husband, and there left.

   Voltore.   Most true.

   Celia. How ready is heaven to those that pray!

   1st Avocatore.   But that
Volpone would have ravished her, he holds
Utterly false, knowing his impotence.

   Corvino. Grave fathers, he is possessed; again, I say,
Possessed——nay, if there be possession,
And obsession, he has both.

   3rd Avocatore.   Here comes our officer.   10

[*Enter Volpone*]

   Volpone. The parasite will straight be here, grave fathers.

   4th Avocatore. You might invent some other name, sir varlet.

   3rd Avocatore. Did not the notary meet him?

   Volpone.   Not that I know.

   4th Avocatore. His coming will clear all.

   2nd Avocatore.   Yet it is misty.

   Voltore. May it please your fatherhoods——

   Volpone. (*Whispers the Advocate*)   Sir, the parasite
Willed me to tell you that his master lives;
That you are still the man; your hopes the same;
And this was only a jest——

   Voltore.   How?

   Volpone.   Sir, to try
If you were firm, and how you stood affected.

   Voltore. Art sure he lives?

   Volpone.   Do I live, sir?

   Voltore.   Oh me!   20
I was too violent.

   Volpone.   Sir, you may redeem it,
They said you were possessed: fall down, and seem so;

I'll help to make it good. (*Voltore falls*) God bless the man!
[*To Voltore*] Stop your wind hard, and swell—— See, see, see, see!
He vomits crooked pins! his eyes are set,
Like a dead hare's, hung in a poulter's shop!
His mouth's running away! do you see, signior?
Now 'tis in his belly.
    Corvino.   Aye, the devil!
    Volpone. Now, in his throat.
    Corvino.   Aye, I perceive it plain.
    Volpone. 'Twill out, 'twill out——stand clear. See, where it flies!   30
In shape of a blue toad, with a bat's wings!
Do not you see it, sir?
    Corbaccio.   What? I think I do.
    Corvino. 'Tis too manifest.
    Volpone.   Look! he comes to himself!
    Voltore. Where am I?
    Volpone. [*Helping him up*] Take good heart, the worst is past, sir.
You are dispossessed.
    1st Avocatore.   What accident is this?
    2nd Avocatore. Sudden, and full of wonder!
    3rd Avocatore.   If he were
Possessed, as it appears, all this is nothing.
    Corvino. He has been often subject to these fits.
    1st Avocatore. Show him that writing. Do you know it, sir?
    Volpone. [*Aside to Voltore*] Deny it, sir, forswear it, know it not.   40
    Voltore. Yes, I do know it well, it is my hand:
But all that it contains is false.
    Bonario.   Oh practice!
    2nd Avocatore. What maze is this!
    1st Avocatore.   Is he not guilty then,
Whom you there name the parasite?
    Voltore.   Grave fathers,
No more than his good patron old Volpone.
    4th Avocatore. Why, he is dead!
    Voltore.   Oh no, my honoured fathers.
He lives——
    1st Avocatore. How! lives?
    Voltore.   Lives.
    2nd Avocatore.   This is subtler yet!
    3rd Avocatore. You said he was dead?
    Voltore.   Never.

3rd Avocatore.   You said so?

Corvino.   I heard so.

4th Avocatore. Here comes the gentleman, make him way.

[*Enter Mosca as a* Clarissimo]

3rd Avocatore.   A stool.

4th Avocatore. [*Aside*] A proper man! and were Volpone dead,   50
A fit match for my daughter.

    3rd Avocatore.   Give him way.

Volpone. [*Aside*] Mosca, I was almost lost: the advocate
Had betrayed all, but now it is recovered;
All's o' the hinge again——say, I am living.

    Mosca. What busy knave is this! Most reverend fathers,
I sooner had attended your grave pleasures,
But that my order for the funeral
Of my dear patron did require me——

    Volpone. [*Aside*]   Mosca!

    Mosca. Whom I intend to bury like a gentleman.

    Volpone. [*Aside*] Aye, quick, and cozen me of all.

    2nd Avocatore.   Still stranger!   60
More intricate!

    1st Avocatore. And come about again!

    4th Avocatore. [*Aside*] It is a match, my daughter is bestowed.

    Mosca. [*Aside to Volpone*] Will you gi' me half?

    Volpone. [*To Mosca*]   First, I'll be hanged.

    Mosca. [*To Volpone*]   I know,
Your voice is good, cry not so loud.

    1st Avocatore.   Demand
The advocate. Sir, did not you affirm
Volpone was alive?

    Volpone.   Yes, and he is;
This gent'man [*Indicating Mosca*] told me so. [*Aside to Mosca*] Thou shalt
     have half.

    Mosca. Whose drunkard is this same? speak some, that know him;
I never saw his face. [*Aside to Volpone*] I cannot now
Afford it you so cheap.

    Volpone. [*To Mosca*]   No?

    1st Avocatore.   What say you?   70

    Voltore. The officer told me.

    Volpone.   I did, grave fathers,
And will maintain he lives, with mine own life.

And that this creature told me. [*Aside*] I was born
With all good stars my enemies.
    Mosca.   Most grave fathers,
If such an insolence as this must pass
Upon me, I am silent: 'twas not this
For which you sent, I hope.
    2nd Avocatore.   Take him away.
    Volpone. [*Aside to Mosca*] Mosca!
    3rd Avocatore.   Let him be whipped——
    Volpone. [*Aside to Mosca*]   Wilt thou
    betray me?
Cozen me?
    3rd Avocatore. And taught to bear himself
Toward a person of his rank.
    4th Avocatore.   Away!   [*Volpone is seized*] 80
    Mosca. I humbly thank your fatherhoods.
    Volpone. [*Aside*]   Soft, soft: whipped?
And lose all that I have? if I confess,
It cannot be much more.
    4th Avocatore. [*To Mosca*] Sir, are you married?
    Volpone. [*Aside*] They'll be allied anon; I must be resolute.
The Fox shall here uncase. (*He puts off his disguise*)
    Mosca. [*Aside to Volpone*] Patron!
    Volpone. [*To Mosca*]   Nay, now
My ruins shall not come alone; your match
I'll hinder sure; my substance shall not glue you,
Nor screw you, into a family.
    Mosca. [*To Volpone*]   Why, patron!
    Volpone. I am Volpone, and this [*To Mosca*] is my knave;
This, [*To Voltore*] his own knave; this, [*To Corbaccio*] avarice's fool; 90
This, [*To Corvino*] a chimera of wittol, fool, and knave;
And, reverend fathers, since we all can hope
Naught but a sentence, let's not now despair it.
You hear me brief.
    Corvino.   May it please your fatherhoods——
    Commendatore.   Silence.
    1st Avocatore. The knot is now undone, by miracle!
    2nd Avocatore. Nothing can be more clear.
    3rd Avocatore.   Or can more prove
These innocent.
    1st Avocatore. Give 'em their liberty.

Bonario. Heaven could not long let such gross crimes be hid.

2nd Avocatore. If this be held the high way to get riches,
May I be poor.

3rd Avocatore. This's not the gain, but torment.   100

1st Avocatore. These possess wealth as sick men possess fevers,
Which trulier may be said to possess them.

2nd Avocatore. Disrobe that parasite.

Corvino, Mosca   Most honoured fathers——

1st Avocatore. Can you plead aught to stay the course of justice?
If you can, speak.

Corvino, Voltore. We beg favour.

Celia.   And mercy.

1st Avocatore. You hurt your innocence, suing for the guilty.
Stand forth; and first, the parasite. You appear
To have been the chiefest minister, if not plotter,
In all these lewd impostures; and now, lastly,
Have, with your impudence, abused the court   110
And habit of a gentleman of Venice,
Being a fellow of no birth or blood;
For which our sentence is, first thou be whipped;
Then live perpetual prisoner in our galleys.

Volpone. I thank you, for him.

Mosca.   Bane to thy wolfish nature.

1st Avocatore. Deliver him to the Saffi.   [*Mosca is taken out*]
                                             Thou, Volpone,
By blood and rank a gentleman, canst not fall
Under like censure; but our judgement on thee
Is, that thy substance all be straight confiscate
To the hospital of the Incurabili: 120
And since the most was gotten by imposture,
By feigning lame, gout, palsy, and such diseases,
Thou art to lie in prison, cramped with irons,
Till thou be'st sick and lame indeed. Remove him.

Volpone. This is called mortifying of a Fox.   [*He is taken out*]

1st Avocatore. Thou, Voltore, to take away the scandal
Thou hast given all worthy men of thy profession,
Art banished from their fellowship, and our state.
Corbaccio! bring him near. We here possess
Thy son of all thy state; and confine thee   130
To the monastery of San' Spirito,
Where, since thou knewst not how to live well here,

Thou shalt be learned to die well.

   Corbaccio.   Ha! What said he?

   Commendatore. You shall know anon, sir.   [*Taking him aside*]

   1st Avocatore.   Thou, Corvino, shalt

Be straight embarked from thine own house, and rowed

Round about Venice through the Grand Canal,

Wearing a cap with fair, long ass's ears,

Instead of horns; and, so to mount, a paper

Pinned on thy breast, to the *berlino*——

   Corvino.   Yes,

And have mine eyes beat out with stinking fish,   140

Bruised fruit, and rotten eggs——'Tis well. I'm glad

I shall not see my shame, yet.

   1st Avocatore.   And to expiate

Thy wrongs done to thy wife, thou art to send her

Home to her father with her dowry trebled;

And these are all your judgements——

   All   Honoured fathers——

   1st Avocatore. Which may not be revoked. Now you begin——

When crimes are done and past, and to be punished——

To think what your crimes are. Away with them!

Let all that see these vices thus rewarded

Take heart, and love to study 'em. Mischiefs feed   150

Like beasts, till they be fat, and then they bleed.   [*Exeunt*]

                [*Enter Volpone*]

   Volpone. The seasoning of a play is the applause.

Now, though the Fox be punished by the laws,

He yet doth hope there is no suffering due

For any fact which he hath done 'gainst you;

If there be, censure him: here he, doubtful, stands.

If not, fare jovially, and clap your hands.

THE END

THE ALCHEMIST

TO THE LADY MOST
DESERVING HER NAME
AND BLOOD:

Mary,

LA[DY] WROTH.

MADAM,

In the age of sacrifices the truth of religion was not in the greatness and
fat of the offerings, but in the devotion and zeal of the sacrificers; else,
what could a handful of gums have done in the sight of a hecatomb? Or
how might I appear at this altar, except with those affections that no less
love the light and witness than they have the conscience of your virtue? If
what I offer bear an acceptable odour and hold the first strength, it is your
value of it which remembers where, when, and to whom it was kindled.
Otherwise, as the times are, there comes rarely forth that thing so full of
authority or example, but by assiduity and custom grows less, and loses.
This, yet safe in your judgement (which is a Sidney's), is forbidden to 10
speak more, lest it talk or look like one of the ambitious faces of the time:
who, the more they paint, are the less themselves.

Your La[dyship's]
true honourer,
BEN JONSON.

To the Reader

If thou beest more, thou art an understander, and then I trust thee. If thou art one that tak'st up, and but a pretender, beware at what hands thou receiv'st thy commodity; for thou wert never more fair in the way to be cozened than in this age in poetry, especially in plays: wherein now the concupiscence of dances and antics so reigneth, as to run away from nature and be afraid of her is the only point of art that tickles the spectators. But how out of purpose and place do I name art, when the professors are grown so obstinate contemners of it, and presumers on their own naturals, as they are deriders of all diligence that way, and by
10 simple mocking at the terms, when they understand not the things, think to get off wittily with their ignorance. Nay, they are esteemed the more learned and sufficient for this by the many, through their excellent vice of judgement. For they commend writers as they do fencers or wrestlers, who, if they come in robustiously, and put for it with a great deal of violence, are received for the braver fellows; when many times their own rudeness is the cause of their disgrace, and a little touch of their adversary gives all that boisterous force the foil. I deny not but that these men, who always seek to do more than enough, may sometime happen on something that is good and great, but very seldom; and when it comes it
20 doth not recompense the rest of their ill. It sticks out perhaps and is more eminent because all is sordid and vile about it, as lights are more discerned in a thick darkness than a faint shadow. I speak not this out of a hope to do good on any man against his will; for I know, if it were put to the question of theirs and mine, the worse would find more suffrages, because the most favour common errors. But I give thee this warning, that there is a great difference between those that, to gain the opinion of copy, utter all they can, however unfitly, and those that use election and a mean. For it is only the disease of the unskilful to think rude things greater than polished, or scattered more numerous than composed.

The Persons of the Play

Subtle, *the Alchemist*
Face, *the Housekeeper*
Dol Common, *their Colleague*
Dapper, *a Clerk*
Drugger, *a Tobacco-man*
Lovewit, *Master of the House*
Epicure Mammon, *a Knight*
Surly, *a Gamester*

Tribulation, *a Pastor of Amsterdam*
Ananias, *a Deacon there*
Kastril, *the Angry Boy*
Da[me] Pliant, *his Sister, a Widow*
Neighbours
Officers
Mutes

The Scene:

London

THE ALCHEMIST

THE ARGUMENT

T he sickness hot, a master quit, for fear,
H is house in town, and left one servant there.
E ase him corrupted, and gave means to know
A cheater and his punk; who, now brought low,
L eaving their narrow practice, were become
C ozeners at large; and only wanting some
H ouse to set up, with him they here contract
E ach for a share, and all begin to act.
M uch company they draw, and much abuse,
I n casting figures, telling fortunes, news, 10
S elling of flies, flat bawdry, with the stone;
T ill it, and they, and all in fume are gone.

PROLOGUE

Fortune, that favours fools, these two short hours
    We wish away, both for your sakes and ours,
Judging spectators; and desire in place
    To the author justice, to ourselves but grace.
Our scene is London, 'cause we would make known
    No country's mirth is better than our own.
No clime breeds better matter for your whore,
    Bawd, squire, impostor, many persons more,
Whose manners, now called humours, feed the stage;
    And which have still been subject for the rage 10
Or spleen of comic writers. Though this pen
    Did never aim to grieve, but better men,
Howe'er the age he lives in doth endure
    The vices that she breeds, above their cure.
But when the wholesome remedies are sweet,
    And, in their working, gain and profit meet,

He hopes to find no spirit so much diseased,
    But will, with such fair correctives, be pleased.
For here he doth not fear who can apply.
    If there be any that will sit so nigh   20
Unto the stream to look what it doth run,
    They shall find things they'd think, or wish, were done;
They are so natural follies, but so shown,
    As even the doers may see, and yet not own.

Act I, Scene i

[Lovewit's house in Blackfriars]

[Enter Face, Subtle, and Dol Common]

Face. Believe't, I will.
Subtle.   Thy worst. I fart at thee.
Dol. Ha' you your wits? why gentlemen! for love——
Face. Sirrah, I'll strip you——
Subtle.   What to do? lick figs
Out at my——
    Face.   Rogue, rogue, out of all your sleights.
    Dol. Nay, look ye! Sovereign, General, are you madmen?
    Subtle. Oh, let the wild sheep loose. I'll gum your silks
With good strong water, an' you come.   *[Brandishes phial]*
    Dol.   Will you have
The neighbours hear you? will you betray all?
Hark, I hear somebody.
    Face.   Sirrah——
    Subtle.   I shall mar
All that the tailor has made, if you approach.   10
    Face. You most notorious whelp, you insolent slave,
Dare you do this?
    Subtle.   Yes faith, yes faith.
    Face.   Why, who
Am I, my mongrel? who am I?
    Subtle.   I'll tell you,
Since you know not yourself——
    Face.   Speak lower, rogue.
    Subtle. Yes: you were once——time's not long past——the good,
Honest, plain, livery-three-pound-thrum, that kept

Your master's worship's house here in the Friars
For the vacations——
    Face.   Will you be so loud?
    Subtle. Since, by my means, translated suburb-captain.
    Face. By your means, Doctor Dog?
    Subtle.   Within man's memory,   20
All this I speak of.
    Face.   Why, I pray you, have I
Been countenanced by you, or you by me?
Do but collect, sir, where I met you first.
    Subtle. I do not hear well.
    Face.   Not of this, I think it.
But I shall put you in mind, sir: at Pie Corner,
Taking your meal of steam in from cooks' stalls,
Where, like the father of hunger, you did walk
Piteously costive, with your pinched-horn nose,
And your complexion of the Roman wash,
Stuck full of black and melancholic worms,   30
Like powder-corns, shot, at the Artillery Yard.
    Subtle. I wish you could advance your voice a little.
    Face. When you went pinned up in the several rags
You'd raked and picked from dunghills before day,
Your feet in mouldy slippers, for your kibes,
A felt of rug, and a thin threaden cloak,
That scarce would cover your no-buttocks——
    Subtle.   So, sir!
    Face. When all your alchemy and your algebra,
Your minerals, vegetals, and animals,
Your conjuring, cozening, and your dozen of trades,   40
Could not relieve your corpse with so much linen
Would make you tinder, but to see a fire;
I ga' you countenance, credit for your coals,
Your stills, your glasses, your materials,
Built you a furnace, drew you customers,
Advanced all your black arts; lent you, beside,
A house to practise in——
    Subtle.   Your master's house?
    Face. Where you have studied the more thriving skill
Of bawdry, since.
    Subtle.   Yes, in your master's house.
You and the rats here kept possession.   50

Make it not strange. I know you were one could keep
The buttery-hatch still locked, and save the chippings,
Sell the dole-beer to aqua-vitae men,
The which, together with your Christmas vails
At post and pair, your letting out of counters,
Made you a pretty stock, some twenty marks,
And gave you credit to converse with cobwebs
Here, since your mistress' death hath broke up house.
    Face. You might talk softlier, rascal.
    Subtle.   No, you scarab,
I'll thunder you in pieces. I will teach you   60
How to beware to tempt a fury again
That carries tempest in his hand and voice.
    Face. The place has made you valiant.
    Subtle.   No, your clothes.
Thou vermin, have I ta'en thee out of dung,
So poor, so wretched, when no living thing
Would keep thee company but a spider, or worse?
Raised thee from brooms and dust and watering pots?
Sublimed thee, and exalted thee, and fixed thee
I' the third region, called our state of grace?
Wrought thee to spirit, to quintessence, with pains   70
Would twice have won me the philosopher's work?
Put thee in words and fashion? made thee fit
For more than ordinary fellowships?
Given thee thy oaths, thy quarrelling dimensions?
Thy rules to cheat at horse-race, cock-pit, cards,
Dice, or whatever gallant tincture else?
Made thee a second in mine own great art?
And have I this for thank? do you rebel?
Do you fly out i' the projection?
Would you be gone now?
    Dol.   Gentlemen, what mean you?   80
Will you mar all?
    Subtle.   Slave, thou hadst had no name——
    Dol. Will you undo yourselves with civil war?
    Subtle. Never been known, past *equi clibanum*
(The heat of horse-dung), underground in cellars,
Or an ale-house darker than deaf John's; been lost
To all mankind but laundresses and tapsters,
Had not I been.

Dol.   D'you know who hears you, Sovereign?
Face. Sirrah——
Dol.   Nay, General, I thought you were civil——
Face. I shall turn desperate, if you grow thus loud.
Subtle. And hang thyself, I care not.
Face.   Hang thee, collier,   90
And all thy pots and pans, in picture I will,
Since thou hast moved me——
Dol. [*Aside*]   Oh, this'll o'erthrow all.
Face. Write thee up bawd in Paul's; have all thy tricks
Of cozening with a hollow coal, dust, scrapings,
Searching for things lost with a sieve and shears,
Erecting figures in your rows of houses,
Ant taking in of shadows with a glass,
Told in red letters; and a face cut for thee,
Worse than Gamaliel Ratsey's.
Dol.   Are you sound?
Ha' you your senses, masters?
Face.   I will have   100
A book, but barely reckoning thy impostures,
Shall prove a true philosopher's stone to printers.
Subtle. Away, you trencher-rascal!   [*Brandishes phial*]
Face. [*Draws sword*]   Out, you dog-leech,
The vomit of all prisons——
Dol.   Will you be
Your own destructions, gentlemen?
Face.   Still spewed out
For lying too heavy o' the basket.
Subtle.   Cheater!
Face. Bawd!
Subtle.   Cowherd!
Face.   Conjurer!
Subtle.   Cutpurse!
Face.   Witch!
Dol.   Oh me!
We are ruined! lost! ha' you no more regard
To your reputations? where's your judgement? 'Slight,
Have yet some care of me, o' your republic——   110
Face. Away this brach! I'll bring thee, rogue, within
The statute of sorcery, *tricesimo tertio*,
Of Harry the Eight; aye, and perhaps thy neck

Within a noose, for laundering gold and barbing it.
　Dol. You'll bring your head within a cockscomb, will you?

　　　(*She catcheth out Face's sword, and breaks Subtle's glass.*)

And you, sir, with your menstrue, gather it up.
'Sdeath, you abominable pair of stinkards,
Leave off your barking, and grow one again,
Or, by the light that shines, I'll cut your throats.
I'll not be made a prey unto the marshal   120
For ne'er a snarling dog-bolt o' you both.
Ha' you together cozened all this while,
And all the world, and shall it now be said
You've made most courteous shift to cozen yourselves?
[*To Face*] You will accuse him? you will bring him in
Within the statute? who shall take your word?
A whoreson, upstart, apocryphal captain,
Whom not a Puritan in Blackfriars will trust
So much as for a feather! [*To Subtle*] And you, too,
Will give the cause, forsooth? you will insult,   130
And claim a primacy in the divisions?
You must be chief? as if you only had
The powder to project with? and the work
Were not begun out of equality?
The venture tripartite? all things in common?
Without priority? 'Sdeath, you perpetual curs,
Fall to your couples again, and cozen kindly
And heartily and lovingly as you should,
And lose not the beginning of a term,
Or, by this hand, I shall grow factious too,   140
And take my part, and quit you.
　Face.　　　　　　　　　'Tis his fault,
He ever murmurs, and objects his pains,
And says the weight of all lies upon him.
　Subtle. Why, so it does.
　Dol.　　　　　　How does it? do not we
Sustain our parts?
　Subtle.　　　Yes, but they are not equal.
　Dol. Why, if your part exceed today, I hope
Ours may tomorrow match it.
　Subtle.　　　　　　Aye, they may.
　Dol. 'May', murmuring mastiff? Aye, and do. Death on me!

Help me to throttle him. [*Seizes Subtle by the throat*]
    Subtle.   Dorothy, mistress Dorothy,
'Ods precious, I'll do anything! What do you mean?   150
    Dol. Because o' your fermentation and cibation?
    Subtle. Not I, by heaven——
    Dol.   Your Sol and Luna—— [*to Face*] help
me.
    Subtle. Would I were hanged then! I'll conform myself.
    Dol. Will you, sir? Do so then, and quickly! Swear.
    Subtle. What should I swear?
    Dol.   To leave your factions, sir.
And labour kindly in the common work.
    Subtle. Let me not breathe if I meant aught beside.
I only used those speeches as a spur
To him.
    Dol.   I hope we need no spurs, sir. Do we?
    Face. 'Slid, prove today who shall shark best.
    Subtle.   Agreed.   160
    Dol. Yes, and work close, and friendly.
    Subtle.   'Slight, the knot
Shall grow the stronger for this breach, with me.
    Dol. Why so, my good baboons! Shall we go make
A sort of sober, scurvy, precise neighbours,
That scarce have smiled twice sin' the king came in,
A feast of laughter at our follies? Rascals,
Would run themselves from breath to see me ride,
Or you to have but a hole to thrust your heads in,
For which you should pay ear-rent? No, agree.
And may Don Provost ride a-feasting long   170
In his old velvet jerkin and stained scarfs
(My noble Sovereign, and worthy General)
Ere we contribute a new crewel garter
To his most worsted worship.
    Subtle.   Royal Dol!
Spoken like Claridiana, and thyself!
    Face. For which at supper thou shalt sit in triumph,
And not be styled Dol Common, but Dol Proper,
Dol Singular; the longest cut at night
Shall draw thee for his Dol Particular.   [*Bell sounds*]
    Subtle. Who's that? One rings. To the window, Dol. Pray heaven   180
The master do not trouble us this quarter.

 Face. Oh, fear not him. While there dies one a week
O' the plague, he's safe from thinking toward London.
Beside, he's busy at his hop-yards now;
I had a letter from him. If he do,
He'll send such word for airing o' the house
As you shall have sufficient time to quit it.
Though we break up a fortnight, 'tis no matter.
 Subtle. Who is it, Dol?
 Dol.   A fine young quodling.
 Face.   Oh,
My lawyer's clerk, I lighted on last night   190
In Holborn, at the Dagger. He would have
(I told you of him) a familiar,
To rifle with at horses, and win cups.
 Dol. Oh, let him in.
 Subtle.   Stay. Who shall do't?
 Face.   Get you
Your robes on. I will meet him, as going out.
 Dol. And what shall I do?
 Face.   Not be seen, away.   [*Exit Dol*]
Seem you very reserved.
 Subtle.   Enough.   [*Exit*]
 Face.   God b'w'you, sir.
I pray you, let him know that I was here.
His name is Dapper. I would gladly have stayed, but——

Act I, Scene ii

Dapper. [*Within*] Captain, I am here.
 Face.   Who's that? He's come, I think, Doctor.
       [*Enter Dapper*]
Good faith, sir, I was going away.
 Dapper.   In truth,
I'm very sorry, Captain.
 Face.   But I thought
Sure I should meet you.
 Dapper.   Aye, I'm very glad.
I had a scurvy writ or two to make,
And I had lent my watch last night to one

That dines today at the sheriff's, and so was robbed
Of my pass-time.

[Enter Subtle in his robes and velvet cap]

              Is this the cunning man?
   Face. This is his worship.
   Dapper.   Is he a doctor?
   Face.   Yes.
   Dapper. And ha' you broke with him, Captain?
   Face.   Aye.
   Dapper.   And how?   10
   Face. Faith, he does make the matter, sir, so dainty,
I know not what to say——
   Dapper.   Not so, good Captain.
   Face. Would I were fairly rid on't, believe me.
   Dapper. Nay, now you grieve me, sir. Why should you wish so?
I dare assure you, I'll not be ungrateful.
   Face. I cannot think you will, sir. But the law
Is such a thing—— And then, he says, Read's matter
Falling so lately——
   Dapper.   Read? He was an ass,
And dealt, sir, with a fool.
   Face.   It was a clerk, sir.
   Dapper. A clerk?
   Face.   Nay, hear me, sir, you know the law   20
Better, I think——
   Dapper.   I should, sir, and the danger.
You know I showed the statute to you?
   Face.   You did so.
   Dapper. And will I tell, then? By this hand of flesh,
Would it might never write good court-hand more,
If I discover. What do you think of me,
That I am a chiaus?
   Face.   What's that?
   Dapper.   The Turk, was here——
As one would say, do you think I am a Turk?
   Face. I'll tell the Doctor so.
   Dapper.   Do, good sweet Captain.
   Face. Come, noble Doctor, 'pray thee, let's prevail,
This is the gentleman, and he is no chiaus.   30
   Subtle. Captain, I have returned you all my answer.

I would do much, sir, for your love—— But this
I neither may, nor can.
   Face.   Tut, do not say so.
You deal now with a noble fellow, Doctor,
One that will thank you richly, and he's no chiaus:
Let that, sir, move you.
   Subtle.   Pray you, forbear——
   Face.   He has
Four angels, here——
   Subtle.   You do me wrong, good sir.
   Face. Doctor, wherein? To tempt you, with these spirits?
   Subtle. To tempt my art and love, sir, to my peril.
'Fore heaven, I scarce can think you are my friend,   40
That so would draw me to apparent danger.
   Face. I draw you? A horse draw you, and a halter,
You, and your flies together——
   Dapper.   Nay, good Captain.
   Face. That know no difference of men.
   Subtle.   Good words, sir.
   Face. Good deeds, Sir Doctor Dogs-meat. 'Slight, I bring you
No cheating Clim-o'the-Cloughs or Claribels,
That look as big as five-and-fifty and flush,
And spit out secrets like hot custard——
   Dapper.   Captain.
   Face. Nor any melancholic under-scribe,
Shall tell the vicar; but a special gentle,   50
That is the heir to forty marks a year,
Consorts with the small poets of the time,
Is the sole hope of his old grandmother,
That knows the law, and writes you six fair hands,
Is a fine clerk, and has his ciphering perfect;
Will take his oath o' the Greek Xenophon,
If need be, in his pocket; and can court
His mistress out of Ovid.
   Dapper.   Nay, dear Captain.
   Face. Did you not tell me so?
   Dapper.   Yes, but I'd ha' you
Use Master Doctor with some more respect.   60
   Face. Hang him, proud stag, with his broad velvet head.
But for your sake, I'd choke ere I would change
An article of breath with such a puck-fist——

Come, let's be gone.
    Subtle.   Pray you, let me speak with you.
    Dapper. His worship calls you, Captain.
    Face.   I am sorry
I e'er embarked myself in such a business.
    Dapper. Nay, good sir. He did call you.
    Face.   Will he take, then?
    Subtle. First, hear me——
    Face.   Not a syllable, 'less you take.
    Subtle. Pray ye, sir——
    Face.   Upon no terms, but an *assumpsit.*
    Subtle. Your humour must be law. (*He takes the money*)
    Face.   Why now, sir, talk.   70
Now, I dare hear you with mine honour. Speak.
So may this gentleman too.
    Subtle.   Why, sir——
    Face.   No whispering.
    Subtle. 'Fore heaven, you do not apprehend the loss
You do yourself in this.
    Face.   Wherein? for what?
    Subtle. Marry, to be so importunate for one
That, when he has it, will undo you all:
He'll win up all the money i' the town.
    Face. How!
    Subtle.   Yes, and blow up gamester after gamester,
As they do crackers in a puppet play.
If I do give him a familiar,   80
Give you him all you play for; never set him,
For he will have it.
    Face.   You're mistaken, Doctor.
Why, he does ask one but for cups and horses,
A trifling fly; none o' your great familiars.
    Dapper. Yes, Captain, I would have it for all games.
    Subtle. I told you so.
    Face.   'Slight, that's a new business!
I understood you, a tame bird, to fly
Twice in a term, or so, on Friday nights,
When you had left the office, for a nag
Of forty or fifty shillings.
    Dapper.   Aye, 'tis true, sir,   90
But I do think, now, I shall leave the law,

And therefore——
   Face.   Why, this changes quite the case!
D'you think that I dare move him?
   Dapper.   If you please, sir,
All's one to him, I see.
   Face.   What! for that money?
I cannot with my conscience. Nor should you
Make the request, methinks.
   Dapper.   No, sir, I mean
To add consideration.
   Face.   Why then, sir,
I'll try. Say, that it were for all games, Doctor?
   Subtle. I say, then, not a mouth shall eat for him
At any ordinary, but o' the score,   100
That is a gaming mouth, conceive me.
   Face.   Indeed!
   Subtle. He'll draw you all the treasure of the realm,
If it be set him.
   Face.   Speak you this from art?
   Subtle. Aye, sir, and reason too, the ground of art.
He's o' the only best complexion
The Queen of Faery loves.
   Face.   What! is he?
   Subtle.   Peace;
He'll overhear you. Sir, should she but see him——
   Face. What?
   Subtle.   Do not you tell him.
   Face.   Will he win at cards too?
   Subtle. The spirits of dead Holland, living Isaac,
You'd swear were in him; such a vigorous luck   110
As cannot be resisted. 'Slight, he'll put
Six o' your gallants to a cloak, indeed.
   Face. A strange success, that some man shall be born to!
   Subtle. He hears you, man——
   Dapper.   Sir, I'll not be ingrateful.
   Face. Faith, I have a confidence in his good nature;
You hear, he says, he will not be ingrateful.
   Subtle. Why, as you please; my venture follows yours.
   Face. Troth, do it, Doctor. Think him trusty, and make him.
He may make us both happy in an hour:
Win some five thousand pound, and send us two on't.   120

Dapper. Believe it, and I will, sir.
Face.   And you shall, sir.
You have heard all?
Dapper.   No, what was't? nothing, I, sir.
Face. Nothing?
Dapper.   A little, sir. (*Face takes him aside*)
Face.   Well, a rare star
Reigned at your birth.
Dapper.   At mine, sir? No.
Face.   The Doctor
Swears that you are——
Subtle.   Nay, Captain, you'll tell all, now.
Face. Allied to the Queen of Faery.
Dapper.   Who? that I am?
Believe it, no such matter——
Face.   Yes, and that
You were born with a caul o' your head.
Dapper.   Who says so?
Face.   Come,
You know it well enough, though you dissemble it.
Dapper. I' fac, I do not. You are mistaken.
Face.   How!   13
Swear by your fac? and in a thing so known
Unto the Doctor? how shall we, sir, trust you
I' the other matter? can we ever think,
When you have won five or six thousand pound,
You'll send us shares in't, by this rate?
Dapper.   By Jove, sir,
I'll win ten thousand pound, and send you half.
I' fac's no oath.
Subtle.   No, no, he did but jest.
Face. Go to. Go, thank the Doctor. He's your friend
To take it so.
Dapper.   I thank his worship.
Face.   So?
Another angel.
Dapper.   Must I?
Face.   Must you? 'slight,   14
What else is thanks? will you be trivial?   [*Dapper gives him money*]
                Doctor,
When must he come for his familiar?

Dapper. Shall I not ha' it with me?
Subtle.   Oh, good sir!
There must a world of ceremonies pass,
You must be bathed and fumigated first;
Besides, the Queen of Faery does not rise
Till it be noon.
    Face.   Not if she danced tonight.
    Subtle. And she must bless it.
    Face.   Did you never see
Her Royal Grace yet?
    Dapper.   Whom?
    Face.   Your aunt of Faery?
    Subtle. Not since she kissed him in the cradle, Captain,   150
I can resolve you that.
    Face.   Well, see her Grace,
Whate'er it cost you, for a thing that I know!
It will be somewhat hard to compass; but,
However, see her. You are made, believe it,
If you can see her. Her Grace is a lone woman,
And very rich, and if she take a fancy,
She will do strange things. See her, at any hand.
'Slid, she may hap to leave you all she has!
It is the Doctor's fear.
    Dapper.   How will't be done then?
    Face. Let me alone, take you no thought. Do you   160
But say to me, Captain, I'll see her Grace.
    Dapper. Captain, I'll see her Grace.   (*One knocks without*)
    Face.   Enough.
    Subtle.   Who's there?
Anon. [*Aside to Face*] Conduct him forth, by the back way.
[*To Dapper*] Sir, against one o'clock, prepare yourself;
Till when you must be fasting; only, take
Three drops of vinegar in at your nose,
Two at your mouth, and one at either ear;
Then bathe your fingers' ends and wash your eyes,
To sharpen your five senses; and cry 'hum',
Thrice, and then 'buzz' as often; and then, come.   [*Exit*]   170
    Face. Can you remember this?
    Dapper.   I warrant you.
    Face. Well then, away. 'Tis but your bestowing
Some twenty nobles 'mong her Grace's servants,

And put on a clean shirt. You do not know
What grace her Grace may do you in clean linen.   [*Exeunt*]

Act I, Scene iii

Subtle. [*Within*] Come in. (Good wives, I pray you forbear me now;
Troth, I can do you no good, till afternoon.)

[*Enter Subtle with Abel Drugger*]

What is your name, say you? Abel Drugger?
 Drugger.   Yes, sir.
 Subtle. A seller of tobacco?
 Drugger.   Yes sir.
 Subtle.   'Umh.
Free of the Grocers?
 Drugger.   Aye, an't please you.
 Subtle.   Well——
Your business, Abel?
 Drugger.   This, an't please your worship:
I am a young beginner, and am building
Of a new shop, an't like your worship, just
At corner of a street——here's the plot on't——
And I would know by art, sir, of your worship,   10
Which way I should make my door, by necromancy,
And where my shelves; and which should be for boxes;
And which for pots. I would be glad to thrive, sir.
And I was wished to your worship by a gentleman,
One Captain Face, that says you know men's planets,
And their good angels, and their bad.
 Subtle.   I do,
If I do see 'em——

[*Enter Face*]

 Face.   What! my honest Abel?
Thou art well met, here!
 Drugger.   Troth, sir, I was speaking
Just as your worship came here, of your worship.
I pray you, speak for me to Master Doctor.
 Face. He shall do anything. Doctor, do you hear?   20
This is my friend, Abel, an honest fellow,
He lets me have good tobacco, and he does not

Sophisticate it with sack-lees, or oil,
Nor washes it in muscatel and grains,
Nor buries it in gravel underground,
Wrapped up in greasy leather or pissed clouts,
But keeps it in fine lily-pots that, opened,
Smell like conserve of roses, or French beans.
He has his maple block, his silver tongs,   30
Winchester pipes, and fire of juniper.
A neat, spruce, honest, fellow, and no goldsmith.
 Subtle. He's a fortunate fellow, that I am sure on——
 Face. Already, sir, ha' you found it? Lo thee, Abel!
 Subtle. And in right way toward riches——
 Face.   Sir!
 Subtle.   This summer
He will be of the clothing of his company,
And next spring, called to the scarlet. Spend what he can.
 Face. What, and so little beard?
 Subtle.   Sir, you must think,
He may have a receipt to make hair come.
But he'll be wise, preserve his youth——and fine for't: 40
His fortune looks for him another way.
 Face. 'Slid, Doctor, how canst thou know this so soon?
I am amused at that.
 Subtle.   By a rule, Captain,
In metoposcopy, which I do work by:
A certain star i' the forehead, which you see not.
Your chestnut or your olive-coloured face
Does never fail, and your long ear doth promise.
I knew't by certain spots too in his teeth,
And on the nail of his mercurial finger.
 Face. Which finger's that?
 Subtle.   His little finger. Look.   50
You were born upon a Wednesday?
 Drugger.   Yes, indeed, sir.
 Subtle. The thumb, in chiromancy, we give Venus;
The forefinger to Jove; the midst, to Saturn;
The ring to Sol; the least, to Mercury,
Who was the lord, sir, of his horoscope,
His house of life being Libra: which foreshowed
He should be a merchant, and should trade with balance.
 Face. Why, this is strange! is't not, honest Nab?

Subtle. There is a ship now coming from Ormus,
That shall yield him such a commodity   60
Of drugs—— [*Looking at Drugger's plan*] This is the west, and this the
    south?
Drugger. Yes, sir.
Subtle.   And those are your two sides?
Drugger.   Aye, sir.
Subtle. Make me your door, then, south; your broad side, west;
And on the east side of your shop, aloft,
Write *Mathlai, Tarmiel,* and *Baraborat*;
Upon the north part, *Rael, Velel, Thiel.*
They are the names of those Mercurial spirits
That do fright flies from boxes.
Drugger.   Yes, sir.
Subtle.   And
Beneath your threshold, bury me a lodestone
To draw in gallants that wear spurs. The rest,   70
They'll seem to follow.
Face.   That's a secret, Nab!
Subtle. And on your stall, a puppet, with a vice,
And a court-fucus, to call city-dames.
You shall deal much with minerals.
Drugger.   Sir, I have,
At home, already——
Subtle.   Aye, I know, you have arsenic,
Vitriol, sal-tartar, argol, alkali,
Cinnabar: I know all. This fellow, Captain,
Will come in time to be a great distiller,
And give a say——I will not say directly,
But very fair——at the philosopher's stone.   80
Face. Why, how now, Abel! is this true?
Drugger.   Good Captain,
What must I give?
Face.   Nay, I'll not counsel thee.
Thou hear'st, what wealth——he says, spend what thou canst——
Th' art like to come to.
Drugger.   I would gi' him a crown.
Face. A crown! and toward such a fortune? heart,
Thou shalt rather gi' him thy shop. No gold about thee?
Drugger. Yes, I have a portague I ha' kept this half year.
Face. Out on thee, Nab! 'Slight, there was such an offer——

'Shalt keep't no longer. I'll gi' it him for thee?
Doctor, Nab prays your worship to drink this, [*giving coin*] and swears   90
He will appear more grateful, as your skill
Does raise him in the world.
    Drugger.   I would entreat
Another favour of his worship.
    Face.   What is't, Nab?
    Drugger. But to look over, sir, my almanac,
And cross out my ill-days, that I may neither
Bargain nor trust upon them.
    Face.   That he shall, Nab.
Leave it, it shall be done 'gainst afternoon.
    Subtle. And a direction for his shelves.
    Face.   Now, Nab?
Art thou well pleased, Nab?
    Drugger.   Thank sir, both your worships.
    Face.   Away. [*Exit Drugger*]
Why, now, you smoky persecutor of nature!   100
Now do you see that something's to be done
Beside your beech-coal and your corsive waters,
Your crosslets, crucibles, and cucurbits?
You must have stuff brought home to you to work on!
And yet you think I am at no expense
In searching out these veins, then following 'em,
Then trying 'em out. 'Fore God, my intelligence
Costs me more money than my share oft comes to,
In these rare works.
    Subtle.   You're pleasant, sir. [*Enter Dol*] How now?

Act I, Scene iv

    Face. What says my dainty Dolkin?
    Dol.   Yonder fishwife
Will not away. And there's your giantess,
The bawd of Lambeth.
    Subtle.   Heart, I cannot speak with 'em.
    Dol. Not afore night, I have told 'em, in a voice
Thorough the trunk, like one of your familiars.
But I have spied Sir Epicure Mammon——
    Subtle.   Where?

Dol. Coming along at far end of the lane,
Slow of his feet, but earnest of his tongue
To one that's with him.
 Subtle.   Face, go you and shift.   [*Exit Face*]
Dol, you must presently make ready too——   10
 Dol. Why, what's the matter?
 Subtle.   Oh, I did look for him
With the sun's rising; 'marvel he could sleep!
This is the day I am to perfect for him
The magisterium, our great work, the stone,
And yield it, made, into his hands; of which
He has this month talked as he were possessed.
And now he's dealing pieces on't away.
Methinks I see him entering ordinaries,
Dispensing for the pox and plaguy-houses,
Reaching his dose, walking Moorfields for lepers,   20
And offering citizens' wives pomander-bracelets
As his preservative, made of the elixir;
Searching the spital to make old bawds young,
And the highways for beggars to make rich;
I see no end of his labours. He will make
Nature ashamed of her long sleep; when art,
Who's but a step-dame, shall do more than she,
In her best love to mankind, ever could.
If his dream last, he'll turn the age to gold.   [*Exeunt*]

Act II, Scene i

[*Lovewit's house. Enter Sir Epicure Mammon and Surly*]

Mammon. Come on, sir. Now you set your foot on shore
In *novo orbe*; here's the rich Peru,
And there within, sir, are the golden mines,
Great Solomon's Ophir! He was sailing to't
Three years, but we have reached it in ten months.
This is the day wherein to all my friends,
I will pronounce the happy word, 'Be rich'.
This day you shall be *spectatissimi*.
You shall no more deal with the hollow die
Or the frail card. No more be at charge of keeping   10

The livery-punk, for the young heir, that must
Seal, at all hours, in his shirt. No more,
If he deny, ha' him beaten to't, as he is
That brings him the commodity. No more
Shall thirst of satin, or the covetous hunger
Of velvet entrails for a rude-spun cloak,
To be displayed at Madam Augusta's, make
The sons of sword and hazard fall before
The golden calf, and on their knees, whole nights,
Commit idolatry with wine and trumpets,   20
Or go a-feasting after drum and ensign.
No more of this. You shall start up young viceroys,
And have your punks and punketees, my Surly.
And unto thee I speak it first, 'Be rich'.
Where is my Subtle, there? Within, ho!
  Face. (*Within*)   Sir,
He'll come to you, by and by.
  Mammon.   That's his fire-drake,
His lungs, his Zephyrus, he that puffs his coals
Till he firk nature up in her own centre.
You are not faithful, sir. This night I'll change
All that is metal in my house to gold,   30
And early in the morning will I send
To all the plumbers and the pewterers
And buy their tin and lead up; and to Lothbury,
For all the copper.
  Surly.   What, and turn that too?
  Mammon. Yes, and I'll purchase Devonshire and Cornwall,
And make them perfect Indies! You admire now?
  Surly. No, faith.
  Mammon.   But when you see the effects of the great medicine,
Of which one part projected on a hundred
Of Mercury, or Venus, or the Moon,
Shall turn it to as many of the Sun,   40
Nay, to a thousand, so *ad infinitum*,
You will believe me.
  Surly.   Yes, when I see't, I will.
But if my eyes do cozen me so, and I
Giving 'em no occasion, sure, I'll have
A whore shall piss 'em out next day.
  Mammon.   Ha! Why?

Do you think I fable with you? I assure you,
He that has once the flower of the sun,
The perfect ruby, which we call elixir,
Not only can do that, but by its virtue,
Can confer honour, love, respect, long life,   50
Give safety, valour, yea, and victory,
To whom he will. In eight and twenty days,
I'll make an old man of fourscore a child.
   Surly. No doubt he's that already.
   Mammon.   Nay, I mean
Restore his years, renew him like an eagle
To the fifth age, make him get sons and daughters,
Young giants, as our philosophers have done
(The ancient patriarchs afore the flood)
But taking, once a week, on a knife's point,
The quantity of a grain of mustard of it;   60
Become stout Marses, and beget young Cupids.
   Surly. The decayed vestals of Pict-hatch would thank you,
That keep the fire alive there.
   Mammon.   'Tis the secret
Of nature naturized 'gainst all infections,
Cures all diseases coming of all causes:
A month's grief in a day, a year's in twelve,
And of what age soever, in a month——
Past all the doses of your drugging doctors.
I'll undertake, withal, to fright the plague
Out o' the kingdom in three months.
   Surly.   And I'll   70
Be bound, the players shall sing your praises then,
Without their poets.
   Mammon.   Sir, I'll do't. Meantime,
I'll give away so much unto my man
Shall serve the whole city with preservative
Weekly, each house his dose, and at the rate——
   Surly. As he that built the waterwork does with water?
   Mammon. You are incredulous.
   Surly.   Faith, I have a humour,
I would not willingly be gulled. Your stone
Cannot transmute me.
   Mammon.   Pertinax, my Surly,
Will you believe antiquity? records?   80

I'll show you a book where Moses and his sister
And Solomon have written of the art;
Aye, and a treatise penned by Adam.
   Surly. How!
   Mammon. O' the philosopher's stone, and in High Dutch.
   Surly. Did Adam write, sir, in High Dutch?
   Mammon. He did;
Which proves it was the primitive tongue.
   Surly. What paper?
   Mammon. On cedar board.
   Surly. Oh, that indeed, they say,
Will last 'gainst worms.
   Mammon. 'Tis like your Irish wood
'Gainst cobwebs. I have a piece of Jason's fleece, too,
Which was no other than a book of alchemy, 90
Writ in large sheepskin, a good fat ram-vellum.
Such was Pythagoras' thigh, Pandora's tub;
And all that fable of Medea's charms
The manner of our work: the bulls, our furnace,
Still breathing fire; our *argent-vive*, the dragon;
The dragon's teeth, mercury sublimate
That keeps the whiteness, hardness, and the biting;
And they are gathered into Jason's helm,
(The alembic) and then sowed in Mars his field,
And thence sublimed so often, till they are fixed. 100
Both this, the Hesperian garden, Cadmus' story,
Jove's shower, the boon of Midas, Argus' eyes,
Boccace his Demogorgon, thousands more,
All abstract riddles of our stone. How now?

Act II, Scene ii

[Enter Face, as Lungs]

   Mammon. Do we succeed? is our day come? and holds it?
   Face. The evening will set red upon you, sir;
You have colour for it, crimson: the red ferment
Has done his office. Three hours hence, prepare you
To see projection.
   Mammon. Pertinax, my Surly,
Again I say to thee, aloud, 'Be rich'.

This day thou shalt have ingots, and tomorrow
Give lords the affront. Is it, my Zephyrus, right?
Blushes the bolt's head?
    Face.   Like a wench with child, sir,
That were but now discovered to her master.   10
    Mammon. Excellent witty Lungs! My only care is
Where to get stuff enough now to project on;
This town will not half serve me.
    Face.   No, sir? Buy
The covering off o' churches.
    Mammon.   That's true.
    Face.   Yes.
Let 'em stand bare, as do their auditory,
Or cap 'em new with shingles.
    Mammon.   No, good thatch;
Thatch will lie light upo' the rafters, Lungs.
Lungs, I will manumit thee from the furnace;
I will restore thee thy complexion, Puff,
Lost in the embers; and repair this brain,   20
Hurt wi' the fume o' the metals.
    Face.   I have blown, sir,
Hard, for your worship; thrown by many a coal,
When 'twas not beech; weighed those I put in, just,
To keep your heat still even. These bleared eyes
Have waked to read your several colours, sir,
Of the pale citron, the green lion, the crow,
The peacock's tail, the plumèd swan.
    Mammon.   And lastly,
Thou hast descried the flower, the *sanguis agni*?
    Face. Yes, sir.
    Mammon.   Where's master?
    Face.   At's prayers, sir; he,
Good man, he's doing his devotions   30
For the success.
    Mammon.   Lungs, I will set a period
To all thy labours; thou shalt be the master
Of my seraglio.
    Face.   Good, sir.
    Mammon.   But do you hear?
I'll geld you, Lungs.
    Face.   Yes, sir.

Mammon.   For I do mean
To have a list of wives and concubines
Equal with Solomon, who had the stone
Alike with me; and I will make me a back
With the elixir that shall be as tough
As Hercules, to encounter fifty a night.
Th' art sure thou saw'st it blood?
   Face.   Both blood and spirit, sir.   40
Mammon. I will have all my beds blown up, not stuffed;
Down is too hard. And then, mine oval room
Filled with such pictures as Tiberius took
From Elephantis, and dull Aretine
But coldly imitated. Then, my glasses
Cut in more subtle angles, to disperse
And multiply the figures, as I walk
Naked between my *succubae*. My mists
I'll have of perfume, vapoured 'bout the room
To lose ourselves in; and my baths like pits   50
To fall into; from whence we will come forth
And roll us dry in gossamer and roses.
(Is it arrived at ruby?)—— Where I spy
A wealthy citizen or rich lawyer
Have a sublimed pure wife, unto that fellow
I'll send a thousand pound to be my cuckold.
   Face. And I shall carry it?
   Mammon.   No: I'll ha' no bawds
But fathers and mothers——they will do it best,
Best of all others. And my flatterers
Shall be the pure and gravest of divines   60
That I can get for money. My mere fools,
Eloquent burgesses; and then my poets
The same that writ so subtly of the fart,
Whom I will entertain still for that subject.
The few that would give out themselves to be
Court and town stallions, and each-where belie
Ladies who are known most innocent for them,
Those will I beg to make me eunuchs of,
And they shall fan me with ten ostrich tails
Apiece made in a plume to gather wind.   70
We will be brave, Puff, now we ha' the medicine.
My meat shall all come in in Indian shells,

Dishes of agate set in gold, and studded
With emeralds, sapphires, hyacinths, and rubies.
The tongues of carps, dormice, and camels' heels,
Boiled i' the spirit of Sol, and dissolved pearl
(Apicius' diet, 'gainst the epilepsy);
And I will eat these broths with spoons of amber,
Headed with diamond and carbuncle.
My footboy shall eat pheasants, calvered salmons,   80
Knots, godwits, lampreys. I myself will have
The beards of barbels served instead of salads;
Oiled mushrooms; and the swelling unctuous paps
Of a fat pregnant sow, newly cut off,
Dressed with an exquisite and poignant sauce;
For which, I'll say unto my cook, 'There's gold;
Go forth, and be a knight'.
    Face.   Sir, I'll go look
A little how it heightens.   [*Exit*]
    Mammon.   Do. My shirts
I'll have of taffeta-sarsenet, soft and light
As cobwebs; and for all my other raiment,   90
It shall be such as might provoke the Persian,
Were he to teach the world riot anew.
My gloves of fishes' and birds' skins, perfumed
With gums of paradise, and eastern air——
    Surly. And do you think to have the stone, with this?
    Mammon. No, I do think to have all this with the stone.
    Surly. Why, I have heard he must be *homo frugi*,
A pious, holy, and religious man,
One free from mortal sin, a very virgin.
    Mammon. That makes it, sir, he is so. But I buy it;   100
My venture brings it me. He, honest wretch——
A notable, superstitious, good soul——
Has worn his knees bare and his slippers bald
With prayer and fasting for it; and sir, let him
Do it alone, for me, still. Here he comes:
Not a profane word afore him; 'tis poison.

Act II, Scene iii

[Enter Subtle]

Mammon. Good morrow, father.

Subtle.   Gentle son, good morrow,
And to your friend there. What is he is with you?

Mammon. An heretic that I did bring along
In hope, sir, to convert him.

Subtle.   Son, I doubt
You're covetous, that thus you meet your time
I' the just point; prevent your day at morning.
This argues something worthy of a fear
Of importune and carnal appetite.
Take heed you do not cause the blessing leave you
With your ungoverned haste. I should be sorry   10
To see my labours, now e'en at perfection,
Got by long watching and large patience,
Not prosper where my love and zeal hath placed 'em.
Which (heaven I call to witness, with yourself,
To whom I have poured my thoughts) in all my ends,
Have looked no way but unto public good,
To pious uses, and dear charity,
No[w] grown a prodigy with men. Wherein
If you, my son, should now prevaricate,
And to your own particular lusts employ   20
So great and catholic a bliss, be sure
A curse will follow, yea, and overtake
Your subtle and most secret ways.

Mammon.   I know, sir,
You shall not need to fear me. I but come,
To ha' you confute this gentleman.

Surly.   Who is,
Indeed, sir, somewhat costive of belief
Toward your stone; would not be gulled.

Subtle.   Well, son,
All that I can convince him in, is this:
The work is done; bright Sol is in his robe.
We have a medicine of the triple soul,   30
The glorified spirit. Thanks be to heaven,
And make us worthy of it. Ulenspiegel!

Face. [*Within*] Anon, sir.

                          [*Enter Face*]

    Subtle.   Look well to the register,
And let your heat still lessen by degrees,
To the aludels.
    Face.   Yes, sir.
    Subtle.   Did you look
O' the bolt's head yet?
    Face.   Which? On D sir?
    Subtle.   Aye.
What's the complexion?
    Face.   Whitish.
    Subtle.   Infuse vinegar,
To draw his volatile substance, and his tincture;
And let the water in glass E be filtered,
And put into the gripe's egg. Lute him well,   40
And leave him closed in *balneo.*
    Face.   I will, sir.   [*Exit*]
    Surly. What a brave language here is! next to canting!
    Subtle. I have another work you never saw, son,
That three days since passed the philosopher's wheel,
In the lent heat of Athanor, and's become
Sulphur o' nature.
    Mammon.   But 'tis for me?
    Subtle.   What need you?
You have enough in that is perfect.
    Mammon.   Oh, but——
    Subtle. Why, this is covetise!
    Mammon.   No, I assure you,
I shall employ it all in pious uses,
Founding of colleges and grammar schools,   50
Marrying young virgins, building hospitals,
And now and then a church.

                          [*Enter Face*]

    Subtle.   How now?
    Face.   Sir, please you,
Shall I not change the filter?
    Subtle.   Marry, yes.
And bring me the complexion of glass B.   [*Exit Face*]
    Mammon. Ha' you another?

Subtle.   Yes, son; were I assured
Your piety were firm, we would not want
The means to glorify it. But I hope the best:
I mean to tinct C in sand-heat tomorrow,
And give him imbibition.
    Mammon.   Of white oil?
    Subtle. No, sir, of red. F is come over the helm too,   60
I thank my Maker, in St Mary's bath,
And shows *lac virginis*. Blessèd be heaven.
I sent you of his faeces there, calcined.
Out of that calx I ha' won the salt of mercury.
    Mammon. By pouring on your rectifièd water?
    Subtle. Yes, and reverberating in Athanor.

[Enter Face]

How now? What colour says it?
    Face.   The ground black, sir.
    Mammon. That's your crow's head?
    Surly.   Your cockscomb's, is it not?
    Subtle. No, 'tis not perfect, would it were the crow.
That work wants something.
    Surly. [*Aside*]   Oh, I looked for this.   70
The hay is a-pitching.
    Subtle.   Are you sure you loosed 'em
I' their own menstrue?
    Face.   Yes, sir, and then married 'em,
And put 'em in a bolt's head nipped to digestion,
According as you bade me, when I set
The liquor of Mars to circulation
In the same heat.
    Subtle.   The process then was right.
    Face. Yes, by the token, sir, the retort brake,
And what was saved was put into the pelican,
And signed with Hermes' seal.
    Subtle.   I think 'twas so.
We should have a new amalgama.
    Surly. [*Aside*]   Oh, this ferret   80
Is rank as any polecat.
    Subtle.   But I care not.
Let him e'en die; we have enough beside
In embrion. H has his white shirt on?

Face.   Yes, sir,
He's ripe for inceration; he stands warm
In his ash-fire. I would not you should let
Any die now, if I might counsel, sir,
For luck's sake to the rest. It is not good.
    Mammon. He says right.
    Surly. [*Aside*]   Aye, are you bolted?
    Face.   Nay, I know't, sir,
I've seen the ill fortune. What is some three ounces
Of fresh materials?
    Mammon.   Is't no more?
    Face.   No more, sir,   90
Of gold t' amalgam with some six of mercury.
    Mammon. Away, here's money. What will serve?
    Face.   Ask him, sir.
    Mammon. How much?
    Subtle.   Give him nine pound; you may gi' him ten.
    Surly. Yes, twenty, and be cozened; do.
    Mammon.   There 'tis.
    Subtle. This needs not, but that you will have it so
To see conclusions of all. For two
Of our inferior works are at fixation,
A third is in ascension. Go your ways.
Ha' you set the oil of Luna in kemia?
    Face. Yes, sir.
    Subtle.   And the philosopher's vinegar?
    Face.   Aye.   [*Exit*] 10
    Surly. We shall have a salad.
    Mammon.   When do you make projection?
    Subtle. Son, be not hasty; I exalt our medicine
By hanging him in *balneo vaporoso*,
And giving him solution; then congeal him;
And then dissolve him; then again congeal him:
For look, how oft I iterate the work,
So many times, I add unto his virtue.
As, if at first one ounce convert a hundred,
After his second loose, he'll turn a thousand;
His third solution, ten; his fourth, a hundred.   11
After his fifth, a thousand thousand ounces
Of any imperfect metal, into pure
Silver or gold, in all examinations,

As good as any of the natural mine.
Get you your stuff here against afternoon:
Your brass, your pewter, and your andirons.
   Mammon. Not those of iron?
   Subtle.   Yes, you may bring them, too;
We'll change all metals.
   Surly.   I believe you in that.
   Mammon. Then I may send my spits?
   Subtle.   Yes, and your racks.
   Surly. And dripping-pans, and pot-hangers, and hooks?   120
Shall he not?
   Subtle.   If he please.
   Surly.   To be an ass.
   Subtle. How, sir!
   Mammon.   This gent'man, you must bear withal;
I told you he had no faith.
   Surly.   And little hope, sir,
But much less charity, should I gull myself.
   Subtle. Why, what have you observed, sir, in our art
Seems so impossible?
   Surly.   But your whole work, no more.
That you should hatch gold in a furnace, sir,
As they do eggs in Egypt!
   Subtle.   Sir, do you
Believe that eggs are hatched so?
   Surly.   If I should?
   Subtle. Why, I think that the greater miracle.   130
No egg but differs from a chicken more
Than metals in themselves.
   Surly.   That cannot be.
The egg's ordained by nature to that end,
And is a chicken in *potentia.*
   Subtle. The same we say of lead and other metals,
Which would be gold, if they had time.
   Mammon.   And that
Our art doth further.
   Subtle.   Aye, for 'twere absurd
To think that nature in the earth bred gold
Perfect, i' the instant. Something went before.
There must be remote matter.
   Surly.   Aye, what is that?   140

Subtle. Marry, we say——
Mammon.   Aye, now it heats: stand, father.
Pound him to dust——
    Subtle.   It is, of the one part,
A humid exhalation, which we call
Materia liquida, or the unctuous water;
On the other part, a certain crass and viscous
Portion of earth; both which, concorporate,
Do make the elementary matter of gold:
Which is not yet *propria materia*,
But common to all metals and all stones.
For where it is forsaken of that moisture,   150
And hath more dryness, it becomes a stone;
Where it retains more of the humid fatness,
It turns to sulphur or to quicksilver,
Who are the parents of all other metals.
Nor can this remote matter suddenly
Progress so from extreme unto extreme,
As to grow gold, and leap o'er all the means.
Nature doth first beget the imperfect, then
Proceeds she to the perfect. Of that airy
And oily water, mercury is engendered,   160
Sulphur o' the fat and earthy part: the one
Which is the last supplying the place of male,
The other of the female, in all metals.
Some do believe hermaphrodeity,
That both do act and suffer. But these two
Make the rest ductile, malleable, extensive.
And even in gold they are; for we do find
Seeds of them by our fire, and gold in them;
And can produce the species of each metal
More perfect thence than nature doth in earth.   170
Beside, who doth not see in daily practice
Art can beget bees, hornets, beetles, wasps,
Out of the carcasses and dung of creatures;
Yea, scorpions, of an herb, being ritely placed;
And these are living creatures, far more perfect
And excellent than metals.
    Mammon.   Well said, father!
Nay, if he take you in hand, sir, with an argument
He'll bray you in a mortar.

Surly.   'Pray you, sir, stay.
Rather than I'll be brayed, sir, I'll believe
That alchemy is a pretty kind of game,   180
Somewhat like tricks o' the cards, to cheat a man
With charming.
    Subtle.   Sir?
    Surly.   What else are all your terms,
Whereon no one o' your writers 'grees with other?
Of your elixir, your *lac virginis*,
Your stone, your medicine, and your chrysosperm,
Your sal, your sulphur, and your mercury,
Your oil of height, your tree of life, your blood,
Your marcasite, your tutty, your magnesia,
Your toad, your crow, your dragon, and your panther,
Your sun, your moon, your firmament, your adrop,   190
Your lato, azoch, zarnich, chibrit, heautarit,
And then, your red man and your white woman,
With all your broths, your menstrues and materials
Of piss and eggshells, women's terms, man's blood,
Hair o' the head, burnt clouts, chalk, merds, and clay,
Powder of bones, scalings of iron, glass,
And worlds of other strange ingredients
Would burst a man to name?
    Subtle.   And all these, named,
Intending but one thing; which art our writers
Used to obscure their art.
    Mammon.   Sir, so I told him,   200
Because the simple idiot should not learn it,
And make it vulgar.
    Subtle.   Was not all the knowledge
Of the Egyptians writ in mystic symbols?
Speak not the Scriptures oft in parables?
Are not the choicest fables of the poets
That were the fountains and first springs of wisdom
Wrapped in perplexèd allegories?
    Mammon.   I urged that,
And cleared to him, that Sisyphus was damned
To roll the ceaseless stone only because
He would have made ours common. (*Dol is seen*) Who is this?   210
    Subtle. God's precious——what do you mean? Go in, good lady,
Let me entreat you. [*Exit Dol*] Where's this varlet?

[*Enter Face*]

Face.   Sir?

Subtle. You very knave! do you use me thus?

Face.   Wherein, sir?

Subtle. Go in and see, you traitor. Go!   [*Exit Face*]

Mammon.   Who is it, sir?

Subtle. Nothing, sir; nothing.

Mammon.   What's the matter, good sir?

I have not seen you thus distempered; who is't?

Subtle. All arts have still had, sir, their adversaries,

But ours the most ignorant. (*Face returns*) What now?

Face. 'Twas not my fault, sir, she would speak with you.

Subtle. Would she, sir? Follow me.   [*Exit*]

Mammon.   Stay, Lungs.

Face.   I dare not, sir.   220

Mammon. Stay man; what is she?

Face.   A lord's sister, sir.

Mammon. How! 'Pray thee, stay.

Face.   She's mad, sir, and sent hither——

He'll be mad too.

Mammon.   I warrant thee.—— Why sent hither?

Face. Sir, to be cured.

Subtle. [*Within*]   Why, rascal!

Face.   Lo you!——here, sir!

                                        (*He goes out*)

Mammon. 'Fore God, a Bradamante, a brave piece.

Surly. Heart, this is a bawdy house! I'll be burnt else.

Mammon. Oh, by this light, no! Do not wrong him. He's

Too scrupulous that way. It is his vice.

No, he's a rare physician, do him right;

An excellent Paracelsian! and has done   230

Strange cures with mineral physic. He deals all

With spirits, he. He will not hear a word

Of Galen, or his tedious recipes.

How now, Lungs!   (*Face again*)

Face.   Softly, sir, speak softly. I meant

To ha' told your worship all. This must not hear.

Mammon. No, he will not be gulled; let him alone.

Face. You're very right, sir, she is a most rare scholar;

And is gone mad with studying Broughton's works.

If you but name a word touching the Hebrew,

She falls into her fit, and will discourse   240
So learnedly of genealogies
As you would run mad, too, to hear her, sir.
    Mammon. How might one do to have conference with her, Lungs?
    Face. Oh, divers have run mad upon the conference.
I do not know, sir; I am sent in haste,
To fetch a vial.
    Surly.   Be not gulled, Sir Mammon.
    Mammon. Wherein? 'Pray ye, be patient.
    Surly.   Yes, as you are.
And trust confederate knaves, and bawds, and whores.
    Mammon. You are too foul, believe it. Come here, Ulen.
One word.
    Face.   I dare not, in good faith. [*Going*]
    Mammon.   Stay, knave.   250
    Face. He's extreme angry that you saw her, sir.
    Mammon. Drink that. [*Gives him money*] What is she when she's out of
    her fit?
    Face. Oh, the most affablest creature, sir! so merry!
So pleasant! she'll mount you up like quicksilver
Over the helm, and circulate like oil,
A very vegetal; discourse of state,
Of mathematics, bawdry, anything——
    Mammon. Is she no way accessible? no means,
No trick, to give a man a taste of her . . . wit——
Or so?——
    Subtle. [*Within*] Ulen!
    Face.   I'll come to you again, sir.   [*Exit*] 260
    Mammon. Surly, I did not think one o' your breeding
Would traduce personages of worth.
    Surly.   Sir Epicure,
Your friend to use; yet still loath to be gulled.
I do not like your philosophical bawds.
Their stone is lechery enough to pay for,
Without this bait.
    Mammon.   'Heart, you abuse yourself.
I know the lady, and her friends, and means,
The original of this disaster. Her brother
Has told me all.
    Surly.   And yet you ne'er saw her
Till now?

Mammon. Oh, yes, but I forgot. I have (believe it)   270
One o' the treacherou'st memories, I do think,
Of all mankind.
  Surly.   What call you her——brother?
  Mammon.   My Lord——
He wi' not have his name known, now I think on't.
  Surly. A very treacherous memory!
  Mammon.   O' my faith——
  Surly. Tut, if you ha' it not about you, pass it
Till we meet next.
  Mammon.   Nay, by this hand, 'tis true.
He's one I honour, and my noble friend,
And I respect his house.
  Surly.   Heart! can it be,
That a grave sir, a rich, that has no need,
A wise sir, too, at other times, should thus   280
With his own oaths and arguments make hard means
To gull himself? And this be your elixir,
Your *lapis mineralis*, and your lunary,
Give me your honest trick yet at primero
Or gleek; and take your *lutum sapientis*,
Your *menstruum simplex*! I'll have gold before you,
And with less danger of the quicksilver,
Or the hot sulphur.

        [*Enter Face*]

  Face. (*To Surly*) Here's one from Captain Face, sir,
Desires you meet him i' the Temple church,
Some half hour hence, and upon earnest business.   290
           (*He whispers Mammon*)
Sir, if you please to quit us now, and come
Again within two hours, you shall have
My master busy examining o' the works;
And I will steal you in unto the party,
That you may see her converse. Sir, shall I say
You'll meet the Captain's worship?
  Surly.   Sir, I will.
[*Aside*] But by attorney, and to a second purpose.
Now I am sure it is a bawdy-house;
I'll swear it, were the marshal here to thank me:
The naming this commander doth confirm it.   300

Don Face! why, he's the most authentic dealer
I' these commodities! the superintendent
To all the quainter traffickers in town.
He is their visitor, and does appoint
Who lies with whom, and at what hour, what price,
Which gown, and in what smock, what fall, what tire.
Him will I prove, by a third person, to find
The subtleties of this dark labyrinth;
Which, if I do discover, dear Sir Mammon,
You'll give your poor friend leave, though no philosopher,   310
To laugh; for you that are, 'tis thought, shall weep.
 Face. Sir, he does pray you'll not forget.
 Surly.   I will not, sir.
Sir Epicure, I shall leave you?
 Mammon.   I follow you, straight. [*Exit Surly*]
 Face. But do so, good sir, to avoid suspicion.
This gent'man has a parlous head.
 Mammon.   But wilt thou, Ulen,
Be constant to thy promise?
 Face.   As my life, sir.
 Mammon. And wilt thou insinuate what I am? and praise me?
And say I am a noble fellow?
 Face.   Oh, what else, sir?
And that you'll make her royal with the stone,
An empress; and yourself king of Bantam.   320
 Mammon. Wilt thou do this?
 Face.   Will I, sir?
 Mammon.   Lungs, my Lungs!
I love thee.
 Face. Send your stuff, sir, that my master
May busy himself about projection.
 Mammon. Th' hast witched me, rogue: take, go. [*Gives him money*]
 Face.   Your jack and all, sir.
 Mammon. Thou art a villain——I will send my jack,
And the weights too. Slave, I could bite thine ear.
Away, thou dost not care for me.
 Face.   Not I, sir?
 Mammon. Come, I was born to make thee, my good weasel;
Set thee on a bench, and ha' thee twirl a chain
With the best lord's vermin of 'em all.
 Face.   Away, sir.   330

Mammon. A Count, nay, a Count Palatine——
Face.   Good sir, go.
Mammon. ——shall not advance thee better: no, nor faster.   [*Exit*]

Act II, Scene iv

[*Enter Subtle and Dol*]

Subtle. Has he bit? has he bit?
Face.   And swallowed too, my Subtle.
I ha' given him line, and now he plays, i' faith.
Subtle. And shall we twitch him?
Face.   Thorough both the gills.
A wench is a rare bait, with which a man
No sooner's taken, but he straight firks mad.
Subtle. Dol, my Lord What's'hum's sister, you must now
Bear yourself *statelich.*
Dol.   Oh, let me alone.
I'll not forget my race, I warrant you.
I'll keep my distance, laugh, and talk aloud,
Have all the tricks of a proud scurvy lady,   10
And be as rude as her woman.
Face.   Well said, Sanguine.
Subtle. But will he send his andirons?
Face.   His jack too;
And's iron shoeing-horn: I ha' spoke to him. Well,
I must not lose my wary gamester, yonder.
Subtle. Oh Monsieur Caution, that will not be gulled?
Face. Aye, if I can strike a fine hook into him now——
The Temple church, there I have cast mine angle.
Well, pray for me. I'll about it.   (*One knocks*)
Subtle.   What, more gudgeons!
Dol, scout, scout! Stay Face, you must go to the door:
'Pray God it be my Anabaptist. [*Dol looks out*] Who is't, Dol?   20
Dol. I know him not. He looks like a gold-end man.
Subtle. Gods so! 'tis he, he said he would send. What call you him?
The sanctified elder, that should deal
For Mammon's jack and andirons! Let him in.
Stay, help me off first with my gown. Away
Madam, to your withdrawing chamber. [*Exit Dol; Face goes to door*] Now,

In a new tune, new gesture, but old language.
This fellow is sent from one negotiates with me
About the stone, too, for the holy Brethren
Of Amsterdam, the exiled Saints, that hope   30
To raise their discipline by it. I must use him
In some strange fashion now, to make him admire me.

Act II, Scene v

[*Face opens to Ananias; he enters*]

Subtle. Where is my drudge?
Face.   Sir!
Subtle.   Take away the recipient,
And rectify your menstrue from the phlegma.
Then pour it o' the Sol, in the cucurbite,
And let 'em macerate together.
Face.   Yes, sir.
And save the ground?
Subtle.   No. *Terra damnata*
Must not have entrance in the work. [*To Ananias*] Who are you?
Ananias. A faithful Brother, if it please you.
Subtle.   What's that?
A Lullianist? a Ripley? *Filius artis*?
Can you sublime and dulcify? calcine?
Know you the *sapor pontic? sapor stiptic?*   10
Or what is homogene, or heterogene?
Ananias. I understand no heathen language, truly.
Subtle. Heathen, you Knipper-Doling? Is *ars sacra*,
Or chrysopoeia, or spagyrica,
Or the pamphysic, or panarchic knowledge,
A heathen language?
Ananias.   Heathen Greek, I take it.
Subtle. How! heathen Greek?
Ananias.   All's heathen but the Hebrew.
Subtle. Sirrah, my varlet, stand you forth, and speak to him
Like a philosopher: answer, i' the language.
Name the vexations and the martyrizations   20
Of metals in the work.
Face.   Sir, putrefaction,

Solution, ablution, sublimation,
Cohobation, calcination, ceration, and
Fixation.
    Subtle. This is heathen Greek to you now?
And when comes vivification?
    Face.   After mortification.
    Subtle. What's cohobation?
    Face.   'Tis the pouring on
Your *aqua regis*, and then drawing him off
To the trine circle of the seven spheres.
    Subtle. What's the proper passion of metals?
    Face.   Malleation.
    Subtle. What's your *ultimum supplicium auri*?
    Face.   Antimonium.   30
    Subtle. This's heathen Greek to you? And what's your mercury?
    Face. A very fugitive: he will be gone, sir.
    Subtle. How know you him?
    Face.   By his viscosity,
His oleosity, and his suscitability.
    Subtle. How do you sublime him?
    Face.   With the calce of eggshells,
White marble, talc.
    Subtle.   Your magisterium, now,
What's that?
    Face.   Shifting, sir, your elements,
Dry into cold, cold into moist, moist into hot,
Hot into dry.
    Subtle.   This's heathen Greek to you, still?
Your *lapis philosophicus*?
    Face.   'Tis a stone, and not   40
A stone; a spirit, a soul, and a body,
Which, if you do dissolve, it is dissolved,
If you coagulate, it is coagulated,
If you make it to fly, it flieth.
    Subtle.   Enough.   [*Exit Face*]
This's heathen Greek to you? What are you, sir?
    Ananias. Please you, a servant of the exiled Brethren,
That deal with widows' and with orphans' goods,
And make a just account unto the Saints:
A deacon.
    Subtle. Oh, you are sent from Master Wholesome,

Your teacher?

Ananias.   From Tribulation Wholesome,   50
Our very zealous Pastor.

Subtle.   Good. I have
Some orphans' goods to come here.

Ananias.   Of what kind, sir?

Subtle. Pewter, and brass, andirons, and kitchenware,
Metals that we must use our medicine on;
Wherein the Brethren may have a penn'orth,
For ready money.

Ananias.   Were the orphans' parents
Sincere professors?

Subtle.   Why do you ask?

Ananias.   Because
We then are to deal justly, and give, in truth,
Their utmost value.

Subtle.   'Slid, you'd cozen else,
And if their parents were not of the faithful?   60
I will not trust you, now I think on't,
Till I ha' talked with your Pastor. Ha' you brought money
To buy more coals?

Ananias.   No, surely.

Subtle.   No? how so?

Ananias. The Brethren bid me say unto you, sir,
Surely they will not venture any more,
Till they may see projection.

Subtle.   How!

Ananias.   You've had
For the instruments——as bricks, and loam, and glasses——
Already thirty pound; and for materials,
They say, some ninety more; and they have heard, since,
That one at Heidelberg made it of an egg   70
And a small paper of pin-dust.

Subtle.   What's your name?

Ananias. My name is Ananias.

Subtle.   Out, the varlet
That cozened the Apostles! Hence, away!
Flee, mischief! Had your holy consistory
No name to send me of another sound
Than wicked Ananias? Send your elders
Hither to make atonement for you quickly,

And gi' me satisfaction; or out goes
The fire, and down the alembics and the furnace,
Piger Henricus, or what not. Thou wretch! 80
Both sericon and bufo shall be lost——
Tell 'em. All hope of rooting out the bishops
Or the antichristian hierarchy shall perish,
If they stay threescore minutes. The aqueity,
Terreity, and sulphureity
Shall run together again, and all be annulled,
Thou wicked Ananias! [*Exit Ananias*] This will fetch 'em,
And make 'em haste towards their gulling more.
A man must deal like a rough nurse, and fright
Those that are froward to an appetite. 90

Act II, Scene vi

[*Enter Face in his Captain's uniform, with Drugger*]

Face. He's busy with his spirits, but we'll upon him.
Subtle. How now! What mates, what Bayards ha' we here?
Face. I told you he would be furious. Sir, here's Nab
Has brought you another piece of gold to look on——
[*To Drugger*] We must appease him. Give it me——and prays you,
You would devise——what is it Nab?
Drugger.   A sign, sir.
Face. Aye, a good lucky one, a thriving sign, Doctor.
Subtle. I was devising now.
Face. [*To Subtle*]   'Slight, do not say so,
He will repent he ga' you any more.
What say you to his constellation, Doctor? 10
The balance?
Subtle.   No, that way is stale and common.
A townsman, born in Taurus, gives the bull,
Or the bull's head; in Aries, the ram——
A poor device! No, I will have his name
Formed in some mystic character, whose radii,
Striking the senses of the passers-by,
Shall, by a virtual influence, breed affections
That may result upon the party owns it:
As thus——

Face.   Nab!
Subtle.   He first shall have a bell, that's Abel;
And, by it, standing one whose name is Dee,   20
In a rug gown; there's D and rug, that's Drug;
And right anenst him, a dog snarling 'er':
There's Drugger, Abel Drugger. That's his sign.
And here's now mystery and hieroglyphic!
Face. Abel, thou art made.
Drugger.   Sir, I do thank his worship.   [*Bows*]
Face. Six o' thy legs more will not do it, Nab.
He has brought you a pipe of tobacco, Doctor.
Drugger.   Yes, sir;
I have another thing I would impart——
Face. Out with it, Nab.
Drugger.   Sir, there is lodged, hard by me,
A rich young widow——
Face.   Good! A *bona roba*?   30
Drugger. But nineteen, at the most.
Face.   Very good, Abel.
Drugger. Marry, she's not in fashion yet; she wears
A hood, but't stands a cop.
Face.   No matter, Abel.
Drugger. And I do now and then give her a fucus——
Face. What! dost thou deal, Nab?
Subtle.   I did tell you, Captain.
Drugger. And physic too sometime, sir, for which she trusts me
With all her mind. She's come up here of purpose
To learn the fashion.
Face.   Good—— [*Aside*] his match too!—— on, Nab.
Drugger. And she does strangely long to know her fortune.
Face. God's lid, Nab, send her to the Doctor, hither.   40
Drugger. Yes, I have spoke to her of his worship already,
But she's afraid it will be blown abroad,
And hurt her marriage.
Face.   Hurt it? 'tis the way
To heal it, if 'twere hurt; to make it more
Followed and sought. Nab, thou shalt tell her this.
She'll be more known, more talked of, and your widows
Are ne'er of any price till they be famous:
Their honour is their multitude of suitors.
Send her, it may be thy good fortune. What?

Thou dost not know?

Drugger.   No, sir, she'll never marry   50
Under a knight. Her brother has made a vow.

Face. What, and dost thou despair, my little Nab,
Knowing what the Doctor has set down for thee,
And seeing so many o' the city dubbed?
One glass o' thy water, with a madam I know
Will have it done, Nab. What's her brother? a knight?

Drugger. No, sir, a gentleman, newly warm in his land, sir.
Scarce cold in his one-and-twenty, that does govern
His sister here, and is a man himself
Of some three thousand a year, and is come up   60
To learn to quarrel and to live by his wits,
And will go down again and die i' the country.

Face. How! to quarrel?

Drugger.   Yes, sir, to carry quarrels
As gallants do, and manage 'em by line.

Face. 'Slid, Nab! the Doctor is the only man
In Christendom for him. He has made a table,
With mathematical demonstrations,
Touching the art of quarrels. He will give him
An instrument to quarrel by. Go, bring 'em, both,
Him and his sister. And, for thee, with her   70
The Doctor happ'ly may persuade. Go to.
'Shalt give his worship a new damask suit
Upon the premises.

Subtle.   Oh, good Captain.

Face.   He shall,
He is the honestest fellow, Doctor. Stay not——
No offers; bring the damask, and the parties.

Drugger. I'll try my power, sir.

Face.   And thy will too, Nab.

Subtle. 'Tis good tobacco this! What is't an ounce?

Face. He'll send you a pound, Doctor.

Subtle.   Oh, no.

Face.   He will do't.
It is the goodest soul. Abel, about it.
Thou shalt know more anon. Away, be gone   *[Exit Drugger]* 80
A miserable rogue, and lives with cheese,
And has the worms. That was the cause indeed
Why he came now. He dealt with me in private

To get a medicine for 'em.
    Subtle.   And shall, sir. This works.
    Face. A wife, a wife, for one on us, my dear Subtle!
We'll e'en draw lots, and he that fails shall have
The more in goods, the other has in tail.
    Subtle. Rather the less. For she may be so light
She may want grains.
    Face.   Aye, or be such a burden,
A man would scarce endure her for the whole.   90
    Subtle. Faith, best let's see her first, and then determine.
    Face. Content. But Dol must ha' no breath on't.
    Subtle.   Mum.
Away, you to your Surly yonder, catch him.
    Face. 'Pray God I ha' not stayed too long.
    Subtle.   I fear it.   [*Exeunt*]

Act III, Scene i

[*Outside Lovewit's house. Enter Tribulation Wholesome and Ananias*]

    Tribulation. These chastisements are common to the Saints,
And such rebukes we of the Separation
Must bear with willing shoulders, as the trials
Sent forth to tempt our frailties.
    Ananias.   In pure zeal,
I do not like the man: he is a heathen.
And speaks the language of Canaan, truly.
    Tribulation. I think him a profane person, indeed.
    Ananias.   He bears
The visible mark of the Beast in his forehead.
And for his stone, it is a work of darkness,
And with philosophy blinds the eyes of man.   10
    Tribulation. Good Brother, we must bend unto all means
That may give furtherance to the holy cause.
    Ananias. Which his cannot; the sanctified cause
Should have a sanctified course.
    Tribulation.   Not always necessary.
The children of perdition are oft-times
Made instruments even of the greatest works.
Beside, we should give somewhat to man's nature,

The place he lives in, still about the fire
And fume of metals, that intoxicate
The brain of man and make him prone to passion.   20
Where have you greater atheists than your cooks?
Or more profane or choleric than your glassmen?
More antichristian than your bell-founders?
What makes the devil so devilish, I would ask you——
Satan, our common enemy——but his being
Perpetually about the fire, and boiling
Brimstone and ars'nic? We must give, I say,
Unto the motives and the stirrers-up
Of humours in the blood. It may be so,
When as the work is done, the stone is made,   30
This heat of his may turn into a zeal
And stand up for the beauteous discipline
Against the menstruous cloth and rag of Rome.
We must await his calling, and the coming
Of the good spirit. You did fault to upbraid him
With the Brethren's blessing of Heidelberg, weighing
What need we have to hasten on the work
For the restoring of the silenced Saints,
Which ne'er will be but by the philosopher's stone.
And so a learnèd elder, one of Scotland,   40
Assured me; *aurum potabile* being
The only medicine for the civil magistrate
To incline him to a feeling of the cause;
And must be daily used in the disease.
     Ananias. I have not edified more, truly, by man,
Not since the beautiful light first shone on me;
And I am sad my zeal hath so offended.
     Tribulation. Let us call on him, then.
     Ananias.   The motion's good,
And of the spirit; I will knock first. [*Knocks*] Peace be within!

Act III, Scene ii

[Subtle opens to them; they enter]

     Subtle. Oh, are you come? 'twas time. Your threescore minutes
Were at the last thread, you see, and down had gone

Furnus acediae, turris circulatorius;
Limbeck, bolt's head, retort, and pelican
Had all been cinders. Wicked Ananias!
Art thou returned? Nay then, it goes down yet.
   Tribulation. Sir, be appeased, he is come to humble
Himself in spirit, and to ask your patience
If too much zeal hath carried him aside
From the due path.
   Subtle.   Why, this doth qualify!   10
   Tribulation. The Brethren had no purpose, verily,
To give you the least grievance, but are ready
To lend their willing hands to any project
The spirit and you direct.
   Subtle.   This qualifies more!
   Tribulation. And for the orphans' goods, let them be valued,
Or what is needful else to the holy work,
It shall be numbered; here, by me, the Saints
Throw down their purse before you.
   Subtle.   This qualifies most!
Why, thus it should be; now you understand.
Have I discoursed so unto you of our stone?   20
And of the good that it shall bring your cause?
Showed you——beside the main of hiring forces
Abroad, drawing the Hollanders, your friends,
From the Indies, to serve you, with all their fleet——
That even the med'cinal use shall make you a faction,
And party in the realm? As, put the case,
That some great man in state, he have the gout,
Why, you but send three drops of your elixir,
You help him straight: there you have made a friend.
Another has the palsy or the dropsy,   30
He takes of your incombustible stuff,
He's young again: there you have made a friend.
A lady that is past the feat of body,
Though not of mind, and hath her face decayed
Beyond all cure of paintings, you restore
With the oil of talc: there you have made a friend,
And all her friends. A lord that is a leper,
A knight that has the bone-ache, or a squire
That hath both these, you make 'em smooth and sound
With a bare fricace of your medicine: still   40

You increase your friends.
   Tribulation.   Aye, 'tis very pregnant.
   Subtle. And, then the turning of this lawyer's pewter
To plate at Christmas——
   Ananias.   Christ-tide, I pray you.
   Subtle. Yet, Ananias?
   Ananias.   I have done.
   Subtle.   Or changing
His parcel gilt to massy gold. You cannot
But raise you friends. Withal, to be of power
To pay an army in the field, to buy
The king of France out of his realms, or Spain
Out of his Indies; what can you not do
Against lords spiritual or temporal,   50
That shall oppone you?
   Tribulation.   Verily, 'tis true.
We may be temporal lords ourselves, I take it.
   Subtle. You may be anything, and leave off to make
Long-winded exercises, or suck up
Your 'ha' and 'hum' in a tune. I not deny
But such as are not gracèd in a state
May, for their ends, be adverse in religion,
And get a tune to call the flock together;
For, to say sooth, a tune does much with women,
And other phlegmatic people: it is your bell.   60
   Ananias. Bells are profane; a tune may be religious.
   Subtle. No warning with you? Then farewell my patience.
'Slight, it shall down! I will not be thus tortured.
   Tribulation. I pray you, sir.
   Subtle.   All shall perish. I have spoke it.
   Tribulation. Let me find grace, sir, in your eyes; the man
He stands corrected; neither did his zeal,
But as yourself, allow a tune somewhere,
Which now, being toward the stone, we shall not need.
   Subtle. No, nor your holy vizard, to win widows
To give you legacies, or make zealous wives   70
To rob their husbands for the common cause;
Nor take the start of bonds, broke but one day,
And say they were forfeited by providence.
Nor shall you need o'er night to eat huge meals
To celebrate your next day's fast the better,

The whilst the Brethren and the Sisters, humbled,
Abate the stiffness of the flesh. Nor cast
Before your hungry hearers scrupulous bones
As whether a Christian may hawk or hunt,
Or whether matrons of the holy assembly   80
May lay their hair out, or wear doublets,
Or have that idol starch about their linen.
   Ananias. It is, indeed, an idol.
   Tribulation.   Mind him not, sir.
I do command thee, spirit of zeal, but trouble,
To peace within him! Pray you, sir, go on.
   Subtle. Nor shall you need to libel 'gainst the prelates,
And shorten so your ears against the hearing
Of the next wire-drawn grace. Nor of necessity
Rail against plays to please the alderman
Whose daily custard you devour. Nor lie   90
With zealous rage till you are hoarse. Not one
Of these so singular arts. Nor call yourselves
By names of Tribulation, Persecution,
Restraint, Long-Patience, and such like, affected
By the whole family or wood of you
Only for glory, and to catch the ear
Of the disciple.
   Tribulation.   Truly, sir, they are
Ways that the godly Brethren have invented
For propagation of the glorious cause,
As very notable means, and whereby also   100
Themselves grow soon and profitably famous.
   Subtle. Oh, but the stone, all's idle to it! nothing!
The art of angels, nature's miracle,
The divine secret that doth fly in clouds,
From east to west, and whose tradition
Is not from men, but spirits.
   Ananias.   I hate traditions;
I do not trust them——
   Tribulation.   Peace.
   Ananias.   They are Popish, all.
I will not peace. I will not——
   Tribulation.   Ananias!
   Ananias. Please the profane, to grieve the godly; I may not.
   Subtle. Well, Ananias, thou shalt overcome.   110

Tribulation. It is an ignorant zeal that haunts him, sir.
But truly, else, a very faithful Brother,
A botcher, and a man by revelation
That hath a competent knowledge of the truth.
 Subtle. Has he a competent sum there i' the bag
To buy the goods within? I am made guardian,
And must, for charity and conscience' sake,
Now see the most be made for my poor orphan;
Though I desire the Brethren, too, good gainers.
There they are within. When you have viewed and bought 'em, 120
And ta'en the inventory of what they are,
They're ready for projection; there's no more
To do; cast on the medicine so much silver
As there is tin there, so much gold as brass,
I'll gi' it you in by weight.
 Tribulation.   But how long time,
Sir, must the Saints expect, yet?
 Subtle.   Let me see,
How's the moon now? Eight, nine, ten days hence
He will be silver potate; then three days
Before he citronize: some fifteen days
The magisterium will be perfected. 130
 Ananias. About the second day of the third week
In the ninth month?
 Subtle.   Yes, my good Ananias.
 Tribulation. What will the orphans' goods arise to, think you?
 Subtle. Some hundred marks; as much as filled three cars,
Unladed now; you'll make six millions of 'em.
But I must ha' more coals laid in.
 Tribulation.   How!
 Subtle.   Another load,
And then we ha' finished. We must now increase
Our fire to *ignis ardens*, we are past
Fimus equinus, balnei, cineris,
And all those lenter heats. If the holy purse 140
Should, with this draught, fall low, and that the Saints
Do need a present sum, I have [a] trick
To melt the pewter you shall buy now, instantly,
And with a tincture make you as good Dutch dollars,
As any are in Holland.
 Tribulation.   Can you so?

Subtle. Aye, and shall bide the third examination.
Ananias. It will be joyful tidings to the Brethren.
Subtle. But you must carry it secret.
Tribulation.   Aye, but stay;
This act of coining, is it lawful?
Ananias.   Lawful?
We know no magistrate. Or, if we did,   150
This's foreign coin.
Subtle.   It is no coining, sir.
It is but casting.
Tribulation.   Ha? you distinguish well.
Casting of money may be lawful.
Ananias.   'Tis, sir.
Tribulation. Truly, I take it so.
Subtle.   There is no scruple,
Sir, to be made of it; believe Ananias:
This case of conscience he is studied in.
Tribulation. I'll make a question of it to the Brethren.
Ananias. The Brethren shall approve it lawful, doubt not.
Where shall't be done?   *(Knock without)*
Subtle.   For that we'll talk anon.
There's some to speak with me. Go in, I pray you,   160
And view the parcels. That's the inventory.
I'll come to you straight.   *[Exeunt Tribulation and Ananias]*
          Who is it? Face! Appear.

Act III, Scene iii

[Enter Face in Captain's uniform]

Subtle. How now? good prize?
Face.   Good pox! yond' costive cheater
Never came on.
Subtle.   How then?
Face.   I ha' walked the round
Till now, and no such thing.
Subtle.   And ha' you quit him?
Face. Quit him? and hell would quit him too, he were happy.
'Slight would you have me stalk like a mill-jade

All day for one that will not yield us grains?
I know him of old.
    Subtle.   Oh, but to ha' gulled him,
Had been a mastery.
    Face.   Let him go, black boy,
And turn thee, that some fresh news may possess thee.
A noble Count, a Don of Spain (my dear   10
Delicious compeer, and my party-bawd)
Who is come hither, private, for his conscience,
And brought munition with him, six great slops
Bigger than three Dutch hoys, beside round trunks,
Furnished with pistolets, and pieces of eight,
Will straight be here, my rogue, to have thy bath——
That is the colour——and to make his battery
Upon our Dol, our castle, our Cinque Port,
Our Dover pier, our what thou wilt. Where is she?
She must prepare perfumes, delicate linen,   20
The bath in chief, a banquet, and her wit,
For she must milk his epididymis.
Where is the doxy?
    Subtle.   I'll send her to thee;
And but dispatch my brace of little John Leydens
And come again myself.
    Face.   Are they within then?
    Subtle. Numbering the sum.
    Face.   How much?
    Subtle.   A hundred marks, boy.
                         [*Exit*]

    Face. Why, this's a lucky day! Ten pounds of Mammon!
Three o' my clerk! a portague o' my grocer!
This o' the Brethren! beside reversions
And states to come i' the widow, and my Count!   30
My share today will not be bought for forty——

             [*Enter Dol*]

    Dol.   What?
    Face. Pounds, dainty Dorothy! art thou so near?
    Dol. Yes. Say Lord General, how fares our camp?
    Face. As with the few that had entrenched themselves
Safe, by their discipline, against a world, Dol,
And laughed within those trenches, and grew fat

With thinking on the booties, Dol, brought in
Daily, by their small parties. This dear hour
A doughty Don is taken with my Dol,
And thou mayst make his ransom what thou wilt,   40
My Dousabel; he shall be brought here, fettered
With thy fair looks, before he sees thee, and thrown
In a down-bed, as dark as any dungeon;
Where thou shalt keep him waking, with thy drum——
Thy drum, my Dol, thy drum——till he be tame
As the poor blackbirds were i' the great frost,
Or bees are with a basin; and so hive him
I' the swan-skin coverlid and cambric sheets,
Till he work honey and wax, my little God's-gift.
   Dol. What is he, General?
   Face.   An *Adelantado*,   50
A grandee, girl. Was not my Dapper here yet?
   Dol. No.
   Face.   Nor my Drugger?
   Dol.   Neither.
   Face.   A pox on 'em,
They are so long a-furnishing! Such stinkards
Would not be seen upon these festival days.

                 [*Enter Subtle*]

How now! ha' you done?
   Subtle.   Done. They are gone. The sum
Is here in bank, my Face. I would we knew
Another chapman now would buy 'em outright.
   Face. 'Slid, Nab shall do't, against he ha' the widow,
To furnish household.
   Subtle.   Excellent, well thought on.
Pray God he come.
   Face.   I pray he keep away   60
Till our new business be o'er-past.
   Subtle.   But Face,
How cam'st thou by this secret Don?
   [*Face.*]   A spirit
Brought me the intelligence in a paper, here,
As I was conjuring yonder in my circle
For Surly; I ha' my flies abroad. Your bath
Is famous, Subtle, by my means. Sweet Dol,

You must go tune your virginal, no losing
O' the least time. And do you hear? good action.
Firk like a flounder; kiss like a scallop, close;
And tickle him with thy mother-tongue. His great   70
Verdugoship has not a jot of language:
So much the easier to be cozened, my Dolly.
He will come here in a hired coach, obscure,
And our own coachman, whom I have sent as guide,
No creature else. (*One knocks*) Who's that?

     Subtle.   It i' not he?
     Face. Oh no, not yet this hour.
     Subtle.   Who is't?
     Dol. [*At window*]   Dapper,
Your clerk.
     Face.   God's will, then—— Queen of Faery,
On with your tire; and, Doctor, with your robes.
Let's dispatch him for God's sake.   [*Exit Dol*]
     Subtle.   'Twill be long.
     Face. I warrant you, take but the cues I give you,   80
I shall be brief enough. [*At window*] 'Slight, here are more!
Abel, and I think the angry boy, the heir,
That fain would quarrel.
     Subtle.   And the widow?
     Face.   No,
Not that I see. Away.   [*Exit Subtle; Face opens door*]
     Oh, sir, you are welcome.

Act III, Scene iv

[Enter Dapper]

     Face. The Doctor is within, a-moving for you——
I have had the most ado to win him to it——
He swears you'll be the darling o' the dice;
He never heard her Highness dote till now, he says.
Your aunt has given you the most gracious words
That can be thought on.
     Dapper.   Shall I see her Grace?
     Face. See her, and kiss her, too.

            [Enter Drugger with Kastril]

What? honest Nab!
Hast brought the damask?
    [*Drugger.*]   No, sir, here's tobacco.
    Face. 'Tis well done, Nab. Thou'lt bring the damask too?
    Drugger. Yes, here's the gentleman, Captain——Master Kastril——   10
I have brought to see the Doctor.
    Face.   Where's the widow?
    Drugger. Sir, as he likes, his sister (he says) shall come.
    Face. Oh, is it so? 'good time. Is your name Kastril, sir?
    Kastril. Aye, and the best o' the Kastrils, I'd be sorry else,
By fifteen hundred a year. Where is this Doctor?
My mad tobacco boy here tells me of one
That can do things. Has he any skill?
    Face.   Wherein, sir?
    Kastril. To carry a business, manage a quarrel fairly,
Upon fit terms.
    Face.   It seems, sir, you're but young
About the town, that can make that a question!   20
    Kastril. Sir, not so young but I have heard some speech
Of the angry boys, and seen 'em take tobacco,
And in his shop; and I can take it too.
And I would fain be one of 'em, and go down
And practise i' the country.
    Face.   Sir, for the duello,
The Doctor, I assure you, shall inform you
To the least shadow of a hair, and show you
An instrument he has of his own making,
Wherewith no sooner shall you make report
Of any quarrel but he will take the height on't   30
Most instantly, and tell in what degree
Of safety it lies in, or mortality;
And how it may be borne, whether in a right line
Or a half-circle; or may else be cast
Into an angle blunt, if not acute;
All this he will demonstrate. And then, rules
To give and take the lie by.
    Kastril.   How? to take it?
    Face. Yes, in oblique, he'll show you, or in circle,
But never in diameter. The whole town
Study his theorems, and dispute them ordinarily   40
At the eating academies.

Kastril.   But does he teach
Living by the wits too?
  Face.   Anything whatever.
You cannot think that subtlety but he reads it.
He made me a captain. I was a stark pimp
Just o' your standing, 'fore I met with him;
It i' not two months since. I'll tell you his method.
First, he will enter you at some ordinary——
  Kastril. No, I'll not come there. You shall pardon me.
  Face.   For why, sir?
  Kastril. There's gaming there, and tricks.
  Face.   Why, would you be
A gallant, and not game?
  Kastril.   Aye, 'twill spend a man.
  Face. Spend you? It will repair you, when you are spent.   50
How do they live by their wits there, that have vented
Six times your fortunes?
  Kastril.   What, three thousand a year!
  Face. Aye, forty thousand.
  Kastril.   Are there such?
  Face.   Aye, sir.
And gallants, yet. Here's a young gentleman,
Is born to nothing——forty marks a year,
Which I count nothing. He's to be initiated,
And have a fly o' the Doctor. He will win you
By unresistable luck, within this fortnight,
Enough to buy a barony. They will set him   60
Upmost, at the groom-porter's, all the Christmas!
And for the whole year through at every place
Where there is play, present him with the chair,
The best attendance, the best drink, sometimes
Two glasses of canary, and pay nothing;
The purest linen, and the sharpest knife,
The partridge next his trencher, and somewhere
The dainty bed, in private, with the dainty.
You shall ha' your ordinaries bid for him,
As play-houses for a poet; and the master   70
Pray him aloud to name what dish he affects,
Which must be buttered shrimps; and those that drink
To no mouth else, will drink to his, as being
The goodly, president mouth of all the board.

Kastril. Do you not gull one?

Face.   'Od's my life! do you think it?
You shall have a cast commander——can but get
In credit with a glover, or a spurrier,
For some two pair of either's ware, aforehand——
Will, by most swift posts, dealing with him,
Arrive at competent means to keep himself,   80
His punk, and naked boy, in excellent fashion,
And be admired for't.

    Kastril.   Will the Doctor teach this?

    Face. He will do more, sir. When your land is gone
(As men of spirit hate to keep earth long)
In a vacation, when small money is stirring,
And ordinaries suspended till the term,
He'll show a perspective, where on one side
You shall behold the faces and the persons
Of all sufficient young heirs in town,
Whose bonds are current for commodity;   90
On the other side, the merchants' forms, and others,
That, without help of any second broker
(Who would expect a share) will trust such parcels;
In the third square, the very street and sign
Where the commodity dwells, and does but wait
To be delivered, be it pepper, soap,
Hops or tobacco, oatmeal, woad or cheeses.
All which you may so handle, to enjoy
To your own use, and never stand obliged.

    Kastril. I' faith! is he such a fellow?

    Face.   Why, Nab here knows him.   100
And then for making matches for rich widows,
Young gentlewomen, heirs, the fortunat'st man!
He's sent to, far and near, all over England,
To have his counsel, and to know their fortunes.

    Kastril. God's will, my suster shall see him.

    Face.   I'll tell you, sir,
What he did tell me of Nab. It's a strange thing!
(By the way you must eat no cheese, Nab, it breeds melancholy:
And that same melancholy breeds worms, but pass it)——
He told me, honest Nab here was ne'er at tavern
But once in's life.

    Drugger.   Truth, and no more I was not.   110

Face. And then he was so sick——

Drugger.   Could he tell you that, too?

Face. How should I know it?

Drugger.   In troth we had been a-shooting,
And had a piece of fat ram-mutton to supper,
That lay so heavy o' my stomach——

    Face.   And he has no head
To bear any wine; for what with the noise o' the fiddlers,
And care of his shop, for he dares keep no servants——

Drugger. My head did so ache——

    Face.   As he was fain to be brought home,
The Doctor told me. And then a good old woman——

Drugger. Yes, faith, she dwells in Seacoal Lane——did cure me,
With sodden ale, and pellitory o' the wall——   120
Cost me but twopence. I had another sickness
Was worse than that.

    Face.   Aye, that was with the grief
Thou took'st for being 'sessed at eighteen pence
For the waterwork.

    Drugger.   In truth, and it was like
To have cost me almost my life.

    Face.   Thy hair went off?

Drugger. Yes, sir, 'twas done for spite.

    Face.   Nay, so says the Doctor.

Kastril. Pray thee, tobacco boy, go fetch my suster,
I'll see this learned boy before I go,
And so shall she.

    Face.   Sir, he is busy now;
But if you have a sister to fetch hither,   130
Perhaps your own pains may command her sooner,
And he by that time will be free.

    Kastril.   I go.   [*Exit*]

Face. Drugger, she's thine: the damask! [*Exit Drugger*] [*Aside*] Subtle
    and I
Must wrestle for her.—— Come on, Master Dapper;
You see, how I turn clients here away
To give your cause dispatch. Ha' you performed
The ceremonies were enjoined you?

    Dapper.   Yes, o' the vinegar,
And the clean shirt.

    Face.   'Tis well; that shirt may do you

More worship than you think. Your aunt's afire,
But that she will not show it, to have a sight on you.   140
Ha' you provided for her Grace's servants?
    Dapper. Yes, here are six-score Edward shillings.
    Face.   Good.
    Dapper. And an old Harry's sovereign.
    Face.   Very good.
    Dapper. And three James shillings, and an Elizabeth groat,
Just twenty nobles.
    Face.   Oh, you are too just.
I would you had had the other noble in Maries.
    Dapper. I have some Philip and Maries.
    Face.   Aye, those same
Are best of all. Where are they? Hark, the Doctor.

Act III, Scene v

([Enter] Subtle disguised like a Priest of Faery)

    Subtle. Is yet her Grace's cousin come?
    Face.   He is come.
    Subtle. And is he fasting?
    Face.   Yes.
    Subtle.   And hath cried 'hum'?
    Face. Thrice, you must answer.
    Dapper.   Thrice.
    Subtle.   And as oft 'buzz'?
    Face. If you have, say.
    Dapper.   I have.
    Subtle.   Then, to her coz,
Hoping, that he hath vinegared his senses,
As he was bid, the Faery Queen dispenses,
By me, this robe, the petticoat of Fortune;
Which that he straight put on, she doth importune.
And though to Fortune near be her petticoat,
Yet nearer is her smock, the Queen doth note: 10
And therefore, even of that a piece she hath sent,
Which, being a child, to wrap him in, was rent;
And prays him, for a scarf, he now will wear it,
With as much love, as then her Grace did tear it,

About his eyes, to show he is fortunate.

(They blind him with a rag)

And trusting unto her to make his state,
He'll throw away all wordly pelf about him;
Which that he will perform, she doth not doubt him.
   Face. She need not doubt him, sir. Alas, he has nothing
But what he will part withal as willingly   20
Upon her Grace's word——throw away your purse——
As she would ask it——handkerchiefs, and all——
She cannot bid that thing but he'll obey——

(He throws away, as they bid him)

If you have a ring about you, cast it off,
Or a silver seal at your wrist. Her Grace will send
Her faeries here to search you, therefore deal
Directly with her Highness. If they find
That you conceal a mite, you are undone.
   Dapper. Truly, there's all.
   Face.   All what?
   Dapper.   My money, truly.
   Face. Keep nothing that is transitory about you.   30
[*To Subtle*] Bid Dol play music.—— Look, the elves are come

(Dol enters with a cithern; they pinch him)

To pinch you, if you tell not truth. Advise you.
   Dapper. Oh, I have a paper with a spur-rial in't.
   Face.   *Ti, ti,*
They knew't, they say.
   Subtle.   *Ti, ti, ti, ti,* he has more yet.
   Face. Ti, ti-ti-ti. I' the tother pocket?
   Subtle.   *Titi, titi, titi, titi.*
They must pinch him, or he will never confess, they say.
   Dapper. Oh, oh!
   Face.   Nay, 'pray you hold. He is her Grace's nephew.
Ti, ti, ti? What care you? Good faith, you shall care:
Deal plainly, sir, and shame the faeries. Show
You are an innocent.
   Dapper.   By this good light, I ha' nothing.   40
   Subtle. Ti ti, ti ti to ta. He does equivocate, she says——
Ti, ti do ti, ti ti do, ti da——and swears by the light, when he is blinded.
   Dapper. By this good dark, I ha' nothing but a half-crown
Of gold about my wrist, that my love gave me,
And a leaden heart I wore sin' she forsook me.   [*Dol goes to window*]

Face. I thought 'twas something. And would you incur
Your aunt's displeasure for these trifles? Come,
I had rather you had thrown away twenty half-crowns.
You may wear your leaden heart still.

[*Dol signals*]

How now?

Subtle. What news, Dol?
Dol.   Yonder's your knight, Sir Mammon.   50
Face. God's lid, we never thought of him, till now.
Where is he?
Dol.   Here, hard by. He's at the door.
Subtle. [*To Face*] And you are not ready, now? Dol, get his suit.

[*Exit Dol*]

He must not be sent back.
Face.   Oh, by no means.
What shall we do with this same puffin here,
Now he's o' the spit?
Subtle.   Why, lay him back a while,
With some device.

[*Enter Dol with Face's suit*]

        Ti, ti ti, ti ti ti. Would her Grace speak with me?
I come. Help, Dol.
Face.   (*He speaks through the keyhole, the other knocking*)
                Who's there? Sir Epicure;
My master's i' the way. Please you to walk
Three or four turns, but till his back be turned,   60
And I am for you.—— Quickly, Dol!
Subtle.   Her Grace
Commends her kindly to you, Master Dapper.
Dapper. I long to see her Grace.
Subtle.   She now is set
At dinner in her bed, and she has sent you
From her own private trencher, a dead mouse
And a piece of gingerbread, to be merry withal,
And stay your stomach, lest you faint with fasting;
Yet if you could hold out till she saw you, she says,
It would be better for you.
Face.   Sir, he shall
Hold out, and 'twere this two hours, for her Highness;   70

I can assure you that. We will not lose
All we ha' done——
    Subtle.   He must nor see nor speak
To anybody till then.
    Face.   For that we'll put, sir,
A stay in's mouth.
    Subtle.   Of what?
    Face.   Of gingerbread.
Make you it fit. He that hath pleased her Grace,
Thus far, shall not now crinkle for a little.
Gape sir, and let him fit you.   [*Thrusting gingerbread into his mouth*]
    Subtle.   Where shall we now
Bestow him?
    Dol.   I' the privy.
    Subtle.   Come along, sir,
I now must show you Fortune's privy lodgings.
    Face. Are they perfumed, and his bath ready?
    Subtle.   All.   80
Only the fumigation's somewhat strong.
                          [*Exeunt Subtle, Dol, Dapper*]
    Face. Sir Epicure, I am yours, sir, by and by.

Act IV, Scene i

[*Face, as Lungs, admits Sir Epicure Mammon*]

    Face. Oh, sir, you're come i' the only finest time——
    Mammon. Where's master?
    Face.   Now preparing for projection, sir.
Your stuff will be all changed shortly.
    Mammon.   Into gold?
    Face. To gold and silver, sir.
    Mammon.   Silver I care not for.
    Face. Yes, sir, a little to give beggars.
    Mammon.   Where's the lady?
    Face. At hand here. I ha' told her such brave things o' you,
Touching your bounty and your noble spirit——
    Mammon.   Hast thou?
    Face. As she is almost in her fit to see you.

But, good sir, no divinity i' your conference,
For fear of putting her in rage——
 Mammon.   I warrant thee.   10
 Face. Six men will not hold her down. And then,
If the old man should hear, or see you——
 Mammon.   Fear not.
 Face. The very house, sir, would run mad. You know it,
How scrupulous he is, and violent
'Gainst the least act of sin. Physic or mathematics,
Poetry, state, or bawdry (as I told you)
She will endure and never startle, but
No word of controversy.
 Mammon.   I am schooled, good Ulen.
 Face. And you must praise her house, remember that,
And her nobility.
 Mammon. Let me alone: 20
No herald, no, nor antiquary, Lungs,
Shall do it better. Go.
 Face. [*Aside*]   Why, this is yet
A kind of modern happiness, to have
Dol Common for a great lady.   [*Exit*]
 Mammon.   Now, Epicure,
Heighten thyself, talk to her, all in gold;
Rain her as many showers, as Jove did drops
Unto his Danaë; show the god a miser
Compared with Mammon. What? the stone will do't.
She shall feel gold, taste gold, hear gold, sleep gold;
Nay, we will *concumbere* gold. I will be puissant 30
And mighty in my talk to her! [*Enter Face with Dol*] Here she comes.
 Face. [*Aside*] To him, Dol, suckle him.—— This is the noble knight
I told your ladyship——
 Mammon.   Madam, with your pardon,
I kiss your vesture.
 Dol.   Sir, I were uncivil
If I would suffer that; my lip to you, sir.
 Mammon. I hope my lord your brother be in health, lady?
 Dol. My lord my brother is, though I no lady, sir.
 Face. [*Aside*] Well said my Guinea bird.
 Mammon.   Right noble madam——
 Face. [*Aside*] Oh, we shall have most fierce idolatry!
 Mammon. 'Tis your prerogative.

Dol.   Rather your courtesy.   40

Mammon. Were there naught else to enlarge your virtues to me,
These answers speak your breeding and your blood.

Dol. Blood we boast none, sir; a poor baron's daughter.

Mammon. Poor! and gat you? Profane not. Had your father
Slept all the happy remnant of his life
After the act, lain but there still, and panted,
He'd done enough to make himself, his issue,
And his posterity noble.

Dol.   Sir, although
We may be said to want the gilt and trappings,
The dress of honour, yet we strive to keep   50
The seeds and the materials.

Mammon.   I do see
The old ingredient, virtue, was not lost,
Nor the drug, money, used to make your compound.
There is a strange nobility i' your eye:
This lip, that chin! Methinks you do resemble
One o' the Austriac princes.

Face. [*Aside*]   Very like,
Her father was an Irish costermonger.

Mammon. The house of Valois just had such a nose.
And such a forehead yet the Medici
Of Florence boast.

Dol.   Troth, and I have been likened   60
To all these princes.

Face. [*Aside*]   I'll be sworn, I heard it.

Mammon. I know not how! it is not any one,
But e'en the very choice of all their features.

Face. [*Aside*] I'll in, and laugh.   [*Exit*]

Mammon.   A certain touch, or air,
That sparkles a divinity beyond
An earthly beauty!

Dol.   Oh, you play the courtier.

Mammon. Good lady, gi' me leave——

Dol.   In faith, I may not,
To mock me, sir.

Mammon.   To burn i' this sweet flame;
The phoenix never knew a nobler death.

Dol. Nay, now you court the courtier, and destroy   70
What you would build. This art, sir, i' your words,

Calls your whole faith in question.

Mammon.   By my soul——

Dol. Nay, oaths are made o' the same air, sir.

Mammon.   Nature

Never bestowed upon mortality

A more unblamed, a more harmonious feature:

She played the step-dame in all faces, else.

Sweet madam, let me be particular——

Dol. Particular, sir? I pray you, know your distance.

Mammon. In no ill sense, sweet lady, but to ask

How your fair graces pass the hours? I see   80

You're lodged here i' the house of a rare man,

An excellent artist; but what's that to you?

Dol. Yes, sir. I study here the mathematics,

And distillation.

Mammon.   Oh, I cry your pardon.

He's a divine instructor! can extract

The souls of all things, by his art; call all

The virtues and the miracles of the sun,

Into a temperate furnace, teach dull nature

What her own forces are. A man the emperor

Has courted above Kelley; sent his medals   90

And chains to invite him.

Dol.   Aye, and for his physic, sir——

Mammon. Above the art of Aesculapius,

That drew the envy of the Thunderer!

I know all this, and more.

Dol.   Troth, I am taken, sir,

Whole, with these studies, that contemplate nature.

Mammon. It is a noble humour. But this form

Was not intended to so dark a use!

Had you been crooked, foul, of some coarse mould,

A cloister had done well; but such a feature

That might stand up the glory of a kingdom,   100

To live recluse is a mere solecism,

Though in a nunnery. It must not be.

I muse my lord your brother will permit it!

You should spend half my land first, were I he.

Does not this diamond better on my finger

Than i' the quarry?

Dol.   Yes.

Mammon.   Why, you are like it.
You were created, lady, for the light!
Here, you shall wear it; take it, the first pledge
Of what I speak, to bind you to believe me.
    Dol. In chains of adamant?
    Mammon.   Yes, the strongest bands.   110
And take a secret, too: here by your side
Doth stand this hour the happiest man in Europe.
    Dol. You are contented, sir?
    Mammon.   Nay, in true being,
The envy of princes, and the fear of states.
    Dol. Say you so, Sir Epicure!
    Mammon.   Yes, and thou shalt prove it,
Daughter of honour. I have cast mine eye
Upon thy form, and I will rear this beauty,
Above all styles.
    Dol.   You mean no treason, sir!
    Mammon. No, I will take away that jealousy.
I am the lord of the philosopher's stone,   120
And thou the lady.
    Dol.   How sir! ha' you that?
    Mammon. I am the master of the mastery.
This day the good old wretch here o' the house
Has made it for us. Now he's at projection.
Think therefore thy first wish, now: let me hear it,
And it shall rain into thy lap no shower,
But floods of gold, whole cataracts, a deluge,
To get a nation on thee!
    Dol.   You are pleased, sir,
To work on the ambition of our sex.
    Mammon. I'm pleased the glory of her sex should know   130
This nook here of the Friars is no climate
For her to live obscurely in, to learn
Physic and surgery for the constable's wife
Of some odd hundred in Essex; but come forth
And taste the air of palaces; eat, drink
The toils of emp'rics, and their boasted practice;
Tincture of pearl and coral, gold, and amber;
Be seen at feasts and triumphs, have it asked
What miracle she is, set all the eyes
Of court afire, like a burning glass,   140

And work 'em into cinders; when the jewels
Of twenty states adorn thee, and the light
Strikes out the stars; that, when thy name is mentioned,
Queens may look pale; and, we but showing our love,
Nero's Poppaea may be lost in story!
Thus will we have it.
   Dol.   I could well consent, sir.
But in a monarchy, how will this be?
The prince will soon take notice, and both seize
You and your stone, it being a wealth unfit
For any private subject.
   Mammon.   If he knew it.   150
   Dol. Yourself do boast it, sir.
   Mammon.   To thee, my life.
   Dol. Oh, but beware, sir! You may come to end
The remant of your days in a loath'd prison,
By speaking of it.
   Mammon.   'Tis no idle fear!
We'll therefore go with all, my girl, and live
In a free state, where we will eat our mullets
Soused in high-country wines, sup pheasants' eggs,
And have our cockles boiled in silver shells;
Our shrimps to swim again as when they lived,
In a rare butter made of dolphins' milk,   160
Whose cream does look like opals: and with these
Delicate meats set ourselves high for pleasure,
And take us down again, and then renew
Our youth and strength with drinking the elixir,
And so enjoy a perpetuity
Of life and lust. And thou shalt ha' thy wardrobe
Richer than Nature's, still, to change thyself,
And vary oftener for thy pride than she,
Or Art, her wise and almost-equal servant.

[Enter Face]

   Face. Sir, you are too loud. I hear you, every word,   170
Into the laboratory. Some fitter place——
The garden, or great chamber above. How like you her?
   Mammon. Excellent, Lungs! There's for thee.   [*Gives him money*]
   Face.   But do you hear?
Good sir, beware; no mention of the Rabbins.

Mammon. We think not on 'em.
Face.   Oh, it is well, sir.
                                    [*Exeunt Mammon and Dol*]
                                        Subtle!

Act IV, Scene ii

[*Enter Subtle*]

Face. Dost thou not laugh?
Subtle.   Yes. Are they gone?
Face.   All's clear.
Subtle. The widow is come.
Face.   And your quarrelling disciple?
Subtle. Aye.
Face.   I must to my captainship again then.
Subtle. Stay, bring 'em in first.
Face.   So I meant. What is she?
A bonnibel?
Subtle.   I know not.
Face.   We'll draw lots;
You'll stand to that?
Subtle.   What else?
Face.   Oh, for a suit
To fall now like a curtain, flap!
Subtle.   To the door, man.
Face. You'll ha' the first kiss, 'cause I am not ready.
Subtle. [*Aside*] Yes, and perhaps hit you through both the nostrils.
Face. [*At door*] Who would you speak with?
Kastril.   Where's the Captain?
Face.   Gone, sir,
About some business.   10
Kastril.   Gone?
Face.   He'll return straight.
But Master Doctor, his lieutenant, is here.
                    [*Enter Kastril and Dame Pliant; exit Face*]
    Subtle. Come near, my worshipful boy, my *terrae fili*——
That is, my boy of land——make thy approaches:
Welcome! I know thy lusts and thy desires,
And I will serve and satisfy 'em. Begin,
Charge me from thence, or thence, or in this line;

Here is my centre: ground thy quarrel.
 Kastril.   You lie!
 Subtle. How, child of wrath, and anger! the loud lie?
For what, my sudden boy?
 Kastril.   Nay, that look you to;   20
I am aforehand.
 Subtle. Oh, this's no true grammar,
And as ill logic! You must render causes, child:
Your first and second intentions; know your canons,
And your divisions, modes, degrees and differences,
Your predicaments, substance, and accident,
Series extern, and intern, with their causes
Efficient, material, formal, final,
And ha' your elements perfect——
 Kastril.   What is this
The angry tongue he talks in?
 Subtle.   That false precept,
Of being aforehand, has deceived a number;   30
And made 'em enter quarrels often-times
Before they were aware, and afterward,
Against their wills.
 Kastril. How must I do then, sir?
 Subtle. I cry this lady mercy. She should first
Have been saluted. I do call you lady,
Because you are to be one ere't be long,
My soft and buxom widow.   *(He kisses her)*
 Kastril.   Is she, i' faith?
 Subtle. Yes, or my art is an egregious liar.
 Kastril. How know you?
 Subtle.   By inspection on her forehead
And subtlety of her lip, which must be tasted   40
Often, to make a judgement. *(He kisses her again)* 'Slight, she melts
Like a myrobalan! Here is yet a line
In *rivo frontis* tells me he is no knight.
 Pliant. What is he then, sir?
 Subtle.   Let me see your hand.
Oh, your *linea fortunae* makes it plain;
And *stella*, here, in *monte Veneris*:
But most of all, *junctura annularis*.
He is a soldier or a man of art, lady,
But shall have some great honour shortly.

Pliant.   Brother,
He's a rare man, believe me!
   Kastril.   Hold your peace.   50
Here comes the t'other rare man.

               [Enter Face in Captain's uniform]

                     'Save you, Captain.
   Face. Good Master Kastril. Is this your sister?
   Kastril.   Aye, sir.
Please you to kuss her, and be proud to know her?
   Face. I shall be proud to know you, lady.
   Pliant.   Brother,
He calls me lady, too.
   Kastril.   Aye, peace. I heard it.
   Face. [Aside] The Count is come.
   Subtle. [Aside]   Where is he?
   Face. [Aside]   At the door.
   *Subtle. [Aside]*Why, you must entertain him.
   Face. [Aside]   What'll you do
With these the while?
   Subtle. [Aside]   Why, have 'em up, and show 'em
Some fustian book, or the dark glass.
   Face. [Aside]   'Fore God,
She is a delicate dabchick! I must have her.   *[Exit]*   60
   Subtle. [Aside] Must you? aye, if your fortune will, you must.
[To Kastril] Come sir, the Captain will come to us presently.
I'll ha' you to my chamber of demonstrations,
Where I'll show you both the grammar and logic
And rhetoric of quarrelling, my whole method
Drawn out in tables, and my instrument
That hath the several scale upon't, shall make you
Able to quarrel at a straw's breadth, by moonlight.
And, lady, I'll have you look in a glass
Some half an hour, but to clear your eyesight   70
Against you see your fortune; which is greater
Than I may judge upon the sudden; trust me.   *[Exeunt]*

Act IV, Scene iii

[*Enter Face*]

Face. Where are you, Doctor?
Subtle. [*Within*]   I'll come to you presently.
Face. I will ha' this same widow, now I ha' seen her,
On any composition.

[*Enter Subtle*]

Subtle.   What do you say?
Face. Ha' you disposed of them?
Subtle.   I ha' sent 'em up.
Face. Subtle, in troth, I needs must have this widow.
Subtle. Is that the matter?
Face.   Nay, but hear me——
Subtle.   Go to,
If you rebel once, Dol shall know it all.
Therefore be quiet, and obey your chance.
Face. Nay, thou art so violent now——do but conceive:
Thou art old, and canst not serve——
Subtle.   Who cannot? I?   10
'Slight, I will serve her with thee, for a——
Face.   Nay,
But understand; I'll gi' you composition.
Subtle. I will not treat with thee; what, sell my fortune?
'Tis better than my birthright. Do not murmur.
Win her, and carry her. If you grumble, Dol
Knows it directly.
Face.   Well sir, I am silent.
Will you go help to fetch in Don, in state?
Subtle. I follow you, sir. [*Exit Face*] We must keep Face in awe,
Or he will overlook us like a tyrant.
Brain of a tailor! who comes here? Don John!   20

(*Surly like a Spaniard* [*enters with Face*])

Surly. Señores, beso las manos a vuestras mercedes.
Subtle. Would you had stooped a little, and kissed our *anos*.
Face. Peace, Subtle.
Subtle.   Stab me; I shall never hold, man.
He looks in that deep ruff like a head in a platter,
Served in by a short cloak upon two trestles!

Face. Or what do you say to a collar of brawn, cut down
Beneath the souse, and wriggled with a knife?

Subtle. 'Slud, he does look too fat to be a Spaniard.

Face. Perhaps some Fleming or some Hollander got him
In D'Alva's time: Count Egmont's bastard.

Subtle.   Don,   30
Your scurvy, yellow, Madrid face is welcome.

Surly. Gracias.

Subtle.   He speaks out of a fortification.
'Pray God he ha' no squibs in those deep sets.

Surly. ¡Por Dios, señores, muy linda casa!

Subtle. What says he?

Face.   Praises the house, I think;
I know no more but's action.

Subtle.   Yes, the *casa*,
My precious Diego, will prove fair enough,
To cozen you in. Do you mark? You shall
Be cozened, Diego.

Face.   Cozened, do you see?
My worthy Donzel, cozened.

Surly.   *Entiendo.*   40

Subtle. Do you intend it? So do we, dear Don. *(He feels his pockets)*
Have you brought pistolets or portagues
My solemn Don? *[To Face]* Dost thou feel any?

   Face. [Also feeling]   Full.

Subtle. You shall be emptied, Don; pumped and drawn
Dry, as they say.

Face.   Milked, in troth, sweet Don.

Subtle. See all the monsters; the great lion of all, Don.

Surly. ¿Con licencia, se puede ver a esta señora?

Subtle. What talks he now?

Face.   O' the *señora.*

Subtle.   Oh, Don,
That is the lioness, which you shall see
Also, my Don.

Face.   'Slid, Subtle, how shall we do?   50

Subtle. For what?

Face.   Why, Dol's employed, you know.

Subtle.   That's true!
'Fore heaven I know not; he must stay, that's all.

Face. Stay? that he must not by no means.

Subtle.   No, why?

Face. Unless you'll mar all. 'Slight, he'll suspect it.

And then he will not pay, not half so well.

This is a travelled punk-master, and does know

All the delays; a notable hot rascal,

And looks already rampant.

Subtle.   'Sdeath, and Mammon

Must not be troubled.

Face.   Mammon! in no case.

Subtle. What shall we do then?

Face.   Think: you must be sudden.   60

Surly. Entiendo que la señora es tan hermosa que codicio tan a verla como la bien aventuranza de mi vida.

Face. Mi vida? 'Slid, Subtle, he puts me in mind o' the widow.

What dost thou say to draw her to it, ha?

And tell her it is her fortune? All our venture

Now lies upon't. It is but one man more,

Which on's chance to have her; and beside,

There is no maidenhead to be feared or lost.

What dost thou think on't, Subtle?

Subtle.   Who, I? why——

Face. The credit of our house too is engaged.   70

Subtle. You made me an offer for my share erewhile.

What wilt thou gi' me, i' faith?

Face.   Oh, by that light,

I'll not buy now. You know your doom to me.

E'en take your lot, obey your chance, sir; win her

And wear her, out for me.

Subtle.   'Slight, I'll not work her then.

Face. It is the common cause, therefore bethink you.

Dol else must know it, as you said.

Subtle.   I care not.

Surly. ¿Señores, porqué se tarda tanto?

Subtle. Faith, I am not fit, I am old.

Face.   That's now no reason, sir.

Surly. Puede ser de hacer burla de mi amor.   80

Face. You hear the Don, too? By this air, I call,

And loose the hinges. Dol!

Subtle.   A plague of hell——

Face. Will you then do?

Subtle.   You're a terrible rogue!

I'll think of this. Will you, sir, call the widow?
   Face. Yes, and I'll take her too, with all her faults,
Now I do think on't better.
   Subtle.   With all my heart, sir,
Am I discharged o' the lot?
   Face.   As you please.
   Subtle.   Hands.
                            (*They shake hands*)
   Face. Remember now, that upon any change
You never claim her.
   Subtle.   Much good joy and health to you, sir.
Marry a whore? Fate, let me wed a witch first.   90
   Surly. Por estas honradas barbas——
   Subtle.   He swears by his beard.
Dispatch, and call the brother too.   [*Exit Face*]
   Surly.   *Tengo duda, señores,*
Que no me hagan alguna traición.
   Subtle. How, issue on? Yes, *praesto señor.* Please you
Enthratha the *chambratha*, worthy Don;
Where if it please the Fates, in your *bathada,*
You shall be soaked, and stroked, and tubbed, and rubbed,
And scrubbed, and fubbed, dear Don, before you go.
You shall, in faith, my scurvy babion Don,
Be curried, clawed, and flawed, and tawed, indeed.   100
I will the heartilier go about it now,
And make the widow a punk, so much the sooner,
To be revenged on this impetuous Face:
The quickly doing of it is the grace.   [*Exeunt*]

Act IV, Scene iv

[*Enter Face, Dame Pliant, Kastril*]

   Face. Come lady. [*To Kastril*] I knew the Doctor would not leave
Till he had found the very nick of her fortune.
   Kastril. To be a countess, say you?
   Face.   A Spanish countess, sir.
   Pliant. Why? is that better than an English countess?
   Face. Better? 'slight, make you that a question, lady?
   Kastril. Nay, she is a fool, Captain, you must pardon her.

Face. Ask from your courtier, to your inns-of-court-man,
To your mere milliner: they will tell you all
Your Spanish jennet is the best horse; your Spanish
Stoop is the best garb; your Spanish beard   10
Is the best cut; your Spanish ruffs are the best
Wear; your Spanish pavan the best dance;
Your Spanish titillation in a glove
The best perfume; and for your Spanish pike
And Spanish blade, let your poor Captain speak.
Here comes the Doctor.

[*Enter Subtle, with a paper*]

Subtle.   My most honoured lady——
For so I am now to style you, having found
By this my scheme, you are to undergo
An honourable fortune very shortly——
What will you say now, if some——
Face.   I ha' told her all, sir,   20
And her right worshipful brother, here, that she shall be
A countess——do not delay 'em, sir——a Spanish countess.
Subtle. Still, my scarce worshipful Captain, you can keep
No secret. Well, since he has told you, madam,
Do you forgive him, and I do.
Kastril.   She shall do that, sir.
I'll look to't, 'tis my charge.
Subtle.   Well then. Naught rests
But that she fit her love now to her fortune.
Pliant. Truly, I shall never brook a Spaniard.
Subtle.   No?
Pliant. Never sin' eighty-eight could I abide 'em,
And that was some three year afore I was born, in truth.   30
Subtle. Come, you must love him, or be miserable;
Choose which you will.
Face.   By this good rush, persuade her;
She will cry strawberries else within this twelve-month.
Subtle. Nay, shads and mackerel, which is worse.
Face.   Indeed, sir?
Kastril. God's lid, you shall love him, or I'll kick you.
Pliant.   Why,
I'll do as you will ha' me, brother.
Kastril.   Do,

Or by this hand, I'll maul you.
   Face.   Nay, good sir,
Be not so fierce.
   Subtle.   No, my enragèd child,
She will be ruled. What, when she comes to taste
The pleasures of a countess! to be courted——   40
   Face. And kissed, and ruffled!
   Subtle.   Aye, behind the hangings.
   Face. And then come forth in pomp!
   Subtle.   And know her state!
   Face. Of keeping all the idolaters o' the chamber
Barer to her, than at their prayers!
   Subtle.   Is served
Upon the knee!
   Face.   And has her pages, ushers,
Footmen, and coaches——
   Subtle.   Her six mares——
   Face.   Nay, eight!
   Subtle. To hurry her through London, to the Exchange,
Bedlam, the China-houses——
   Face.   Yes, and have
The citizens gape at her, and praise her tires!
And my lord's goose-turd bands, that rides with her!   50
   Kastril. Most brave! by this hand, you are not my suster,
If you refuse.
   Pliant.   I will not refuse, brother.

               [*Enter Surly*]

   Surly. ¿Qué es esto, señores, que no se venga?
¡Esta tardanza me mata!
   Face.   It is the Count come!
The Doctor knew he would be here, by his art.
   Subtle. ¡En gallanta Madama, Don! ¡Gallantissima!
   Surly. ¡Por todos los dioses, la más acabada
Hermosura que he visto en mi vida!
   Face. Is't not a gallant language that they speak?
   Kastril. An admirable language! is't not French?   60
   Face. No, Spanish, sir.
   Kastril.   It goes like law-French,
And that, they say, is the courtliest language.
   Face.   List, sir.

Surly. El Sol ha perdido su lumbre, con el
Resplandor, que trae esta dama. ¡Válgame Dios!
    Face. He admires your sister.
    Kastril.   Must not she make curtsey?
    Subtle. 'Ods will, she must go to him, man, and kiss him!
It is the Spanish fashion for the women
To make first court.
    Face.   'Tis true he tells you, sir;
His art knows all.
    Surly.   *¿Porqué no se acude?*
    Kastril. He speaks to her, I think?
    Face.   That he does sir.   70
    Surly. Por el amor de Dios, que es esto, que se tarda?
    Kastril. Nay, see, she will not understand him! Gull,
Noddy!
    Pliant. What say you brother?
    Kastril.   Ass, my suster,
Go kuss him, as the cunning man would ha' you;
I'll thrust a pin i' your buttocks else.
    Face.   Oh, no sir.
    Surly. Señora mía, mi persona muy indigna está
A llegar a tanta hermosura.
    Face. Does he not use her bravely?
    Kastril.   Bravely, i' faith!
    Face. Nay, he will use her better.
    Kastril.   Do you think so?
    Surly. Señora, si será servida, entremos.   [*Exit with Dame Pliant*]   80
    Kastril. Where does he carry her?
    Face.   Into the garden, sir;
Take you no thought. I must interpret for her.
    Subtle. Give Dol the word. [*Exit Face*] Come, my fierce child, advance;
We'll to our quarrelling lesson again.
    Kastril.   Agreed.
I love a Spanish boy with all my heart.
    Subtle. Nay, and by this means, sir, you shall be brother
To a great Count.
    Kastril.   Aye, I knew that at first.
This match will advance the house of the Kastrils.
    Subtle. 'Pray God your sister prove but pliant.
    Kastril.   Why,
Her name is so, by her other husband.

Subtle.   How!   90
Kastril. The widow Pliant. Knew you not that?
Subtle.   No faith, sir.
Yet by erection of her figure I guessed it.
Come, let's go practise.
     Kastril.   Yes, but do you think, Doctor,
I e'er shall quarrel well?
     Subtle.   I warrant you.   [*Exeunt*]

Act IV, Scene v

[*Enter Dol (in her fit of talking) with Sir Epicure Mammon*]

Dol. For, after Alexander's death——
Mammon.   Good lady——
Dol. That Perdiccas and Antigonus were slain,
The two that stood, Seleuc' and Ptolemy——
Mammon. Madam——
     Dol.   Made up the two legs, and the fourth beast.
That was Gog-north and Egypt-south, which after
Was called Gog-iron-leg and South-iron-leg——
     Mammon.   Lady——
Dol. And then Gog-hornèd. So was Egypt, too;
Then Egypt-clay-leg, and Gog-clay-leg——
Mammon.   Sweet madam——
Dol. And last Gog-dust and Egypt-dust, which fall
In the last link of the fourth chain. And these   10
Be stars in story, which none see, or look at——
Mammon. What shall I do?
     Dol.   For, as he says, except
We call the Rabbins and the heathen Greeks——
Mammon. Dear lady——
     Dol.   To come from Salem and from Athens,
And teach the people of Great Britain——

[*Enter Face, as Lungs*]

Face.   What's the matter, sir?
Dol. To speak the tongue of Eber and Javan——
Mammon.   Oh,
She's in her fit.
     Dol.   We shall know nothing——
     Face.   Death, sir,

We are undone!

   Dol.   Where then a learnèd linguist

Shall see the ancient used communion

Of vowels and consonants——

   Face.   My master will hear!   20

   Dol. A wisdom which Pythagoras held most high——

   Mammon. Sweet honourable lady——

   Dol.   To comprise

All sounds of voices in few marks of letters——

   Face. Nay, you must never hope to lay her now.

                      (They speak together)

Dol. And so we may arrive by Talmud skill,	*Face.* How did you put her into't?
	Mammon. Alas, I talked
And profane Greek, to raise the building up	Of a fifth monarchy I would erect,
Of Helen's house against the Ismaelite,	With the philosopher's stone, by chance, and she
King of Thogarma, and his habergeons	Falls on the other four, straight.
	Face. Out of Broughton!
Brimstony, blue, and fiery; and the force	I told you so. 'Slid, stop her mouth.
	Mammon. Is't best?
Of King Abaddon, and the Beast of Cittim;	*Face.* She'll never leave else. If the old man hear her, 30
Which Rabbi David Kimchi, Onkelos,	We are but faeces, ashes.
	Subtle. [*Within*]
	What's to do there?
And Aben-Ezra do interpret Rome.	*Face.* Oh, we are lost. Now she hears him, she is quiet.

        (Upon Subtle's entry they disperse) [*Exeunt Dol and Face*]

   Mammon. Where shall I hide me?

   Subtle.   How! What sight is here!

Close deeds of darkness, and that shun the light!

Bring him again. Who is he? What, my son!

Oh, I have lived too long.

   Mammon.   Nay good, dear father,

There was no unchaste purpose.

   Subtle.   Not? and flee me,

When I come in?

   Mammon.   That was my error.

Subtle. Error?
Guilt, guilt, my son; give it the right name. No marvel
If I found check in our great work within,   40
When such affairs as these were managing!
   Mammon. Why, have you so?
   Subtle. It has stood still this half hour,
And all the rest of our less works gone back.
Where is the instrument of wickedness,
My lewd false drudge?
   Mammon. Nay, good sir, blame not him.
Believe me, 'twas against his will or knowledge.
I saw her by chance.
   Subtle. Will you commit more sin,
To excuse a varlet?
   Mammon. By my hope, 'tis true, sir.
   Subtle. Nay, then I wonder less, if you, for whom
The blessing was prepared, would so tempt heaven,   50
And lose your fortunes.
   Mammon. Why, sir?
   Subtle. This'll retard
The work a month at least.
   Mammon. Why, if it do,
What remedy? But think it not, good father;
Our purposes were honest.
   Subtle. As they were,
So the reward will prove. (*A great crack and noise within*) How now! Ay me.
God, and all saints be good to us.

             [*Enter Face*]

               What's that?
   Face. Oh sir, we are defeated! All the works
Are flown *in fumo*: every glass is burst;
Furnace and all rent down, as if a bolt
Of thunder had been driven through the house!   60
Retorts, receivers, pelicans, bolt heads,
All struck in shivers! (*Subtle falls down as in a swoon*) Help, good sir! Alas,
Coldness, and death invades him. Nay, Sir Mammon,
Do the fair offices of a man! You stand
As you were readier to depart than he.   (*One knocks*)
Who's there? [*Looking out*] My lord her brother is come.
   Mammon. Ha, Lungs?

Face. His coach is at the door. Avoid his sight,
For he's as furious as his sister is mad.
   Mammon. Alas!
   Face.   My brain is quite undone with the fume, sir,
I ne'er must hope to be mine own man again.   70
   Mammon. Is all lost, Lungs? Will nothing be preserved
Of all our cost?
   Face.   Faith, very little, sir.
A peck of coals or so, which is cold comfort, sir.
   Mammon. Oh, my voluptuous mind! I am justly punished.
   Face. And so am I, sir.
   Mammon.   Cast from all my hopes——
   Face. Nay, certainties, sir.
   Mammon.   By mine own base affections.
                     (Subtle seems to come to himself)
   Subtle. Oh, the cursèd fruits of vice and lust!
   Mammon.   Good father,
It was my sin. Forgive it.
   Subtle.   Hangs my roof
Over us still, and will not fall? Oh, justice
Upon us, for this wicked man!
   Face.   Nay, look, sir,   80
You grieve him now with staying in his sight;
Good sir, the nobleman will come too, and take you,
And that may breed a tragedy.
   Mammon.   I'll go.
   Face. Aye, and repent at home, sir. It may be,
For some good penance, you may ha' it yet:
A hundred pound to the box at Bedlam——
   Mammon.   Yes.
   Face. For the restoring such as ha' their wits.
   Mammon.   I'll do't.
   Face. I'll send one to you to receive it.
   Mammon.   Do.
Is no projection left?
   Face.   All flown, or stinks, sir.
   Mammon. Will naught be saved that's good for medicine, thinkst thou? 90
   Face. I cannot tell, sir. There will be, perhaps,
Something about the scraping of the shards
Will cure the itch—— [*Aside*] though not your itch of mind, sir——
It shall be saved for you, and sent home. Good sir,

This way, for fear the lord should meet you.   [*Exit Mammon*]
   Subtle.   Face!
   Face. Aye.
   Subtle.   Is he gone?
   Face.   Yes, and as heavily
As all the gold he hoped for were in his blood.
Let us be light, though.
   Subtle. [*Leaping up*]   Aye, as balls, and bound
And hit our heads against the roof for joy;
There's so much of our care now cast away.   100
   Face. Now to our Don.
   Subtle.   Yes, your young widow by this time
Is made a Countess, Face; she's been in travail
Of a young heir for you.
   Face.   Good, sir.
   Subtle.   Off with your case,
And greet her kindly, as a bridegroom should,
After these common hazards.
   Face.   Very well, sir.
Will you go fetch Don Diego off the while?
   Subtle. And fetch him over too, if you'll be pleased, sir.
Would Dol were in her place, to pick his pockets now!
   Face. Why, you can do it as well, if you would set to't.
I pray you prove your virtue.
   Subtle.   For your sake, sir.   [*Exeunt*] 110

Act IV, Scene vi

[*Enter Surly and Dame Pliant*]

   Surly. Lady, you see into what hands you are fallen,
'Mongst what a nest of villains! and how near
Your honour was to have catched a certain clap,
Through your credulity, had I but been
So punctually forward, as place, time,
And other circumstance would ha' made a man;
For you're a handsome woman; would you were wise, too.
I am a gentleman, come here disguised
Only to find the knaveries of this citadel;
And where I might have wronged your honour, and have not,   10

I claim some interest in your love. You are,
They say, a widow, rich; and I am a bachelor
Worth naught. Your fortunes may make me a man,
As mine ha' preserved you a woman. Think upon it,
And whether I have deserved you, or no.
    Pliant.   I will, sir.
    Surly. And for these household-rogues, let me alone
To treat with them.

[Enter Subtle]

    Subtle.   How doth my noble Diego,
And my dear madam Countess? Hath the Count
Been courteous, lady? liberal and open?
Donzel, methinks you look melancholic   20
After your *coitum*, and scurvy! Truly,
I do not like the dullness of your eye:
It hath a heavy cast, 'tis upsee Dutch,
And says you are a lumpish whore-master.
Be lighter, I will make your pockets so.   (*He falls to picking of them*)
    Surly. Will you, Don Bawd, and Pick-purse? [*Knocks him down*] How
         now? reel you?
Stand up sir: you shall find since I am so heavy,
I'll gi' you equal weight.
    Subtle.   Help, murder!
    Surly.   No, sir,
There's no such thing intended. A good cart
And a clean whip shall ease you of that fear.   30
I am the Spanish Don, that should be cozened,
Do you see? cozened? Where's your Captain Face,
That parcel-broker, and whole-bawd, all rascal?

[Enter Face in his Captain's uniform]

    Face. How, Surly!
    Surly.   Oh, make your approach, good Captain.
I've found from whence your copper rings and spoons
Come now, wherewith you cheat abroad in taverns.
'Twas here you learned to anoint your boot with brimstone,
Then rub men's gold on't for a kind of touch,
And say 'twas naught, when you had changed the colour,
That you might ha't for nothing! And this Doctor,   40
Your sooty, smoky-bearded compeer, he
Will close you so much gold in a bolt's head,

And, on a turn, convey i' the stead another
With sublimed mercury, that shall burst i' the heat
And fly out all *in fumo*? [*Exit Face*] Then weeps Mammon;
Then swoons his worship. Or he is the Faustus
That casteth figures, and can conjure, cures
Plague, piles, and pox by the ephemerides,
And holds intelligence with all the bawds
And midwives of three shires, while you send in——   50
Captain——what is he gone?——damsels with child,
Wives that are barren, or the waiting-maid
With the green-sickness?—— Nay, sir, you must tarry,

[*Seizes Subtle*]

Though he be 'scaped; and answer by the ears, sir.

Act IV, Scene vii

[*Enter Face and Kastril*]

Face. Why, now's the time, if ever you will quarrel
Well, as they say, and be a true-born child.
The Doctor and your sister both are abused.
    Kastril. Where is he? which is he? he is a slave
Whate'er he is, and the son of a whore. Are you
The man, sir, I would know?
    Surly.   I should be loath, sir,
To confess so much.
    Kastril.   Then you lie i' your throat!
    Surly.   How?
    Face. A very arrant rogue, sir, and a cheater,
Employed here by another conjurer
That does not love the Doctor, and would cross him   10
If he knew how——
    Surly.   Sir, you are abused.
    Kastril.   You lie,
And 'tis no matter.
    Face.   Well said, sir! He is
The impudentest rascal——
    Surly.   You are indeed. Will you hear me, sir?
    Face. By no means; bid him be gone.
    Kastril.   Be gone, sir, quickly.

Surly. This's strange! Lady, do you inform your brother.

> [*Dame Pliant talks to Kastril*]

Face. There is not such a foist in all the town.
The Doctor had him presently; and finds yet
The Spanish Count will come here. Bear up, Subtle.

Subtle. Yes, sir, he must appear within this hour.

Face. And yet this rogue would come in a disguise,   20
By the temptation of another spirit,
To trouble our art, though he could not hurt it.

Kastril.   Aye,
I know——[*To Dame Pliant*] Away, you talk like a foolish mauther.

> [*Exit Dame Pliant*]

Surly. Sir, all is truth, she says.

Face.   Do not believe him, sir;
He is the lyingest swabber! Come your ways, sir.

Surly. You are valiant, out of company.

Kastril.   Yes, how then, sir?

> [*Enter Drugger with a piece of damask*]

Face. Nay, here's an honest fellow, too, that knows him
And all his tricks. [*Aside to Drugger*] Make good what I say, Abel;
This cheater would ha' cozened thee o' the widow.——
He owes this honest Drugger here seven pound   30
He has had on him in two-penny'orths of tobacco.

Drugger. Yes sir. And he's damned himself three terms to pay me.

Face. And what does he owe for lotium?

Drugger.   Thirty shillings, sir;
And for six syringes.

Surly.   Hydra of villainy!

Face. Nay, sir, you must quarrel him out o' the house.

Kastril.   I will.
Sir, if you get not out o' doors, you lie,
And you are a pimp.

Surly.   Why, this is madness, sir,
Not valour in you; I must laugh at this.

Kastril. It is my humour; you are a pimp, and a trig,
And an Amadis de Gaul, or a Don Quixote.   40

Drugger. Or a Knight o' the Curious Coxcomb. Do you see?

> [*Enter Ananias*]

Ananias. Peace to the household!

Kastril.   I'll keep peace for no man.

Ananias. Casting of dollars is concluded lawful.

Kastril. Is he the constable?

Subtle.   Peace, Ananias.

Face.   No, sir.

Kastril. Then you are an otter, and a shad, a whit,
A very tim.

Surly.   You'll hear me, sir?

Kastril.   I will not.

Ananias. What is the motive?

Subtle.   Zeal in the young gentleman,
Against his Spanish slops——

Ananias.   They are profane,
Lewd, superstitious, and idolatrous breeches.

Surly. New rascals!

Kastril.   Will you be gone, sir?

Ananias.   Avoid Satan,   50
Thou art not of the light. That ruff of pride
About thy neck betrays thee, and is the same
With that which the unclean birds, in seventy-seven,
Were seen to prank it with on divers coasts.
Thou look'st like Antichrist in that lewd hat.

Surly. I must give way.

Kastril.   Be gone, sir.

Surly.   But I'll take
A course with you——

Ananias.   Depart, proud Spanish fiend!

Surly. Captain and Doctor——

Ananias.   Child of perdition!

Kastril.   Hence, sir!

                                        [*Exit Surly*]

Did I not quarrel bravely?

Face.   Yes, indeed, sir.

Kastril. Nay, and I give my mind to't, I shall do't.   60

Face. Oh, you must follow, sir, and threaten him tame.
He'll turn again else.

Kastril.   I'll re-turn him, then.   [*Exit*]

Face. Drugger, this rogue prevented us for thee.
We had determined that thou shouldst ha' come
In a Spanish suit, and ha' carried her so; and he,
A brokerly slave, goes puts it on himself.
Hast brought the damask?

Drugger.   Yes sir.

Face.   Thou must borrow

A Spanish suit. Hast thou no credit with the players?

    Drugger. Yes, sir; did you never see me play the fool?

    Face. I know not, Nab; thou shalt, if I can help it.   70

Hieronimo's old cloak, ruff, and hat will serve;

I'll tell thee more when thou bringst 'em.   [*Exit Drugger*]

    Ananias. (Subtle hath whispered with him this while)

                       Sir, I know

The Spaniard hates the Brethren, and hath spies

Upon their actions; and that this was one

I make no scruple. But the holy synod

Have been in prayer and meditation for it;

And 'tis revealed no less to them than me,

That casting of money is most lawful.

    Subtle.   True.

But here I cannot do it; if the house

Should chance to be suspected, all would out,   80

And we be locked up in the tower for ever,

To make gold there for the state, never come out;

And then are you defeated.

    Ananias.   I will tell

This to the elders and the weaker Brethren,

That the whole company of the Separation

May join in humble prayer again.

    Subtle.   And fasting.

    Ananias. Yea, for some fitter place. The peace of mind

Rest with these walls.

    Subtle.   Thanks, courteous Ananias.   [*Exit Ananias*]

    Face. What did he come for?

    Subtle.   About casting dollars,

Presently, out of hand. And so I told him   90

A Spanish minister came here to spy,

Against the faithful——

    Face.   I conceive. Come Subtle,

Thou art so down upon the least disaster!

How wouldst thou ha' done if I had not helped thee out?

    Subtle. I thank thee Face, for the angry boy, i' faith.

    Face. Who would ha' looked it should ha' been that rascal

Surly? He had dyed his beard, and all. Well, sir,

Here's damask come to make you a suit.

Subtle.   Where's Drugger?

Face. He is gone to borrow me a Spanish habit;
I'll be the Count now.

Subtle.   But where's the widow?

Face. Within, with my lord's sister——Madam Dol   100
Is entertaining her.

Subtle.   By your favour, Face:
Now she is honest, I will stand again.

Face. You will not offer it?

Subtle.   Why?

Face.   Stand to your word,
Or——here comes Dol. She knows——

Subtle.   You're tyrannous still.

                                        [*Enter Dol*]

Face. Strict for my right. How now, Dol? Hast told her
The Spanish Count will come?

Dol.   Yes, but another is come
You little looked for!

Face.   Who's that?

Dol.   Your master;
The master of the house.

Subtle.   How, Dol!

Face.   She lies.
This is some trick. Come, leave your quiblins, Dorothy.   110

Dol. Look out, and see.   [*Face goes to the window*]

Subtle.   Art thou in earnest?

Dol.   'Slight,
Forty o' the neighbours are about him, talking.

Face. 'Tis he, by this good day.

Dol.   'Twill prove ill day,
For some on us.

Face.   We are undone, and taken.

Dol. Lost, I'm afraid.

Subtle.   You said he would not come
While there died one a week within the liberties.

Face. No: 'twas within the walls.

Subtle.   Was't so? cry you mercy:
I thought the liberties. What shall we do now, Face?

Face. Be silent; not a word, if he call or knock.
I'll into mine old shape again and meet him,   120
Of Jeremy the butler. I' the meantime,

Do you two pack up all the goods and purchase,
That we can carry i' the two trunks. I'll keep him
Off for today, if I cannot longer, and then
At night I'll ship you both away to Ratcliff,
Where we'll meet tomorrow, and there we'll share.
Let Mammon's brass and pewter keep the cellar;
We'll have another time for that. But, Dol,
'Pray thee, go heat a little water quickly,
Subtle must shave me. [*Exit Dol*] All my Captain's beard   130
Must off, to make me appear smooth Jeremy.
You'll do't?
    Subtle.   Yes, I'll shave you as well as I can.
    Face. And not cut my throat, but trim me?
    Subtle.   You shall see, sir.
                                    [*Exeunt*]

Act V, Scene i

[Outside Lovewit's house; Lovewit with Neighbours]

Lovewit. Has there been such resort, say you?
    1st Neighbour.   Daily, sir.
    2nd Neighbour. And nightly, too.
    3rd Neighbour.   Aye, some as brave as lords.
    4th Neighbour. Ladies and gentlewomen.
    5th Neighbour.   Citizens' wives.
    1st Neighbour. And knights.
    6th Neighbour.   In coaches.
    2nd Neighbour.   Yes, and oyster-women.
    1st Neighbour. Beside other gallants.
    3rd Neighbour.   Sailors' wives.
    4th Neighbour.   Tobacco-men.
    5th Neighbour. Another Pimlico!
    Lovewit.   What should my knave advance
To draw this company? He hung out no banners
Of a strange calf with five legs to be seen?
Or a huge lobster with six claws?
    6th Neighbour.   No, sir.
    3rd Neighbour. We had gone in then, sir.
    Lovewit.   He has no gift   10

Of teaching i' the nose that e'er I knew of!
You saw no bills set up that promised cure
Of agues or the toothache?
    2nd Neighbour.   No such thing, sir.
    Lovewit. Nor heard a drum struck for baboons or puppets?
    5th Neighbour. Neither, sir.
    Lovewit.   What device should he bring forth now?
I love a teeming wit as I love my nourishment.
'Pray God he ha' not kept such open house
That he hath sold my hangings and my bedding;
I left him nothing else. If he have eat 'em,
A plague o' the moth, say I. Sure he has got   20
Some bawdy pictures, to call all this ging:
The friar and the nun, or the new motion
Of the knight's courser covering the parson's mare,
The boy of six year old with the great thing;
Or't may be he has the fleas that run at tilt
Upon a table, or some dog to dance?
When saw you him?
    1st Neighbour.   Who, sir, Jeremy?
    2nd Neighbour.   Jeremy butler?
We saw him not this month.
    Lovewit.   How?
    4th Neighbour.   Not these five weeks, sir.
    [*1st*] *Neighbour.* These six weeks, at the least.
    Lovewit.   You amaze me, neighbours!
    5th Neighbour. Sure, if your worship know not where he is,
He's slipped away.   30
    6th Neighbour.   Pray God, he be not made away!
    Lovewit. Ha? It's no time to question, then.   (*He knocks*)
    6th Neighbour.   About
Some three weeks' since I heard a doleful cry,
As I sat up a-mending my wife's stockings.
    Lovewit. This's strange, that none will answer! Didst thou hear
A cry, sayst thou?
    6th Neighbour. Yes, sir, like unto a man
That had been strangled an hour, and could not speak.
    2nd Neighbour. I heard it too, just this day three weeks, at two o'clock
Next morning.
    Lovewit.   These be miracles, or you make 'em so!
A man an hour strangled, and could not speak,   40

And both you heard him cry?
   3rd Neighbour.   Yes, downward, sir.
   Lovewit. Thou art a wise fellow; give me thy hand, I pray thee.
What trade art thou on?
   3rd Neighbour.   A smith, and't please your worship.
   Lovewit. A smith? Then lend me thy help to get this door open.
   3rd Neighbour. That I will presently, sir, but fetch my tools——
                                                           [*Exit*]

   1st Neighbour. Sir, best to knock again, afore you break it.

Act V, Scene ii

   Lovewit. I will.   [*Knocks*]
      [*Face, dressed as Jeremy the butler, opens the door*]
   Face.   What mean you, sir?
   1st, 2nd, 4th Neighbours.   Oh, here's Jeremy!
   Face. Good sir, come from the door.
   Lovewit.   Why! what's the matter?
   Face. Yet farther, you are too near, yet.
   Lovewit.   I' the name of wonder!
What means the fellow?
   Face.   The house, sir, has been visited.
   Lovewit. What, with the plague? Stand thou then farther.
   Face.   No, sir,
I had it not.
   Lovewit.   Who had it then? I left
None else but thee i' the house.
   Face.   Yes, sir. My fellow
The cat that kept the buttery had it on her
A week before I spied it, but I got her
Conveyed away i' the night. And so I shut   10
The house up for a month——
   Lovewit.   How!
   Face.   Purposing then, sir,
To have burnt rose-vinegar, treacle, and tar,
And ha' made it sweet, that you should ne'er ha' known it;
Because I knew the news would but afflict you, sir.
   Lovewit. Breathe less, and farther off. Why, this is stranger!

The neighbours tell me all, here, that the doors
Have still been open——
  Face.   How, sir!
  Lovewit.   Gallants, men and women
And of all sorts, tag-rag, been seen to flock here
In threaves, these ten weeks, as to a second Hogsden
In days of Pimlico and Eye-bright.
  Face.   Sir,   20
Their wisdoms will not say so.
  Lovewit.   Today they speak
Of coaches and gallants; one in a French hood,
Went in, they tell me; and another was seen
In a velvet gown at the window. Divers more
Pass in and out.
  Face.   They did pass through the doors then,
Or walls, I assure their eyesights and their spectacles:
For here, sir, are the keys, and here have been
In this my pocket now above twenty days!
And for before, I kept the fort alone there.
But that 'tis yet not deep i' the afternoon,   30
I should believe my neighbours had seen double
Through the black-pot, and made these apparitions!
For on my faith to your worship, for these three weeks
And upwards the door has not been opened.
  Lovewit.   Strange!
  1st Neighbour. Good faith, I think I saw a coach!
  2nd Neighbour.   And I too,
I'd ha' been sworn!
  Lovewit. Do you but think it now?
And but one coach?
  4th Neighbour. We cannot tell, sir; Jeremy
Is a very honest fellow.
  Face.   Did you see me at all?
  1st Neighbour. No; that we are sure on.
  2nd Neighbour.   I'll be sworn o' that.
  Lovewit. Fine rogues, to have your testimonies built on! 40

     [Enter 3rd Neighbour with tools]

  3rd Neighbour. Is Jeremy come?
  1st Neighbour.   Oh, yes, you may leave your tools;
We were deceived, he says.

2nd Neighbour.   He's had the keys,
And the door has been shut these three weeks.
   3rd Neighbour.   Like enough.
   Lovewit. Peace, and get hence, you changelings.

                [*Surly and Mammon approach*]

   Face. [*Aside*]   Surly come!
And Mammon made acquainted? They'll tell all.
How shall I beat them off? What shall I do?
Nothing's more wretched than a guilty conscience.

Act V, Scene iii

[Enter Surly and Sir Epicure Mammon]

   Surly. No, sir, he was a great physician. This,
It was no bawdy-house, but mere chancel.
You knew the lord and his sister.
   Mammon.   Nay, good Surly——
   Surly. The happy word, 'Be rich'——
   Mammon.   Play not the tyrant——
   Surly. Should be today pronounced to all your friends.
And where be your andirons now? and your brass pots,
That should ha' been golden flagons and great wedges?
   Mammon. Let me but breathe.—— What! They ha' shut their doors,
Methinks!
   Surly.   Aye, now 'tis holiday with them.
   Mammon.   Rogues,
Cozeners, impostors, bawds!   (*Mammon and Surly knock*)
   Face.   What mean you, sir?   10
   Mammon. To enter if we can.
   Face.   Another man's house?
Here is the owner, sir: turn you to him,
And speak your business.
   Mammon.   Are you, sir, the owner?
   Lovewit Yes, sir.
   Mammon.   And are those knaves within your cheaters?
   Lovewit. What knaves? what cheaters?
   Mammon.   Subtle and his Lungs.
   Face. The gentleman is distracted, sir! No lungs
Nor lights ha' been seen here these three weeks, sir,

Within these doors, upon my word!

Surly.   Your word,
Groom arrogant?

Face.   Yes, sir, I am the housekeeper,
And know the keys ha' not been out o' my hands.

Surly. This's a new Face?

Face.   You do mistake the house, sir!
What sign was't at?

Surly.   You rascal! this is one
O' the confederacy. Come, let's get officers,
And force the door.

Lovewit.   'Pray you stay, gentlemen.

Surly. No, sir, we'll come with warrant.

Mammon.   Aye, and then,
We shall ha' your doors open.   [*Exeunt Mammon and Surly*]

Lovewit.   What means this?

Face. I cannot tell, sir!

1st Neighbour.   These are two o' the gallants
That we do think we saw.

Face.   Two o' the fools?
You talk as idly as they. Good faith, sir,
I think the moon has crazed 'em all!

[*Enter Kastril*]

      [*Aside*] Oh me,
The angry boy come too? He'll make a noise,
And ne'er away till he have betrayed us all.   (*Kastril knocks*)

Kastril. What, rogues, bawds, slaves! you'll open the door anon.
Punk, cockatrice, my suster! By this light,
I'll fetch the marshal to you. You are a whore
To keep your castle——

Face.   Who would you speak with, sir?

Kastril. The bawdy Doctor, and the cozening Captain,
And Puss my suster.

Lovewit.   This is something, sure!

Face. Upon my trust, the doors were never open, sir.

Kastril. I have heard all their tricks told me twice over,
By the fat knight and the lean gentleman.

Lovewit. Here comes another.

[*Enter Ananias and Tribulation*]

Face. [Aside]   Ananias too?
And his pastor?
    Tribulation.   The doors are shut against us.
                                        (*They beat, too, at the door*)
    Ananias. Come forth, you seed of sulphur, sons of fire!
Your stench, it is broke forth; abomination
Is in the house.
    Kastril.   Aye, my suster's there.
    Ananias.   The place,
It is become a cage of unclean birds.
    Kastril. Yes, I will fetch the scavenger and the constable.
    Tribulation. You shall do well.
    Ananias.   We'll join to weed them out.
    Kastril. You will not come then? Punk device, my suster!   50
    Ananias. Call her not sister. She is a harlot, verily.
    Kastril. I'll raise the street.
    Lovewit.   Good gentlemen, a word.
    Ananias. Satan, avoid, and hinder not our zeal!
                            [*Exeunt Ananias, Tribulation, Kastril*]
    Lovewit. The world's turned Bedlam.
    Face.   These are all broke loose
Out of St Katherine's, where they use to keep
The better sort of mad-folks.
    1st Neighbour.   All these persons
We saw go in and out here.
    2nd Neighbour.   Yes, indeed, sir.
    3rd Neighbour. These were the parties.
    Face.   Peace, you drunkards. Sir,
I wonder at it! Please you to give me leave
To touch the door; I'll try an' the lock be changed.   60
    Lovewit. It 'mazes me!
    Face.   Good faith, sir, I believe
There's no such thing. 'Tis all *deceptio visus*.
[*Aside*] Would I could get him away.

                    (*Dapper cries out within*)

    Dapper.   Master Captain, Master Doctor!
    Lovewit. Who's that?
    Face. [Aside]   Our clerk within, that I forgot!——I know not,
        sir.
    Dapper. [Within] For God's sake, when will her Grace be at leisure?

Face.   Ha!
Illusions, some spirit o' the air——[*Aside*] His gag is melted,
And now he sets out the throat.
    Dapper. [*Within*]   I am almost stifled——
    Face. [*Aside*] Would you were altogether.
    Lovewit.   'Tis i' the house.
Ha! list.
    Face. Believe it, sir, i' the air!
    Lovewit.   Peace, you——
    Dapper. [*Within*] Mine aunt's Grace does not use me well.
    Subtle. [*Within*]   You fool,   70
Peace, you'll mar all.
    Face. [*Whispering to Subtle within*] Or you will else, you rogue.
    Lovewit. [*Overhearing*] Oh, is it so? then you converse with spirits!
Come sir. No more o' your tricks, good Jeremy;
The truth, the shortest way.
    Face.   Dismiss this rabble, sir.
[*Aside*] What shall I do? I am catched.
    Lovewit.   Good neighbours,
I thank you all. You may depart. [*Exeunt Neighbours*] Come sir,
You know that I am an indulgent master;
And therefore conceal nothing. What's your medicine
To draw so many several sorts of wildfowl?
    Face. Sir, you were wont to affect mirth and wit——   80
But here's no place to talk on't i' the street.
Give me but leave to make the best of my fortune,
And only pardon me the abuse of your house;
It's all I beg. I'll help you to a widow,
In recompense, that you shall gi' me thanks for,
Will make you seven years younger, and a rich one.
'Tis but your putting on a Spanish cloak;
I have her within. You need not fear the house;
It was not visited.
    Lovewit.   But by me, who came
Sooner than you expected.
    Face.   It is true, sir.   90
'Pray you forgive me.
    Lovewit.   Well; let's see your widow.   [*Exeunt*]

Act V, Scene iv

[Enter Subtle with Dapper, still blindfolded]

Subtle. How! ha' you eaten your gag?

Dapper.   Yes faith, it crumbled
Away i' my mouth.

    Subtle.   You ha' spoiled all then.

    Dapper.   No:
I hope my aunt of Faery will forgive me.

    Subtle. Your aunt's a gracious lady; but in troth
You were to blame.

    Dapper.   The fume did overcome me,
And I did do't to stay my stomach. 'Pray you
So satisfy her Grace. Here comes the Captain.

[Enter Face in his Captain's uniform]

    Face. How now! is his mouth down?

    Subtle.   Aye! he has spoken!

    Face. [*To Subtle*] A pox, I heard him, and you too.—— [*Aloud*] He's
    undone, then.

[*Talking to one side with Subtle*] I have been fain to say the house is
    haunted   10
With spirits, to keep churl back.

    Subtle.   And hast thou done it?

    Face. Sure, for this night.

    Subtle.   Why, then triumph, and sing
Of Face so famous, the precious king
Of present wits.

    Face.   Did you not hear the coil
About the door?

    Subtle.   Yes, and I dwindled with it.

    Face. Show him his aunt, and let him be dispatched:
I'll send her to you.   [*Exit*]

    Subtle.   Well sir, your aunt her Grace
Will give you audience presently, on my suit
And the Captain's word that you did not eat your gag
In any contempt of her Highness. [*Unties Dapper's blindfold*]

    Dapper.   Not I, in troth, sir.   20

([Enter] Dol like the Queen of Faery)

    Subtle. Here she is come. Down o' your knees, and wriggle;

She has a stately presence. [*Dapper advances on his knees*] Good. Yet
   nearer,
And bid, 'God save you'.
   Dapper.   Madam!
   Subtle.   And your aunt.
   Dapper. And my most gracious aunt, God save your Grace.
   Dol. Nephew, we thought to have been angry with you;
But that sweet face of yours hath turned the tide,
And made it flow with joy, that ebbed of love.
Arise, and touch our velvet gown.
   Subtle.   The skirts,
And kiss 'em. So.
   Dol.   Let me now stroke that head,
Much, nephew, shalt thou win, much shalt thou spend;   30
Much shalt thou give away; much shalt thou lend.
   Subtle. [*Aside*] Aye, much, indeed. Why do you not thank her Grace?
   Dapper. I cannot speak for joy.
   Subtle.   See, the kind wretch!
Your Grace's kinsman right.
   Dol.   Give me the bird.
Here is your fly in a purse, about your neck, cousin;
Wear it, and feed it about this day sen'night,
On your right wrist——
   Subtle.   Open a vein with a pin,
And let it suck but once a week; till then,
You must not look on't.
   Dol.   No. And, kinsman,
Bear yourself worthy of the blood you come on.   40
   Subtle. Her Grace would ha' you eat no more Woolsack pies,
Nor Dagger frumenty.
   Dol.   Nor break his fast
In Heaven and Hell.
   Subtle.   She's with you everywhere!
Nor play with costermongers at mumchance, tray-trip,
God-make-you-rich (whenas your aunt has done it), but keep
The gallant'st company, and the best games——
   Dapper.   Yes, sir.
   Subtle. Gleek and primero: and what you get, be true to us.
   Dapper. By this hand, I will.
   Subtle.   You may bring's a thousand pound
Before tomorrow night, if but three thousand

Be stirring, an' you will.

Dapper.   I swear I will then.   50

Subtle. Your fly will learn you all games.

Face. [Within]   Ha' you done there?

Subtle. Your Grace will command him no more duties?

Dol.   No;

But come and see me often. I may chance

To leave him three or four hundred chests of treasure,

And some twelve thousand acres of Faeryland,

If he game well and comely with good gamesters.

Subtle. There's a kind aunt! Kiss her departing part.

But you must sell your forty mark a year now.

Dapper. Aye, sir, I mean.

Subtle.   Or, gi't away; pox on't!

Dapper. I'll gi't mine aunt. I'll go and fetch the writings.   60

Subtle. 'Tis well, away.   [*Exit Dapper*]

[Enter Face]

Face.   Where's Subtle?

Subtle.   Here. What news?

Face. Drugger is at the door; go take his suit,

And bid him fetch a parson presently;

Say he shall marry the widow. Thou shalt spend

A hundred pound by the service!   [*Exit Subtle*]

       Now, Queen Dol,

Ha' you packed up all?

Dol.   Yes.

Face.   And how do you like

The lady Pliant?

Dol.   A good dull innocent.

[Enter Subtle]

Subtle. Here's your Hieronimo's cloak and hat.

Face.   Give me 'em.

Subtle. And the ruff too?

Face.   Yes, I'll come to you presently.   [*Exit*]

Subtle. Now he is gone about his project, Dol,   70

I told you of, for the widow.

Dol.   'Tis direct

Against our articles.

Subtle.   Well, we'll fit him, wench.

Hast thou gulled her of her jewels or her bracelets?

Dol. No, but I will do't.

Subtle.   Soon at night, my Dolly,
When we are shipped and all our goods aboard,
Eastward for Ratcliff, we will turn our course
To Brentford, westward, if thou sayst the word,
And take our leaves of this o'er-weening rascal,
This peremptory Face.

    Dol.   Content, I'm weary of him.

    Subtle. Thou'st cause, when the slave will run a-wiving, Dol,   80
Against the instrument that was drawn between us.

    Dol. I'll pluck his bird as bare as I can.

    Subtle.   Yes, tell her
She must by any means address some present
To the cunning man, make him amends for wronging
His art with her suspicion; send a ring
Or chain of pearl; she will be tortured else
Extremely in her sleep, say, and ha' strange things
Come to her. Wilt thou?

    Dol.   Yes.

    Subtle.   My fine flitter-mouse,
My bird o' the night; we'll tickle it at the Pigeons
When we have all, and may unlock the trunks,   90
And say, this's mine, and thine, and thine, and mine——

                                (*They kiss*)

                [*Enter Face*]

    Face. What now, a-billing?

    Subtle.   Yes, a little exalted
In the good passage of our stock-affairs.

    Face. Drugger has brought his parson; take him in, Subtle,
And send Nab back again to wash his face.

    Subtle. I will; and shave himself?

    Face.   If you can get him.

                                  [*Exit Subtle*]

    Dol. You are hot upon it, Face, whate'er it is!

    Face. A trick that Dol shall spend ten pound a month by.

                [*Enter Subtle*]

Is he gone?

    Subtle.   The chaplain waits you i' the hall, sir.

    Face. I'll go bestow him.   [*Exit*]

    Dol.   He'll now marry her instantly.   100

Subtle. He cannot yet, he is not ready. Dear Dol,
Cozen her of all thou canst. To deceive him
Is no deceit, but justice, that would break
Such an inextricable tie as ours was.
    Dol. Let me alone to fit him.

                    [*Enter Face*]

Face.   Come, my venturers,
You ha' packed up all? Where be the trunks? Bring forth.
    Subtle. Here.
    Face.   Let's see 'em. Where's the money?
    Subtle.   Here,
In this.
    Face. Mammon's ten pound; eight score before.
The Brethren's money, this. Drugger's, and Dapper's.
What paper's that?
    Dol.   The jewel of the waiting maid's,   110
That stole it from her lady, to know certain——
    Face. If she should have precedence of her mistress?
    Dol.   Yes.
    Face. What box is that?
    Subtle.   The fishwife's rings, I think,
And the alewife's single money. Is't not Dol?
    Dol. Yes, and the whistle that the sailor's wife
Brought you to know and her husband were with Ward.
    Face. We'll wet it tomorrow, and our silver beakers
And tavern cups. Where be the French petticoats
And girdles, and hangers?
    Subtle.   Here, i' the trunk,
And the bolts of lawn.
    Face.   Is Drugger's damask there?   120
And the tobacco?
    Subtle.   Yes.
    Face.   Give me the keys.
    Dol. Why you the keys?
    Subtle.   No matter, Dol, because
We shall not open 'em before he comes.
    Face. 'Tis true, you shall not open them, indeed,
Nor have 'em forth. Do you see? Not forth, Dol.
    Dol.   No!
    Face. No, my smock-rampant. The right is, my master

Knows all, has pardoned me, and he will keep 'em.
Doctor, 'tis true——you look——for all your figures;
I sent for him, indeed. Wherefore, good partners,
Both he and she, be satisfied; for here   130
Determines the indenture tripartite
Twixt Subtle, Dol, and Face. All I can do
Is to help you over the wall o' the back-side,
Or lend you a sheet to save your velvet gown, Dol.
Here will be officers, presently; bethink you
Of some course suddenly to 'scape the dock,
For thither you'll come else. (*Some knock*) Hark you, thunder.
    Subtle. You are a precious fiend!
    Officers. [*Without*]   Open the door!
    Face. Dol, I am sorry for thee i' faith. But hear'st thou?
It shall go hard, but I will place thee somewhere: 140
Thou shalt ha' my letter to Mistress Amo——
    Dol.   Hang you——
    Face. Or Madam Caesarean.
    Dol.   Pox upon you, rogue;
Would I had but time to beat thee!
    Face.   Subtle,
Let's know where you set up next; I'll send you
A customer now and then, for old acquaintance.
What new course ha' you?
    Subtle.   Rogue, I'll hang myself,
That I may walk a greater devil than thou,
And haunt thee i' the flock-bed and the buttery.   [*Exeunt*]

Act V, Scene v

[*Loud knocking at the door. Enter Lovewit in Spanish dress, with the Parson*]
    Lovewit. What do you mean, my masters?
    Mammon. [*Without*]   Open your door,
Cheaters, bawds, conjurors!
    Officer. [*Without*]   Or we'll break it open.
    Lovewit. What warrant have you?
    Officer. [*Without*]   Warrant enough, sir, doubt not,
If you'll not open it.
    Lovewit.   Is there an officer there?

Officer [*Without*] Yes, two or three for failing.
Lovewit.   Have but patience,
And I will open it straight.

[*Enter Face as Jeremy*]

Face.   Sir, ha' you done?
Is it a marriage? Perfect?
Lovewit.   Yes, my brain.
Face. Off with your ruff, and cloak then; be yourself, sir.
Surly. [*Without*] Down with the door!
Kastril. [*Without*]   'Slight, ding it open!

[*Lovewit throws off his disguise and opens the door. Enter Mammon, Surly,
        Ananias, Tribulation, Kastril, and Officers*]

                                                        Hold,
Hold, gentlemen, what means this violence?   10
Mammon. Where is this collier?
Surly.   And my Captain Face?
Mammon. These day-owls——
Surly.   That are birding in men's purses.
Mammon. Madam Suppository——
Kastril.   Doxy, my suster——
Ananias.   Locusts
Of the foul pit——
Tribulation.   Profane as Bel, and the Dragon——
Ananias. Worse than the grasshoppers, or the lice of Egypt!
Lovewit. Good gentlemen, hear me. Are you officers,
And cannot stay this violence?
Officers.   Keep the peace!
Lovewit. Gentlemen, what is the matter? Whom do you seek?
Mammon. The chemical cozener——
Surly.   And the Captain Pandar.
Kastril. The nun my suster——
Mammon.   Madam Rabbi——
Ananias.   Scorpions,   20
And caterpillars!
Lovewit.   Fewer at once, I pray you.
Officer. One after another, gentlemen, I charge you,
By virtue of my staff——
Ananias.   They are the vessels
Of pride, lust, and the cart!

Lovewit. Good zeal, lie still
A little while.
　Tribulation. Peace, Deacon Ananias!
　Lovewit. The house is mine here, and the doors are open;
If there be any such persons as you seek for,
Use your authority: search on o' God's name.
I am but newly come to town, and finding
This tumult 'bout my door——to tell you true——　　　　30
It somewhat 'mazed me; till my man here, fearing
My more displeasure, told me [he] had done
Somewhat an insolent part, let out my house
(Belike presuming on my known aversion
From any air o' the town while there was sickness)
To a Doctor and a Captain; who, what they are,
Or where they be, he knows not.
　Mammon. Are they gone?
　Lovewit. You may go in and search, sir. (*They enter [the interior of the
　　house; Kastril and Surly remain]*) Here, I find
The empty walls worse than I left 'em, smoked;
A few cracked pots and glasses, and a furnace,　　　　40
The ceiling filled with poesies of the candle,
And madam with a dildo writ o' the walls.
Only one gentlewoman I met here,
That is within, that said she was a widow——
　Kastril. Aye, that's my suster. I'll go thump her. Where is she?
　　　　　　　　　　　　　　　　　　　　　[*Goes inside*]
　Lovewit. And should ha' married a Spanish Count, but he,
When he came to't, neglected her so grossly
That I, a widower, am gone through with her.
　Surly. How! have I lost her then?
　Lovewit. Were you the Don, sir?
Good faith, now, she does blame you extremely, and says　　50
You swore and told her you had ta'en the pains
To dye your beard, and umber o'er your face,
Borrowed a suit and ruff, all for her love;
And then did nothing. What an oversight
And want of putting forward, sir, was this!
Well fare an old harquebusier yet,
Could prime his powder, and give fire, and hit
All in a twinkling!　　　　　　　　(*Mammon comes forth*)
　Mammon. The whole nest are fled!

Lovewit. What sort of birds were they?

Mammon.   A kind of choughs

Or thievish daws, sir, that have picked my purse   60
Of eight-score and ten pounds within these five weeks,
Beside my first materials, and my goods
That lie i' the cellar, which I am glad they ha' left,
I may have home yet.

Lovewit.   Think you so, sir?

Mammon.   Aye.

Lovewit. By order of law, sir, but not otherwise.

Mammon. Not mine own stuff?

Lovewit.   Sir, I can take no knowledge
That they are yours, but by public means.
If you can bring certificate that you were gulled of 'em,
Or any formal writ out of a court
That you did cozen yourself, I will not hold them.   70

Mammon. I'll rather lose 'em.

Lovewit.   That you shall not, sir,
By me, in troth. Upon these terms they're yours.
What should they ha' been, sir: turned into gold all?

Mammon.   No——
I cannot tell——it may be they should——what then?

Lovewit. What a great loss in hope have you sustained!

Mammon. Not I, the commonwealth has.

Face.   Aye, he would ha' built
The city new, and made a ditch about it
Of silver, should have run with cream from Hogsden,
That every Sunday in Moorfields the younkers
And tits and tomboys should have fed on, *gratis*.   80

Mammon. I will go mount a turnip-cart, and preach
The end o' the world within these two months.——Surly——
What! in a dream?

Surly.   Must I needs cheat myself
With that same foolish vice of honesty!
Come let us go, and hearken out the rogues.
That Face I'll mark for mine, if e'er I meet him.

Face. If I can hear of him, sir, I'll bring you word
Unto your lodging; for in troth, they were strangers
To me; I thought 'em honest, as myself, sir.

       [*Exeunt Surly and Mammon*] (*Tribulation and Ananias come forth*)

Tribulation. 'Tis well, the Saints shall not lose all yet. Go   90

And get some carts——

Lovewit. For what, my zealous friends?

Ananias. To bear away the portion of the righteous
Out of this den of thieves.

Lovewit. What is that portion?

Ananias. The goods, sometimes the orphans', that the Brethren
Bought with their silver pence.

Lovewit. What, those i' the cellar,
The knight Sir Mammon claims?

Ananias. I do defy
The wicked Mammon, so do all the Brethren,
Thou profane man! I ask thee with what conscience
Thou canst advance that idol against us
That have the seal? Were not the shillings numbered 100
That made the pounds? Were not the pounds told out
Upon the second day of the fourth week,
In the eight month, upon the table dormant,
The year of the last patience of the Saints
Six hundred and ten?

Lovewit. Mine earnest vehement botcher,
And deacon also, I cannot dispute with you,
But if you get you not away the sooner,
I shall confute you with a cudgel.

Ananias. Sir!

Tribulation. Be patient, Ananias.

Ananias. I am strong,
And will stand up, well girt, against an host 110
That threaten Gad in exile.

Lovewit. I shall send you
To Amsterdam, to your cellar.

Ananias. I will pray there
Against thy house: may dogs defile thy walls,
And wasps and hornets breed beneath thy roof;
This seat of falsehood, and this cave of cozenage!

[*Exeunt Ananias and Tribulation*]

Lovewit. Another too?

(*Drugger enters, and he beats him away*)

Drugger. Not I, sir, I am no Brother.

Lovewit. Away you Harry Nicholas, do you talk?

[*Exit Drugger*]

Face. No, this was Abel Drugger. (*To the Parson*) Good sir, go

And satisfy him; tell him all is done:
He stayed too long a-washing of his face.   120
The Doctor, he shall hear of him at Westchester,
And of the Captain, tell him, at Yarmouth, or
Some good port-town else, lying for a wind.   [*Exit Parson*]

        [*Enter Kastril with Dame Pliant*]

If you get off the angry child, now, sir——
    Kastril. (*To his sister*) Come on, you ewe, you have matched most
      sweetly, ha' you not?
Did not I say I would never ha' you tupped
But by a dubbed boy, to make you a lady-tom?
'Slight, you are a mammet! Oh, I could touse you now.
Death, mun' you marry with a pox?
    Lovewit.   You lie, boy!
As sound as you, and I am aforehand with you.
    Kastril.   Anon?   130
    Lovewit. Come, will you quarrel? I will feize you, sirrah.
Why do you not buckle to your tools?
    Kastril.   God's light!
This is a fine old boy as e'er I saw!
    Lovewit. What, do you change your copy, now? Proceed:
Here stands my dove, stoop at her if you dare.
    Kastril. 'Slight I must love him! I cannot choose, i' faith,
And I should be hanged for't! Suster, I protest,
I honour thee, for this match.
    Lovewit.   Oh, do you so, sir?
    Kastril. Yes, and thou canst take tobacco and drink, old boy,
I'll give her five hundred pound more to her marriage   140
Than her own state.
    Lovewit.   Fill a pipe-full, Jeremy.
    Face. Yes, but go in, and take it, sir.
    Lovewit.   We will.
I will be ruled by thee in anything, Jeremy.
    Kastril. 'Slight, thou art not hidebound! Thou art a Jovy boy!
Come let's in, I pray thee, and take our whiffs.
    Lovewit. Whiff in with your sister, brother boy. [*Exeunt Kastril with
    Dame Pliant*] That master
That had received such happiness by a servant,
In such a widow, and with so much wealth,
Were very ungrateful if he would not be

A little indulgent to that servant's wit,   150
And help his fortune, though with some small strain
Of his own candour. Therefore, gentlemen,
And kind spectators, if I have outstripped
An old man's gravity, or strict canon, think
What a young wife and a good brain may do:
Stretch age's truth sometimes, and crack it too.
Speak for thyself, knave.
  Face.   So I will, sir. Gentlemen,
My part a little fell in this last scene,
Yet 'twas decorum. And though I am clean
Got off from Subtle, Surly, Mammon, Dol,   160
Hot Ananias, Dapper, Drugger, all
With whom I traded; yet I put myself
On you, that are my country; and this pelf,
Which I have got, if you do quit me, rests
To feast you often, and invite new guests.   [*Exeunt*]

THE END

EPIGRAMS

TO THE
GREAT EXAMPLE OF
HONOUR AND VIRTUE,
THE MOST NOBLE WILLIAM,
EARL OF PEMBROKE,
L[ORD] CHAMBERLAIN,
ETC.

My Lord: While you cannot change your merit, I dare not change your title; it was that made it, and not I. Under which name, I here offer to your Lo[rdship] the ripest of my studies, my *Epigrams*, which, though they carry danger in the sound, do not therefore seek your shelter; for when I made them I had nothing in my conscience to expressing of which I did need a cipher. But if I be fallen into those times wherein, for the likeness of vice and facts, everyone thinks another's ill deeds objected to him, and that in their ignorant and guilty mouths the common voice is, for their security, 'Beware the poet'—confessing therein so much love to their diseases as they would rather make a party for them than be either 10 rid or told of them—I must expect at your Lo[rdship's] hand the protection of truth and liberty while you are constant to your own goodness. In thanks whereof I return you the honour of leading forth so many good and great names as my verses mention on the better part, to their remembrance with posterity; amongst whom if I have praised, unfortunately, anyone that doth not deserve, or if all answer not in all numbers the pictures I have made of them, I hope it will be forgiven me, that they are no ill pieces, though they be not like the persons. But I foresee a nearer fate to my book than this: that the vices therein will be owned before the virtues (though there I have avoided all particulars, as I 20 have done names) and that some will be so ready to discredit me as they will have the impudence to belie themselves; for if I meant them not, it is so. Nor can I hope otherwise; for why should they remit anything of their riot, their pride, their self-love, and other inherent graces, to consider truth or virtue? but with the trade of the world lend their long ears against men they love not, and hold their dear mountebank or jester in far better condition than all the study or studiers of humanity. For such, I would

rather know them by their vizards still, than they should publish their
faces at their peril in my theatre, where Cato, if he lived, might enter
without scandal.

30

Your Lo[rdship's] most faithful honourer,
Ben Jonson.

I

To the Reader

Pray thee take care, that tak'st my book in hand,
To read it well; that is, to understand.

2

To My Book

It will be looked for, book, when some but see
    Thy title, *Epigrams*, and named of me,
Thou shouldst be bold, licentious, full of gall,
    Wormwood and sulphur, sharp and toothed withal;
Become a petulant thing, hurl ink and wit
    As madmen stones, not caring whom they hit.
Deceive their malice who could wish it so.
    And by thy wiser temper let men know
Thou are not covetous of least self-fame
    Made from the hazard of another's shame;   10
Much less with lewd, profane and beastly phrase,
    To catch the world's loose laughter or vain gaze.
He that departs with his own honesty
    For vulgar praise, doth it too dearly buy.

3

To My Bookseller

Thou that mak'st gain thy end, and wisely well
    Call'st a book good or bad, as it doth sell,

Use mine so, too; I give thee leave; but crave
   For the luck's sake it thus much favour have:
To lie upon thy stall till it be sought;
   Not offered, as it made suit to be bought;
Nor have my title-leaf on posts or walls
   Or in cleft-sticks, advancèd to make calls
For termers or some clerk-like serving-man
   Who scarce can spell the hard names; whose   10
      knight less can.
If, without these vile arts, it will not sell,
   Send it to Bucklersbury: there 'twill, well.

4

To King James

How, best of kings, dost thou a sceptre bear!
   How, best of poets, dost thou laurel wear!
But two things rare the fates had in their store,
   And gave thee both, to show they could no more.
For such a poet, while thy days were green
   Thou wert, as chief of them are said to have been.
And such a prince thou art, we daily see,
   As chief of those still promise they will be.
Whom should my muse then fly to, but the best
   Of kings for grace, of poets for my test?   10

5

On the Union

When was there contract better driven by fate?
   Or celebrated with more truth of state?
The world the temple was, the priest a king,
   The spousèd pair two realms, the sea the ring.

6

To Alchemists

If all you boast of your great art be true,
Sure, willing poverty lives most in you.

7

On the New Hot-House

Where lately harboured many a famous whore,
    A purging bill now fixed upon the door
Tells you it is a hot-house; so it ma',
    And still be a whore-house: they're synonima.

8

On a Robbery

Ridway robbed Duncote of three hundred pound;
    Ridway was ta'en, arraigned, condemned to die;
But for this money was a courtier found,
    Begged Ridway's pardon. Duncote now doth cry,
Robbed both of money and the law's relief:
    The courtier is become the greater thief.

9

To All to Whom I Write

May none whose scattered names honour my book
    For strict degrees of rank or title look;
'Tis 'gainst the manners of an epigram;
    And I a poet here, no herald am.

10

To My Lord Ignorant

Thou call'st me poet, as a term of shame;
But I have my revenge made in thy name.

11

On Something that Walks Somewhere

At court I met it, in clothes brave enough
    To be a courtier, and looks grave enough
To seem a statesman. As I near it came,
    It made me a great face; I asked the name;
A lord, it cried, buried in flesh and blood,
    And such from whom let no man hope least good,
For I will do none; and as little ill,
    For I will dare none. Good lord, walk dead still.

12

On Lieutenant Shift

Shift, here in town not meanest among squires
    That haunt Pickt-hatch, Marsh-Lambeth, and Whitefriars,
Keeps himself, with half a man, and defrays
    The charge of that state with this charm: God pays.
By that one spell he lives, eats, drinks, arrays
    Himself; his whole revénue is, God pays.
The quarter-day is come; the hostess says
    She must have money; he returns, God pays.
The tailor brings a suit home; he it 'ssays,
    Looks o'er the bill, likes it, and says, God pays.   10
He steals to ordinaries; there he plays
    At dice his borrowed money; which God pays.
Then takes up fresh commodity for days,
    Signs to new bond, forfeits, and cries, God pays.

That lost, he keeps his chamber, reads essays,
   Takes physic, tears the papers; still God pays.
Or else by water goes, and so to plays,
   Calls for his stool, adorns the stage; God pays.
To every cause he meets, this voice he brays:
   His only answer is to all, God pays.   20
Not his poor cockatrice but he betrays
   Thus; and for his lechery scores: God pays.
But see! the old bawd hath served him in his trim,
   Lent him a pocky whore. She hath paid him.

13

To Doctor Empiric

When men a dangerous disease did 'scape
   Of old, they gave a cock to Aesculape.
Let me give two, that doubly am got free
   From my disease's danger, and from thee.

14

To William Camden

Camden, most reverend head, to whom I owe
   All that I am in arts, all that I know,
(How nothing's that?) to whom my country owes
   The great renown and name wherewith she goes;
Than thee the age sees not that thing more grave,
   More high, more holy, that she more would crave.
What name, what skill, what faith hast thou in things!
   What sight in searching the most ántique springs!
What weight, and what authority in thy speech!
   Man scarce can make that doubt, but thou canst teach.   10
Pardon free truth, and let thy modesty,
   Which conquers all, be once overcome by thee.
Many of thine this better could than I;
   But for their powers accept my piety.

15

On Court-Worm

All men are worms: but this no man. In silk
   'Twas brought to court first wrapped, and white as milk;
Where afterwards it grew a butterfly,
   Which was a caterpillar. So 'twill die.

16

To Brain-Hardy

Hardy, thy brain is valiant, 'tis confessed;
   Thou more, that with it every day dar'st jest
Thyself into fresh brawls; when called upon,
   Scarce thy week's swearing brings thee off of one.
So in short time thou art in arrearage grown
   Some hundred quarrels, yet dost thou fight none;
Nor need'st thou; for those few, by oath released,
   Make good what thou dar'st do in all the rest.
Keep thyself there, and think thy valour right;
   He that dares damn himself dares more than fight.   10

17

To the Learned Critic

May others fear, fly, and traduce thy name
   As guilty men do magistrates; glad I,
That wish my poems a legitimate fame,
   Charge them, for crown, to thy sole censure hie;
And but a sprig of bays, given by thee,
   Shall outlive garlands stolen from the chaste tree.

18

To My Mere English Censurer

To thee my way in epigrams seems new,
   When both it is the old way and the true.
Thou say'st that cannot be: for thou hast seen
   Davies and Weever, and the best have been,
And mine come nothing like. I hope so. Yet,
   As theirs did with thee, mine might credit get,
If thou'dst but use thy faith as thou didst then
   When thou wert wont to admire, not censure men.
Prithee believe still, and not judge so fast;
   Thy faith is all the knowledge that thou hast.   10

19

On Sir Cod the Perfumed

That Cod can get no widow, yet a knight,
I scent the cause: he woos with an ill sprite.

20

To the Same Sir Cod

The expense in odours is a most vain sin,
Except thou couldst, Sir Cod, wear them within.

21

On Reformed Gamester

Lord, how is Gamester changed! His hair close cut,
   His neck fenced round with ruff, his eyes half shut!
His clothes two fashions off, and poor; his sword
   Forbid' his side; and nothing but the word

Quick in his lips! Who hath this wonder wrought?
   The late-ta'en bastinado. So I thought,
What several ways men to their calling have!
   The body's stripes, I see, the soul may save.

22

On My First Daughter

Here lies, to each her parents' ruth,
Mary, the daughter of their youth;
Yet, all heaven's gifts being heaven's due,
It makes the father less to rue.
At six months' end she parted hence
With safety of her innocence;
Whose soul heaven's Queen (whose name she bears),
In comfort of her mother's tears,
Hath placed amongst her virgin train;
Where, while that severed doth remain,   10
This grave partakes the fleshly birth;
Which cover lightly, gentle earth.

23

To John Donne

Donne, the delight of Phoebus and each muse,
   Who, to thy one, all other brains refuse;
Whose every work of thy most early wit
   Came forth example, and remains so yet;
Longer a-knowing than most wits do live;
   And which no affection praise enough can give!
To it, thy language, letters, arts, best life,
   Which might with half mankind maintain a strife;
All which I meant to praise, and yet I would,
   But leave, because I cannot as I should.   10

24

To the Parliament

There's reason good that you good laws should make:
Men's manners ne'er were viler, for your sake.

25

On Sir Voluptuous Beast

While Beast instructs his fair and innocent wife
    In the past pleasures of his sensual life,
Telling the motions of each petticoat,
    And how his Ganymede moved, and how his goat,
And now her, hourly, her own cuckquean makes
    In varied shapes, which for his lust she takes;
What doth he else but say: leave to be chaste,
    Just wife, and, to change me, make woman's haste?

26

On the Same Beast

Than his chaste wife though Beast now know no more,
He adulters still: his thoughts lie with a whore.

27

On Sir John Roe

In place of scutcheons that should deck thy hearse,
Take better ornaments, my tears and verse.
    If any sword could save from fates, Roe's could;
    If any muse outlive their spite, his can;
    If any friend's tears could restore, his would;
    If any pious life e'er lifted man
To heaven, his hath. O happy state! wherein
We, sad for him, may glory and not sin.

28

On Don Surly

Don Surly, to aspire the glorious name
  Of a great man, and to be thought the same,
Makes serious use of all great trade he knows.
  He speaks to men with a rhinocerote's nose,
Which he thinks great; and so reads verses, too;
  And that is done as he saw great men do.
He has tympanies of business in his face,
  And can forget men's names with a great grace.
He will both argue and discourse in oaths,
  Both which are great; and laugh at ill-made clothes—   10
That's greater yet—to cry his own up neat.
  He doth, at meals, alone, his pheasant eat,
Which is main greatness. And at his still board
  He drinks to no man; that's, too, like a lord.
He keeps another's wife, which is a spice
  Of solemn greatness. And he dares at dice
Blaspheme God, greatly; or some poor hind beat
  That breathes in his dog's way; and this is great.
Nay more, for greatness' sake, he will be one
  May hear my epigrams, but like of none.   20
Surly, use other arts; these only can
  Style thee a most great fool, but no great man.

29

To Sir Annual Tilter

Tilter, the most may admire thee, though not I;
  And thou, right guiltless, mayst plead to it: why?
For thy late sharp device. I say 'tis fit
  All brains, at times of triumph, should run wit,
For then our water-conduits do run wine;
  But that's put in, thou'lt say. Why, so is thine.

30

To Person Guilty

Guilty, be wise; and though thou know'st the crimes
  Be thine I tax, yet do not own my rhymes;
'Twere madness in thee to betray thy fame
  And person to the world, ere I thy name.

31

On Bank the Usurer

Bank feels no lameness of his knotty gout;
  His moneys travel for him, in and out;
And though the soundest legs go every day,
  He toils to be at hell as soon as they.

32

On Sir John Roe

What two brave perils of the private sword
  Could not effect, not all the furies do
That self-divided Belgia did afford;
  What not the envy of the seas reached to,
The cold of Moscow, and fat Irish air,
  His often change of clime (though not of mind)
What could not work; at home in his repair
  Was his blest fate, but our hard lot, to find.
Which shows, wherever death doth please to appear,
  Seas, serenes, swords, shot, sickness, all are there.   10

33

To the Same

I'll not offend thee with a vain tear more,
  Glad-mentioned Roe; thou art but gone before

Whither the world must follow. And I now
   Breathe to expect my when, and make my how;
Which if most gracious heaven grant like thine,
   Who wets my grave can be no friend of mine.

34

Of Death

He that fears death, or mourns it in the just,
Shows of the resurrection little trust.

35

To King James

Who would not be thy subject, James, to obey
   A prince that rules by example more than sway?
Whose manners draw, more than thy powers constrain;
   And in this short time of thy happiest reign
Hast purged thy realms, as we have now no cause
   Left us of fear, but first our crimes, then laws.
Like aids 'gainst treasons who hath found before?
   And than in them, how could we know God more?
First thou preserved wert, our king to be,
   And since, the whole land was preservèd for thee.   10

36

To the Ghost of Martial

Martial, thou gav'st far nobler epigrams
   To thy Domitian, than I can my James;
But in my royal subject I pass thee:
   Thou flattered'st thine, mine cannot flattered be.

37

On Cheverel the Lawyer

No cause nor client fat will Cheverel leese,
  But as they come, on both sides he takes fees,
And pleaseth both: for while he melts his grease
  For this, that wins, for whom he holds his peace.

38

To Person Guilty

Guilty, because I bade you late be wise,
  And to conceal your ulcers did advise,
You laugh when you are touched, and long before
  Any man else, you clap your hands, and roar,
And cry, 'Good, good!' This quite perverts my sense,
  And lies so far from wit, 'tis impudence.
Believe it, Guilty, if you lose your shame,
  I'll lose my modesty, and tell your name.

39

On Old Colt

For all night-sins with others' wives, unknown,
Colt now doth daily penance in his own.

40

On Margaret Radcliffe

M arble, weep, for thou dost cover
A dead beauty underneath thee,
R ich as nature could bequeath thee;
G rant, then, no rude hand remove her.
A ll the gazers on the skies
R ead not in fair heaven's story
E xpresser truth or truer glory
T han they might in her bright eyes.

R are as wonder was her wit,
A nd like nectar ever flowing;   10
T ill time, strong by her bestowing,
C onquered hath both life and it.
L ife, whose grief was out of fashion
I n these times: few so have rued
F ate, in a brother. To conclude,
F or wit, feature, and true passion,
E arth, thou hast not such another.

41

On Gypsy

Gypsy, new bawd, is turned physician,
  And gets more gold than all the College can.
Such her quaint practice is, so it allures,
  For what she gave, a whore, a bawd, she cures.

42

On Giles and Joan

Who says that Giles and Joan at discord be?
  The observing neighbours no such mood can see.
Indeed, poor Giles repents he married ever:
  But that his Joan doth too. And Giles would never,
By his free will, be in Joan's company;
  No more would Joan he should. Giles riseth early,
And having got him out of doors is glad—
  The like is Joan—but turning home, is sad;
And so is Joan. Oft-times, when Giles doth find
  Harsh sights at home, Giles wisheth he were blind: 10
All this doth Joan. Or that his long-yarned life
  Were quite out-spun; the like wish hath his wife.
The children that he keeps, Giles swears are none
  Of his begetting; and so swears his Joan:
In all affections she concurreth still.
  If now, with man and wife, to will and nill

The self-same things a note of concord be,
　　I know no couple better can agree!

43

To Robert, Earl of Salisbury

What need hast thou of me, or of my muse,
　　Whose actions so themselves do celebrate?
Which should thy country's love to speak refuse,
　　Her foes enough would fame thee, in their hate.
'Tofore, great men were glad of poets; now
　　I, not the worst, am covetous of thee;
Yet dare not to my thought least hope allow
　　Of adding to thy fame: thine may to me,
When in my book men read but Cecil's name;
　　And what I write thereof find far and free   10
From servile flattery (common poets' shame)
　　As thou stand'st clear of the necessity.

44

On Chuff, Bank's the Usurer's Kinsman

Chuff, lately rich in name, in chattels, goods,
　　And rich in issue to inherit all,
　　Ere blacks were bought for his own funeral,
Saw all his race approach the blacker floods.
　　He meant they thither should make swift repair,
　　When he made him executor, might be heir.

45

On My First Son

Farewell, thou child of my right hand, and joy;
　　My sin was too much hope of thee, loved boy.

Seven years thou wert lent to me, and I thee pay,
   Exacted by thy fate, on the just day.
Oh, could I lose all father now! For why
   Will man lament the state he should envy?
To have so soon 'scaped world's and flesh's rage,
   And, if no other misery, yet age?
Rest in soft peace, and, asked, say here doth lie
   Ben Jonson his best piece of poetry;   10
For whose sake, henceforth, all his vows be such,
   As what he loves may never like too much.

46

To Sir Luckless Woo-All

Is this the sir, who, some waste wife to win,
   A knighthood bought, to go a-wooing in?
'Tis Luckless he, that took up one on band
   To pay at's day of marriage. By my hand,
The knight-wright's cheated, then: he'll never pay.
   Yes, now he wears his knighthood every day.

47

To the Same

Sir Luckless, troth, for luck's sake pass by one:
He that woos every widow will get none.

48

On Mongrel Esquire

His bought arms Mong not liked; for his first day
Of bearing them in field, he threw 'em away;
And hath no honour lost, our duellists say.

49

To Playwright

Playwright me reads, and still my verses damns:
   He says I want the tongue of epigrams;
I have no salt: no bawdry, he doth mean;
   For witty, in his language, is obscene.
Playwright, I loathe to have thy manners known
   In my chaste book: profess them in thine own.

50

To Sir Cod

Leave, Cod, tobacco-like, burnt gums to take,
Or fumy clysters, thy moist lungs to bake:
Arsenic would thee fit for society make.

51

To King James

Upon the Happy False Rumour of His Death,
the Two-and-Twentieth Day of March, 1607

That we thy loss might know, and thou our love,
   Great heaven did well to give ill fame free wing;
Which, though it did but panic terror prove,
   And far beneath least pause of such a king,
Yet give thy jealous subjects leave to doubt,
   Who this thy 'scape from rumour gratulate
No less than if from peril; and, devout,
   Do beg thy care unto thy after-state.
For we, that have our eyes still in our ears,
   Look not upon thy dangers, but our fears.   10

52

To Censorious Courtling

Courtling, I rather thou shouldst utterly
    Dispraise my work than praise it frostily:
When I am read thou feign'st a weak applause,
    As if thou wert my friend, but lack'dst a cause.
This but thy judgement fools; the other way
    Would both thy folly and thy spite betray.

53

To Old-End Gatherer

Long-gathering Old-End, I did fear thee wise
    When, having pilled a book which no man buys,
Thou wert content the author's name to lose;
    But when, in place, thou didst the patron's choose,
It was as if thou printed hadst an oath,
    To give the world assurance thou wert both;
And that, as Puritans at baptism do,
    Thou art the father and the witness too.
For, but thyself, where, out of motley, is he
    Could save that line to dedicate to thee?   10

54

On Cheverel

Cheverel cries out my verses libels are,
    And threatens the Star Chamber and the Bar.
What are thy petulant pleadings, Cheverel, then,
    That quitt'st the cause so oft, and rail'st at men?

55

To Francis Beaumont

How I do love thee, Beaumont, and thy muse,
    That unto me dost such religion use!
How I do fear myself, that am not worth
    The least indulgent thought thy pen drops forth!
At once thou mak'st me happy, and unmak'st;
    And giving largely to me, more thou tak'st.
What fate is mine that so itself bereaves?
    What art is thine that so thy friend deceives?
When even there where most thou praisest me
    For writing better, I must envy thee.   10

56

On Poet-Ape

Poor Poet-Ape, that would be thought our chief,
    Whose works are e'en the frippery of wit,
From brokage is become so bold a thief
    As we, the robbed, leave rage, and pity it.
At first he made low shifts, would pick and glean,
    Buy the reversion of old plays; now grown
To a little wealth and credit in the scene,
    He takes up all, makes each man's wit his own;
And, told of this, he slights it: Tut, such crimes
    The sluggish gaping auditor devours;   10
He marks not whose 'twas first; and after-times
    May judge it to be his as well as ours.
Fool, as if half-eyes will not know a fleece
    From locks of wool, or shreds from the whole piece!

57

On Bawds and Usurers

If, as their ends, their fruits were so the same,
Bawdry and usury were one kind of game.

58

To Groom Idiot

Idiot, last night I prayed thee but forbear
   To read my verses; now I must to hear:
For offering with thy smiles my wit to grace,
   Thy ignorance still laughs in the wrong place.
And so my sharpness thou no less disjoints
   Than thou didst late my sense, losing my points.
So have I seen at Christmas sports one lost,
   And, hoodwinked, for a man, embrace a post.

59

On Spies

Spies, you are lights in state, but of base stuff,
Who, when you've burnt yourselves down to the snuff,
Stink, and are thrown away. End fair enough.

60

To William, Lord Monteagle

Lo, what my country should have done—have raised
   An obelisk or column to thy name,
Or, if she would but modestly have praised
   Thy fact, in brass or marble writ the same—
I, that am glad of thy great chance, here do!
   And, proud my work shall outlast common deeds,
Durst think it great, and worthy wonder, too:
   But thine, for which I do it, so much exceeds!
My country's parents I have many known,
   But saver of my country thee alone. 10

61

To Fool or Knave

Thy praise or dispraise is to me alike;
One doth not stroke me, nor the other strike.

62

To Fine Lady Would-Be

Fine Madam Would-Be, wherefore should you fear,
    That love to make so well, a child to bear?
The world reputes you barren; but I know
    Your 'pothecary, and his drug says no.
Is it the pain affrights? That's soon forgot.
    Or your complexion's loss? You have a pot
That can restore that. Will it hurt your feature?
    To make amends, you're thought a wholesome creature.
What should the cause be? Oh, you live at court:
    And there's both loss of time and loss of sport   10
In a great belly. Write, then, on thy womb:
    Of the not born, yet buried, here's the tomb.

63

To Robert, Earl of Salisbury

Who can consider thy right courses run,
    With what thy virtue on the times hath won,
And not thy fortune; who can clearly see
    The judgement of the king so shine in thee;
And that thou seek'st reward of thy each act
    Not from the public voice, but private fact;
Who can behold all envy so declined
    By constant suffering of thy equal mind;
And can to these be silent, Salisbury,
    Without his, thine, and all time's injury?   10

Cursed be his muse that could lie dumb or hid
  To so true worth, though thou thyself forbid.

64

To the Same

Upon the accession of the Treasurership to him

Not glad, like those that have new hopes or suits
  With thy new place, bring I these early fruits
Of love, and what the golden age did hold
  A treasure, art: contemned in the age of gold;
Nor glad as those that old dependants be
  To see thy father's rites new laid on thee;
Nor glad for fashion; nor to show a fit
  Of flattery to thy titles; nor of wit.
But I am glad to see that time survive
  Where merit is not sepulchred alive;   10
Where good men's virtues them to honours bring,
  And not to dangers; when so wise a king
Contends to have worth enjoy, from his regard,
  As her own conscience, still the same reward.
These, noblest Cecil, laboured in my thought,
  Wherein what wonder, see, thy name hath wrought:
That whilst I meant but thine to gratulate
  I've sung the greater fortunes of our state.

65

To My Muse

Away, and leave me, thou thing most abhorred,
  That hast betrayed me to a worthless lord,
Made me commit most fierce idolatry
  To a great image through thy luxury.
Be thy next master's more unlucky muse,
  And, as thou hast mine, his hours and youth abuse.

Get him the time's long grudge, the court's ill-will;
  And, reconciled, keep him suspected still.
Make him lose all his friends; and, which is worse,
  Almost all ways to any better course.   10
With me thou leav'st an happier muse than thee,
  And which thou brought'st me, welcome poverty;
She shall instruct my after-thoughts to write
  Things manly, and not smelling parasite.
But I repent me: stay. Whoe'er is raised
  For worth he has not, he is taxed, not praised.

66

To Sir Henry Cary

That neither fame nor love might wanting be
  To greatness, Cary, I sing that, and thee;
Whose house, if it no other honour had,
  In only thee might be both great and glad;
Who, to upbraid the sloth of this our time,
  Durst valour make almost, but not a crime.
Which deed I know not whether were more high
  Or thou more happy, it to justify
Against thy fortune: when no foe that day
  Could conquer thee but chance, who did betray.   10
Love thy great loss, which a renown hath won
  To live when Broick not stands, nor Ruhr doth run.
Love honours, which of best example be
  When they cost dearest and are done most free;
Though every fortitude deserves applause,
  It may be much or little in the cause.
He's valiant'st that dares fight, and not for pay;
  That virtuous is when the reward's away.

67

To Thomas, Earl of Suffolk

Since men have left to do praiseworthy things,
  Most think all praises flatteries. But truth brings

That sound and that authority with her name,
    As to be raised by her is only fame.
Stand high, then, Howard, high in eyes of men,
    High in thy blood, thy place, but highest then
When, in men's wishes, so thy virtues wrought
    As all thy honours were by them first sought,
And thou designed to be the same thou art,
    Before thou wert it, in each good man's heart: 10
Which, by no less confirmed than thy king's choice,
    Proves that is God's, which was the people's, voice.

68

On Playwright

Playwright, convict of public wrongs to men,
    Takes private beatings, and begins again.
Two kinds of valour he doth show at once:
    Active in's brain, and passive in his bones.

69

To Pertinax Cob

Cob, thou nor soldier, thief, nor fencer art,
Yet by thy weapon liv'st! Thou hast one good part.

70

To William Roe

When Nature bids us leave to live, 'tis late
    Then to begin, my Roe; he makes a state
In life that can employ it, and takes hold
    On the true causes ere they grow too old.
Delay is bad, doubt worse, depending worst;
    Each best day of our life escapes us first.
Then, since we (more than many) these truths know,
    Though life be short, let us not make it so.

71

On Court-Parrot

To pluck down mine, Poll sets up new wits still;
Still, 'tis his luck to praise me 'gainst his will.

72

To Courtling

I grieve not, Courtling, thou are started up
  A chamber-critic, and dost dine and sup
At madam's table, where thou mak'st all wit
  Go high or low as thou wilt value it.
'Tis not thy judgement breeds the prejudice:
  Thy person only, Courtling, is the vice.

73

To Fine Grand

What is't, fine Grand, makes thee my friendship fly,
  Or take an epigram so fearfully,
As 'twere a challenge, or a borrower's letter?
  The world must know your greatness is my debtor.
In primis, Grand, you owe me for a jest
  I lent you, on mere acquaintance, at a feast;
Item, a tale or two some fortnight after,
  That yet maintains you and your house in laughter;
Item, the Babylonian song you sing;
  Item, a fair Greek posy for a ring,   10
With which a learnèd madam you belie.
  Item, a charm surrounding fearfully
Your *partie-per-pale* picture, one half drawn
  In solemn cypress, the other cobweb-lawn;
Item, a gulling impres' for you, at tilt;
  Item, your mistress' anagram, i' your hilt;

Item, your own, sewed in your mistress' smock;
   Item, an epitaph on my lord's cock,
In most vile verses, and cost me more pain
   Than had I made 'em good, to fit your vain.   20
Forty things more, dear Grand, which you know true:
   For which or pay me quickly, or I'll pay you.

74

To Thomas, Lord Chancellor [Egerton]

Whilst thy weighed judgements, Egerton, I hear,
   And know thee then a judge not of one year;
Whilst I behold thee live with purest hands;
   That no affection in thy voice commands;
That still thou'rt present to the better cause,
   And no less wise than skilful in the laws;
Whilst thou art certain to thy words, once gone,
   As is thy conscience, which is always one:
The Virgin, long since fled from earth, I see,
   To our times returned, hath made her heaven in thee.   10

75

On Lippe, the Teacher

I cannot think there's that antipathy
   'Twixt Puritans and players as some cry;
Though Lippe, at Paul's, ran from his text away
   To inveigh 'gainst plays, what did he then but play?

76

On Lucy, Countess of Bedford

This morning, timely rapt with holy fire,
   I thought to form unto my zealous muse
What kind of creature I could most desire
   To honour, serve and love, as poets use.

I meant to make her fair, and free, and wise,
   Of greatest blood, and yet more good than great;
I meant the day-star should not brighter rise,
   Nor lend like influence from his lucent seat.
I meant she should be courteous, facile, sweet,
   Hating that solemn vice of greatness, pride;   10
I meant each softest virtue there should meet,
   Fit in that softer bosom to reside.
Only a learnèd and a manly soul
   I purposed her, that should, with even powers,
The rock, the spindle and the shears control
   Of destiny, and spin her own free hours.
Such when I meant to feign and wished to see,
   My muse bade, *Bedford* write, and that was she.

77

To One that Desired Me Not to Name Him

Be safe, nor fear thyself so good a fame
   That any way my book should speak thy name:
For if thou shame, ranked with my friends, to go,
   I'm more ashamed to have thee thought my foe.

78

To Hornet

Hornet, thou hast thy wife dressed for the stall
To draw thee custom: but herself gets all.

79

To Elizabeth, Countess of Rutland

That poets are far rarer births than kings
   Your noblest father proved: like whom, before

Or then or since, about our muses' springs,
   Came not that soul exhausted so their store.
Hence was it that the destinies decreed
   (Save that most masculine issue of his brain)
No male unto him, who could so exceed
   Nature, they thought, in all that he would feign;
At which she, happily displeased, made you:
   On whom, if he were living now, to look,   10
He should those rare and absolute numbers view
   As he would burn, or better far, his book.

80

Of Life and Death

The ports of death are sins; of life, goods deeds,
   Through which our merit leads us to our meeds.
How wilful blind is he, then, that would stray,
   And hath it in his powers to make his way!
This world death's region is, the other life's;
   And here it should be one of our first strifes
So to front death, as men might judge us past it:
   For good men but see death, the wicked taste it.

81

To Prowl the Plagiary

Forbear to tempt me, Prowl, I will not show
   A line unto thee till the world it know,
Or that I've by two good sufficient men
   To be the wealthy witness of my pen:
For all thou hear'st, thou swear'st thyself didst do;
   Thy wit lives by it, Prowl, and belly too.
Which if thou leave not soon (though I am loath)
   I must a libel make, and cozen both.

82

On Cashiered Captain Surly

Surly's old whore in her new silks doth swim:
He cast, yet keeps her well! No, she keeps him.

83

To a Friend

To put out the word 'whore' thou dost me woo,
Throughout my book. Troth, put out 'woman' too.

84

To Lucy, Countess of Bedford

Madam, I told you late how I repented,
    I asked a lord a buck, and he denied me;
And, ere I could ask you, I was prevented:
    For your most noble offer had supplied me.
Straight went I home; and there, most like a poet,
    I fancied to myself what wine, what wit
I would have spent; how every muse should know it,
    And Phoebus' self should be at eating it.
O madam, if your grant did thus transfer me,
    Make it your gift: see whither that will bear me.   10

85

To Sir Henry Goodyere

Goodyere, I'm glad and grateful to report
    Myself a witness of thy few days' sport,
Where I both learned why wise men hawking follow,
    And why that bird was sacred to Apollo:

She doth instruct men by her gallant flight
   That they to knowledge so should tower upright,
And never stoop but to strike ignorance;
   Which, if they miss, they yet should re-advance
To former height, and there in circle tarry
   Till they be sure to make the fool their quarry.   10
Now, in whose pleasures I have this discerned,
   What would his serious actions me have learned?

86

To the Same

When I would know thee, Goodyere, my thought looks
   Upon thy well-made choice of friends and books;
Then do I love thee, and behold thy ends
   In making thy friends books, and thy books friends.
Now I must give thy life and deed the voice
   Attending such a study, such a choice:
Where, though it be love that to thy praise doth move,
   It was a knowledge that begat that love.

87

On Captain Hazard the Cheater

Touched with the sin of false play in his punk,
   Hazard a month forswore his, and grew drunk
Each night, to drown his cares. But when the gain
   Of what she had wrought came in, and waked his brain,
Upon the account, hers grew the quicker trade;
   Since when, he's sober again, and all play's made.

88

On English Monsieur

Would you believe, when you this monsieur see,
   That his whole body should speak French, not he?

That so much scarf of France, and hat, and feather,
   And shoe, and tie, and garter should come hither
And land on one whose face durst never be
   Toward the sea, farther than half-way tree?
That he, untravelled, should be French so much,
   As Frenchmen in his company should seem Dutch?
Or had his father, when he did him get,
   The French disease, with which he labours yet?   10
Or hung some monsieur's picture on the wall,
   By which his dam conceived him, clothes and all?
Or is it some French statue? No: it doth move,
   And stoop, and cringe. Oh, then it needs must prove
The new French tailor's motion, monthly made,
   Daily to turn in Paul's and help the trade.

89

To Edward Alleyn

If Rome so great, and in her wisest age,
   Feared not to boast the glories of her stage,
As skilful Roscius and grave Aesop, men
   Yet crowned with honours as with riches then,
Who had no less a trumpet of their name
   Than Cicero, whose every breath was fame:
How can so great example die in me,
   That, Alleyn, I should pause to publish thee?
Who both their graces in thyself hast more
   Out-stripped, than they did all that went before;   10
And present worth in all dost so contract,
   As other speak, but only thou dost act.
Wear this renown. 'Tis just that who did give
   So many poets life, by one should live.

90

On Mill, My Lady's Woman

When Mill first came to court, the unprofiting fool,
   Unworthy such a mistress, such a school,

Was dull and long ere she would go to man.
  At last ease, appetite and example wan
The nicer thing to taste her lady's page;
  And, finding good security in his age,
Went on; and proving him still day by day,
  Discerned no difference of his years or play,
Not though that hair grew brown which once was amber,
  And he, grown youth, was called to his lady's chamber.   10
Still Mill continued: nay, his face growing worse,
  And he removed to gent'man of the horse,
Mill was the same. Since, both his body and face
  Blown up, and he (too unwieldy for that place)
Hath got the steward's chair, he will not tarry
  Longer a day, but with his Mill will marry.
And it is hoped that she, like Milo, wull,
  First bearing him a calf, bear him a bull.

91

To Sir Horace Vere

Which of thy names I take, not only bears
  A Roman sound, but Roman virtue wears:
Illustrous Vere, or Horace, fit to be
  Sung by a Horace, or a muse as free;
Which thou art to thyself, whose fame was won
  In the eye of Europe, where thy deeds were done,
When on thy trumpet she did sound a blast
  Whose relish to eternity shall last.
I leave thy acts, which should I prosecute
  Throughout, might flattery seem; and to be mute   10
To any one were envy, which would live
  Against my grave, and time could not forgive.
I speak thy other graces, not less shown
  Nor less in practice, but less marked, less known:
Humanity and piety, which are
  As noble in great chiefs as they are rare;
And best become the valiant man to wear,
  Who more should seek men's reverence than fear.

92

The New Cry

Ere Cherries ripe! and Strawberries! be gone,
   Unto the cries of London I'll add one:
Ripe statesmen, ripe! They grow in every street;
   At six-and-twenty, ripe; you shall 'em meet
And have 'em yield no savour but of state.
   Ripe are their ruffs, their cuffs, their beards, their gait,
And grave as ripe, like mellow as their faces.
   They know the states of Christendom, not the places;
Yet have they seen the maps, and bought 'em too,
   And understand 'em, as most chapmen do.   10
The counsels, projects, practices they know,
   And what each prince doth for intelligence owe,
And unto whom; they are the almanacs
   For twelve years yet to come, what each state lacks.
They carry in their pockets Tacitus,
   And the *Gazetti*, or *Gallo-Belgicus*;
And talk reserved, locked up, and full of fear,
   Nay, ask you how the day goes, in your ear;
Keep a Star-Chamber sentence close, twelve days,
   And whisper what a proclamation says.   20
They meet in sixes, and at every mart
   Are sure to con the catalogue by heart;
Or every day someone at Rimee's looks,
   Or Bill's, and there he buys the names of books.
They all get Porta, for the sundry ways
   To write in cipher, and the several keys
To ope the character. They've found the sleight
   With juice of lemons, onions, piss, to write,
To break up seals, and close 'em. And they know,
   If the States make peace, how it will go   30
With England. All forbidden books they get;
   And of the Powder Plot they will talk yet.
At naming the French king, their heads they shake,
   And at the Pope and Spain slight faces make;
Or 'gainst the bishops, for the brethren, rail,
   Much like those brethren, thinking to prevail
With ignorance on us, as they have done
   On them; and therefore do not only shun

Others more modest, but contemn us too,
   That know not so much state, wrong, as they do.   40

93

To Sir John Radcliffe

How like a column, Radcliffe, left alone
   For the great mark of virtue—those being gone
Who did, alike with thee, thy house up-bear—
   Stand'st thou, to show the times what you all were!
Two bravely in the battle fell, and died,
   Upbraiding rebels' arms and barbarous pride;
And two that would have fallen as great as they,
   The Belgic fever ravished away.
Thou, that art all their valour, all their spirit,
   And thine own goodness to increase thy merit;   10
Than whose I do not know a whiter soul,
   Nor could I, had I seen all Nature's roll:
Thou yet remain'st, unhurt in peace or war,
   Though not unproved: which shows thy fortunes are
Willing to expiate the fault in thee
   Wherewith, against thy blood, they offenders be.

94

To Lucy, Countess of Bedford, with Mr Donne's Satires

Lucy, you brightness of our sphere, who are
   Life of the muses' day, their morning-star!
If works, not the authors, their own grace should look,
   Whose poems would not wish to be your book?
But these, desired by you, the maker's ends
   Crown with their own. Rare poems ask rare friends.
Yet satires, since the most of mankind be
   Their unavoided subject, fewest see:
For none e'er took that pleasure in sin's sense
   But, when they heard it taxed, took more offence.   10

They, then, that living where the matter is bred
　　Dare for these poems yet both ask and read,
And like them, too, must needfully, though few,
　　Be of the best; and 'mongst those, best are you.
Lucy, you brightness of our sphere, who are
　　The muses' evening- as their morning-star.

95

To Sir Henry Savile

If, my religion safe, I durst embrace
　　That stranger doctrine of Pythagoras,
I should believe the soul of Tacitus
　　In thee, most weighty Savile, lived to us:
So hast thou rendered him in all his bounds
　　And all his numbers, both of sense and sounds.
But when I read that special piece, restored,
　　Where Nero falls and Galba is adored,
To thine own proper I ascribe then more,
　　And gratulate the breach I grieved before:　　　　10
Which fate, it seems, caused in the history
　　Only to boast thy merit in supply.
Oh, wouldst thou add like hand to all the rest!
　　Or (better work!) were thy glad country blest
To have her story woven in thy thread,
　　Minerva's loom was never richer spread.
For who can master those great parts like thee,
　　That liv'st from hope, from fear, from faction free;
That hast thy breast so clear of present crimes
　　Thou need'st not shrink at voice of after-times;　　20
Whose knowledge claimeth at the helm to stand,
　　But wisely thrusts not forth a forward hand,
No more than Sallust in the Roman state.
　　As, then, his cause, his glory emulate.
Although to write be lesser than to do,
　　It is the next deed, and a great one too.
We need a man that knows the several graces
　　Of history, and how to apt their places:
Where brevity, where splendour, and where height,
　　Where sweetness is required, and where weight;　　30

We need a man can speak of the intents,
   The counsels, actions, orders and events
Of state, and censure them; we need his pen
   Can write the things, the causes, and the men.
But most we need his faith (and all have you)
   That dares nor write things false, nor hide things true.

96

To John Donne

Who shall doubt, Donne, whe'er I a poet be,
   When I dare send my epigrams to thee?
That so alone canst judge, so alone dost make;
   And in thy censures, evenly dost take
As free simplicity to disavow
   As thou hast best authority to allow.
Read all I send; and if I find but one
   Marked by thy hand, and with the better stone,
My title's sealed. Those that for claps do write,
   Let puisnes', porters', players' praise delight,   10
And till they burst, their backs, like asses', load:
   A man should seek great glory, and not broad.

97

On the New Motion

See you yond motion? Not the old fa-ding,
   Nor Captain Pod, nor yet the Eltham thing,
But one more rare, and in the case so new:
   His cloak with orient velvet quite lined through,
His rosy ties and garters so o'er-blown,
   By his each glorious parcel to be known!
He wont was to encounter me, aloud,
   Where'er he met me; now he's dumb, or proud.
Know you the cause? he has neither land nor lease,
   Nor bawdy stock that travails for increase,   10
Nor office in the town, nor place in court
   Nor 'bout the bears, nor noise to make lords sport.

He is no favourite's favourite, no dear trust
   Of any madam's, hath need squires and must.
Nor did the king of Denmark him salute
   When he was here. Nor hath he got a suit,
Since he was gone, more than the one he wears.
   Nor are the Queen's most honoured maids by the ears
About his form. What then so swells each limb?
   Only his clothes have over-leavened him.   20

98

To Sir Thomas Roe

Thou hast begun well, Roe, which stand well to,
   And I know nothing more thou hast to do.
He that is round within himself, and straight,
   Need seek no other strength, no other height;
Fortune upon him breaks herself, if ill,
   And what would hurt his virtue makes it still.
That thou at once, then, nobly mayst defend
   With thine own course the judgement of thy friend,
Be always to thy gathered self the same,
   And study conscience more than thou wouldst fame.   10
Though both be good, the latter yet is worst,
   And ever is ill-got without the first.

99

To the Same

That thou hast kept thy love, increased thy will,
   Bettered thy trust to letters; that, thy skill;
Hast taught thyself worthy thy pen to tread,
   And that to write things worthy to be read:
How much of great example wert thou, Roe,
   If time to facts, as unto men, would owe?
But much it now avails what's done, of whom:
   The self-same deeds, as diversely they come

From place or fortune, are made high or low,
　　And even the praiser's judgement suffers so.   10
Well, though thy name less than our great ones be,
　　Thy fact is more: let truth encourage thee.

100

On Playwright

Playwright, by chance, hearing some toys I'd writ,
　　Cried to my face, they were the elixir of wit;
And I must now believe him: for today
　　Five of my jests, then stolen, passed him a play.

101

Inviting a Friend to Supper

Tonight, grave sir, both my poor house and I
　　Do equally desire your company;
Not that we think us worthy such a guest,
　　But that your worth will dignify our feast
With those that come; whose grace may make that seem
　　Something, which else could hope for no esteem.
It is the fair acceptance, sir, creates
　　The entertainment perfect, not the cates.
Yet shall you have, to rectify your palate,
　　An olive, capers, or some better salad   10
Ushering the mutton; with a short-legged hen,
　　If we can get her, full of eggs, and then
Lemons, and wine for sauce; to these, a coney
　　Is not to be despaired of, for our money;
And though fowl now be scarce, yet there are clerks,
　　The sky not falling, think we may have larks.
I'll tell you of more, and lie, so you will come:
　　Of partridge, pheasant, woodcock, of which some
May yet be there; and godwit, if we can;
　　Knat, rail and ruff, too. Howsoe'er, my man   20
Shall read a piece of Virgil, Tacitus,
　　Livy, or of some better book to us,

Of which we'll speak our minds, amidst our meat;
   And I'll profess no verses to repeat;
To this, if aught appear which I not know of,
   That will the pastry, not my paper, show of.
Digestive cheese and fruit there sure will be;
   But that which most doth take my muse and me
Is a pure cup of rich Canary wine,
   Which is the Mermaid's now, but shall be mine;   30
Of which had Horace or Anacreon tasted,
   Their lives, as do their lines, till now had lasted.
Tobacco, nectar, or the Thespian spring
   Are all but Luther's beer to this I sing.
Of this we will sup free, but moderately;
   And we will have no Poley or Parrot by;
Nor shall our cups make any guilty men,
   But at our parting we will be as when
We innocently met. No simple word
   That shall be uttered at our mirthful board   40
Shall make us sad next morning, or affright
   The liberty that we'll enjoy tonight.

102

To William, Earl of Pembroke

I do but name thee, Pembroke, and I find
   It is an epigram on all mankind,
Against the bad, but of and to the good;
   Both which are asked, to have thee understood.
Nor could the age have missed thee, in this strife
   Of vice and virtue, wherein all great life,
Almost, is exercised; and scarce one knows
   To which yet of the sides himself he owes.
They follow virtue for reward today,
   Tomorrow vice, if she give better pay;   10
And are so good and bad, just at a price,
   As nothing else discerns the virtue or vice.
But thou, whose noblesse keeps one stature still,
   And one true posture, though besieged with ill

Of what ambition, faction, pride can raise,
  Whose life even they that envy it must praise,
That art so reverenced, as thy coming in
  But in the view doth interrupt their sin:
Thou must draw more; and they that hope to see
  The commonwealth still safe must study thee.   20

103

To Mary, Lady Wroth

How well, fair crown of your fair sex, might he
  That but the twilight of your sprite did see,
And noted for what flesh such souls were framed,
  Know you to be a Sidney, though unnamed?
And, being named, how little doth that name
  Need any muse's praise to give it fame?
Which is itself the imprese of the great,
  And glory of them all, but to repeat!
Forgive me, then, if mine but say you are
  A Sidney; but in that extend as far   10
As loudest praisers, who perhaps would find
  For every part a character assigned.
My praise is plain, and wheresoe'er professed
  Becomes none more than you, who need it least.

104

To Susan, Countess of Montgomery

Were they that named you prophets? Did they see,
  Even in the dew of grace, what you would be?
Or did our times require it, to behold
  A new Susanna equal to that old?
Or, because some scarce think that story true,
  To make those faithful did the fates send you?
And to your scene lent no less dignity
  Of birth, of match, of form, of chastity?
Or, more than born for the comparison
  Of former age, or glory of our one,   10

Were you advancèd past those times, to be
   The light and mark unto posterity?
Judge they that can; here I have raised to show
   A picture which the world for yours must know,
And like it, too, if they look equally;
   If not, 'tis fit for you some should envy.

105

To Mary, Lady Wroth

Madam, had all antiquity been lost,
   All history sealed up and fables crossed;
That we had left us, nor by time nor place,
   Least mention of a nymph, a muse, a grace,
But even their names were to be made anew:
   Who could not but create them all from you?
He that but saw you wear the wheaten hat
   Would call you more than Ceres, if not that;
And, dressed in shepherd's 'tire, who would not say
   You were the bright Oenone, Flora, or May?   10
If dancing, all would cry the Idalian queen
   Were leading forth the graces on the green;
And, armèd to the chase, so bare her bow
   Diana alone, so hit, and hunted so.
There's none so dull that for your style would ask
   That saw you put on Pallas' plumèd casque;
Or, keeping your due state, that would not cry
   There Juno sat, and yet no peacock by.
So are you nature's index, and restore
   In yourself all treasure lost of the age before.   20

106

To Sir Edward Herbert

If men get name for some one virtue, then
   What man art thou, that art so many men,
All-virtuous Herbert! on whose every part
   Truth might spend all her voice, fame all her art.

Whether thy learning they would take, or wit,
   Or valour, or thy judgement seasoning it,
Thy standing upright to thyself, thy ends
   Like straight, thy piety to God and friends:
Their latter praise would still the greatest be,
   And yet they, all together, less than thee.   10

107

To Captain Hungry

Do what you come for, Captain, with your news,
   That's sit and eat; do not my ears abuse.
I oft look on false coin, to know't from true:
   Not that I love it more than I will you.
Tell the gross Dutch those grosser tales of yours,
   How great you were with their two emperors,
And yet are with their princes; fill them full
   Of your Moravian horse, Venetian bull.
Tell them what parts you've ta'en, whence run away,
   What states you've gulled, and which yet keeps you in pay.   10
Give them your services and embassies
   In Ireland, Holland, Sweden (pompous lies),
In Hungary and Poland, Turkey too;
   What at Leghorn, Rome, Florence you did do;
And, in some year, all these together heaped,
   For which there must more sea and land be leaped
—If but to be believed you have the hap—
   Than can a flea at twice skip in the map.
Give your young statesmen (that first make you drunk
   And then lie with you, closer than a punk,   20
For news) your Villecroys and Silleries,
   Janins, your nuncios and your Tuileries,
Your archduke's agents and your Beringhams,
   That are your words of credit. Keep your names
Of Hannow, Shieter-huissen, Popenheim,
   Hans-spiegle, Rotteinberg and Boutersheim
For your next meal: this you are sure of. Why
   Will you part with them here, unthriftily?

Nay, now you puff, tusk, and draw up your chin,
    Twirl the poor chain you run a-feasting in.   30
Come, be not angry, you are Hungry: eat;
    Do what you come for, Captain: there's your meat.

108

To True Soldiers

Strength of my country, whilst I bring to view
    Such as are mis-called captains, and wrong you
And your high names, I do desire that thence
    Be nor put on you, nor you take offence.
I swear by your true friend, my muse, I love
    Your great profession; which I once did prove,
And did not shame it with my actions then,
    No more than I dare now do with my pen.
He that not trusts me, having vowed thus much,
    But's angry for the Captain still, is such.   10

109

To Sir Henry Neville

Who now calls on thee, Neville, is a muse
    That serves nor fame nor titles, but doth choose
Where virtue makes them both, and that's in thee,
    Where all is fair, beside thy pedigree.
Thou art not one seek'st miseries with hope,
    Wrestlest with dignities, or feign'st a scope
Of service to the public when the end
    Is private gain, which hath long guilt to friend.
Thou rather striv'st the matter to possess,
    And elements of honour, than the dress;   10
To make thy lent life good against the fates;
    And first to know thine own state, then the State's;
To be the same in root thou art in height,
    And that thy soul should give thy flesh her weight.

Go on, and doubt not what posterity,
  Now I have sung thee thus, shall judge of thee.
Thy deeds unto thy name will prove new wombs,
  Whilst others toil for titles to their tombs.

110

To Clement Edmondes, on His
Caesar's Commentaries Observed and Translated

Not Caesar's deeds, nor all his honours won
  In these west parts; nor when that war was done,
The name of Pompey for an enemy,
  Cato's to boot, Rome and her liberty
All yielding to his fortune; nor, the while,
  To have engraved these acts with his own style,
And that so strong and deep as't might be thought
  He wrote with the same spirit that he fought;
Nor that his work lived in the hands of foes,
  Unargued then, and yet hath fame from those: 10
Not all these, Edmondes, or what else put to,
  Can so speak Caesar as thy labours do.
For, where his person lived but one just age,
  And that midst envy and parts, then fell by rage:
His deeds too dying, but in books (whose good
  How few have read, how fewer understood!)
Thy learnèd hand and true Promethean art
  (As by a new creation) part by part,
In every counsel, stratagem, design,
  Action or engine worth a note of thine,   20
To all future time not only doth restore
  His life, but makes that he can die no more.

111

To the Same, on the Same

Who, Edmondes, reads thy book and doth not see
  What the antique soldiers were, the modern be?

Wherein thou show'st how much the latter are
    Beholding to this master of the war;
And that in action there is nothing new,
    More than to vary what our elders knew:
Which all but ignorant captains will confess,
    Nor to give Caesar this, makes ours the less.
Yet thou, perhaps, shalt meet some tongues will grutch
    That to the world thou shouldst reveal so much,   10
And thence deprave thee and thy work. To those
    Caesar stands up, as from his urn late rose,
By thy great help, and doth proclaim by me,
    They murder him again that envy thee.

112

To a Weak Gamester in Poetry

With thy small stock, why art thou venturing still
    At this so subtle sport, and play'st so ill?
Think'st thou it is mere fortune that can win?
    Or thy rank setting? That thou dar'st put in
Thy all, at all; and whatsoe'er I do,
    Art still at that, and think'st to blow me up too?
I cannot for the stage a drama lay,
    Tragic or comic, but thou writ'st the play.
I leave thee there, and, giving way, intend
    An epic poem: thou hast the same end.   10
I modestly quit that, and think to write,
    Next morn, an ode: thou mak'st a song ere night.
I pass to elegies: thou meet'st me there;
    To satires: and thou dost pursue me. Where,
Where shall I 'scape thee? in an epigram?
    Oh (thou criest out), that is thy proper game.
Troth, if it be, I pity thy ill luck,
    That both for wit and sense so oft dost pluck,
And never art encountered, I confess;
    Nor scarce dost colour for it, which is less.   20
Prithee yet save thy rest; give o'er in time:
    There's no vexation that can make thee prime.

113

To Sir Thomas Overbury

So Phoebus makes me worthy of his bays
    As but to speak thee, Overbury, is praise;
So, where thou liv'st, thou mak'st life understood,
    Where what makes others great doth keep thee good!
I think the fate of court thy coming craved,
    That the wit there and manners might be saved;
For since, what ignorance, what pride is fled,
    And letters and humanity in the stead!
Repent thee not of thy fair precedent,
    Could make such men and such a place repent;   10
Nor may any fear to lose of their degree
    Who in such ambition can but follow thee.

114

To Mistress Philip Sidney

I must believe some miracles still be
    When Sidney's name I hear, or face I see;
For Cupid, who at first took vain delight
    In mere out-forms, until he lost his sight,
Hath changed his soul, and made his object you:
    Where finding so much beauty met with virtue,
He hath not only gained himself his eyes,
    But, in your love, made all his servants wise.

115

On the Town's Honest Man

You wonder who this is, and why I name
    Him not aloud that boasts so good a fame,
Naming so many, too! But this is one
    Suffers no name but a description:
Being no vicious person, but the vice
    About the town; and known too, at that price.

A subtle thing that doth affections win
      By speaking well o' the company it's in.
Talks loud and bawdy, has a gathered deal
      Of news and noise to s[tr]ow out a long meal.   10
Can come from Tripoli, leap stools, and wink,
      Do all that 'longs to the anarchy of drink,
Except the duel. Can sing songs and catches,
      Give everyone his dose of mirth; and watches
Whose name's unwelcome to the present ear,
      And him it lays on—if he be not there.
Tells of him all the tales itself then makes;
      But if it shall be questioned, undertakes
It will deny all, and forswear it, too:
      Not that it fears, but will not have to do   20
With such a one. And therein keeps its word.
      'Twill see its sister naked, ere a sword.
At every meal where it doth dine or sup,
      The cloth's no sooner gone but it gets up
And, shifting of its faces, doth play more
      Parts than the Italian could do with his door.
Acts old Iniquity, and in the fit
      Of miming gets the opinion of a wit.
Executes men in picture. By defect,
      From friendship, is its own fame's architect.   30
An engineer in slanders of all fashions,
      That, seeming praises, are yet accusations.
Described, it's thus; defined would you it have?
      Then the town's honest man's her arrant'st knave.

116

To Sir William Jephson

Jephson, thou man of men, to whose loved name
      All gentry yet owe part of their best flame!
So did thy virtue inform, thy wit sustain
      That age when thou stood'st up the master-brain;
Thou wert the first mad'st merit know her strength,
      And those that lacked it to suspect at length

'Twas not entailed on title; that some word
   Might be found out as good, and not My Lord;
That Nature no such difference had impressed
   In men, but every bravest was the best;   10
That blood not minds, but minds did blood adorn;
   And to live great was better than great born.
These were thy knowing arts: which who doth now
   Virtuously practise must at least allow
Them in, if not from, thee; or must commit
   A desperate solecism in truth and wit.

117

On Groin

Groin, come of age, his 'state sold out of hand
For his whore: Groin doth still occupy his land.

118

On Gut

Gut eats all day, and lechers all the night,
   So all his meat he tasteth over, twice;
And striving so to double his delight,
   He makes himself a thoroughfare of vice.
Thus in his belly can he change a sin:
   Lust it comes out, that gluttony went in.

119

To Sir Ralph Sheldon

Not he that flies the court for want of clothes,
   At hunting rails, having no gift in oaths,
Cries out 'gainst cocking, since he cannot bet,
   Shuns press for two main causes, pox and debt,
With me can merit more than that good man,
   Whose dice not doing well, to a pulpit ran.

No, Sheldon, give me thee, canst want all these,
    But dost it out of judgement, not disease;
Dar'st breathe in any air, and with safe skill,
    Till thou canst find the best, choose the least ill;   10
That to the vulgar canst thyself apply,
    Treading a better path, not contrary;
And in their error's maze thine own way know:
    Which is to live to conscience, not to show.
He that but living half his age, dies such,
    Makes the whole longer than 'twas given him, much.

120

Epitaph on S[alomon] P[avy], a Child of Q[ueen] El[izabeth's] Chapel

Weep with me all you that read
    This little story,
And know, for whom a tear you shed,
    Death's self is sorry.
'Twas a child that so did thrive
    In grace and feature,
As heaven and nature seemed to strive
    Which owned the creature.
Years he numbered scarce thirteen
    When fates turned cruel,   10
Yet three filled zodiacs had he been
    The stage's jewel,
And did act (what now we moan)
    Old men so duly
As, sooth, the Parcae thought him one,
    He played so truly.
So, by error, to his fate
    They all consented,
But viewing him since (alas, too late)
    They have repented;   20
And have sought, to give new birth,
    In baths to steep him;
But being so much too good for earth,
    Heaven vows to keep him.

121

To Benjamin Rudyerd

Rudyerd, as lesser dames to great ones use,
   My lighter comes to kiss thy learnèd muse,
Whose better studies while she emulates,
   She learns to know long difference of their states.
Yet is the office not to be despised,
   If only love should make the action prized;
Nor he for friendship to be thought unfit
   That strives his manners should precede his wit.

122

To the Same

If I would wish, for truth and not for show,
   The agèd Saturn's age and rites to know;
If I would strive to bring back times, and try
   The world's pure gold and wise simplicity;
If I would virtue set as she was young,
   And hear her speak with one and her first tongue;
If holiest friendship naked to the touch
   I would restore, and keep it ever such;
I need no other arts but study thee,
   Who prov'st all these were, and again may be.   10

123

To the Same

Writing thyself or judging others' writ,
   I know not which thou'st most, candour or wit;
But both thou'st so, as who affects the state
   Of the best writer and judge should emulate.

124

Epitaph on Elizabeth, L.H.

Wouldst thou hear what man can say
   In a little? Reader, stay.
Underneath this stone doth lie
   As much beauty as could die;
Which in life did harbour give
   To more virtue than doth live.
If at all she had a fault,
   Leave it buried in this vault.
One name was Elizabeth,
   The other let it sleep with death: 10
Fitter where it died to tell,
   Than that it lived at all. Farewell.

125

To Sir William Uvedale

Uvedale, thou piece of the first times, a man
   Made for what nature could, or virtue can;
Both whose dimensions, lost, the world might find
   Restorèd in thy body and thy mind!
Who sees a soul in such a body set
   Might love the treasure for the cabinet.
But I, no child, no fool, respect the kind,
   The full, the flowing graces there enshrined;
Which (would the world not miscall't flattery)
   I could adore, almost to idolatry.   10

126

To His Lady, then Mistress Cary

Retired, with purpose your fair worth to praise,
   'Mongst Hampton shades and Phoebus' grove of bays,

I plucked a branch: the jealous god did frown,
   And bade me lay the usurpèd laurel down;
Said I wronged him, and, which was more, his love.
   I answered, Daphne now no pain can prove.
Phoebus replied, Bold head, it is not she:
   Cary my love is, Daphne but my tree.

127

To Esmé, Lord Aubigny

Is there a hope that man would thankful be
   If I should fail in gratitude to thee,
To whom I am so bound, loved Aubigny?
   No; I do therefore call posterity
Into the debt, and reckon on her head
   How full of want, how swallowed up, how dead
I and this muse had been if thou hadst not
   Lent timely succours, and new life begot:
So all reward or name that grows to me
   By her attempt, shall still be owing thee.   10
And than this same I know no abler way
   To thank thy benefits: which is, to pay.

128

To William Roe

Roe (and my joy to name) thou'rt now to go
   Countries and climes, manners and men to know,
To extract and choose the best of all these known,
   And those to turn to blood and make thine own.
May winds as soft as breath of kissing friends
   Attend thee hence; and there may all thy ends,
As the beginnings here, prove purely sweet,
   And perfect in a circle always meet.
So when we, blest with thy return, shall see
   Thyself, with thy first thoughts, brought home by thee,   10

We each to other may this voice inspire:
   This is that good Aeneas, passed through fire,
Through seas, storms, tempests; and embarked for hell,
   Came back untouched. This man hath travailed well.

129

To Mime

That not a pair of friends each other see,
   But the first question is, when one saw thee?
That there's no journey set or thought upon
   To Brentford, Hackney, Bow, but thou mak'st one;
That scarce the town designeth any feast
   To which thou'rt not a week bespoke a guest;
That still thou'rt made the supper's flag, the drum,
   The very call, to make all others come:
Think'st thou, Mime, this is great? or that they strive
   Whose noise shall keep thy miming most alive   10
Whilst thou dost raise some player from the grave,
   Out-dance the babion, or out-boast the brave?
Or (mounted on a stool) thy face doth hit
   On some new gesture, that's imputed wit?
Oh, run not proud of this. Yet take thy due:
   Thou dost out-zany Cokeley, Pod, nay, Gue,
And thine own Coryate too. But, wouldst thou see,
   Men love thee not for this: they laugh at thee.

130

To Alphonso Ferrabosco, on His Book

To urge, my loved Alphonso, that bold fame
   Of building towns, and making wild beasts tame,
Which music had; or speak her known effects:
   That she removeth cares, sadness ejects,
Declineth anger, persuades clemency,
   Doth sweeten mirth and heighten piety,

And is to a body, often ill-inclined,
   No less a sovereign cure than to the mind;
To allege that greatest men were not ashamed
   Of old, even by her practice to be famed;   10
To say indeed she were the soul of heaven,
   That the eighth sphere, no less than planets seven,
Moved by her order, and the ninth more high,
   Including all, were thence called harmony:
I yet had uttered nothing on thy part,
   When these were but the praises of the art.
But when I have said, The proofs of all these be
   Shed in thy songs, 'tis true: but short of thee.

131

To the Same

When we do give, Alphonso, to the light
   A work of ours, we part with our own right;
For then all mouths will judge, and their own way:
   The learned have no more privilege than the lay.
And though we could all men, all censures hear,
   We ought not give them taste we had an ear.
For if the humorous world will talk at large,
   They should be fools, for me, at their own charge.
Say this or that man they to thee prefer;
   Even those for whom they do this know they err: 10
And would, being asked the truth, ashamèd say
   They were not to be named on the same day.
Then stand unto thyself, not seek without
   For fame, with breath soon kindled, soon blown out.

132

To Mr Joshua Sylvester

If to admire were to commend, my praise
   Might then both thee, thy work and merit raise;
But as it is (the child of ignorance,
   And utter stranger to all air of France)

How can I speak of thy great pains, but err,
   Since they can only judge that can confer?
Behold! the reverend shade of Bartas stands
   Before my thought, and, in thy right, commands
That to the world I publish for him this:
   Bartas doth wish thy English now were his.   10
So well in that are his inventions wrought
   As his will now be the translation thought,
Thine the original; and France shall boast
   No more those maiden glories she hath lost.

133

On the Famous Voyage

No more let Greece her bolder fables tell
   Of Hercules or Theseus going to hell,
Orpheus, Ulysses; or the Latin muse
   With tales of Troy's just knight our faiths abuse:
We have a Sheldon and a Heydon got,
   Had power to act what they to feign had not.
All that they boast of Styx, of Acheron,
   Cocytus, Phlegethon, our have proved in one:
The filth, stench, noise; save only what was there
   Subtly distinguished, was confusèd here.   10
Their wherry had no sail, too; ours had none;
   And in it two more horrid knaves than Charon.
Arses were heard to croak instead of frogs,
   And for one Cerberus, the whole coast was dogs.
Furies there wanted not; each scold was ten;
   And for the cries of ghosts, women and men
Laden with plague-sores and their sins were heard,
   Lashed by their consciences; to die, afeared.
Then let the former age with this content her:
   She brought the poets forth, but ours the adventer.   20

The Voyage Itself

I sing the brave adventure of two wights,
And pity 'tis I cannot call 'em knights:

One was; and he for brawn and brain right able
To have been stylèd of King Arthur's table.
The other was a squire of fair degree,
But in the action greater man than he,
Who gave, to take at his return from hell,
His three for one. Now, lordings, listen well.
    It was the day, what time the powerful moon
Makes the poor Bankside creature wet it' shoon   30
In it' own hall, when these (in worthy scorn
Of those that put out moneys on return
From Venice, Paris, or some inland passage
Of six times to and fro without embassage,
Or him that backward went to Berwick, or which
Did dance the famous morris unto Norwich)
At Bread Street's Mermaid having dined, and merry,
Proposed to go to Holborn in a wherry:
A harder task than either his to Bristo',
Or his to Antwerp. Therefore, once more, list ho!   40
    A dock there is that callèd is Avernus,
Of some, Bridewell, and may in time concern us
All that are readers; but methinks 'tis odd
That all this while I have forgot some god
Or goddess to invoke, to stuff my verse,
And with both bombard-style and phrase rehearse
The many perils of this port, and how
Sans help of sibyl or a golden bough
Or magic sacrifice, they passed along.
Alcides, be thou succouring to my song!   50
Thou hast seen hell, some say, and know'st all nooks there,
Canst tell me best how every fury looks there,
And art a god, if fame thee not abuses,
Always at hand to aid the merry muses.
Great Club-fist, though thy back and bones be sore
Still, with thy former labours, yet once more
Act a brave work, call it thy last adventry;
But hold my torch while I describe the entry
To this dire passage. Say thou stop thy nose:
'Tis but light pains: indeed this dock's no rose.   60
    In the first jaws appeared that ugly monster
Yclepèd Mud, which when their oars did once stir,
Belched forth an air as hot as at the muster

Of all your night-tubs, when the carts do cluster,
Who shall discharge first his merd-urinous load:
Thorough her womb they make their famous road
Between two walls, where on one side, to scar men
Were seen your ugly centaurs ye call car-men,
Gorgonian scolds and harpies; on the other
Hung stench, diseases, and old filth, their mother,   70
With famine, wants and sorrows many a dozen,
The least of which was to the plague a cousin.
But they unfrighted pass, though many a privy
Spake to 'em louder than the ox in Livy,
And many a sink poured out her rage anenst 'em;
But still their valour and their virtue fenced 'em,
And on they went, like Castor brave and Pollux,
Ploughing the main. When see (the worst of all lucks)
They met the second prodigy, would fear a
Man that had never heard of a Chimaera.   80
One said it was bold Briareus, or the beadle
(Who hath the hundred hands when he doth meddle);
The other thought it Hydra, or the rock
Made of the trull that cut her father's lock;
But coming near, they found it but a lighter,
So huge, it seemed, they could by no means quite her.
Back, cried their brace of Charons; they cried, No,
No going back! On still, you rogues, and row.
How hight the place? A voice was heard: Cocytus.
Row close then, slaves! Alas, they will beshite us.   90
No matter, stinkards, row! What croaking sound
Is this we hear? of frogs? No, guts wind-bound,
Over your heads. Well, row! At this a loud
Crack did report itself, as if a cloud
Had burst with storm, and down fell *ab excelsis*
Poor Mercury, crying out on Paracelsus
And all his followers, that had so abused him,
And in so shitten sort so long had used him;
For (where he was the god of eloquence,
And subtlety of metals) they dispense   100
His spirits now in pills and eke in potions,
Suppositories, cataplasms and lotions.
But many moons there shall not wane, quoth he,
(In the meantime, let 'em imprison me)

But I will speak—and know I shall be heard—
Touching this cause, where they will be afeared
To answer me. And sure, it was the intent
Of the grave fart, late let in parliament,
Had it been seconded, and not in fume
Vanished away: as you must all presume   110
Their Mercury did now. By this, the stem
Of the hulk touched and, as by Polypheme
The sly Ulysses stole in a sheepskin,
The well-greased wherry now had got between,
And bade her farewell sough unto the lurdan.
Never did bottom more betray her burden:
The meat-boat of Bears' College, Paris Garden,
Stunk not so ill; nor, when she kissed, Kate Arden.
Yet one day in the year for sweet 'tis voiced,
And that is when it is the Lord Mayor's foist.   120
   By this time had they reached the Stygian pool
By which the masters swear when, on the stool
Of worship, they their nodding chins do hit
Against their breasts. Here several ghosts did flit
About the shore, of farts but late departed,
White, black, blue, green, and in more forms out-started
Than all those atomi ridiculous
Whereof old Democrite and Hill Nicholas,
One said, the other swore, the world consists.
These be the cause of those thick frequent mists   130
Arising in that place, through which who goes
Must try the unused valour of a nose:
And that ours did. For yet no nare was tainted,
Nor thumb nor finger to the stop acquainted,
But open and unarmed encountered all.
Whether it languishing stuck upon the wall
Or were precipitated down the jakes,
And after swom abroad in ample flakes,
Or that it lay heaped like an usurer's mass,
All was to them the same: they were to pass,   140
And so they did, from Styx to Acheron,
The ever-boiling flood; whose banks upon
Your Fleet Lane furies and hot cooks do dwell,
That with still-scalding steams make the place hell.
The sinks ran grease, and hair of measled hogs,

The heads, houghs, entrails, and the hides of dogs:
For, to say truth, what scullion is so nasty
To put the skins and offal in a pasty?
Cats there lay divers had been flayed and roasted
And, after mouldy grown, again were toasted;   150
Then selling not, a dish was ta'en to mince 'em,
But still, it seemed, the rankness did convince 'em.
For here they were thrown in wi' the melted pewter,
Yet drowned they not. They had five lives in future.
   But 'mongst these Tiberts, who d'you think there was?
Old Banks the juggler, our Pythagoras,
Grave tutor to the learnèd horse: both which
Being, beyond sea, burned for one witch,
Their spirits transmigrated to a cat;
And now, above the pool, a face right fat,   160
With great grey eyes, are lifted up, and mewed;
Thrice did it spit, thrice dived. At last it viewed
Our brave heroes with a milder glare,
And in a piteous tune began: How dare
Your dainty nostrils (in so hot a season,
When every clerk eats artichokes and peason,
Laxative lettuce, and such windy meat)
'Tempt such a passage? When each privy's seat
Is filled with buttock, and the walls do sweat
Urine and plasters? When the noise doth beat   170
Upon your ears of discords so unsweet,
And outcries of the damnèd in the Fleet?
Cannot the plague-bill keep you back? nor bells
Of loud Sepulchre's, with their hourly knells,
But you will visit grisly Pluto's hall?
Behold where Cerberus, reared on the wall
Of Holborn (three sergeants' heads) looks o'er,
And stays but till you come unto the door!
Tempt not his fury; Pluto is away,
And Madam Caesar, great Proserpina,   180
Is now from home. You lose your labours quite,
Were you Jove's sons, or had Alcides' might.
They cried out, Puss! He told them he was Banks,
That had so often showed 'em merry pranks.
They laughed at his laugh-worthy fate; and passed
The triple head without a sop. At last,

Calling for Rhadamanthus, that dwelt by,
A soap-boiler, and Aeacus him nigh,
Who kept an ale-house, with my little Minos,
An ancient purblind fletcher with a high nose,   190
They took 'em all to witness of their action,
And so went bravely back, without protraction.
   In memory of which most liquid deed,
The city since hath raised a pyramid.
And I could wish for their eternized sakes,
My muse had ploughed with his that sung A-jax.

THE FOREST

Why I Write Not of Love

Some act of Love's bound to rehearse,
I thought to bind him in my verse;
Which when he felt, Away! quoth he,
Can poets hope to fetter me?
It is enough they once did get
Mars and my mother in their net:
I wear not these my wings in vain.
With which he fled me; and again
Into my rhymes could ne'er be got
By any art. Then wonder not   10
That since, my numbers are so cold,
When Love is fled, and I grow old.

2

To Penshurst

Thou art not, Penshurst, built to envious show
   Of touch or marble, nor canst boast a row
Of polished pillars, or a roof of gold;
   Thou hast no lantern whereof tales are told,
Or stair, or courts; but stand'st an ancient pile,
   And these grudged at, art reverenced the while.
Thou joy'st in better marks, of soil, of air,
   Of wood, of water; therein thou art fair.
Thou hast thy walks for health as well as sport:
   Thy Mount, to which the dryads do resort,   10
Where Pan and Bacchus their high feasts have made,
   Beneath the broad beech and the chestnut shade;
That taller tree, which of a nut was set
   At his great birth, where all the muses met.

There, in the writhèd bark, are cut the names
   Of many a sylvan taken with his flames;
And thence the ruddy satyrs oft provoke
   The lighter fauns to reach thy lady's oak.
Thy copse, too, named of Gamage, thou hast there,
   That never fails to serve thee seasoned deer   20
When thou wouldst feast or exercise thy friends.
   The lower land, that to the river bends,
Thy sheep, thy bullocks, kine and calves do feed;
   The middle grounds thy mares and horses breed.
Each bank doth yield thee conies, and the tops,
   Fertile of wood, Ashour and Sidney's copse,
To crown thy open table, doth provide
   The purpled pheasant with the speckled side;
The painted partridge lies in every field,
   And for thy mess is willing to be killed.   30
And if the high-swoll'n Medway fail thy dish,
   Thou hast thy ponds that pay thee tribute fish:
Fat, agèd carps, that run into thy net;
   And pikes, now weary their own kind to eat,
As loath the second draught or cast to stay,
   Officiously, at first, themselves betray;
Bright eels, that emulate them, and leap on land
   Before the fisher, or into his hand.
Then hath thy orchard fruit, thy garden flowers,
   Fresh as the air and new as are the hours: 40
The early cherry, with the later plum,
   Fig, grape and quince, each in his time doth come;
The blushing apricot and woolly peach
   Hang on thy walls, that every child may reach.
And though thy walls be of the country stone,
   They're reared with no man's ruin, no man's groan;
There's none that dwell about them wish them down,
   But all come in, the farmer and the clown,
And no one empty-handed, to salute
   Thy lord and lady, though they have no suit.   50
Some bring a capon, some a rural cake,
   Some nuts, some apples; some that think they make
The better cheeses, bring 'em; or else send
   By their ripe daughters, whom they would commend
This way to husbands; and whose baskets bear

An emblem of themselves, in plum or pear.
But what can this (more than express their love)
Add to thy free provisions, far above
The need of such? whose liberal board doth flow
With all that hospitality doth know! 60
Where comes no guest but is allowed to eat
Without his fear, and of thy lord's own meat;
Where the same beer and bread and self-same wine
That is his lordship's shall be also mine;
And I not fain to sit, as some this day
At great men's tables, and yet dine away.
Here no man tells my cups, nor, standing by,
A waiter, doth my gluttony envy,
But gives me what I call, and lets me eat;
He knows below he shall find plenty of meat, 70
Thy tables hoard not up for the next day.
Nor, when I take my lodging, need I pray
For fire or lights or livery: all is there,
As if thou then wert mine, or I reigned here;
There's nothing I can wish, for which I stay.
That found King James, when, hunting late this way
With his brave son, the Prince, they saw thy fires
Shine bright on every hearth as the desires
Of thy Penates had been set on flame
To entertain them; or the country came 80
With all their zeal to warm their welcome here.
What (great, I will not say, but) sudden cheer
Didst thou then make 'em! and what praise was heaped
On thy good lady then! who therein reaped
The just reward of her high housewifery:
To have her linen, plate, and all things nigh
When she was far; and not a room but dressed
As if it had expected such a guest!
These, Penshurst, are thy praise, and yet not all.
Thy lady's noble, fruitful, chaste withal; 90
His children thy great lord may call his own,
A fortune in this age but rarely known.
They are and have been taught religion; thence
Their gentler spirits have sucked innocence.
Each morn and even they are taught to pray
With the whole household, and may every day

Read in their virtuous parents' noble parts
    The mysteries of manners, arms and arts.
Now, Penshurst, they that will proportion thee
    With other edifices, when they see   100
Those proud, ambitious heaps, and nothing else,
    May say, their lords have built, but thy lord dwells.

3

To Sir Robert Wroth

How blest art thou canst love the country, Wroth,
    Whether by choice, or fate, or both;
And, though so near the city and the court,
    Art ta'en with neither's vice nor sport;
That at great times art no ambitious guest
    Of sheriff's dinner or mayor's feast;
Nor com'st to view the better cloth of state,
    The richer hangings, or crown-plate;
Nor throng'st, when masquing is, to have a sight
    Of the short bravery of the night,   10
To view the jewels, stuffs, the pains, the wit
    There wasted, some not paid for yet!
But canst at home in thy securer rest
    Live with unbought provision blest;
Free from proud porches or their gilded roofs,
    'Mongst lowing herds and solid hoofs;
Alongst the curlèd woods and painted meads,
    Through which a serpent river leads
To some cool, courteous shade, which he calls his,
    And makes sleep softer than it is!   20
Or, if thou list the night in watch to break,
    A-bed canst hear the loud stag speak,
In spring oft rousèd for thy master's sport,
    Who for it makes thy house his court;
Or with thy friends the heart of all the year
    Divid'st upon the lesser deer;
In autumn at the partridge makes a flight,
    And giv'st thy gladder guests the sight;

And in the winter hunt'st the flying hare,
   More for thy exercise than fare;   30
While all that follow, their glad ears apply
   To the full greatness of the cry;
Or hawking at the river, or the bush,
   Or shooting at the greedy thrush,
Thou dost with some delight the day out-wear,
   Although the coldest of the year!
The whilst, the several seasons thou hast seen
   Of flowery fields, of copses green,
The mowèd meadows, with the fleecèd sheep,
   And feasts that either shearers keep;   40
The ripened ears, yet humble in their height,
   And furrows laden with their weight;
The apple-harvest, that doth longer last;
   The hogs returned home fat from mast;
The trees cut out in log, and those boughs made
   A fire now, that lent a shade!
Thus Pan and Silvane having had their rites,
   Comus puts in for new delights,
And fills thy open hall with mirth and cheer,
   As if in Saturn's reign it were;   50
Apollo's harp and Hermes' lyre resound,
   Nor are the muses strangers found.
The rout of rural folk come thronging in
   (Their rudeness then is thought no sin);
Thy noblest spouse affords them welcome grace,
   And the great heroes of her race
Sit mixed with loss of state or reverence:
   Freedom doth with degree dispense.
The jolly wassail walks the often round,
   And in their cups their cares are drowned;   60
They think not then which side the cause shall leese,
   Nor how to get the lawyer fees.
Such and no other was that age of old,
   Which boasts to have had the head of gold.
And such, since thou canst make thine own content,
   Strive, Wroth, to live long innocent.
Let others watch in guilty arms, and stand
   The fury of a rash command,
Go enter breaches, meet the cannon's rage,

That they may sleep with scars in age,   70
And show their feathers shot, and colours torn,
   And brag that they were therefore born.
Let this man sweat and wrangle at the bar
   For every price in every jar,
And change possessions oftener with his breath
   Than either money, war or death;
Let him than hardest sires more disinherit,
   And each-where boast it as his merit
To blow up orphans, widows, and their states,
   And think his power doth equal fate's.   80
Let that go heap a mass of wretched wealth
   Purchased by rapine, worse than stealth,
And brooding o'er it sit, with broadest eyes,
   Not doing good, scarce when he dies.
Let thousands more go flatter vice, and win
   By being organs to great sin,
Get place and honour, and be glad to keep
   The secrets that shall break their sleep;
And, so they ride in purple, eat in plate,
   Though poison, think it a great fate.   90
But thou, my Wroth, if I can truth apply,
   Shalt neither that nor this envy:
Thy peace is made; and when man's state is well,
   'Tis better if he there can dwell.
God wisheth none should wrack on a strange shelf;
   To him man's dearer than to himself;
And howsoever we may think things sweet,
   He always gives what he knows meet,
Which who can use is happy: such be thou.
   Thy morning's and thy evening's vow   100
Be thanks to him, and earnest prayer, to find
   A body sound, with sounder mind;
To do thy country service, thyself right;
   That neither want do thee affright,
Nor death; but when thy latest sand is spent,
   Thou mayst think life a thing but lent.

4

To the World
A Farewell for a Gentlewoman, Virtuous and Noble

False world, good night. Since thou hast brought
   That hour upon my morn of age,
Henceforth I quit thee from my thought;
   My part is ended on thy stage.
Do not once hope that thou canst tempt
   A spirit so resolved to tread
Upon thy throat and live exempt
   From all the nets that thou canst spread.
I know thy forms are studied arts,
   Thy subtle ways be narrow straits,   10
Thy courtesy but sudden starts,
   And what thou call'st thy gifts are baits.
I know too, though thou strut and paint,
   Yet art thou both shrunk up and old;
That only fools make thee a saint,
   And all thy good is to be sold.
I know thou whole art but a shop
   Of toys and trifles, traps and snares,
To take the weak, or make them stop;
   Yet art thou falser than thy wares.   20
And knowing this, should I yet stay,
   Like such as blow away their lives
And never will redeem a day,
   Enamoured of their golden gyves?
Or, having 'scaped, shall I return
   And thrust my neck into the noose
From whence so lately I did burn
   With all my powers myself to loose?
What bird or beast is known so dull
   That, fled his cage, or broke his chain,   30
And tasting air and freedom, wull
   Render his head in there again?
If these, who have but sense, can shun
   The engines that have them annoyed,
Little for me had reason done,
   If I could not thy gins avoid.

Yes, threaten, do. Alas, I fear
   As little as I hope from thee;
I know thou canst nor show nor bear
   More hatred than thou hast to me.   40
My tender, first, and simple years
   Thou didst abuse, and then betray;
Since stirredst up jealousies and fears,
   When all the causes were away.
Then in a soil hast planted me
   Where breathe the basest of thy fools,
Where envious arts professèd be,
   And pride and ignorance the schools;
Where nothing is examined, weighed,
   But, as 'tis rumoured, so believed;   50
Where every freedom is betrayed,
   And every goodness taxed or grieved.
But what we're born for we must bear:
   Our frail condition it is such
That, what to all may happen here,
   If't chance to me, I must not grutch.
Else I my state should much mistake,
   To harbour a divided thought
From all my kind; that, for my sake,
   There should a miracle be wrought.   60
No, I do know that I was born
   To age, misfortune, sickness, grief;
But I will bear these with that scorn
   As shall not need thy false relief.
Nor for my peace will I go far,
   As wanderers do that still do roam,
But make my strengths, such as they are,
   Here in my bosom, and at home.

5

Song
To Celia

Come, my Celia, let us prove,
While we may, the sports of love;

Time will not be ours for ever;
He at length our good will sever.
Spend not then his gifts in vain.
Suns that set may rise again;
But if once we lose this light,
'Tis with us perpetual night.
Why should we defer our joys?
Fame and rumour are but toys.   10
Cannot we delude the eyes
Of a few poor household spies?
Or his easier ears beguile,
So removèd by our wile?
'Tis no sin love's fruit to steal,
But the sweet theft to reveal:
To be taken, to be seen,
These have crimes accounted been.

6

To the Same

Kiss me, sweet: the wary lover
Can your favours keep and cover,
When the common courting jay
All your bounties will betray.
Kiss again: no creature comes.
Kiss, and score up wealthy sums
On my lips, thus hardly sundered,
While you breathe. First give a hundred,
Then a thousand, then another
Hundred, then unto the t'other   10
Add a thousand, and so more,
Till you equal with the store
All the grass that Romney yields,
Or the sands in Chelsea fields,
Or the drops in silver Thames,
Or the stars that gild his streams
In the silent summer nights,
When youths ply their stol'n delights:

That the curious may not know
How to tell 'em as th[e]y flow,   20
And the envious, when they find
What their number is, be pined.

7

Song
That Women Are but Men's Shadows

Follow a shadow, it still flies you;
    Seem to fly it, it will pursue:
So court a mistress, she denies you;
    Let her alone, she will court you.
Say, are not women truly then
    Styled but the shadows of us men?

At morn and even shades are longest;
    At noon they are or short or none:
So men at weakest, they are strongest,
    But grant us perfect, they're not known.   10
Say, are not women truly then
    Styled but the shadows of us men?

8

To Sickness

Why, disease, dost thou molest
Ladies, and of them the best?
Do not men enough of rites
To thy altars, by their nights
Spent in surfeits, and their days
And nights too, in worser ways?
Take heed, sickness, what you do:
I shall fear you'll surfeit too.
Live not we as all thy stalls,
Spitals, pest-house, hospitals,   10
Scarce will take our present store?
And this age will build no more;

Pray thee feed contented, then,
Sickness, only on us men.
Or if needs thy lust will taste
Woman-kind, devour the waste
Livers, round about the town.
But, forgive me, with thy crown
They maintain the truest trade,
And have more diseases made.   20
What should yet thy palate please?
Daintiness, and softer ease,
Sleekèd limbs, and finest blood?
If thy leanness love such food,
There are those that for thy sake
Do enough, and who would take
Any pains—yea, think it price
To become thy sacrifice;
That distil their husbands' land
In decoctions; and are manned   30
With ten emp'rics in their chamber,
Lying for the spirit of amber;
That for the oil of talc dare spend
More than citizens dare lend
Them, and all their officers;
That, to make all pleasure theirs,
Will by coach and water go,
Every stew in town to know;
Dare entail their loves on any,
Bald or blind or ne'er so many;   40
And for thee, at common game
Play away health, wealth and fame.
These, disease, will thee deserve;
And will, long ere thou shouldst starve,
On their beds, most prostitute,
Move it as their humblest suit,
In thy justice to molest
None but them, and leave the rest.

9
Song
To Celia

Drink to me only with thine eyes,
    And I will pledge with mine;
Or leave a kiss but in the cup,
    And I'll not look for wine.
The thirst that from the soul doth rise
    Doth ask a drink divine;
But might I of Jove's nectar sup,
    I would not change for thine.
I sent thee late a rosy wreath,
    Not so much honouring thee   10
As giving it a hope that there
    It could not withered be.
But thou thereon didst only breathe,
    And sent'st it back to me;
Since when it grows, and smells, I swear,
    Not of itself, but thee.

10

And must I sing? What subject shall I choose?
Or whose great name in poets' heaven use
For the more countenance to my active muse?

Hercules? Alas, his bones are yet sore
With his old earthly labours. To exact more
Of his dull godhead were sin. I'll implore

Phoebus. No, tend thy cart still: envious day
Shall not give out that I have made thee stay,
And foundered thy hot team, to tune my lay.

Nor will I beg of thee, lord of the vine,   10
To raise my spirits with thy conjuring wine,
In the green circle of thy ivy twine.

Pallas, nor thee I call on, mankind maid,
That at thy birth mad'st the poor smith afraid,
Who with his axe thy father's midwife played.

Go, cramp dull Mars, light Venus, when he snorts,
Or with thy tribade trine invent new sports;
Thou nor thy looseness with my making sorts.

Let the old boy, your son, ply his old task,
Turn the stale prologue to some painted masque;   20
His absence in my verse is all I ask.

Hermes, the cheater, shall not mix with us,
Though he would steal his sisters' Pegasus
And riffle him, or pawn his petasus.

Nor all the ladies of the Thespian lake
(Though they were crushed into one form) could make
A beauty of that merit that should take

My muse up by commission: no, I bring
My own true fire. Now my thought takes wing,
And now an epode to deep ears I sing.   30

Proludium

An elegy? No, muse; it asks a strain
Too loose and capering for thy stricter vein.
Thy thoughts did never melt in amorous fire,
Like glass blown up and fashioned by desire.
The skilful mischief of a roving eye
Could ne'er make prize of thy white chastity.
Then leave these lighter numbers to light brains
In whom the flame of every beauty reigns,
Such as in lust's wild forest love to range,
Only pursuing constancy in change;   10
Let these in wanton feet dance out their souls.
A farther fury my raised spirit controls,
Which raps me up to the true heaven of love,
And conjures all my faculties to approve
The glories of it. Now our muse takes wing,
And now an epode to deep ears we sing.

11

Epode

Not to know vice at all, and keep true state,
    Is virtue, and not fate;
Next to that virtue, is to know vice well
    And her black spite expel.
Which to effect, since no breast is so sure
    Or safe but she'll procure
Some way of entrance, we must plant a guard
    Of thoughts to watch and ward
At the eye and ear, the ports unto the mind,
    That no strange or unkind   10
Object arrive there, but the heart, our spy,
    Give knowledge instantly
To wakeful reason, our affections' king;
    Who, in the examining,
Will quickly taste the treason and commit
    Close the close cause of it.
'Tis the securest policy we have
    To make our sense our slave.
But this true course is not embraced by many—
    By many? scarce by any.   20
For either our affections do rebel,
    Or else the sentinel,
That should ring larum to the heart, doth sleep,
    Or some great thought doth keep
Back the intelligence, and falsely swears
    They're base and idle fears
Whereof the loyal conscience so complains.
    Thus, by these subtle trains,
Do several passions [still] invade the mind
    And strike our reason blind.   30
Of which usurping rank some have thought love
    The first, as prone to move
Most frequent tumults, horrors and unrests
    In our inflamèd breasts;
But this doth from the[ir] cloud of error grow
    Which thus we overblow:

The thing they here call love is blind desire,
    Armed with bow, shafts and fire;
Inconstant like the sea, of whence 'tis born,
    Rough, swelling, like a storm;   40
With whom who sails, rides on the surge of fear,
    And boils as if he were
In a continual tempest. Now true love
    No such effects doth prove;
That is an essence far more gentle, fine,
    Pure, perfect, nay divine;
It is a golden chain let down from heaven,
    Whose links are bright and even,
That falls like sleep on lovers, and combines
    The soft and sweetest minds   50
In equal knots. This bears no brands nor darts
    To murther different hearts,
But in a calm and god-like unity
    Preserves community.
Oh, who is he that, in this peace, enjoys
    The elixir of all joys?
A form more fresh than are the Eden bowers,
    And lasting as her flowers;
Richer than time, and as time's virtue rare;
    Sober as saddest care;   60
A fixèd thought, an eye untaught to glance.
    Who, blest with such high chance,
Would at suggestion of a steep desire
    Cast himself from the spire
Of all his happiness? But soft, I hear
    Some vicious fool draw near
That cries, we dream, and swears there's no such thing
    As this chaste love we sing.
Peace, luxury, thou art like one of those
    Who, being at sea, suppose   70
Because they move, the continent doth so;
    No, vice, we let thee know,
Though thy wild thoughts with sparrows' wings do fly,
    Turtles can chastely die.
And yet, in this to express ourselves more clear,
    We do not number here
Such spirits as are only continent

Because lust's means are spent;
Or those who doubt the common mouth of fame,
   And for their place and name   80
Cannot so safely sin: their chastity
   Is mere necessity.
Nor mean we those whom vows and conscience
   Have filled with abstinence:
Though we acknowledge, who can so abstain
   Makes a most blessèd gain.
He that for love of goodness hateth ill
   Is more crown-worthy still
Than he which for sin's penalty forbears;
   His heart sins, though he fears.   90
But we propose a person like our dove,
   Graced with a phoenix' love;
A beauty of that clear and sparkling light
   Would make a day of night,
And turn the blackest sorrows to bright joys;
   Whose odorous breath destroys
All taste of bitterness, and makes the air
   As sweet as she is fair.
A body so harmoniously composed
   As if nature disclosed   100
All her best symmetry in that one feature!
   Oh, so divine a creature
Who could be false to? chiefly, when he knows
   How only she bestows
The wealthy treasure of her love on him,
   Making his fortunes swim
In the full flood of her admired perfection?
   What savage, brute affection
Would not be fearful to offend a dame
   Of this excelling frame?   110
Much more a noble and right generous mind,
   To virtuous moods inclined,
That knows the weight of guilt: he will refrain
   From thoughts of such a strain,
And to his sense object this sentence ever:
   Man may securely sin, but safely, never.

12

Epistle
To Elizabeth, Countess of Rutland

MADAM,
Whilst that for which all virtue now is sold
   And almost every vice, almighty gold;
That which, to boot with hell, is thought worth heaven,
   And for it life, conscience, yea souls, are given;
Toils by grave custom up and down the court
   To every squire or groom that will report
Well or ill only, all the following year,
   Just to the weight their this day's presents bear;
While it makes ushers serviceable men,
   And someone apteth to be trusted then,   10
Though never after; whiles it gains the voice
   Of some grand peer, whose air doth make rejoice
The fool that gave it, who will want and weep
   When his proud patron's favours are asleep;
While thus it buys great grace and hunts poor fame,
   Runs between man and man, 'tween dame and dame;
Solders cracked friendship, makes love last a day
   Or perhaps less: whilst gold bears all this sway,
I, that have none to send you, send you verse.
   A present which, if elder writs rehearse   20
The truth of times, was once of more esteem
   Than this, our gilt, nor golden age can deem;
When gold was made no weapon to cut throats
   Or put to flight Astraea, when her ingots
Were yet unfound, and better placed in earth
   Than here, to give pride fame, and peasants birth.
But let this dross carry what price it will
   With noble ignorants, and let them still
Turn upon scornèd verse their quarter-face;
   With you, I know, my offering will find grace.   30
For what a sin 'gainst your great father's spirit
   Were it to think that you should not inherit
His love unto the muses, when his skill
   Almost you have, or may have, when you will?

Wherein wise nature you a dowry gave
    Worth an estate treble to that you have.
Beauty, I know, is good, and blood is more;
    Riches thought most. But, madam, think what store
The world hath seen, which all these had in trust
    And now lie lost in their forgotten dust.   40
It is the muse alone can raise to heaven,
    And, at her strong arm's end, hold up and even
The souls she loves. Those other glorious notes,
    Inscribed in touch or marble, or the coats
Painted or carved upon our great men's tombs,
    Or in their windows, do but prove the wombs
That bred them graves; when they were born, they died
    That had no muse to make their fame abide.
How many equal with the Argive Queen
    Have beauty known, yet none so famous seen?   50
Achilles was not first that valiant was,
    Or, in an army's head, that, locked in brass,
Gave killing strokes. There were brave men before
    Ajax, or Idomen, or all the store
That Homer brought to Troy; yet none so live,
    Because they lacked the sacred pen could give
Like life unto 'em. Who heaved Hercules
    Unto the stars? or the Tyndarides?
Who placed Jason's Argo in the sky,
    Or set bright Ariadne's crown so high?   60
Who made a lamp of Berenice's hair,
    Or lifted Cassiopeia in her chair,
But only poets, rapt with rage divine?
    And such, or my hopes fail, shall make you shine.
You, and that other star, that purest light
    Of all Lucina's train, Lucy the bright;
Than which a nobler, heaven itself knows not.
    Who, though she have a better verser got
(Or 'poet', in the court account) than I,
    And who doth me, though I not him, envy   70
Yet, for the timely favours she hath done
    To my less sanguine muse, wherein she hath won
My grateful soul, the subject of her powers,
    I have already used some happy hours
To her remembrance; which, when time shall bring

To curious light, the notes I then shall sing
Will prove old Orpheus' act no tale to be;
   For I shall move stocks, stones no less than he.
Then all that have but done my muse least grace
   Shall thronging come, and boast the happy place   80
They hold in my strange poems, which, as yet,
   Had not their form touched by an English wit.
There like a rich and golden pyramid,
   Borne up by statues shall I rear your head
Above your under-carvèd ornaments,
   And show how, to the life, my soul presents
Your form impressed there: not with tickling rhymes,
   Or commonplaces, filched, that take these times,
But high and noble matter, such as flies
   From brains entranced and filled with ecstasies,   90
Moods which the god-like Sidney oft did prove,
   And your brave friend and mine so well did love.
Who, wheresoe'er he be . . .

The rest is lost

    [Who, wheresoe'er he be, on what dear coast,
    Now thinking on you, though to England lost,
    For that firm grace he holds in your regard,
    I, that am grateful for him, have prepared
    This hasty sacrifice; wherein I rear
    A vow as new and ominous as the year:
    Before his swift and circled race be run,
    My best of wishes, may you bear a son.]   100

13

Epistle
To Katherine, Lady Aubigny

'Tis grown almost a danger to speak true
   Of any good mind now, there are so few.
The bad, by number, are so fortified,
   As, what they've lost to expect, they dare deride.
So both the praised and praisers suffer: yet,
   For others' ill, ought none their good forget.

I, therefore, who profess myself in love
  With every virtue, wheresoe'er it move,
And howsoever; as I am at feud
  With sin and vice, though with a throne endued,   10
And, in this name, am given out dangerous
  By arts and practice of the vicious,
Such as suspect themselves, and think it fit
  For their own capital crimes to indict my wit;
I, that have suffered this, and though forsook
  Of fortune, have not altered yet my look,
Or so myself abandoned, as, because
  Men are not just, or keep no holy laws
Of nature and society, I should faint,
  Or fear to draw true lines, 'cause others paint: 20
I, madam, am become your praiser. Where,
  If it may stand with your soft blush to hear
Yourself but told unto yourself, and see
  In my character what your features be,
You will not from the paper slightly pass;
  No lady but, at some time, loves her glass.
And this shall be no false one, but as much
  Removed, as you from need to have it such.
Look then, and see yourself. I will not say
  Your beauty, for you see that every day,   30
And so do many more. All which can call
  It perfect, proper, pure and natural,
Not taken up o' the doctors, but as well
  As I can say, and see, it doth excel.
That asks but to be censured by the eyes,
  And in those outward forms all fools are wise.
Nor that your beauty wanted not a dower
  Do I reflect. Some alderman has power,
Or cozening farmer of the customs, so
  To advance his doubtful issue, and o'erflow   40
A prince's fortune: these are gifts of chance,
  And raise not virtue; they may vice enhance.
My mirror is more subtle, clear, refined,
  And takes and gives the beauties of the mind;
Though it reject not those of fortune, such
  As blood and match. Wherein, how more than much
Are you engagèd to your happy fate

For such a lot! that mixed you with a state
Of so great title, birth, but virtue most;
    Without which all the rest were sounds, or lost.   50
'Tis only that can time and chance defeat,
    For he that once is good is ever great.
Wherewith, then, madam, can you better pay
    This blessing of your stars, than by that way
Of virtue, which you tread? What if alone,
    Without companions? 'Tis safe to have none.
In single paths dangers with ease are watched;
    Contagion in the press is soonest catched.
This makes, that wisely you decline your life
    Far from the maze of custom, error, strife,   60
And keep an even and unaltered gait,
    Not looking by, or back (like those that wait
Times and occasions, to start forth and seem);
    Which though the turning world may disesteem,
Because that studies spectacles and shows,
    And after varied, as fresh, objects goes,
Giddy with change, and therefore cannot see
    Right the right way; yet must your comfort be
Your conscience; and not wonder if none asks
    For truth's complexion, where they all wear masks.   70
Let who will, follow fashions and attires;
    Maintain their liegers forth; for foreign wires
Melt down their husbands' land, to pour away
    On the close groom and page on New Year's Day
And almost all days after, while they live
    (They find it both so witty and safe to give).
Let 'em on powders, oils, and paintings spend
    Till that no usurer nor his bawds dare lend
Them or their officers; and no man know
    Whether it be a face they wear, or no.   80
Let 'em waste body and state, and after all,
    When their own parasites laugh at their fall,
May they have nothing left, whereof they can
    Boast, but how oft they have gone wrong to man,
And call it their brave sin. For such there be
    That do sin only for the infamy,
And never think how vice doth every hour
    Eat on her clients and some one devour.

You, madam, young have learned to shun these shelves,
   Whereon the most of mankind wrack themselves,   90
And, keeping a just course, have early put
   Into your harbour, and all passage shut
'Gainst storms, or pirates, that might charge your peace;
   For which you worthy are the glad increase
Of your blessed womb, made fruitful from above,
   To pay your lord the pledges of chaste love,
And raise a noble stem, to give the fame
   To Clifton's blood that is denied their name.
Grow, grow fair tree, and as thy branches shoot,
   Hear what the muses sing about thy root,   100
By me, their priest (if they can aught divine):
   Before the moons have filled their triple trine,
To crown the burthen which you go withal,
   It shall a ripe and timely issue fall,
To expect the honours of great Aubigny,
   And greater rites, yet writ in mystery,
But which the fates forbid me to reveal.
   Only thus much, out of a ravished zeal
Unto your name and goodness of your life,
   They speak; since you are truly that rare wife   110
Other great wives may blush at, when they see
   What your tried manners are, what theirs should be.
How you love one, and him you should; how still
   You are depending on his word and will;
Not fashioned for the court, or strangers' eyes,
   But to please him, who is the dearer prize
Unto himself, by being so dear to you.
   This makes, that your affections still be new,
And that your souls conspire, as they were gone
   Each into other, and had now made one.   120
Live that one still; and as long years do pass,
   Madam, be bold to use this truest glass,
Wherein your form you still the same shall find,
   Because nor it can change, nor such a mind.

14

Ode
To Sir William Sidney, on His Birthday

Now that the hearth is crowned with smiling fire,
   And some do drink, and some do dance,
       Some ring,
       Some sing,
   And all do strive to advance
The gladness higher;
     Wherefore should I
     Stand silent by,
       Who not the least
       Both love the cause and authors of the feast?   10

Give me my cup, but from the Thespian well,
   That I may tell to Sidney what
       This day
       Doth say,
   And he may think on that
Which I do tell;
     When all the noise
     Of these forced joys
       Are fled and gone,
       And he with his best genius left alone.   20

This day says, then, the number of glad years
   Are justly summed, that make you man;
       Your vow
       Must now
   Strive all right ways it can
To outstrip your peers:
     Since he doth lack
     Of going back
       Little, whose will
       Doth urge him to run wrong, or to stand still.   30

Nor can a little of the common store
  Of nobles' virtue show in you;
       Your blood
       So good
  And great must seek for new,
And study more;
    Not, weary, rest
    On what's deceased.
      For they that swell
      With dust of ancestors, in graves but dwell.   40

'Twill be exacted of your name, whose son,
  Whose nephew, whose grandchild you are;
      And men
      Will then
  Say you have followed far,
When well begun;
    Which must be now:
    They teach you how.
      And he that stays
      To live until tomorrow hath lost two days.   50

So may you live in honour as in name,
  If with this truth you be inspired;
      So may
      This day
  Be more, and long desired;
And with the flame
    Of love be bright,
    As with the light
      Of bonfires. Then
      The birthday shines, when logs not burn, but men. 60

15

To Heaven

Good and great God, can I not think of thee,
  But it must straight my melancholy be?

Is it interpreted in me disease
    That, laden with my sins, I seek for ease?
Oh, be thou witness, that the reins dost know
    And hearts of all, if I be sad for show;
And judge me after, if I dare pretend
    To aught but grace, or aim at other end.
As thou art all, so be thou all to me,
    First, midst, and last; converted one and three;   10
My faith, my hope, my love; and in this state,
    My judge, my witness, and my advocate.
Where have I been this while exiled from thee?
    And whither rapt, now thou but stoop'st to me?
Dwell, dwell here still: Oh, being everywhere,
    How can I doubt to find thee ever here?
I know my state, both full of shame and scorn,
    Conceived in sin, and unto labour born,
Standing with fear, and must with horror fall,
    And destined unto judgement, after all.   20
I feel my griefs too, and there scarce is ground
    Upon my flesh to inflict another wound.
Yet dare I not complain, or wish for death
    With holy Paul, lest it be thought the breath
Of discontent; or that these prayers be
    For weariness of life, not love of thee.

THE UNDERWOOD

TO THE READER

With the same leave, the ancients called that kind of body *sylva*, or *῞Υλη*, in which there were works of diverse nature and matter congested, as the multitude call timber-trees, promiscuously growing, a wood or forest; so am I bold to entitle these lesser poems of later growth by this of *Underwood*, out of the analogy they hold to *The Forest* in my former book, and no otherwise.

Ben Jonson

I

Poems of Devotion

i

The Sinner's Sacrifice
To the Holy Trinity

1. O holy, blessèd, glorious Trinity
Of persons, still one God in unity,
The faithful man's believèd mystery,
    Help, help to lift

2. Myself up to thee, harrowed, torn, and bruised
By sin and Satan; and my flesh misused,
As my heart lies in pieces, all confused,
    Oh, take my gift.

3. All-gracious God, the sinner's sacrifice,
A broken heart thou wert not wont despise,   10
But 'bove the fat of rams, or bulls, to prize
    An offering meet

4. For thy acceptance. Oh, behold me right,
And take compassion on my grievous plight.
What odour can be, than a heart contrite,
    To thee more sweet?

5. Eternal Father, God who didst create
This all of nothing, gavest it form and fate,
And breath'st into it life and light, with state
      To worship thee;   20

6. Eternal God the Son, who not denied'st
To take our nature, becam'st man, and died'st
To pay our debts, upon thy cross, and cried'st
      All's done in me;

7. Eternal Spirit, God from both proceeding,
Father and Son, the comforter in breeding
Pure thoughts in man; with fiery zeal them feeding
      For acts of grace:

8. Increase those acts, O glorious Trinity
Of persons, still one God in unity,   30
Till I attain the longed-for mystery
      Of seeing your face,

9. Beholding one in three, and three in one,
A Trinity, to shine in union;
The gladdest light dark man can think upon,
      O grant it me!

10. Father, and Son, and Holy Ghost, you three
All coeternal in your majesty,
Distinct in persons, yet in unity
      One God to see,   40

11. My Maker, Saviour, and my Sanctifier,
To hear, to meditate, sweeten my desire
With grace, with love, with cherishing entire;
      Oh, then how blest,

12. Among thy saints elected to abide,
And with thy angels placèd side by side,
But in thy presence truly glorified,
      Shall I there rest!

I. ii
A Hymn to God the Father

Hear me, O God!
   A broken heart
   Is my best part;
Use still thy rod,
   That I may prove
   Therein thy love.

If thou hadst not
   Been stern to me,
   But left me free,
I had forgot   10
   Myself and thee.

For sin's so sweet,
   As minds ill bent
   Rarely repent,
Until they meet
   Their punishment.

Who more can crave
   Than thou hast done?
   That gav'st a Son,
To free a slave,   20
   First made of naught;
   With all since bought.

Sin, death, and hell
   His glorious name
   Quite overcame,
Yet I rebel,
   And slight the same.

But I'll come in,
   Before my loss
   Me farther toss,   30
As sure to win
   Under his cross.

I. iii

A Hymn
On the Nativity of My Saviour

I sing the birth was born tonight,
The author both of life and light;
    The angels so did sound it,
And like, the ravished shepherds said,
Who saw the light and were afraid,
    Yet searched, and true they found it.

The Son of God, the Eternal King,
That did us all salvation bring,
    And freed the soul from danger;
He whom the whole world could not take,   10
The Word, which heaven and earth did make,
    Was now laid in a manger.

The Father's wisdom willed it so,
The Son's obedience knew no No,
    Both wills were in one stature;
And as that wisdom had decreed,
The Word was now made flesh indeed,
    And took on him our nature.

What comfort by him do we win,
Who made himself the price of sin,   20
    To make us heirs of glory!
To see this babe, all innocence,
A martyr born in our defence,
    Can man forget this story?

2

A Celebration of Charis in Ten Lyric Pieces

i

His Excuse for Loving

Let it not your wonder move,
Less your laughter, that I love.

Though I now write fifty years,
I have had, and have, my peers;
Poets, though divine, are men:
Some have loved as old again.
And it is not always face,
Clothes, or fortune gives the grace,
Or the feature, or the youth;
But the language, and the truth,   10
With the ardour and the passion,
Gives the lover weight and fashion.
If you then will read the story,
First prepare you to be sorry
That you never knew till now
Either whom to love, or how;
But be glad as soon with me,
When you know that this is she,
Of whose beauty it was sung,
She shall make the old man young,   20
Keep the middle age at stay,
And let nothing high decay,
Till she be the reason why
All the world for love may die.

2. ii
How He Saw Her

I beheld her, on a day,
When her look out-flourished May,
And her dressing did outbrave
All the pride the fields then have;
Far I was from being stupid,
For I ran and called on Cupid:
Love, if thou wilt ever see
Mark of glory, come with me.
Where's thy quiver? Bend thy bow!
Here's a shaft—thou art too slow!   10
And (withal) I did untie
Every cloud about his eye;
But he had not gained his sight
Sooner than he lost his might

Or his courage; for away
Straight he ran, and durst not stay,
Letting bow and arrow fall,
Nor for any threat or call
Could be brought once back to look.
I, foolhardy, there up-took   20
Both the arrow he had quit
And the bow, with thought to hit
This my object. But she threw
Such a lightning, as I drew,
At my face, that took my sight
And my motion from me quite;
So that there I stood a stone,
Mocked of all, and called of one
(Which with grief and wrath I heard)
Cupid's statue with a beard,   30
Or else one that played his ape
In a Hercules's shape.

2. iii
What He Suffered

After many scorns like these,
Which the prouder beauties please,
She content was to restore
Eyes and limbs, to hurt me more.
And would, on conditions, be
Reconciled to Love and me.
First, that I must kneeling yield
Both the bow and shaft I held
Unto her; which Love might take
At her hand, with oath, to make   10
Me the scope of his next draught,
Aimed with that self-same shaft.
He no sooner heard the law,
But the arrow home did draw,
And, to gain her by his art,
Left it sticking in my heart;
Which when she beheld to bleed,
She repented of the deed,

And would fain have changed the fate,
But the pity comes too late.   20
Loser-like, now, all my wreak
Is that I have leave to speak,
And in either prose, or song,
To revenge me with my tongue;
Which how dexterously I do,
Hear, and make example too.

2. iv
Her Triumph

See the chariot at hand here of Love,
    Wherein my lady rideth!
Each that draws is a swan or a dove,
    And well the car Love guideth.
As she goes, all hearts do duty
                Unto her beauty;
And enamoured, do wish, so they might
                But enjoy such a sight,
    That they still were to run by her side,
Through swords, through seas, whither she would ride.   10

Do but look on her eyes, they do light
    All that Love's world compriseth!
Do but look on her hair, it is bright
    As Love's star when it riseth!
Do but mark, her forehead's smoother
                Than words that soothe her!
And from her arched brows, such a grace
                Sheds itself through the face,
    As alone there triumphs to the life
All the gain, all the good, of the elements' strife.   20

Have you seen but a bright lily grow,
    Before rude hands have touched it?
Have you marked but the fall o' the snow,
    Before the soil hath smutched it?
Have you felt the wool o' the beaver?
                Or swan's down ever?

Or have smelled o' the bud o' the briar?
Or the nard i' the fire?
Or have tasted the bag o' the bee?
O so white! O so soft! O so sweet is she!   30

2. V

His Discourse with Cupid

Noblest Charis, you that are
Both my fortune and my star!
And do govern more my blood
Than the various moon the flood!
Hear what late discourse of you
Love and I have had, and true.
'Mongst my muses finding me,
Where he chanced your name to see
Set, and to this softer strain:
Sure, said he, if I have brain,   10
This, here sung, can be no other
By description but my mother!
So hath Homer praised her hair,
So Anacreon drawn the air
Of her face, and made to rise,
Just above her sparkling eyes,
Both her brows, bent like my bow.
By her looks I do her know,
Which you call my shafts. And see!
Such my mother's blushes be,   20
As the bath your verse discloses
In her cheeks, of milk and roses;
Such as oft I wanton in!
And, above her even chin,
Have you placed the bank of kisses,
Where, you say, men gather blisses,
Ripened with a breath more sweet,
Than when flowers and west winds meet.
Nay, her white and polished neck,
With the lace that doth it deck,   30
Is my mother's! Hearts of slain
Lovers, made into a chain!

And between each rising breast
Lies the valley called my nest,
Where I sit and proyne my wings
After flight, and put new stings
To my shafts! Her very name
With my mother's is the same.
I confess all, I replied,
And the glass hangs by her side,   40
And the girdle 'bout her waist:
All is Venus, save unchaste.
But alas, thou seest the least
Of her good, who is the best
Of her sex; but could'st thou, Love,
Call to mind the forms that strove
For the apple, and those three
Make in one, the same were she.
For this beauty yet doth hide
Something more than thou hast spied.   50
Outward grace weak love beguiles;
She is Venus, when she smiles,
But she's Juno, when she walks,
And Minerva, when she talks.

2. vi
Claiming a Second Kiss by Desert

Charis, guess, and do not miss,
Since I drew a morning kiss
From your lips, and sucked an air
Thence as sweet as you are fair,
What my muse and I have done:
Whether we have lost, or won,
If by us the odds were laid
That the bride, allowed a maid,
Looked not half so fresh and fair,
With the advantage of her hair   10
And her jewels, to the view
Of the assembly, as did you!

Or, that did you sit, or walk,
You were more the eye and talk
Of the court, today, than all
Else that glistered in Whitehall;
So as those that had your sight
Wished the bride were changed tonight,
And did think such rites were due
To no other grace but you!   20
Or, if you did move tonight
In the dances, with what spite
Of your peers you were beheld,
That at every motion swelled
So to see a lady tread,
As might all the graces lead,
And was worthy, being so seen,
To be envied of the queen.
Or if you would yet have stayed,
Whether any would upbraid   30
To himself his loss of time,
Or have charged his sight of crime
To have left all sight for you.
Guess of these which is the true:
And if such a verse as this
May not claim another kiss.

2. vii
Begging Another, on Colour of Mending the Former

For Love's sake, kiss me once again,
  I long, and should not beg in vain,
    Here's none to spy, or see:
      Why do you doubt, or stay?
    I'll taste as lightly as the bee,
That doth but touch his flower, and flies away.
  Once more, and (faith) I will be gone;
  Can he that loves ask less than one?
    Nay, you may err in this,
      And all your bounty wrong: 10
    This could be called but half a kiss.
What we are but once to do, we should do long.

I will but mend the last, and tell
Where, how, it would have relished well;
   Join lip to lip, and try;
      Each suck [the] other's breath.
And whilst our tongues perplexèd lie,
Let who will think us dead, or wish our death.

2. viii
Urging Her of a Promise

   Charis one day in discourse
Had of Love and of his force,
Lightly promised she would tell
What a man she could love well;
And that promise set on fire
All that heard her, with desire.
With the rest I long expected
When the work would be effected;
But we find that cold delay
And excuse spun every day,   10
As, until she tell her one,
We all fear she loveth none.
Therefore, Charis, you must do it,
For I will so urge you to it,
You shall neither eat, nor sleep,
No, nor forth your window peep
With your emissary eye
To fetch in the forms go by,
And pronounce which band or lace
Better fits him than his face;   20
Nay, I will not let you sit
'Fore your idol glass a whit,
To say over every purl
There or to reform a curl;
Or with secretary Cis
To consult, if fucus this
Be as good as was the last:
All your sweet of life is past,
Make account, unless you can
(And that quickly) speak your man.   30

2. ix
Her Man Described by Her Own Dictamen

Of your trouble, Ben, to ease me,
I will tell what man would please me.
I would have him, if I could,
Noble, or of greater blood;
Titles, I confess, do take me,
And a woman God did make me;
French to boot, at least in fashion,
And his manners of that nation.

   Young I'd have him too, and fair,
Yet a man; with crispèd hair   10
Cast in thousand snares and rings
For Love's fingers and his wings:
Chestnut colour, or more slack
Gold, upon a ground of black.
Venus' and Minerva's eyes,
For he must look wanton-wise.

   Eyebrows bent like Cupid's bow,
Front an ample field of snow;
Even nose, and cheek (withal)
Smooth as is the billard ball;   20
Chin as woolly as the peach,
And his lip should kissing teach,
Till he cherished too much beard,
And make Love or me afeared.

   He would have a hand as soft
As the down, and show it oft;
Skin as smooth as any rush,
And so thin to see a blush
Rising through it ere it came;
All his blood should be a flame   30
Quickly fired as in beginners
In Love's school, and yet no sinners.
'Twere too long to speak of all;
What we harmony do call
In a body should be there.
Well he should his clothes, too, wear,
Yet no tailor help to make him;
Dressed, you still for man should take him,

And not think he'd ate a stake
Or were set up in a brake. 40
　Valiant he should be as fire,
Showing danger more than ire.
Bounteous as the clouds to earth,
And as honest as his birth.
All his actions to be such,
As to do no thing too much.
Nor o'erpraise, nor yet condemn,
Nor out-value, nor contemn;
Nor do wrongs, nor wrongs receive;
Nor tie knots, nor knots unweave; 50
And from baseness to be free,
As he durst love truth and me.
　Such a man, with every part,
I could give my very heart;
But of one, if short he came,
I can rest me where I am.

2. X
Another Lady's Exception, Present at the Hearing

For his mind I do not care,
That's a toy that I could spare;
Let his title be but great,
His clothes rich, and band sit neat,
Himself young, and face be good,
All I wish is understood.
What you please you parts may call,
'Tis one good part I'd lie withal.

3

The Musical Strife; in a Pastoral Dialogue

She
Come, with our voices let us war,
　And challenge all the spheres,
Till each of us be made a star
　And all the world turn ears.

He

At such a call what beast or fowl
  Of reason empty is?
What tree or stone doth want a soul?
  What man but must lose his?

She

Mix then your notes, that we may prove
  To stay the running floods,   10
To make the mountain quarries move,
  And call the walking woods.

He

What need of me? Do you but sing,
  Sleep and the grave will wake;
No tunes are sweet, nor words have sting,
  But what those lips do make.

She

They say the angels mark each deed
  And exercise below,
And out of inward pleasure feed
  On what they viewing know.   20

He

O sing not you then, lest the best
  Of angels should be driven
To fall again, at such a feast
  Mistaking earth for heaven.

She

Nay, rather both our souls be strained
  To meet their high desire;
So they in state of grace retained
  May wish us of their choir.

4

A Song

Oh, do not wanton with those eyes
    Lest I be sick with seeing;
Nor cast them down, but let them rise,
    Lest shame destroy their being.

Oh, be not angry with those fires,
    For then their threats will kill me;
Nor look too kind on my desires,
    For then my hopes will spill me.

Oh, do not steep them in thy tears,
    For so will sorrow slay me;   10
Nor spread them as distract with fears,
    Mine own enough betray me.

5

In the Person of Womankind
A Song Apologetic

Men, if you love us, play no more
    The fools or tyrants with your friends,
To make us still sing o'er and o'er
    Our own false praises, for your ends;
        We have both wits and fancies too,
        And if we must, let's sing of you.

Nor do we doubt but that we can,
    If we would search with care and pain,
Find some one good in some one man;
    So going thorough all your strain   10
        We shall, at last, of parcels make
        One good enough for a song's sake.

And as a cunning painter takes
    In any curious piece you see
More pleasure while the thing he makes
    Than when 'tis made, why so will we.
        And having pleased our art, we'll try
        To make a new, and hang that by.

6

Another: in Defence of Their Inconstancy
A Song

Hang up those dull and envious fools
    That talk abroad of woman's change,
We were not bred to sit on stools,
    Our proper virtue is to range;
        Take that away, you take our lives,
        We are no women then, but wives.

Such as in valour would excel
    Do change, though man, and often fight,
Which we in love must do as well,
    If ever we will love aright.   10
        The frequent varying of the deed
        Is that which doth perfection breed.

Nor is't inconstancy to change
    For what is better, or to make,
By searching, what before was strange
    Familiar, for the use's sake;
        The good from bad is not descried
        But as 'tis often vexed and tried.

And this profession of a store
    In love, doth not alone help forth   20
Our pleasure, but preserves us more
    From being forsaken than doth worth;
        For were the worthiest woman cursed
        To love one man, he'd leave her first.

7

A Nymph's Passion

I love and he loves me again,
    Yet dare I not tell who;
For if the nymphs should know my swain,
    I fear they'd love him too;
        Yet if it be not known
      The pleasure is as good as none,
For that's a narrow joy is but our own.

I'll tell, that if they be not glad,
    They yet may envy me;
But then if I grow jealous mad
    And of them pitied be,   10
        It were a plague 'bove scorn;
      And yet it cannot be forborne,
Unless my heart would as my thought be torn.

He is, if they can find him, fair,
    And fresh and fragrant too
As summer's sky or purgèd air,
    And looks as lilies do
        That were this morning blown;
      Yet, yet I doubt he is not known,   20
And fear much more that more of him be shown.

But he hath eyes so round and bright
    As make away my doubt,
Where Love may all his torches light
    Though hate had put them out;
        But then, to increase my fears,
      What nymph soe'er his voice but hears
Will be my rival, though she have but ears.

I'll tell no more, and yet I love,
    And he loves me; yet no   30
One unbecoming thought doth move
    From either heart, I know;
        But so exempt from blame,
      As it would be to each a fame,
If love, or fear, would let me tell his name.

8

The Hour-Glass

Do but consider this small dust
   Here running in the glass,
     By atoms moved:
Could you believe that this
   The body [ever] was
     Of one that loved?
And in his mistress' flame, playing like a fly,
   Turned to cinders by her eye?
   Yes; and in death, as life, unblest,
     To have't expressed,   10
Even ashes of lovers find no rest.

9

My Picture Left in Scotland

I now think Love is rather deaf than blind,
   For else it could not be
     That she
Whom I adore so much should so slight me,
   And cast my love behind;
I'm sure my language to her was as sweet,
     And every close did meet
     In sentence of as subtle feet,
     As hath the youngest he
   That sits in shadow of Apollo's tree.   10

   Oh, but my conscious fears
     That fly my thoughts between,
     Tell me that she hath seen
     My hundred of grey hairs,
     Told seven-and-forty years,
Read so much waste, as she cannot embrace
   My mountain belly, and my rocky face;
And all these through her eyes have stopped her ears.

10

Against Jealousy

Wretched and foolish jealousy
How cam'st thou thus to enter me?
   I ne'er was of thy kind,
  Nor have I yet the narrow mind
   To vent that poor desire
That others should not warm them at my fire;
   I wish the sun should shine
On all men's fruit and flowers, as well as mine.

But under the disguise of love
Thou say'st thou only cam'st to prove   10
   What my affections were.
  Think'st thou that love is helped by fear?
   Go, get thee quickly forth,
Love's sickness and his noted want of worth,
   Seek doubting men to please;
I ne'er will owe my health to a disease.

11

The Dream

Or scorn, or pity on me take,
I must the true relation make:
   I am undone tonight;
  Love in a subtle dream disguised
  Hath both my heart and me surprised,
Whom never yet he durst attempt awake;
Nor will he tell me for whose sake
   He did me the delight,
    Or spite,
  But leaves me to inquire,   10
  In all my wild desire
   Of sleep again, who was his aid;
   And sleep so guilty and afraid
As, since, he dares not come within my sight.

12

An Epitaph on Master Vincent Corbett

I have my piety too, which could
It vent itself but as it would,
    Would say as much as both have done
    Before me here, the friend and son;
For I both lost a friend and father,
Of him whose bones this grave doth gather:
    Dear Vincent Corbett, who so long
    Had wrestled with diseases strong
That though they did possess each limb,
Yet he broke them, ere they could him,   10
    With the just canon of his life;
    A life that knew nor noise nor strife,
But was, by sweetening so his will,
All order and disposure still.
    His mind as pure, and neatly kept,
    As were his nurseries, and swept
So of uncleanness or offence,
That never came ill odour thence;
    And add his actions unto these,
    They were as specious as his trees.   20
'Tis true, he could not reprehend;
His very manners taught to amend,
    They were so even, grave, and holy;
    No stubbornness so stiff, nor folly
To licence ever was so light
As twice to trespass in his sight;
    His looks would so correct it, when
    It chid the vice, yet not the men.
Much from him I profess I won,
And more and more I should have done,   30
    But that I understood him scant.
    Now I conceive him by my want,
And pray, who shall my sorrows read,
That they for me their tears will shed;
    For truly, since he left to be,
    I feel I'm rather dead than he!

Reader, whose life and name did e'er become
   An epitaph, deserved a tomb;
Nor wants it here, through penury or sloth;
   Who makes the one, so it be first, makes both.   40

13

An Epistle to Sir Edward Sackville, now Earl of Dorset

If, Sackville, all that have the power to do
Great and good turns, as well could time them too,
And knew their how and where, we should have then
Less list of proud, hard, or ungrateful men.
For benefits are owed with the same mind
As they are done, and such returns they find.
You then whose will not only, but desire
To succour my necessities took fire,
Not at my prayers, but your sense, which laid
The way to meet what others would upbraid,   10
And in the act did so my blush prevent,
As I did feel it done as soon as meant;
You cannot doubt but I, who freely know
This good from you, as freely will it owe.
And though my fortune humble me to take
The smallest courtesies with thanks, I make
Yet choice from whom I take them, and would shame
To have such do me good I durst not name.
They are the noblest benefits, and sink
Deepest in man, of which, when he doth think,   20
The memory delights him more from whom
Than what he hath received. Gifts stink from some,
They are so long a-coming, and so hard;
Where any deed is forced, the grace is marred.
   Can I owe thanks for courtesies received
Against his will that does 'em; that hath weaved
Excuses or delays; or done 'em scant,
That they have more oppressed me than my want?
Or if he did it not to succour me
But by mere chance, for interest, or to free   30

Himself of farther trouble, or the weight
Of pressure, like one taken in a strait?
All this corrupts the thanks; less hath he won
That puts it in his debt-book ere it be done;
Or that doth sound a trumpet, and doth call
His grooms to witness; or else lets it fall
In that proud manner, as a good so gained
Must make me sad for what I have obtained.
   No! Gifts and thanks should have one cheerful face,
So each that's done and ta'en becomes a brace.   40
He neither gives, or does, that doth delay
A benefit, or that doth throw it away;
No more than he doth thank that will receive
Naught but in corners, and is loath to leave
Least air or print, but flies it: such men would
Run from the conscience of it, if they could.
   As I have seen some infants of the sword,
Well known and practised borrowers on their word,
Give thanks by stealth, and whispering in the ear,
For what they straight would to the world forswear;   50
And speaking worst of those from whom they went
But then, fist-filled, to put me off the scent:
Now, damn me, sir, if you shall not command
My sword ('tis but a poor sword, understand)
As far as any poor sword in the land.
Then turning unto him is next at hand,
Damns whom he damned too is the veriest gull
Has feathers, and will serve a man to pull.
   Are they not worthy to be answered so,
That to such natures let their full hands flow,   60
And seek not wants to succour, but inquire,
Like money-brokers, after names, and hire
Their bounties forth to him that last was made,
Or stands to be, [i]n commission of the blade?
Still, still the hunters of false fame apply
Their thoughts and means to making loud the cry;
But one is bitten by the dog he fed,
And, hurt, seeks cure: the surgeon bids take bread
And sponge-like with it dry up the blood quite,
Then give it to the hound that did him bite.   70
Pardon, says he, that were a way to see

All the town curs take each their snatch at me.
Oh, is it so? Knows he so much? And will
Feed those at whom the table points at still?
I not deny it, but to help the need
Of any is a great and generous deed:
Yea, cf the ungrateful; and he forth must tell
Many a pound and piece, will p[l]ace one well.
But these men ever want: their very trade
Is borrowing; that but stopped, they do invade   80
All as their prize, turn pirates here at land,
Have their Bermudas, and their straits i' the Strand;
Man out their boats to the Temple; and not shift
Now, but command, make tribute what was gift;
And it is paid 'em with a trembling zeal,
And superstition I dare scarce reveal
If it were clear; but being so in cloud
Carried and wrapped, I only am allowed
My wonder why the taking a clown's purse,
Or robbing the poor market-folks should nurse   90
Such a religious horror in the breasts
Of our town gallantry! Or why there rests
Such worship due to kicking of a punk,
Or swaggering with the watch, or drawer, drunk,
Or feats of darkness acted in mid-sun,
And told of with more licence than they were done!
Sure there is mystery in it I not know,
That men such reverence to such actions show!
And almost deify the authors: make
Loud sacrifice of drink for their health's sake,   100
Rere-suppers in their names, and spend whole nights
Unto their praise in certain swearing rites!
Cannot a man be reckoned in the state
Of valour, but at this idolatrous rate?
I thought that fortitude had been a mean
'Twixt fear and rashness; not a lust obscene,
Or appetite of offending, but a skill
Or science of discerning good and ill.
And you, sir, know it well, to whom I write,
That with these mixtures we put out her light.   110
Her ends are honesty and public good,
And where they want, she is not understood.

No more are these of us, let them then go;
I have the list of mine own faults to know,
Look to, and cure. He's not a man hath none,
But like to be, that every day mends one
And feels it; else he tarries by the beast.
Can I discern how shadows are decreased
Or grown, by height or lowness of the sun,
And can I less of substance? When I run,   120
Ride, sail, am coached, know I how far I have gone,
And my mind's motion not? Or have I none?
No! he must feel and know that will advance.
Men have been great, but never good, by chance
Or on the sudden. It were strange that he
Who was this morning such a one should be
Sidney ere night! Or that did go to bed
Coryate should rise the most sufficient head
Of Christendom! And neither of these know,
Were the rack offered them, how they came so;   130
'Tis by degrees that men arrive at glad
Profit in aught; each day some little add,
In time 'twill be a heap; this is not true
Alone in money, but in manners too.
Yet we must more than move still, or go on,
We must accomplish: 'tis the last keystone
That makes the arch. The rest that there were put
Are nothing till that comes to bind and shut.
Then stands it a triumphal mark! Then men
Observe the strength, the height, the why, and when   140
It was erected; and still walking under
Meet some new matter to look up and wonder!
Such notes are virtuous men: they live as fast
As they are high; are rooted, and will last.
They need no stilts, nor rise upon their toes.
As if they would belie their stature; those
Are dwarfs of honour, and have neither weight
Nor fashion; if they chance aspire to height,
'Tis like light canes, that first rise big and brave,
Shoot forth in smooth and comely spaces, have   150
But few and fair divisions; but being got
Aloft, grow less and straitened, full of knot,
And last, go out in nothing; you that see

Their difference cannot choose which you will be.
You know (without my flattering you) too much
For me to be your indice. Keep you such,
That I may love your person (as I do)
Without your gift, though I can rate that too,
By thanking thus the courtesy to life,
Which you will bury; but therein the strife   160
May grow so great to be example, when
(As their true rule or lesson) either men,
Donors or donees, to their practice shall
Find you to reckon nothing, me owe all.

14

An Epistle to Master John Selden

I know to whom I write. Here, I am sure,
Though I am short, I cannot be obscure;
Less shall I for the art or dressing care,
Truth and the graces best when naked are.
Your book, my Selden, I have read, and much
Was trusted, that you thought my judgement such
To ask it; though in most of works it be
A penance, where a man may not be free,
Rather than office, when it doth or may
Chance that the friend's affection proves allay   10
Unto the censure. Yours all need doth fly
Of this so vicious humanity.
Than which there is not unto study a more
Pernicious enemy; we see before
A many of books, even good judgements wound
Themselves through favouring what is there not found.
But I on yours far otherwise shall do,
Not fly the crime, but the suspicion too;
Though I confess (as every muse hath erred,
And mine not least) I have too oft preferred   20
Men past their terms, and praised some names too much;
But 'twas with purpose to have made them such.
Since being deceived, I turn a sharper eye
Upon myself, and ask to whom, and why,

And what I write? And vex it many days
Before men get a verse, much less a praise;
So that my reader is assured I now
Mean what I speak, and still will keep that vow.
Stand forth my object, then, you that have been
Ever at home, yet have all countries seen;   30
And like a compass keeping one foot still
Upon your centre, do your circle fill
Of general knowledge; watched men, manners too,
Heard what times past have said, seen what ours do.
Which grace shall I make love to first: your skill,
Or faith in things? Or is't your wealth and will
To instruct and teach, or your unwearied pain
Of gathering, bounty in pouring out again?
What fables have you vexed, what truth redeemed,
Antiquities searched, opinions disesteemed,   40
Impostures branded, and authorities urged!
What blots and errors have you watched and purged
Records and authors of! How rectified
Times, manners, customs! Innovations spied!
Sought out the fountains, sources, creeks, paths, ways,
And noted the beginnings and decays!
Where is that nominal mark, or real rite,
Form, art, or ensign that hath 'scaped your sight?
How are traditions there examined, how
Conjectures retrieved! And a story now   50
And then of times, besides the bare conduct
Of what it tells us, weaved in to instruct!
I wondered at the richness, but am lost
To see the workmanship so exceed the cost;
To mark the excellent seasoning of your style,
And manly elocution, not one while
With horror rough, then rioting with wit:
But to the subject still the colours fit
In sharpness of all search, wisdom of choice,
Newness of sense, antiquity of voice!   60
　　I yield, I yield, the matter of your praise
Flows in upon me, and I cannot raise
A bank against it. Nothing but the round
Large clasp of nature such a wit can bound.
Monarch in letters! 'mongst thy titles shown

Of others' honours, thus enjoy thine own.
I first salute thee so, and gratulate,
With that thy style, thy keeping of thy state,
In offering this thy work to no great name
That would, perhaps, have praised and thanked the same,   70
But naught beyond. He thou hast given it to,
Thy learnèd chamber-fellow, knows to do
It true respects. He will not only love,
Embrace, and cherish, but he can approve
And estimate thy pains, as having wrought
In the same mines of knowledge, and thence brought
Humanity enough to be a friend,
And strength to be a champion and defend
Thy gift 'gainst envy. O how I do count
Among my comings-in, and see it mount,   80
The gain of your two friendships! Hayward and
Selden: two names that so much understand;
On whom I could take up, and ne'er abuse
The credit, what would furnish a tenth muse!
But here's no time, nor place, my wealth to tell;
You both are modest: so am I. Farewell.

15

An Epistle to a Friend, to Persuade Him to the Wars

Wake, friend, from forth thy lethargy; the drum
Beats brave and loud in Europe, and bids come
All that dare rouse, or are not loath to quit
Their vicious ease and be o'erwhelmed with it.
It is a call to keep the spirits alive
That gasp for action, and would yet revive
Man's buried honour in his sleepy life,
Quickening dead nature to her noblest strife.
All other acts of worldlings are but toil
In dreams, begun in hope, and end in spoil.   10
Look on the ambitious man, and see him nurse
His unjust hopes with praises begged, or (worse)
Bought flatteries, the issue of his purse,
Till he become both their and his own curse!

Look on the false and cunning man, that loves
No person, nor is loved; what ways he proves
To gain upon his belly, and at last
Crushed in the snaky brakes that he had passed!
See the grave, sour, and supercilious sir—
In outward face, but, inward, light as fur   20
Or feathers—lay his fortune out to show,
Till envy wound or maim it at a blow!
See him, that's called and thought the happiest man,
Honoured at once and envied (if it can
Be honour is so mixed) by such as would,
For all their spite, be like him if they could.
No part or corner man can look upon,
But there are objects bid him to be gone
As far as he can fly, or follow day,
Rather than here, so bogged in vices, stay.   30
The whole world here, leavened with madness, swells,
And being a thing blow out of naught, rebels
Against his Maker; high alone with weeds
And impious rankness of all sects and seeds;
Not to be checked or frighted now with fate,
But more licentious made, and desperate!
Our delicacies are grown capital,
And even our sports are dangers; what we call
Friendship is now masked hatred; justice fled,
And shamefastness together; all laws dead   40
That kept man living; pleasures only sought!
Honour and honesty as poor things thought
As they are made; pride and stiff clownage mixed
To make up greatness! And man's whole good fixed
In bravery, or gluttony, or coin,
All which he makes the servants of the groin:
Thither it flows! How much did Stallion spend
To have his court-bred filly there commend
His lace and starch, and fall upon her back
In admiration, stretched upon the rack   50
Of lust, to his rich suit and title, lord?
Aye, that's a charm and half! She must afford
That all respect; she must lie down—nay, more,
'Tis there civility to be a whore.
He's one of blood and fashion! and with these

The bravery makes; she can no honour leese.
To do't with cloth, or stuffs, lust's name might merit;
With velvet, plush, and tissues, it is spirit.
Oh, these so ignorant monsters! light, as proud;
Who can behold their manners and not cloud- 60
Like upon them lighten? If nature could
Not make a verse, anger or laughter would,
To see 'em aye discoursing with their glass
How they may make someone that day an ass;
Planting their purls, and curls spread forth like net,
And every dressing for a pitfall set
To catch the flesh in, and to pound a prick.
Be at their visits: see 'em squeamish, sick,
Ready to cast, at one whose band sits ill,
And then leap mad on a neat piccadill, 70
As if a breeze were gotten in their tail;
And firk and jerk, and for the coachman rail,
And jealous each of other, yet think long
To be abroad chanting some bawdy song,
And laugh, and measure thighs, then squeak, spring, itch,
Do all the tricks of a salt lady bitch;
For t'other pound of sweetmeats, he shall feel
That pays, or what he will: the dame is steel.
For these with her young company she'll enter
Where Pitts, or Wright, or Modet would not venter, 80
And comes by these degrees the style to inherit
Of woman of fashion, and a lady of spirit;
Nor is the title questioned with our proud,
Great, brave, and fashioned folk; these are allowed
Adulteries, now, are not so hid, or strange:
They're grown commodity upon exchange.
He that will follow but another's wife
Is loved, though he let out his own for life;
The husband now's called churlish, or a poor
Nature, that will not let his wife be a whore; 90
Or use all arts, or haunt all companies
That may corrupt her, even in his eyes.
The brother trades a sister, and the friend
Lives to the lord, but to the lady's end.
Less must not be thought on than mistress, or,
If it be thought, killed like her embryons; for,

Whom no great mistress hath as yet infamed,
A fellow of coarse lechery is named;
The servant of the serving-woman, in scorn,
Ne'er came to taste the plenteous marriage-horn.   100
    Thus they do talk. And are these objects fit
For man to spend his money on? His wit,
His time, health, soul? Will he for these go throw
Those thousands on his back, shall after blow
His body to the Counters, or the Fleet?
Is it for these that Fine-man meets the street
Coached, or on foot-cloth, thrice changed every day,
To teach each suit he has the ready way
From Hyde Park to the stage, where at the last
His dear and borrowed bravery he must cast?   110
When not his combs, his curling irons, his glass,
Sweet bags, sweet powders, nor sweet words will pass
For less security? O [God], for these
Is it that man pulls on himself disease,
Surfeit, and quarrel; drinks the t'other health,
Or by damnation voids it, or by stealth?
What fury of late is crept into our feasts!
What honour given to the drunkenest guests!
What reputation to bear one glass more,
When oft the bearer is borne out of door!   120
This hath our ill-used freedom and soft peace
Brought on us, and will every hour increase.
Our vices do not tarry in a place,
But being in motion still, or rather in race,
Tilt one upon another, and now bear
This way, now that, as if their number were
More than themselves, or than our lives, could take,
But both fell pressed under the load they make.
    I'll bid thee look no more, but flee, flee, friend,
This precipice and rocks that have no end   130
Or side, but threatens ruin. The whole day
Is not enough now, but the night's to play;
And whilst our states, strength, body, and mind we waste,
Go make ourselves the usurer's at a cast.
He that no more for age, cramps, palsies can
Now use the bones, we see doth hire a man
To take the box up for him, and pursues

The dice with glassen eyes to the glad views
Of what he throws: like lechers grown content
To be beholders, when their powers are spent.   140
   Can we not leave this worm? Or will we not?
Is that the truer excuse, or have we got
In this, and like, an itch of vanity,
That scratching now's our best felicity?
Well, let it go. Yet this is better than
To lose the forms and dignities of men,
To flatter my good lord, and cry his bowl
Runs sweetly as it had his lordship's soul;
Although perhaps it has: what's that to me,
That may stand by and hold my peace? Will he,   150
When I am hoarse with praising his each cast,
Give me but that again, that I must waste
In sugar candied or in buttered beer,
For the recovery of my voice? No, there
Pardon his lordship. Flattery's grown so cheap
With him, for he is followed with that heap
That watch and catch at what they may applaud,
As a poor single flatterer, without bawd,
Is nothing; such scarce meat and drink he'll give;
But he that's both, and slave to boot, shall live   160
And be beloved, while the whores last. O times!
Friend, fly from hence, and let these kindled rhymes
Light thee from hell on earth; where flatterers, spies,
Informers, masters both of arts and lies,
Lewd slanderers, soft whisperers that let blood
The life and fame-veins (yet not understood
Of the poor sufferers); where the envious, proud,
Ambitious, factious, superstitious, loud
Boasters, and perjured, with the infinite more
Prevaricators swarm. Of which the store   170
(Because they are everywhere amongst mankind
Spread through the world) is easier far to find
Than once to number, or bring forth to hand,
Though thou wert muster-master of the land.
   Go, quit 'em all. And take along with thee
Thy true friend's wishes, Colby, which shall be
That thine be just and honest; that thy deeds
Not wound thy conscience, when thy body bleeds;

That thou dost all things more for truth than glory,
And never but for doing wrong be sorry;   180
That by commanding first thyself, thou mak'st
Thy person fit for any charge thou tak'st;
That fortune never make thee to complain,
But what she gives thou dar'st give her again;
That whatsoever face thy fate puts on,
Thou shrink or start not, but be always one;
That thou think nothing great but what is good,
And from that thought strive to be understood.
So, 'live or dead, thou wilt preserve a fame
Still precious with the odour of thy name.   190
And last, blaspheme not; we did never hear
Man thought the valianter 'cause he durst swear,
No more than we should think a lord had had
More honour in him 'cause we have known him mad:
These take, and now go seek thy peace in war;
Who falls for love of God shall rise a star.

16

An Epitaph on Master Philip Gray

Reader, stay,
And if I had no more to say
But here doth lie, till the last day,
All that is left of Philip Gray,
It might thy patience richly pay:
For if such men as he could die,
What surety of life have thou, and I?

17

Epistle to a Friend

They are not, sir, worst owers, that do pay
    Debts when they can; good men may break their day,
And yet the noble nature never grudge;
    'Tis then a crime, when the usurer is judge,

And he is not in friendship. Nothing there
    Is done for gain; if't be, 'tis not sincere.
Nor should I at this time protested be,
    But that some greater names have broke with me,
And their words too, where I but break my band.
    I add that 'but' because I understand   10
That as the lesser breach; for he that takes
    Simply my band, his trust in me forsakes
And looks unto the forfeit. If you be
    Now so much friend as you would trust in me,
Venture a longer time, and willingly;
    All is not barren land doth fallow lie.
Some grounds are made the richer for the rest,
    And I will bring a crop, if not the best.

18

An Elegy

Can beauty that did prompt me first to write,
    Now threaten with those means she did invite?
Did her perfections call me on to gaze,
    Then like, then love, and now would they amaze?
Or was she gracious afar off, but near
    A terror? Or is all this but my fear?
That as the water makes things put in't straight,
    Crooked appear, so that doth my conceit;
I can help that with boldness; and love sware,
    And fortune once, to assist the spirits that dare.   10
But which shall lead me on? Both these are blind;
    Such guides men use not, who their way would find,
Except the way be error to those ends,
    And then the best are, still, the blindest friends!
Oh how a lover may mistake! To think
    Or love or fortune blind, when they but wink
To see men fear; or else, for truth and state,
    Because they would free justice imitate,
Veil their own eyes, and would impartially
    Be brought by us to meet our destiny.   20

If it be thus, come love, and fortune go;
  I'll lead you on; or if my fate will so
That I must send one first, my choice assigns
  Love to my heart, and fortune to my lines.

19

An Elegy

By those bright eyes, at whose immortal fires
  Love lights his torches to inflame desires;
By that fair stand, your forehead, whence he bends
  His double bow, and round his arrows sends;
By that tall grove, your hair, whose globy rings
  He flying curls and crispeth with his wings;
By those pure baths your either cheek discloses,
  Where he doth steep himself in milk and roses;
And lastly by your lips, the bank of kisses,
  Where men at once may plant and gather blisses: 10
Tell me, my loved friend, do you love, or no,
  So well as I may tell in verse, 'tis so?
You blush, but do not; friends are either none,
  Though they may number bodies, or but one.
I'll therefore ask no more, but bid you love;
  And so, that either may example prove
Unto the other, and live patterns how
  Others in time may love, as we do now.
Slip no occasion; as time stands not still,
  I know no beauty, nor no youth that will.   20
To use the present, then, is not abuse,
  You have a husband is the just excuse
Of all that can be done him; such a one
  As would make shift to make himself, alone,
That which we can; who both in you, his wife,
  His issue, and all circumstance of life,
As in his place, because he would not vary,
  Is constant to be extraordinary.

20

A Satirical Shrub

A woman's friendship! God whom I trust in,
  Forgive me this one foolish deadly sin,
Amongst my many other, that I may
  No more (I am sorry for so fond cause) say
At fifty years, almost, to value it
  That ne'er was known to last above a fit!
Or have the least of good, but what it must
  Put on for fashion, and take up on trust.
Knew I all this afore? Had I perceived
  That their whole life was wickedness, though weaved   10
Of many colours; outward, fresh from spots,
  But their whole inside full of ends and knots?
Knew I that all their dialogues and discourse
  Were such as I will now relate, or worse?
         Here something is wanting.
   *   *   *   *   *   *
   *   *   *   *   *   *
Knew I this woman? Yes; and you do see
  How penitent I am, or I should be!
Do not you ask to know her; she is worse
  Than all ingredients made into one curse,
And that poured out upon mankind, can be!
  Think but the sin of all her sex, 'tis she!   20
I could forgive her being proud, a whore,
  Perjured, and painted, if she were no more:
But she is such, as she might yet forestall
  The devil, and be the damning of us all.

21

A Little Shrub Growing By

Ask not to know this man. If fame should speak
  His name in any metal, it would break.
Two letters were enough the plague to tear
  Out of his grave, and poison every ear.

A parcel of court dirt, a heap and mass
   Of all vice hurled together; there he was
Proud, false, and treacherous, vindictive, all
   That thought can add: unthankful, the lay-stall
Of putrid flesh alive; of blood the sink;
   And so I leave to stir him, lest he stink.   10

22

An Elegy

Though beauty be the mark of praise,
   And yours of whom I sing be such
   As not the world can praise too much,
Yet is't your virtue now I raise.

A virtue, like alloy, so gone
   Throughout your form, as though that move,
   And draw, and conquer all men's love,
This subjects you to love of one.

Wherein you triumph yet, because
   'Tis of yourself, and that you use   10
   The noblest freedom, not to choose
Against or faith, or honour's laws.

But who should less expect from you,
   In whom alone Love lives again?
   By whom he is restored to men,
And kept, and bred, and brought up true.

His falling temples you have reared,
   The withered garlands ta'en away,
   His altars kept from the decay
That envy wished, and nature feared.   20

And on them burn so chaste a flame
   With so much loyalty's expense,
   As Love, to acquit such excellence,
Is gone himself into your name.

And you are he, the deity
   To whom all lovers are designed
   That would their better objects find;
Among which faithful troop am I.

Who, as an offering at your shrine,
   Have sung this hymn, and here entreat   30
   One spark of your diviner heat
To light upon a love of mine.

Which if it kindle not, but scant
   Appear, and that to shortest view,
   Yet give me leave to adore in you
What I, in her, am grieved to want.

23

An Ode. To Himself

Where dost thou careless lie,
   Buried in ease and sloth?
Knowledge that sleeps doth die;
And this security,
   It is the common moth
That eats on wits and arts, and [oft] destroys them both.

Are all the Aonian springs
   Dried up? Lies Thespia waste?
Doth Clarius' harp want strings,
That not a nymph now sings?   10
   Or droop they, as disgraced
To see their seats and bowers by chattering pies defaced?

If hence thy silence be,
   As 'tis too just a cause,
Let this thought quicken thee:
Minds that are great and free,
   Should not on fortune pause;
'Tis crown enough to virtue still, her own applause.

What though the greedy fry
   Be taken with false baits   20
Of worded balladry,
   And think it poesy?
      They die with their conceits,
And only piteous scorn upon their folly waits.

Then take in hand thy lyre,
   Strike in thy proper strain;
With Japhet's line, aspire
   Sol's chariot for new fire
      To give the world again;
Who aided him, will thee, the issue of Jove's brain.   30

And since our dainty age
   Cannot endure reproof,
Make not thyself a page
   To that strumpet, the stage;
      But sing high and aloof,
Safe from the wolf's black jaw, and the dull ass's hoof.

24

The Mind of the Frontispiece to a Book

From death and dark oblivion (near the same)
   The mistress of man's life, grave history,
Raising the world to good or evil fame
   Doth vindicate it to eternity.
Wise providence would so, that nor the good
   Might be defrauded, nor the great secured,
But both might know their ways were understood,
   When vice alike in time with virtue dured.
Which makes that, lighted by the beamy hand
   Of truth that searcheth the most [hidden] springs,   10
And guided by experience, whose straight wand
   Doth mete, whose line doth sound the depth of things,
She cheerfully supporteth what she rears,
   Assisted by no strengths but are her own;

The frontispiece to Sir Walter Raleigh's *History of the World* (1614), engraved by
Renold Elstracke from a design by Raleigh

Some note of which each varied pillar bears;
   By which, as proper titles, she is known
Time's witness, herald of antiquity,
   The light of truth, and life of memory.

25

An Ode to James, Earl of Desmond.
Writ in Queen Elizabeth's Time,
Since Lost, and Recovered

Where art thou, genius? I should use
   Thy present aid; arise invention,
Wake, and put on the wings of Pindar's muse,
   To tower with my intention
   High as his mind, that doth advance
Her upright head above the reach of chance,
     Or the time's envy;
     Cinthius, I apply
My bolder numbers to thy golden lyre:
     Oh, then inspire   10
Thy priest in this strange rapture; heat my brain
     With Delphic fire,
That I may sing my thoughts in some unvulgar strain.

   Rich beam of honour, shed your light
   On these dark rhymes, that my affection
May shine through every chink, to every sight,
   Graced by your reflection!
   Then shall my verses, like strong charms,
Break the knit circle of her stony arms
     That hold[s] your spirit,   20
     And keeps your merit
Locked in her cold embraces, from the view
     Of eyes more true,
Who would with judgement search, searching conclude
     (As proved in you)
True noblesse. Palm grows straight, though handled ne'er
     so rude.

Nor think yourself unfortunate,
If subject to the jealous errors
Of politic pretext, that wries a state;
    Sink not beneath these terrors,   30
    But whisper, O glad innocence,
Where only a man's birth is his offence;
      Or the disfavour,
      Of such as savour
Nothing, but practise upon honour's thrall.
      O virtue's fall!
When her dead essence, like the anatomy
      In Surgeons' Hall,
Is but a statist's theme, to read phlebotomy.

    Let Brontes and black Steropes   40
    Sweat at the forge, their hammers beating;
Pyracmon's hour will come to give them ease,
    Though but while metal's heating;
    And after all the Aetnean ire
Gold that is perfect will outlive the fire.
      For fury wasteth,
      As patience lasteth.
No armour to the mind! He is shot-free
      From injury
That is not hurt, not he that is not hit;   50
      So fools, we see,
Oft 'scape an imputation more through luck than wit.

    But to yourself, most loyal lord,
    Whose heart in that bright sphere flames clearest,
Though many gems be in your bosom stored,
    Unknown which is the dearest,
    If I auspiciously divine,
As my hope tells, that our fair Phoeb[e]'s shine
      Shall light those places
      With lustrous graces,   60
Where darkness with her gloomy-sceptred hand
      Doth now command;
O then, my best-best loved, let me importune,
      That you will stand
As far from all revolt, as you are now from fortune.

26

An Ode

High-spirited friend,
I send nor balms nor corsives to your wound;
Your fate hath found
A gentler and more agile hand to tend
The cure of that, which is but corporal,
And doubtful days (which were named critical)
Have made their fairest flight,
And now are out of sight.
Yet doth some wholesome physic for the mind
Wrapped in this paper lie,   10
Which in the taking, if you misapply,
You are unkind.

Your covetous hand,
Happy in that fair honour it hath gained,
Must now be reined.
True valour doth her own renown command
In one full action; nor have you now more
To do than be a husband of that store.
Think but how dear you bought
This fame which you have caught;   20
Such thoughts will make you more in love with truth.
'Tis wisdom, and that high,
For men to use their fortune reverently,
Even in youth.

27

An Ode

Helen, did Homer never see
Thy beauties, yet could write of thee?
Did Sappho, on her seven-tongued lute,
So speak, as yet it is not mute,
Of Phao[n]'s form? Or doth the boy
In whom Anacreon once did joy,

Lie drawn to life in his soft verse,
As he whom Maro did rehearse?
Was Lesbia sung by learn'd Catullus,
Or Delia's graces by Tibullus?   10
Doth Cinthia in Propertius' song
Shine more than she the stars among?
Is Horace his each love so high,
Rapt from the earth, as not to die;
With bright Lycoris, Gallus' choice,
Whose fame hath an eternal voice?
Or hath Corinna, by the name
Her Ovid gave her, dimmed the fame
Of Caesar's daughter, and the line
Which all the world then styled divine?   20
Hath Petrarch since his Laura raised
Equal with her; or Ronsard praised
His new Cassandra 'bove the old
Which all the fate of Troy foretold?
Hath our great Sidney Stella set,
Where never star shone brighter yet;
Or Constable's ambrosiac muse
Made Dian not his notes refuse?
Have all these done—and yet I miss
The swan that so relished Pancharis—   30
And shall not I my Celia bring
Where men may see whom I do sing?
Though I, in working of my song,
Come short of all this learnèd throng,
Yet sure my tunes will be the best,
So much my subject drowns the rest.

28

A Sonnet
to the Noble Lady, the Lady Mary Worth

I, that have been a lover, and could show it,
   Though not in these, in rhymes not wholly dumb,
   Since I exscribe your sonnets, am become
A better lover, and much better poet.

Nor is my muse or I ashamed to owe it
  To those true numerous graces, whereof some
  But charm the senses, others overcome
Both brains and hearts; and mine now best do know it:
For in your verse all Cupid's armory,
  His flames, his shafts, his quiver, and his bow,   10
  His very eyes are yours to overthrow.
But then his mother's sweets you so apply,
Her joys, her smiles, her loves, as readers take
For Venus' ceston every line you make.

29

A Fit of Rhyme against Rhyme

Rhyme, the rack of finest wits
That expresseth but by fits
            True conceit;
Spoiling senses of their treasure,
Cozening judgement with a measure
            But false weight.
Wresting words from their true calling,
Propping verse for fear of falling
            To the ground.
Jointing syllabes, drowning letters,   10
Fastening vowels, as with fetters
            They were bound!
Soon as lazy thou wert known,
All good poetry hence was flown,
            And art banished.
For a thousand years together
All Parnassus' green did wither,
            And wit vanished.
Pegasus did fly away,
At the well no muse did stay,   20
            But bewailed
So to see the fountain dry,
And Apollo's music die,
            All light failed!

Starveling rhymes did fill the stage,
Not a poet in an age
         Worth [a-]crowning.
Not a work deserving bays,
Nor a line deserving praise,
         Pallas frowning.   30
Greek was free from rhyme's infection,
Happy Greek by this protection,
         Was not spoiled.
Whilst the Latin, queen of tongues,
Is not yet free from rhyme's wrongs,
         But rests foiled.
Scarce the hill again doth flourish,
Scarce the world a wit doth nourish,
         To restore
Phoebus to his crown again,   40
And the muses to their brain,
         As before.
Vulgar languages that want
Words and sweetness, and be scant
         Of true measure,
Tyrant rhyme hath so abused,
That they long since have refused
         Other caesure.
He that first invented thee,
May his joints tormented be,   50
         Cramped for ever;
Still may syllabes jar with time,
Still may reason war with rhyme,
         Resting never.
May his sense, when it would meet
The cold tumour in his feet,
         Grow unsounder.
And his title be long fool,
That in rearing such a school,
         Was the founder.   60

30

An Epigram
on Will[i]am, Lord Burghl[ey],
Lo[rd] High Treasurer of England

If thou wouldst know the virtues of mankind,
   Read here in one, what thou in all canst find,
And go no farther; let this circle be
   Thy universe, though his epitome.
Cecil, the grave, the wise, the great, the good:
   What is there more that can ennoble blood?
The orphan's pillar, the true subject's shield,
   The poor's full store-house, and just servant's field.
The only faithful watchman for the realm,
   That in all tempests never quit the helm,   10
But stood unshaken in his deeds and name,
   And laboured in the work, not with the fame;
That still was good for goodness' sake, nor thought
   Upon reward, till the reward him sought.
Whose offices and honours did surprise
   Rather than meet him; and before his eyes
Closed to their peace, he saw his branches shoot,
   And in the noblest families took root
Of all the land. Who now at such a rate
   Of divine blessing, would not serve a state?   20

31

An Epigram
to Thomas, Lo[rd] Ellesmere,
the Last Term He Sat Chancellor

So, justest lord, may all your judgements be
   Laws, and no change e'er come to one decree;
So may the king proclaim your conscience is
   Law to his law, and think your enemies his;
So from all sickness may you rise to health,
   The care and wish still of the public wealth;

So may the gentler muses, and good fame
   Still fly about the odour of your name:
As, with the safety and honour of the laws,
   You favour truth, and me, in this man's cause.   10

32

Another to Him

The judge his favour timely then extends
   When a good cause is destitute of friends,
Without the pomp of counsel, or more aid
   Than to make falsehood blush, and fraud afraid,
When those good few that her defenders be
   Are there for charity, and not for fee.
Such shall you hear today, and find great foes,
   Both armed with wealth and slander to oppose,
Who, thus long safe, would gain upon the times
   A right by the prosperity of their crimes;   10
Who, though their guilt and perjury they know,
   Think—yea, and boast—that they have done it so,
As, though the court pursues them on the scent,
   They will come off, and 'scape the punishment.
When this appears, just lord, to your sharp sight,
   He does you wrong that craves you to do right.

33

An Epigram to the Counsellor that Pleaded and Carried the Cause

That I, hereafter, do not think the Bar
   The seat made of a more than civil war,
Or the Great Hall at Westminster the field
   Where mutual frauds are fought, and no side yield;
That, henceforth, I believe nor books nor men
   Who 'gainst the law weave calumnies, my [Benn],
But when I read or hear the names so rife
   Of hirelings, wranglers, stitchers-to of strife,

Hook-handed harpies, gownèd vultures, put
   Upon the reverend pleaders; do now shut   10
All mouths that dare entitle them (from hence)
   To the wolf's study, or dog's eloquence:
Thou art my cause; whose manners since I knew,
   Have made me to conceive a lawyer new.
So dost thou study matter, men, and times,
   Mak'st it religion to grow rich by crimes;
Dar'st not abuse thy wisdom in the laws,
   Or skill, to carry out an evil cause,
But first dost vex and search it. If not sound,
   Thou prov'st the gentler ways to cleanse the wound,   20
And make the scar fair; if that will not be,
   Thou hast the brave scorn to put back the fee.
But in a business that will bide the touch,
   What use, what strength of reason! and how much
Of books, of precedents hast thou at hand!
   As if the general store thou didst command
Of argument, still drawing forth the best,
   And not being borrowed by thee, but possessed.
So com'st thou like a chief into the court,
   Armed at all pieces, as to keep a fort   30
Against a multitude, and (with thy style
   So brightly brandished) wound'st, defend'st—the while
Thy adversaries fall, as not a word
   They had, but were a reed unto thy sword.
Then com'st thou off with victory and palm,
   Thy hearers' nectar, and thy client's balm,
The court's just honour, and thy judge's love.
   And (which doth all achievements get above)
Thy sincere practice breeds not thee a fame
   Alone, but all thy rank a reverend name.   40

34

An Epigram to the Smallpox

Envious and foul disease, could there not be
   One beauty in an age, and free from thee?

What did she worth thy spite? Were there not store
   Of those that set by their false faces more
Than this did by her true? She never sought
   Quarrel with nature, or in balance brought
Art, her false servant; nor, for Sir Hugh Platt
   Was drawn to practise other hue than that
Her own blood gave her; she ne'er had, nor hath
   Any belief in Madam Bawd-be's bath,   10
Or Turner's oil of talc; nor ever got
   Spanish receipt to make her teeth to rot.
What was the cause, then? Thought'st thou in disgrace
   Of beauty so to nullify a face
That heaven should make no more; or should amiss
   Make all hereafter, hadst thou ruined this?
Aye, that thy aim was: but her fate prevailed;
   And, scorned, thou hast shown thy malice, but hast failed.

35

An Epitaph [on Elizabeth Chute]

What beauty would have lovely styled,
What manners pretty, nature mild,
What wonder perfect, all were filed,
Upon record, in this blest child.
   And till the coming of the soul
   To fetch the flesh, we keep the roll.

36

A Song

Lover
Come, let us here enjoy the shade,
For love in shadow best is made.
Though envy oft his shadow be,
None brooks the sunlight worse than he.

Mistress

Where love doth shine, there needs no sun,
All lights into his one doth run;
Without which all the world were dark,
Yet he himself is but a spark.

Arbiter

A spark to set whole world[s] afire,
Who more they burn, they more desire,   10
And have their being their waste to see,
And waste still, that they still might be.

Chorus

Such are his powers, whom time hath styled
Now swift, now slow, now tame, now wild;
Now hot, now cold, now fierce, now mild;
The eldest god, yet still a child.

37

An Epistle to a Friend

Sir, I am thankful, first to heaven for you;
   Next to yourself, for making your love true;
   Then to your love and gift. And all's but due.

You have unto my store added a book,
   On which with profit I shall never look
   But must confess from whom what gift I took.

Not like your country neighbours, that commit
   Their vice of loving for a Christmas fit,
   Which is indeed but friendship of the spit;

But as a friend, which name yourself receive,   10
   And which you, being the worthier, gave me leave
   In letters, that mix spirits, thus to weave.

Which, how most sacred I will ever keep,
   So may the fruitful vine my temples steep,
   And fame wake for me, when I yield to sleep.

Though you sometimes proclaim me too severe,
   Rigid, and harsh, which is a drug austere
   In friendship, I confess: but, dear friend, hear:

Little know they that profess amity,
   And seek to scant her comely liberty,   20
   How much they lame her in her property.

And less they know, who being free to use
   That friendship which no chance, but love, did choose,
   Will unto licence that fair leave abuse.

It is an act of tyranny, not love,
   In practised friendship wholly to reprove,
   As flattery with friends' humours still to move.

From each of which I labour to be free;
   Yet if with either's vice I tainted be,
   Forgive it as my frailty, and not me.   30

For no man lives so out of passion's sway,
   But shall sometimes be tempted to obey
   Her fury, yet no friendship to betray.

38

An Elegy

'Tis true, I'm broke! Vows, oaths, and all I had
   Of credit lost. And I am now run mad,
Or do upon myself some desperate ill;
   This sadness makes no approaches but to kill.
It is a darkness hath blocked up my sense,
   And drives it in to eat on my offence,
Or there to starve it. Help, O you that may
   Alone lend succours, and this fury stay,
Offended mistress; you are yet so fair,
   As light breaks from you that affrights despair,   10
And fills my powers with persuading joy
   That you should be too noble to destroy.

There may some face or menace of a storm
   Look forth, but cannot last in such [a] form.
If there be nothing worthy you can see
   Of graces, or your mercy here in me,
Spare your own goodness yet, and be not great
   In will and power, only to defeat.
God, and the good, know to forgive and save;
   The ignorant and fools no pity have.   20
I will not stand to justify my fault,
   Or lay the excuse upon the vintner's vault,
Or in confessing of the crime be nice,
   Or go about to countenance the vice,
By naming in what company 'twas in,
   As I would urge authority for sin.
No, I will stand arraigned and cast, to be
   The subject of your grace in pardoning me,
And, styled your mercy's creature, will live more
   Your honour now than your disgrace before.   30
Think it was frailty, mistress, think me man,
   Think that yourself, like heaven, forgive me can;
Where weakness doth offend, and virtue grieve,
   There greatness takes a glory to relieve.
Think that I once was yours, or may be now;
   Nothing is vile that is a part of you.
Error and folly in me may have crossed
   Your just commands, yet those, not I, be lost.
I am regenerate now, become the child
   Of your compassion. Parents should be mild;   40
There is no father that for one demerit,
   Or two, or three, a son will disinherit;
That as the last of punishments is meant:
   No man inflicts that pain till hope be spent.
An ill-affected limb, whate'er it ail,
   We cut not off till all cures else do fail;
And then with pause; for severed once, that's gone
   Would live his glory, that could keep it on.
Do not despair my mending; to distrust
   Before you prove a medicine, is unjust.   50
You may so place me, and in such an air,
   As not alone the cure, but scar be fair.
That is, if still your favours you apply,

And not the bounties you have done, deny.
Could you demand the gifts you gave again?
   Why was't? Did e'er the clouds ask back their rain?
The sun his heat and light, the air his dew,
   Or winds the spirit by which the flower so grew?
That were to wither all, and make a grave
   Of that wise nature would a cradle have.   60
Her order is to cherish and preserve;
   Consumption's nature to destroy and starve.
But to exact again what once is given
   Is nature's mere obliquity!—as heaven
Should ask the blood and spirits he hath infused
   In man, because man hath the flesh abused.
O may your wisdom take example hence:
   God lightens not at man's each frail offence;
He pardons slips, goes by a world of ills,
   And then his thunder frights more than it kills.   70
He cannot angry be, but all must quake,
   It shakes even him that all things else doth shake.
And how more fair and lovely looks the world
   In a calm sky, than when the heaven is hurled
About in clouds, and wrapped in raging weather,
   As all with storm and tempest ran together.
O imitate that sweet serenity
   That makes us live, not that which calls to die.
In dark and sullen morns, do we not say,
   This looketh like an execution day?   80
And with the vulgar doth it not obtain
   The name of cruel weather, storm, and rain?
Be not affected with these marks too much
   Of cruelty, lest they do make you such.
But view the mildness of your Maker's state,
   As I the penitent's here emulate:
He, when he sees a sorrow such as this,
   Straight puts off all his anger, and doth kiss
The contrite soul, who hath no thought to win
   Upon the hope to have another sin   90
Forgiven him. And in that line stand I
   Rather than once displease you more, to die;
To suffer tortures, scorn, and infamy;
   What fools, and all their parasites can apply,

The wit of ale and genius of the malt
 Can pump for, or a libel without salt
Produce; though threatening with a coal or chalk
 On every wall, and sung where'er I walk.
I number these as being of the chore
 Of contumely, and urge a good man more   100
Than sword, or fire, or what is of the race
 To carry noble danger in the face:
There is not any punishment, or pain,
 A man should fly from, as he would disdain.
Then mistress, here, here let your rigour end,
 And let your mercy make me ashamed to offend.
I will no more abuse my vows to you
 Than I will study falsehood, to be true.
Oh, that you could but by dissection see
 How much you are the better part of me;   110
How all my fibres by your spirit do move;
 And that there is no life in me, but love.
You would be then most confident, that though
 Public affairs command me now to go
Out of your eyes, and be awhile away,
 Absence or distance shall not breed decay.
Your form shines here, here fixèd in my heart:
 I may dilate myself, but not depart.
Others by common stars their courses run,
 When I see you, then I do see my sun,   120
Till then 'tis all but darkness that I have;
 Rather than want your light, I wish a grave.

[For *Und.* 39, see *Dubia*, 1]

40

An Elegy

That love's a bitter sweet I ne'er conceive
 Till the sour minute comes of taking leave,
And then I taste it. But as men drink up
 In haste the bottom of a medicined cup,

And take some syrup after, so do I,
  To put all relish from my memory
Of parting, drown it in the hope to meet
  Shortly again, and make our absence sweet.
This makes me, mistress, that sometime by stealth,
  Under another name, I take your health,   10
And turn the ceremonies of those nights
  I give or owe my friends, into your rites:
But ever without blazon, or least shade
  Of vows so sacred, and in silence made;
For though love thrive, and may grow up with cheer
  And free society, he's born elsewhere,
And must be bred so to conceal his birth,
  As neither wine do rack it out, or mirth.
Yet should the lover still be airy and light,
  In all his actions rarefied to sprite;   20
Not, like a Midas, shut up in himself,
  And turning all he toucheth into pelf,
Keep in, reserved, in his dark-lantern face,
  As if that excellent dullness were love's grace;
No, mistress, no, the open merry man
  Moves like a sprightly river, and yet can
Keep secret in his channels what he breeds,
  'Bove all your standing waters, choked with weeds.
They look at best like cream bowls, and you soon
  Shall find their depth: they're sounded with a spoon. 30
They may say grace, and for love's chaplains pass,
  But the grave lover ever was an ass;
Is fixed upon one leg, and dares not come
  Out with the other, for he's still at home;
Like the dull wearied crane that, come on land,
  Doth, while he keeps his watch, betray his stand.
Where he that knows will, like a lapwing, fly
  Far from the nest, and so himself belie
To others as he will deserve the trust
  Due to that one that doth believe him just.   40
And such your servant is, who vows to keep
  The jewel of your name as close as sleep
Can lock the sense up, or the heart a thought,
  And never be by time or folly brought,
Weakness of brain, or any charm of wine,

The sin of boast, or other countermine
   (Made to blow up love's secrets) to discover
     That article may not become [y]our lover:
   Which in assurance to your breast I tell,
     If I had writ no word but Dear, farewell.   50

41

An Elegy

Since you must go, and I must bid farewell,
   Hear, mistress, your departing servant tell
What it is like, and do not think they can
   Be idle words, though of a parting man:
It is as if a night should shade noonday,
   Or that the sun was here, but forced away,
And we were left under that hemisphere
   Where we must feel it dark for half a year.
What fate is this, to change men's days and hours,
   To shift their seasons and destroy their powers!   10
Alas, I ha' lost my heat, my blood, my prime,
   Winter is come a quarter ere his time;
My health will leave me; and when you depart
   How shall I do, sweet mistress, for my heart?
You would restore it? No, that's worth a fear
   As if it were not worthy to be there:
Oh, keep it still, for it had rather be
   Your sacrifice than here remain with me.
And so I spare it. Come what can become
   Of me, I'll softly tread unto my tomb;   20
Or like a ghost walk silent amongst men,
   Till I may see both it and you again.

42

An Elegy

Let me be what I am: as Virgil cold,
   As Horace fat, or as Anacreon old;

No poet's verses yet did ever move,
  Whose readers did not think he was in love.
Who shall forbid me then in rhyme to be
  As light and active as the youngest he
That from the muses' fountains doth endorse
  His lines, and hourly sits the poet's horse?
Put on my ivy garland; let me see
  Who frowns, who jealous is, who taxeth me.   10
Fathers and husbands, I do claim a right
  In all that is called lovely: take my sight
Sooner than my affection from the fair.
  No face, no hand, proportion, line, or air
Of beauty, but the muse hath interest in;
  There is not worn that lace, purl, knot, or pin,
But is the poet's matter; and he must,
  When he is furious, love, although not lust.
But then consent, your daughters and your wives,
  If they be fair and worth it, have their lives   20
Made longer by our praises. Or, if not,
  Wish you had foul ones and deformèd got,
Cursed in their cradles, or there changed by elves,
  So to be sure you do enjoy yourselves.
Yet keep those up in sackcloth too, or leather,
  For silk will draw some sneaking songster thither.
It is a rhyming age, and verses swarm
  At every stall; the city cap's a charm.
But I who live, and have lived, twenty year
  Where I may handle silk as free and near   30
As any mercer, or the whale-bone man
  That quilts those bodies, I have leave to span;
Have eaten with the beauties and the wits
  And braveries of court, and felt their fits
Of love and hate, and came so nigh to know
  Whether their faces were their own or no;
It is not likely I should now look down
  Upon a velvet petticoat or a gown,
Whose like I have known the tailor's wife put on
  To do her husband's rites in, ere 'twere gone   40
Home to the customer; his lechery
  Being, the best clothes still to preoccupy.
Put a coach-mare in tissue, must I horse

Her presently? or leap thy wife of force,
When by thy sordid bounty she hath on
    A gown of that was the caparison?
So I might dote upon thy chairs and stools
    That are like clothed: must I be of those fools
Of race accounted, that no passion have
    But when thy wife, as thou conceiv'st, is brave?   50
Then ope thy wardrobe, think me that poor groom
    That from the footman, when he was become
An officer there, did make most solemn love
    To every petticoat he brushed, and glove
He did lay up, and would adore the shoe
    Or slipper was left off, and kiss it too;
Court every hanging gown, and after that
    Lift up some one and do I tell not what.
Thou didst tell me, and wert o'erjoyed to peep
    In at a hole, and see these actions creep   60
From the poor wretch, which, though he played in prose,
    He would have done in verse with any of those
Wrung on the withers by Lord Love's despite,
    Had he'd the faculty to read and write!
Such songsters there are store of: witness he
    That chanced the lace laid on a smock to see
And straightway spent a sonnet; with that other
    That (in pure madrigal) unto his mother
Commended the French hood and scarlet gown
    The Lady Mayoress passed in through the town   70
Unto the Spittle sermon. Oh, what strange
    Variety of silks were on the Exchange,
Or in Moorfields this other night! sings one;
    Another answers, 'las, those silks are none,
In smiling l'envoy, as he would deride
    Any comparison had with his Cheapside.
And vouches both the pageant and the day,
    When not the shops but windows do display
The stuffs, the velvets, plushes, fringes, lace,
    And all the original riots of the place.   80
Let the poor fools enjoy their follies, love
    A goat in velvet, or some block could move
Under that cover, an old midwife's hat,
    Or a close-stool so cased, or any fat

Bawd in a velvet scabbard! I envy
  None of their pleasures, nor will ask thee why
Thou art jealous of thy wife's or daughter's case:
  More than of either's manners, wit, or face.

43

An Execration upon Vulcan

And why to me this, thou lame lord of fire,
  What had I done that might call on thine ire?
Or urge thy greedy flame thus to devour
  So many my years' labours in an hour?
I ne'er attempted, Vulcan, 'gainst thy life,
  Nor made least line of love to thy loose wife,
Or in remembrance of thy affront and scorn,
  With clowns and tradesmen, kept thee closed in horn.
'Twas Jupiter that hurled thee headlong down,
  And Mars that gave thee a lanthorn for a crown.   10
Was it because thou wert of old denied
  By Jove to have Minerva for thy bride
That, since, thou tak'st all envious care and pain
  To ruin any issue of the brain?
Had I wrote treason there, or heresy,
  Imposture, witchcraft, charms, or blasphemy,
I had deserved, then, thy consuming looks;
  Perhaps to have been burnèd with my books.
But, on thy malice, tell me, didst thou spy
  Any least loose or s[c]urrile paper lie   20
Concealed or kept there, that was fit to be,
  By thy own vote, a sacrifice to thee?
Did I there wound the honour of the crown,
  Or tax the glories of the church and gown,
Itch to defame the state, or brand the times,
  And myself most, in some self-boasting rhymes?
If none of these, then why this fire? Or find
  A cause before, or leave me one behind.
Had I compiled from Amadis de Gaul,
  The Esplandians, Arthurs, Palmerins, and all   30
The learnèd library of Don Quixote,
  And so some goodlier monster had begot;

Or spun out riddles, and weaved fifty tomes
    Of logogriphs, and curious palindromes;
Or pumped for those hard trifles, anagrams,
    Or eteostics, or those finer flams
Of eggs, and halberds, cradles and a hearse,
    A pair of scissors and a comb in verse,
Acrostics and telestichs on jump names,
    Thou then hadst had some colour for thy flames   40
On such my serious follies. But, thou'lt say,
    There were some pieces of as base allay,
And as false stamp there: parcels of a play,
    Fitter to see the fire-light than the day,
Adulterate moneys, such as might not go;
    Thou shouldst have stayed till public fame said so.
She is the judge, thou executioner;
    Or if thou needs wouldst trench upon her power,
Thou mightst have yet enjoyed thy cruelty
    With some more thrift and more variety: 50
Thou mightst have had me perish piece by piece,
    To light tobacco, or save roasted geese,
Singe capons, or poor pigs, dropping their eyes;
    Condemned me to the ovens with the pies,
And so have kept me dying a whole age,
    Not ravished all hence in a minute's rage.
But that's a mark whereof thy rites do boast,
    To make consumption ever, where thou goest.
Had I foreknown of this thy least desire
    To have held a triumph or a feast of fire,   60
Especially in paper, that that steam
    Had tickled your large nostril, many a ream
To redeem mine I had sent in: Enough!
    Thou shouldst have cried, and all been proper stuff.
The Talmud and the Alcoran had come,
    With pieces of the *Legend*; the whole sum
Of errant knighthood, with the dames and dwarfs,
    The charmèd boats, and the enchanted wharves;
The Tristrams, Lancelots, Turpins and the Peers,
    All the mad Rolands, and sweet Olivers,   70
To Merlin's marvels and his cabal's loss,
    With the chimera of the Rosy Cross,
Their seals, their characters, hermetic rings,

Their gem of riches, and bright stone that brings
Invisibility, and strength, and tongues;
  The Art of Kindling the True Coal, by Lungs:
With Nicholas Pasquill's *Meddle With Your Match*,
  And the strong lines, that so the time do catch;
Or Captain Pamp[h]let's horse and foot, that sally
  Upon the Exchange, still, out of Pope's Head Alley; 80
The weekly *Courants*, with Paul's seal, and all
  The admired discourses of the prophet Ball:
These, hadst thou pleased either to dine or sup,
  Had made a meal for Vulcan to lick up.
But in my desk what was there to accite
  So ravenous and vast an appetite?
I dare not say a body, but some parts
  There were of search, and mastery in the arts.
All the old Venusine in poetry,
  And lighted by the Stagirite, could spy 90
Was there mad[e] English; with a Grammar too,
  To teach some that their nurses could [not] do,
The purity of language; and among
  The rest, my journey into Scotland sung,
With all the adventures; three books not afraid
  To speak the fate of the Sicilian maid
To our own ladies; and in story there
  Of our fifth Henry, eight of his nine year;
Wherein was oil, beside the succour, spent
  Which noble Carew, Cotton, Selden lent; 100
And twice twelve years' stored-up humanity,
  With humble gleanings in divinity,
After the fathers, and those wiser guides
  Whom faction had not drawn to study sides.
How in these ruins, Vulcan, thou dost lurk,
  All soot and embers, odious as thy work!
I now begin to doubt if ever grace
  Or goddess could be patient of thy face.
Thou woo Minerva! or to wit aspire!
  'Cause thou canst halt, with us, in arts and fire! 110
Son of the wind—for so thy mother, gone
  With lust, conceived thee; father thou hadst none;
When thou wert born and that thou look'st at best,
  She durst not kiss, but flung thee from her breast.

And so did Jove, who ne'er meant thee his cup:
   Nor mar'l the clowns of Lemnos took thee up,
For none but smiths would have made thee a god.
   Some alchemist there may be yet, or odd
Squire of the squibs, against the pageant day
   May to thy name a *Vulcanale* say,   120
And for it lose his eyes with gunpowder,
   As the other may his brains with quicksilver.
Well fare the wise men yet, on the Bankside,
   My friends the watermen! They could provide
Against thy fury, when to serve their needs
   They made a Vulcan of a sheaf of reeds,
Whom they durst handle in their holiday coats,
   And safely trust to dress, not burn, their boats.
But, O those reeds! Thy mere disdain of them
   Made thee beget that cruel stratagem   130
(Which some are pleased to style but thy mad prank)
   Against the Globe, the glory of the Bank.
Which, though it were the fort of the whole parish,
   Flanked with a ditch and forced out of a marish,
I saw with two poor chambers taken in
   And razed, ere thought could urge, This might have been!
See the world's ruins, nothing but the piles
   Left! and wit since to cover it with tiles.
The brethren, they straight noised it out for news,
   'Twas verily some relic of the stews   140
And this a sparkle of that fire let loose
   That was raked up in the Winchestrian goose
Bred on the Bank, in time of Popery,
   When Venus there maintained the mystery.
But others fell with that conceit by the ears,
   And cried, it was a threatening to the bears,
And that accursèd ground, the Parish Garden;
   Nay, sighed a sister, 'twas the nun, Kate Arden,
Kindled the fire! But then, did one return,
   No fool would his own harvest spoil or burn!   150
If that were so, thou rather wouldst advance
   The place that was thy wife's inheritance.
O no! cried all, Fortune, for being a whore,
   'Scaped not his justice any jot the more;
He burnt that idol of the revels too:

Nay, let Whitehall with revels have to do,
Though but in dances, it shall know his power;
    There was a judgement shown too in an hour.
He is true Vulcan still! He did not spare
    Troy, though it were so much his Venus' care.   160
Fool, wilt thou let that in example come?
    Did not she save from thence to build a Rome?
And what hast thou done in these petty spites,
    More than advanced the houses and their rites?
I will not argue thee, from those, of guilt,
    For they were burnt but to be better built.
'Tis true that in thy wish they were destroyed,
    Which thou hast only vented, not enjoyed.
So wouldst th[ou] have run upon the Rolls by stealth,
    And didst invade part of the commonwealth   170
In those records which, were all chronicle[r]s gone,
    Will be remembered by six clerks to one.
But say, all six good men, what answer ye?
    Lies there no writ out of the Chancery
Against this Vulcan, no injunction,
    No order, no decree? Though we be gone
At common-law, methinks in his despite
    A court of Equity should do us right,
But to confine him to the brew-houses,
    The glass-house, dye-vats, and their furnaces;   180
To live in sea-coal and go forth in smoke,
    Or—lest that vapour might the city choke—
Condemn him to the brick-kilns, or some hill-
    Foot (out in Sussex) to an iron mill;
Or in small faggots have him blaze about
    Vile taverns, and the drunkards piss him out;
Or in the bellman's lanthorn, like a spy,
    Burn to a snuff, and then stink out and die.
I could invent a sentence yet were worse,
    But I'll conclude all in a civil curse: 190
Pox on your flameship, Vulcan; if it be
    To all as fatal as it hath been to me,
And to Paul's steeple, which was unto us
    'Bove all your fireworks had at Ephesus
Or Alexandria; and though a divine
    Loss, remains yet as unrepaired as mine.

Would you had kept your forge at Aetna still,
   And there made swords, bills, glaives, and arms your fill,
Maintained the trade at Bilbo, or elsewhere,
   Struck in at Milan with the cutlers there,   200
Or stayed but where the friar and you first met,
   Who from the Devil's Arse did guns beget,
Or fixed in the Low Countries, where you might
   On both sides do your mischiefs with delight,
Blow up and ruin, mine and countermine,
   Make your petards and granats, all your fine
Engines of murder, and receive the praise
   Of massacring mankind so many ways.
We ask your absence here, we all love peace,
   And pray the fruits thereof and the increase;   210
So doth the king, and most of the king's men
   That have good places: therefore once again
Pox on thee, Vulcan, thy Pandora's pox,
   And all the evils that flew out of her box
Light on thee; of if those plagues will not do,
   Thy wife's pox on thee, and B[ess] B[roughton]'s too.

44

A Speech according to Horace

Why yet, my noble hearts, they cannot say
   But we have powder still for the King's Day,
And ordnance too; so much as from the Tower
   To have waked, if sleeping, Spain's ambassador,
Old Aesop Gondomar: the French can tell,
   For they did see it the last tilting well,
That we have trumpets, armour, and great horse,
   Lances, and men, and some a breaking force.
They saw too store of feathers, and more may,
   If they stay here but till Saint George's Day.   10
All ensigns of a war are not yet dead,
   Nor marks of wealth so from our nation fled
But they may see gold chains and pearl worn then,
   Lent by the London dames to the lords' men;

Withal, the dirty pains those citizens take
    To see the pride at court their wives do make;
And the return those thankful courtiers yield
    To have their husbands drawn forth to the field,
And coming home, to tell what acts were done
    Under the auspice of young Swinnerton.   20
What a strong fort old Pimlico had been,
    How it held out, how (last) 'twas taken in!
Well, I say, thrive; thrive, brave Artillery Yard,
    Thou seed-plot of the war, that hast not spared
Powder or paper to bring up the youth
    Of London in the military truth
These ten years' day, as all may swear that look
    But on thy practice and the posture-book;
He that but saw thy curious captain's drill
    Would think no more of Flushing or the Brill,   30
But give them over to the common ear
    For that unnecessary charge they were.
Well did thy crafty clerk and knight, Sir Hugh,
    Supplant bold Panton, and brought there to view
Translated Aelian['s] *Tactics* to be read
    And the Greek discipline, with the modern, shed
So in that ground, as soon it grew to be
    The City question whether Tilly or he
Were now the greater captain; for they saw
    The Bergen siege, and taking in Breda,   40
So acted to the life, as Maurice might
    And Spinola, have blushèd at the sight.
O happy art, and wise epitome
    Of bearing arms, most civil soldiery!
Thou canst draw forth thy forces, and fight dry
    The battles of thy aldermanity,
Without the hazard of a drop of blood
    More than the surfeits in thee that day stood.
Go on, increase in virtue and in fame,
    And keep the glory of the English name   50
Up among nations. In the stead of bold
    Beauchamps, and Nevilles, Cliffords, Audleys old,
Insert thy Hodges, and those newer men,
    As Styles, Dyke, Ditchfield, Millar, Crips, and Fenn;
That keep the war, though now it be grown more tame,

Alive yet in the noise, and still the same;
And could, if our great men would let their sons
   Come to their schools, show 'em the use of guns,
And there instruct the noble English heirs
   In politic and militar affairs.   60
But he that should persuade to have this done
   For education of our lordings, soon
Should he hear of billow, wind, and storm
   From the tempestuous grandlings: Who'll inform
Us in our bearing, that are thus and thus
   Born, bred, allied? What's he dare tutor us?
Are we by bookworms to be awed? Must we
   Live by their scale that dare do nothing free?
Why are we rich or great, except to show
   All licence in our lives? What need we know   70
More than to praise a dog, or horse, or speak
   The hawking language; or our day to break
With citizens? Let clowns and tradesmen breed
   Their sons to study arts, the laws, the creed;
We will believe, like men of our own rank
   In so much land a year, or such a bank
That turns us so much moneys, at which rate
   Our ancestors imposed on prince and state.
Let poor nobility be virtuous; we,
   Descended in a rope of titles, be   80
From Guy, or Bevis, Arthur, or from whom
   The herald will. Our blood is now become
Past any need of virtue. Let them care
   That in the cradle of their gentry are,
To serve the state by counsels and by arms;
   We neither love the troubles nor the harms.
What love you then? Your whore. What study? Gait,
   Carriage, and dressing. There is up of late
The Academy, where the gallants meet—
   What, to make legs? Yes, and to smell most sweet: 90
All that they do at plays. Oh, but first here
   They learn and study, and then practise there.
But why are all these irons in the fire
   Of several makings? Helps, helps, to attire
His lordship. That is for his band, his hair
   This, and that box his beauty to repair,

This other for his eyebrows—hence, away!
  I may no longer on these pictures stay:
These carcasses of honour, tailors' blocks
  Covered with tissue, whose prosperity mocks   100
The fate of things; whilst tottered virtue holds
  Her broken arms up to their empty moulds.

45

An Epistle to Master Arth[ur] Squib

What I am not, and what I fain would be,
  Whilst I inform myself, I would teach thee,
My gentle Arthur, that it might be said
  One lesson we have both learned and well read.
I neither am, nor art thou, one of those
  That hearkens to a jack's pulse, when it goes;
Nor ever trusted to that friendship yet
  Was issue of the tavern or the spit:
Much less a name would we bring up or nurse
  That could but claim a kindred from the purse.   10
Those are poor ties depend on those false ends,
  'Tis virtue alone, or nothing, that knits friends.
And as within your office you do take
  No piece of money, but you know or make
Inquiry of the worth, so must we do:
  First weigh a friend, then touch, and try him too;
For there are many slips and counterfeits.
  Deceit is fruitful. Men have masks and nets,
But these with wearing will themselves unfold:
  They cannot last. No lie grew ever old.   20
Turn him, and see his threads; look if he be
  Friend to himself, that would be friend to thee.
For that is first required, a man be his own.
  But he that's too much that is friend of none.
Then rest, and a friend's value understand:
  It is a richer purchase than of land.

46

An Epigram
on Sir Edward Coke,
When He Was Lord Chief Justice of England

He that should search all glories of the gown,
  And steps of all raised servants of the crown,
He could not find, than thee, of all that store,
  Whom fortune aided less, or virtue more.
Such Coke, were thy beginnings, when thy good
  In others' evil best was understood;
When, being the stranger's help, the poor man's aid,
  Thy just defences made the oppressor afraid.
Such was thy process, when integrity
  And skill in thee now grew authority;   10
That clients strove, in question of the laws,
  More for thy patronage than for their cause,
And that thy strong and manly eloquence
  Stood up thy nation's fame, her crown's defence.
And now such is thy stand; while thou dost deal
  Desirèd justice to the public weal
Like Solon's self, explait'st the knotty laws
  With endless labours, whilst thy learning draws
No less of praise than readers in all kinds
  Of worthiest knowledge that can take men's minds.   20
Such is thy all, that (as I sung before)
  None fortune aided less, or virtue more.
Or if chance must, to each man that doth rise,
  Needs lend an aid, to thine she had her eyes.

47

An Epistle Answering to One that Asked to be
Sealed of the Tribe of Ben

Men that are safe and sure in all they do
Care not what trials they are put unto;

They meet the fire, the test, as martyrs would,
   And though opinion stamp them not, are gold.
I could say more of such, but that I fly
   To speak myself out too ambitiously,
And showing so weak an act to vulgar eyes,
   Put conscience and my right to compromise.
Let those that merely talk, and never think,
   That live in the wild anarchy of drink,   10
Subject to quarrel only, or else such
   As make it their proficiency how much
They have glutted in and lechered out that week,
   That never yet did friend or friendship seek
But for a sealing: let these men protest.
   Or the other on their borders, that will jest
On all souls that are absent, even the dead,
   Like flies or worms which man's corrupt parts fed:
That to speak well, think it above all sin,
   Of any company but that they are in;   20
Call every night to supper in these fits,
   And are received for the covey of wits;
That censure all the town, and all the affairs,
   And know whose ignorance is more than theirs;
Let these men have their ways, and take their times
   To vent their libels, and to issue rhymes,
I have no portion in them, nor their deal
   Of news they get to strew out the long meal;
I study other friendships, and more one
   Than these can ever be; or else wish none.   30
What is't to me whether the French design
   Be, or be not, to get the Valtelline?
Or the States' ships sent forth belike to meet
   Some hopes of Spain in their West Indian Fleet?
Whether the dispensation yet be sent,
   Or that the match from Spain was ever meant?
I wish all well, and pray high heaven conspire
   My prince's safety and my king's desire;
But if, for honour, we must draw the sword,
   And force back that which will not be restored,   40
I have a body yet that spirit draws
   To live, or fall a carcass in the cause.
So far without inquiry what the States,

Brunsfield, and Mansfeld, do this year, my fates
Shall carry me at call, and I'll be well,
    Though I do neither hear these news, nor tell
Of Spain or France, or were not pricked down one
    Of the late mystery of reception,
Although my fame to his not under-hears,
    That guides the motions and directs the bears.   50
But that's a blow by which in time I may
    Lose all my credit with my Christmas clay
And animated porcelain of the court;
    Aye, and for this neglect, the coarser sort
Of earthen jars there may molest me too:
    Well, with mine own frail pitcher, what to do
I have decreed; keep it from waves and press,
    Lest it be jostled, cracked, made naught, or less;
Live to that point I will, for which I am man,
    And dwell as in my centre as I can,   60
Still looking to, and ever loving, heaven;
    With reverence using all the gifts thence given.
'Mongst which, if I have any friendships sent,
    Such as are square, well-tagged, and permanent,
Not built with canvas, paper, and false lights,
    As are the glorious scenes at the great sights,
And that there be no fevery heats, nor colds,
    Oily expansions, or shrunk dirty folds,
But all so clear and led by reason's flame,
    As but to stumble in her sight were shame;   70
These I will honour, love, embrace, and serve,
    And free it from all question to preserve.
So short you read my character, and theirs
    I would call mine, to which not many stairs
Are asked to climb. First give me faith, who know
    Myself a little. I will take you so,
As you have writ yourself. Now stand, and then,
    Sir, you are sealèd of the tribe of Ben.

48

The Dedication of the King's New Cellar.
To Bacchus

Since, Bacchus, thou art father
Of wines, to thee the rather
We dedicate this cellar,
Where now, thou art made dweller,
And seal thee thy commission;
But 'tis with a condition
That thou remain here taster
Of all to the great master.
And look unto their faces,
Their qualities, and races,   10
That both their odour take him
And relish merry make him.
   For, Bacchus, thou art freer
Of cares, and overseer
Of feast and merry meeting,
And still begin'st the greeting;
See then thou dost attend him,
Lyaeus, and defend him
By all the arts of gladness
From any thought like sadness.   20
   So mayst thou still be younger
Than Phoebus, and much stronger
To give mankind their eases,
And cure the world's diseases;
   So may the muses follow
Thee still, and leave Apollo,
And think thy stream more quicker
Than Hippocrene's liquor:
And thou make many a poet
Before his brain do know it;   30
So may there never quarrel
Have issue from the barrel;
But Venus and the graces
Pursue thee in all places,
And not a song be other
Than Cupid and his mother.

That when King James, above here,
Shall feast it, thou mayst love there
The causes and the guests too,
And have thy tales and jests too,   40
Thy circuits and thy rounds free
As shall the feast's fair grounds be.
    Be it he hold communion
In great Saint George's union,
Or gratulates the passage
Of some well-wrought embassage,
Whereby he may knit sure up
The wishèd peace of Europe;
Or else a health advances,
To put his court in dances,   50
And set us all on skipping,
When with his royal shipping
The narrow seas are shady,
And Charles brings home the lady.

Accessit fervor capiti, numerusque lucernis.

49

An Epigram
on the Court Pucelle

Does the court pucelle then so censure me,
    And thinks I dare not her? Let the world see.
What though her chamber be the very pit
    Where fight the prime cocks of the game, for wit?
And that as any are struck, her breath creates
    New in their stead, out of the candidates?
What though with tribade lust she force a muse,
    And in an epicoene fury can write news
Equal with that which for the best news goes,
    As airy light, and as like wit as those?   10
What though she talk, and can at once with them
    Make state, religion, bawdry, all a theme?
And as lip-thirsty, in each word's expense,
    Doth labour with the phrase more than the sense?

What though she ride two mile on holidays
   To church, as others do to feasts and plays,
To show their 'tires, to view and to be viewed?
   What though she be with velvet gowns endued,
And spangled petticoats brought forth to eye,
   As new rewards of her old secrecy?   20
What though she hath won on trust, as many do,
   And that her truster fears her: must I too?
I never stood for any place: my wit
   Thinks itself naught, though she should value it.
I am no statesman, and much less divine;
   For bawdry, 'tis her language, and not mine.
Farthest I am from the idolatry
   To stuffs and laces: those my man can buy.
And trust her I would least, that hath forswore
   In contract twice; what can she perjure more?   30
Indeed, her dressing some man might delight,
   Her face there's none can like by candle-light.
Not he that should the body have, for case
   To his poor instrument, now out of grace.
Shall I advise thee, pucelle? Steal away
   From court, while yet thy fame hath some small day;
The wits will leave you, if they once perceive
   You cling to lords, and lords, if them you leave
For sermoneers: of which now one, now other
   They say you weekly invite with fits of the mother,   40
And practise for a miracle; take heed
   This age would lend no faith to Darrel's deed:
Or if it would, the court is the worst place,
   Both for the mothers and the babes of grace;
For there the wicked in the chair of scorn
   Will call it a bastard, when a prophet's born.

50

An Epigram
to the Honoured [Elizabeth,] Countess of [Rutland]

   The wisdom, madam, of your private life
      Wherewith this while you live a widowed wife,

And the right ways you take unto the right,
  To conquer rumour and triumph on spite;
Not only shunning by your act to do
  Aught that is ill, but the suspicion too,
Is of so brave example, as he were
  No friend to virtue could be silent here.
The rather when the vices of the time
  Are grown so fruitful, and false pleasures climb   10
By all oblique degrees that killing height
  From whence they fall, cast down with their own weight.
And though all praise bring nothing to your name,
  Who, herein studying conscience and not fame,
Are in yourself rewarded; yet 'twill be
  A cheerful work to all good eyes, to see
Among the daily ruins that fall foul,
  Of state, of fame, of body, and of soul,
So great a virtue stand upright to view,
  As makes Penelope's old fable true: 20
Whilst your Ulysses hath ta'en leave to go,
  Countries and climes, manners and men to know.
Only your time you better entertain,
  Than the great Homer's wit for her could feign;
For you admit no company but good,
  And when you want those friends, or near in blood,
Or your allies, you make your books your friends,
  And study them unto the noblest ends,
Searching for knowledge, and to keep your mind
  The same it was inspired, rich, and refined.   30
These graces, when the rest of ladies view,
  Not boasted in your life, but practised true,
As they are hard for them to make their own,
  So are they profitable to be known:
For when they find so many meet in one,
  It will be shame for them, if they have none.

51

Lord Bacon's Birthday

Hail, happy genius of this ancient pile!
How comes it all things so about thee smile?

The fire, the wine, the men! and in the midst
Thou stand'st as if some mystery thou didst!
Pardon, I read it in thy face, the day
For whose returns, and many, all these pray:
And so do I. This is the sixtieth year
Since Bacon, and thy lord was born, and here;
Son to the grave wise Keeper of the Seal,
Fame and foundation of the English weal.   10
What then his father was, that since is he,
Now with a title more to the degree;
England's high Chancellor: the destined heir
In his soft cradle to his father's chair;
Whose even thread the fates spin round and full,
Out of their choicest and their whitest wool.
   'Tis a brave cause of joy, let it be known,
For 'twere a narrow gladness, kept thine own.
Give me a deep-crowned bowl, that I may sing,
In raising him, the wisdom of my king.   20

52

A Poem Sent Me by Sir William Burlase
The Painter to the Poet

To paint thy worth, if rightly I did know it,
And were but painter half like thee, a poet,
     Ben, I would show it;
But in this skill my unskilful pen will tire,
Thou, and thy worth, will still be found far higher,
     And I a liar.
Then what a painter's here! or what an eater
Of great attempts! when as his skill's no greater,
     And he a cheater!
Then what a poet's here! whom, by confession   10
Of all with me, to paint without digression,
     There's no expression.

My Answer
The Poet to the Painter

Why? though I seem of a prodigious waist,
I am not so voluminous and vast
But there are lines wherewith I might be embraced.

'Tis true, as my womb swells, so my back stoops,
And the whole lump grows round, deformed, and droops,
But yet the tun at Heidelberg had hoops.

You were not tied by any painter's law
To square my circle, I confess, but draw
My superficies: that was all you saw.

Which if in compass of no art it came   10
To be describèd by a monogram,
With one great blot, you had formed me as I am.

But whilst you curious were to have it be
An archetype for all the world to see,
You made it a brave piece, but not like me.

Oh, had I now your manner, mastery, might,
Your power of handling shadow, air, and sprite,
How I would draw, and take hold and delight.

But you are he can paint; I can but write:
A poet hath no more but black and white,   20
Ne knows he flattering colours, or false light.

Yet when of friendship I would draw the face,
A lettered mind and a large heart would place
To all posterity: I will write *Burlase*.

53

An Epigram
to William, Earl of Newcastle

When first, my lord, I saw you back your horse,
   Provoke his mettle, and command his force
To all the uses of the field and race,
   Methought I read the ancient art of Thrace,
And saw a centaur, past those tales of Greece;
   So seemed your horse and you both of a piece!
You showed like Perseus upon Pegasus,
   Or Castor mounted on his Cyllarus,
Or what we hear our home-born legend tell
   Of bold Sir Bevis and his Arundel;   10
Nay, so your seat his beauties did endorse
   As I began to wish myself a horse.
And surely had I but your stable seen
   Before, I think my wish absolved had been.
For never saw I yet the muses dwell,
   Nor any of their household, half so well.
So well, as when I saw the floor and room,
   I looked for Hercules to be the groom,
And cried, Away with the Caesarian bread!
   At these immortal mangers Virgil fed.   20

54

Epistle
to Mr Arthur Squib

I am to dine, friend, where I must be weighed
   For a just wager, and that wager paid
If I do lose it: and, without a tale,
   A merchant's wife is regent of the scale.
Who, when she heard the match, concluded straight,
   An ill commodity! It must make good weight.
So that upon the point my corporal fear
   Is she will play Dame Justice too severe,
And hold me to it close; to stand upright
   Within the balance, and not want a mite,   10

Bur rather with advantage to be found
    Full twenty stone, of which I lack two pound:
That's six in silver; now within the socket
    Stinketh my credit, if into the pocket
It do not come. One piece I have in store;
    Lend me, dear Arthur, for a week five more
And you shall make me good, in weight and fashion,
    And then to be returned; or protestation
To go out after—till when, take this letter
    For your security. I can no better.   20

55

To Mr John Burgess

Would God, my Burgess, I could think
Thoughts worthy of thy gift, this ink;
Then would I promise here to give
Verse that should thee and me outlive.
But since the wine hath steeped my brain
I only can the paper stain;
Yet with a dye that fears no moth,
But scarlet-like outlasts the cloth.

56

Epistle
to My Lady Covell

You won not verses, madam, you won me,
    When you would play so nobly, and so free.
A book to a few lines; but it was fit
    You won them too, your odds did merit it.
So have you gained a servant and a muse:
    The first of which, I fear, you will refuse;
And you may justly, being a tardy, cold,
    Unprofitable chattel, fat and old,
Laden with belly, and doth hardly approach
    His friends, but to break chairs or crack a coach.   10

His weight is twenty stone, within two pound,
   And that's made up as doth the purse abound.
Marry, the muse is one can tread the air,
   And stroke the water: nimble, chaste and fair;
Sleep in a virgin's bosom without fear,
   Run all the rounds in a soft lady's ear,
Widow or wife, without the jealousy
   Of either suitor or a servant by.
Such, if her manners like you, I do send:
   And can for other graces her commend,   20
To make you merry on the dressing stool
   A-mornings, and at afternoons to fool
Away ill company, and help in rhyme
   Your Joan to pass her melancholy time.
By this, although you fancy not the man,
   Accept his muse; and tell (I know you can)
How many verses, madam, are your due!
   I can lose none in tendering these to you.
I gain in having leave to keep my day,
   And should grow rich, had I much more to pay.   30

57

To Master John Burgess

Father John Burgess
Necessity urges
My woeful cry,
To Sir Robert Pye:
And that he will venture
To send my debenture.
Tell him his Ben
Knew the time, when
He loved the muses;
Though now he refuses   10
To take apprehension
Of a year's pension,
And more is behind:
Put him in mind

Christmas is near;
And neither good cheer,
Mirth, fooling, nor wit,
Nor any least fit
Of gambol or sport
Will come at the court,   20
If there be no money;
No plover, or coney
Will come to the table,
Or wine to enable
The muse or the poet,
The parish will know it;
Nor any quick warming-pan help him to bed,
If the 'chequer be empty, so will be his head.

58

Epigram
to My Bookseller

Thou friend, wilt hear all censures; unto thee
    All mouths are open, and all stomachs free:
Be thou my book's intelligencer, note
    What each man says of it, and of what coat
His judgement is; if he be wise and praise,
    Thank him; if other, he can give no bays.
If his wit reach no higher but to spring
    Thy wife a fit of laughter, a cramp-ring
Will be reward enough, to wear like those
    That hang their richest jewels in their nose,   10
Like a rung bear or swine: grunting out wit
    As if that part lay for a —— most fit!
        If they go on, and that thou lov'st alife
        Their perfumed judgements, let them kiss thy wife.

59

An Epigram
to William, Earl of Newcastle

They talk of fencing and the use of arms,
　The art of urging and avoiding harms,
The noble science and the mastering skill
　Of making just approaches, how to kill,
To hit in angles, and to clash with time:
　As all defence or offence were a chime!
I hate such measured, give me mettled! fire,
　That trembles in the blaze, but then mounts higher,
A quick and dazzling motion! When a pair
　Of bodies meet like rarefied air!　　　　　　　10
Their weapons shot out with that flame and force
　As they outdid the lightning in the course;
This were a spectacle! A sight to draw
　Wonder to valour! No; it is the law
Of daring not to do a wrong is true
　Valour: to slight it, being done to you;
To know the heads of danger, where 'tis fit
　To bend, to break, provoke, or suffer it!
All this, my lord, is valour. This is yours,
　And was your father's, all your ancestors'!　　20
Who durst live great 'mongst all the colds and heats
　Of human life, as all the frosts and sweats
Of fortune, when or death appeared, or bands;
　And valiant were with, or without, their hands.

60

An Epitaph on Henry, L[ord] La Warr.
To the Passer-by

　　If, passenger, thou canst but read,
　　Stay, drop a tear for him that's dead:
　　Henry, the brave young Lord La Warr,
　　Minerva's and the muses' care!

What could their care do 'gainst the spite
Of a disease that loved no light
Of honour, nor no air of good,
But crept like darkness through his blood,
Offended with the dazzling flame
Of virtue, got above his name?   10
No noble furniture of parts,
No love of action and high arts,
No aim at glory, or, in war,
Ambition to become a star
Could stop the malice of this ill,
That spread his body o'er, to kill:
And only his great soul envied
Because it durst have noblier died.

61

An Epigram

That you have seen the pride, beheld the sport,
   And all the games of fortune played at court;
Viewed there the market, read the wretched rate
   At which there are would sell the prince and state;
That scarce you hear a public voice alive,
   But whispered councils, and those only, thrive:
Yet are got off thence with clear mind and hands
   To lift to heaven: who is't not understands
Your happiness, and doth not speak you blest,
   To see you set apart, thus, from the rest,   10
To obtain of God what all the land should ask?
   A nation's sin got pardoned—'twere a task
Fit for a bishop's knees! O bow them oft,
   My lord, till felt grief make our stone hearts soft,
And we do weep to water for our sin.
   He that in such a flood as we are in
Of riot and consumption, knows the way
   To teach the people how to fast and pray,
And do their penance, to avert God's rod:
   He is the man, and favourite of God.   20

62

An Epigram to K[ing] Charles,
for a Hundred Pounds He Sent Me in My Sickness. 1629

Great Charles, among the holy gifts of grace
    Annexèd to thy person and thy place,
'Tis not enough (thy piety is such)
    To cure the called king's evil with thy touch;
But thou wilt yet a kinglier mastery try,
    To cure the poet's evil, poverty;
And in these cures dost so thyself enlarge
    As thou dost cure our evil at thy charge.
Nay, and in this thou show'st to value more
    One poet, than of other folk ten score.   10
O piety, so to weigh the poor's estates!
    O bounty, so to difference the rates!
What can the poet wish his king may do,
    But that he cure the people's evil too?

63

To K[ing] Charles and Q[ueen] Mary.
For the Loss of Their First-Born; an Epigram Consolatory

Who dares deny that all first fruits are due
    To God, denies the Godhead to be true;
Who doubts those fruits God can with gain restore,
    Doth by his doubt distrust his promise more.
He can, he will, and with large interest, pay
    What, at his liking, he will take away.
Then, royal Charles and Mary, do not grutch
    That the Almighty's will to you is such;
But thank his greatness, and his goodness too,
    And think all still the best that he will do.   10
That thought shall make he will this loss supply
    With a long, large, and blest posterity!
For God, whose essence is so infinite,
    Cannot but heap that grace he will requite.

64

An Epigram
to Our Great and Good K[ing] Charles,
on His Anniversary Day, 1629

How happy were the subject, if he knew
   Most pious king, but his own good in you!
How many times, Live long, Charles! would he say,
   If he but weighed the blessings of this day,
And as it turns our joyful year about,
   For safety of such majesty, cry out?
Indeed, when had Great Britain greater cause
   Than now, to love the sovereign and the laws?
When you that reign are her example grown,
   And what are bounds to her, you make your own?   10
When your assiduous practice doth secure
   That faith which she professeth to be pure?
When all your life's a precedent of days,
   And murmur cannot quarrel at your ways?
How is she barren grown of love, or broke,
   That nothing can her gratitude provoke!
O times! O manners! surfeit bred of ease,
   The truly epidemical disease!
'Tis not alone the merchant, but the clown
   Is bankrupt turned; the cassock, cloak, and gown   20
Are lost upon account! and none will know
   How much to heaven for thee, great Charles, they owe!

65

An Epigram on the Prince's Birth, 1630

And art thou born, brave babe? Blest be thy birth,
   That so hath crowned our hopes, our spring, and earth,
The bed of the chaste lily and the rose!
   What month than May was fitter to disclose
This prince of flowers? Soon shoot thou up, and grow
   The same that thou art promised; but be slow

And long in changing. Let our nephews see
   Thee quickly [come] the garden's eye to be,
And there to stand so. Haste now, envious moon,
   And interpose thyself ('care not how soon)   10
And threat' the great eclipse. Two hours but run,
   Sol will re-shine. If not, Charles hath a son.

      ——*Non displicuisse meretur,*
      Festinat, Caesar, qui placuisse tibi.

66

An Epigram to the Queen, then Lying In, 1630

Hail Mary, full of grace! it once was said,
   And by an angel, to the blessed'st maid,
The mother of our Lord: why may not I
   Without profaneness, yet, a poet, cry
Hail Mary, full of honours! to my queen,
   The mother of our prince? When was there seen,
Except the joy that the first Mary brought,
   Whereby the safety of mankind was wrought,
So general a gladness to an isle,
   To make the hearts of a whole nation smile,   10
As in this prince? Let it be lawful so
   To compare small with great, as still we owe
Glory to God. Then, Hail to Mary! spring
   Of so much safety to the realm and king!

67

An Ode, or Song, by All the Muses,
in Celebration of Her Majesty's Birthday, 1630

1. *Clio*   Up public joy, remember
                This sixteenth of November,
                  Some brave uncommon way;
                And though the parish steeple
                Be silent, to the people
                  Ring thou it holiday.

2. *Mel[pomene]*   What though the thrifty Tower
          And guns there spare to pour
            Their noises forth in thunder;
          As fearful to awake   10
          This city, or to shake
            Their guarded gates asunder?

3. *Thal[ia]*   Yet let our trumpets sound,
          And cleave both air and ground
            With beating of our drums;
          Let every lyre be strung,
          Harp, lute, theorbo sprung
            With touch of dainty thumbs!

4. *Eut[erpe]*   That when the choir is full
          The harmony may pull   20
            The angels from their spheres;
          And each intelligence
          May wish itself a sense
            Whilst it the ditty hears.

5. *Terp[sichore]*   Behold the royal Mary,
          The daughter of great Harry
            And sister to just Louis,
          Comes in the pomp and glory
          Of all her brother's story
            And of her father's prowess!   30

6. *Erat[o]*   She shows so far above
          The feignèd queen of love,
            This sea-girt isle upon,
          As here no Venus were;
          But that she reigning here
            Had got the ceston on!

7. *Calli[ope]*   See, see our active king
          Hath taken twice the ring
            Upon his pointed lance;
          Whilst all the ravished rout   40
          Do mingle in a shout,
            Hey! for the flower of France!

8. *Ura*[*nia*]   This day the court doth measure
                   Her joy in state and pleasure,
                       And with a reverend fear
                   The revels and the play
                   Sum up this crownèd day,
                       Her two-and-twentieth year!

9. *Poly*[*hymnia*] Sweet, happy Mary! All
                   The people her do call.   50
                       And this the womb divine,
                   So fruitful and so fair,
                   Hath brought the land an heir,
                       And Charles a Caroline!

68

An Epigram
to the Household, 1630

What can the cause be, when the k[ing] hath given
    His poet sack, the household will not pay?
Are they so scanted in their store, or driven,
    For want of knowing the poet, to say him nay?
Well, they should know him, would the k[ing] but grant
    His poet leave to sing his household true;
He'd frame such ditties of their store and want
    Would make the very Greencloth to look blue;
And rather wish, in their expense of sack,
    So the allowance from the king to use,   10
As the old bard should no Canary lack.
    'Twere better spare a butt than spill his muse.
For in the genius of a poet's verse
    The king's fame lives. Go now, deny his tierce!

69

Epigram
to a Friend, and Son

Son, and my friend, I had not called you so
   To me, or been the same to you, if show,
Profit, or chance had made us; but I know
   What by that name we each to other owe—
Freedom and truth, with love from those begot:
   Wise crafts, on which the flatterer ventures not.
His is more safe commodity, or none;
   Nor dares he come in the comparison.
But as the wretched painter, who so ill
   Painted a dog that now his subtler skill   10
Was to have a boy stand with a club, and fright
   All live dogs from the lane and his shop's sight,
Till he had sold his piece, drawn so unlike;
   So doth the flatterer with fair cunning strike
At a friend's freedom, proves all circling means
   To keep him off, and howsoe'er he gleans
Some of his forms, he lets him not come near
   Where he would fix, for the distinction's fear;
For as at distance few have faculty
   To judge, so all men coming near can spy.   20
Though now of flattery, as of picture, are
   More subtle works and finer pieces far
Than knew the former ages: yet to life
   All is but web and painting; be the strife
Never so great to get them; and the ends
   Rather to boast rich hangings than rare friends.

70

To the Immortal Memory and Friendship of That Noble Pair,
Sir Lucius Cary and Sir H. Morison

The Turn
Brave infant of Saguntum, clear
Thy coming forth in that great year

When the prodigious Hannibal did crown
His rage with razing your immortal town.
Thou, looking then about,
Ere thou wert half got out,
Wise child, didst hastily return,
And mad'st thy mother's womb thine urn.
How summed a circle didst thou leave mankind
Of deepest lore, could we the centre find!   10

The Counter-Turn

Did wiser nature draw thee back
From out the horror of that sack?
Where shame, faith, honour, and regard of right
Lay trampled on; the deeds of death and night
Urged, hurried forth, and hurled
Upon the affrighted world:
Sword, fire, and famine with fell fury met,
And all on utmost ruin set;
As, could they but life's miseries foresee,
No doubt all infants would return like thee.   20

The Stand

For what is life, if measured by the space,
Not by the act?
Or maskèd man, if valued by his face
Above his fact?
Here's one outlived his peers
And told forth fourscore years;
He vexèd time, and busied the whole state;
Troubled both foes and friends,
But ever to no ends;
What did this stirrer, but die late?   30
How well at twenty had he fallen or stood!
For three of his fourscore he did no good.

The Turn

He entered well by virtuous parts,
Got up and thrived with honest arts;
He purchased friends and fame and honours then,
And had his noble name advanced with men;

But weary of that flight,
He stooped in all men's sight
To sordid flatteries, acts of strife,
And sunk in that dead sea of life   40
So deep, as he did then death's waters sup,
But that the cork of title buoyed him up.

The Counter-Turn

Alas, but Morison fell young!
He never fell: thou fall'st, my tongue.
He stood, a soldier to the last right end,
A perfect patriot, and a noble friend;
But most, a virtuous son.
All offices were done
By him so ample, full, and round,
In weight, in measure, number, sound,   50
As, though his age imperfect might appear,
His life was of humanity the sphere.

The Stand

Go now, and tell out days summed up with fears;
And make them years;
Produce thy mass of miseries on the stage,
To swell thine age;
Repeat of things a throng,
To show thou hast been long,
Not lived; for life doth her great actions spell
By what was done and wrought   60
In season, and so brought
To light: her measures are, how well
Each syllabe answered, and was formed, how fair;
These make the lines of life, and that's her air.

The Turn

It is not growing like a tree
In bulk, doth make man better be;
Or standing long an oak, three hundred year,
To fall a log at last, dry, bald, and sere:
A lily of a day
Is fairer far, in May,   70

Although it fall and die that night;
It was the plant and flower of light.
In small proportions we just beauty see,
And in short measures life may perfect be.

The Counter-Turn

Call, noble Lucius, then for wine,
And let thy looks with gladness shine;
Accept this garland, plant it on thy head;
And think, nay know, thy Morison's not dead.
He leaped the present age,
Possessed with holy rage   80
To see that bright eternal day,
Of which we priests and poets say
Such truths as we expect for happy men;
And there he lives with memory, and Ben

The Stand

Jonson, who sung this of him, ere he went
Himself to rest,
Or taste a part of that full joy he meant
To have expressed
In this bright asterism;
Where it were friendship's schism   90
(Were not his Lucius long with us to tarry)
To separate these twi-
Lights, the Dioscuri;
And keep the one half from his Harry.
But fate doth so alternate the design,
Whilst that in heaven, this light on earth must shine.

The Turn

And shine as you exalted are;
Two names of friendship, but one star:
Of hearts the union. And those not by chance
Made, or indentured, or leased out to advance   100
The profits for a time.
No pleasures vain did chime,
Of rhymes, or riots, at your feasts,
Orgies of drink, or feigned protests:

But simple love of greatness, and of good;
That knits brave minds and manners, more than blood.

The Counter-Turn
This made you first to know the why
You liked; then after to apply
That liking; and approach so one the t'other,
Till either grew a portion of the other: 110
Each stylèd, by his end,
The copy of his friend.
You lived to be the great surnames
And titles by which all made claims
Unto the virtue. Nothing perfect done
But as a Cary, or a Morison.

The Stand
And such a force the fair example had,
As they that saw
The good and durst not practise it, were glad
That such a law   120
Was left yet to mankind;
Where they might read and find
Friendship in deed was written, not in words;
And with the heart, not pen,
Of two so early men
Whose lines her rolls were, and records.
Who, ere the first down bloomèd on the chin,
Had sowed these fruits, and got the harvest in.

71

To the Right Honourable,
the Lord High Treasurer of England
an Epistle Mendicant, 1631

MY LORD,
Poor wretched states, pressed by extremities,
Are fain to seek for succours and supplies
Of princes' aids, or good men's charities.

Disease, the enemy, and his engineers,
Want, with the rest of his concealed compeers,
Have cast a trench about me, now, five years;

And made those strong approaches, by faussebraies,
Redoubts, half-moons, horn-works, and such close ways,
The muse not peeps out one of hundred days;

But lies blocked up and straitened, narrowed in,   10
Fixed to the bed and boards, unlike to win
Health, or scarce breath, as she had never been.

Unless some saving honour of the crown
Dare think it, to relieve, no less renown
A bed-rid wit than a besiegèd town.

72

To the King, on His Birthday
19 November 1632
an Epigram Anniversary

This is King Charles's day. Speak it, thou Tower,
    Unto the ships, and they from tier to tier,
Discharge it 'bout the island in an hour,
    As loud as thunder, and as swift as fire.
Let Ireland meet it out at sea, half-way,
    Repeating all Great Britain's joy, and more,
Adding her own glad accents to this day,
    Like echo playing from the other shore.
What drums or trumpets, or great ordnance can,
    The poetry of steeples, with the bells,   10
Three kingdoms' mirth, in light and airy man,
    Made lighter with the wind. All noises else,
At bonfires, rockets, fireworks, with the shouts
    That cry that gladness, which their hearts would pray,

Had they but grace of thinking at these routs
  On the often coming of this holiday:
    And ever close the burden of the song,
    Still to have such a Charles, but this Charles long.

    The wish is great, but where the prince is such,
    What prayers, people, can you think too much?   20

73

On the Right Honourable and Virtuous Lord Weston,
L[ord] High Treasurer of England,
upon the Day He Was Made Earl of Portland,
17 February 1632.
To the Envious

Look up, thou seed of envy, and still bring
  Thy faint and narrow eyes to read the king
In his great actions: view whom his large hand
  Hath raised to be the port unto his land!
Weston! That waking man, that eye of state,
  Who seldom sleeps, whom bad men only hate!
Why do I irritate or stir up thee,
  Thou sluggish spawn, that canst, but wilt not, see?
Feed on thyself for spite, and show thy kind:
  To virtue and true worth be ever blind.   10
Dream thou couldst hurt it; but before thou wake
  To effect it, feel thou hast made thine own heart ache.

74

To the Right Hon[ourable] Jerome, L[ord] Weston
An Ode Gratulatory,
for His Return from His Embassy, 1632

Such pleasure as the teeming earth
Doth take in easy nature's birth,
    When she puts forth the life of every thing,
And in a dew of sweetest rain
She lies delivered, without pain,
    Of the prime beauty of the year, the spring;
The rivers in their shores do run,
The clouds rack clear before the sun,
    The rudest winds obey the calmest air;
Rare plants from every bank do rise,   10
And every plant the sense surprise,
    Because the order of the whole is fair!
The very verdure of her nest,
Wherein she sits so richly dressed,
    As all the wealth of season there was spread,
Doth show the graces and the hours
Have multiplied their arts and powers
    In making soft her aromatic bed.
Such joys, such sweets doth your return
Bring all your friends, fair lord, that burn   20
    With love, to hear your modesty relate
The business of your blooming wit,
With all the fruit shall follow it,
    Both to the honour of the king and state.
O how will then our court be pleased,
To see great Charles of travail eased,
    When he beholds a graft of his own hand
Shoot up an olive fruitful, fair,
To be a shadow to his heir,
    And both a strength and beauty to his land!   30

75

Epithalamion;
or, a Song, Celebrating the Nuptials
of that Noble Gentleman, Mr Jerome Weston,
Son and Heir of the Lord Weston, Lord High Treasurer of
England,
with the Lady Frances Stuart,
Daughter of Esmé, D[uke] of Lennox, Deceased,
and Sister of the Surviving Duke of the Same Name

Though thou hast passed thy summer standing, stay
 Awhile with us, bright sun, and help our light;
Thou canst not meet more glory on the way
 Between thy tropics, to arrest thy sight,
  Than thou shalt see today:
   We woo thee, stay
  And see what can be seen,
The bounty of a king, and beauty of his queen!

See the procession! What a holy day
 (Bearing the promise of some better fate)   10
Hath filled with caroches all the way
 From Greenwich hither to Roehampton gate!
  When looked the year, at best,
   So like a feast?
   Or were affairs in tune,
By all the spheres' consent, so in the heart of June?

What bevy of beauties, and bright youths at charge
 Of summer's liveries and gladding green,
Do boast their loves and braveries so at large
 As they came all to see, and to be seen!   20
  When looked the earth so fine,
   Or so did shine,
   In all her bloom and flower
To welcome home a pair, and deck the nuptial bower?

It is the kindly season of the time,
   The month of youth, which calls all creatures forth
To do their offices in nature's chime,
    And celebrate (perfection at the worth)
        Marriage, the end of life,
          That holy strife,   30
        And the allowèd war:
Through which not only we, but all our species are.

Hark how the bells upon the waters play
   Their sister-tunes from Thames's either side!
As they had learned new changes for the day,
    And all did ring the approaches of the bride;
        The Lady Frances, dressed
          Above the rest
        Of all the maidens fair,
In graceful ornament of garland, gems, and hair.   40

See how she paceth forth in virgin white,
   Like what she is, the daughter of a duke,
And sister; darting forth a dazzling light
    On all that come her simplesse to rebuke!
        Her tresses trim her back,
          As she did lack
        Naught of a maiden queen,
With modesty so crowned, and adoration seen.

Stay, thou wilt see what rites the virgins do!
   The choicest virgin-troop of all the land;   50
Porting the ensigns of united two,
    Both crowns and kingdoms in their either hand;
        Whose majesties appear,
          To make more clear
        This feast than can the day,
Although that thou, O sun, at our entreaty stay!

See, how with roses and with lilies shine
   (Lilies and roses, flowers of either sex)
The bright bride's paths, embellished more than thine
    With light of love, this pair doth intertex!   60

Stay, see the virgins sow
      Where she shall go
The emblems of their way:
Oh, now thou smil'st, fair sun, and shin'st, as thou
            wouldst stay!

With what full hands, and in how plenteous showers,
   Have they bedewed the earth where she doth tread,
As if her airy steps did spring the flowers,
   And all the ground were garden, where she led!
         See, at another door,
            On the same floor,   70
         The bridegroom meets the bride
With all the pomp of youth, and all our court beside.

Our court, and all the grandees; now, sun, look,
   And looking with thy best inquiry, tell,
In all thy age of journals thou hast took
   Saw'st thou that pair became these rites so well,
         Save the preceding two?
            Who, in all they do,
         Search, sun, and thou wilt find,
They are the exampled pair, and mirror of their kind.   80

Force from the phoenix, then, no rarity
   Of sex, to rob the creature; but from man,
The king of creatures, take his parity
   With angels, muse, to speak these: nothing can
         Illustrate these, but they
            Themselves today,
         Who the whole act express;
All else we see beside are shadows, and go less.

It is their grace and favour that makes seen
   And wondered at the bounties of this day: 90
All is a story of the king and queen!
   And what of dignity and honour may
         Be duly done to those
            Whom they have chose,
         And set the mark upon
To give a greater name and title to: their own!

Weston, their treasure, as their treasurer,
    That mine of wisdom and of counsels deep,
Great say-master of state, who cannot err,
    But doth his carat and just standard keep   100
            In all the proved assays,
                And legal ways
            Of trials, to work down
Men's loves unto the laws, and laws to love the crown.

And this well moved the judgement of the king
    To pay with honours to his noble son,
Today, the father's service, who could bring
    Him up to do the same himself had done.
            That far all-seeing eye
                Could soon espy   110
            What kind of waking man
He had so highly set, and in what Barbican.

Stand there; for when a noble nature's raised
    It brings friends joy, foes grief, posterity fame;
In him the times, no less than prince, are praised,
    And by his rise, in active men his name
            Doth emulation stir;
                To the dull, a spur
            It is: to the envious meant
A mere upbraiding grief, and torturing punishment.   120

See, now the chapel opens, where the king
    And bishop stay to consummate the rites:
The holy prelate prays, then takes the ring,
    Asks first, Who gives her? (I, Charles): then he plights
            One in the other's hand,
                Whilst they both stand
            Hearing their charge, and then
The solemn choir cries, Joy, and they return, Amen.

O happy bands! and thou more happy place,
    Which to this use wert built and consecrate!   130
To have thy God to bless, thy king to grace,
    And this their chosen bishop celebrate

And knit the nuptial knot,
   Which time shall not,
   Or cankered jealousy,
With all corroding arts, be able to untie!

The chapel empties, and thou mayst be gone
   Now, sun, and post away the rest of day:
These two, now holy church hath made them one,
   Do long to make themselves so, another way: 140
      There is a feast behind
      To them of kind,
   Which their glad parents taught
One to the other, long ere these to light were brought.

Haste, haste, officious sun, and send them night
   Some hours before it should, that these may know
All that their fathers and their mothers might
   Of nuptial sweets, at such a season, owe,
      To propagate their names,
      And keep their fames   150
   Alive, which else would die,
For fame keeps virtue up, and it posterity.

The ignoble never lived, they were awhile
   Like swine, or other cattle here on earth:
Their names are not recorded on the file
   Of life, that fall so; Christians know their birth
      Alone, and such a race
      We pray may grace
   Your fruitful spreading vine,
But dare not ask our wish in language fescennine.   160

Yet, as we may, we will with chaste desires
   (The holy perfumes of the marriage bed)
Be kept alive those sweet and sacred fires
   Of love between you and your lovelihead:
      That when you both are old,
      You find no cold
   There; but, renewèd, say
(After the last child born), This is our wedding day.

Till you behold a race to fill your hall,
    A Richard, and a Jerome, by their names   170
Upon a Thomas, or a Francis call;
    A Kate, a Frank, to honour their granddames,
        And 'tween their grandsires' thighs,
            Like pretty spies,
          Peep forth a gem; to see
How each one plays his part of the large pedigree.

And never may there want one of the stem
    To be a watchful servant for this state;
But like an arm of eminence, 'mongst them
    Extend a reaching virtue, early and late: 180
        Whilst the main tree, still found
            Upright and sound,
          By this sun's noonstead's made
So great; his body now alone projects the shade.

They both are slipped to bed; shut fast the door,
    And let him freely gather love's first fruits;
He's master of the office; yet no more
    Exacts than she is pleased to pay: no suits,
        Strifes, murmurs, or delay,
            Will last till day;   190
          Night and the sheets will show
The longing couple all that elder lovers know.

76

The Humble Petition of Poor Ben.
To the Best of Monarchs, Masters, Men,
King Charles

    —Doth most humbly show it,
    To your Majesty your poet:

    That whereas your royal father,
    James the blessèd, pleased the rather,
    Of his special grace to letters,
    To make all the muses debtors

To his bounty; by extension
Of a free poetic pension,   10
A large hundred marks' annuity,
To be given me in gratuity
For done service, and to come:
    And that this so accepted sum
Or dispensed in books, or bread,
(For with both the muse was fed)
Hath drawn on me from the times
All the envy of the rhymes
And the rattling pit-pat noise
Of the less poetic boys;   20
When their pot-guns aim to hit,
With their pellets of small wit,
Parts of me they judged decayed,
But we last out, still unlaid.
    Please your majesty to make
Of your grace, for goodness' sake,
Those your father's marks, your pounds;
Let their spite, which now abounds,
Then go on and do its worst;
This would all their envy burst,   30
And so warm the poet's tongue
You'd read a snake in his next song.

77

To the Right Honourable, the Lord Treasurer of England an Epigram

If to my mind, great lord, I had a state,
    I would present you now with curious plate
Of Nuremburg, or Turkey; hang your rooms
    Not with the Arras, but the Persian looms.
I would, if price or prayer could them get,
    Send in what or Romano, Tintoret,
Titian, or Raphael, Michelangelo,
    Have left in fame to equal, or outgo
The old Greek hands in picture, or in stone.
    This I would do, could I think Weston one   10

Catched with these arts, wherein the judge is wise
   As far as sense, and only by the eyes.
But you I know, my lord, and know you can
   Discern between a statue and a man,
Can do the things that statues do deserve,
   And act the business which they paint, or carve.
What you have studied are the arts of life:
   To compose men and manners, stint the strife
Of murmuring subjects, make the nations know
   What worlds of blessings to good kings they owe,   20
And mightiest monarchs feel what large increase
   Of sweets and safeties they possess by peace.
These I look up at with a reverent eye,
   And strike religion in the standers-by;
Which, though I cannot as an architect
   In glorious piles or pyramids erect
Unto your honour: I can tune in song
   Aloud; and (haply) it may last as long.

78

An Epigram
to My Muse, the Lady Digby
on Her Husband, Sir Kenelm Digby

Though, happy muse, thou know my Digby well,
   Yet read him in these lines: he doth excel
In honour, courtesy, and all the parts
   Court can call hers, or man could call his arts.
He's prudent, valiant, just, and temperate;
   In him all virtue is beheld in state:
And he is built like some imperial room
   For that to dwell in, and be still at home.
His breast is a brave palace, a broad street,
   Where all heroic ample thoughts do meet;   10
Where nature such a large survey hath ta'en,
   As other souls, to his, dwell in a lane:
Witness his action done at Scanderoon,
   Upon my birthday, the eleventh of June;

When the apostle Barnaby the bright
    Unto our year doth give the longest light;
In sign the subject and the song will live,
    Which I have vowed posterity to give.
Go, muse, in, and salute him. Say he be
    Busy, or frown at first, when he sees thee   20
He will clear up his forehead, think thou bring'st
    Good omen to him in the note thou sing'st,
For he doth love my verses, and will look
    Upon them (next to Spenser's noble book)
And praise them too. Oh, what a fame 't will be!
    What reputation to my lines and me,
When he shall read them at the Treasurer's board
    (The knowing Weston) and that learnèd lord
Allows them! Then, what copies shall be had,
    What transcripts begged; how cried up, and how glad   30
Wilt thou be, muse, when this shall them befall!
    Being sent to one, they will be read of all.

79

New Years expect new gifts: sister, your harp,
    Lute, lyre, theorbo, all are called today;
Your change of notes, the flat, the mean, the sharp,
    To show the rites and to usher forth the way
Of the New Year, in a new silken warp,
    To fit the softness of our Year's-gift, when
    We sing the best of monarchs, masters, men;
For, had we here said less, we had sung nothing then.

A New Year's Gift Sung to King Charles, 1635

Rector chori
Today old Janus opens the New Year
    And shuts the old. Haste, haste, all loyal swains,   10
That know the times and seasons when to appear,
    And offer your just service on these plains;
Best kings expect first-fruits of your glad gains.
    1. Pan is the great preserver of our bounds,
    2. To him we owe all profits of our grounds:

3. Our milk, 4. Our fells, 5. Our fleeces, 6. And first lambs;
7. Our teeming ewes, 8. And lusty-mounting rams.
9. See where he walks, [10.] With Mira by his side;
Chorus
Sound, sound his praises loud, and with his, hers divide.
Shepherds
Of Pan we sing, the best of hunters, Pan,   20
   That drives the hart to seek unusèd ways,
And in the chase more than Silvanus can;
Chorus
   Hear, O you groves, and hills resound his praise.
Nymphs
Of brightest Mira do we raise our song,
   Sister of Pan, and glory of the spring;
Who walks on earth as May still went along;
Chorus
   Rivers and valleys, echo what we sing.
Shepherds
Of Pan we sing, the chief of leaders, Pan,
   That leads our flocks and us, and calls both forth
To better pastures than great Pales can;   30
Chorus
   Hear, O you groves, and hills, resound his worth.
Nymphs
Of brightest Mira is our song, the grace
   Of all that nature yet to life did bring;
And were she lost, could best supply her place;
Chorus
   Rivers and valleys, echo what we sing.
   1. Where'er they tread the enamoured ground
      The fairest flowers are always found;
   2. As if the beauties of the year
      Still waited on them where they were.
   1. He is the father of our peace;   40
   2. She to the crown hath brought increase.
   1. We know no other power than his,
      Pan only our great shepherd is,
Chorus
Our great, our good. Where one's so dressed
In truth of colours, both are best.
Haste, haste you hither, all you gentler swains,

That have a flock, or herd, upon these plains;
This is the great preserver of our bounds,
To whom you owe all duties of your grounds;
Your milks, your fells, your fleeces, and first lambs,   50
Your teeming ewes, as well as mounting rams.
Whose praises let's report unto the woods,
That they may take it echoed by the floods.
    'Tis he, 'tis he; in singing, he,
    And hunting, Pan, exceedeth thee.
    He gives all plenty, and increase,
    He is the author of our peace.

Where'er he goes upon the ground,
The better grass and flowers are found.
To sweeter pastures lead he can,   60
Than ever Pales could, or Pan;
He drives diseases from our folds,
The thief from spoil his presence holds.
Pan knows no other power than his,
This only the great shepherd is.
    'Tis he, 'tis he, &c.

[For *Und.* 80 and 81, see *Dubia*, 2 and 3]

82

To My L[ord] the King,
on the Christening His Second Son, James

That thou art loved of God, this work is done,
    Great king, thy having of a second son;
And by thy blessing may thy people see
    How much they are beloved of God, in thee;
Would they would understand it! Princes are
    Great aids to empire, as they are great care
To pious parents, who would have their blood
    Should take first seisin of the public good,

As hath thy James; cleansed from original dross
   This day by baptism, and his Saviour's cross: 10
Grow up, sweet babe, as blessèd in thy name,
   As in renewing thy good grandsire's fame;
Methought Great Britain in her sea before
   Sat safe enough, but now securèd more.
At land she triumphs in the triple shade
   Her rose and lily, intertwined, have made.

     Oceano secura meo, securior umbris.

83

An Elegy
on the Lady Jane Paulet,
Marchion[ess] of Winton

What gentle ghost, besprent with April dew,
   Hails me so solemnly to yonder yew,
And beckoning woos me, from the fatal tree
   To pluck a garland for herself, or me?
I do obey you, beauty! for in death
   You seem a fair one. Oh, that you had breath
To give your shade a name! Stay, stay, I feel
   A horror in me, all my blood is steel!
Stiff, stark, my joints 'gainst one another knock!
   Whose daughter?—ha! Great Savage of the Rock?   10
He's good as great. I am almost a stone!
   And ere I can ask more of her, she's gone.
Alas, I am all marble! Write the rest
   Thou wouldst have written, fame, upon my breast:
It is a large fair table, and a true,
   And the disposure will be something new,
When I, who would her poet have become,
   At least may bear the inscription to her tomb.
She was the Lady Jane, and Marchioness
   Of Winchester—the heralds can tell this: 20
Earl Rivers' grandchild—serve not forms, good fame,
   Sound thou her virtues, give her soul a name.

Had I a thousand mouths, as many tongues,
  And voice to raise them from my brazen lungs,
I durst not aim at that: the dotes were such
  Thereof, no notion can express how much
Their carat was! I or my trump must break,
  But rather I, should I of that part speak!
It is too near of kin to heaven, the soul,
  To be described; fame's fingers are too foul   30
To touch these mysteries. We may admire
  The blaze and splendour, but not handle fire!
What she did here by great example well
  To enlive posterity, her fame may tell;
And, calling truth to witness, make that good
  From the inherent graces in her blood!
Else, who doth praise a person by a new
  But a feigned way, doth rob it of the true.
Her sweetness, softness, her fair courtesy,
  Her wary guards, her wise simplicity,   40
Were like a ring of virtues 'bout her set,
  And piety the centre, where all met.
A reverend state she had, an awful eye,
  A dazzling, yet inviting majesty:
What nature, fortune, institution, fact
  Could sum to a perfection, was her act!
How did she leave the world, with what contempt!
  Just as she in it lived, and so exempt
From all affection. When they urged the cure
  Of her disease, how did her soul assure   50
Her sufferings, as the body had been away!
  And to the torturers, her doctors, say,
Stick on your cupping-glasses, fear not, put
  Your hottest caustics to, burn, lance, or cut:
'Tis but a body which you can torment,
  And I into the world all soul was sent!
Then comforted her lord, and blessed her son
  Cheered her fair sisters in her race to run,
With gladness tempered her sad parents' tears,
  Made her friends' joys to get above their fears,   60
And, in her last act, taught the standers-by
  With admiration and applause to die.
Let angels sing her glories, who did call

Her spirit home to her original;
Who saw the way was made it, and were sent
    To carry and conduct the complement
'Twixt death and life; where her mortality
    Became her birthday to eternity.
And now, through circumfusèd light, she looks
    On nature's secrets, there, as her own books: 70
Speaks heaven's language, and discourseth free
    To every order, every hierarchy;
Beholds her Maker, and in him doth see
    What the beginnings of all beauties be,
And all beatitudes that thence do flow:
    Which they that have the crown are sure to know.
Go now, her happy parents, and be sad,
    If you not understand what child you had;
If you dare grudge at heaven, and repent
    To have paid again a blessing was but lent 80
And trusted so, as it deposited lay
    At pleasure to be called for, every day;
If you can envy your own daughter's bliss
    And wish her state less happy than it is;
If you can cast about your either eye,
    And see all dead here, or about to die;
The stars, that are the jewels of the night,
    And day, deceasing with the prince of light,
The sun; great kings and mightiest kingdoms fall;
    Whole nations, nay mankind, the world, with all 90
That ever had beginning there, to have end!
    With what injustice should one soul pretend
To escape this common known necessity;
    When we were all born, we began to die;
And, but for that contention and brave strife
    The Christian hath to enjoy the future life,
He were the wretched'st of the race of men:
    But as he soars at that, he bruiseth then
The serpent's head; gets above death and sin,
    And, sure of heaven, rides triumphing in. 100

84

Eupheme;
or, the Fair Fame Left to Posterity
of that Truly Noble Lady, the Lady Venetia Digby,
Late Wife of Sir Kenelm Digby, Knight:
A Gentleman Absolute in All Numbers.

Consisting of These Ten Pieces:
The Dedication of Her Cradle;
The Song of Her Descent;
The Picture of Her Body;
Her Mind;
Her Being Chosen a Muse;
Her Fair Offices;
Her Happy Match;
Her Hopeful Issue;
Her 'Αποθέωσις, or Relation to the Saints;
Her Inscription, or Crown.

Vivam amare voluptas, defunctam religio.

Stat[ius].

84. i

The Dedication of Her Cradle

Fair fame, who art ordained to crown
With evergreen, and great renown,
Their heads that envy would hold down
      With her, in shade

Of death and darkness, and deprive
Their names of being kept alive
By thee and conscience, both who thrive
      By the just trade

Of goodness still: vouchsafe to take
This cradle, and for goodness' sake,   10
A dedicated ensign make
      Thereof, to time.

That all posterity, as we,
Who read what the crepundia be,
May something by that twilight see
              'Bove rattling rhyme.

For though that rattles, timbrels, toys
Take little infants with their noise,
As properest gifts to girls and boys
              Of light expense;   20

Their corals, whistles, and prime coats,
Their painted masks, their paper boats,
With sails of silk, as the first notes
              Surprise their sense:

Yet here are no such trifles brought,
No cobweb cauls, no surcoats wrought
With gold or clasps, which might be bought
              On every stall.

But here's a song of her descent,
And call to the high parliament   30
Of heaven, where seraphim take tent
              Of ordering all.

This uttered by an ancient bard,
Who claims (of reverence) to be heard,
As coming with his harp, prepared
              To chant her gree,

Is sung; as also her getting up
By Jacob's ladder to the top
Of that eternal port kept ope
              For such as she.   40

84. ii

The Song of Her Descent

I sing the just and uncontrolled descent
   Of Dame Venetia Digby, styled the fair;
For mind and body the most excellent
   That ever nature, or the later air,

Gave two such houses as Northumberland
   And Stanley, to the which she was co-heir.
Speak it, you bold Penates, you that stand
   At either stem, and know the veins of good
Run from your roots; tell, testify the grand
   Meeting of graces, that so swelled the flood   10
Of virtues in her as, in short, she grew
   The wonder of her sex and of your blood.
And tell thou, Alderley, none can tell more true
   Thy niece's line than thou that gav'st thy name
Into the kindred, whence thy Adam drew
   Meschin's honour with the Cestrian fame
Of the first Lupus, to the family
   By Ranulf . . .

The rest of this song is lost

84. iii

The Picture of the Body

Sitting, and ready to be drawn,
   What make these velvets, silks, and lawn,
   Embroideries, feathers, fringes, lace,
   Where every limb takes like a face?

Send these suspected helps to aid
   Some form defective, or decayed;
   This beauty without falsehood fair
   Needs naught to clothe it but the air.

Yet something, to the painter's view,
   Were fitly interposed; so new,   10
   He shall, if he can understand,
   Work with my fancy his own hand.

Draw first a cloud, all save her neck,
   And out of that make day to break;
   Till, like her face it do appear,
   And men may think all light rose there.

Then let the beams of that disperse
   The cloud, and show the universe;
   But at such distance as the eye
   May rather yet adore than spy.   20

The heaven designed, draw next a spring,
   With all that youth or it can bring:
   Four rivers branching forth like seas,
   And Paradise confining these.

Last, draw the circles of this globe,
   And let there be a starry robe
   Of constellations 'bout her hurled;
   And thou hast painted beauty's world.

But, painter, see thou do not sell
   A copy of this piece, nor tell   30
   Whose 'tis: but if it favour find,
   Next sitting we will draw her mind.

84. iv

The Mind

Painter, you're come, but may be gone;
   Now I have better thought thereon,
   This work I can perform alone;
   And give you reasons more than one.

Not that your art I do refuse;
   But here I may no colours use.
   Beside, your hand will never hit
   To draw a thing that cannot sit.

You could make shift to paint an eye,
   An eagle towering in the sky,   10
   The sun, a sea, or soundless pit,
   But these are like a mind, not it.

No, to express a mind to sense
  Would ask a heaven's intelligence;
  Since nothing can report that flame
  But what's of kin to whence it came.

Sweet mind, then speak yourself, and say
  As you go on, by what brave way
  Our sense you do with knowledge fill
  And yet remain our wonder still.   20

I call you muse, now make it true:
  Henceforth may every line be you;
  That all may say that see the frame,
  This is no picture, but the same.

A mind so pure, so perfect fine,
  As 'tis not radiant, but divine:
  And so disdaining any trier;
  'Tis got where it can try the fire.

There, high exalted in the sphere,
  As it another nature were,   30
  It moveth all, and makes a flight
  As circular as infinite.

Whose notions when it will express
  In speech, it is with that excess
  Of grace, and music to the ear,
  As what it spoke, it planted there.

The voice so sweet, the words so fair,
  As some soft chime had stroked the air;
  And though the sound were parted thence,
  Still left an echo in the sense.   40

But that a mind so rapt, so high,
  So swift, so pure, should yet apply
  Itself to us, and come so nigh
  Earth's grossness: there's the how and why.

Is it because it sees us dull,
    And stuck in clay here, it would pull
    Us forth by some celestial sleight
    Up to her own sublimèd height?

Or hath she here, upon the ground
    Some paradise, or palace found   50
    In all the bounds of beauty fit,
    For her to inhabit? There is it.

Thrice happy house, that hast receipt
    For this so lofty form, so straight,
    So polished, perfect, round, and even,
    As it slid moulded off from heaven.

Not swelling like the ocean proud,
    But stooping gently as a cloud,
    As smooth as oil poured forth, and calm
    As showers, and sweet as drops of balm.   60

Smooth, soft, and sweet, in all a flood
    Where it may run to any good;
    And where it stays, it there becomes
    A nest of odorous spice and gums.

In action, wingèd as the wind;
    In rest, like spirits left behind
    Upon a bank, or field of flowers,
    Begotten by that wind, and showers.

In thee, fair mansion, let it rest,
    Yet know with what thou art possessed: 70
    Thou entertaining in thy breast
    But such a mind, mak'st God thy guest.

84. [viii]

A whole quaternion in the midst of this poem is lost, containing entirely the three
next pieces of it, and all of the fourth (which in the order of the whole, is the

eighth) excepting the very end: which at the top of the next quaternion goeth on thus:

But for you, growing gentlemen, the happy branches of two so illustrious houses as these, wherefrom your honoured mother is in both lines descended, let me leave you this last legacy of counsel; which, so soon as you arrive at years of mature understanding, open you, sir, that are the eldest, and read it to your brethren, for it will concern you all alike. Vowed by a faithful servant and client of your family, with his latest breath expiring it,   B.J.

To Kenelm, John, George

Boast not these titles of your ancestors,
    Brave youths, they're their possessions, none of yours;   10
When your own virtues equalled have their names,
    'Twill be but fair to lean upon their fames,
For they are strong supporters; but till then,
    The greatest are but growing gentlemen.
It is a wretched thing to trust to reeds,
    Which all men do that urge not their own deeds
Up to their ancestors'; the river's side
    By which you're planted shows your fruit shall bide.
Hang all your rooms with one large pedigree:
    'Tis virtue alone is true nobility.   20
Which virtue from your father, ripe, will fall;
    Study illustrious him, and you have all.

84. ix

Elegy on My Muse,
the Truly Honoured Lady, the Lady Venetia Digby:
who, Living, Gave Me Leave to Call Her So.
Being Her Ἀποθέωσις, *or Relation to the Saints.*

Sera quidem tanto struitur medicina dolori.

'Twere time that I died too, now she is dead,
    Who was my muse, and life of all I said,
The spirit that I wrote with, and conceived;

All that was good or great in me she weaved,
And set it forth; the rest were cobwebs fine,
  Spun out in name of some of the old nine,
To hang a window or make dark the room,
  Till, swept away, they were cancelled with a broom:
Nothing that could remain, or yet can stir
  A sorrow in me, fit to wait to her!   10
Oh, had I seen her laid out a fair corse
  By death on earth, I should have had remorse
On nature for her, who did let her lie,
  And saw that portion of herself to die.
Sleepy, or stupid nature, couldst thou part
  With such a rarity, and not rouse art
With all her aids to save her from the seize
  Of vulture death, and those relentless clees?
Thou wouldst have lost the phoenix, had the kind
  Been trusted to thee, not to itself assigned.   20
Look on thy sloth, and give thyself undone:
  For so thou art with me, now she is gone.
My wounded mind cannot sustain this stroke;
  It rages, runs, flies, stands, and would provoke
The world to ruin with it; in her fall,
  I sum up mine own breaking, and wish all.
Thou hast no more blows, fate, to drive at one:
  What's left a poet, when his muse is gone?
Sure, I am dead, and know it not! I feel
  Nothing I do, but like a heavy wheel,   30
Am turned with another's powers. My passion
  Whirls me about, and to blaspheme in fashion,
I murmur against God, for having ta'en
  Her blessèd soul hence, forth this valley vain
Of tears, and dungeon of calamity.
  I envy it the angels' amity!
The joy of saints, the crown for which it lives,
  The glory and gain of rest which the place gives!
Dare I profane, so irreligious be
  To greet or grieve her soft euthanasy?   40
So sweetly taken to the court of bliss,
  As spirits had stolen her spirit, in a kiss,
From off her pillow and deluded bed,
  And left her lovely body unthought dead!

Indeed, she is not dead, but laid to sleep
   In earth, till the last trump awake the sheep
And goats together, whither they must come
   To hear their judge and his eternal doom;
To have that final retribution,
   Expected with the flesh's restitution.   50
For, as there are three natures, schoolmen call
   One corporal only, the other spiritual,
Like single; so there is a third, commixt
   Of body and spirit together, placed betwixt
Those other two; which must be judged or crowned:
   This, as it guilty is, or guiltless found,
Must come to take a sentence, by the sense
   Of that great evidence, the conscience,
Who will be there, against that day prepared,
   To accuse, or quit all parties to be heard.   60
O day of joy and surety to the just,
   Who in that feast of resurrection trust!
That great eternal holy-day of rest
   To body and soul, where love is all the guest,
And the whole banquet is full sight of God:
   Of joy the circle and sole period!
All other gladness with the thought is barred,
   Hope hath her end, and faith hath her reward.
This being thus, why should my tongue or pen
   Presume to interpel that fulness, when   70
Nothing can more adorn it than the seat
   That she is in, or make it more complete?
Better be dumb, than superstitious;
   Who violates the godhead is most vicious
Against the nature he would worship. He
   Will honoured be in all simplicity,
Have all his actions wondered at, and viewed
   With silence and amazement, not with rude,
Dull, and profane, weak, and imperfect eyes,
   Have busy search made in his mysteries.   80
He knows what work he hath done to call this guest
   Out of her noble body to this feast,
And give her place, according to her blood,
   Amongst her peers, those princes of all good:
Saints, martyrs, prophets, with those hierarchies,

Angels, archangels, principalities,
The dominations, virtues, and the powers,
    The thrones, the cherub, and seraphic bowers,
That planted round, there sing before the Lamb
    A new song to his praise, and great *I am*.   90
And she doth know, out of the shade of death,
    What 'tis to enjoy an everlasting breath!
To have her captived spirit freed from flesh,
    And on her innocence a garment fresh
And white as that, put on; and in her hand
    With boughs of palm, a crownèd victrix stand!
And will you, worthy son, sir, knowing this,
    Put black and mourning on, and say you miss
A wife, a friend, a lady, or a love,
    Whom her redeemer honoured hath above   100
Her fellows, with the oil of gladness, bright
    In heaven's empyrean, with a robe of light?
Thither you hope to come, and there to find
    That pure, that precious and exalted mind
You once enjoyed; a short space severs ye
    Compared unto that long eternity
That shall rejoin ye. Was she then so dear
    When she departed? You will meet her there
Much more desired, and dearer than before,
    By all the wealth of blessings, and the store   110
Accumulated on her by the Lord
    Of life and light, the Son of God, the Word!
There all the happy souls that ever were
    Shall meet with gladness in one theatre;
And each shall know, there, one another's face,
    By beatific virtue of the place.
There shall the brother with the sister walk,
    And sons and daughters with their parents talk,
But all of God; they still shall have to say,
    But make him all in all, their theme that day,   120
That happy day, that never shall see night!
    Where he will be all beauty to the sight,
Wine or delicious fruits unto the taste,
    A music in the ears, will ever last,
Unto the scent a spicery or balm,
    And to the touch a flower like soft as palm.

He will all glory, all perfection be,
   God, in the Union, and the Trinity!
That holy, great, and glorious mystery
   Will there revealèd be in majesty!   130
By light and comfort of spiritual grace,
   The vision of our Saviour, face to face
In his humanity! To hear him preach
   The price of our redemption, and to teach
Through his inherent righteousness, in death,
   The safety of our souls, and forfeit breath:
What fulness of beatitude is here!
   What love with mercy mixèd doth appear!
To style us friends, who were by nature foes;
   Adopt us heirs by grace, who were of those   140
Had lost ourselves, and prodigally spent
   Our native portions and possessèd rent;
Yet have all debts forgiven us, and advance
   By imputed right to an inheritance
In his eternal kingdom, where we sit
   Equal with angels, and co-heirs of it!
Nor dare we under blasphemy conceive
   He that shall be our supreme judge should leave
Himself so uninformed of his elect,
   Who knows the hearts of all, and can dissect   150
The smallest fibre of our flesh; he can
   Find all our atoms from a point to a span,
Our closest creeks and corners, and can trace
   Each line, as it were graphic, in the face.
And best he knew her noble character,
   For 'twas himself who formed and gave it her.
And to that form lent two such veins of blood,
   As nature could not more increase the flood
Of title in her. All nobility
   (But pride, that schism of incivility)   160
She had, and it became her; she was fit
   To have known no envy but by suffering it.
She had a mind as calm as she was fair,
   Not tossed or troubled with light lady-air,
But kept an even gait; as some straight tree
   Moved by the wind, so comely movèd she.
And by the awful manage of her eye

She swayed all business in the family!
To one she said, Do this; he did it. So
    To another, Move; he went. To a third, Go;   170
He run. And all did strive with diligence
    To obey and serve her sweet commandéments.
She was, in one, a many parts of life;
    A tender mother, a discreeter wife,
A solemn mistress, and so good a friend,
    So charitable to religious end,
In all her petty actions so devote,
    As her whole life was now become one note
Of piety and private holiness.
    She spent more time in tears herself to dress   180
For her devotions, and those sad essays
    Of sorrow, than all pomp of gaudy days:
And came forth ever cheerèd with the rod
    Of divine comfort, when she'd talked with God.
Her broken sighs did never miss whole sense,
    Nor can the bruisèd heart want eloquence:
For prayer is the incense most perfumes
    The holy altars, when it least presumes.
And hers were all humility; they beat
    The door of grace, and found the mercy-seat.   190
In frequent speaking by the pious psalms
    Her solemn hours she spent, or giving alms,
Or doing other deeds of charity,
    To clothe the naked, feed the hungry. She
Would sit in an infirmary whole days
    Poring, as on a map, to find the ways
To that eternal rest, where now she hath place
    By sure election, and predestined grace.
She saw her Saviour, by an early light,
    Incarnate in the manger, shining bright   200
On all the world. She saw him on the cross,
    Suffering and dying to redeem our loss.
She saw him rise, triumphing over death
    To justify, and quicken us in breath.
She saw him too in glory to ascend
    For his designèd work, the perfect end
Of raising, judging, and rewarding all
    The kind of man, on whom his doom should fall.

All this by faith she saw, and framed a plea,
   In manner of a daily apostrophe,   210
To him should be her judge, true God, true man,
   Jesus, the only-gotten Christ, who can
(As being redeemer, and repairer too
   Of lapsèd nature) best know what to do,
In that great act of judgement: which the Father
   Hath given wholly to the Son (the rather
As being the Son of Man) to show his power,
   His wisdom, and his justice, in that hour,
The last of hours, and shutter-up of all;
   Where first his power will appear, by call   220
Of all are dead to life; his wisdom show
   In the discerning of each conscience, so;
And most his justice, in the fitting parts
   And giving dues to all mankind's deserts.
In this sweet ecstasy she was rapt hence.
   Who reads, will pardon my intelligence,
That thus have ventured these true strains upon,
   To publish her a saint. My muse is gone.

In pietatis memoriam
quam praestas
Venetiae *tuae illustrissim.*
marit. dign. Digbeie
Hanc Ἀποθέωσιν, *tibi, tuisque sacro.*

The tenth, being her Inscription, or Crown, is lost.

85

[Horace, Epode ii]
The Praises of a Country Life

Happy is he, that from all business clear
   As the old race of mankind were,
With his own oxen tills his sire's left lands,
   And is not in the usurer's bands;
Nor, soldier-like, started with rough alarms,
   Nor dreads the sea's enragèd harms;

But flees the bar and courts, with the proud boards
   And waiting-chambers of great lords.
The poplar tall he then doth marrying twine
   With the grown issue of the vine;   10
And with his hook lops off the fruitless race,
   And sets more happy in the place;
Or in the bending vale beholds afar
   The lowing herds there grazing are;
Or the pressed honey in pure pots doth keep
   Of earth, and shears the tender sheep;
Or when that autumn through the fields lifts round
   His head, with mellow apples crowned,
How, plucking pears his own hand grafted had,
   And purple-matching grapes, he's glad!   20
With which, Priapus, he may thank thy hands,
   And, Silvane, thine, that kept'st his lands.
Then, now beneath some ancient oak he may,
   Now in the rooted grass, him lay,
Whilst from the higher banks do slide the floods;
   The soft birds quarrel in the woods,
The fountains murmur as the streams do creep,
   And all invite to easy sleep.
Then when the thundering Jove his snow and showers
   Are gathering by the wintry hours,   30
Or hence, or thence, he drives with many a hound
   Wild boars into his toils pitched round;
Or strains on his small fork his subtle nets
   For the eating thrush, or pitfalls sets;
And snares the fearful hare and new-come crane,
   And 'counts them sweet rewards so ta'en.
Who, amongst these delights, would not forget
   Love's cares so evil, and so great?
But if, to boot with these, a chaste wife, meet
   For household aid and children sweet,   40
Such as the Sabines'; or a sun-burnt blowze,
   Some lusty, quick Apulian's spouse,
To deck the hallowed hearth with old wood fired
   Against the husband comes home tired;
That penning the glad flock in hurdles by,
   Their swelling udders doth draw dry;
And from the sweet tub wine of this year takes,

And unbought viands ready makes:
Not Locrine oysters I could then more prize,
  Nor turbot, nor bright golden-eyes;   50
If with bright floods, the winter troubled much,
  Into our seas send any such,
The Ionian godwit, nor the Guinea-hen
  Could not go down my belly then
More sweet than olives that new-gathered be
  From fattest branches of the tree;
Or the herb sorrel that loves meadows still,
  Or mallows, loosing body's ill;
Or at the feast of bounds, the lamb then slain,
  Or kid forced from the wolf again.   60
Among these cates how glad the sight doth come
  Of the fed flocks approaching home!
To view the weary oxen draw, with bare
  And fainting necks, the turnèd share!
The wealthy household swarm of bondmen met,
  And 'bout the steaming chimney set!
These thoughts when usurer Alfius, now about
  To turn mere farmer, had spoke out,
'Gainst the ides his moneys he gets in with pain
  At the calends, puts all out again.   70

86

[*Horace,*] *Ode the First, the Fourth Book:*
To Venus

  Venus, again thou mov'st a war
Long intermitted: pray thee, pray thee, spare;
  I am not such as in the reign
Of the good Cinara I was; refrain,
  Sour mother of sweet loves, forbear
To bend a man, now at his fiftieth year
  Too stubborn for commands, so slack;
Go where youth's soft entreaties call thee back.
  More timely hie thee to the house,
With thy bright swans, of Paulus Maximus: 10
  There jest and feast, make him thine host,
If a fit liver thou dost seek to toast;

For he's both noble, lovely, young,
And for the troubled client files his tongue,
   Child of a hundred arts, and far
Will he display the ensigns of thy war.
   And when he smiling finds his grace
With thee 'bove all his rivals' gifts take place,
   He'll thee a marble statue make
Beneath a sweet-wood roof, near Alba lake: 20
   There shall thy dainty nostril take
In many a gum, and for thy soft ear's sake
   Shall verse be set to harp and lute,
And Phrygian hautboy, not without the flute.
   There twice a day in sacred lays
The youths and tender maids shall sing thy praise;
   And in the Salian manner meet
Thrice 'bout thy altar with their ivory feet.
   Me now nor wench, nor wanton boy,
Delights, nor credulous hope of mutual joy,   30
   Nor care I now healths to propound,
Or with flesh flowers to girt my temple round.
   But why, O why, my Ligurine,
Flow my thin tears down these pale cheeks of mine?
   Or why, my well-graced words among,
With an uncomely silence fails my tongue?
   Hard-hearted, I dream every night
I hold thee fast! but fled hence, with the light,
   Whether in Mars's field thou be,
Or Tiber's winding streams, I follow thee.   40

87

[Horace,] Ode ix, 3rd Book:
To Lydia
Dialogue of Horace and Lydia

Horace   Whilst, Lydia, I was loved of thee,
And, 'bout thy ivory neck, no youth did fling
   His arms more acceptable free,
I thought me richer than the Persian king.

Lydia   Whilst Horace loved no mistress more,
       Nor after Chloe did his Lydia sound,
         In name I went all names before,
       The Roman Ilia was not more renowned.

Horace   'Tis true, I'm Thracian Chloe's, I,
       Who sings so sweet, and with such cunning plays,   10
         As, for her, I'd not fear to die,
       So fate would give her life, and longer days.

Lydia   And I am mutually on fire
       With gentle Calais, Thurine Ornith's son;
         For whom I doubly would expire,
       So fates would let the boy a long thread run.

Horace   But say old love return should make,
       And us disjoined, force to her brazen yoke,
         That I bright Chloe off should shake,
       And to left Lydia now the gate stood ope?   20

Lydia   Though he be fairer than a star,
       Thou lighter than the bark of any tree,
         And than rough Adria angrier far,
       Yet would I wish to love, live, die with thee.

88

[*A Fragment of Petronius Arbiter*]

Doing a filthy pleasure is, and short;
And done, we straight repent us of the sport;
Let us not then rush blindly on unto it,
Like lustful beasts that only know to do it:
For lust will languish, and that heat decay.
But thus, thus, keeping endless holiday,
Let us together closely lie, and kiss,
There is no labour, nor no shame in this;
This hath pleased, doth please, and long will please; never
Can this decay, but is beginning ever.   10

89

[*Martial, Epigram lxxvii, Book VIII*]

Liber, of all thy friends, thou sweetest care,
    Thou worthy in eternal flower to fare,
If thou be'st wise, with Syrian oil let shine
    Thy locks, and rosy garlands crown thy head;
Dark thy clear glass with old Falernian wine,
    And heat with softest love thy softer bed.
He that but living half his days, dies such,
    Makes his life longer than 'twas given him, much.

90

Martial, [*Epigram xlvii, Book X*]

The things that make the happier life are these,
Most pleasant Martial: substance got with ease,
Not laboured for, but left thee by thy sire;
A soil not barren; a continual fire;
Never at law; seldom in office gowned;
A quiet mind; free powers; and body sound;
A wise simplicity; friends alike-stated;
Thy table without art, and easy rated;
Thy night not drunken, but from cares laid waste,
No sour or sullen bed-mate, yet a chaste;   10
Sleep that will make the darkest hours swift-paced.
Will to be what thou art, and nothing more;
Nor fear thy latest day, nor wish therefore.

UNGATHERED VERSE

I

From Thomas Palmer's The Sprite of Trees and Herbs, *1598–9*

When late, grave Palmer, these thy grafts and flowers,
So well disposed by thy auspicious hand,
Were made the objects to my weaker powers,
I could not but in admiration stand.
First, thy success did strike my sense with wonder,
That 'mongst so many plants transplanted hither
Not one but thrives, in spite of storms and thunder,
Unseasoned frosts, or the most envious weather.
Then I admired the rare and precious use
Thy skill hath made of rank despisèd weeds,   10
Whilst other souls convert to base abuse
The sweetest simples, and most sovereign seeds.
Next, that which rapt me was, I might behold
How, like the carbuncle in Aaron's breast,
The seven-fold flower of art, more rich than gold,
Did sparkle forth in centre of the rest;
Thus, as a ponderous thing in water cast
Extendeth circles into infinites,
Still making that the greatest that is last,
Till the one hath drowned the other in our sights: 20
So in my brain the strong impression
Of thy rich labours worlds of thoughts created,
Which thoughts being circumvol[v]ed in gyre-like motion
Were spent with wonder as they were dilated,
Till giddy with amazement I fell down
In a deep trance; * * * * *
* * * * * when, lo! to crown thy worth
I struggled with this passion that did drown
My abler faculties; and thus brake forth:
    Palmer, thy travails well become thy name,   30
    And thou in them shalt live as long as fame.

    Dignum laude virum musa vetat mori.

2

From Nicholas Breton's Melancholic Humours, *1600*
In Authorem

Thou that wouldst find the habit of true passion,
    And see a mind attired in perfect strains;
Not wearing modes, as gallants do a fashion
    In these pied times, only to show their brains:

Look here on Breton's work, the master print,
    Where such perfections to the life do rise.
If they seem wry to such as look asquint
    The fault's not in the object, but their eyes.

For as one coming with a lateral view
    Unto a cunning piece wrought pérspective   10
Wants faculty to make a censure true;
    So with this author's readers will it thrive:

Which, being eyed directly, I divine,
His proof their praise will meet, as in this line.

3

Fragments from England's Parnassus, *1600*

Murder
Those that in blood such violent pleasure have,
Seldom descend but bleeding to their grave.

Peace
War's grea[t]est woes, and misery's increase,
Flows from the surfeits which we take in peace.

Riches
Gold is a suitor never took repulse;
It carries palm with it where'er it goes,
Respect, and observation; it uncovers
The knotty heads of the most surly grooms,

Enforcing iron doors to yield it way,
Were they as strong rammed-up as Aetna gates.   10
It bends the hams of Gossip Vigilance,
And makes her supple feet as swift as wind.
It thaws the frostiest and most stiff disdain,
Muffles the clearness of election,
Strains fancy unto foul apostasy,
And strikes the quickest-sighted judgement blind.
Then why should we despair? Despair, away!
Where gold's the motive, women have no nay.

4

From Love's Martyr, *1601*
The Phoenix Analysed

Now, after all, let no man
    Receive it for a fable
    If a bird so amiable
Do turn into a woman.

Or, by our turtle's augur,
    That nature's fairest creature
    Prove of his mistress' feature
But a bare type and figure.

5

From Love's Martyr, *1601*
Ode ἐνθουσιαστικὴ

Splendour, O more than mortal!
For other forms come short all
Of her illustrate brightness,
As far as sin's from lightness.

Her wit as quick and sprightful
As fire, and more delightful
Than the stol'n sports of lovers,
When night their meeting covers.

Judgement adorned with learning
Doth shine in her discerning,   10
Clear as a naked vestal
Closed in an orb of crystal.

Her breath for sweet exceeding
The phoenix' place of breeding,
But, mixed with sound, transcending
All nature of commending.

Alas! Then whither wade I
In thought to praise this lady,
When seeking her renowning,
Myself am so near drowning?   20

Retire and say: Her graces
Are deeper than their faces;
Yet she's nor nice to show them,
Nor takes she pride to know them.

6

From Pancharis, *1603*
Ode ἀλληγορικὴ

Who saith our times nor have, nor can
   Produce us a black swan?
  Behold, where one doth swim:
    Whose note and hue,
Besides the other swans' admiring him,
    Betray it true;
  A gentler bird than this
Did never dint the breast of Tamesis.

Mark, mark, but when his wing he takes
   How fair a flight he makes,   10
  How upward and direct!
    Whilst pleased Apollo
Smiles in his sphere to see the rest affect
    In vain to follow;

This swan is only his
And Phoebus' love cause of his blackness is.

He showed him first the hoof-cleft spring
   Near which the Thespiades sing;
   The clear Dircaean fount
     Where Pindar swam,   20
The pale Pyrene, and the forkèd mount;
     And when they came
   To brooks and broader streams
From Zephyr's rape would close him with his beams.

This changed his down, till this, as white
   As the whole herd in sight,
   And still is in the breast:
     That part nor wind
Nor sun could make to vary from the rest,
     Or alter kind.   30
    So much doth virtue hate,
For style of rareness, to degenerate.

Be then both rare and good, and long
   Continue thy sweet song.
   Nor let one river boast
     Thy tunes alone;
But prove the air, and sail from coast to coast:
     Salute old Mon;
   But first to Clwyd stoop low,
The vale that bred thee pure as her hills' snow.   40

From thence display thy wing again,
   Over Iërna main
   To the Eugenian dale;
     There charm the rout
With thy soft notes, and hold them within pale
     That late were out.
    Music hath power to draw,
Where neither force can bend, nor fear can awe.

Be proof, the glory of his hand,
   Charles Mountjoy, whose command   50

Hath all been harmony;
   And more hath won
Upon the kerne, and wildest Irishry
    Than time hath done,
   Whose strength is above strength,
And conquers all things (yea, itself) at length.

Whoever sipped at Baphyre river,
   That heard but spite deliver
   His far-admirèd acts,
    And is not rapt   60
With entheate rage to publish their bright tracts?
    (But this more apt
   When him alone we sing);
Now must we ply our aim: our swan's on wing.

Who (see!) already hath o'er-flown
   The Hebrid isles, and known
   The scattered Orcades;
    From thence is gone
To utmost Thule; whence he backs the seas
    To Caledon,   70
   And over Grampius mountain
To Lomond lake, and Tweed's black-springing fountain.

Haste, haste, sweet singer, nor to Tyne,
   Humber, or Ouse decline,
   But overland to Trent;
    There cool thy plumes,
And up again in skies and air to vent
    Their reeking fumes;
   Till thou at Thames alight,
From whose proud bosom thou began'st thy flight.   80

Thames, proud of thee, and of his fate
   In entertaining late
   The choice of Europe's pride:
    The nimble French;
The Dutch whom wealth, not hatred, doth divide;
    The Danes that drench

Their cares in wine; with sure
Though slower Spain, and Italy mature.

All which, when they but hear a strain
   Of thine, shall think the main   90
   Hath sent her mermaids in
      To hold them here;
Yet looking in thy face, they shall begin
      To lose that fear;
   And, in the place, envy
So black a bird, so bright a quality.

But should they know (as I) that this,
   Who warbleth *Pancharis*,
   Were Cygnus, once high flying
      With Cupid's wing,   100
Though now by love transformed, and daily dying
      (Which makes him sing
   With more delight and grace);
Or thought they Leda's white adulterer's place

Among the stars should be resigned
   To him, and he there shrined;
   Or Thames be rapt from us
      To dim and drown
In heaven the sign of old Eridanus:
      How they would frown!   110
   But these are mysteries
Concealed from all but clear prophetic eyes.

It is enough, their grief shall know
   At their return, nor Po,
   Iberus, Tagus, Rhine,
      Scheldt, nor the Maas,
Slow Arar nor swift Rhone, the Loire nor Seine,
      With all the race
   Of Europe's waters can
Set out a like, or second, to our swan.   120

7

From Thomas Wright's
The Passions of the Mind in General, *1604*
To the Author

In picture, they which truly understand
Require (besides the likeness of the thing)
Light, posture, heightening, shadow, colouring,
All which are parts commend the cunning hand;
And all your book, when it is throughly scanned,
Will well confess: presenting, limiting
Each subtlest passion, with her source and spring,
So bold, as shows your art you can command.
But now your work is done, if they that view
The several figures languish in suspense   10
To judge which passion's false and which is true,
Between the doubtful sway of reason and sense;
'Tis not your fault if they shall sense prefer,
Being told there, reason cannot, sense may, err.

8

From The Faithful Shepherdess
To the Worthy Author, M[r] John Fletcher

The wise and many-headed bench that sits
    Upon the life and death of plays and wits
(Composed of gamester, captain, knight, knight's man,
    Lady or pucelle, that wears mask or fan,
Velvet or taffeta cap, ranked in the dark
    With the shop's foreman, or some such brave spark
That may judge for his sixpence) had, before
    They saw it half, damned thy whole play, and more;
Their motives were, since it had not to do
    With vices, which they looked for, and came to.   10
I, that am glad thy innocence was thy guilt,
    And wish that all the muses' blood were spilt

In such a martyrdom, to vex their eyes
  Do crown thy murdered poem: which shall rise
A glorified work to time, when fire
  Or moths shall eat what all these fools admire.

9

Epitaph on Cecilia Bulstrode

Stay, view this stone; and if thou beest not such,
Read here a little, that thou mayst know much.
It covers, first, a virgin; and then one
That durst be that in court: a virtue alone
To fill an epitaph. But she had more:
She might have claimed to have made the graces four,
Taught Pallas language, Cynthia modesty,
As fit to have increased the harmony
Of spheres, as light of stars; she was earth's eye;
The sole religious house and votary,   10
With rites not bound, but conscience. Wouldst thou all?
She was Cil Bulstrode. In which name, I call
Up so much truth as, could I it pursue,
Might make the fable of good women true.

10

From Coryate's Crudities, *1611*
Certain Opening and Drawing Distichs

To be applied as mollifying cataplasms to the
tumours, carnosities, or difficult pimples full of
matter appearing in the author's front, conflated of styptic and glutinous vapours arising
out of the *Crudities*; the heads whereof are particularly pricked and pointed out by letters
for the reader's better understanding. . . .

Here follow certain other verses, as charms to
unlock the mystery of the *Crudities*.

The title-page of Coryate's *Crudities* (1611), engraved by William Hole

A

Here, like Arion, our Coryate doth draw   10
All sorts of fish with music of his maw.

B

Here, not up Holborn, but down a steep hill,
He's carried 'twixt Montreuil and Abbeville.

C

A horse here is saddled, but no Tom him to back:
It should rather have been Tom that a horse did lack.

D

Here, up the Alps (not so plain as to Dunstable)
He's carried like a cripple, from constable to constable.

E

A punk here pelts him with eggs. How so?
For he did but kiss her, and so let her go.

F

Religiously here he bids, Row from the stews!   20
He will expiate this sin with converting the Jews.

G

And there, while he gives the zealous bravado,
A rabbin confutes him with the bastinado.

H

Here, by a boor too, he's like to be beaten,
For grapes he had gathered before they were eaten.

I

Old hat here, torn hose, with shoes full of gravel,
And louse-dropping case, are the arms of his travel.

K

Here, finer than coming from his punk you him see,
F shows what he was, K what he will be.

L

Here France and Italy both to him shed   30
Their horns, and Germany pukes on his head.

M

And here he disdained not, in a foreign land,
To lie at livery, while the horses did stand.

N

But here, neither trusting his hands nor his legs,
Being in fear to be robbed, he most learnedly begs.

11

From Coryate's Crudities . . . *To the Right Noble
Tom, Tell-Troth of his Travails, the Coryate of
Odcombe, and his Book, Now Going to Travel.*

T ry and trust *Roger* was the word, but now   [80]
H onest Tom Tell-Troth puts down Roger: how?
O f travel he discourseth so at large,
M arry, he sets it out at his own charge;
A nd therein (which is worth his valour too)
S hows he dares more than Paul's Churchyard durst do.

C ome forth thou bonny bouncing book then, daughter
O f Tom of Odcombe, that odd jovial author;
R ather his son, I should have called thee: why?
Y es, thou wert born out of his travelling thigh
A s well as from his brains, and claim'st thereby   [90]
T o be his Bacchus as his Pallas: be
E ver his thighs male then, and his brains she.

12

From Coryate's Crambe, *1611*
Certain Verses Written upon Coryate's Crudities

Which should have been printed with the other panegyric lines, but then were upon some occasions omitted, and now communicated to the world.

> *Incipit* Ben Jonson
> To the London Reader, on the Odcombian Writer,
>   Polytopian Thomas the Traveller.

> Whoever he be, would write a story at
> The height, let him learn of Mr Tom Coryate;
> Who, because his matter in all should be meet
> To his strength, hath measured it out with his feet.
> And that, say philosophers, is the best model.
> Yet who could have hit on't but the wise noddle
> Of our Odcombian, that literate elf,
> To line out no stride, but paced by himself,
> And allow you for each particular mile
> By the scale of his book, a yard of his style?   10
> Which unto all ages for his will be known,
> Since he treads in no other man's steps but his own.
> And that you may see he most luckily meant
> To write it with the self-same spirit he went,
> He says to the world, Let any man mend it!
> In five months he went it, in five months he penned it.
> But who will believe this, that chanceth to look
> The map of his journey, and sees in his book
> France, Savoy, Italy, and Helvetia,
> The Low Countries, Germany and Rhoetia   20
> There named to be travelled? For this our Tom saith:
> Pize on't! You have his historical faith.
> Each leaf of his journal and line doth unlock
> The truth of his heart there, and tells what a-clock
> He went out at each place, and at what he came in,
> How long he did stay, at what sign he did inn.
> Besides he tried ship, cart, waggon, and chair,
> Horse, foot, and all but flying in the air;

And therefore, however the travelling nation
Or builders of story have oft imputation   30
Of lying, he fears so much the reproof
Of his foot or his pen, his brain or his hoof,
That he dares to inform you (but somewhat meticulous)
How scabbèd, how raggèd, and how pediculous
He was in his travail, how like to be beaten
For grapes he had gathered before they were eaten.
How fain for his venery he was to cry *tergum o!*
And lay in straw with the horses at Bergamo;
How well and how often his shoes too were mended,
That sacred to Odcombe are there now suspended: 40
I mean that one pair wherewith he so hobbled
From Venice to Flushing; were not they well cobbled?
Yes. And thanks God in his pistle or his book
How many learnèd men he have drawn with his hook
Of Latin and Greek, to his friendship. And seven
He there doth protest he saw of the eleven.
Nay, more in his wardrobe, if you will laugh at a
Jest, he says: *item*, one suit of black taffeta
(Except a doublet), and bought of the Jews.
So that not them, his scabs, lice, or the stews,   50
Or anything else that another should hide
Doth he once dissemble, but tells he did ride
In a cart 'twixt Montreuil and Abbeville.
And being at Flushing enforcèd to feel
Some want, they say in a sort he did crave:
I writ he only his tail there did wave;
Which he not denies. Now, being so free,
Poor Tom, have we cause to suspect just thee?
No! As I first said, who would write a story at
The height, let him learn of Mr Tom Coryate.   60

[*UV* 13, 14, 15—three short poems in Latin—are omitted from this
edition: see H & S, viii. 381–2.]

16

A Speech Presented unto King James at a Tilting, in the Behalf of the Two Noble Brothers, S[i]r Robert and S[i]r Henry Rich, Now Earls of Warwick and Holland

Two noble knights, whom true desire and zeal
Hath armed at all points, charge me humbly kneel
Unto thee, king of men, their noblest parts
To tender thus: their lives, their loves, their hearts!
The elder of these two, rich hope's increase,
Presents a royal altar of fair peace;
And as an everlasting sacrifice
His life, his love, his honour which ne'er dies
He freely brings; and on this altar lays
As true oblations. His brother's emblem says   10
Except your gracious eye, as through a glass
Made prospective, behold him, he must pass
Still that same little point he was; but when
Your royal eye, which still creates new men,
Shall look, and on him so, then art's a liar
If from a little spark he rise not fire.

17

From Cynthia's Revenge, *or* Menander's Ecstasy, *1613*
To His Much and Worthily Esteemed Friend, the Author

Who takes thy volume to his virtuous hand
Must be intended still to understand;
Who bluntly doth but look upon the same
May ask, What author would conceal his name?
Who reads may rove, and call the passage dark,
Yet may, as blind men, sometimes hit the mark.
Who reads, who roves, who hopes to understand
May take thy volume to his virtuous hand.
Who cannot read, but only doth desire
To understand, he may at length admire.   10

18

To the Most Noble, and Above His Titles,
Robert, Earl of Somerset

They are not those, are present with their face
    And clothes, and gifts, that only do thee grace
At these thy nuptials; but whose heart and thought
    Do wait upon thee: and their love not bought.
Such wear true wedding robes, and are true friends
    That bid, God give thee joy! and have no ends.
Which I do, early, virtuous Somerset,
    And pray thy joys as lasting be as great.
Not only this, but every day of thine
    With the same look, or with a better, shine.   10
May she whom thou for spouse today dost take
    Out-be that wife in worth thy friend did make;
And thou to her, that husband, may exalt
    Hymen's amends, to make it worth his fault.
So be there never discontent or sorrow
    To rise with either of you on the morrow.
So be your concord still as deep, as mute,
    And every joy in marriage turn a fruit.
So may those marriage-pledges comforts prove,
    And every birth increase the heat of love.   20
So in their number may [you] never see
    Mortality, till you [im]mortal be.
And when your years rise more than would be told,
    Yet neither of you seem to th'other old.
Th[a]t all that view you then and late may say,
    Sure, this glad pair were married but this day!

19

From The Ghost of Richard the Third, *1614*
To His Friend the Author,
Upon His Richard

When these, and such, their voices have employed,
    What place is for my testimony void?

Or to so many and so broad seals had
  What can one witness, and a weak one, add
To such a work, as could not need theirs? Yet
  If praises, when they're full, heaping admit,
My suffrage brings thee all increase, to crown
  Thy *Richard*, raised in song, past pulling down.

20

From The Husband, *1614*
To the Worthy Author, on The Husband

It fits not only him that makes a book
  To see his work be good, but that he look
Who are his test, and what their judgement is,
  Lest a false praise do make their dotage his.
I do not feel that ever yet I had
  The art of uttering wares if they were bad,
Or skill of making matches in my life;
  And therefore I commend unto *The Wife*
That went before, a *Husband*. She, I'll swear,
  Was worthy of a good one; and this, here,   10
I know for such, as (if my word will weigh)
  She need not blush upon the marriage-day.

21

From Britannia's Pastorals, *The Second Book, 1616*
To My Truly-Beloved Friend, Mr Browne, On His Pastorals

Some men, of books or friends not speaking right,
  May hurt them more with praise, than foes with spite.
But I have seen thy work, and I know thee:
  And, if thou list thyself, what thou canst be.
For though but early in these paths thou tread,
  I find thee write most worthy to be read.
It must be thine own judgement, yet, that sends
  This thy work forth: that judgement mine commends.

And where the most read books on authors' fames,
    Or, like our money-brokers, take up names   10
On credit, and are cozened, see that thou
    By offering not more sureties than enow
Hold thine own worth unbroke: which is so good
    Upon the exchange of letters, as I would
More of our writers would, like thee, not swell
    With the *how much* they set forth, but the *how well.*

22

Charles Cavendish to His Posterity

Sons, seek not me among these polished stones,
These only hide part of my flesh and bones,
Which, did they ne'er so neat or proudly dwell,
Will all turn dust, and may not make me swell.
Let such as justly have outlived all praise
Trust in the tombs their careful friends do raise;
I made my life my monument, and yours,
To which there's no material that endures,
Nor yet inscription like it. Write but that,
And teach your nephews it to emulate: 10
It will be matter loud enough to tell
Not when I died, but how I lived. Farewell.

23

From George Chapman's The Georgics of Hesiod, *1618* *To My Worthy and Honoured Friend, Mr George Chapman, On His Translation of Hesiod's* Works and Days

Whose work could this be, Chapman, to refine
Old Hesiod's ore and give it us, but thine,
Who hadst before wrought in rich Homer's mine?

What treasure hast thou brought us! And what store
Still, still, dost thou arrive with at our shore,
To make thy honour and our wealth the more!

If all the vulgar tongues that speak this day
Were asked of thy discoveries, they must say
To the Greek coast thine only knew the way.

Such passage hast thou found, such returns made,   10
As now, of all men, it is called thy trade:
And who make thither else, rob or invade.

24

From The Rogue, *1622*
On the Author, Work, and Translator

Who tracks this author's or translator's pen
Shall find that either hath read books and men:
To say but one, were single. Then it chimes
When the old words do strike on the new times,
As in this Spanish Proteus; who, though writ
But in one tongue, was formed with the world's wit;
And hath the noblest mark of a good book,
That an ill man dares not securely look
Upon it, but will loathe, or let it pass,
As a deformèd face doth a true glass.   10
Such books deserve translators of like coat
As was the genius wherewith they were wrote;
And this hath met that one that may be styled
More than the foster-father of this child;
For though Spain gave him his first air and vogue
He would be called henceforth the English *Rogue*,
But that he's too well-suited, in a cloth
Finer than was his Spanish, if my oath
Will be received in court; if not, would I
Had clothed him so. Here's all I can supply   20
To your desert, who've done it, friend. And this
Fair emulation and no envy is;
When you behold me wish myself the man
That would have done that which you only can.

25

From Mr William Shakespeare's Comedies, Histories, and Tragedies, *1623*
To the Reader

This figure that thou here seest put,
    It was for gentle Shakespeare cut;
Wherein the graver had a strife
    With nature, to out-do the life.
Oh, could he but have drawn his wit
    As well in brass as he hath hit
His face, the print would then surpass
    All that was ever writ in brass.
But since he cannot, reader, look
    Not on his picture but his book.   10

26

From Mr William Shakespeare's Comedies, Histories, and Tragedies, *1623*
To the Memory of My Beloved,
The Author, Mr William Shakespeare,
And What He Hath Left Us

To draw no envy, Shakespeare, on thy name,
    Am I thus ample to thy book and fame;
While I confess thy writings to be such
    As neither man nor muse can praise too much:
'Tis true, and all men's suffrage. But these ways
    Were not the paths I meant unto thy praise:
For silliest ignorance on these may light,
    Which, when it sounds at best, but echoes right;
Or blind affection, which doth ne'er advance
    The truth, but gropes, and urgeth all by chance;   10
Or crafty malice might pretend this praise,
    And think to ruin where it seemed to raise.
These are as some infamous bawd or whore
    Should praise a matron: what could hurt her more?

But thou art proof against them, and indeed
   Above the ill fortune of them, or the need.
I therefore will begin. Soul of the age!
   The applause, delight, the wonder of our stage!
My Shakespeare, rise: I will not lodge thee by
   Chaucer or Spenser, or bid Beaumont lie   20
A little further, to make thee a room;
   Thou art a monument without a tomb,
And art alive still while thy book doth live,
   And we have wits to read, and praise to give.
That I not mix thee so, my brain excuses:
   I mean with great, but disproportioned, muses;
For if I thought my judgement were of years
   I should commit thee surely with thy peers:
And tell how far thou didst our Lyly outshine,
   Or sporting Kyd, or Marlowe's mighty line.   30
And though thou hadst small Latin, and less Greek,
   From thence to honour thee I would not seek
For names, but call forth thundering Aeschylus,
   Euripides, and Sophocles to us,
Pacuvius, Accius, him of Cordova dead,
   To life again, to hear thy buskin tread
And shake a stage; or, when thy socks were on,
   Leave thee alone for the comparison
Of all that insolent Greece or haughty Rome
   Sent forth, or since did from their ashes come.   40
Triumph, my Britain, thou hast one to show
   To whom all scenes of Europe homage owe.
He was not of an age, but for all time!
   And all the muses still were in their prime
When like Apollo he came forth to warm
   Our ears, or like a Mercury to charm!
Nature herself was proud of his designs,
   And joyed to wear the dressing of his lines,
Which were so richly spun and woven so fit
   As, since, she will vouchsafe no other wit.   50
The merry Greek, tart Aristophanes,
   Neat Terence, witty Plautus, now not please,
But antiquated and deserted lie
   As they were not of nature's family.
Yet must I not give nature all: thy art,

My gentle Shakespeare, must enjoy a part.
For though the poet's matter nature be,
    His art doth give the fashion. And that he
Who casts to write a living line must sweat
    (Such as thine are) and strike the second heat   60
Upon the muses' anvil: turn the same
    (And himself with it) that he thinks to frame;
Or for the laurel he may gain a scorn:
    For a good poet's made, as well as born;
And such wert thou. Look how the father's face
    Lives in his issue: even so, the race
Of Shakespeare's mind and manners brightly shines
    In his well-turnèd and true-filèd lines:
In each of which he seems to shake a lance,
    As brandished at the eyes of ignorance.   70
Sweet swan of Avon! What a sight it were
    To see thee in our waters yet appear,
And make those flights upon the banks of Thames
    That so did take Eliza, and our James!
But stay, I see thee in the hemisphere
    Advanced, and made a constellation there!
Shine forth, thou star of poets, and with rage
    Or influence chide or cheer the drooping stage;
Which, since thy flight from hence, hath mourned like night,
    And despairs day, but for thy volume's light.   80

[For *UV* 27, see *Dubia*, 4]

28

To the Memory of That Most Honoured Lady Jane,
Eldest Daughter to Cuthbert, Lord Ogle,
And Countess of Shrewsbury

I could begin with that grave form, *Here lies*,
And pray thee, reader, bring thy weeping eyes
To see who 'tis: a noble countess, great
In blood, in birth, by match, and by her seat;

Religious, wise, chaste, loving, gracious, good;
And number attributes unto a flood:
But every table in this church can say
A list of epithets, and praise this way.
No stone in any wall here but can tell
Such things of everybody, and as well.   10
Nay, they will venture one's descent to hit,
And Christian name, too, with a herald's wit.
But I would have thee to know something new,
Not usual in a lady, and yet true:
At least so great a lady. She was wife
But of one husband; and since he left life,
But sorrow, she desired no other friend:
And her she made her inmate to the end,
To call on sickness still to be her guest,
Whom she with sorrow first did lodge, then feast,   20
Then entertain, and as death's harbinger;
So wooed at last, that he was won to her
Importune wish, and by her loved lord's side
To lay her here, enclosed, his second bride.
Where, spite of death, next life, for her love's sake,
This second marriage will eternal make.

29

From Lucan's Pharsalia, *1627*
To My Chosen Friend,
The Learned Translator of Lucan,
Thomas May Esq.

When, Rome, I read thee in thy mighty pair,
And see both climbing up the slippery stair
Of fortune's wheel, by Lucan driven about,
And the world in it, I begin to doubt:
At every line some pin thereof should slack
At least, if not the general engine crack.
But when again I view the parts so peised,
And those in number so, and measure raised,
As neither Pompey's popularity,
Caesar's ambition, Cato's liberty,   10

Calm Brutus' tenor start, but all along
Keep due proportion in the ample song,
It makes me, ravished with just wonder, cry
What muse, or rather god of harmony
Taught Lucan these true modes? Replies my sense:
What gods but those of arts and eloquence,
Phoebus and Hermes? They whose tongue or pen
Are still the interpreters 'twixt gods and men!
But who hath them interpreted, and brought
Lucan's whole frame unto us, and so wrought   20
As not the smallest joint or gentlest word
In the great mass or machine there is stirred?
The self-same genius! so the work will say:
The sun translated, or the son of May.

30

From The Battle of Agincourt, *1627*
The Vision of Ben Jonson,
On the Muses of His Friend
M. Drayton

It hath been questioned, Michael, if I be
A friend at all; or, if at all, to thee:
Because who make the question have not seen
Those ambling visits pass in verse between
Thy muse and mine, as they expect. 'Tis true;
You have not writ to me, nor I to you;
And though I now begin, 'tis not to rub
Haunch against haunch, or raise a rhyming club
About the town; this reckoning I will pay
Without conferring symbols. This is my day.   10
    It was no dream: I was awake, and saw!
Lend me thy voice, O fame, that I may draw
Wonder to truth, and have my vision hurled,
Hot from thy trumpet, round about the world!
    I saw a beauty from the sea to rise
That all earth looked on: and that earth, all eyes!

It cast a beam as when the cheerful sun
Is fair got up, and day some hours begun,
And filled an orb as circular as heaven.
The orb was cut forth into regions seven,   20
And those so sweet and well-proportioned parts
As it had been the circle of the arts!
When, by thy bright *Ideas* standing by,
I found it pure and perfect poesy;
There read I straight thy learnèd *Legends* three,
Heard the soft airs between our swains and thee,
Which made me think the old Theocritus
Or rural Virgil come to pipe to us!
But then thy epistolar *Heroic Songs*,
Their loves, their quarrels, jealousies, and wrongs   30
Did all so strike me, as I cried, Who can
With us be called the Naso, but this man?
And looking up, I saw Minerva's fowl
Perched overhead, the wise Athenian *Owl*;
I thought thee then our Orpheus, that wouldst try
Like him, to make the air one volary;
And I had styled thee Orpheus: but before
My lips could form the voice, I heard that roar
And rouse, the marching of a mighty force,
Drums against drums, the neighing of the horse,   40
The fights, the cries; and, wondering at the jars,
I saw and read it was thy *Barons' Wars*!
Oh, how in those dost thou instruct these times
That rebels' actions are but valiant crimes;
And, carried, though with shout and noise, confess
A wild and an authorized wickedness!
Say'st thou so, Lucan? But thou scorn'st to stay
Under one title. Thou hast made thy way
And flight about the isle well-near by this
In thy admirèd periegesis.   50
Or universal circumduction
Of all that read thy *Poly-Olbion*.
That read it? That are ravished! Such was I
With every song, I swear, and so would die;
But that I hear again thy drum to beat
A better cause, and strike the bravest heat
That ever yet did fire the English blood:

Our right in France! (if rightly understood).
There, thou art Homer! Pray thee, use the style
Thou hast deserved, and let me read the while   60
Thy catalogue of ships, exceeding his;
Thy list of aids and force, for so it is
The poet's act; and for his country's sake
Brave are the musters that the muse will make.
And when he ships them where to use their arms,
How do his trumpets breathe! What loud alarms!
Look how we read the Spartans were inflamed
With bold Tyrtaeus' verse: when thou art named,
So shall our English youth urge on, and cry
An Agincourt! An Agincourt! Or die.   70
This book, it is a catechism to fight,
And will be bought of every lord and knight
That can but read; who cannot, may in prose
Get broken pieces, and fight well by those.
The *Miseries of Margaret the Queen*
Of tender eyes will more be wept, than seen;
I feel it by mine own, that overflow
And stop my sight in every line I go.
But then refreshèd with thy *Fairy Court*,
I look on *Cynthia*, and *Sirena's* sport,   80
As on two flowery carpets that did rise
And with their grassy green restored mine eyes.
Yet give me leave to wonder at the birth
Of thy strange *Mooncalf*, both thy strain of mirth
And gossip-got acquaintance, as to us
Thou hadst brought Lapland, or old Cobalus,
Empusa, Lamia, or some monster more
Than Afric knew, or the full Grecian store!
I gratulate it to thee, and thy *Ends*,
To all thy virtuous and well-chosen friends;   90
Only my loss is that I am not there:
And till I worthy am to wish I were,
I call the world that envies me to see
If I can be a friend, and friend to thee.

31

[Epitaph on Katherine, Lady Ogle]
ʽΟ Ζεὺς κατεῖδε χρόνιος εἰς τὰς διφθέρας.

'Tis a record in heaven. You, that were
Her children and grandchildren, read it here!
Transmit it to your nephews, friends, allies,
Tenants and servants, have they hearts and eyes
To view the truth and own it. Do but look
With pause upon it: make this page your book;
Your book? Your volume! Nay, the state and story,
Code, digests, pandects of all female glory!

Dip[h]thera Jovis

She was the light (without reflex
Upon herself) to all her sex;   10
The best of women: her whole life
Was the example of a wife,
Or of a parent, or a friend!
All circles had their spring and end
In her, and what could perfect be
Or without angles, it was she.
All that was solid in the name
Of virtue, precious in the frame,
Or else magnetic in the force,
Or sweet or various in the course;   20
What was proportion, or could be
By warrant called just symmetry
In number, measure, or degree
Of weight or fashion, it was she.
Her soul possessed her flesh's state
In fair freehold, not an inmate;
And when the flesh here shut up day,
Fame's heat upon the grave did stay;
And hourly brooding o'er the same
Keeps warm the spice of her good name,   30
Until the dust returnèd be
Into a phoenix, which is she.

For this did Katherine, Lady Ogle, die
To gain the crown of immortality,
Eternity's great charter; which became
Her right, by gift and purchase of the Lamb:
Sealed and delivered to her in the sight
Of angels and all witnesses of light,
Both saints and martyrs, by her lovèd Lord.
And this a copy is of the record.

32

From Bosworth Field, *1629*
On the Honoured Poems of His Honoured Friend,
Sir John Beaumont, Baronet

This book will live: it hath a genius; this
  Above his reader or his praiser is.
Hence, then, profane! Here needs no words' expense
  In bulwarks, ravelins, ramparts, for defence,
Such as the creeping common pioneers use
  When they do sweat to fortify a muse.
Though I confess a Beaumont's book to be
  The bound and frontier of our poetry;
And doth deserve all muniments of praise
  That art or engine on the strength can raise.   10
Yet who dares offer a redoubt to rear,
  To cut a dike, or stick a stake up here
Before this work, where envy hath not cast
  A trench against it, nor a battery placed?
Stay till she make her vain approaches: then
  If, maimed, she come off, 'tis not of men
This fort of so impregnable access,
  But higher power, as spite could not make less
Nor flattery; but, secured by the author's name,
  Defies what's cross to piety or good fame;   20
And like a hallowed temple free from taint
  Of ethnicism, makes his muse a saint.

33

From French Court Airs, *1629*
To My Worthy Friend, Master Edward Filmer,
On His Work Published

What charming peals are these,
That, while they bind the senses, do so please?
They are the marriage-rites
Of two, the choicest pair of man's delights,
Music and poesy:
French air and English verse here wedded lie.
Who did this knot compose
Again hath brought the lily to the rose;
And, with their chainèd dance,
Re-celebrates the joyful match with France.   10
They are a school to win
The fair French daughter to learn English in;
And, gracèd with her song,
To make the language sweet upon her tongue.

34

An Expostulation w[i]th Inigo Jones

M[aste]r Survey[o]r, you that first began
From thirty pound in pipkins, to the man
You are: from them leaped forth an architect
Able to talk of Euclid, and correct
Both him and Archimede; damn Archytas,
The noblest engineer that ever was;
Control Ctesibius, overbearing us
With mistook names out of Vitruvius;
Drawn Aristotle on us: and thence shown
How much architectonike is your own!   10
(Whether the building of the stage or scene,
Or making of the properties it mean,
Vizors or antics, or it comprehend
Something your sirship doth not yet intend!)

By all your titles and whole style at once
Of Tire-man, Mountebank, and Justice Jones
I do salute you! Are you fitted yet?
Will any of these express your place or wit?
Or are you so ambitious 'bove your peers,
You would be an asinigo, by your ears? 20
Why, much good do't you! Be what beast you will,
You'll be, as Langley said, an Inigo still.
   What makes your wretchedness to bray so loud
In town and court; are you grown rich and proud?
Your trappings will not change you: change your mind.
No velvet sheath you wear will alter kind;
A wooden dagger is a dagger of wood,
Though gold or ivory hafts would make it good.
What is the cause you pomp it so? (I ask)
And all men echo, You have made a masque. 30
I chime that too; and I have met with those
That do cry up the machine, and the shows,
The majesty of Juno in the clouds,
And peering-forth of Iris in the shrouds!
The ascent of Lady Fame, which none could spy,
Not they that sided her, Dame Poetry,
Dame History, Dame Architecture, too,
And Goody Sculpture, brought with much ado
To hold her up. O shows! Shows! Mighty shows!
The eloquence of masques! What need of prose, 40
Or verse, or sense, to express immortal you?
You are the spectacles of state! 'Tis true
Court hieroglyphics, and all arts afford
In the mere perspective of an inch-board.
You ask no more than certain politic eyes,
Eyes that can pierce into the mysteries
Of many colours, read them, and reveal
Mythology there painted on slit deal.
Oh, to make boards to speak! There is a task!
Painting and carpentry are the soul of masque. 50
Pack with your peddling poetry to the stage:
This is the money-get, mechanic age!
To plant the music where no ear can reach,
Attire the persons as no thought can teach
Sense what they are: which, by a specious, fine

Term of the architects, is called *design*!
But in the practised truth destruction is
Of any art beside what he calls his.
Whither, O whither will this tire-man grow?
His name is Σκευοποιός we all know,   60
The maker of the properties, in sum,
The scene, the engine! But he now is come
To be the music-master, fabler, too;
He is, or would be, the main Dominus Do-
All in the work! And so shall still, for Ben:
Be Inigo the whistle, and his men.
He's warm on his feet now, he says, and can
Swim without cork: why, thank the good Queen Anne.
I am too fat to envy him; he too lean
To be worth envy. Henceforth I do mean   70
To pity him, as smiling at his feat
Of lantern-lurry: with fuliginous heat
Whirling his whimsies, by a subtlety
Sucked from the veins of shop-philosophy.
What would he do now, giving his mind that way,
In presentation of some puppet-play
Should but the king his justice-hood employ
In setting-forth of such a solemn toy?
How would he firk, like Adam Overdo,
Up and about, dive into cellars, too,   80
Disguised, and thence drag forth enormity:
Discover vice, commit absurdity
Under the moral? Show he had a pate
Moulded, or stroked up, to survey a state?
O wise surveyor! Wiser architect!
But wisest Inigo! Who can reflect
On the new priming of thy old sign-posts,
Reviving with fresh colours the pale ghosts
Of thy dead standards; or (with miracle) see
Thy twice-conceived, thrice-paid-for imagery   90
And not fall down before it, and confess
Almighty architecture: who no less
A goddess is, than painted cloth, deal-boards,
Vermilion, lake, or cinnabar affords
Expression for; with that unbounded line
Aimed at in thy omnipotent design.

What poesy e'er was painted on a wall
That might compare with thee? What story shall,
Of all the Worthies, hope to outlast thy one,
So the materials be of Purbeck stone?   100
Live long the Feasting Room! And ere thou burn
Again, thy architect to ashes turn!
Whom not ten fires nor a parliament can,
Will all remonstrance, make an honest man.

35

To Inigo, Marquis Would-Be
A Corollary

But 'cause thou hear'st the mighty k[ing] of Spain
Hath made his Inigo marquis, wouldst thou fain
Our Charles should make thee such? 'Twill not become
All kings to do the self-same deeds with some;
Besides, his man may merit it, and be
A noble honest soul: what's this to thee?
He may have skill and judgement to design
Cities and temples: thou, a cave for wine
Or ale! He build a palace: thou a shop
With sliding windows, and false lights a-top;   10
He draw a forum with quadrivial streets:
Thou paint a lane, where Thumb the pygmy meets!
He, some Colossus to bestride the seas
From the famed pillars of old Hercules:
Thy canvas giant at some channel aims,
Or Dowgate torrent, falling into Thames,
And, straddling, shows the boys' brown-paper fleet,
Yearly set out there, to sail down the street.
Your works thus differing, troth, let so your style:
Content thee to be Pancridge earl the while;   20
An earl of show, for all thy work is show.
But when thou turn'st a real Inigo,
Or canst of truth the least entrenchment pitch,
We'll have thee styled the Marquis of New Ditch.

36

To a Friend
An Epigram of Him

Sir Inigo doth fear it, as I hear,
And labours to seem worthy of that fear,
That I should write upon him some sharp verse
Able to eat into his bones, and pierce
The marrow. Wretch, I quit thee of thy pain:
Thou'rt too ambitious, and dost fear in vain!
The Libyan lion hunts no butterflies,
He makes the camel and dull ass his prize.
If thou be so desirous to be read
Seek out some hungry painter, that for bread   10
With rotten chalk or coal upon a wall
Will well design thee, to be viewed of all
That sit upon the common draught or strand:
Thy forehead is too narrow for my brand.

37

To My Detractor

My verses were commended, thou dar'st say,
  And they were very good: yet thou think'st nay.
For thou objectest (as thou hast been told)
  The envied return of forty pound in gold.
Fool, do not rate my rhymes: I've found thy vice
  Is to make cheap the lord, the lines, the price.
But bawl thou on; I pity thee, poor cur,
  That thou hast lost thy noise, thy foam, thy stir,
To be known what thou art, a blatant beast,
  By barking against me. Thou look'st at least   10
I now would write on thee? No, wretch, thy name
  Shall not work out unto it such a fame.
Thou art not worth it. Who will care to know
  If such a tyke as thou e'er wert or no,
A mongrel cur? Thou shouldst stink forth and die
  Nameless and noisome as thy infamy.

No man will tarry by thee as he goes
   To ask thy name, if he have half his nose,
But fly thee, like the pest! Walk not the street
   Out in the dog-days, lest the killer meet   20
Thy noddle, with his club; and dashing forth
   Thy dirty brains, men smell thy want of worth.

38

From The Northern Lass, *1632*
To My Old Faithful Servant,
And, By His Continued Virtue, My Loving Friend,
The Author of This Work, Mr Rich[ard] Brome

I had you for a servant once, Dick Brome,
   And you performed a servant's faithful parts;
Now you are got into a nearer room
   Of fellowship, professing my old arts.
And you do do them well, with good applause,
   Which you have justly gainèd from the stage
By observation of those comic laws
   Which I, your master, first did teach the age.
You learned it well, and for it, served your time
   A 'prenticeship, which few do nowadays.   10
Now each court hobby-horse will wince in rhyme;
   Both learnèd and unlearnèd, all write plays.
It was not so of old: men took up trades
   That knew the crafts they had been bred in, right:
An honest Bilbo smith would make good blades,
   And the physician teach men spew or shite;
     The cobbler kept him to his awl; but now
     He'll be a pilot, scarce can guide a plough.

39

[An Answer to Alexander Gill]

Shall the prosperity of a pardon still
Secure thy railing rhymes, infamous Gill,

At libelling? Shall no Star Chamber peers,
Pillory, nor whip, nor want of ears
(All which thou hast incurred deservedly)
Nor degradation from the ministry
To be the Denis of thy father's school,
Keep in thy barking wit, thou bawling fool?
Thinking to stir me, thou hast lost thy end:
I'll laugh at thee, poor wretched tyke; go send   10
Thy blatant muse abroad, and teach it rather
A tune to drown the ballads of thy father;
For thou hast naught [in thee] to cure his fame,
But tune and noise, the echo of thy shame.
A rogue by statute, censured to be whipped,
Cropped, branded, slit, neck-stocked: go, you are stripped!

40

From Meditation of Man's Mortality, *1634*
To Mrs Alice Sutcliffe,
on Her Divine Meditations

When I had read
          Your holy *Meditations*,
And in them viewed
          The uncertainty of life,
The motives and true spurs
          To all good nations;
The peace of conscience
          And the godly's strife,
The danger of delaying
          To repent,   10
And the deceit of pleasures
          By consent;
The comfort of weak Christians,
          With their warning
From fearful back-slides;
          And the debt we're in
To follow goodness
          By our own discerning

Our great reward,
      The eternal crown to win: 20
I said, Who'd supped so deep
      Of this sweet chalice
Must Celia be:
      The anagram of Alice.

41

From The Female Glory, *1635*
The Garland of the Blessed Virgin Marie

Here are five letters in this blessèd name,
  Which, changed, a five-fold mystery design:
The M, the myrtle, A, the almonds claim,
  R, rose, I, ivy, E, sweet eglantine.

These form thy garland. Whereof myrtle green,
  The gladdest ground to all the numbered five,
Is so implexèd and laid in between
  As love here studied to keep grace alive.

The second string is the sweet almond bloom
  Ymounted high upon Selinus' crest;   10
As it alone, and only it, had room
  To knit thy crown, and glorify the rest.

The third is from the garden culled, the rose,
  The eye of flowers, worthy for his scent
To top the fairest lily now that grows
  With wonder on the thorny regiment.

The fourth is humble ivy, intersert,
  But lowly laid, as on the earth asleep,
Preservèd in her antique bed of vert:
  No faith's more firm or flat than where't doth creep. 20

But that which sums all is the eglantine,
  Which of the field is clept the sweetest briar,
Inflamed with ardour to that mystic shine
  In Moses' bush, unwasted in the fire.

Thus love and hope and burning charity
    (Divinest graces) are so intermixed
With odorous sweets and soft humility,
    As if they adored the head whereon they're fixed.

The Reverse: on the Back Side

These mysteries do point to three more great
    On the reverse of this your circling crown,   30
    All pouring their full shower of graces down,
The glorious Trinity in Union met.

Daughter and mother and the spouse of God,
    Alike of kin to that most blessèd Trine
    Of persons, yet in Union one, divine;
How are thy gifts and graces blazed abroad!

Most holy and pure virgin, blessèd maid,
    Sweet tree of life, King David's strength and tower,
    The house of gold, the gate of heaven's power,
The morning-star, whose light our fall hath stayed.   40

Great queen of queens, most mild, most meek, most wise,
    Most venerable, cause of all our joy;
    Whose cheerful look our sadness doth destroy,
And art the spotless mirror to man's eyes.

The seat of sapience, the most lovely mother,
    And most to be admirèd of thy sex,
    Who mad'st us happy all, in thy reflex,
By bringing forth God's only Son, no other.

Thou throne of glory, beauteous as the moon,
    The rosy morning, or the rising sun,   50
    Who, like a giant, hastes his course to run,
Till he hath reached his two-fold point of noon.

How are thy gifts and graces blazed abroad,
    Through all the lines of this circumference
    To imprint in all purged hearts this virgin sense,
Of being daughter, mother, spouse of God!

42

From The Shepherds' Holiday, *1635*
To My Dear Son and Right-Learned Friend,
Master Joseph Rutter

You look, my Joseph, I should something say
Unto the world in praise of your first play;
And truly, so I would, could I be heard.
You know I never was of truth afeared
And less ashamed; not when I told the crowd
How well I loved truth: I was scarce allowed
By those deep-grounded, understanding men
That sit to censure plays, yet know not when
Or why to like; they found it all was new,
And newer than could please them, because true.   10
Such men I met withal, and so have you.
Now for mine own part, and it is but due
(You have deserved it from me), I have read
And weighed your play: untwisted every thread,
And know the woof and warp thereof; can tell
Where it runs round and even; where so well,
So soft and smooth it handles, the whole piece,
As it were spun by nature off the fleece:
This is my censure. Now there is a new
Office of wit, a mint (and this is true)   20
Cried up of late; whereto there must be first
A master-worker called, the old standard burst
Of wit, and a new made: a warden, then,
And a comptroller, two most rigid men
For order, and for governing the pyx;
A say-master, hath studied all the tricks
Of fineness and alloy: follow his hint,
You've all the mysteries of wit's new mint,
    The valuations, mixtures, and the same
    Concluded from a carat to a dram.   30

43

From Annalia Dubrensia, *1635*
An Epigram to My Jovial Good Friend
Mr Robert Dover,
on His Great Instauration of His Hunting and Dancing
at Cotswold

I cannot bring my muse to drop [her] vies
'Twixt Cotswold and the Olympic exercise;
But I can tell thee, Dover, how thy games
Renew the glories of our blessèd James:
How they do keep alive his memory
With the glad country, and posterity;
How they advance true love, and neighbourhood,
And do both church and commonwealth the good,
In spite of hypocrites, who are the worst
Of subjects: let such envy, till they burst.   10

44

[A Song of Welcome to King Charles]

Fresh as the day, and new as are the hours,
Our first of fruits, that is the prime of flowers
Bred by your breath on this low bank of ours,
Now in a garland by the graces knit,
Upon this obelisk advanced for it,
We offer as a circle the most fit
To crown the years which you begin, great king,
And you with them, as father of our spring.

45

[A Song of the Moon]

To the wonders of the Peak
I am come to add and speak,
Or, as some would say, to break
My mind unto you:

And I swear by all the light
At my back, I am no sprite,
But a very merry wight
      Pressed in to see you.

I had somewhat else to say,
But have lost it by the way,   10
I shall think on't ere't be day.
      The moon commends her
To the merry beards in hall,
Those turned up, and those that fall,
Morts and merkins that wag all,
      Tough, foul, or tender.

And as either news or mirth
Rise or fall upon the earth,
She desires of every birth
      Some taste to send her.   20
Specially the news of Derby:
For if there or peace or war be,
To the Peak it is so hard by,
      She soon will hear it.

If there be a cuckold major
That the wife heads for a wager
As the standard shall engage her,
      The moon will bear it.
Though she change as oft as she,
And of circle be as free,   30
Or her quarters lighter be,
      Yet do not fear it.

Or if any strife betide
For the breeches with the bride,
'Tis but the next neighbour ride
      And she is pleasèd.
Or if't be the gossips' hap
Each to pawn her husband's cap
At Pem Waker's good ale-tap,
      Her mind is easèd.   40

Or by chance if in their grease,
Or their ale, they break the peace,
Forfeiting their drinking lease:
    She will not seize it.

46

To Mr Ben Jonson in His Journey
By Mr Craven

When wit and learning are so hardly set
That from their needful means they must be barred,
Unless by going hard they maintenance get,
Well may Ben Jonson say the world goes hard.

This Was Mr Ben Jonson's Answer Of The Sudden

Ill may Ben Jonson slander so his feet,
For when the profit with the pain doth meet,
Although the gate were hard, the gain is sweet.

47

A Grace by Ben Jonson
Extempore before King James

Our king and queen the Lord God bless,
The Palsgrave and the Lady Bess,
And God bless every living thing
That lives and breathes and loves the king.
God bless the Council of Estate,
And Buckingham the fortunate;
God bless them all, and keep them safe:
And God bless me, and God bless Ralph.

Another Version
A Form of a Grace

The king, the queen, the prince, God bless,
The Palsgrave and the Lady Bess;

God bless the Council and the State,
And Buckingham the fortunate;
God bless every living thing
That the king loves, and loves the king.
God bless us all, Bedford keep safe:
God bless me, and God bless Ralph.

48

Ode

If men and times were now
    Of that true face
As when they both were great, and both knew how
    That fortune to embrace
By cherishing the spirits that gave their greatness grace:
    I then could raise my notes
    Loud to the wondering throng
And better blazon them than all their coats,
That were the happy subject of my song.

But clownish pride hath got   10
    So much the start
Of civil virtue, that he now is not
    Nor can be of desert
That hath not country impudence enough to laugh at art:
    Whilst like a blaze of straw
    He dies with an ill scent
To every sense, and scorn to those that saw
How soon with a self-tickling he was spent.

Break then thy quills, blot out
    Thy long-watch[ed] verse,   20
And rather to the fire than to the rout
    Thy laboured tunes rehearse,
Whose air will sooner hell, than their dull senses, pierce:
    Thou that dost spend thy days
    To get thee a lean face
And come forth worthy ivy or the bays,
And, in this age, canst hope no [other] grace.

Yet since the bright and wise
    Minerva deigns
Upon so humbled earth to cast her eyes,   30
    We'll rip our richest veins
And once more strike the ear of time with those fresh strains
    As shall, besides delight
    And cunning of their ground,
Give cause to some of wonder, some despite,
But unto more, despair to imitate their sound.

Throw, holy virgin, then
    Thy crystal shield
About this isle, and charm the round, as when
    Thou mad'st in open field   40
The rebel giants stoop, and gorgon envy yield;
    Cause reverence, if not fear,
    Throughout their general breasts,
And, by their taking, let it once appear
Who worthy win, who not, to be wise Pallas' guests.

49

[An Epistle to a Friend]

    'Censure not sharply then, but me advise,
    Before I write more verse, to be more wise.'

So ended your epistle; mine begins:
He that so censureth or adviseth, sins;
The empty carper scorn, not credit, wins.

I have, with strict advantage of free time,
O'er-read, examined, tried, and proved your rhyme
As clear and distant as yourself from crime;

And though your virtue, as becomes it, still
Deigns mine the power to find, yet want I will   10
Or malice to make faults, which now is skill.

Little know they that profess amity,
And seek to scant her comely liberty,
How much they lame her in her property;

And less they know, that being free to use
That friendship which no chance, but love, did choose,
Will unto licence that free leave abuse.

It is an act of tyranny, not love,
In course of friendship wholly to reprove,
And flattery, with friends' humours still to move.   20

From each of which I labour to [be] free;
Yet if with either's vice I tainted be,
Forgive it as my frailty, and not me.

For no man lives so out of passion's sway
But sometimes shall be tempted to obey
Her fury, though no friendship he betray.

50

A Speech out of Lucan

Just and fit actions, Ptolemy (he saith),
Make many hurt themselves; a praisèd faith
Is her own scourge, when it sustains their states
Whom fortune hath depressed. Come near the fates
And the immortal gods: love only those
Whom thou seest happy; wretches flee as foes.
Look how the stars from earth or seas from flames
Are distant: so is profit from just aims.
The main command of sceptres soon doth perish
If it begin religious thoughts to cherish;   10
Whole armies fall, swayed by those nice respects.
It is a licence to do ill protects
Even states most hated, when no laws resist
The sword, but that it acteth what it list.
Yet 'ware: thou mayst do all things cruelly;
Not safe, but when thou dost them thoroughly;

He that will honest be may quit the court:
Virtue and sovereignty, they not consort.
That prince that shames a tyrant's name to bear,
Shall never dare do anything but fear.   20

SONGS AND POEMS FROM THE PLAYS AND MASQUES

1

To Lucy, Countess of Bedford
In a Gift-Copy of Cynthia's Revels, *1601*
Author ad Librum

Go, little book, go, little fable
   Unto the bright and amiable
Lucy of Bedford; she, that bounty
   Appropriates still unto that county;
Tell her, his muse that did invent thee
   To Cynthia's fairest nymph hath sent thee,
And sworn that he will quite discard thee
   If any way she doth reward thee
But with a kiss (if thou canst dare it)
   Of her white hand; or she can spare it.   10

2

From Cynthia's Revels, *I. ii. 65–75*
Echo's Song

Slow, slow, fresh fount, keep time with my salt tears;
Yet slower yet, O faintly gentle springs;
List to the heavy part the music bears:
   Woe weeps out her division when she sings.
     Droop, herbs and flowers,
     Fall, grief, in showers;
     Our beauties are not ours:
       Oh, I could still
(Like melting snow upon some craggy hill)
     Drop, drop, drop, drop   10
Since nature's pride is now a withered daffodil.

3

From Cynthia's Revels, *II. v (F & Q)*
Beggar's Song

Come follow me, my wags, and say as I say:
There's no riches but in rags: hey day, hey day!
You that profess this art, come away, come away,
And help to bear a part: hey day, hey day!

    Bear-wards and blacking-men,
    Corn-cutters and car-men,
    Sellers of marking-stones,
    Gatherers-up of marrow-bones,
    Pedlars and puppet-players,
    Sow-gelders and sooth-sayers,   10
    Gypsies and gaolers,
    Rat-catchers and railers,
    Beadles and ballad-singers,
    Fiddlers and fadingers,
    Thomalins and tinkers,
    Scavengers and skinkers:
    There goes the hare away!
          Hey day, hey day!

    Bawds and blind doctors,
    Paritors and spittle proctors,   20
    Chemists and cuttlebungs,
    Hookers and horn-thumbs,
    With all cast commanders
    Turned post-knights or panders;
    Jugglers and jesters,
    Borrowers of testers,
    And all the troop of trash
    That are allied to the lash:
    Come and join with your jags,
    Shake up your muscle-bags,   30
    For beggary bears the sway;
    Then sing: cast care away!
          Hey day, hey day!

4

From Cynthia's Revels, *IV. iii. 242–53*
Hedon's Song

Oh, that joy so soon should waste!
   Or so sweet a bliss
     As a kiss
Might not for ever last!
So sugared, so melting, so soft, so delicious:
   The dew that lies on roses
   When the morn herself discloses
     Is not so precious.
Oh, rather than I would it smother,
Were I to taste such another;   10
   It should be my wishing
   That I might die, kissing.

5

From Cynthia's Revels, *IV. iii. 305–16*
Amorphus' Song

Thou more than most sweet glove
  Unto my more sweet love,
  Suffer me to store with kisses
  This empty lodging, that now misses
    The pure rosy hand that ware thee,
    Whiter than the kid that bare thee,
      Thou art soft, but that was softer;
      Cupid's self hath kissed it ofter
      Than e'er he did his mother's doves,
      Supposing her the queen of loves   10
        That was thy mistress,
          Best of gloves.

6

From Cynthia's Revels, *V. vi. 1–18*
Hymn to Cynthia

Queen and huntress, chaste and fair,
Now the sun is laid to sleep,
Seated in thy silver chair,
State in wonted manner keep:
    Hesperus entreats thy light,
    Goddess excellently bright.

Earth, let not thy envious shade
Dare itself to interpose;
Cynthia's shining orb was made
Heaven to clear, when day did close: 10
    Bless us then with wishèd sight,
    Goddess excellently bright.

Lay thy bow of pearl apart,
And thy crystal-shining quiver;
Give unto the flying hart
Space to breathe, how short soever:
    Thou that mak'st a day of night,
    Goddess excellently bright.

7

From Poetaster, *II. ii. 163–72, 179–88*
Crispinus' and Hermogenes' Song

Crispinus   If I freely may discover
What would please me in my lover,
    I would have her fair and witty,
    Savouring more of court than city:
    A little proud, but full of pity:
    Light and humorous in her toying,
    Oft building hopes, and soon destroying,
    Long but sweet in the enjoying,
Neither too easy, nor too hard:
All extremes I would have barred.   10

Hermogenes She should be allowed her passions,
      So they were but used as fashions;
          Sometimes froward, and then frowning,
          Sometimes sickish, and then swowning,
          Every fit with change still crowning.
          Purely jealous I would have her,
          Then only constant when I crave her:
          'Tis a virtue should not save her.
      Thus, nor her delicates would cloy me,
      Neither her peevishness annoy me.   20

8

From Poetaster, *III. i. 8–12*
Horace's Ode

  Swell me a bowl with lusty wine,
  Till I may see the plump Lyaeus swim.
          Above the brim:
  I drink as I would write,
  In flowing measure, filled with flame and spright.

9

From Poetaster, *IV. iii. 67–78*
Crispinus' Song

    Love is blind and a wanton;
    In the whole world there is scant one
      Such another:
      No, not his mother.
    He hath plucked her doves and sparrows
    To feather his sharp arrows,
      And alone prevaileth
      Whilst sick Venus waileth.
    But if Cypris once recover
    The wag, it shall behove her   10
      To look better to him;
      Or she will undo him.

10

From Poetaster, *IV. v. 176–83, 188–99*
Feasting Song

Wake, our mirth begins to die;
Quicken it with tunes and wine:
Raise your notes—you're out: fie, fie!
This drowsiness is an ill sign.
We banish him the choir of gods
    That droops again:
    Then all are men,
For here's not one but nods.

Hermogenes	Then in a free and lofty strain	
	Our broken tunes we thus repair;	10
Crispinus	And we answer them again,	
	Running division on the panting air:	
Both	To celebrate this feast of sense,	
	As free from scandal as offence.	
Hermogenes	Here is beauty for the eye;	
Crispinus	For the ear, sweet melody;	
Hermogenes	Ambrosiac odours for the smell;	
Crispinus	Delicious nectar for the taste;	
Both	For the touch, a lady's waist,	
	Which doth all the rest excel!	20

11

From Poetaster, *V. iii. 626–30*
Final Song

Blush, folly, blush, here's none that fears
The wagging of an ass's ears,
Although a wolvish case he wears.
Detraction is but baseness' varlet,
And apes are apes, though clothed in scarlet.

12

From The Entertainment at Althorp, *53–100*
The Satyr's Verses

Satyr   This is Mab the mistress-fairy,
             That doth nightly rob the dairy,
             And can hurt, or help, the churning,
             As she please, without discerning.

Elf   Pug, you will anon take warning?

Satyr   She that pinches country wenches
             If they rub not clean their benches,
             And with sharper nails remembers
             When they rake not up their embers;
             But if so they chance to feast her,   10
             In a shoe she drops a tester.

Elf   Shall we strip the skipping jester?

Satyr   This is she that empties cradles,
             Takes out children, puts in ladles,
             Trains forth midwives in their slumber
             With a sieve the holes to number;
             And then leads them from her boroughs
             Home through ponds and water-furrows.

Elf   Shall not all this mocking stir us?

Satyr   She can start our franklins' daughters   20
             In their sleep, with shrieks and laughters;
             And on sweet St Anne's night
             Feed them with a promised sight,
             Some of husbands, some of lovers,
             Which an empty dream discovers.

Elf   Satyr, vengeance near you hovers.

Satyr   And in hope that you would come here
          Yester-eve, the Lady Summer
          She invited to a banquet:
          But, in sooth, I can you thank yet   30
          That you could so well deceive her
          Of the pride which 'gan up-heave her,
          And, by this, would so have blown her,
          As no wood-god should have known her.

Here he skipped into the wood.

Elf   Mistress, this is only spite:
          For you would not yester-night
          Kiss him in the cock-shut light.

And came again.

Satyr   By Pan, and thou hast hit it right.   40

There they laid hold on him, and nipped him.

Fairy   Fairies, pinch him black and blue:
          Now you have him, make him rue.

Satyr   Oh, hold, Mab: I sue.

Elf   Nay, the devil shall have his due.

13

From The Masque of Blackness, *306–23*

          Daughters of the subtle flood,
            Do not let earth longer entertain you;
1st Echo   Let earth longer entertain you.
2nd Echo   Longer entertain you.

          'Tis to them enough of good
           That you give this little hope to gain you.
1st Echo   Give this little hope to gain you.
2nd Echo   Little hope to gain you.

If they love,
        You shall quickly see;   10
    For when to flight you move,
They'll follow you, the more you flee.
1st Echo   Follow you, the more you flee.
2nd Echo   The more you flee.

    If not, impute it each to other's matter;
They are but earth,
1st Echo   But earth,
2nd Echo   Earth—
                        And what you vowed was water.
1st Echo   And what you vowed was water.
2nd Echo   You vowed was water.

14

From Hymenaei, *387–98*

O know to end, as to begin;
A minute's loss in love is sin.
These humours will the night outwear
In their own pastimes here;
You do our rites much wrong
In seeking to prolong
These outward pleasures:
The night hath other treasures
Than these, though long concealed,
Ere day to be revealed.   10
Then know to end, as to begin;
A minute's loss in love is sin.

15

From The Masque of Beauty, *325–32*

So beauty on the waters stood
When Love had severed earth from flood!
So when he parted air from fire,
He did with concord all inspire!

And then a motion he them taught
That elder than himself was thought,
Which thought was, yet, the child of earth,
For Love is elder than his birth.

16

From The Masque of Beauty, *369–74*

Had those that dwell in error foul,
And hold that women have no soul,
But seen these move, they would have then
Said women were the souls of men.
  So they do move each heart and eye
  With the world's soul, true harmony.

17

Epithalamion from The Haddington Masque, *370–447*

Up, youths and virgins, up, and praise
  The god whose nights outshine his days,
    Hymen, whose hallowed rites
  Could never boast of brighter lights;
    Whose bands pass liberty.
Two of your troop that with the morn were free
  Are now waged to his war;
    And what they are,
    If you'll perfection see,
      Yourselves must be.   10
Shine, Hesperus, shine forth, thou wishèd star.

What joy or honours can compare
  With holy nuptials when they are
    Made out of equal parts
  Of years, of states, of hands, of hearts?
    When in the happy choice,
The spouse and spousèd have the foremost voice.

Such, glad of Hymen's war,
    Live what they are,
And long perfection see;   20
    And such ours be.
Shine, Hesperus, shine forth, thou wishèd star.

The solemn state of this one night
    Were fit to last an age's light,
        But there are rites behind
    Have less of state but more of kind:
        Love's wealthy crop of kisses,
And fruitful harvest of his mother's blisses.
    Sound then to Hymen's war,
        That what these are,   30
Who will perfection see
    May haste to be.
Shine, Hesperus, shine forth, thou wishèd star.

Love's commonwealth consists of toys;
    His council are those antic boys,
        Games, laughter, sports, delights,
    That triumph with him on these nights,
        To whom we must give way;
For now their reign begins, and lasts till day.
    They sweeten Hymen's war,   40
        And in that jar
Make all that married be
    Perfection see.
Shine, Hesperus, shine forth, thou wishèd star.

Why stays the bridegroom to invade
    Her that would be a matron made?
        Goodnight, whilst yet we may
    Goodnight to you a virgin, say;
        Tomorrow, rise the same
Your mother is, and use a nobler name.   50
    Speed well in Hymen's war,
        That what you are
By your perfection we
    And all may see.
Shine, Hesperus, shine forth, thou wishèd star.

Tonight is Venus' vigil kept.
  This night no bridegroom ever slept;
    And if the fair bride do,
  The married say 'tis his fault too.
    Wake then, and let your lights   60
Wake too; for they'll tell nothing of your nights,
  But that in Hymen's war
    You perfect are.
  And such perfection we
    Do pray should be.
Shine, Hesperus, shine forth, thou wishèd star.

That ere the rosy-fingered morn
  Behold nine moons, there may be born
    A babe to uphold the fame
  Of Radcliffe's blood and Ramsey's name;   70
    That may in his great seed
Wear the long honours of his father's deed.
  Such fruits of Hymen's war
    Most perfect are;
  And all perfection we
    Wish you should see.
Shine, Hesperus, shine forth, thou wishèd star.

18

From The Masque of Queens, *75–94*
The Witches' Charm

The owl is abroad, the bat and the toad,
  And so is the cat-o'-mountain;
The ant and the mole sit both in a hole,
  And frog peeps out o' the fountain;
The dogs they do bay, and the timbrels play,
  The spindle is now a-turning;
The moon it is red, and the stars are fled,
  But all the sky is a-burning:
The ditch is made, and our nails the spade,
With pictures full, of wax and of wool;   10
Their livers I stick with needles quick:

There lacks but the blood, to make up the flood.
  Quickly, dame, then, bring your part in,
  Spur, spur upon little Martin,
  Merrily, merrily, make him sail,
  A worm in his mouth, and a thorn in's tail,
  Fire above and fire below,
  With a whip i' your hand to make him go.
  Oh, now she's come!
  Let all be dumb.   20

19

From The Silent Woman, *I. i. 91–102*
Clerimont's Song

    Still to be neat, still to be dressed,
    As you were going to a feast;
    Still to be powdered, still perfumed:
    Lady, it is to be presumed,
    Though art's hid causes are not found,
    All is not sweet, all is not sound.

    Give me a look, give me a face,
    That makes simplicity a grace;
    Robes loosely flowing, hair as free:
    Such sweet neglect more taketh me   10
    Than all the adulteries of art:
    They strike mine eyes, but not my heart.

20

From Oberon, The Fairy Prince, *210–17*
Satyrs' Catch

      Buzz, quoth the blue fly,
        Hum, quoth the bee:
      Buzz and hum, they cry,
        And so do we.

In his ear, in his nose,
Thus, do you see?
He ate the dormouse,
Else it was he.

21

From Love Freed From Ignorance and Folly, *358–69*

What just excuse had agèd Time
His weary limbs now to have eased,
And sat him down without his crime,
While every thought was so much pleased!
For he so greedy to devour
His own, and all that he brings forth,
Is eating every piece of hour
Some object of the rarest worth.
Yet this is rescued from his rage,
As not to die by time or age.   10
For beauty hath a living name,
And will to heaven, from whence it came.

22

From Love Restored, *273–8*

This motion was of love begot,
It was so airy, light and good,
His wings into their feet he shot,
Or else himself into their blood.
But ask not how. The end will prove
That love's in them, or they're in love.

23

From Love Restored, *280–91*

Have men beheld the graces dance,
Or seen the upper orbs to move?

So these did turn, return, advance,
 Drawn back by doubt, put on by love.
And now, like earth, themselves they fix,
Till greater powers vouchsafe to mix
 Their motions with them. Do not fear,
 You brighter planets of this sphere:
  Not one male heart you see
   But rather to his female eyes   10
  Would die a destined sacrifice
Than live at home and free.

24

From Love Restored, *293–300*

Give end unto thy pastimes, Love,
 Before they labours prove;
A little rest between
Will make thy next shows better seen.
 Now let them close their eyes and see
 If they can dream of thee,
Since morning hastes to come in view,
And all the morning dreams are true.

25

From Bartholomew Fair, *III. v. 69 ff.*
Nightingale's Song

My masters and friends and good people, draw near,
And look to your purses, for that I do say:
And though little money in them you do bear,
It cost more to get than to lose in a day.
 You oft have been told,
 Both the young and the old,
 And bidden beware of the cutpurse so bold:
Then if you take heed not, free me from the curse,
Who both give you warning for and the cutpurse.
Youth, youth, thou hadst better been starved by thy nurse 10
Than live to be hanged for cutting a purse.

It hath been upbraided to men of my trade
That often-times we are the cause of this crime:
Alack and for pity, why should it be said?
As if they regarded or places or time.
        Examples have been
        Of some that were seen
In Westminster Hall, yea, the pleaders between:
Then why should the judges be free from this curse,
More than my poor self, for cutting the purse?   20
Youth, youth, &c.

At Worcester 'tis known well, and even i' the gaol,
A knight of good worship did there show his face
Against the foul sinners, in zeal for to rail:
And lost, *ipso facto*, his purse in the place.
        Nay, once from the seat
        Of judgement so great
A judge there did lose a fair pouch of velvet.
O Lord for thy mercy, how wicked or worse
Are those that so venture their necks for a purse!   30
Youth, youth, &c.

At plays and at sermons and at the sessions
'Tis daily their practice such booty to make:
Yea, under the gallows at executions
They stick not the stare-abouts' purses to take.
        Nay, one without grace
        At a [far] better place
At court, and in Christmas, before the king's face:
Alack then for pity, must I bear the curse
That only belongs to the cunning cutpurse?   40
Youth, youth, &c.

But O you vile nation of cutpurses all,
Relent and repent and amend and be sound:
And know that you ought not by honest men's fall
Advance your own fortunes, to die above ground;
        And though you go gay
        In silks as you may,
It is not the highway to heaven, as they say:

Repent then, repent you, for better, for worse,
And kiss not the gallows for cutting a purse: 50
Youth, youth, thou hadst better been starved by thy nurse
Than live to be hanged for cutting a purse.

26

From Mercury Vindicated, *6–17*
Cyclope's Song

Soft, subtle fire, thou soul of art,
   Now do thy part
On weaker nature, that through age is lamed.
   Take but thy time, now she is old,
   And the sun her friend grown cold,
She will no more in strife with thee be named.

Look but how few confess her now
   In cheek or brow!
From every head, almost, how she is frighted!
   The very age abhors her so, 10
   That it learns to speak and go
As if by art alone it could be righted.

27

From The Vision of Delight, *237–46*
Epilogue

[*Aurora*]   I was not wearier where I lay
    By frozen Tithon's side tonight,
    Than I am willing now to stay
    And be a part of your delight:
      But I am urgèd by the day,
    Against my will, to bid you come away.

The Choir   They yield to time, and so must all:
    As night to sport, day doth to action call,
      Which they the rather do obey
    Because the morn with roses strews the way. 10

28

From Pleasure Reconciled to Virtue, *13–36*
Song for Comus

Room, room, make room for the bouncing belly!
First father of sauce, and deviser of jelly:
Prime master of arts and the giver of wit,
That found out the excellent engine, the spit,
The plough and the flail, the mill and the hopper,
The hutch and the bolter, the furnace and copper:
The oven, the bavin, the mawkin and peel,
The hearth and the range, the dog and the wheel.
He, he first invented both hogshead and tun,
The gimlet and vice, too, and taught 'em to run;   10
And since, with the funnel, an hippocras bag
He's made of himself, that now he cries swag.
Which shows, though the pleasure be but of four inches,
Yet he is a weezle, the gullet that pinches,
Of any delight; and not spares from the back
Whatever, to make of the belly a sack.
Hail, hail, plump paunch! O the founder of taste
For fresh meats or powdered or pickle or paste;
Devourer of broilèd, baked, roasted or sod,
And emptier of cups, be they even or odd.   20
All which have now made thee so wide i' the waist
As scarce with no pudding thou art to be laced:
But eating and drinking until thou dost nod,
Thou break'st all thy girdles, and break'st forth a god.

29

From Pleasure Reconciled to Virtue, *253–72*
Daedalus's Song

Come on, come on, and where you go
    So interweave the curious knot
As even th' observer scarce may know
    Which lines are pleasure's, and which not.

First, figure out the doubtful way
   At which a while all youth should stay,
Where she and virtue did contend
   Which should have Hercules to friend.
Then, as all actions of mankind
   Are but a labyrinth or maze,   10
So let your dances be entwined,
   Yet not perplex men unto gaze;
But measured, and so numerous, too,
   As men may read each act you do.
And when they see the graces meet,
   Admire the wisdom of your feet.
For dancing is an exercise
   Not only shows the mover's wit
But maketh the beholder wise,
   As he hath power to rise to it.   20

30

From The Gypsies Metamorphosed, *121–44*
The Jackman's Song

From the famous Peak of Derby
   And the Devil's Arse there hard by
   Where we yearly keep our musters,
   Thus the Egyptians throng in clusters.

Be not frighted with our fashion,
   Though we seem a tattered nation:
   We account our rags our riches,
   So our tricks exceed our stitches.

Give us bacon, rinds of walnuts,
   Shells of cockles and of small nuts,   10
   Ribbons, bells, and saffron linen,
   All the world is ours to win in.

Knacks we have that will delight you,
   Sleights of hand that will invite you
   To endure our tawny faces,
   And not cause you cut your laces.

All your fortunes we can tell ye,
   Be they for your back or belly,
   In the moods too, and the tenses,
   That may fit your fine five senses.   20

Draw but then your gloves, we pray you,
   And sit still, we will not fray you:
   For though we be here at Burley,
   We'd be loath to make a hurly.

31

From The Gypsies Metamorphosed, *262–71*
The Patrico's Song

The fairy beam upon you,
The stars to glister on you,
   A moon of light
   In the noon of night,
Till the firedrake hath o'er-gone you.

The wheel of fortune guide you,
The boy with the bow beside you
   Run aye in the way
   Till the bird of day.
And the luckier lot betide you.   10

32

From The Gypsies Metamorphosed, *1329–89*
Blessing the Sovereign and His Senses

From a gypsy in the morning,
   Or a pair of squint eyes turning,
From the goblin and the spectre,
   Or a drunkard, though with nectar;
From a woman true to no man,
   And is ugly, beside common,

A smock rampant, and that itches
   To be putting on the breeches:
Wheresoe'er they have their being,
Bless the sovereign and his seeing.   10

From a fool, and serious toys,
   From a lawyer three-parts noise,
From impertinence, like a drum
   Beat at dinner in his room;
From a tongue without a file,
   Heaps of phrases, and no style,
From a fiddle out of tune,
   As the cuckoo is in June;
From the candlesticks of Lothbury,
   And the loud, pure, wives of Banbury,   20
[Or a long pretended fit
   Meant for mirth, but is not it,]
Only time and ears out-wearing:
Bless the sovereign and his hearing.

From a strolling tinker's sheet,
   And a pair of carrier's feet,
From a lady that doth breathe
   Worse above than underneath;
From the diet, and the knowledge,
   Of the students in Bears' College;   30
From tobacco, with the type
   Of the devil's clyster-pipe;
Or a stink all stinks excelling,
   A fishmonger's dwelling;
Bless the sovereign and his smelling.

From an oyster and fried fish,
   A sow's baby in a dish,
Any portion of a swine;
   From bad venison, and worse wine,
Ling, what cook soe'er it boil,   40
   Though with mustard sauce and oil;
Or what else would keep man fasting:
Bless the sovereign and his tasting.

Both from birdlime and from pitch,
  From a doxy and her itch,
From the bristles of a hog,
  Or the ringworm in a dog;
From the courtship of a briar,
  From St Anthony's old fire;
From a needle or a thorn   50
  I' the bed at even or morn,
Or from any gout's least grutching,
Bless the sovereign and his touching.

Bless him, too, from all offences
  In his sports, as in his senses:
From a boy to cross his way,
  From a fall, or a foul day.

Bless him, O bless him, heaven, and lend him long
  To be the sacred burthen of all song:
The acts and years of all our kings to outgo,   60
  And, while he's mortal, we not think him so.

33
From Neptune's Triumph, *472–95*
Song to the Ladies

Proteus   Come, noble nymphs, and do not hide
            The joys for which you so provide.

Saron   If not to mingle with the men
            What do you here? Go home again.

Portunus Your dressings do confess
            By what we see, so curious parts
            Of Pallas' and Arachne's arts,
              That you could mean no less.

Proteus   Why do you wear the silkworm's toils,
            Or glory in the shellfish spoils,   10

Or strive to show the grains of ore
That you have gathered on the shore
   Whereof to make a stock
To graft the greener emerald on,
Or any better-watered stone?

Saron   Or ruby of the rock?

Proteus Why do you smell of ambergris,
Of which was formèd Neptune's niece,
The queen of love, unless you can,
Like sea-born Venus, love a man?   20

Saron   Try, put yourselves unto't.

Chorus Your looks, your smiles and thoughts that meet,
Ambrosian hands and silver feet,
   Do promise you will do't.

34

From The New Inn, *IV. iv. 4–13*
A Vision of Beauty

It was a beauty that I saw
So pure, so perfect, as the frame
Of all the universe was lame;
To that one figure, could I draw,
Or give least line of it a law!

A skein of silk without a knot!
A fair march made without a halt!
A curious form without a fault!
A printed book without a blot!
All beauty, and without a spot!   10

35

On The New Inn
Ode. To Himself

Come, leave the loathèd stage,
  And the more loathsome age,
Where pride and impudence, in faction knit,
    Usurp the chair of wit:
Indicting and arraigning every day
    Something they call a play.
  Let their fastidious, vain
  Commission of the brain
Run on and rage, sweat, censure, and condemn:
They were not made for thee, less thou for them.   10

  Say that thou pour'st them wheat,
  And they will acorns eat:
'Twere simple fury still thyself to waste
    On such as have no taste:
To offer them a surfeit of pure bread
    Whose appetites are dead.
  No, give them grains their fill,
  Husks, draff to drink, and swill;
If they love lees, and leave the lusty wine,
Envy them not, their palate's with the swine.   20

  No doubt some mouldy tale
  Like *Pericles*, and stale
As the shrieve's crusts, and nasty as his fish-
    Scraps out [of] every dish,
Thrown forth, and raked into the common tub,
    May keep up the play club:
  There sweepings do as well
  As the best-ordered meal.
For who the relish of these guests will fit
Needs set them but the alms-basket of wit.   30

  And much good do't you then:
  Brave plush and velvet men

Can feed on orts; and safe in your stage-clothes
    Dare quit, upon your oaths,
The stagers and the stage-wrights too (your peers)
    Or larding your large ears
  With their foul comic socks,
  Wrought upon twenty blocks:
Which, if they're torn and turned and patched enough,
The gamesters share your guilt, and you their stuff.   40

    Leave things so prostitute,
    And take the Alcaic lute,
Or thine own Horace, or Anacreon's lyre;
    Warm thee by Pindar's fire:
And though thy nerves be shrunk and blood be cold
    Ere years have made thee old,
  Strike that disdainful heat
  Throughout, to their defeat:
As curious fools, and envious of thy strain,
May, blushing, swear no palsy's in thy brain.   50

    But when they hear thee sing
    The glories of thy king,
His zeal to God, and his just awe o'er men:
    They may, blood-shaken, then
Feel such a flesh-quake to possess their powers,
    As they shall cry: Like ours
  In sound of peace or wars
  No harp e'er hit the stars,
In tuning forth the acts of his sweet reign:
And raising Charles's chariot 'bove his wain.   60

36

From The Sad Shepherd, *I. v. 65–80*
Karolin's Song

    Though I am young and cannot tell
    Either what death or love is well,
  Yet I have heard they both bear darts,
    And both do aim at human hearts;

And then again I have been told
   Love wounds with heat, as death with cold:
So that I fear they do but bring
   Extremes to touch, and mean one thing.

As in a ruin, we it call
   One thing to be blown up, or fall;   10
Or to our end like way may have
   By a flash of lightning, or a wave;
So love's inflamèd shaft or brand
   May kill as soon as death's cold hand:
Except love's fires the virtue have
   To fright the frost out of the grave.

A PANEGYRE

On the Happy Entrance of
James, Our Sovereign, to His First High Session of
Parliament in This Kingdom, the 19 of March, 1603

Mart[ial], *Licet toto nunc Helicone frui.*

Heaven now not strives, alone, our breasts to fill
With joys, but urgeth his full favours still.
Again, the glory of our western world
Unfolds himself, and from his eyes are hurled,
Today, a thousand radiant lights, that stream
To every nook and angle of his realm.
His former rays did only clear the sky,
But these his searching beams are cast to pry
Into those dark and deep concealèd vaults
Where men commit black incest with their faults,   10
And snore supinely in the stall of sin;
Where murder, rapine, lust do sit within,
Carousing human blood in iron bowls,
And make their den the slaughter-house of souls;
From whose foul reeking caverns first arise
Those damps that so offend all good men's eyes;
And would, if not dispersed, infect the crown,
And in their vapour her bright metal drown.
    To this so clear and sanctified an end,
I saw, when reverend Themis did descend   20
Upon his state, let down in that rich chain
That fasteneth heavenly power to earthly reign.
Beside her, stooped on either hand, a maid:
Fair Dice and Eunomia, who were said
To be her daughters, and but faintly known
On earth till now they came to grace his throne.
Her third, Irene, helped to bear his train;
And in her office vowed she would remain
Till foreign malice or unnatural spite—
Which fates avert—should force her from her right.   30
With these he passed, and with his people's hearts
Breathed in his way, and souls (their better parts)

Hasting to follow forth in shouts and cries,
Upon his face all threw their covetous eyes
As on a wonder: some amazèd stood,
As if they felt, but had not known, their good;
Others would fain have shown it in their words;
But when their speech so poor a help affords
Unto their zeal's expression, they are mute,
And only with red silence him salute.   40
Some cry from tops of houses, thinking noise
The fittest herald to proclaim true joys;
Others on ground run gazing by his side,
All as unwearied as unsatisfied;
And every window grieved it could not move
Along with him, and the same trouble prove.
They that had seen but four short days before
His gladding look, now longed to see it more.
And as of late, when he through London went,
The amorous city spared no ornament   50
That might her beauties heighten, but so dressed
As our ambitious dames when they make feast,
And would be courted, so this town put on
Her brightest tire; and in it, equal shone
To her great sister, save that modesty,
Her place and years, gave her precedency.
     The joy of either was alike, and full;
No age nor sex so weak, or strongly dull,
That did not bear a part in this consent
Of hearts and voices. All the air was rent   60
As with the murmur of a moving wood;
The ground beneath did seem a moving flood;
Walls, windows, roofs, towers, steeples, all were set
With several eyes, that in this object met.
Old men were glad their fates till now did last;
And infants, that the hours had made such haste
To bring them forth; whilst riper aged, and apt
To understand the more, the more were rapt.
This was the people's love, with which did strive
The nobles' zeal, yet either kept alive   70
The other's flame, as doth the wick and wax,
That, friendly tempered, one pure taper makes.
Meanwhile the reverend Themis draws aside

The king's obeying will from taking pride
In these vains stirs, and to his mind suggests
How he may triumph in his subjects' breasts
With better pomp. She tells him first that kings
Are here on earth the most conspicuous things;
That they by Heaven are placed upon his throne,
To rule like Heaven; and have no more their own,   80
As they are men, than men. That all they do
Though hid at home, abroad is searched into;
And, being once found out, discovered lies
Unto as many envies there as eyes.
That princes, since they know it is their fate,
Oft-times, to have the secrets of their state
Betrayed to fame, should take more care, and fear
In public acts what face and form they bear.
She then remembered to his thought the place
Where he was going, and the upward race   90
Of kings preceding him in that high court;
Their laws, their ends, the men she did report;
And all so justly as his ear was joyed
To hear the truth, from spite or flattery void.
She showed him who made wise, who honest acts;
Who both, who neither; all the cunning tracts
And thriving statutes she could promptly note;
The bloody, base, and barbarous she did quote;
Where laws were made to serve the tyrant will;
Where sleeping they could save, and waking kill;   100
Where acts gave licence to impetuous lust
To bury churches in forgotten dust,
And with their ruins raise the pandar's bowers;
When, public justice borrowed all her powers
From private chambers, that could then create
Laws, judges, councillors, yea prince and state.
All this she told and more, with bleeding eyes,
For right is as compassionate as wise.
Nor did he seem their vices so to love
As once defend what Themis did reprove.   110
For though by right and benefit of times
He owned their crowns, he would not so their crimes.
He knew that princes who had sold their fame
To their voluptuous lusts had lost their name;

And that no wretch was more unblest than he
Whose necessary good 'twas now to be
An evil king, and so must such be still,
Who once have got the habit to do ill.
One wickedness another must defend;
For vice is safe, while she hath vice to friend.   120
He knew that those who would with love command
Must with a tender, yet a steadfast, hand
Sustain the reins, and in the check forbear
To offer cause of injury or fear.
That kings by their example more do sway
Than by their power, and men do more obey
When they are led than when they are compelled.
    In all these knowing arts our prince excelled.
And now the dame had dried her dropping eyne,
When, like an April Iris, flew her shine   130
About the streets, as it would force a spring
From out the stones to gratulate the king.
She blessed the people that in shoals did swim
To hear her speech; which still began in him
And ceased in them. She told them what a fate
Was gently fallen from heaven upon this state;
How dear a father they did now enjoy
That came to save, what discord would destroy;
And entering with the power of a king,
The temperance of a private man did bring,   140
That won affections ere his steps won ground;
And was not hot or covetous to be crowned
Before men's hearts had crowned him. Who—unlike
Those greater bodies of the sky, that strike
The lesser fires dim—in his access,
Brighter than all, hath yet made no one less,
Though many greater; and the most, the best.
Wherein his choice was happy with the rest
Of his great actions first to see and do
What all men's wishes did aspire unto.   150
    Hereat the people could no longer hold
Their bursting joys, but through the air was rolled
The lengthened shout, as when the artillery
Of heaven is discharged along the sky,
And this confession flew from every voice:

'Never had land more reason to rejoice.
Nor to her bliss could aught now added be,
Save that she might the same perpetual see.'
Which when time, nature, and the fates denied,
With a twice louder shout again they cried,   160
'Yet, let blest Britain ask, without your wrong,
Still to have such a king, and this king long.'

Solus rex et poeta non quotannis nascitur.

LEGES CONVIVALES

Quod felix, faustumque in Apolline sit.

1. Nemo asymbolus, nisi umbra, huc venito.
2. Idiota insulsus, tristis, turpis, abesto.
3. Eruditi, urbani, hilares, honesti, adsciscuntor.
4. Nec lectae foeminae repudiantor.
5. In apparatu, quod convivis corruget nares, nil esto.
6. Epulae delectu potiùs, quam sumptu, parantor.
7. Opsonator et coquus, convivarum gulae periti sunto.
8. De discubitu non contenditor.
9. Ministri à dapibus oculati et muti; à poculis auriti, et celeres, sunto.
10. Vina puris fontibus ministrantor; aut vapulet hospes.
11. Moderatis poculis provocare sodales, fas esto.
12. At fabulis magis, quam vino, velitatio fiat.
13. Convivae nec muti, nec loquaces sunto.
14. De seriis, aut sacris, poti et saturi ne disserunto.
15. Fidicen, nisi accersitus, non venito.
16. Admisso; risu, tripudiis, choreis, cantu, salibus, omni gratiarum festivitate, sacra celebrantor.
17. Joci sine felle sunto.
18. Insipida poëmata nulla recitantor.
19. Versus scribere, nullus cogitor.
20. Argumentationis totus strepitus abesto.
21. Amatoriis querelis, ac suspiriis, liber angulus esto.
22. Lapitharum more scyphis pugnare, vitrea collidere, fenestras excutere, supellectilem dilacerare, nefas esto.
23. Qui foràs vel dicta, vel facta, eliminat, eliminator.
24. Neminen reum pocula faciunto.

Focus perennis esto.

Alexander Brome's Translation of the Leges Convivales
Ben Jonson's Sociable Rules for the Apollo

Let none but guests or clubbers hither come;
Let dunces, fools, sad, sordid men keep home;
Let learnèd, civil, merry men be invited,
And modest, too; nor the choice ladies slighted.
Let nothing in the treat offend the guests;
More for delight than cost prepare the feasts;
The cook and purveyor must our palates know;
And none contend who shall sit high or low.
Our waiters must quick-sighted be, and dumb;
And let the drawers quickly hear and come.
Let not our wine be mixed, but brisk and neat,   10
Or else the drinkers may the vintners beat.
And let our only emulation be
Not drinking much, but talking wittily.
Let it be voted lawful to stir up
Each other with a moderate chirping cup;
Let none of us be mute, or talk too much;
On serious things or sacred let's not touch
With sated heads and bellies. Neither may
Fiddlers, unasked, obtrude themselves to play.
With laughing, leaping, dancing, jests, and songs   20
And whate'er else to grateful mirth belongs
Let's celebrate our feasts. And let us see
That all our jests without reflection be;
Insipid poems let no man rehearse,
Nor any be compelled to write a verse.
All noise of vain disputes must be forborne,
And let no lover in a corner mourn.
To fight and brawl like Hectors let none dare,
Glasses or windows break, or hangings tear.
Whoe'er shall publish what's here done or said   30
From our society must be banishèd.
Let none by drinking do or suffer harm,
And while we stay let us be always warm.

Over the Door at the Entrance into the Apollo

Welcome, all who lead or follow
To the oracle of Apollo:
Here he speaks out of his pottle,
Or the tripos, his tower bottle;
All his answers are divine:
Truth itself doth flow in wine.
Hang up all the poor hop-drinkers!
Cries old Sim, the king of skinkers;
He the half of life abuses
That sits watering with the muses.   10
Those dull girls no good can mean us;
Wine, it is the milk of Venus
And the poets' horse accounted:
Ply it, and you all are mounted.
'Tis the true Phoebeian liquor,
Cheers the brains, makes wit the quicker,
Pays all debts, cures all diseases,
And at once three senses pleases.
Welcome, all who lead or follow
To the oracle of Apollo!   20

DUBIA

I

An Elegy

To make the doubt clear that no woman's true,
  Was it my fate to prove it full in you?
Thought I but one had breathed the purer air,
  And must she needs be false, because she's fair?
Is it your beauty's mark, or of your youth,
  Or your perfection, not to study truth?
Or think you heaven is deaf, or hath no eyes,
  Or those it has wink at your perjuries?
Are vows so cheap with women, or the matter
  Whereof they are made, that they are writ in water,   10
And blown away with wind? Or doth their breath,
  Both hot and cold at once, threat life and death?
Who could have thought so many accents sweet
  Tuned to our words, so many sighs should meet,
Blown from our hearts: so many oaths and tears
  Sprinkled among, all sweeter by our fears,
And the divine impression of stolen kisses,
  That sealed the rest, could now prove empty blisses?
Did you draw bonds to forfeit? Sign, to break?
  Or must we read you quite from what you speak,   20
And find the truth out the wrong way? Or must
  He first desire you false, would wish you just?
Oh, I profane! Though most of women be
  The common monster, love shall except thee,
My dearest love, however jealousy
  With circumstance might urge the contrary.
Sooner I'll think the sun would cease to cheer
  The teeming earth, and that forget to bear;
Sooner that rivers would run back, or Thames
  With ribs of ice in June would bind his streams;   30
Or nature, by whose strength the world endures,
  Would change her course, before you alter yours.
But, oh, that treacherous breast to whom weak you
  Did trust our counsels! And we both may rue,

Having his falsehood found too late. 'Twas he
   That made me cast you guilty, and you me;
Whilst he, black wretch, betrayed each simple word
   We spake unto the cunning of a third!
Cursed may he be, that so our love hath slain,
   And wander wretched on the earth as Cain: 40
Wretched as he, and not deserve least pity;
   In plaguing him, let misery be witty.
Let all eyes shun him, and he shun each eye,
   Till he be noisesome as his infamy;
May he without remorse deny God thrice,
   And not be trusted more, on his soul's price;
And after all self-torment, when he dies,
   May wolves tear out his heart, vultures his eyes,
Swine eat his bowels; and his falser tongue,
   That uttered all, be to some raven flung;   50
And let his carrion corse be a longer feast
   To the king's dogs than any other beast.
Now I have cursed, let us our love revive;
   In me the flame was never more alive.
I could begin again to court and praise,
   And in that pleasure lengthen the short days
Of my life's lease, like painters that do take
   Delight, not in made works, but whilst they make.
I could renew those times when first I saw
   Love in your eyes that gave my tongue the law   60
To like what you liked; and at masques or plays
   Commend the self-same actors, the same ways;
Ask how you did? And often, with intent
   Of being officious, grow impertinent:
All which were such soft pastimes, as in these
   Love was as softly catched as a disease.
But being got, it is a treasure sweet,
   Which to defend is harder than to get;
And ought not be profaned on either part,
   For though 'tis got by chance, 'tis kept by art.   70

2

Fair friend, 'tis true your beauties move
    My heart to a respect,
Too little to be paid with love,
    Too great for your neglect.

I neither love nor yet am free,
    For though the flame I find
Be not intense in the degree
    'Tis of the purest kind.

It little wants of love, but pain:
    Your beauty takes my sense;   10
And lest you should that price disdain,
    My thoughts, too, feel the influence.

'Tis not a passion's first access
    Ready to multiply,
But like love's calmest state it is
    Possessed with victory.

It is like love to truth reduced,
    All the false values gone,
Which were created and induced
    By fond imagination.   20

'Tis either fancy or 'tis fate
    To love you more than I:
I love you at your beauty's rate,
    Less were an injury.

Like unstamped gold, I weigh each grace,
    So that you may collect
Th' intrinsic value of your face
    Safely from my respect.

And this respect would merit love,
    Were not so fair a sight   30
Payment enough: for who dare move
    Reward for his delight?

3

On the King's Birthday

Rouse up thyself, my gentle muse,
   Though now our green conceits be grey,
And yet once more do not refuse
   To take thy Phrygian harp, and play
   In honour of this cheerful day:
      Long may they both contend to prove
      That best of crowns is such a love.

Make first a song of joy and love
   Which chastely flames in royal eyes,
Then tune it to the spheres above,   10
   When the benignest stars do rise
   And sweet conjunctions grace the skies.
      Long may, &c.

To this let all good hearts resound,
   Whilst diadems invest his head;
Long may he live, whose life doth bound
   More than his laws, and better lead
   By high example than by dread.
      Long may, &c.

Long may he round about him see   20
   His roses and his lilies blown:
Long may his only dear and he
   Joy in ideas of their own,
   And kingdom's hopes, so timely sown.
      Long may they both contend to prove
      That best of crowns is such a love.

4

From The Touchstone of Truth, *1624*

Truth is the trial of itself,
   And needs no other touch;
And purer than the purest gold,
   Refine it ne'er so much.

It is the life and light of love,
    The sun that ever shineth,
And spirit of that special grace,
    That faith and love defineth.
It is the warrant of the word,
    That yields a scent so sweet,   10
As gives a power to faith, to tread
    All falsehood under feet.
It is the sword that doth divide
    The marrow from the bone,
And in effect of heavenly love
    Doth show the holy one.
This, blessèd Warre, thy blessèd book
    Unto the world doth prove:
A worthy work, and worthy well
    Of the most worthy love.   20

5

Another [*Epigram*] *On the Birth of the Prince*

Another phoenix! though the first is dead:
A second's flown from his immortal bed,
To make this our Arabia to be
The nest of an eternal progeny.
Choice nature framed the former but to find
What error might be mended in mankind;
Like some industrious workmen, which affect
Their first endeavours only to correct:
So this the building, that the model was,
The type of all that now is come to pass: 10
That but the shadow, this the substance is.
All that was but a prophecy of this:
And when it did this after-birth fore-run
'Twas but the morning-star unto this sun;
The dawning of this day, when Sol did think
We having such a light, that he might wink
And we ne'er miss his lustre: nay, so soon
As Charles was born, he and the pale-faced moon

With envy then did copulate, to try
If such a birth might be produced i' the sky.   20
What heavenly favour made a star appear
To bid wise kings to do their homage here
And prove him truly Christian? Long remain
On earth, sweet prince, that when great Charles shall reign
In heaven above, our little Charles may be
As great on earth, because as good, as he.

6

A Petition of the Infant Prince Charles
The Prince's Verses for One of His Rockers

Read, royal father, mighty king,
What my little hands do bring:
I, whose happy birth imparts
Joy to all good subjects' hearts,
Though an infant, do not break
Nature's laws whilst thus I speak
By this interpreter for one
Whose face doth blush, whose heart doth groan
For her acknowledgèd offence,
And only hath my innocence   10
To gain her mercy. Though thus bold
Yet some proportion it may hold
That to the father she may run
Through mediation of the son.
If therefore now, O royal sir,
My first request may purchase her
Restoring unto grace, to me
(Though prince) it will an honour be
That in my cradle 'twill be said
I Master of Requests was made.   20

7

Ode

Scorn, or some humbler fate
Light thick, and long endure
On the ridiculous state
Of our pied courtlings and secure
Race of self-loving lords,
That wallow in the flood
Of their great birth and blood;
Whiles their whole life affords
No other graces
But pride, lust, oaths, and faces: 10
And yet would have me deem
Of them at that high rate
As they themselves esteem.
Perish such surquedry,
O'erwhelmed with dust:
'Tis only virtue must
Blazon nobility.

8

Horace, Odes, II. iii

Remember when blind fortune knits her brow,
Thy mind be not dejected over-low;
Nor let thy thoughts too insolently swell,
Though all thy hopes do prosper ne'er so well.
For drink thy tears, with sorrow still oppressed,
Or taste pure vine, secure and ever blest,
In those remote and pleasant shady fields
Where stately pine and poplar shadow yields,
Or circling streams that warble, passing by;
All will not help, sweet friend: for thou must die.   10
   The house thou hast thou once must leave behind thee,
And those sweet babes thou often kissest kindly:
And when thou'st gotten all the wealth thou can,
Thy pains is taken for another man.

Alas! What poor advantage doth it bring
To boast thyself descended of a king!
When those that have no house to hide their heads
Find in their grave as warm and easy beds.

TIMBER,
OR,
DISCOVERIES,

Made upon men and matter, as they have flowed
out of his daily readings, or had their reflux
to his peculiar notion of the times,

By

Ben Jonson

Tecum habita, ut noris quam sit tibi curta supellex.
Pers[ius], *Sat.* iv.

SILVA

Rerum et sententiarum, quasi "Υλη *dicta a multiplici materia et varietate in iis
contenta. Quemadmodum enim vulgo solemus infinitam arborum nascentium
indiscriminatim multitudinem* Silvam *dicere: ita etiam libros suos in quibus
variae et diversae materiae opuscula temere congesta erant,* Silvas *appellabant
antiqui:* timber-trees.

EXPLORATA:
OR,
DISCOVERIES

Ill fortune never crushed that man whom good fortune *Fortuna*
deceived not. I therefore have counselled my friends
never to trust to her fairer side, though she seemed to
make peace with them, but to place all things she gave
them so as she might ask them again without their
trouble: she might take them from them, not pull them;

to keep always a distance between her and themselves. He knows not his own strength that hath not met adversity. Heaven prepares good men with crosses; but no ill can happen to a good man. Contraries are not 10 mixed. Yet that which happens to any man, may to every man. But it is in his reason what he accounts it, and will make it.

Casus

Change into extremity is very frequent and easy. As when a beggar suddenly grows rich, he commonly becomes a prodigal; for to obscure his former obscurity, he puts on riot and excess.

Consilia

No man is so foolish, but may give another good counsel sometimes; and no man is so wise, but may easily err if he will take no others' counsel but his own. But 20 very few men are wise by their own counsel, or learned by
Αὐτοδίδακτος their own teaching. For he that was only taught by himself, had a fool to his master.

Fama

A fame that is wounded to the world would be better cured by another's apology than its own; for few can apply medicines well themselves. Besides, the man that is once hated, both his good and his evil deeds oppress him: he is not easily emergent.

Negotia

In great affairs it is a work of difficulty to please all. And oft-times we lose the occasion of carrying a business 30 well and thoroughly by our too much haste. For passions are spiritual rebels, and raise sedition against the understanding.

Amor patriae

There is a necessity all men should love their country; he that professeth the contrary, may be delighted with his words, but his heart is there.

Ingenia

Natures that are hardened to evil you shall sooner break than make straight; they are like poles that are crooked and dry: there is no attempting them.

Applausus

We praise the things we hear with much more willing- 40

ness than those we see; because we envy the present and
reverence the past; thinking ourselves instructed by the
one, and overlaid by the other.

Opinion is a light, vain, crude, and imperfect thing, *Opinio*
settled in the imagination, but never arriving at the
understanding, there to obtain the tincture of reason. We
labour with it more than truth. There is much more
holds us than presseth us. An ill fact is one thing, an ill
fortune is another; yet both often-times sway us alike, by
50 the error of our thinking.

Many men believe not themselves what they would *Impostura*
persuade others; and less do the things which they would
impose on others: but least of all know what they
themselves most confidently boast. Only they set the sign
of the cross over their outer doors, and sacrifice to their
gut and their groin in their inner closets.

What a deal of cold business doth a man misspend the *Jactura vitae*
better part of life in! In scattering compliments, tendering visits, gathering and venting news, following feasts
60 and plays, making a little winter-love in a dark corner.

Puritanus hypocrita est haereticus, quem opinio propriae *Hypocrita*
perspicaciae, qua sibi videtur, cum paucis, in ecclesiae dog-
matibus errores quosdam animadvertisse, de statu mentis
deturbavit: unde sacro furore percitus, phrenetice pugnat
contra magistratus, sic ratus, obedientiam praestare Deo.

Learning needs rest: sovereignty gives it. Sovereignty *Mutua auxilia*
needs counsel: learning affords it. There is such a
consociation of offices between the prince and whom his
favour breeds, that they may help to sustain his power, as
70 he their knowledge. It is the greatest part of his liberality,
his favour; and from whom doth he hear discipline more
willingly, or the arts discoursed more gladly, than from
those whom his own bounty and benefits have made able
and faithful?

In being able to counsel others, a man must be *Cognit[io]*
furnished with an universal store in himself, to the *universi*

knowledge of all nature: that is the matter and seed-plot; there are the seats of all argument and invention. But especially you must be cunning in the nature of man: there is the variety of things, which are as the elements 80 and letters which his art and wisdom must rank and order to the present occasion. For we see not all letters in single words, nor all places in particular discourses. That cause seldom happens wherein a man will use all arguments.

Consiliarii   The two chief things that give a man reputation in
adjunct[i]:   counsel are the opinion of his honesty and the opinion of
probitas,   his wisdom. The authority of those two will persuade,
sapientia   when the same counsels, uttered by other persons less qualified, are of no efficacy or working.   90

Wisdom without honesty is mere craft and cozenage. And therefore the reputation of honesty must first be
Vita recta   gotten, which cannot be but by living well. A good life is a main argument.

Obsequentia   Next a good life, to beget love in the persons we counsel, by dissembling our knowledge of ability in ourselves, and avoiding all suspicion of arrogance; ascribing all to their instruction, as an ambassador to his master, or a subject to his sovereign; seasoning all with
humanitas,   humanity and sweetness, only expressing care and solici- 100
sollicitudo   tude. And not to counsel rashly, or on the sudden, but with advice and meditation. *Dat nox consilium.* For many foolish things fall from wise men if they speak in haste, or be extemporal. It therefore behoves the giver of counsel to be circumspect; especially to beware of those with whom he is not thoroughly acquainted, lest any spice of rashness, folly, or self-love appear, which will be marked by new persons and men of experience in affairs.

And to the prince, or his superior, to behave himself
Modestia,   modestly and with respect; yet free from flattery or 110
parrhesia   empire. Not with insolence or precept; but as the prince were already furnished with the parts he should have,

especially in affairs of state. For in other things they will
more easily suffer themselves to be taught, or reprehended; they will not willingly contend. But hear (with
Alexander) the answer the musician gave him: *Absit, o
rex, ut tu melius haec scias, quam ego.*

*Plutarc[h] in
vita
Alex[andri]*

A man should so deliver himself to the nature of the
subject whereof he speaks, that his hearer may take
120 knowledge of his discipline with some delight; and so
apparel fair and good matter, that the studious of elegancy be not defrauded; redeem arts from their rough
and braky seats where they lay hid and overgrown with
thorns, to a pure, open, and flowery light, where they may
take the eye, and be taken by the hand.

*Perspicuitas
elegantia*

I cannot think nature is so spent and decayed that she
can bring forth nothing worth her former years. She is
always the same, like herself; and when she collects her
strength, is abler still. Men are decayed, and studies: she
130 is not.

*Natura non
effeta*

I know nothing can conduce more to letters than to
examine the writings of the ancients, and not to rest in
their sole authority, or take all upon trust from them;
provided the plagues of judging and pronouncing against
them be away: such as are envy, bitterness, precipitation,
impudence, and scurrile scoffing. For to all the observations of the ancients, we have our own experience;
which, if we will use and apply, we have better means to
pronounce. It is true they opened the gates and made the
140 way, that went before us; but as guides, not commanders:
non domini nostri, sed duces fuere. Truth lies open to all; it is
no man's several. *Patet omnibus veritas, nondum est
occupata. Multum ex illa etiam futuris relictum est.*

*Non nimium
credendum
antiquitati*

If in some things I dissent from others, whose wit,
industry, diligence and judgement I look up at, and
admire, let me not therefore hear presently of ingratitude
and rashness. For I thank those that have taught me, and
will ever; but yet dare not think the scope of their labour

Dissentire licet

sed cum ratione

and enquiry was to envy their posterity what they also 150
could add and find out.

Non mihi
cedendum,

If I err, pardon me: *nulla ars simul et inventa est et absoluta.*
I do not desire to be equal to those that went before, but
to have my reason examined with theirs, and so much
faith to be given them, or me, as those shall evict. I am
neither author, or fautor of any sect. I will have no man
addict himself to me; but if I have anything right, defend
it as truth's, not mine (save as it conduceth to a common
good). It profits not me to have any man fence or fight for

sed veritati

me, to flourish, or take a side. Stand for truth, and 'tis 160
enough.

Scientiae
liberales

Arts that respect the mind were ever reputed nobler
than those that serve the body, though we less can be
without them. As tillage, spinning, weaving, building,
etc. without which we could scarce sustain life a day. But
these were the works of every hand; the other of the brain
only, and those the most generous and exalted wits, and
spirits that cannot rest, or acquiesce. The mind of man is
still fed with labour: *opere pascitur.*

non vulgi sunt

There is a more secret cause; and the power of liberal 170
studies lies more hid than that it can be wrought out by
profane wits. It is not every man's way to hit. They are
men (I confess) that set the carat and value upon things
as they love them; but science is not every man's mistress. It is as great a spite to be praised in the wrong place,
and by a wrong person, as can be done to a noble nature.

Honesta
ambitio

If divers men seek fame or honour by divers ways, so
both be honest, neither is to be blamed; but they that
seek immortality, are not only worthy of leave, but of
praise.

                                                              180

Maritus
improbus

He hath a delicate wife, a fair fortune, and family to go
to [to] be welcome, yet he had rather be drunk with mine
host and the fiddlers of such a town, than go home.

Afflictio pia
magistra

Affliction teacheth a wicked person sometime to pray:
prosperity never.

Many might go to heaven with half the labour they go *Deploratis* to hell, if they would venture their industry the right way; *facilis descensus* but 'The devil take all!' (quoth he) that was choked i' the *Averni.* mill-dam, with his four last words in his mouth. *The devil take all*

190   A cripple in the way out-travels a footman or a post out *Aegidius cursu* of the way. *superat*

Bags of money to a prodigal person are the same that *Prodigo nummi* cherry stones are with some boys, and so thrown away. *nauci*

A woman, the more curious she is about her face, is *Munda et* commonly the more careless about her house. *sordida*

Of this spilt water, there is little to be gathered up: it is *Debitum* a desperate debt. *deploratum*

The thief (with a great belly) that had a longing at the *Latro* gallows to commit one robbery more before he was *sesquipedalis* 200   hanged.

And like the German lord, when he went out of *Com[es] de* Newgate into the cart, took order to have his arms set up *Schortenhien* in the last harborough; said he was taken and committed upon suspicion of treason, no witness appearing against him; but the judges entertained him most civilly, discoursed with him, offered him the courtesy of the rack; but he confessed, etc.

I am beholden to calumny, that she hath so en- *Calumniae* deavoured and taken pains to belie me. It shall make me *fructus* 210   set a surer guard on myself, and keep a better watch upon my actions.

A tedious person is one a man would leap a steeple *Impertinens* from, gallop down any steep hill to avoid him; forsake his meat, sleep, nature itself, with all her benefits, to shun him. A mere impertinent; one that touched neither heaven nor earth in his discourse. He opened an entry into a fair room, but shut it again presently. I spake to him of garlic, he answered asparagus; consulted him of

marriage, he tells me of hanging: as if they went by one
and the same destiny.   220

*Bellum
scribentium*

What a sight it is to see writers committed together by
the ears for ceremonies, syllables, points, colons, com-
mas, hyphens, and the like! Fighting as for their fires and
their altars, and angry that none are frighted at their
noises and loud brayings under their asses' skins!

There is hope of getting a fortune without digging in
these quarries. *Sed meliore (in omne) ingenio, animoque
quam fortuna sum usus.*
Pingue solum lassat, sed iuvat ipse labor.

*Differentia
inter doctos et
sciolos*

Wits made out their several expeditions then for the   230
discovery of truth to find out great and profitable knowledges; had their several instruments for the disquisition
of arts. Now there are certain *scioli*, or smatterers, that
are busy in the skirts and outsides of learning, and have
scarce anything of solid literature to commend them.
They may have some edging or trimming of a scholar, a
welt or so; but it is no more.

*Impostorum
fucus*

Imposture is a specious thing, yet never worse than
when it feigns to be best, and to none discovered sooner
than the simplest. For truth and goodness are plain and   240
open; but imposture is ever ashamed of the light.

*Icuncularum
motio*

A puppet-play must be shadowed, and seen in the
dark; for draw the curtain, *et sordet gesticulatio.*

*Principes et
administri*

There is a great difference in the understanding of
some princes, as in the quality of their ministers about
them. Some would dress their masters in gold, pearl, and
all true jewels of majesty; others furnish them with
feathers, bells, and ribbons: and are therefore esteemed
the fitter servants. But they are ever good men that must
make good the times; if the men be naught, the times will   250
be such. *Finis expectandus est in unoquoque hominum;
animali ad mutationem promptissimo.*

It is a quick saying with the Spaniards, *artes inter haeredes non dividi*. Yet these have inherited their fathers' lying, and they brag of it. He is a narrow-minded man that affects a triumph in any glorious study; but to triumph in a lie, and a lie themselves have forged, is frontless. Folly often goes beyond her bounds; but impudence knows none.

Scitum Hispanicum

260   Envy is no new thing, nor was it born only in our times. The ages past have brought it forth, and the coming ages will. So long as there are men fit for it, *quorum odium virtute relicta placet*, it will never be wanting. It is a barbarous envy to take from those men's virtues, which, because thou canst not arrive at, thou impotently des-paires[t] to imitate. Is it a crime in me that I know that which others had not yet known but from me? Or that I am the author of many things which would never have come in thy thought but that I taught them? It is a new but
270   a foolish way you have found out, that whom you cannot equal or come near in doing, you would destroy or ruin with evil speaking; as if you had bound both your wits and nature's prentices to slander, and then came forth the best artificers, when you could form the foulest calumnies.

Non nova res livor

Indeed, nothing is of more credit or request now, than a petulant paper, or scoffing verses; and it is but con- venient to the times and manners we live with, to have then the worst writings and studies flourish, when the
280   best begin to be despised. Ill arts begin where good end.

Nil gratius protervo lib[ro]

The time was when men would learn and study good things, not envy those that had them. Then men were had in price for learning; now letters only make men vile. He is upbraidingly called a poet, as if it were a most contemptible nickname. But the professors, indeed, have made the learning cheap: railing and tinkling rhymers, whose writings the vulgar more greedily read, as being taken with the scurrility and petulancy of such wits. He shall not have a reader now unless he jeer and
290   lie. It is the food of men's natures; the diet of the times!

Jam litterae sordent

Pastus hodier[ni] ingen[ii]

Gallants cannot sleep else. The writer must lie, and the gentle reader rests happy, to hear the worthiest works misinterpreted, the clearest actions obscured, the innocentest life traduced; and in such a licence of lying, a field so fruitful of slanders, how can there be matter wanting to his laughter? Hence comes the epidemical infection. For how can they escape the contagion of the writings, whom the virulency of the calumnies hath not staved off from reading?

Sed seculi morbus

Nothing doth more invite a greedy reader than an 300 unlooked-for subject. And what more unlooked-for than to see a person of an unblamed life made ridiculous or odious by the artifice of lying? But it is the disease of the age; and no wonder if the world, growing old, begin to be infirm; old age itself is a disease. It is long since the sick world began to dote and talk idly; would she had but doted still! but her dotage is now broke forth into a madness, and become a mere frenzy.

Alastoris malitia

This Alastor, who hath left nothing unsearched or unassailed by his impudent and licentious lying in his 310 aguish writings—for he was in his cold quaking fit all the while—what hath he done more than a troublesome base cur: barked, and made a noise afar off; had a fool or two to spit in his mouth, and cherish him with a musty bone? But they are rather enemies of my fame than me, these barkers.

Mali choragi fuere

It is an art to have so much judgement as to apparel a lie well, to give it a good dressing; that though the nakedness would show deformed and odious, the suiting of it might draw their readers. Some love any strumpet, 320 be she never so shop-like or meritorious, in good clothes. But these, nature could not have formed them better to destroy their own testimony, and overthrow their calumny.

Hearsay news

That an elephant, 630, came hither ambassador from the Great Mogul, who could both write and read, and was every day allowed twelve cast of bread, twenty quarts

of Canary sack, besides nuts and almonds the citizens'
wives sent him. That he had a Spanish boy to his
330 interpreter, and his chief negotiation was to confer or
practise with Archy, the principal fool of state, about
stealing hence Windsor Castle and carrying it away on
his back if he can.

A wise tongue should not be licentious and wandering;   *Lingua*
but moved and, as it were, governed with certain reins   *sapientis,*
from the heart and bottom of the breast; and it was   *potius quam*
excellently said of that philosopher, that there was a wall *loquentis*
or parapet of teeth set in our mouth, to restrain the   *optanda*
petulancy of our words; that the rashness of talking
340 should not only be retarded by the guard and watch of
our heart, but be fenced in and defended by certain
strengths placed in the mouth itself, and within the lips.
But you shall see some so abound with words without any
seasoning or taste of matter, in so profound a security, as
while they are speaking, for the most part they confess to
speak they know not what.

Of the two (if either were to be wished) I would rather
have a plain downright wisdom than a foolish and
affected eloquence. For what is so furious and Bedlam-
350 like as a vain sound of chosen and excellent words,
without any subject of sentence or science mixed?

Whom the disease of talking still once possesseth, he
can never hold his peace. Nay, rather than he will not
discourse, he will hire men to hear him. And so heard,
not hearkened unto, he comes off most times like a
mountebank, that when he hath praised his medicines,
finds none will take them or trust him. He is like
Homer's Thersites, Ἀμετροεπὴς, Ἀκριτόμυθος, without   *Thersites,*
judgement or measure. *Loquax magis, quam facundus.*   *Homeri,*
                                                        Sallust
360 *Satis loquentiae, sapientiae parum.*

    Γλώσσης τοι θησαυρὸς ἐν ἀνθρώποισιν ἄριστος   *Hesiodus*
Φειδωλῆς, πλείστη δὲ χάρις κατὰ μέτρον ἰούσης.
Optimus est homini linguae thesaurus, et ingens
Gratia, quae parcis mensurat singula verbis.

Ulysses, in Homer, is made a long-thinking man before he speaks; and Epaminondas is celebrated by Pindar to be a man that, though he knew much, yet he spoke but little. Demaratus, when on the bench he was long silent and said nothing, one asking him if it were folly in him or want of language, he answered, 'A fool 370 could never hold his peace.' For too much talking is ever the indice of a fool.

> *Dum tacet indoctus, poterit cordatus haberi;*
> *Is morbos animi namque tacendo tegit.*

Nor is that worthy speech of Zeno the philosopher to be passed over without the note of ignorance; who being invited to a feast in Athens, where a great Prince's ambassadors were entertained, and was the only person had said nothing at the table; one of them with courtesy asked him, 'What shall we return from thee, Zeno, to the 380 prince our master, if he ask us of thee?' 'Nothing', he replied, 'more, but that you found an old man in Athens that knew to be silent amongst his cups.' It was near a miracle to see an old man silent, since talking is the disease of age; but amongst cups makes it fully a wonder.

It was wittily said upon one that was taken for a great and grave man so long as he held his peace: this man might have been a counsellor of state, till he spoke; but having spoken, not a beadle of the ward. Ἐχεμυθία *Pythag[orae] quam laudabilis!* γλωσσῆς πρὸ τῶν ἄλλων 390 χράτει, θεοῖς ἐπόμενος. *Linguam cohibe, prae aliis omnibus, ad deorum exemplum. *Digito compesce labellum.*

There is almost no man but he sees clearlier and sharper the vices in a speaker, than the virtues. And there are many that with more ease will find fault with what is spoken foolishly, than that can give allowance to that wherein you are wise silently. The treasure of a fool is always in his tongue (says the witty comic poet) and it appears not in anything more than in that nation; whereof one, when he had got the inheritance of an 400 unlucky old grange, would needs sell it; and to draw

buyers, proclaimed the virtues of it. 'Nothing ever *Trin[ummus],*
thrived on it', saith he. 'No owner of it ever died in his *Act 2,*
bed: some hung, some drowned themselves, some were *scaen[a] 6*
banished, some starved; the trees were all blasted; the
swine died of the measles, the cattle of the murrain, the
sheep of the rot; they that stood were ragged, bare, and
bald as your hand; nothing was ever reared there, not a *Sim[iliter]*
duckling, or a goose.' *Hospitium fuerat calamitatis.* Was *Mart[ial], lib.*
410 not this man like to sell it?   *I, ep. 85*

Expectation of the vulgar is more drawn and held with *Vulgi expectatio*
newness than goodness: we see it in fencers, in players,
in poets, in preachers, in all where fame promiseth
anything; so it be new, though never so naught and
depraved, they run to it and are taken. Which shows that
the only decay or hurt of the best men's reputation with
the people is, their wits have outlived the people's
palates. They have been too much or too long a
feast.

420 Greatness of name in the father, oft-times helps not *Claritas patria*
forth, but o'erwhelms the son; they stand too near one
another. The shadow kills the growth; so much, that we
see the grandchild come more and oftener to be the heir
of the first, than doth the second. He dies between: the
possession is the third's.

Eloquence is a great and diverse thing; nor did she yet *Eloquentia*
ever favour any man so much as to become wholly his.
He is happy that can arrive to any degree of her grace.
Yet there are who prove themselves masters of her, and
430 absolute lords; but I believe they may mistake their
evidence: for it is one thing to be eloquent in the schools
or in the hall, another at the bar or in the pulpit. There is
a difference between mooting and pleading; between
fencing and fighting. To make arguments in my study
and confute them is easy, where I answer myself, not an
adversary. So I can see whole volumes dispatched by the
umbratical doctors on all sides. But draw these forth into
the just lists: let them appear *sub dio,* and they are
changed with the place, like bodies bred i' the shade;

they cannot suffer the sun or a shower, nor bear the open 440
air; they scarce can find themselves, they that were wont
to domineer so among their auditors. But indeed I would
no more choose a rhetorician for reigning in a school,
than I would a pilot for rowing in a pond.

Amor et odium   Love that is ignorant, and hatred, have almost the
same ends. Many foolish lovers wish the same to their
friends, which their enemies would: as to wish a friend
banished, that they might accompany him in exile; or
some great want, that they might relieve him; or a
disease, that they might sit by him. They make a cause- 450
way to their courtesy by injury; as if it were not honester
to do nothing, than to seek a way to do good by a
mischief.

Injuriae   Injuries do not extinguish courtesies; they only suffer
them not to appear fair. For a man that doth me an injury
after a courtesy, takes not away the courtesy, but defaces
it; as he that writes other verses upon my verses, takes not
away the first letters, but hides them.

Beneficia   Nothing is a courtesy unless it be meant us; and that
friendly and lovingly. We owe no thanks to rivers, that 460
they carry our boats; or winds, that they be favouring, and
fill our sails; or meats, that they be nourishing. For these
are what they are necessarily. Horses carry us, trees
shade us, but they know it not. It is true, some man may
receive a courtesy, and not know it; but never any man
received it from him that knew it not. Many men have
been cured of diseases by accidents, but they were not
remedies. I myself have known one helped of an ague by
falling into a water; another whipped out of a fever: but
no man would ever use these for medicines. It is the 470
mind, and not the event, that distinguisheth the courtesy
from wrong. My adversary may offend the judge with his
pride and impertinences, and I win my cause; but he
meant it not me as a courtesy. I 'scaped pirates by being
ship-wrecked: was the wreck a benefit therefore? No; the
doing of courtesies aright is the mixing of the respects for
his own sake and for mine. He that doth them merely for

his own sake is like one that feeds his cattle to sell them; he hath his horse well-dressed for Smithfield.

480   The price of many things is far above what they are *Valor rerum* bought and sold for. Life and health, which are both inestimable, we have of the physician; as learning and knowledge, the true tillage of the mind, from our schoolmasters. But the fees of the one or the salary of the other never answer the value of what we received, but serve to gratify their labours.

Memory, of all the powers of the mind, is the most *Memoria* delicate and frail; it is the first of our faculties that age invades. Seneca, the father, the rhetorician, confesseth
490   of himself he had a miraculous one, not only to receive but to hold. I myself could in my youth have repeated all that ever I had made, and so continued till I was past forty; since, it is much decayed in me. Yet I can repeat whole books that I have read, and poems of some selected friends, which I have liked to charge my memory with. It was wont to be faithful to me, but shaken with age now, and sloth, which weakens the strongest abilities, it may perform somewhat, but cannot promise much. By exercise it is to be made better and serviceable. What-
500   soever I pawned with it while I was young and a boy, it offers me readily and without stops; but what I trust to it now, or have done of later years, it lays up more negligently, and often-times loses; so that I receive mine own (though frequently called for) as if it were new and borrowed. Nor do I always find presently from it what I do seek; but while I am doing another thing, that I laboured for will come; and what I sought with trouble will offer itself when I am quiet. Now in some men I have found it as happy as nature, who, whatsoever they read or
510   pen, they can say without book presently, as if they did then write in their mind. And it is more a wonder in such as have a swift style, for their memories are commonly slowest; such as torture their writings, and go into council for every word, must needs fix somewhat, and make it their own at last, though but through their own vexation.

Comit[iorum]
suffragia

Suffrages in Parliament are numbered, not weighed; nor can it be otherwise in these public councils, where nothing is so unequal as the equality: for there, how odd soever men's brains or wisdoms are, their power is 520 always even and the same.

Stare a
partibus

Some actions, be they never so beautiful and generous, are often obscured by base and vile misconstructions, either out of envy or ill nature, that judgeth of others as of itself. Nay, the times are so wholly grown to be either partial or malicious, that if he be a friend, all sits well about him, his very vices shall be virtues; if an enemy, or of the contrary faction, nothing is good or tolerable in him; insomuch that we care not to discredit and shame our judgements to soothe our passions.   530

Deus in
creaturis

Man is read in his face, God in his creatures; but not as the philosopher, the creature of glory, reads him, but as the divine, the servant of humility; yet even he must take care not to be too curious. For to utter truth of God but as he thinks only may be dangerous, who is best known by our not knowing. Some things of him, so much as he hath revealed or commanded, it is not only lawful but necessary for us to know; for therein our ignorance was the first cause of our wickedness.

Veritas
proprium
hominis

Truth is man's proper good, and the only immortal 540 thing was given to our mortality to use. No good Christian or ethnic, if he be honest, can miss it; no statesman, or patriot should. For without truth all the actions of mankind are craft, malice, or what you will, rather than wisdom. Homer says he hates him worse than hell-mouth that utters one thing with his tongue, and keeps another in his breast. Which high expression was grounded on divine reason; for a lying mouth is a stinking pit, and murders with the contagion it venteth. Beside, nothing is lasting that is feigned; it will have 550 another face than it had, ere long. As Euripides saith, 'No lie ever grows old.'

Nullum vitium
sine patrocinio

It is strange there should be no vice without his patronage, that when we have no other excuse, we will

say, we love it, we cannot forsake it; as if that made it not
more a fault. We cannot, because we think we cannot,
and we love it, because we will defend it. We will rather
excuse it than be rid of it. That we cannot, is pretended;
but that we will not is the true reason. How many have I
560 known that would not have their vices hid? Nay, and to be
noted, live like antipodes to others in the same city; never
see the sun rise or set in so many years, but be as they
were watching a corpse by torchlight; would not sin the
common way, but held that a kind of rusticity: they would
do it new, or contrary, for the infamy? They were
ambitious of living backward; and at last arrived at that,
as they would love nothing but the vices, not the vicious
customs. It was impossible to reform these natures; they
were dried and hardened in their ill. They may say they
570 desired to leave it, but do not trust them; and they may
think they desired it, but they may lie for all that. They
are a little angry with their follies now and then: marry,
they come into grace with them again quickly. They will
confess they are offended with their manner of living;
like enough, who is not? When they can put me in
security that they are more than offended, that they hate
it, then I'll hearken to them, and perhaps, believe them;
but many nowadays love and hate their ill together.

I do hear them say often, some men are not witty, *De vere argutis*
580 because they are not everywhere witty; than which
nothing is more foolish. If an eye or a nose be an
excellent part in the face, therefore, be all eye or nose? I
think the eyebrow, the forehead, the cheek, chin, lip, or
any part else are as necessary and natural in the place.
But now nothing is good that is natural; right and natural
language seem[s] to have least of the wit in it; that which
is writhed and tortured is counted the more exquisite.
Cloth of baudekin or tissue must be embroidered; as if
no face were fair that were not powdered or painted! No
590 beauty to be had but in wresting and writhing our own
tongue! Nothing is fashionable till it be deformed; and
this is to write like a gentleman. All must be as affected
and preposterous as our gallants' clothes, sweet bags,

and night-dressings, in which you would think our men
lay in, like ladies, it is so curious.

Censura de
poetis

Nothing in our age, I have observed, is more preposterous than the running judgements upon poetry and
poets; when we shall hear those things commended and
cried up for the best writings which a man would scarce
vouchsafe to wrap any wholesome drug in; he would   600
never light his tobacco with them. And those men almost
named for miracles, who yet are so vile that if a man
should go about to examine and correct them, he must
make all they have done but one blot. Their good is so
entangled with their bad, as forcibly one must draw on
the other's death with it. A sponge dipped in ink will do
all:

Mart[ial],
l[ib.]4, epig.
10

—*comitetur Punica librum*
spongea.—

Et paulo post,   610

Non possunt . . . multae [. . .] una litura potest.

Yet their vices have not hurt them; nay, a great many
they have profited, for they have been loved for nothing
else. And this false opinion grows strong against the best
Cestius
Cicero
men, if once it take root with the ignorant. Cestius in
his time was preferred to Cicero, so far as the ignorant
durst. They learned him without book, and had him
often in their mouths. But a man cannot imagine that
thing so foolish or rude but will find and enjoy an
admirer; at least a reader or spectator. The puppets are   620
Heath
Taylor
seen now in despite of the players; Heath's epigrams and
the Sculler's poems have their applause. There are never
wanting that dare prefer the worst preachers, the worst
pleaders, the worst poets; not that the better have left to
write or speak better, but that they that hear them judge
worse: *non illi pejus dicunt, sed hi corruptius judicant.* Nay,
if it were put to the question of the water-rhymer's works
Spenser
against Spenser's, I doubt not but they would find more
suffrages; because the most favour common vices, out of
a prerogative the vulgar have to lose their judgements   630
and like that which is naught.

Poetry in this latter age hath proved but a mean mistress to such as have wholly addicted themselves to her, or given their names up to her family. They who have but saluted her on the by, and now and then tendered their visits, she hath done much for, and advanced in the way of their own professions—both the law, and the gospel—beyond all they could have hoped or done for themselves without her favour. Wherein she
640 doth emulate the judicious but preposterous bounty of the time's grandees, who accumulate all they can upon the parasite or freshman in their friendship, but think an old client or honest servant bound by his place to write and starve.

Indeed, the multitude commend writers as they do fencers or wrestlers, who, if they come in robustiously, and put for it with a deal of violence, are received for the braver fellows; when many times their own rudeness is a cause of their disgrace, and a slight touch of their
650 adversary gives all that boisterous force the foil. But in these things the unskilful are naturally deceived, and judging wholly by the bulk, think rude things greater than polished, and scattered more numerous than composed. Nor think this only to be true in the sordid multitude, but the neater sort of our gallants; for all are the multitude, only they differ in clothes, not in judgement or understanding.

I remember the players have often mentioned it as an honour to Shakespeare, that in his writing, whatsoever
660 he penned, he never blotted out line. My answer hath been, 'Would he had blotted a thousand'; which they thought a malevolent speech. I had not told posterity this but for their ignorance, who choose that circumstance to commend their friend by wherein he most faulted; and to justify mine own candour: for I loved the man, and do honour his memory, on this side idolatry, as much as any. He was, indeed, honest, and of an open and free nature; had an excellent fantasy, brave notions, and gentle expressions; wherein he flowed with that facility that
670 sometime it was necessary he should be stopped. '*Suf-flaminandus erat*', as Augustus said of Haterius. His wit

De Shakespeare nostrat[i]

Augustus in Hat[erium]

was in his own power; would the rule of it had been so too. Many times he fell into those things, could not escape laughter: as when he said in the person of Caesar, one speaking to him, 'Caesar, thou dost me wrong'; he replied, 'Caesar did never wrong, but with just cause'; and such like: which were ridiculous. But he redeemed his vices with his virtues. There was ever more in him to be praised than to be pardoned.

Ingeniorum discrimina. Not[a] 1

In the difference of wits I have observed there are 680 many notes, and it is a little mastery to know them: to discern what every nature, every disposition will bear; for before we sow our land we should plough it. There are no fewer forms of minds than of bodies amongst us. The variety is incredible, and therefore we must search. Some are fit to make divines, some poets, some lawyers, some physicians; some to be sent to the plough, and trades.

There is no doctrine will do good where nature is wanting. Some wits are swelling and high, others low and 690 still, some hot and fiery, others cold and dull; one must have a bridle, the other a spur.

Not[a] 2

There be some that are forward and bold, and these will do every little thing easily—I mean, that is hard by and next them: which they will utter, unretarded, without any shamefastness. These never perform much, but quickly. They are what they are on the sudden; they show presently, like grain that, scattered on the top of the ground, shoots up but takes no root, has a yellow blade, but the ear empty. They are wits of good promise at first, 700 but there is an *ingeni-stitium*: they stand still at sixteen, they get no higher.

*A wit-stand.

Not[a] 3

You have others that labour only to ostentation, and are ever more busy about the colours and surface of a work, than in the matter and foundation: for that is hid, the other is seen.

Not[a] 4 Martial, lib. 11, epig. 9[o]

Others, that in composition are nothing but what is rough and broken: *quae per salebras altaque saxa cadunt.* And if it would come gently, they trouble it of purpose. They would not have it run without rubs, as if that style 710 were more strong and manly that struck the ear with a

kind of uneven[n]ess. These men err not by chance, but
knowingly and willingly; they are like men that affect a
fashion by themselves, have some singularity in a ruff,
cloak, or hatband; or their beards specially cut to provoke
beholders, and set a mark upon themselves. They would
be reprehended while they are looked on. And this vice,
one that is in authority with the rest, loving, delivers over
to them to be imitated; so that oft-times the faults which
720 he fell into, the others seek for. This is the danger, when
vice becomes a precedent.

   Others there are that have no composition at all, but a   *Not[a] 5*
kind of tuning and rhyming fall in what they write. It runs
and slides and only makes a sound. Women's poets they
are called, as you have women's tailors.

>   They write a verse as smooth, as soft, as cream,
>   In which there is not torrent, nor scarce stream.

You may sound these wits, and find the depth of them,
with your middle finger. They are cream-bowl- or but
730 puddle-deep.

   Some that turn over all books, and are equally search-   *Not[a] 6*
ing in all papers, that write out of what they presently find
or meet, without choice: by which means it happens that
what they have discredited and impugned in one work,
they have before or after extolled the same in another.
Such are all the essayists, even their master Montaigne.   *Mic[hel] de*
These, in all they write, confess still what books they   *Montaigne*
have read last, and therein their own folly, so much, that
they bring it to the stake raw and undigested; not that the
740 place did need it neither, but that they thought themselves furnished, and would vent it.

   Some again, who, after they have got authority, or,   *Not[a] 7*
which is less, opinion, by their writings, to have read
much, dare presently to feign whole books and authors,
and lie safely. For what never was, will not easily be
found, not by the most curious.

   And some, by a cunning protestation against all read-   *Not[a] 8*
ing, and false venditation of their own naturals, think to
divert the sagacity of their readers from themselves, and
750 cool the scent of their own fox-like thefts; when yet they
are so rank, as a man may find whole pages together

usurped from one author; their necessities compelling
them to read for present use, which could not be in many
books; and so come forth more ridiculously and palpably
guilty than those who, because they cannot trace, they yet
would slander their industry.

Not[a] 9   But the wretcheder are the obstinate contemners of all
helps and arts; such as presuming on their own naturals
(which perhaps are excellent) dare deride all diligence,
and seem to mock at the terms when they understand not   760
the things, thinking that way to get off wittily with their
ignorance. These are imitated often by such as are their
peers in negligence, though they cannot be in nature;
and they utter all they can think with a kind of violence
and indisposition; unexamined, without relation either to
person, place, or any fitness else; and the more wilful and
stubborn they are in it, the more learned they are
esteemed of the multitude, through their excellent vice
of judgement, who think those things the stronger that
have no art; as if to break were better than to open, or to   770
rend asunder, gentler than to loose.

Not[a] 10   It cannot but come to pass that these men who
commonly seek to do more than enough may sometimes
happen on something that is good and great, but very
seldom; and when it comes, it doth not recompense the
rest of their ill. For their jests and their sentences
—which they only and ambitiously seek for—stick out
and are more eminent, because all is sordid and vile
about them, as lights are more discerned in a thick
darkness than a faint shadow. Now because they speak   780
all they can, however unfitly, they are thought to have the
greater copy; where the learned use ever election and a
mean, they look back to what they intended at first, and
make all an even and proportioned body. The true
artificer will not run away from nature, as he were afraid
of her, or depart from life and the likeness of truth, but
speak to the capacity of his hearers. And though his
language differ from the vulgar somewhat, it shall not fly
from all humanity, with the Tamerlanes and Tamer-
chams of the late age, which had nothing in them but the   790
scenical strutting and furious vociferation to warrant
them to the ignorant gapers. He knows it is his only art so

to carry it, as none but artificers perceive it. In the meantime, perhaps, he is called barren, dull, lean, a poor writer, or by what contumelious word can come into their cheeks, by these men, who without labour, judgement, knowledge, or almost sense, are received or preferred before him. He gratulates them and their fortune. Another age, or juster men, will acknowledge the virtues of his studies: his wisdom in dividing, his subtlety in arguing, with what strength he doth inspire his readers; with what sweetness he strokes them; in inveighing, what sharpness; in jest, what urbanity he uses. How he doth reign in men's affections; how invade, and break in upon them, and makes their minds like the thing he writes. Then in his elocution to behold what word is proper, which hath ornament, which height, what is beautifully translated, where figures are fit, which gentle, which strong, to show the composition manly. And how he hath avoided faint, obscure, obscene, sordid, humble, improper, or effeminate phrase; which is not only praised of the most, but commended (which is worse), especially for that it is naught.

I know no disease of the soul but ignorance: not of the *Ignorantia animae* arts and sciences, but of itself; yet relating to those, it is a pernicious evil, the darkener of man's life, the disturber of his reason, and common confounder of truth, with which a man goes groping in the dark no otherwise than if he were blind. Great understandings are most racked and troubled with it; nay, sometimes they will rather choose to die than not to know the things they study for. Think then what an evil it is, and what good the contrary.

Knowledge is the action of the soul, and is perfect *Scientia* without the senses, as having the seeds of all science and virtue in itself; but not without the service of the senses; by those organs, the soul works: she is a perpetual agent, prompt and subtle, but often flexible and erring, entangling herself like a silkworm; but her reason is a weapon with two edges, and cuts through. In her indagations oft-times new scents put her by, and she takes in errors into her by the same conduits she doth truths.

*Otium
studiorum*

Ease and relaxation are profitable to all studies. The mind is like a bow, the stronger by being unbent. But the temper in spirits is all, when to command a man's wit, when to favour it. I have known a man vehement on both sides, that knew no mean, either to intermit his studies or call upon them again. When he hath set himself to wri[t]ing, he would join night to day, press upon himself without release, not minding it, till he fainted; and when he left off, resolve himself into all sports, and looseness 840 again, that it was almost a despair to draw him to his book; but once got to it, he grew stronger and more earnest by the ease. His whole powers were renewed; he would work out of himself what he desired, but with such excess as his study could not be ruled: he knew not how to dispose his own abilities or husband them; he was of that immoderate power against himself. Nor was he only a strong, but an absolute, speaker and writer: but his subtlety did not show itself; his judgement thought that a vice; for the ambush hurts more that is hid. He never 850 forced his language, nor went out of the highway of speaking but for some great necessity or apparent profit. For he denied figures to be invented for ornament, but for aid; and still thought it an extreme madness to bend or wrest that which ought to be right.

*Et stili
eminentia:
Virgil, Tully,
Sallust,
Plato*

It is no wonder men's eminence appears but in their own way. Virgil's felicity left him in prose, as Tully's forsook him in verse. Sallust's orations are read in the honour of story, yet the most eloquent Plato's speech, which he made for Socrates, is neither worthy of the 860 patron or the person defended. Nay, in the same kind of oratory, and where the matter is one, you shall have him that reasons strongly, open negligently; another that prepares well, not fit so well; and this happens not only to brains but to bodies. One can wrestle well, another run well, a third leap or throw the bar, a fourth lift, or stop a cart going; each hath his way of strength. So in other creatures: some dogs are for the deer, some for the wild boar, some are foxhounds, some otter-hounds. Nor are all horses for the coach or saddle; some are for the cart 870 and panniers.

I have known many excellent men that would speak *De claris*
suddenly to the admiration of their hearers who upon *oratoribus*
study and premeditation have been forsaken by their own
wits, and no way answered their fame; their eloquence
was greater than their reading, and the things they
uttered better than those they knew. Their fortune
deserved better of them than their care. For men of
present spirits, and of greater wits than study, do please
880 more in the things they invent than in those they bring.
And I have heard some of them compelled to speak, out
of necessity, that have so infinitely exceeded themselves,
as it was better both for them and their auditory that they
were so surprised, not prepared. Nor was it safe then to
cross them, for their adversary: their anger made them
more eloquent. Yet these men I could not but love and
admire, that they returned to their studies. They left not
diligence (as many do) when their rashness prospered.
For diligence is a great aid, even to an indifferent wit;
890 when we are not contented with the examples of our own
age, but would know the face of the former. Indeed, the
more we confer with, the more we profit by, if the
persons be chosen.

One, though he be excellent and the chief, is not to be *Dominus*
imitated alone. For never no imitator ever grew up to his *Verulamius*
author; likeness is always on this side truth. Yet there
happened in my time one noble speaker who was full of
gravity in his speaking. His language, where he could
spare or pass by a jest, was nobly censorious. No man
900 ever spake more neatly, more pressly, more weightily, or
suffered less emptiness, less idleness, in what he uttered.
No member of his speech but consisted of the own
graces: his hearers could not cough, or look aside from
him, without loss. He commanded where he spoke, and
had his judges angry and pleased at his devotion. No man
had their affections more in his power. The fear of every
man that heard him was lest he should make an end.

Cicero is said to be the only wit that the people of *Scriptorum*
Rome had equalled to their empire: *ingenium par imperio.* *catalogus: Sir*
Thomas More,
910 We have had many, and in their several ages—to take in *Sir Thomas*
but the former seculum—Sir Thomas More, the elder *Wyatt,*

Hen[ry],
Earl of Surrey,
Sir Thomas
Chaloner, Sir
Thomas Smith,
Sir Thomas
Elyot,
B[ishop]
Gardiner,
Sir Nic[holas]
Bacon, L.K.,
Sir Philip
Sidney,
M[r] Richard
Hooker, Rob[ert],
Earl of Essex,
Sir Walter
Raleigh, Sir
Henry Savile,
Sir Edwin
Sandys,
Sir Thomas
Egerton, L.C.,
Sir Francis
Bacon, L.C.

Wyatt, Henry, Earl of Surrey, Chaloner, Smith, Elyot, B[ishop] Gardiner, were for their times admirable; and the more, because they began eloquence with us. Sir Nicho[las] Bacon was singular, and almost alone, in the beginning of Queen Elizabeth's times. Sir Philip Sidney and Mr Hooker, in different matter, grew great masters of wit and language, and in whom all vigour of invention and strength of judgement met. The Earl of Essex, noble and high; and Sir Walter Raleigh, not to be contemned, 920 either for judgement, or style; Sir Henry Savile, grave, and truly lettered; Sir Edwin Sandys, excellent in both; Lo[rd] Egerton, the Chancellor, a grave and great orator, and best when he was provoked. But his learned and able (though unfortunate) successor is he who hath filled up all numbers, and performed that in our tongue which may be compared or preferred either to insolent Greece or haughty Rome. In short, within his view, and about his times, were all the wits born that could honour a language or help study. Now things daily fall: wits grow 930 downward, and eloquence grows backward; so that he may be named and stand as the mark and ἀκμὴ of our language.

De augmentis
scientiarum

I have ever observed it to have been the office of a wise patriot, among the greatest affairs of the state, to take care of the commonwealth of learning. For schools, they are the seminaries of state; and nothing is worthier the study of a statesman than that part of the republic which we call the advancement of letters. Witness the care of

Julius Caesar

Julius Caesar, who in the heat of the civil war, writ his 940 books of *Analogy*, and dedicated them to Tully. This

Lord S[t]
Alban[s]

made the late Lord S[t] Alban[s] entitle his work *Novum Organum*; which though by the most of superficial men, who cannot get beyond the title of nominals, it is not penetrated, nor understood, it really openeth all defects of learning whatsoever, and is a book,

Horat[ius]
De Art[e]
Poetica

   Qui longum noto scriptori porriget aevum.

My conceit of his person was never increased toward him by his place or honours. But I have and do reverence him for the greatness that was only proper to himself, in 950 that he seemed to me ever, by his work, one of the greatest men, and most worthy of admiration, that had been in many ages. In his adversity I ever prayed that God would give him strength; for greatness he could not want. Neither could I condole in a word or syllable for him, as knowing no accident could do harm to virtue, but rather help to make it manifest.

There cannot be one colour of the mind, another of *De corruptela* the wit. If the mind be staid, grave, and composed, the *morum*
960 wit is so; that vitiated, the other is blown and deflowered. Do we not see, if the mind languish, the members are dull? Look upon an effeminate person: his very gait confesseth him. If a man be fiery, his motion is so; if angry, 'tis troubled and violent. So that we may conclude, wheresoever manners and fashions are corrupted, language is. It imitates the public riot. The excess of feasts and apparel are the notes of a sick state, and the wantonness of language, of a sick mind.

If we would consider what our affairs are indeed, not *De rebus*
970 what they are called, we should find more evils belong to *mundanis* us, than happen to us. How often doth that which was called a calamity prove the beginning and cause of a man's happiness? And on the contrary, that which happened or came to another with great gratulation and applause, how it hath lifted him but a step higher to his ruin! As if he stood before where he might fall safely.

Do but ask of nature why all living creatures are less delighted with meat and drink, that sustains them, than
980 with venery, that wastes them. And she will tell thee, the first respects but a private, the other a common, good: propagation.

The vulgar are commonly ill-natured, and always *Vulgi mores* grudging against their governors; which makes that a prince has more business and trouble with them than ever Hercules had with the bull or any other beast; by how much they have more heads than will be reined with one bridle. There was not that variety of beasts in the ark, as is of beastly natures in the multitude; especially when they come to that iniquity to censure their sovereign's actions. Then all the counsels are made good or bad by the events. And it falleth out that the same facts receive from them the names, now of diligence, now of vanity, now of majesty, now of fury; where they ought wholly to hang on his mouth, as he to consist of himself, and not others' counsels.

Morbus comitialis (margin, lines 990)

After God, nothing is to be loved of man like the prince; he violates nature that doth it not with his whole heart. For when he hath put on the care of the public good and common safety, I am a wretch, and put off man, if I do not reverence and honour him, in whose charge all things divine and human are placed.

Princeps (margin); 1000

He is the arbiter of life and death; when he finds no other subject for his mercy, he should spare himself. All his punishments are rather to correct than to destroy. Why are prayers with Orpheus said to be the daughters of Jupiter, but that princes are thereby admonished that the petitions of the wretched ought to have more weight with them than the laws themselves?

De eodem (margin)

Orpheus hymn[i] (margin)

It was a great accu[mu]lation to his majesty's deserved praise that men might openly visit and pity those whom his greatest prisons had at any time received, or his laws condemned. 1010

De opt[imo] rege Jacobo (margin)

Wise is rather the attribute of a prince than learned or good. The learned man profits others rather than himself; the good man, rather himself than others; but the prince commands others, and doth himself. The wise Lycurgus gave no law but what himself kept. Sulla and Lysander did not so; the one, living extremely dissolute himself, enforced frugality by the laws; the other permit- ted those licences to others which himself abstained from. But the prince's prudence is his chief art and safety. In his counsels and deliberations he foresees the future times. In the equity of his judgement he hath remembrance of the past, and knowledge of what is to be done or avoided for the present. Hence the Persians gave out their Cyrus to have been nursed by a bitch, a creature 1020

De princ[ipum] adjunctis. —Sed vere prudens haud concipi possit princeps, nisi simul et bonus. Lycurgus, Sulla, Lysander (margin)

Cyrus (margin)

to encounter ill, as of sagacity to seek out good; showing
that wisdom may accompany fortitude, or it leaves to be,
1030 and puts on the name of rashness.

There be some men are born only to suck out the *De malign[itate]*
poison of books: *habent venenum pro victu; imo, pro deliciis.* *studentium*
And such are they that only relish the obscene and foul
things in poets, which makes the profession taxed. But by
whom? Men that watch for it, and—had they not had this
hint—are so unjust valuers of letters as they think no
learning good but what brings in gain. It shows they
themselves would never have been of the professions
they are, but for the profits and fees. But if another
1040 learning, well used, can instruct to good life, inform
manners, no less persuade and lead men than they
threaten and compel, and have no reward, is it therefore
the worse study? I could never think the study of wisdom
confined only to the philosopher, or of piety to the divine,
or of state to the politic. But that he which can feign a
commonwealth, which is the poet, can govern it with
counsels, strengthen it with laws, correct it with judgements, inform it with religion and morals, is all these. We
do not require in him mere elocution, or an excellent
1050 faculty in verse, but the exact knowledge of all virtues and
their contraries; with ability to render the one loved, the
other hated, by his proper embattling them. The philosophers did insolently, to challenge only to themselves
that which the greatest generals, and gravest counsellors
never durst. For such had rather do than promise the
best things.

Some controverters in divinity are like swaggerers in a *Controvers[iales]*
tavern, that catch that which stands next them, the *scriptores*
candlestick or pots; turn everything into a weapon; oft-
1060 times they fight blindfold, and both beat the air. The one *More*
milks a he-goat, the other holds under a sieve. Their *andabatarum,*
arguments are as fluxive as liquor spilt upon a table, *qui clausis*
which with your finger you may drain as you will. Such *oculis pugnant*
controversies or disputations, carried with more labour
than profit, are odious; where most times the truth is lost
in the midst, or left untouched. And the fruit of their

fight is that they spit one upon another, and are both defiled. These fencers in religion I like not.

Morbi

The body hath certain diseases that are with less evil tolerated than removed. As if to cure a leprosy a man 1070 should bathe himself with the warm blood of a murdered child, so in the church some errors may be dissimuled with less inconvenience than can be discovered.

Jactantia intempestiva

Men that talk of their own benefits are not believed to talk of them because they have done them, but to have done them because they might talk of them. That which had been great if another had reported it of them, vanisheth, and is nothing, if he that did it speak of it. For men, when they cannot destroy the deed, will yet be glad to take advantage of the boasting, and lessen 1080 it.

I have seen that poverty makes men do unfit things; but honest men should not do them: they should gain otherwise. Though a man be hungry, he should not play the parasite. That hour wherein I would repent me to be honest, there were ways enough open for me to be rich.

Adulatio

But flattery is a fine pick-lock of tender ears, especially of those whom fortune hath borne high upon their wings, that submit their dignity and authority to it, by a soothing of themselves. For indeed men could never be taken in 1090 that abundance with the springes of others' flattery, if they began not there; if they did but remember how much more profitable the bitterness of truth were than all the honey distilling from a whorish voice, which is not praise, but poison. But now it is come to that extreme folly, or rather madness, with some, that he that flatters them modestly or sparingly is thought to malign them. If their friend consent not to their vices, though he do not contradict them, he is nevertheless an enemy. When they do all things the worst way, even then they look for praise. 1100 Nay, they will hire fellows to flatter them with suits and suppers, and to prostitute their judgements. They have livery-friends, friends of the dish and of the spit, that wait their turns, as my lord has his feasts and guests.

I have considered our whole life is like a play: wherein *De vita*
every man, forgetful of himself, is in travail with expres- *humana*
sion of another. Nay, we so insist in imitating others, as
we cannot, when it is necessary, return to ourselves; like
children that imitate the vices of stammerers so long, till
1110 at last they become such, and make the habit to another
nature, as it is never forgotten.

Good men are the stars, the planets of the ages *De piis et*
wherein they live, and illustrate the times. God did never *probis*
let them be wanting to the world: as Abel, for an example
of innocency, Enoch of purity, Noah of trust in God's
mercies, Abraham of faith, and so of the rest. These,
sensual men thought mad, because they would not be
partakers or practisers of their madness. But they, placed
high on the top of all virtue, looked down on the stage of
1120 the world, and contemned the play of fortune. For
though the most be players, some must be spectators.

I have discovered that a feigned familiarity in great *Mores aulici*
ones is a note of certain usurpation on the less. For great
and popular men feign themselves to be servants to
others to make those slaves to them. So the fisher
provides baits for the trout, roach, dace etc., that they
may be food to him.

The complaint of Caligula was most wicked of the *Impiorum*
condition of his times, when he said they were not *querela*
1130 famous by any public calamity, as the reign of Augustus *Augustus*
was by the defeat of Varus and the legions; and that of *Varus*
Tiberius, by the falling of the theatre at Fidenae; whilst *Tiberius*
his oblivion was imminent, through the prosperity of his
affairs. As that other voice of his was worthier a heads-
man than a head, when he wished the people of Rome
had but one neck. But he found (when he fell) they had
many hands. A tyrant, how great and mighty soever he
may seem to cowards and sluggards, is but one creature,
one animal.

1140 I have marked among the nobility some are so addic- *Nobilium*
ted to the service of the prince and commonwealth, as *ingenia*

they look not for spoil; such are to be honoured and loved. There are others which no obligation will fasten on, and they are of two sorts. The first are such as love their own ease; or, out of vice of nature or self-direction, avoid business and care. Yet these the prince may use with safety. The other remove themselves upon craft, and design (as the architects say) with a premeditated thought to their own, rather than their prince's, profit. Such let the prince take heed of, and not doubt to reckon in the list of his open enemies.

Principum varia[tio]— Firmissima vero omnium basis jus haereditarium principis

There is a great variation between him that is raised to the sovereignty by the favour of his peers, and him that comes to it by the suffrage of the people. The first holds with more difficulty, because he hath to do with many that think themselves his equals, and raised him for their own greatness, and oppression of the rest. The latter hath no upbraiders, but was raised by them that sought to be defended from oppression; whose end is both the easier and the honester to satisfy. Beside, while he hath the people to friend, who are a multitude, he hath the less fear of the nobility, who are but few. Nor let the common proverb of 'He that builds on the people, builds on the dirt' discredit my opinion: for that hath only place where an ambitious and private person, for some popular end, trusts in them against the public justice and magistrate. There they will leave him. But when a prince governs them, so as they have still need of his administration —for that is his art—he shall ever make and hold them faithful.

Clementia

A prince should exercise his cruelty not by himself, but by his ministers; so he may save himself and his dignity with his people by sacrificing those when he list, saith the great doctor of state, Machiavel. But I say he puts off man and goes into a beast, that is cruel. No virtue is a prince's own, or becomes him more, than his clemency; and no glory is greater than to be able to save with his power. Many punishments sometimes and in some cases as much discredit a prince as many funerals a physician. The state of things is secured by clemency; severity represseth a few, but it irritates more.* The lopping of trees makes the boughs shoot out thicker; and the taking

Machiavel

*Haud infima ars in principe,

1150

1160

1170

1180

DISCOVERIES 553

away of some kind of enemies increaseth the number. It is then most gracious in a prince to pardon when many about him would make him cruel; to think then how much he can save when others tell him how much he can destroy; not to consider what the impotence of others hath demolished, but what his own greatness can sustain. These are a prince's virtues; and they that give him other counsels are but the hangman's factors.

He that is cruel to halves (saith the said St Nicholas) loseth no less the opportunity of his cruelty than of his benefits; for then to use his cruelty is too late, and to use his favours will be interpreted fear and necessity; and so he loseth the thanks. Still the counsel is cruelty. But princes, by hearkening to cruel counsels, become in time obnoxious to the authors, their flatterers and ministers; and are brought to that, that when they would, they dare not change them; they must go on and defend cruelty with cruelty; they cannot alter the habit. It is then grown necessary, they must be as ill as those have made them; and in the end they will grow more hateful to themselves than to their subjects. Whereas, on the contrary, the merciful prince is safe in love, not in fear. He needs no emissaries, spies, intelligencers, to entrap true subjects. He fears no libels, no treasons. His people speak what they think, and talk openly what they do in secret. They have nothing in their breasts that they need a cipher for. He is guarded with his own benefits.

The strength of empire is in religion. What else is the Palladium (with Homer) that kept Troy so long from sacking? Nothing more commends the sovereign to the subject than it. For he that is religious must be merciful and just necessarily; and they are two strong ties upon mankind. Justice is the virtue that innocence rejoiceth in. Yet even that is not always so safe, but it may love to stand in the sight of mercy. For sometimes misfortune is made a crime, and then innocence is succoured no less than virtue. Nay, often-times virtue is made capital; and through the condition of the times it may happen that that may be punished with our praise. Let no man therefore murmur at the actions of the prince, who is placed so far above him. If he offend, he hath his

190

200

210

220

ubi lenitas, ubi severitas, plus polleat in commune bonum callere

Clementia tutela optima

St Nicholas

Religio Palladium Homeri

discoverer. God hath a height beyond him. But where
Euripides   the prince is good, Euripides saith, God is a guest in a
human body.

Tyranni   There is nothing with some princes sacred above their
majesty; or profane, but what violates their sceptres. But
a prince with such counsel is like the God Terminus, of
stone, his own landmark; or (as it is in the fable) a   1230
crowned lion. It is dangerous offending such a one, who,
being angry, knows not how to forgive; that cares not to
do anything for maintaining or enlarging of empire; kills
not men or subjects, but destroyeth whole countries,
armies, mankind, male and female, guilty or not guilty,
holy or profane; yea, some that have not seen the light.
All is under the law of their spoil and licence. But princes
that neglect their proper office thus, their fortune is
Sejanus   often-times to draw a Sejanus to be near about them,
who will at last affect to get above them, and put them in a   1240
worthy fear of rooting both them out and their family.
For no men hate an evil prince more than they that
helped to make him such; and none more boastingly
weep his ruin than they that procured and practised it.
The same path leads to ruin which did to rule, when men
profess a licence in governing. A good king is a public
servant.

Illiteratus   A prince without letters is a pilot without eyes. All his
princeps   government is groping. In sovereignty it is a most happy
thing not to be compelled; but so it is the most miserable   1250
not to be counselled. And how can he be counselled that
cannot see to read the best counsellors, which are books:
for they neither flatter us nor hide from us? He may hear,
you will say; but how shall he always be sure to hear truth,
or be counselled the best things, not the sweetest? They
say princes learn no art truly but the art of horsemanship.
The reason is the brave beast is no flatterer. He will
throw a prince as soon as his groom. Which is an
argument that the good counsellors to princes are the
best instruments of a good age. For though the prince   1260
himself be of most prompt inclination to all virtue, yet the
best pilots have need of mariners, besides sails, anchor,
Character   and other tackle.
principis   If men did know what shining fetters, gilded miseries,

and painted happiness thrones and sceptres were, there would not be so frequent strife about the getting or holding of them; there would be more principalities than princes. For a prince is the pastor of the people. He ought to shear, no[t] to flay his sheep; to take their

1270 fleeces, not their fells. Who were his enemies before, being a private man, become his children, now he is public. He is the soul of the commonwealth, and ought to cherish it as his own body. Alexander the Great was wont *Alexander* to say, he hated that gardener that plucked his herbs or *magnus* flowers up by the roots. A man may milk a beast till the blood come; churn milk, and it yieldeth butter; but wring the nose, and the blood followeth. He is an ill prince that so pulls his subjects' feathers as he would not have them grow again; that makes his exchequer a receipt for the

1280 spoils of those he governs. No, let him keep his own, not affect his subjects'; strive rather to be called just than powerful. Not, like the Roman tyrants, affect the surnames that grow by human slaughters; neither to seek war in peace, or peace in war, but to observe faith given, though to an enemy. Study piety toward the subject; show care to defend him. Be slow to punish in divers cases, but be a sharp and severe revenger of open crimes. Break no decrees or dissolve no orders to slacken the strength of laws. Choose neither magistrates civil or

1290 ecclesiastic by favour or price, but with long disquisition and report of their worth by all suffrages. Sell no honours, nor give them hastily, but bestow them with counsel and for reward; if he do, acknowledge it, though late, and mend it. For princes are easy to be deceived. And what wisdom can escape it, where so many court-arts are studied? But above all, the prince is to remember that when the great day of account comes, which neither magistrate nor prince can shun, there will be required of him a reckoning for those whom he hath trusted, as for

1300 himself, which he must provide. And if piety be wanting in the priests, equity in the judges, or the magistrate be found rated at a price, what justice or religion is to be expected?—which are the only two attributes make kings akin to gods, and is the Delphic sword, both to kill sacrifices, and to chastise offenders.

De gratiosis   When a virtuous man is raised, it brings gladness to his friends, grief to his enemies, and glory to his posterity. Nay, his honours are a great part of the honour of the times; when by this means he is grown to active men an example, to the slothful a spur, to the envious a 1310 punishment.

Divites   He which is sole heir to many rich men, having —beside his father's and uncles'—the states of divers his kindred come to him by accession, must needs be richer *Heredes* than father or grandfather; so they which are left heirs *ex* *ex asse* *asse* of all their ancestors' vices, and by their good husbandry improve the old and daily purchase new, must needs be wealthier in vice, and have a greater revenue or stock of ill to spend on.

Fures publici   The great thieves of a state are lightly the officers of 1320 the crown; they hang the less still, play the pikes in the pond, eat whom they list. The net was never spread for the hawk or buzzard that hurt us, but the harmless birds: they are good meat.

Juvenalis   *Dat veniam corvis, vexat censura columbas.*

Plautus   *Non rete accipitri ten[n]itur, neque miluo.*

But they are not always safe, though, especially when they meet with wise masters. They can take down all the huff and swelling of their looks, and, like dexterous auditors, place the counter where he shall value nothing. 1330 *Louis XI* Let them but remember Louis the eleventh, who to a clerk of the Exchequer that came to be Lord Treasurer, and had for his device represented himself sitting upon Fortune's wheel, told him he might do well to fasten it with a good strong nail, lest, turning about, it might bring him where he was again. As indeed it did.

De bonis et   A good man will avoid the spot of any sin. The very *malis* aspersion is grievous, which makes him choose his way in his life as he would in his journey. The ill man rides through all confidently; he is coated and booted for it. 1340 The oftener he offends, the more openly; and the fouler, the fitter in fashion. His modesty, like a riding coat, the more it is worn is the less cared for. It is good enough for the dirt still, and the ways he travels in. An innocent man *De innocentia* needs no eloquence: his innocence is instead of it; else I had never come off so many times from these precipices whither men's malice hath pursued me. It is true I have been accused to the lords, to the king, and by great ones; but it happened my accusers had not thought of the

1350 accusation with themselves, and so were driven, for want of crimes, to use invention, which was found slander; or too late (being entered so far) to seek starting-holes for their rashness, which were not given them. And then they may think what accusation that was like to prove, when they that were the engineers feared to be the authors. Nor were they content to feign things against me, but to urge things, feigned by the ignorant, against my profession; which though from their hired and mercenary impudence I might have passed by, as granted

1360 to a nation of barkers that let out their tongues to lick others' sores, yet I durst not leave myself undefended, having a pair of ears unskilful to hear lies, or have those things said of me which I could truly prove of them. They objected making of verses to me, when I could object to most of them their not being able to read them, but as worthy of scorn. Nay, they would offer to urge mine own writings against me, but by pieces, which was an excellent way of malice: as if any man's context might not seem dangerous and offensive if that which was knit to what

1370 went before were defrauded of his beginning, or that things by themselves uttered might not seem subject to calumny, which read entire would appear most free. At last they upbraided my poverty. I confess she is my domestic: sober of diet, simple of habit, frugal, painful, a good counsellor to me, that keeps me from cruelty, pride, or other more delicate impertinences, which are the nurse-children of riches. But let them look over all the great and monstrous wickednesses, they shall never find those in poor families. They are the issue of the wealthy

1380 giants and the mighty hunters; whereas no great work or worthy of praise or memory but came out of poor cradles. It was the ancient poverty that founded commonweals,

built cities, invented arts, made wholesome laws, armed
men against vices, rewarded them with their own virtues,
and preserved the honour and state of nations, till they
betrayed themselves to riches.

Amor nummi   Money never made any man rich, but his mind. He
that can order himself to the law of nature is not only
without the sense but the fear of poverty. Oh, but to
strike blind the people with our wealth and pomp, is the   1390
thing! What a wretchedness is this, to thrust all our
riches outward, and be beggars within; to contemplate
nothing but the little, vile, and sordid things of the world,
not the great, noble, and precious! We serve our avarice,
and not content with the good of the earth that is offered
us, we search and dig for the evil that is hidden. God
offered us those things, and placed them at hand and
near us, that he knew were profitable for us; but the
hurtful he laid deep and hid. Yet do we seek only the
things whereby we may perish, and bring them forth,   1400
when God and nature hath buried them. We covet
superfluous things, when it were more honour for us if
we could contemn necessary. What need hath nature of
silver dishes, multitudes of waiters, delicate pages, perfumed napkins? She requires meat only, and hunger is
not ambitious. Can we think no wealth enough but such a
state for which a man may be brought into a praemunire,
begged, proscribed, or poisoned? Oh, if a man could
restrain the fury of his gullet and groin, and think how
many fires, how many kitchens, cooks, pastures, and   1410
ploughed lands; what orchards, stews, ponds, and parks,
coops, and garners he could spare; what velvets, tissues,
embroideries, laces he could lack; and then how short,
and uncertain his life is; he were in a better way to
happiness than to live the emperor of these delights, and
be the dictator of fashions! But we make ourselves slaves
to our pleasures, and we serve fame and ambition, which
is an equal slavery. Have I not seen the pomp of a whole
kingdom, and what a foreign king could bring hither also
to make himself gazed and wondered at, laid forth as it   1420
were to the show, and vanish all away in a day? And shall
that which could not fill the expectation of few hours,
entertain and take up our whole lives, when even it

appeared as superfluous to the possessors, as to me that was a spectator? The bravery was shown, it was not possessed; while it boasted itself, it perished. It is vile and a poor thing to place our happiness on these desires. Say we wanted them all: famine ends famine.

There is nothing valiant or solid to be hoped for from *De mollibus et* such as are always kempt and perfumed, and every day *effeminatis* smell of the tailor; the exceedingly curious, that are wholly in mending such an imperfection in the face, in taking away the morphew in the neck, or bleaching their hands at midnight, gumming and bridling their beards, or making the waist small: binding it with hoops, while the mind runs at waste; too much pickedness is not manly. Nor from those that will jest at their own outward imperfections, but hide their ulcers within—their pride, lust, envy, ill nature—with all the art and authority they can. These persons are in danger; for whilst they think to justify their ignorance by impudence, and their persons by clothes and outward ornaments, they use but a commission to deceive themselves; where, if we will look with our understanding and not our senses, we may behold virtue and beauty (though covered with rags) in their brightness; and vice and deformity so much the fouler, in having all the splendour of riches to gild them, or the false light of honour and power to help them. Yet this is that wherewith the world is taken, and runs mad to gaze on: clothes and titles, the birdlime of fools.

What petty things they are we wonder at, like children *De stultitia* that esteem every trifle, and prefer a fairing before their fathers! What difference is between us and them but that we are dearer fools, coxcombs at a higher rate? They are pleased with cockleshells, whistles, hobby-horses, and such like; we with statues, marble pillars, pictures, gilded roofs, where underneath is lath and lime, perhaps loam. Yet we take pleasure in the lie, and are glad we can cozen ourselves. Nor is it only in our walls and ceilings, but all that we call happiness is mere painting and gilt, and all for money: what a thin membrane of honour that is! And how hath all true reputation fallen, since money began to have any! Yet the great herd, the multitude, that in all other things are divided, in this alone conspire and agree: to love money. They wish for it, they embrace it, they adore it, while yet it is possessed with greater stir and torment than it is gotten.

De sibi molestis   Some men, what losses soever they have, they make them greater; and if they have none, even all that is not 1470 gotten is a loss. Can there be creatures of more wretched condition than these, that continually labour under their own misery and others' envy? A man should study other things, not to covet, not to fear, not to repent him; to make his base such as no tempest shall shake him; to be secure of all opinion; and pleasing to himself, even for that wherein he displeaseth others. For the worst opinion gotten for doing well should delight us. Wouldst not thou be just, but for fame, thou oughtest to be it with infamy. He that would have his virtue published is not the servant 1480 of virtue, but glory.

Periculosa   It is a dangerous thing when men's minds come to
melancholia   sojourn with their affections, and their diseases eat into their strength; that when too much desire and greediness of vice hath made the body unfit or unprofitable, it is yet gladded with the sight and spectacle of it in others; and for want of ability to be an actor, is content to be a witness. It enjoys the pleasure of sinning in beholding others sin, as in dicing, drinking, drabbing, etc. Nay, when it cannot do all these, it is offended with his own 1490 narrowness, that excludes it from the universal delights of mankind, and oft-times dies of a melancholy, that it cannot be vicious enough.

Falsae species   I am glad when I see any man avoid the infamy of a
fugiendae   vice; but to shun the vice itself were better. Till he do that he is but like the prentice, who, being loath to be spied by his master coming forth of Black Lucy's, went in again; to whom his master cried, 'The more thou runnest that way to hide thyself, the more thou art in the place.' So are those that keep a tavern all day, that they may not be seen 1500

at night. I have known lawyers, divines—yea great
ones—of this heresy.

There is a greater reverence had of things remote or *Decipimur*
strange to us than of much better, if they be nearer and *specie*
fall under our sense. Men, and almost all sort of
creatures, have their reputation by distance. Rivers, the
farther they run and more from their spring, the broader
they are and greater. And where our original is known,
we are the less confident; among strangers we trust
1510 fortune. Yet a man may live as renowned at home in his
own country, or a private village, as in the whole world.
For it is virtue that gives glory; that will endenizen a man
everywhere. It is only that can naturalize him. A native, if
he be vicious, deserves to be a stranger, and cast out of
the commonwealth as an alien.

A dejected countenance and mean clothes beget often *Dejectio*
a contempt, but it is with the shallowest creatures: *aulic[orum]*
courtiers commonly. Look up even with them in a new
suit, you get above them straight. Nothing is more short-
1520 lived than [their] pride; it is but while their clothes last:
stay but while these are worn out, you cannot wish the
thing more wretched or dejected.

Poetry and picture are arts of a like nature, and both *Poesis et*
are busy about imitation. It was excellently said of *pictura*
Plutarch, poetry was a speaking picture, and picture a *Plutarch*
mute poesy. For they both invent, feign, and devise many
things, and accommodate all they invent to the use and
service of nature. Yet of the two, the pen is more noble
than the pencil; for that can speak to the understanding,
1530 the other, but to the sense. They both behold pleasure
and profit as their common object; but should abstain
from all base pleasures, lest they should err from their
end, and while they seek to better men's minds, destroy
their manners. They both are born artificers, not made.
Nature is more powerful in them than study.
Whosoever loves not picture is injurious to truth, and *De pictura*
all the wisdom of poetry. Picture is the invention of
heaven: the most ancient, and most akin to nature. It is

itself a silent work, and always of one and the same habit;
yet it doth so enter and penetrate the inmost affection   1540
—being done by an excellent artificer—as sometimes it
o'ercomes the power of speech and oratory. There are
divers graces in it, so are there in the artificers. One
excels in care, another in reason, a third in easiness, a
fourth in nature and grace. Some have diligence and
comeliness, but they want majesty. They can express a
human form in all the graces, sweetness, and elegancy,
but they miss the authority. They can hit nothing but
smooth cheeks; they cannot express roughness or
gravity. Others aspire to truth so much as they are rather   1550
lovers of likeness than beauty. Zeuxis and Parrhasius are
said to be contemporaries; the first found out the reason
of lights and shadows in picture; the other more subtly
examined the lines.

De stilo In picture light is required no less than shadow; so in
Pliny style, height as well as humbleness. But beware they be
not too humble: as Pliny pronounced of Regulus' writings, you would think them written not on a child, but by
a child. Many, out of their own obscene apprehensions,
refuse proper and fit words, as 'occupy', 'nature', and the   1560
like; so the curious industry in some, of having all alike
good, hath come nearer a vice than a virtue.

De Picture took her feigning from poetry; from geometry
progress[ione] her rule, compass, lines, proportion, and the whole
picturae symmetry. Parrhasius was the first won reputation by
Parrhasius adding symmetry to picture; he added subtlety to the
countenance, elegancy to the hair, loveliness to the face,
and by the public voice of all artificers, deserved honour
Eupompus in the outer lines. Eupompus gave it splendour by
numbers and other elegancies. From the optics it drew   1570
reasons by which it considered how things placed at
distance and afar off should appear less; how above or
beneath the head should deceive the eye, etc. So from
thence it took shadows, recessor, light, and heightenings.
From moral philosophy it took the soul, the expression of
senses, perturbations, manners, when they would paint
Plin[y], lib. an angry person, a proud, an inconstant, an ambitious, a
35, c. 2, 5, 6, brave, a magnanimous, a just, a merciful, a compassion-
& 7 ate, an humble, a dejected, a base, and the like. They

1580 made all heightenings bright, all shadows dark, all swellings from a plane; all solids from breaking. See *where
he complains of their painting chimaeras, by the vulgar
unaptly called grotesque, saying that men who were born
truly to study and emulate nature did nothing but make
monsters against nature; which ᵃHorace so laughed at.
The art plastic was moulding in clay or potters' earth
anciently. This is the parent of statuary: sculpture,
graving, and picture, cutting in brass and marble, all
serve under her. ᵇSocrates taught Parrhasius and Clito,
1590 two noble statuaries, first to express manners by their
looks in imagery. ᶜPolygnotus and Aglaophon were
ancienter. After them ᵈZeuxis, who was the lawgiver to
all painters, after ᵉParrhasius. They were contemporaries, and lived both about Philip's time, the
father of Alexander the Great.

　　There lived in this latter age six famous painters in
Italy, who were excellent and emulous of the ancients:
ᶠRaphael de Urbino, Michelangelo Buonarota, Titian,
Antonio of Correggio, Sebastian of Venice, Giulio
1600 Romano, and Andrea Sartorio.

*Vitruv[ius],
li[b.] [3] & 7

ᵃHorat[ius] in
Arte Poet[ica]
ᵇSocrates,
Parrhasius,
Clito,
ᶜPolygnotus,
Aglaophon,
ᵈZeuxis,
ᵉParrhasius
ᶠRaphael de
Urbino,
Mich[el]-
ange[lo]
Buonarota,
Titian, Antonio
de Correg[gio],
Sebast[ian] de
Venet[ia],
Giulio
Romano,
Andrea
Sartorio

*There are flatterers for their bread, that praise all my
oraculous lord does or says, be it true or false; invent
tales that shall please; make baits for his lordship's ears;
and if they be not received in what they offer at, they shift
a point of the compass, and turn their tale, presently tack
about, deny what they confessed and confess what they
denied, fit their discourse to the persons and occasions.
What they snatch up and devour at one table, utter at
another; and grow suspected of the master, hated of the
1610 servants, while they enquire, and reprehend, and compound, and delate business of the house they have
nothing to do with. They praise my lord's wine and the
sauce he likes; observe the cook and bottleman; while
they stand in my lord's favour, speak for a pension for
them, but pound them to dust upon my lord's least
distaste, or change of his palate.

*Parasiti ad
mensam

　　How much better is it to be silent, or at least to speak
sparingly! For it is not enough to speak good, but timely,

things. If a man be asked a question, to answer; but to repeat the question before he answer is well, that he be sure to understand it, to avoid absurdity. For it is less dishonour to hear imperfectly than to speak imperfectly: the ears are excused, the understanding is not. And in things unknown to a man, not to give his opinion, lest by affectation of knowing too much he lose the credit he hath by speaking or knowing the wrong way what he utters. Nor seek to get his patron's favour by embarking himself in the factions of the family, to enquire after domestic simulties, their sports or affections. They are an odious and vile kind of creatures that fly about the house all day, and, picking up the filth of the house like pies or swallows, carry it to their nest—the lord's ears —and often-times report the lies they have feigned, for what they have seen and heard.

Immo serviles   These are called instruments of grace and power with great persons, but they are indeed the organs of their impotency, and marks of weakness. For sufficient lords are able to make these discoveries themselves. Neither will an honourable person enquire who eats and drinks together, what that man plays, whom this man loves, with whom such a one walks, what discourse they held, who sleeps with whom. They are base and servile natures that busy themselves about these disquisitions. How often have I seen (and worthily) these censors of the family undertaken by some honest rustic, and cudgelled thriftily? These are commonly the off-scouring and dregs of men that do these things, or calumniate others. Yet I know not truly which is worse: he that maligns all, or that praises all. There is as great a vice in praising, and as frequent, as in detracting.

[De liberis educandis]   It pleased your lordship of late to ask my opinion touching the education of your sons, and especially to the advancement of their studies. To which, though I returned somewhat for the present, which rather manifested a will in me than gave any just resolution to the thing propounded, I have upon better cogitation called those aids about me, both of mind and memory,

1620

1630

1640

1650

which shall venture my thoughts clearer, if not fuller, to
your lordship's demand. I confess, my lord, they will
1660 seem but petty and minute things I shall offer to you,
being writ for children, and of them. But studies have
their infancy, as well as creatures. We see in men even
the strongest compositions had their beginnings from
milk and the cradle; and the wisest tarried sometimes
about apting their mouths to letters and syllables. In their
education, therefore, the care must be the greater had of
their beginnings, to know, examine, and weigh their
natures; which, though they be proner in some children
to some disciplines, yet are they naturally prompt to taste
1670 all by degrees, and with change. For change is a kind of
refreshing in studies, and infuseth knowledge by way of
recreation. Thence the school itself is called a play or
game, and all letters are so best taught to scholars. They
should not be affrighted or deterred in their entry, but
drawn on with exercise and emulation. A youth should
not be made to hate study before he know the causes to
love it, or taste the bitterness before the sweet; but called
on and allured, entreated and praised; yea, when he
deserves it not. For which cause I wish them sent to the
1680 best school, and a public, which I think the best. Your
lordship, I fear, hardly hears of that, as willing to breed
them in your eye and at home, and doubting their
manners may be corrupted abroad. They are in more
danger in your own family, among ill servants (allowing
they be safe in their schoolmaster) than amongst a
thousand boys, however immodest. Would we did not
spoil our own children, and overthrow their manners
ourselves by too much indulgence! To breed them at
home is to breed them in a shade, where in a school they
1690 have the light and heat of the sun. They are used and
accustomed to things and men. When they come forth
into the commonwealth, they find nothing new, or to
seek. They have made their friendships and aids, some to
last till their age. They hear what is commanded to
others, as well as themselves, much approved, much
corrected: all which they bring to their own store and
use, and learn as much as they hear. Eloquence would be
but a poor thing if we should only converse with

singulars, speak but man and man together. Therefore I like no private breeding. I would send them where their industry should be daily increased by praise, and that kindled by emulation. It is a good thing to inflame the mind; and though ambition itself be a vice, it is often the cause of great virtue. Give me that wit whom praise excites, glory puts on, or disgrace grieves: he is to be nourished with ambition, pricked forward with honour, checked with reprehension, and never to be suspected of sloth. Though he be given to play, it is a sign of spirit and liveliness, so there be a mean had of their sports and relaxations. And from the rod or ferule, I would have them free, as from the menace of them; for it is both deformed and servile.

De stilo, et optimo scribendi genere   For a man to write well, there are required three necessaries: to read the best authors, observe the best speakers, and much exercise of his own style. In style, to consider what ought to be written, and after what manner, he must first think and excogitate his matter; then choose his words, and examine the weight of either. Then take care in placing and ranking both matter and words, that the composition be comely; and to do this with diligence and often. No matter how slow the style be at first, so it be laboured, and accurate; seek the best, and be not glad of the forward conceits or first words that offer themselves to us, but judge of what we invent, and order what we approve. Repeat often what we have formerly written; which beside that it helps the consequence, and makes the juncture better, it quickens the heat of imagination, that often cools in the time of setting down, and gives it new strength, as if it grew lustier by the going back. As we see in the contention of leaping, they jump farthest, that fetch their race largest; or, as in throwing a dart or javelin, we force back our arms to make our loose the stronger. Yet if we have a fair gale of wind, I forbid not the steering out of our sail, so the favour of the gale deceive us not. For all that we invent doth please us in the conception or birth, else we would never set it down. But the safest is to return to our judgement, and handle over again those things, the

easiness of which might make them justly suspected. So
1740 did the best writers in their beginnings: they imposed
upon themselves care and industry. They did nothing
rashly. They obtained first to write well, and then custom
made it easy and a habit. By little and little, their matter
showed itself to 'em more plentifully; their words
answered, their composition followed, and all, as in a
well-ordered family, presented itself in the place. So that
the sum of all is: ready writing makes not good writing,
but good writing brings on ready writing; yet when we
think we have got the faculty, it is even then good to resist
1750 it, as to give a horse a check sometimes with [a] bit, which
doth not so much stop his course as stir his mettle. Again,
whither a man's genius is best able to reach thither it
should more and more contend, lift and dilate itself; as
men of low stature raise themselves on their toes, and so
oft-times get even, if not eminent. Besides, as it is fit for
grown and able writers to stand of themselves, and work
with their own strength, to trust and endeavour by their
own faculties, so it is fit for the beginner and learner to
study others and the best. For the mind and memory are
1760 more sharply exercised in comprehending another man's
things than our own; and such as accustom themselves,
and are familiar with the best authors, shall ever and
anon find somewhat of them in themselves, and in the
expression of their minds, even when they feel it not; be
able to utter something like theirs, which hath an authority above their own. Nay, sometimes it is the reward of
a man's study, the praise of quoting another man fitly:
and though a man be more prone, and able for one kind
of writing than another, yet he must exercise all. For as in
1770 an instrument, so in style, there must be a harmony and
concent of parts.

   I take this labour in teaching others, that they should *Praecipiendi*
not be always to be taught, and I would bring my precepts *modi*
into practice; for rules are ever of less force and value
than experiments. Yet with this purpose, rather to show
the right way to those that come after, than to detect any
that have slipped before by error; and I hope it will be
more profitable: for men do more willingly listen, and

with more favour, to precept than reprehension. Among divers opinions of an art (and most of them contrary in 1780 themselves) it is hard to make election; and therefore, though a man cannot invent new things after so many, he may do a welcome work yet to help posterity to judge rightly of the old. But arts and precepts avail nothing, except nature be beneficial and aiding. And therefore these things are no more written to a dull disposition, than rules of husbandry to a barren soil. No precepts will profit a fool, no more than beauty will the blind, or music the deaf. As we should take care that our style in writing by neither dry nor empty, we should look again it be not 1790 winding or wanton with far-fetched descriptions: either is a vice. But that is worse which proceeds out of want, than that which riots out of plenty. The remedy of fruitfulness is easy, but no labour will help the contrary. I will like and praise some things in a young writer, which yet if he continue in, I cannot but justly hate him for the same. There is a time to be given all things for maturity, and that even your country husbandman can teach, who to a young plant will not put the pruning knife, because it seems to fear the iron, as not able to admit the scar. No 1800 more would I tell a green writer all his faults, lest I should make him grieve and faint, and at last despair. For nothing doth more hurt than to make him so afraid of all things as he can endeavour nothing. Therefore youth ought to be instructed betimes, and in the best things; for we hold those longest we take soonest, as the first scent of a vessel lasts, and that tinct the wool first receives. Therefore a master should temper his own powers, and descend to the other's infirmity. If you pour a glut of water upon a bottle, it receives little of it; but with a 1810 funnel, and by degrees, you shall fill many of them, and spill little of your own; to their capacity they will all receive and be full. And as it is fit to read the best authors to youth first, so let them be of the openest and clearest, as Livy before Sallust, Sidney before Donne. And beware of letting them taste Gower or Chaucer at first, lest falling too much in love with antiquity, and not apprehending the weight, they grow rough and barren in language only. When their judgements are firm and out

Livy, Sallust, Sidney, Donne, Gower, Chaucer

1820 of danger, let them read both the old and the new; but no less take heed that their new flowers and sweetness do not as much corrupt as the other's dryness and squalor, if they choose not carefully. Spenser, in affecting the ancients, writ no language; yet I would have him read for his matter; but as Virgil read Ennius. The reading of Homer and Virgil is counselled by Quintilian as the best way of informing youth and confirming man. For besides that the mind is raised with the height and sublimity of such a verse, it takes spirit from the greatness of the 1830 matter, and is tincted with the best things. Tragic and lyric poetry is good too, and comic with the best, if the manners of the reader be once in safety. In the Greek poets, as also in Plautus, we shall see the economy and disposition of poems better observed than in Terence and the later, who thought the sole grace and virtue of their fable the sticking in of sentences, as ours do the forcing in of jests.

Spenser

Virgil, Ennius,
Homer, Virgil,
Quintilian

Plautus
Terence

We should not protect our sloth with the patronage of difficulty. It is a false quarrel against nature, that she 1840 helps understanding but in a few; when the most part of mankind are inclined by her thither, if they would take the pains, no less than birds to fly, horses to run, etc.: which if they lose, it is through their own sluggishness, and by that means [they] become her prodigies, not her children. I confess, nature in children is more patient of labour in study than in age; for the sense of the pain, the judgement of the labour is absent: they do not measure what they have done. And it is the thought and consideration that affects us more than the weariness itself. 1850 Plato was not content with the learning that Athens could give him, but sailed into Italy for Pythagoras' knowledge; and yet not thinking himself sufficiently informed, went into Egypt to the priests, and learned their mysteries. He laboured, so must we. Many things may be learned together, and performed in one point of time; as musicians exercise their memory, their voice, their fingers, and sometime their head and feet at once. And so a preacher, in the invention of matter, election of words, composition of gesture, look, pronunciation, motion,

Fals[a]
querel[a]
fugiend[a]

Platonis
peregrinatio
in Italiam

useth all these faculties at once. And if we can express   1860
this variety together, why should not divers studies at
divers hours delight, when the variety is able alone to
refresh and repair us? As when a man is weary of writing,
to read; and then again of reading, to write. Wherein,
howsoever we do many things, yet are we (in a sort) still
fresh to what we begin; we are recreated with change, as
the stomach is with meats. But some will say this variety
breeds confusion, and makes, that either we lose all, or
hold no more than the last. Why do we not then persuade
husbandmen that they should not till land, help it with   1870
marl, lime, and compost, plant hop-gardens, prune
trees, look to bee-hives, rear sheep, and all other cattle at
once? It is easier to do many things and continue, than to
do one thing long.

Praecept[a]
element[aria]

It is not the passing through these learnings that hurts
us, but the dwelling and sticking about them. To
descend to those extreme anxieties and foolish cavils of
grammarians, is able to break a wit in pieces, being a
work of manifold misery and vainness, to be *elementarii
senes.* Yet even letters are, as it were, the bank of words,   1880
and restore themselves to an author as the pawns of
language. But talking and eloquence are not the same: to
speak, and to speak well, are two things. A fool may talk,
but a wise man speaks, and out of the observation,
knowledge, and use of things. Many writers perplex their
readers and hearers with mere nonsense. Their writings
need sunshine. Pure and neat language I love, yet plain
and customary. A barbarous phrase hath often made me
out of love with a good sense, and doubtful writing hath
racked me beyond my patience. The reason why a poet is   1890
said that he ought to have all knowledges is that he
should not be ignorant of the most, especially of those he
will handle. And indeed, when the attaining of them is
possible, it were a sluggish and base thing to despair; for
frequent imitation of anything becomes a habit quickly.
If a man should prosecute as much as could be said of
everything, his work would find no end.

De orationis
dignitate

Speech is the only benefit man hath to express his
excellency of mind above other creatures. It is the

1900 instrument of society. Therefore Mercury, who is the president of language, is called *deorum hominumque interpres*. In all speech, words and sense are as the body and the soul. The sense is as the life and soul of language, without which all words are dead. Sense is wrought out of experience, the knowledge of human life and actions, or of the liberal arts, which the Greeks called Ἐγκύκλο παιδείαν. Words are the people's, yet there is a choice of them to be made; for *verborum delectus origo est eloquentiae*. They are to be chose according to the

1910 persons we make speak, or the things we speak of. Some are of the camp, some of the council-board, some of the shop, some of the sheepcote, some of the pulpit, some of the bar, etc. And herein is seen their elegance and propriety, when we use them fitly and draw them forth to their just strength and nature by way of translation or metaphor. But in this translation we must only serve necessity (*nam temere nihil transfertur a prudenti*) or com-modity, which is a kind of necessity: that is, when we either absolutely want a word to express by, and that is

1920 necessity, or when we have not so fit a word, and that is commodity; as when we avoid loss by it, and escape obsceneness, and gain in the grace and property, which helps significance. Metaphors far-fet hinder to be understood; and affected, lose their grace. Or when the person fetcheth his translations from a wrong place: as if a privy councillor should at the table take his metaphor from a dicing house, or ordinary, or a vintner's vault; or a justice of peace draw his similitudes from the mathe-matics; or a divine from a bawdy-house, or taverns; or a

1930 gentleman of Northamptonshire, Warwickshire, or the Midland should fetch all his illustrations to his country neighbours from shipping, and tell them of the main sheet and the bowline. Metaphors are thus many times deformed, as in him that said, *castratam morte Africani rempublicam*; and another, *stercus curiae Glauciam*; and *cana nive conspuit Alpes*. All attempts that are new in this kind are dangerous, and somewhat hard, before they be softened with use. A man coins not a new word without some peril, and less fruit: for if it happen to be received, the praise is but moderate; if refused, the scorn is 1940

Ἐγκύκλο παιδείαν Julius Caesar. Of words, see Hor[ace], De Art[e] Poetic[a], Quintil[ian], l[ib.] 8, Ludov[icus] Vives, pag[inae] 6 & 7 Metaphora

Consuetudo

Perspicuitas

Venustas
Auctoritas

Virgil
Lucretius
Chaucerism

Paronomasia

assured. Yet we must adventure, for things at first hard and rough are by use made tender and gentle. It is an honest error that is committed, following great chiefs.

Custom is the most certain mistress of language, as the public stamp makes the current money. But we must not be too frequent with the mint, every day coining, nor fetch words from the extreme and utmost ages; since the chief virtue of a style is perspicuity, and nothing so vicious in it as to need an interpreter. Words borrowed of antiquity do lend a kind of majesty to style, and are 1950 not without their delight sometimes; for they have the authority of years, and out of their intermission do win to themselves a kind of grace like newness. But the eldest of the present and newest of the past language is the best. For what was the ancient language, which some men so dote upon, but the ancient custom? Yet when I name custom, I understand not the vulgar custom; for that were a precept no less dangerous to language than life, if we should speak or live after the manners of the vulgar; but that I call custom of speech, which is the consent of 1960 the learned; as custom of life, which is the consent of the good. Virgil was most loving of antiquity; yet how rarely doth he insert *aquai*, and *pictai*! Lucretius is scabrous and rough in these: he seeks them, as some do Chaucerisms with us, which were better expunged and banished. Some words are to be culled out for ornament and colour, as we gather flowers to strew houses, or make garlands; but they are better when they grow to our style as in a meadow, where though the mere grass and greenness delights, yet the variety of flowers doth 1970 heighten and beautify. Marry, we must not play or riot too much with them, as in paronomasies, nor use too swelling or ill-sounding words; *quae per salebras altaque saxa cadunt*. It is true, there is no sound but shall find some lovers, as the bitterest confections are grateful to some palates. Our composition must be more accurate in the beginning and end than in the midst, and in the end more than in the beginning; for through the midst the stream bears us. And this is attained by custom, more than care or diligence. We must express readily and fully, 1980

not profusely. There is difference between a liberal and a prodigal hand. As it is a great point of art, when our matter requires it, to enlarge and veer out all sail; so to take it in, and contract it, is of no less praise when the argument doth ask it: either of them hath their fitness in the place. A good man always profits by his endeavour, by his help, yea, when he is absent; nay, when he is dead, by his example and memory. So good authors in their style. *De stilo*
A strict and succinct style is that where you can take away *Tacitus*
1990 nothing without loss, and that loss to be manifest. The brief style is that which expresseth much in little. The *The laconic* concise style, which expresseth not enough, but leaves *Suetonius* somewhat to be understood. The abrupt style, which *Seneca et* hath many breaches, and doth not seem to end, but fall. *Fabianus* The congruent and harmonious fitting of parts in a sentence hath almost the fastening and force of knitting and connection; as in stones well-squared, which will rise strong a great way without mortar.

Periods are beautiful when they are not too long, for so *Periodi*
2000 they have their strength too, as in a pike or javelin. As we must take the care that our words and sense be clear, so if the obscurity happen through the hearer's or reader's want of understanding, I am not to answer for them, no more than for their not listening or marking: I must neither find them ears nor mind. But a man cannot put a word so in sense but something about it will illustrate it, if the writer understand himself; for order helps much to perspicuity, as confusion hurts. *Rectitudo lucem adfert: obliquitas et circumductio offuscat.* We should therefore
2010 speak what we can the nearest way, so as we keep our gait, not leap; for too short may as well be not let into the memory, as too long not kept in. Whatsoever loseth the grace and clearness, converts into a riddle; the obscurity *Obscuritas* is marked, but not the value. That perisheth, and is *offundit* passed by, like the pearl in the fable. Our style should be *tenebras* like a skein of silk, to be carried and found by the right thread, not ravelled and perplexed: then all is a knot, a heap. There are words that do as much raise a style as others can depress it. Superlation and overmuchness *Superlatio*
2020 amplifies; it may be above faith, but never above a mean. It was ridiculous in Cestius when he said of Alexander, *Cestius*

fremit oceanus, quasi indignetur, quod terras relinquas; but
propitiously from Virgil:

Virgil

> . . . *credas innare revolsas*
> *Cycladas.*

He doth not say it was so, but seemed to be so. Although
it be somewhat incredible, that is excused before it be
spoken. But there are hyperboles which will become one
language, that will by no means admit another. As *eos esse*
P[opuli] R[omani] exercitus, qui coelum possint perrumpere: 203
who would say this with us, but a madman? Therefore we
must consider in every tongue what is used, what
received. Quintilian warns us that in no kind of translation, or metaphor, or allegory, we make a turn from what
we began; as if we fetch the original of our metaphor
from sea and billows, we end not in flames and ashes: it is
a most foul inconsequence. Neither must we draw out
our allegory too long, lest either we make ourselves
obscure, or fall into affectation, which is childish. But
why do men depart at all from the right and natural ways 204
of speaking? Sometimes for necessity, when we are
driven, or think it fitter, to speak that in obscure words or
by circumstance which uttered plainly would offend the
hearers; or to avoid obsceneness, or sometimes for
pleasure and variety: as travellers turn out of the highway, drawn either by the commodity of a footpath, or the
delicacy or freshness of the fields. And all this is called
ἐσχηματισμένη, or figured language.

Language most shows a man: speak, that I may see thee.
It springs out of the most retired and inmost parts of us, 205
and is the image of the parent of it, the mind. No glass
renders a man's form or likeness so true as his speech.
Nay, it is likened to a man; and as we consider feature
and composition in a man, so words in language: in the
greatness, aptness, sound, structure, and harmony of it.
Some men are tall and big, so some language is high and
great. Then the words are chosen, their sound ample,
the composition full, the absolution plenteous, and
poured out, all grave, sinewy, and strong. Some are little
and dwarfs; so of speech, it is humble and low, the words 206

Caesar,
comment[arii],
circa fin[em]

Quintilian

Oratio imago
animi

Structura et
statura:
sublimis,
humilis,
pumila.

poor and flat, the members and periods thin and weak, without knitting or number. The middle are of a just stature. There the language is plain and pleasing, even without stopping, round without swelling; all well-turned, composed, elegant, and accurate. The vicious language is vast and gaping, swelling and irregular; when it contends to be high, full of rock, mountain, and pointedness; as it affects to be low, it is abject and creeps, full of bogs and holes. And according to their subject, these styles vary, and lose their names: for that which is high and lofty, declaring excellent matter, becomes vast and tumorous, speaking of petty and inferior things; so that which was even and apt in a mean and plain subject, will appear most poor and humble in a high argument. Would you not laugh to meet a great councillor of state in a flat cap, with his trunk-hose and a hobby-horse cloak, his gloves under his girdle, and yond haberdasher in a velvet gown, furred with sables? There is a certain latitude in these things, by which we find the degrees. The next thing to the stature is the figure and feature in language: that is, whether it be round and straight, which consists of short and succinct periods, numerous and polished; or square and firm, which is to have equal and strong parts everywhere answerable and weighed. The third is the skin and coat, which rests in the well-joining, cementing, and coagmentation of words: when as it is smooth, gentle and sweet, like a table upon which you may run your finger without rubs, and your nail cannot find a joint; not horrid, rough, wrinkled, gaping, or chapped. After these, the flesh, blood, and bones come in question. We say it is a fleshy style, when there is much periphrasis, and circuit of words; and when with more than enough, it grows fat and corpulent: *arvina orationis*, full of suet and tallow. It hath blood and juice, when the words are proper and apt, their sound sweet, and the phrase neat and picked: *oratio uncta, et bene pasta*. But where there is redundancy, both the blood and juice are faulty and vicious: *redundat sanguine, quae multo plus dicit, quam necesse est.* Juice in language is somewhat less than blood; for if words be but becoming and signifying, and the sense gentle, there is juice; but where that wanteth,

Mediocris: plana et placida

Vitiosa oratio: vasta, tumens, enormis, affectata, abjecta.

Figura

Cutis sive cortex Compositio

Carnosa

Adipata

Redundans

Jejuna,
macilenta,
strigosa

the language is thin, flagging, poor, starved, scarce covering the bone, and shows like stones in a sack. Some men, to avoid redundancy, run into that; and while they strive to have no ill blood or juice, they lose their good. There be some styles, again, that have not less blood, but less flesh and corpulence. These are bony and sinewy: *ossa habent, et nervos.*

Ossea et
nervosa

Notae Domini
S[anc]t[i]
Albani de
doctrin[ae]
intemper[antia]

It was well noted by the late L[ord] St Alban[s], that the study of words is the first distemper of learning; vain   2110 matter the second; and a third distemper is deceit, or the likeness of truth: imposture held up by credulity. All these are the cobwebs of learning, and to let them grow in us is either sluttish or foolish. Nothing is more ridiculous than to make an author a dictator, as the Schools have done Aristotle. The damage is infinite knowledge receives by it; for to many things a man should owe but a temporary belief, and a suspension of his own judgement, not an absolute resignation of himself, or a perpetual captivity. Let Aristotle and others have their   2120 dues, but if we can make farther discoveries of truth and fitness than they, why are we envied? Let us beware, while we strive to add, we do not diminish, or deface; we may improve, but not augment. By discrediting falsehood, truth grows in request. We must not go about like men anguished and perplexed for vicious affectations of praise, but calmly study the separation of opinions, find the errors have intervened, awake antiquity, call former times into question; but make no parties with the present, nor follow any fierce undertakers, mingle no   2130 matter of doubtful credit with the simplicity of truth, but gently stir the mould about the root of the question, and avoid all digladiations, facility of credit, or superstitious simplicity; seek the consonancy and concatenation of truth; stoop only to point of necessity, and what leads to convenience. Then make exact animadversion where style hath degenerated, where flourished and thrived in choiceness of phrase, round and clean composition of sentence, sweet falling of the clause, varying an illustration by tropes and figures, weight of matter, worth of   2140 subject, soundness of argument, life of invention, and depth of judgement. This is *monte potiri*, to get the hill.

Dictator
Aristoteles

For no perfect discovery can be made upon a flat or a level.

Now that I have informed you in the knowing these things, let me lead you by the hand a little farther in the direction of the use, and make you an able writer by practice. The conceits of the mind are pictures of things, and the tongue is the interpreter of those pictures. The order of God's creatures in themselves is not only admirable and glorious, but eloquent; then he who could apprehend the consequence of things in their truth, and utter his apprehensions as truly, were the best writer or speaker. Therefore Cicero said much when he said, *dicere recte nemo potest, nisi qui prudenter intelligit.* The shame of speaking unskilfully were small if the tongue only thereby were disgraced; but as the image of a king, in his seal ill-represented, is not so much a blemish to the wax or the signet that sealed it, as to the prince it representeth, so disordered speech is not so much injury to the lips that give it forth, as to the disproportion and incoherence of things in themselves, so negligently expressed. Neither can his mind be thought to be in tune whose words do jar; nor his reason in frame, whose sentence is preposterous; nor his elocution clear and perfect, whose utterance breaks itself into fragments and uncertainties. Were it not a dishonour to a mighty prince, to have the majesty of his embassage spoiled by a careless ambassador? and is it not as great an indignity that an excellent conceit and capacity, by the indiligence of an idle tongue, should be disgraced? Negligent speech doth not only discredit the person of the speaker, but it discrediteth the opinion of his reason and judgement; it discrediteth the force and uniformity of the matter and substance. If it be so then in words, which fly and escape censure, and where one good phrase begs pardon for many incongruities and faults, how shall he then be thought wise whose penning is thin and shallow? How shall you look for wit from him whose leisure and head, assisted with the examination of his eyes, yield you no life or sharpness in his writing?

De optimo scriptore

Cicero

De stilo
epistolari.
Inventio

In writing [of letters] there is to be regarded the invention and the fashion. For the invention, that ariseth upon your business; whereof there can be no rules of more certainty, or precepts of better direction given, than conjecture can lay down from the several occasions of men's particular lives and vocations. But sometimes men make business of kindness: as 'I could not satisfy myself till I had discharged my remembrance, and charged my   2190
letter with commendations to you'; or 'My business is no other than to testify my love to you, and to put you in mind of my willingness to do you all kind offices'; or 'Sir, have you leisure to descend to the remembering of that assurance you have long possessed in your servant, and upon your next opportunity, make him happy with some commands from you?', or the like, that go a-begging for some meaning, and labour to be delivered of the great burden of nothing. When you have invented, and that your business be matter, and not bare form or mere   2200
ceremony but some earnest, then you are to proceed to the ordering of it, and digesting the parts, which is had out of two circumstances. One is the understanding of the persons to whom you are to write; the other is the coherence of your sentence. For men's capacity, [you are] to weigh what will be apprehended with greatest attention or leisure, what next regarded and longed for especially, and what last will leave [most] satisfaction, and as it were the sweetest memorial and brief of all that is past in his understanding whom you write to. For the   2210
consequence of sentences, you must be sure that every clause do give the cue one to the other, and be bespoken ere it come. So much for invention and order.

Modus:
1. Brevitas

Now for fashion: it consists in four things, which are qualities of your style. The first is brevity. For they must not be treatises or discourses (your letters) except it be to learned men. And even among them there is a kind of thrift and saving of words. Therefore you are to examine the clearest passages of your understanding, and through them to convey the sweetest and most significant words   2220
you can devise, that you may the easier teach them the readiest way to another man's apprehension, and open their meaning fully, roundly, and distinctly, so as the

reader may not think a second view cast away upon your
letter. And though respect be a part following this, yet
now here, and still I must remember it: if you write to a
man whose estate and cense, as senses, you are familiar
with, you may the bolder—to set a task to his brain—venture on a knot. But if to your superior, you are bound to
2230 measure him in three farther points: first, your interest in
him; secondly, his capacity in your letters; thirdly, his
leisure to peruse them. For your interest or favour with
him, you are to be the shorter or longer, more familiar or
submiss, as he will afford you time. For his capacity, you
are to be quicker and fuller of those reaches and glances
of wit or learning as he is able to entertain them. For his
leisure, you are commanded to the greater briefness as
his place is of greater discharges and cares. But with your
betters, you are not to put riddles of wit, by being too
2240 scarce of words; nor to cause the trouble of making
breviates, by writing too riotous and wastingly. Brevity is
attained in matter by avoiding idle compliments, pre-
faces, protestations, parentheses, superfluous circuit of
figures and digressions; in the composition, by omitting
conjunctions, 'not only . . . but also', 'both the one and
the other', 'whereby it cometh to pass', and such-like idle
particles, that have no great business in a serious letter
but breaking of sentences; as often-times a short journey
is made long by unnecessary baits.

2250   But, as Quintilian saith, there is a briefness of the parts *Quintilian*
sometimes that makes the whole long, as 'I came to the
stairs, I took a pair of oars, they launched out, rowed
apace, I landed at the court gate, I paid my fare, went up
to the presence, asked for my lord, I was admitted.' All
this is but 'I went to the court, and spake with my lord.'
This is the fault of some Latin writers within these last
hundred years of my reading, and perhaps Seneca may
be appeached of it; I accuse him not.

The next property of epistolary style is perspicuity, *2. Perspi-*
2260 and is often-times [endangered by the former quality *cu[i]tas*
(brevity), often-times] by affectation of some wit ill-
angled for, or ostentation of some hidden terms of art.
Few words they darken speech, and so do too many, as
well too much light hurteth the eyes, as too little; and a

long bill of chancery confounds the understanding as much as the shortest note. Therefore let not your letters be penned like English statutes, and this is obtained. These vices are eschewed by pondering your business well, and distinctly conceiving yourself, which is much furthered by uttering your thoughts, and letting them as well come forth to the light and judgement of your own outward senses as to the censure of other men's ears; for that is the reason why many good scholars speak but fumblingly: like a rich man, that for want of particular note and difference can bring you no certain ware readily out of his shop. Hence it is that talkative shallow men do often content the hearers more than the wise. But this may find a speedier redress in writing, where all comes under the last examination of the eyes. First mind it well, then pen it, then examine it, then amend it, and you may be in the better hope of doing reasonably well. Under this virtue may come plainness, which is not to be curious in the order, as to answer a letter as if you were to answer to interrogatories: as to the first, first, and to the second, secondly, etc. But both in method [and words] to use, as ladies do in their attire, a diligent kind of negligence, and their sportive freedom; though with some men you are not to jest, or practise tricks, yet the delivery of the most important things may be carried with such a grace as that it may yield a pleasure to the conceit of the reader. There must be store, though no excess of terms; as if you are to name 'store', sometimes you may call it 'choice', sometimes 'plenty', sometimes 'copiousness' or 'variety'; but ever so, that the word which comes in lieu have not such difference of meaning as that it may put the sense of the first in hazard to be mistaken. You are not to cast a ring for the perfumed terms of the time, as 'accommodation', 'compliment', 'spirit' etc., but use them properly in their place, as others.

3. Vigor   There followeth life and quickness, which is the strength and sinews (as it were) of your penning by pithy sayings, similitudes, and conceits, allusions [to] some known history, or other commonplace, such as are in *The Courtier* and the second book of Cicero, *De Oratore*.

4. Discretio   The last is, respect to discern what fits yourself, him to

2270

2280

2290

2300

whom you write, and that which you handle, which is a quality fit to conclude the rest, because it doth include all. And that must proceed from ripeness of judgement, which, as one truly saith, is gotten by four means: God, nature, diligence, and conversation. Serve the first well, and the rest will serve you.

We have spoken sufficiently of oratory: let us now make a diversion to poetry. Poetry, in the primogeniture, had *De Poetica* many peccant humours, and is made to have more now through the levity and inconstancy of men's judgements. Whereas, indeed, it is the most prevailing eloquence, and of the most exalted charact. Now the discredits and disgraces are many it hath received through men's study of depravation or calumny; their practice being to give it diminution of credit by lessening the professors' estimation, and making the age afraid of their liberty; and the age is grown so tender of her fame, as she calls all writings *aspersions*. That is the state-word, the phrase of court, Placentia College, which some call Parasites' Place, the Inn of Ignorance.

Whilst I name no persons, but deride follies, why should any man confess or betray himself? Why doth not that of S[t] Jerome come into their mind: *ubi generalis est* *D[ivus]* *de vitiis disputatio, ibi nullius esse personae injuriam?* Is it *Hieronimus* such an inexpiable crime in poets to tax vices generally, and no offence in them who, by their exception, confess they have committed them particularly? Are we fallen into those times that we must not

Auriculas teneras mordaci rodere vero? *Pers[ius], Sat. 1*

Remedii votum semper verius erat, quam spes. *Livius*

If men may by no means write freely, or speak truth, but when it offends not, why do physicians cure with sharp medicines or corrosives? Is not the same equally lawful in the cure of the mind that is in the cure of the body? Some vices (you will say) are so foul that it is better they should be done than spoken. But they that take offence where no name, character, or signature doth blazon them seem to *Sexus* me like affected as women who, if they hear anything ill *femin[arum]*

spoken of the ill of their sex, are presently moved, as if
the contumely respected their particular; and on the
contrary, when they hear good of good women, conclude
that it belongs to them all. If I see anything that toucheth
me, shall I come forth a betrayer of myself presently? No;
if I be wise, I'll dissemble it; if honest, I'll avoid it, lest I
publish that on my own forehead which I saw there noted   2350
without a title. A man that is on the mending hand will
either ingenuously confess or wisely dissemble his
disease; and the wise and virtuous will never think
anything belongs to themselves that is written, but
rejoice that the good are warned not to be such, and the
ill to leave to be such. The person offended hath no
reason to be offended with the writer, but with himself;
and so to declare that properly to belong to him which
was spoken of all men, as it could be no man's several,
but his that would wilfully and desperately claim it. It   2360
sufficeth I know what kind of persons I displease, men
bred in the declining and decay of virtue, betrothed to
their own vices, that have abandoned or prostituted their
good names; hungry and ambitious of infamy, invested in
all deformity, enthralled to ignorance and malice, of a
hidden and concealed malignity, and that hold a concomitancy with all evil.

What is a poet?

Poeta

A poet is that which by the Greeks is called κατ' ἐξοχ-
ὴν, ὁ Ποιητὴς, a maker or a feigner; his art, an art of   2370
imitation or feigning, expressing the life of man in fit
measure, numbers, and harmony, according to Aristotle:
from the word ποιεῖν, which signifies to make or feign.
Hence he is called a poet, not he which writeth in
measure only, but that feigneth and formeth a fable,
and writes things like the truth. For the fable and fiction
is (as it were) the form and soul of any poetical work or
poem.

What mean you by a poem?

Poema

A poem is not alone any work or composition of the   2380
poet's in many or few verses; but even one alone verse
sometimes makes a perfect poem. As when Aeneas

hangs up and consecrates the arms of Abas with this inscription: *Virgilius, Aeneid, lib. 3*

> *Aeneas haec de Danais victoribus arma,*

and calls it a poem, or *carmen.* Such are those in Martial: *Martial*

> *Omnia, Castor, emis: sic fiet, ut omnia vendas,*

and

> *Pauper videri Cinna vult; et est pauper.* *lib. 8, epigr. 19*

2390 So were Horace's odes called *Carmina*, his lyric songs. *Horatius* And Lucretius designs a whole book in his sixth: *Lucretius*

> *Quod in primo quoque carmine claret.*

And anciently all the oracles were called *carmina*; or whatever sentence was expressed, were it much or little, it was called an epic, dramatic, lyric, elegiac, or epigrammatic poem. *Epicum, dramaticum, lyricum, elegiacum, epigrammat-[icum]*

But how differs a poem from what we call poesy?
A poem, as I have told you, is the work of the poet, the end and fruit of his labour and study. Poesy is his skill or
2400 craft of making; the very fiction itself, the reason or form of the work. And these three voices differ, as the thing done, the doing, and the doer; the thing feigned, the feigning, and the feigner; so the poem, the poesy, and the poet. Now the poesy is the habit or the art; nay, rather the queen of arts, which had her original from heaven, *Artium regina* received thence from the Hebrews, and had in prime estimation with the Greeks, transmitted to the Latins and all nations that professed civility. The study of it (if we will trust Aristotle) offers to mankind a certain rule *Aristotle*
2410 and pattern of living well and happily, disposing us to all civil offices of society. If we will believe Tully, it *M[arcus] T[ullius] Cicero* nourisheth and instructeth our youth, delights our age, adorns our prosperity, comforts our adversity, entertains us at home, keeps us company abroad, travels with us, watches, divides the times of our earnest and sports, shares in our country recesses and recreations, insomuch as the wisest and best learned have thought her the absolute mistress of manners and nearest of kin

to virtue. And whereas they entitle philosophy to be a
rigid and austere poesy, they have (on the contrary)   2420
styled poesy a dulcet and gentle philosophy, which leads
on and guides us by the hand to action with a ravishing
delight and incredible sweetness. But before we handle
the kinds of poems, with their special differences, or
make court to the art itself as a mistress, I would lead you

Poet[ae]
differentiae

to the knowledge of our poet by a perfect information
what he is or should be by nature, by exercise, by
imitation, by study, and so bring him down through the

Grammatica,
logic[a],
rhetoric[a],
ethica

disciplines of grammar, logic, rhetoric, and the ethics,
adding somewhat out of all peculiar to himself and   2430
worthy of your admittance or reception.

1. Ingenium

First, we require in our poet or maker—for that title
our language affords him elegantly with the Greek—a
goodness of natural wit. For whereas all other arts
consist of doctrine and precepts, the poet must be able by
nature and instinct to pour out the treasure of his mind,

Seneca

and as Seneca saith, *aliquando secundum Anacreontem*
insanire jucundum esse: by which he understands the

Plato
Aristotle

poetical rapture. And according to that of Plato, *frustra*
poeticas fores sui compos pulsavit; and of Aristotle, *nullum*   2440
magnum ingenium sine mixtura dementiae fuit. Nec potest
grande aliquid, et supra caeteros loqui, nisi mota mens. Then
it riseth higher, as by a divine instinct, when it contemns
common and known conceptions. It utters somewhat
above a mortal mouth. Then it gets aloft, and flies away
with his rider, whither before it was doubtful to ascend.

Helicon,
Pegasus,
Parnassus,
Ovidius

This the poets understood by their Helicon, Pegasus, or
Parnassus; and this made Ovid to boast:

> *Est deus in nobis; agitante calescimus illo:*
> *Sedibus aetheriis spiritus ille venit.*   2450

Lipsius

And Lipsius, to affirm: *scio poetam neminem praestantem*
fuisse, sine parte quadam uberiore divinae aurae. And hence
it is that the coming up of good poets (for I mind not
mediocres, or *imos*) is so thin and rare among us. Every
beggarly corporation affords the state a mayor or two

Petron[ii] in
fragm[enta]

bailiffs yearly; but *solus rex, aut poeta, non quotannis*
nascitur.

To this perfection of nature in our poet we require

exercise of those parts, and frequent. If his wit will not   *2. Exercitatio*
arrive suddenly at the dignity of the ancients, let him not
yet fall out with it, quarrel, or be over-hastily angry, offer
to turn it away from study in a humour; but come to it
again upon better cogitation, try another time with
labour. If then it succeed not, cast not away the quills yet,
nor scratch the wainscot, beat not the poor desk, but
bring all to the forge, and file again, turn it anew. There
is no statute law of the kingdom bids you be a poet against
your will or the first quarter; if it come in a year or two, it
is well. The common rhymers pour forth verses, such as
they are, extempore, but there never come[s] from them
one sense worth the life of a day. A rhymer and a poet are
two things. It is said of the incomparable Virgil that he   *Virgil*
brought forth his verses like a bear, and after formed
them with licking. Scaliger the father writes it of him,   *Scaliger*
that he made a quantity of verses in the morning which
afore night he reduced to a less number. But that which
Valerius Maximus hath left recorded of Euripides (the   *Valerius*
tragic poet)'s answer to Alcestis (another poet) is as   *Maximus,*
memorable as modest: who, when it was told to Alcestis   *Euripides,*
   Alcestis
that Euripides had in three days brought forth but three
verses, and those with some difficulty and throes,
Alcestis glorying he could with ease have sent forth a
hundred in the space, Euripides roundly repl[i]ed, 'Like
enough. But here is the difference: thy verses will not last
those three days, mine will to all time.' Which was as to
tell him he could not write a verse. I have met many of
these rattles that made a noise and buzzed. They had
their hum, and no more. Indeed, things wrote with labour
deserve so to be read, and will last their age.

The third requisite in our poet or maker is imitation,   *3. Imitatio*
to be able to convert the substance or riches of another
poet to his own use. To make choice of one excellent
man above the rest, and so to follow him till he grow very
he, or so like him as the copy may be mistaken for the
principal. Not as a creature that swallows what it takes in
crude, raw, or indigested, but that feeds with an appetite,
and hath a stomach to concoct, divide, and turn all into
nourishment. Not to imitate servilely (as Horace saith)   *Horatius*
and catch at vices for virtue, but to draw forth out of the

Virgilius,
Statius,
Homer,
Horat[ius],
Archil[ochus],
Alcaeus, etc.

best and choicest flowers, with the bee, and turn all into 2500
honey: work it into one relish and savour, make our
imitation sweet, observe how the best writers have
imitated, and follow them: how Virgil and Statius have
imitated Homer, how Horace, Archilochus; how
Alcaeus, and the other lyrics; and so of the rest.

4. Lectio

But that which we especially require in him is an
exactness of study and multiplicity of reading, which
maketh a full man, not alone enabling him to know the
history or argument of a poem and to report it, but so to
master the matter and style as to show he knows how to 2510
handle, place, or dispose of either with elegancy when
need shall be. And not think he can leap forth suddenly a

Parnassus,
Helicon

poet by dreaming he hath been in Parnassus, or having
washed his lips (as they say) in Helicon. There goes more
to his making than so: for to nature, exercise, imitation,

Ars coron[at]

and study, art must be added, to make all these perfect.
And though these challenge to themselves much in the
making up of our maker, it is art only can lead him to
perfection, and leave him there in possession, as planted
by her hand. It is the assertion of Tully, if to an excellent 2520

M[arcus]
T[ullius]
Cicero

nature there happen an accession or conformation of
learning and discipline, there will then remain somewhat noble and singular. For as Simylus saith in

Simylus,
Stob[aeus]

Stobaeus,

οὔτε φύσις ἱκανὴ γίνεται τέχνης ἄτερ,
οὔτε πᾶν τέχνη μή φύσιν κεκτημένη

—without art, nature can never be perfect; and without
nature, art can claim no being. But our poet must beware
that his study be not only to learn of himself, for he that
shall affect to do that confesseth his ever having a fool to 2530
his master. He must read many, but ever the best and
choicest: those that can teach him anything, he must ever
account his masters, and reverence: among whom

Horatius,
Aristoteles

Horace, and he that taught him, Aristotle, deserve to be
the first in estimation. Aristotle was the first accurate
critic and truest judge, nay, the greatest philosopher, the
world ever had, for he noted the vices of all knowledges
in all creatures, and out of many men's perfections in a
science he formed still one art. So he taught us two

2540 offices together, how we ought to judge rightly of others,
and what we ought to imitate specially in ourselves. But
all this in vain without a natural wit, and a poetical nature
in chief. For no man, so soon as he knows this or reads it,
shall be able to write the better, but as he is adapted to it
by nature, he shall grow the perfect writer. He must have
civil prudence and eloquence, and that whole not taken
up by snatches or pieces, in sentences or remnants when
he will handle business or carry counsels, as if he came
then out of the declaimers' gallery, or shadow, but
2550 furnished out of the body of the state, which commonly is   *Virorum schola*
the school of men. The poet is the nearest borderer upon   *respub[lica]*
the orator, and expresseth all his virtues, though he be
tied more to numbers; is his equal in ornament, and
above him in his strengths. And of the kind, the comic
comes nearest, because in moving the minds of men and
stirring of affections—in which oratory shows and
especially approves her eminence—he chiefly excels.
What figure of a body was Lysippus ever able to form   *Lysippus,*
with his graver, or Apelles to paint with his pencil, as the   *Apelles*
2560 comedy to life expresseth so many and various affections
of the mind? There shall the spectator see some insulting
with joy, others fretting with melancholy, raging with
anger, mad with love, boiling with avarice, undone with
riot, tortured with expectation, consumed with fear; no
perturbation in common life but the orator finds an
example of it in the scene. And then for the elegancy of
language, read but this inscription on the grave of a
comic poet: *Naevius*

>   *Immortales mortales, si fas esset, flere,*
> 2570 *Flerent divae Camoenae Naevium poetam;*
>   *Itaque postquam est Orcino traditus thesauro,*
>   *Obliti sunt Romae lingua loqui Latina.*

Or that modester testimony given by Lucius Aelius Stilo   *L[ucius] Aelius*
upon Plautus, who affirmed, *Musas, si Latine loqui voluis-*   *Stilo, Plautus*
sent, Plautino sermone fuisse locuturas. And that illustrious
judgement by the most learned M. Varro of him, who   *M[arcus] Varro*
pronounced him the prince of letters and elegancy in the
Roman language.
  I am not of that opinion to conclude a poet's liberty

within the narrow limits of laws which either the gram-   2580
marians or philosophers prescribe. For before they
found out those laws there were many excellent poets
that fulfilled them; amongst whom none more perfect
Sophocles   than Sophocles, who lived a little before Aristotle. Which
Demosthenes   of the Greeklings durst ever give precepts to Demos-
Pericles   thenes? or to Pericles, whom the age surnamed
                   'heavenly', because he seemed to thunder and lighten
Alcibiades   with his language? or to Alcibiades, who had rather
                   nature for his guide than art for his master?   2590

But whatsoever nature at any time dictated to the most
happy, or long exercise to the most laborious, that the
Aristotle   wisdom and learning of Aristotle hath brought into an
art, because he understood the causes of things; and
what other men did by chance or custom, he doth by
reason; and not only found out the way not to err, but the
short way we should take not to err.

Euripides,   Many things in Euripides hath Aristophanes wittily
Aristophanes   reprehended: not out of art, but out of truth. For
Euripides is sometimes peccant, as he is most times 2600
perfect. But judgement when it is greatest, if reason doth
not accompany it, is not ever absolute.

Cens[ura]   To judge of poets is only the faculty of poets; and not
Scal[igeri] in   all poets, but the best. *Nemo infelicius de poetis judicavit,*
Lil[ium]
Gre[gorium]   *quam qui de poetis scripsit.* But some will say critics are a
Senec[a], De   kind of tinkers, that make more faults than they mend
Brev[itate]   ordinarily. See their diseases, and those of grammarians.
Vit[ae], cap.   It is true, many bodies are the worse for the meddling
13; &   with; and the multitude of physicians hath destroyed
Epist[olae], 88 many sound patients with their wrong practice. But the
                   office of a true critic or censor is not to throw by a letter 2610
anywhere, or damn an innocent syllabe, but lay the words
together, and amend them; judge sincerely of the author
and his matter, which is the sign of solid and perfect
Horace   learning in a man. Such was Horace, an author of much
civility, and—if any one among the heathen can be—the
best master both of virtue and wisdom; an excellent and
true judge upon cause and reason: not because he
Heins[ius], De   thought so, but because he knew so, out of use and
Sat[yra], [p.]   experience.
26[6]   Cato, the Grammarian, a defender of Lucilius.   2620

Cato grammaticus, Latina Siren,
Qui solus legit et facit poetas.

Quintilian of the same heresy, but rejected. Horace's   *Pag. 267,*
judgement of Choerilus, defended against Joseph Scali-   *pag. 270, 271,*
ger, and of Laberius against Julius. But chiefly his   *pag. 273 et*
opinion of Plautus, vindicated against many that are   *seq.*
offended, and say it is a hard censure upon the parent of   *pag. in*
all conceit and sharpness. And if they wish it had not   *comm[entario]*
fallen from so great a master and censor in the art, whose   *153 et seq.*
2630 bondmen knew better how to judge of Plautus than any
that dare patronize the family of learning in this age; who
could not be ignorant of the judgement of the times in
which he lived, when poetry and the Latin language were
at the height; especially being a man so conversant and
inwardly familiar with the censures of great men that did
discourse of these things daily amongst themselves.
Again, a man so gracious and in high favour with the
emperor, as Augustus often called him his witty manling,
for the littleness of his stature; and, if we may trust
2640 antiquity, had designed him for a secretary of estate, and
invited him to the p[a]lace, which he modestly prayed off
and refused. Horace did so highly esteem Terence's   *Terence*
comedies as he ascribes the art in comedy to him alone
among the Latins, and joins him with Menander. Now   *Menander*
let us see what may be said for either, to defend Horace's
judgement to posterity, and not wholly to condemn
Plautus.

The parts of a comedy are the same with a tragedy, and   *The parts of a*
the end is partly the same. For they both delight and   *comedy and*
2650 teach; the comics are called διδάσκαλοι, of the Greeks, no *tragedy*
less than the tragics.

Nor is the moving of laughter always the end of
comedy; that is rather a fowling for the people's delight,
or their fooling. For as Aristotle says rightly, the moving *Aristotle*
of laughter is a fault in comedy, a kind of turpitude that
depraves some part of a man's nature without a disease.
As a wry face without pain moves laughter, or a deformed
vizard, or a rude clown dressed in a lady's habit and using
her actions; we dislike and scorn such representations,

Plato

Homer

which made the ancient philosophers ever think laughter 2660
unfitting in a wise man. And this induced Plato to esteem
of Homer as a sacrilegious person, because he presented
the gods sometimes laughing. As also it is divinely said of
Aristotle, that to seem ridiculous is a part of dishonesty,
and foolish.

*The wit of the
Old Comedy*

So that what either in the words or sense of an author,
or in the language or actions of men, is awry or depraved
doth strangely stir mean affections, and provoke for the
most part to laughter. And therefore it was clear that all
insolent and obscene speeches, jest[s] upon the best 2670
men, injuries to particular persons, perverse and sinister
sayings—and the rather unexpected—in the Old Comedy
did move laughter, especially where it did imitate any
dishonesty, and scurrility came forth in the place of wit;
which who understands the nature and genius of
laughter cannot but perfectly know.

*Aristophanes
Plautus*

Of which Aristophanes affords an ample harvest,
having not only outgone Plautus or any other in that kind,
but expressed all the moods and figures of what is
ridiculous, oddly. In short, as vinegar is not accounted 2680
good until the wine is corrupted, so jests that are true and
natural seldom raise laughter with the beast, the
multitude. They love nothing that is right and proper.
The farther it runs from reason or possibility with them,
the better it is. What could have made them laugh, like to

Socrates

see Socrates presented—that example of all good life,
honesty, and virtue—to have him hoisted up with a
pulley, and there play the philosopher in a basket;
measure how many foot a flea could skip geometrically by
a just scale, and edify the people from the engine? This 2690

Theatrical wit

was theatrical wit, right stage-jesting, and relishing a
playhouse invented for scorn and laughter; whereas, if it
had savoured of equity, truth, perspicuity, and candour,
to have tasten a wise or a learned palate, spit it out
presently. This is bitter and profitable, this instructs and
would inform us! What need we know anything, that are
nobly born, more than a horse-race or a hunting-match,
our day to break with citizens, and such innate mysteries?

The cart

This is truly leaping from the stage to the tumbril again,
reducing all wit to the original dung-cart.

2700

Of the magnitude and compass of any fable, epic or dramatic
To the resolving of this question we must first agree in
the definition of the fable. The fable is called the
imitation of one entire and perfect action, whose parts
are so joined and knit together as nothing in the structure
can be changed or taken away without impairing or
troubling the whole, of which there is a proportionable
magnitude in the members. As (for example) if a man
would build a house, he would first appoint a place to
710   build it in, which he would define within certain bounds;
so in the constitution of a poem, the action is aimed at by
the poet, which answers place in a building; and that
action hath his largeness, compass, and proportion. But
as a court or king's palace requires other dimensions
than a private house, so the epic asks a magnitude from
other poems. Since what is place in the one is action in
the other, the difference is in space. So that by this
definition we conclude the fable to be the imitation of
one perfect and entire action, as one perfect and entire
2720 place is required to a building. By perfect, we understand
that to which nothing is wanting, as place to the building
that is raised, and action to the fable that is formed. It is
perfect, perhaps, not for a court or king's palace, which
requires a greater ground, but for the structure we would
raise. So the space of the action may not prove large
enough for the epic fable, yet be perfect for the dramatic,
and whole.
    Whole we call that, and perfect, which hath a begin-
ning, a midst, and an end. So the place of any building
730   may be whole and entire for that work, though too little
for a palace. As to a tragedy or a comedy, the action may
be convenient and perfect that would not fit an epic poem
in magnitude. So a lion is a perfect creature in himself,
though it be less than [an elephant. The head of a lion is a
whole, though it be less than] that of a buffalo or a
rhinocerote. They differ but in specie; either in the kind
is absolute: both have their parts, and either the whole.
Therefore as in every body, so in every action which is
the subject of a just work, there is required a certain
740   proportionable greatness, neither too vast nor too
minute. For that which happens to the eyes when we

What the measure of a fable is. The fable or plot of a poem defined

The epic fable

Differing from the dramatic

What we understand by whole

behold a body, the same happens to the memory when
we contemplate an action. I look upon a monstrous giant,
as Tityus, whose body covered nine acres of land, and
mine eye sticks upon every part; the whole that consists
of those parts will never be taken in at one entire view. So
in a fable, if the action be too great, we can never
comprehend the whole together in our imagination.
Again, if it be too little, there ariseth no pleasure out of
the object; it affords the view no stay; it is beheld and
vanisheth at once. As if we should look upon an ant or
pismire, the parts fly the sight, and the whole considered
is almost nothing. The same happens in action, which is
the object of memory, as the body is of sight. Too vast
oppresseth the eyes, and exceeds the memory; too little
scarce admits either.

What the
utmost bound
of a fable

Now in every action it behoves the poet to know which
is his utmost bound, how far with fitness and a necessary
proportion he may produce and determine it; that is, till
either good fortune change into the worse, or the worse
into the better. For as a body without proportion cannot
be goodly, no more can the action, either the comedy or
tragedy, without his fit bounds. And every bound, for the
nature of the subject, is esteemed the best that is largest,
till it can increase no more; so it behoves the action in
tragedy or comedy to be let grow till the necessity ask a
conclusion; wherein two things are to be considered:
first, that it exceed not the compass of one day; next, that
there be place left for digression and art. For the
episodes and digressions in a fable are the same that
household stuff and other furniture are in a house. And
so far for the measure and extent of a fable dramatic.

What by one
and entire

Now that it should be one and entire. One is considerable two ways: either, as it is only separate, and by itself,
or as being composed of many parts, it begins to be one as
those parts grow or are wrought together. That it should
be one the first way alone, and by itself, no man that hath
tasted letters ever would say, especially having required
before a just magnitude and equal proportion of the parts
in themselves. Neither of which can possibly be if the
action be single and separate, not composed of parts
which, laid together in themselves with an equal and

2750

2760

2770

2780

fitting proportion, tend to the same end; which thing out of antiquity itself hath deceived many, and more this day it doth deceive.

So many there be of old that have thought the action of one man to be one, as of Hercules, Theseus, Achilles, Ulysses, and other heroes, which is both foolish and false; since by one and the same person many things may 2790 be severally done which cannot fitly be referred or joined to the same end; which not only the excellent tragic poets, but the best masters of the epic, Homer and Virgil, saw. For though the argument of an epic poem be far more diffused and poured out than that of tragedy, yet Virgil, writing of Aeneas, hath pretermitted many things. He neither tells how he was born, how brought up, how he fought with Achilles, how he was snatched out of the battle by Venus; but that one thing, how he came into Italy, he prosecutes in twelve books. The rest of his 2800 journey, his error by sea, the sack of Troy, are put not as the argument of the work, but episodes of the argument. So Homer laid by many things of Ulysses and handled no more than he saw tended to one and the same end.

Contrary to which and foolishly those poets did, whom the philosopher taxeth: of whom one gathered all the actions of Theseus, another put all the labours of Hercules in one work. So did he whom Juvenal mentions in the beginning, 'hoarse Codrus', that recited a volume compiled, which he called his *Theseid*, not yet finished, to 2810 the great trouble both of his hearers and himself; amongst which there were many parts had no coherence, nor kindred one with another, so far they were from being one action, one fable. For as a house consisting of diverse materials becomes one structure and one dwelling, so an action composed of divers parts may become one fable, epic or dramatic. For example, in a tragedy, look upon Sophocles's *Ajax*: Ajax, deprived of Achilles' armour, which he hoped from the suffrage of the Greeks, disdains; and, growing impatient of the injury, rageth, 2820 and turns mad. In that humour he doth many senseless things, and at last falls upon the Grecian flock, and kills a great ram for Ulysses. Returning to his sense, he grows ashamed of the scorn, and kills himself; and is by the

Hercules, Theseus, Achilles, Ulysses

Homer and Virgil

Aeneas

Venus

Homer

Theseus, Hercules, Juvenal, Codrus

Sophocles, Ajax

Ulysses

chiefs of the Greeks forbidden burial. These things agree and hang together, not as they were done, but as seeming to be done; which made the action whole, entire, and absolute.

The conclusion concerning the whole and the parts

For the whole, as it consisteth of parts, so without all the parts it is not the whole; and to make it absolute is required not only the parts, but such parts as are true. 2830 For a part of the whole was true, which, if you take away, you either change the whole, or it is not the whole. For if it be such a part, as being present or absent, nothing concerns the whole, it cannot be called a part of the

Which are episodes. Ajax and Hector. Homer

whole; and such are the episodes, of which hereafter. For the present, here is one example: the single combat of Ajax with Hector, as it is at large described in Homer, nothing belongs to this *Ajax* of Sophocles.

You admire no poems, but such as run like a brewer's-cart upon the stones, hobbling, 2840

Martial, lib. 11 epig. 9[0]

> *Et quae per salebras altaque saxa cadunt.*
> *Accius et quidquid Pacuviusque vomunt.*
> *Attonitusque legis 'terrai frugiferai'.*

FINIS

CONVERSATIONS
WITH
WILLIAM DRUMMOND OF
HAWTHORNDEN

Informations by Ben Jonson to W.D. when he came to Scotland upon foot, 1619

Certain informations and manners of Ben Jonson's to W. Drummond

1. That he had an intention to perfect an epic poem, entitled *Heroologia*, of the worthies of his country roused by fame, and was to dedicate it to his country. It is all in couplets, for he detesteth all other rhymes. Said he had written a discourse of poesy both against Campion and Daniel, especially this last, where he proves couplets to be the bravest sort of verses, especially when they are broken, like hexameters; and that cross-rhymes and stanzas—because the purpose would lead him beyond eight lines to conclude—were all forced.

2. He recommended to my reading Quintilian (who, he said, would tell me all the faults of my verses as if he had lived with me) and Horace, Plinius secundus' *Epistles*, Tacitus, Juvenal, Martial, whose epigram 'Vitam quae faciunt beatiorem' etc. he hath translated.

3. His censure of the English poets was this: that Sidney did not keep a decorum in making everyone speak as well as himself.

Spenser's stanzas pleased him not, nor his matter, the meaning of which allegory he had delivered in papers to Sir Walter Raleigh.

Samuel Daniel was a good honest man, had no children, but no poet.

That Michael Drayton's *Poly-O[l]bion*, if [he] had performed what he promised to write, the deeds of all the worthies, had been excellent. His long verses pleased him not.

That Sylvester's translation of Du Bartas was not well done, and that he wrote his verses before it ere he understood to confer. Nor that of Fairfax his.

That the translations of Homer and Virgil in long Alexandrines were but prose.

That John Harington's Ariosto under all translations was the worst. That when Sir John Harington desired him to tell the truth of his epigrams, he answered him that he loved not the truth, for they were narrations, and not epigrams.

30   That Warner, since the king's coming to England, [ha]d marred all his *Albion's England*.

That Donne's *Anniversary* was profane and full of blasphemies. That he told Mr Donne, if it had been written of the Virgin Mary it had been something; to which he answered that he described the idea of a woman, and not as she was.

That Donne, for not keeping of accent, deserved hanging.

That Shakespeare wanted art.

That Sharpham, Day, Dekker, were all rogues, and that Minsheu was one.

40   That Abraham Fraunce in his English hexameters was a fool.

That next himself only Fletcher and Chapman could make a masque.

4. His judgement of stranger poets was: that he thought not Bartas a poet but a verser, because he wrote not fiction.

He cursed Petrarch for redacting verses to sonnets, which he said were like that tyrant's bed, where some who were too short were racked, others too long cut short.

That Guarini in his *Pastor Fido* kept not decorum in making shepherds speak as well as himself could.

That Lucan, taken in parts, was good divided; read altogether, 50 merited not the name of a poet.

That Bonefonius' *Vigilium Veneris* was excellent.

That he told Cardinal de Perron (at his being in France, anno 1613) who show[ed] him his translations of Virgil, that they were naught.

That the best pieces of Ronsard were his odes.

All this was to no purpose, for he neither doth understand French nor Italian.

5. He read his translation of that ode of Horace, 'Beatus ille qui procul negotiis', etc. and admired it. Of an epigram of Petronius, 'Foeda et brevis est Veneris voluptas', concluding it was better to lie still and kiss 60 than pant.

To me he read the preface of his *Art of Poesy*, upon Horace['s] *Art of Poesy*, where he hath an apology of a play of his, *St Bartholomew's Fair*. By

Criticus is understood Donne. There is an epigram of Sir Edward
Herbert's before it. The [translation], he said, he had done in my Lord
Aubigny's house ten years since, anno 1604.

The most commonplace of his repetition was a dialogue pastoral
between a shepherd and shepherdess about singing; another,
Parabostes' Parian with his letter; that epigram 'Of Gut'; my Lady
Bedford's buck; his verses of drinking, 'Drink to me but with thine eyes',
'Swell me a bowl', etc.; his verses of a kiss: 70

> But kiss me once, and, faith, I will be gone;
> And I will touch as harmless as the bee
> That doth but taste the flower, and flee away.
> That is but half a one;
> What should be done but once should be done long.

He read a satire of a lady come from the bath; verses on the pucelle of
the court, Mistress Bulstrode, whose epitaph Donne made; a satire,
telling there was no abuses to write a satire of, and [in] which he
repeateth all the abuses in England and the world. He insisted in that of
Martia[l] 'Vitam quae faciunt beatiorem'.   80

6. His censure of my verses was that they were all good, especially my
epitaph of the prince, save that they smelled too much of the schools, and
were not after the fancy of the time; for a child, says he, may write after
the fashion of the Greeks and Latin verses in running; yet that he wished,
to please the king, that piece of 'Forth Feasting' had been his own.

7. He esteemeth John Donne the first poet in the world in some things.
His verses of the lost chain he hath by heart; and that passage of 'The
Calm', that dust and feathers do not stir, all was so quiet. Affirmeth
Donne to have written all his best pieces ere he was twenty-five years old.

Sir Edward Wotton's verses of a happy life he hath by heart, and a   90
piece of Chapman's translation of the thirteen of the *Iliads*, which he
thinketh well done.

That Donne said to him he wrote that epitaph on Prince Henry, 'Look
to me, faith', to match Sir Ed[ward] Herbert in obscureness.

He hath by heart some verses of Spenser's *Calendar*, about wine,
between Colin and Percy.

8. The conceit of Donne's 'Transformation' or μετεμψυχοσις
was that he sought the soul of that apple which Eva pulled, and thereafter
made it the soul of a bitch, then of a she-wolf, and so of a woman. His

100 general purpose was to have brought in all the bodies of the heretics from
the soul of Cain, and at last left it in the body of Calvin. Of this he never
wrote but one sheet, and now, since he was made doctor, repenteth
highly, and seeketh to destroy all his poems.

9. That Petronius, Plinius Secundus, Tacitus, speak best Latin; that
Quintilian's 6, 7, 8 books were not only to be read, but altogether
digested. Juvenal, Pers[ius], Horace, Martial, for delight, and so was
Pindar. For health, Hippocrates.

Of their nation, Hooker's *Ecclesiastical History* (whose children are now
beggars) for church matters. Selden's *Titles of Honour* for antiquities
110 here; and one book of the *Gods of the Gentiles*, whose names are in the
scripture, of Selden's.

Tacitus, he said, wrote the secrets of the council and senate, as
Suetonius did those of the cabinet and court.

10. For a heroic poem, he said, there was no such ground as King
Arthur's fiction, and th[a]t S[ir] P. Sidney had an intention to have
transformed all his *Arcadia* to the stories of King Arthur.

11. His acquaintance and behaviour with poets living with him.
Daniel was at jealousies with him.
Drayton feared him, and he esteemed not of him.
120 That Francis Beaumont loved too much himself and his own verses.
Th[a]t S[i]r John Roe loved him; and when they two were ushered by
my Lord Suffolk from a masque, Roe wrote a moral epistle to him which
began 'That next to plays, the court and the state were the best. God
threateneth kings, kings lords, and lords do us.'
He beat Marston, and took his pistol from him.
Sir W. Alexander was not half kind unto him, and neglected him,
because a friend to Drayton.
That Sir R. Ayton loved him dearly.
Ned Field was his scholar, and he had read to him the satires of
130 Horace, and some epigrams of Martial.
That Markham, who added his *English Arcadia*, was not of the number
of the faithful, i.[e.] poets, and but a base fellow.
That such were Day and Middleton.
That Chapman and Fletcher were loved of him.
Overbury was first his friend, then turned his mortal enemy.

12. Particulars of the actions of other poets, and apothegms.

That the Irish, having robbed Spenser's goods and burnt his house and a little child new-born, he and his wife escaped, and after he died for lack of bread in King Street, and refused twenty pieces sent to him by my Lord of Essex, and said he was sorry he had no time 140 to spend them.

That in th[a]t paper S[ir] W. Raleigh had of the allegories of his *Faerie Queene*, by the Blating Beast the Puritans were understood; by the false Duessa, the Q[ueen] of Scots.

That Southwell was hanged; yet so he had written that piece of his, 'The burning babe', he would have been content to destroy many of his.

Franc[is] Beaumont died ere he was thirty years of age.

Sir John Roe was an infinite spender, and used to say, when he had no more to spend he could die. He died in his arms of the pest, and he furnished his charges, £20; which was given him back. 150

That Drayton was challenged for entitling one book *Mortimeriados*.

That S[ir] J. Davies played in an epigram on Drayton, who in a sonnet concluded his mistress might been the ninth worthy; and said he used a phrase like Dametas in Arcadia, who said, 'For wit his mistress might be a giant.'

Donne's grandfather on the mother side was Heywood the epigrammatist.

That Donne himself, for not being understood, would perish.

That S[i]r W. Raleigh esteemed more of fame than conscience. The best wits of England were employed for making of his *History*. Ben 160 himself had written a piece to him of the Punic War, which he altered and set in his book. S[ir] W. hath written the life of Queen Elizabeth, of which there is copies extant.

Sir P. Sidney had translated some of the psalms which went abroad under the name of the Countess of Pembroke.

Marston wrote his father-in-law's preachings, and his father-in-law his comedies.

Shakespeare in a play brought in a number of men saying they had suffered shipwreck in Bohemia, where th[e]r[e] is no sea near by some 100 miles. 170

Daniel wrote *Civil Wars*, and yet hath not one battle in all his book.

The Countess of Rutland was nothing inferior to her father, S[ir] P. Sidney, in poesy. Sir Th[omas] Overbury was in love with her, and caused Ben to read his 'Wife' to her, which he, with an excellent grace, did, and praised the author. That the morn thereafter he discorded with Overbury, who would have him to intend a suit th[a]t was unlawful. The lines my lady kept in remembrance, 'He comes too near, who comes to be denied'. Beaumont wrote that elegy on the death of the Countess of Rutland, and in effect her husband wanted the half of his in his travels.

180   Owen is a pure pedantic schoolmaster, sweeping his living from the posteriors of little children, and hath nothing good in him, his epigrams being bare narrations.

Chapman hath translated Musaeus in his verses like his Homer.

Fletcher and Beaumont ten years since hath written *The Faithful Shepherdess*, a tragicomedy well done.

Dyer died unmarried.

S[ir] P. Sidney was no pleasant man in countenance, his face being spoiled with pimples, and of high blood, and long. That my lord Lisle (now Earl of Worcester)'s eldest son resembleth him.

190   13. Of his own life, education, birth, actions. His grandfather came from Carlisle, and he thought from Annandale to it; he served Henry VIII, and was a gentleman. His father lost all his estate under Queen Mary; having been cast in prison and forfeited, at last turned minister. So he was a minister's son. He himself was posthumous born a month after his father's decease; brought up poorly, put to school by a friend (his master Camden), after taken from it, and put to another craft (I think was to be a wright or bricklayer), which he could not endure. Then went he to the Low Countries, but returning soon he betook himself to his wonted studies. In his service in the Low Countries he had, in the face of

200   both the camps, killed an enemy and taken *opima spolia* from him; and since his coming to England, being appealed to the fields, he had killed his adversary, which had hurt him in the arm, and whose sword was ten inches longer than his; for the which he was imprisoned, and almost at the gallows. Then took he his religion by trust of a priest who visited him in prison. Thereafter he was twelve years a papist.

He was Master of Arts in both the universities, by th[ei]r favour, not his study.

He married a wife who was a shrew yet honest. Five years he had not bedded w[i]t[h] her, but remained w[i]t[h] my lord Aubigny.

210   In the time of his close imprisonment under Queen Elizabeth, his judges could get nothing of him to all th[ei]r demands but 'aye' and 'no'. They placed two damned villains to catch advantage of him, w[i]t[h] him, but he was advertised by his keeper. Of the spies he hath an epigram.

When the king came in England, at that time the pest was in London. He being in the country at S[i]r Robert Cotton's house with old Camden, he saw in a vision his eldest son, th[e]n a child and at London, appear unto him w[i]t[h] the mark of a bloody cross on his forehead, as if it had been cutted w[i]t[h] a sword; at which, amazed, he prayed unto God; and in the morning he came to Mr Camden's chamber to tell him, who persuaded him it was but an apprehension of his fantasy, at which he should not be disjected. In the meantime comes th[e]r[e] letters from his wife of the death of th[a]t boy in the plague. He appeared to him, he said, of a manly shape, and of th[a]t growth that he thinks he shall be at the resurrection.

He was delated by S[i]r James Murray to the king for writing something against the Scots in a play, *Eastward Ho*, and voluntarily imprisoned himself w[i]t[h] Chapman and Marston, who had written it amongst th[e]m. The report was that they should then had their ears cut and noses. After th[ei]r delivery he banqueted all his friends: th[e]r[e] was Camden, Selden and others. At the midst of the feast his old mother drank to him, and show[ed] him a paper which she had, if the sentence had taken execution, to have mixed in the prison among his drink, which was full of lusty strong poison. And that she was no churl, she told she minded first to have drunk of it herself.

He had many quarrels with Marston: beat him, and took his pistol from him; wrote his *Poetaster* on him. The beginning of th[e]m were that Marston represented him in the stage.

In his youth given to venery. He thought the use of a maid nothing in comparison to the wantonness of a wife, and would never have another mistress. He said two accidents strange befell him: one, that a man made his own wife to court him, whom he enjoyed two years ere he knew of it, and one day finding them by chance, was passingly delighted with it; one other, lay divers times with a woman who show[ed] him all that he wished except the last act, which she would never agree unto.

S[ir] W. Raleigh sent him governor w[i]t[h] his son, anno 1613, to France. This youth, being knavishly inclined, among other pastimes (as the setting of the favours of damsels on a cod-piece), caused him to be drunken and dead drunk, so that he knew not where he was; thereafter laid him on a car which he made to be drawn by pioneers through the streets, at every corner showing his governor stretched out, and telling them that was a more lively image of the crucifix than any they had; at which sport young Raleigh's mother delighted much, saying, his father young was so inclined; though the father abhorred it.

He can set horoscopes, but trusts not in th[e]m. He, with the consent of a friend, cozened a lady with whom he had made an appointment to meet an old astrologer in the suburbs, which she kept; and it was himself disguised in a long gown and a white beard at the light of [a] dim-burning candle, up in a little cabinet reached unto by a ladder.

Every first day of the New Year he had £20 sent him from the Earl of
260 Pembroke to buy books.

After he was reconciled with the church and left off to be a recusant, at
his first communion, in token of true reconciliation, he drank out all the
full cup of wine.

Being at the end of my Lord Salisbury's table with Inigo Jones, and
demanded by my Lord why he was not glad, 'My Lord', said he, 'You
promised I should dine with you, but I do not', for he had none of his
meat. He esteemed only th[a]t his meat which was of his own dish.

He hath consumed a whole night in lying looking to his great toe,
about which he hath seen Tartars and Turks, Romans and Cartha-
270 ginians, fight in his imagination.

Northampton was his mortal enemy for brawling, on a St George's
Day, one of his attenders; he was called before the Council for his
Sejanus, and accused both of popery and treason by him.

Sundry times he hath devoured his books, i.[e.], sold th[e]m all for
necessity.

He hath a mind to be a churchman, and so he might have favour to
make one sermon to the king. He careth not what th[e]r[e]after should
befall him; for he would not flatter, though he saw death.

At his hither coming, S[i]r Francis Bacon said to him he loved not to
280 see poesy go on other feet th[a]n poetical dactyls and spondees.

14. His narrations of great ones.
He never esteemed of a man for the name of a lord.

Queen Elizabeth never saw herself after she became old in a true
glass; they painted her, and sometimes would vermilion her nose. She
had always, about Christmas evens, set dice that threw sixes or five (and
she knew not they were other) to make her win and esteem herself
fortunate. That she had a *membrana* on her which made her uncapable of
man, though for her delight she tried many. At the coming over of
Monsieur, there was a French surgeon who took in hand to cut it, yet fear
290 stayed her, and his death. King Philip had intention by dispensation of
the Pope to have married her.

Sir P. Sidney's mother, Leicester's sister, after she had the little pox
never show[ed] herself in court th[e]r[e]after but masked.

The Earl of Leicester gave a bottle of liquor to his lady which he willed
her to use in any faintness; which she, after his return from court, not
knowing it was poison, gave him; and so he died.

Salisbury never cared for any man longer nor he could make use of
him.

My lord Lisle's daughter, my Lady Wroth, is unworthily married on a
jealous husband.   300

Ben one day being at table with my lady Rutland, her husband coming
in, accused her that she kept table to poets; of which she wrote a letter to
him, which he answered. My lord intercepted the letter, but never
challenged him.

My Lord Chancellor of England wringeth his speeches from the
strings of his band, and other councillors from the picking of th[ei]r
teeth.

Pembroke and his lady discoursing, the Earl said the women were
men's shadows, and she maintained th[e]m. Both appealing to Jonson,
he affirmed it true; for which my lady gave a penance to prove it in verse: 310
hence his epigram.

Essex wrote that epistle or preface before the translation of the last
part of Tacitus, which is A.B. The last book the gentleman durst not
translate for the evil it contains of the Jews.

The king said Sir P. Sidney was no poet; neither did he see ever any
verses in England to the Sculler's.

It was good that half of the preachers of England were plain ignorants,
for that either in their sermons they flatter, or strive to show their own
eloquence.

15. His opinion of verses.   320

That he wrote all his first in prose, for so his master Camden had
learned him.

That verses stood by sense without either colours or accent; which yet
other times he denied.

A great many epigrams were ill because they expressed in the end what
should have been understood by what was said: that of S[ir] John Davies.

Some loved running verses, *plus mihi com[m]a placet.*

He imitated the description of a night from Bonefonius's *Vigilium
Veneris.*

He scorned such verses as could be transponed: 330

> Where is the man that never yet did hear
> Of fair Penelope, Ulysses' queen?
> Of fair Penelope, Ulysses' queen,
> Where is the man that never yet did hear?

16. Of his works.

That the half of his comedies were not in print.

He hath a pastoral entitled *The May Lord.* His own name is Alken;

Ethra, the Countess of Bedford's; Mogibell, Overbury; the old Countess of Suffolk, an enchantress; other names are given to Somerset's lady,
340 Pemb[r]oke, the Countess of Rutland, Lady Wroth. In his first story, Alken cometh in mending his broken pipe. Contrary to all other pastorals, he bringeth the clowns making mirth and foolish sports.

He hath intention to write a fisher or pastoral play, and set the stage of it in the Lomond Lake.

That epithalamium that wants a name in his printed works was made at the Earl of Essex's marriage.

He is to write his foot pilgrimage hither, and to call it *A Discovery*.

In a poem he calleth Edinburgh 'The heart of Scotland, Britain's other eye'.

350 A play of his upon which he was accused, *The Devil is an Ass*: according to *comedia vetus* in England, the devil was brought in either w[i]t[h] one vice or other; the play done, the devil carried away the vice. He brings in the devil so overcome w[i]t[h] the wickedness of this age that [he] thought himself an ass. Πάρεργως is discoursed of the Duke of Drownland. The king desired him to conceal it.

He hath commented and translated Horace[']s *Art of Poesy*. It is in dialogue ways; by Criticus he understandeth Dr Donne. The old book th[a]t goes about, *The Art of English Poesy*, was done twenty years since, and kept long in writ as a secret.

360 He had an intention to have made a play like Plaut[u]s' *Amphitrio*, but left it off for that he could never find two so like others that he could persuade the spectators they were one.

17. Of his jests and apothegms.

At what time Henry the fourth turned Catholic, Pasquil had in his hand a book, and was asked by Morphorius what it was. He told him it was grammar. 'Why do ye study grammar, being so old?' asked Morphorius. 'Because', answered he, 'I have found a positive that hath no superlative, and a superlative that wants a positive: the King of Spain is Rex Catholicus, and is not Catholicissimus; and the French King
370 Christianissimus, yet is not Christianus.'

When they drank on him, he cited th[a]t of Pliny, that they called him *ad prandium, non ad poenam et notam*.

And said of that panegyrist who wrote panegyrics in acrostics, windows, crosses, that he was *homo miserrimae patientiae*.

He scorned anagrams, and had ever in his mouth

> *Turpe est difficiles amare nugas,*
> *Et stultus labor est ineptiarum.*

A cook who was of an evil life, when a minister told him he would go to hell, asked what torment was th[e]r[e]. Being answered 'Fire'—'Fire!' said he, 'that is my play-fellow.' 380

A lord playing at tennis, and having asked those in the gallery whether a stroke was chase or loss, a brother of my lord Northumberland's answered it was loss. The lord demanded if he did say it. 'I say it,' said he; 'what are you?' 'I have played your worth,' said the lord. 'Ye know not the worth of a gentleman!' replied the other. And it proved so, for ere he died he was greater than the other. Another English lord lost all his game, if he had seen a face that liked him not, he struck his balls at th[a]t gallery.

An Englishman who had maintained Democritus' opinion of atoms, being old wrote a book to his son, who was not then six years of age, in which he left him arguments to maintain and answer objections for all 390 that was in his book; only if they objected obscurity against his book, he bid him answer that his father, above all names in the world, hated most the name of Lucifer; and all open writers were Luciferi.

Butler excommunicat[ed] from his table all reporters of long poems, wilful disputers, tedious discoursers. The best banquets were those where they mistered no musicians to chase time.

The greatest sport he saw in France was the picture of our Saviour with the Apostles eating the paschal lamb th[a]t was all larded.

At a supper where a gentlewoman had given him unsavoury wild fowl, and th[e]r[e]after, to wash, sweet water; he commended her that she gave 400 him sweet water, because her flesh stinked.

He said to Prince Charles of Inigo Jones, that when he wanted words to express the greatest villain in the world, he would call him an Inigo.

Jones having accused him for naming him behind his back a fool, he denied it; but, says he , 'I said he was an arrant knave, and I avouch it.'

One who fired a tobacco pipe with a ballad the next day having a sore head, swore he had a great singing in his head, and he thought it was the ballad. A poet should detest a ballad maker.

He saw a picture painted by a bad painter of Esther, Haman, and Ahasuerus; Haman, courting Esther in a bed after the fashion of ours, 410 was only seen by one leg. Ahasuerus' back was turned, with this verse over him, 'And wilt thou, Haman, be so malicious as to lie w[i]t[h] my own wife in mine house?'

He himself being once so taken, the goodman said, 'I would not believe ye would abuse my house so.'

In a profound contemplation a student of Oxford ran over a man in the fields, and walked twelve miles ere he knew what he was doing.

One who wore side hair being asked of another who was bald why he

suffered his hair to grow so long, answered it was to see if his hair would
420 grow to seed, th[a]t he might sow of it on bald plates.

A painter who could paint nothing but a rose, when an inn-keeper had
advised w[i]t[h] him about an ensign, said that a horse was a good one, so
was a hare, but a rose was above th[e]m all.

A little man drinking Prince Henry's health between two tall fellows
said he made up the H.

Sir Henry Wotton, before his Majesty's going to England, being
disguised at Leith on Sunday when all the rest were at church, being
interrupted of his occupation by another wench who came in at the door,
cried out, 'Pox on thee, for thou hast hindered the procreation of a child',
430 and betrayed himself.

A Justice of Peace would have commanded a captain to sit first
at a table, 'Because', says he, 'I am a Justice of Peace.' The other,
drawing his sword, commanded him: 'For', saith he, 'I am a Justice of
War.'

What is that, that the more you cut of it groweth still the longer?—A
ditch.

He used to say that they who delight to fill men extraordinary full in
their own houses loved to have their meat again.

A certain Puritan minister would not give the communion save unto
440 thirteen at once, imitating (as he thought) our Master. Now when they
were set, and one bethinking himself that some of th[e]m must represent
Judas, that it should not be, he returned, and so did all the rest,
understanding his thought.

A gentlewoman fell in such a fantasy or frenzy w[i]t[h] one Mr Dod, a
Puritan preacher, th[a]t she requested her husband that, for the procreation of an angel or saint, he might lie w[i]t[h] her; which having
obtained, it was but an ordinary birth.

Scaliger writes an epistle to Casaubon, where he scorns the English
speak[ing] of Latin, for he thought he had spoken English to him.
450 A gentleman reading a poem th[a]t began with

> Where is that man that never yet did hear
> Of fair Penelope, Ulysses' queen?

calling his cook, asked if he had ever heard of her, who answering 'No',
demonstrate to him,

> Lo, there the man that never yet did hear
> Of fair Penelope, Ulysses' queen!

A waiting woman, having cockered w[i]t[h] muscadel and eggs her mistress' page for a she-meeting in the dark, his mistress invaded; of whom she would of such boldness have a reason. 'Faith, lady,' said he, 'I have no reason, save that such was the good pleasure of muscadel and eggs.'

A Judge coming along a hall and being stopped by a throng, cried, 'Dominum cognoscite vestrum!' One of th[e]m th[e]r[e] said they would if he durst say the beginning of th[a]t verse (for he had a fair wife): 'Actaeon ego sum!' cried he, and went on.

A packet of letters which had fallen overboard was devoured of a fish that was ta'en at Flushing, and the letters were safely delivered to him to whom they were written at London.

He scorned that simplicity of Cardan about the pebble-stone of Dover, which he thought had th[a]t virtue, kept between one's teeth, as to save him from being sick.

A scholar expert in Latin and Greek, but nothing in the English, said of hot broth that he would 'make the danger of it'; for it could not be ill English th[a]t was good Latin, *facere periculum*.

A translator of the *Emperors' Lives* translated Antonius Pius 'Anthony Pye'.

The word 'harlot' was taken from 'Arlott', who was the mother of William the Conqueror; a 'rogue' from the Latin *erro*, by putting a 'g' to it.

S[i]r Josceline Percy asked the Mayor of Plymouth whether it was his own beard or the town's beard that he came to welcome my Lord with, for he thought it was so long that he thought everyone of the town had eked some part to it.

That he struck at S[i]r Jerome Bowes' breast, and asked him if he was within.

An epitaph was made upon one who had a long beard, 'Here lies a man at a beard's end', etc.

He said to the king his master M[r] G. Buchanan had corrupted his ear when young, and learned him to sing verses when he should have read them.

S[i]r Francis Walsingham said of our king, when he was ambassador in Scotland, 'Hic nunquam regnabit super nos.'

Of all his plays he never gained two hundred pounds.

He had oft this verse, though he scorned it:

> So long as we may, let us enjoy this breath,
> For naught doth kill a man so soon as death.

One Mr Gryse told the king of a man who, being consumed, occupied his wife with a dildo, and she never knew of it till one day he all sleepery had there left his.

500   Heywood the epigrammatist, being apparelled in velvet by Queen Mary, with his cap on in the presence in spite of all the gentlemen, till the queen herself asked him what he meant; and then he asked her if he was Heywood, for she had made him so brave that he almost had misknown himself.

His impresa was a compass with one foot in centre, the other broken; the word, *deest quod duceret orbem.*

Essex, after his brother's death (Mr Devereux) in France, at tilt had a black shield void; the word, *par nulla figura dolori.* Another time, when the queen was offended at him, a diamond with its own ashes with which
510   it is cut; about it the word, *dum formas minuis.*

He gave the prince *fax gloria mentis honestae.*

He said to me that I was too good and simple, and that oft a man's modesty made a fool of his wit.

His arms were three spindles or rhombi; his own word about th[e]m, *percontabor* or *perscrutator.*

His epitaph, by a companion written, is:

> Here lies Benjamin Jonson dead,
> And hath no more wit than [a] goose in his head;
> That as he was wont, so doth he still
520   > Live by his wit, and evermore will.

Another:

> Here lies honest Ben
> That had not a beard on his chin.

18. Miscellanies.

John Stow had monstrous observations in his *Chronicle*, and was of his craft a tailor. 'He and I walking alone, he asked two cripples what they would have to take him to their order.'

In his *Sejanus* he hath translated a whole oration of Tacitus. The first four books of Tacit[u]s ignorantly done in English.
530   J. Selden liveth on his own, is the law-book of the judges of England, the bravest man in all languages; his book *Titles of Honour*, written to his chamber-fellow Hayward.

Taylor was sent along here to scorn him.

Camden wrote that book *Remains of Britain*.

Joseph Hall the harbinger to Donne's 'Anniversary'.

The epigram of Martial *In verpum* he vaunts to expone.

Lucan, Sidney, Guarini, make every man speak as well as themselves, forgetting decorum; for Dametas sometimes speaks grave sentences.

Lucan, taken in parts, excellent; altogether, naught.

He dissuaded me from poetry, for that she had beggared him, when he might have been a rich lawyer, physician, or merchant.   540

Questioned about English 'them', 'they', 'those': 'they' is still the nominative, 'those' accusative, 'them' neuter; collective not 'them men', 'them trees', but 'them' by itself referred to many. 'Which', 'who' be relatives, not 'that'. 'Floods', 'hills' he would have masculines.

He was better versed, and knew more in Greek and Latin, than all the poets in England, and quintessence[th] their brains.

He made much of that epistle of Plinius where *ad prandium, non ad notam* is, and th[a]t other of Messalinus, who Pliny made to be removed from the table; and of the gross turbot.   550

One wrote an epigram to his father, and vaunted he had slain ten; the quantity of 'decem' being false, another answered the epigram, telling that 'decem' was false.

S[ir] J. Davies' epigram of the whore's c[unt] compared to a cowl.

Of all styles he loved most to be named honest, and hath of that an hundred letters so naming him.

He had this oft:

> Thy flattering picture, Phryne, is like thee
> Only in this, that ye both painted be.

In his merry humour he was wont to name himself The Poet.   560

He went from Leith homeward the 25 of January, 1619, in a pair of shoes which, he told, lasted him since he came from Darnton, which he minded to take back that far again; they were appearing like Coryate's: the first two days he was all excoriate.

If he died by the way, he promised to send me his papers of this country, hewen as they were.

I have to send him descriptions of Edinburgh borough-laws, of the Lomond.

That piece of the pucelle of the court was stolen out of his pocket by a gentleman who drank him drowsy, and given Mistress Bulstrode; which brought him great displeasure.   570

19. He sent to me this madrigal:

On a lover's dust, made sand for an hour-glass

> Do but consider this small dust
>   Here running in the glass,
>   By atoms moved:
> Could thou believe that this
>   The body ever was
>   Of one that loved?
> And in his mistress' flaming, playing like the fly,
>   Turned to cinders by her eye?
>   Yes; and in death, as life, unblest,
>   To have it expressed,
> Even ashes of lovers find no rest.

And this, which is, as he said, a picture of himself:

> I doubt that Love is rather deaf than blind,
>   For else it could not be
>   That she
> Whom I adore so much should so slight me,
>   And cast my suit behind;
> I'm sure my language to her is as sweet,
>   And all my closes meet
>   In numbers of as subtle feet,
>   As makes the youngest he
> That sits in shadow of Apollo's tree.

> Oh, but my conscious fears
>   That fly my thoughts between,
>   Prompt me that she hath seen
>   My hundred of grey hairs,
>   Told six-and-forty years,
> Read so much waste, as she cannot embrace
>   My mountain belly, and my rocky face;
> And all these through her eyes have stopped her ears.

January 19, 1619

    He is a great lover and praiser of himself, a contemner and scorner of others, given rather to lose a friend than a jest, jealous of every word and action of those about him (especially after drink, which is one of the elements in which he liveth), a dissembler of ill parts which reign in him, a bragger of some good that he wanteth, thinketh nothing well but what either he himself or some of his friends and countrymen hath said or done. He is passionately kind and angry, careless either to gain or keep, vindicative, but, if he be well answered, at himself. 610

For any religion, as being versed in both. Interpreteth best sayings and deeds often to the worst. Oppressed with fantasy, which hath ever mastered his reason, a general disease in many poets. His inventions are smooth and easy; but above all he excelleth in a translation.

When his play of a *Silent Woman* was first acted, there was found verses after on the stage against him, concluding that that play was well named *The Silent Woman*: there was never one man to say *plaudite* to it.

Finis

ABBREVIATIONS

(i) *General works*

DNB	*Dictionary of National Biography*
Donne, *Divine Poems*	John Donne, *The Divine Poems*, edited by Helen Gardner (Oxford, 1952)
Donne, *Epithalamions*	John Donne, *The Epithalamions, Anniversaries, and Epicedes*, edited by W. Milgate (Oxford, 1978)
Donne, *Satires*	John Donne, *The Satires, Epigrams, and Verse Letters*, edited by W. Milgate (Oxford, 1967)
Fleay	F. G. Fleay, *A Biographical Chronicle of the English Drama, 1559–1642*, 2 vols. (London, 1891)
Herrick	Robert Herrick, *The Poetical Works*, edited by L. C. Martin (Oxford, 1956)
OED	*Oxford English Dictionary*
Sugden	E. H. Sugden, *A Topographical Dictionary to the Works of Shakespeare and his Fellow Dramatists* (Manchester, London, and New York, 1925; repr. Hildesheim and New York, 1969)
Tilley	M. P. Tilley, *A Dictionary of the Proverbs in England in the Sixteenth and Seventeenth Centuries* (Ann Arbor, 1950)

(ii) *Journals*

BJRL	*Bulletin of the John Rylands Library*
CP	*Classical Philology*
Crit. Q.	*Critical Quarterly*
E. & S.	*Essays and Studies by Members of the English Association*
E. in C.	*Essays in Criticism*
ELH	*ELH, A Journal of English Literary History*
ELN	*English Language Notes*
ELR	*English Literary Renaissance*
Eng. Misc.	*English Miscellany*
ES	*English Studies*
Expl.	*Explicator*
HLB	*Harvard Library Bulletin*
HSNPL	*Harvard Studies and Notes in Philology and Literature*
JEGP	*Journal of English and Germanic Philology*
JWCI	*Journal of the Warburg and Courtauld Institutes*
MLN	*Modern Language Notes*
MLR	*Modern Language Review*
MP	*Modern Philology*
NQ	*Notes and Queries*
PBSA	*Papers of the Bibliographical Society of America*

PMLA	PMLA, Publication of the Modern Language Association of America
PQ	Philological Quarterly
RES	Review of English Studies
RMS	Renaissance and Modern Studies
RN	Renaissance News
RQ	Renaissance Quarterly
SEL	Studies in English Literature 1500–1900
SLI	Studies in the Literary Imagination
SP	Studies in Philology
SR	Studies in the Renaissance
TLS	Times Literary Supplement

(iii) Works by Jonson

Alch.	The Alchemist (1610)
Augurs	The Masque of Augurs (1622)
Beauty	The Masque of Beauty (1608)
BF	Bartholomew Fair (1614)
Blackness	The Masque of Blackness (1605)
Cat.	Catiline (1611)
Chall. Tilt	A Challenge at Tilt (1613/14)
Chlor.	Chloridia (1631)
Christmas	Christmas his Masque (1616)
C. is A.	The Case is Altered (written c.1598)
Conv. Dr.	Conversations with William Drummond of Hawthornden (1618/19)
CR	Cynthia's Revels (1600)
D. is A.	The Devil is an Ass (1616)
Disc.	Timber, or Discoveries (1640 Folio)
EMI	Every Man in his Humour (1598 version in 1601 Quarto; revision in 1616 Folio)*
EMO	Every Man out of his Humour (1599)
Eng. Gram.	The English Grammar (1640 Folio)
Ent. Alth.	The Entertainment at Althorpe (1603)
Ent. K. & Q. Theob.	The Entertainment of the King and Queen at Theobalds (1607)
Ent. Welb.	The King's Entertainment at Welbeck (1633)
Epig.	Epigrams (1616 Folio)
For.	The Forest (1616 Folio)
Fort. Is.	The Fortunate Isles, and their Union (1625)
G.A. Rest.	The Golden Age Restored (1615)
Gyp. Met.	The Gypsies Metamorphosed (1621)
Haddington	The Haddington Masque (1608)
Hym.	Hymenaei (1606)

* All references to the 1616 Folio text, unless otherwise specified.

King's Ent.	The King's Entertainment in Passing to his Coronation (1604)
Leg. Conv.	Leges Convivales
Love Freed	Love Freed from Ignorance and Folly (1611)
Love's Tr.	Love's Triumph Through Callipolis (1631)
Love's Welc. Bols.	Love's Welcome at Bolsover (1634)
LR	Love Restored (1612)
Merc. Vind.	Mercury Vindicated from the Alchemists at Court (1616)
ML	The Magnetic Lady (1632)
Nept. Tr.	Neptune's Triumph for the Return of Albion (1623/4)
NI	The New Inn (1629)
Oberon	Oberon, the Fairy Prince (1611)
Panegyre	A Panegyre on the King's Opening of Parliament (1604)
P.H. Barr.	The Speeches at Prince Henry's Barriers (1609)
Pleas. Rec.	Pleasure Reconciled to Virtue (1618)
Poet.	Poetaster (1601)
Queens	The Masque of Queens (1609)
Sad Shep.	The Sad Shepherd (unfinished)
Sej.	Sejanus (1603)
S. of N.	The Staple of News (1626)
Songs	Songs and Poems from the Plays and Masques*
SW	Epicoene, or the Silent Woman (1609)
Time Vind.	Time Vindicated to Himself and to his Honours (1623)
T. of T.	A Tale of a Tub (1633)
Und.	The Underwood (1640 Folio)
UV	Ungathered Verse
Vis. Delight	The Vision of Delight (1617)
Volp.	Volpone (1605 or 1606)

(iv) Editions of Jonson and Critical Studies

Castelain	Ben Jonson, Discoveries, edited by Maurice Castelain (Paris and London, n.d. [1906])
Chalfant	F. C. Chalfant, Ben Jonson's London (Athens, Ohio, 1978)
Creaser	Ben Jonson, Volpone or the Fox, edited by John W. Creaser, London Mediaeval and Renaissance Series (London, etc., 1978)
Gifford	The Works of Ben Jonson, edited by W. Gifford, 9 vols. (London, 1816)
Gifford/Cunningham	The Works of Ben Jonson, edited by W. Gifford, with introduction and appendices by Lieut.-Col. F. Cunningham, 9 vols. (London, 1875)
Gollancz	Ben Jonson, Timber: or Discoveries, ed. I. Gollancz (London, 1898)

* This edition.

H & S   *Ben Jonson*, edited by C. H. Herford and Percy and
                 Evelyn Simpson, 11 vols. (Oxford, 1925–52)

Hunter   *The Complete Poetry of Ben Jonson*, edited by William B.
                 Hunter, Jun. (New York, 1963)

Mares   Ben Jonson, *The Alchemist*, edited by F. H. Mares, The
                 Revel Plays (London, 1967)

Miller   Ben Jonson, *Selected Poems*, edited by Anthony Miller
                 (Sydney University, Sydney, 1981)

Newdigate   *The Poems of Ben Jonson*, edited by Bernard H. Newdi-
                 gate (Oxford, 1936)

Parfitt   Ben Jonson, *The Complete Poems*, edited by George
                 Parfitt, Penguin English Poets (Harmondsworth,
                 1975)

Patterson   *Ben Jonson's Conversations with William Drummond of
                 Hawthornden*, edited by R. F. Patterson (London, etc.,
                 1923)

Peterson   Richard S. Peterson, *Imitation and Praise in the Poems of
                 Ben Jonson* (New Haven and London, 1981)

Rea   Ben Jonson, *Volpone*, edited by John D. Rea, Yale
                 Studies in English, 59 (New Haven, 1919)

Schelling   Ben Jonson, *Timber, or Discoveries*, edited by Felix E.
                 Schelling (Boston, 1892)

Trimpi   Wesley Trimpi, *Ben Jonson's Poems: A Study of the Plain
                 Style* (Stanford, 1962)

Whalley   *The Works of Ben Jonson*, edited by Peter Whalley, 7
                 vols. (London, 1756)

Wilkes   Ben Jonson, *The Complete Plays*, edited by G. A. Wilkes,
                 4 vols. (based on the Herford and Simpson edition)
                 (Oxford, 1981–2)

Other editions consulted in the preparation of this edition include, for *Volpone*,
those of J. B. Bamborough (1963), Philip Brockbank (1968), David Cook (1962),
Jay L. Halio (1968), Michael Jamieson (1966), Alvin B. Kernan (1962), and A.
Sale (1951). R. B. Parker's edition (1983) appeared while this edition was at
press. For *The Alchemist*: the editions of J. B. Bamborough (1967), Douglas
Brown (1966), Michael Jamieson (1966), Alvin B. Kernan (1974), and J. B.
Steane (1967). For the poems: the editions of John Hollander (1961) and G. B.
Johnston (1954).

NOTES

Jonson wrote *Volpone* in a period of five weeks, as he reveals with a touch of pleasure in the play's prologue; such speed ran counter to his alleged slowness of composition. The play was performed almost at once by the King's Men at the Globe Theatre, probably with John Lowin in the title role and Richard Burbage as Mosca. According to the title-page of the 1616 Folio, *Volpone* was 'acted in the year 1605'. The discussion between Peregrine and Sir Politic Would-be at the opening of the second act seemingly refers, however, to events which took place in January 1606. It seems likely, then, that '1605' in the title-page is a dating according to the legal year, which ran until 24 March, and that *Volpone* was first performed around mid March 1606. (Arguments for an earlier dating of mid 1605 have been advanced on account of apparent borrowings from *Volpone* in plays by Marston and Middleton, but it is not easy to tell who borrowed from whom.)

Volpone was performed with evident success at Oxford and Cambridge in 1606 or 1607, and revived at frequent intervals throughout the seventeenth and eighteenth centuries. In the late eighteenth century *Volpone* disappeared from the popular repertory. Since its revival by the Phoenix Society in 1921, however, it has become the most frequently revived of all non-Shakespearian plays of this period; notable Volpones in recent times include Donald Wolfit, Leo McKern, and Paul Scofield.

While the plot of *Volpone* is largely original, Jonson could have found in Horace, Juvenal, Pliny, and—more especially—in Lucian some of the ingredients from which to develop his comedy of legacy-hunting (H & S, ii. 49–65). Occasional touches are borrowed from Erasmus. Popular beast lore and fable underlie both plot and sub-plot, as several scholars have shown (see in particular Jonas A. Barish, *MP* li (1953), 83–92; R. B. Parker, *Renaissance Drama*, NS vii, ed. Joel H. Kaplan (Evanston, 1976), pp. 3–42).

Volpone was published by Thomas Thorpe (printer: George Eld) in a Quarto edition dated 1607, and again in the 1616 Folio of William Stansby; both editions were approved by Jonson. The variants between Quarto (Q) and Folio (F) texts are relatively few; the more significant are recorded in the notes of this edition. F adds nearly thirty stage directions, which are printed here within round brackets. Both Q and F title-pages carry a tag from Horace's *Ars Poetica*, I. 334: 'simul et iucunda et idonea dicere vitae', from a passage Jonson himself translated: 'Poets would either profit or delight, | Or mixing sweet and fit, teach life the right.'

[Epistle Dedicatory] *equal.* (i) Of equal merit; (ii) impartial (Lat. *aequus*). *himself.* Q continues: 'There follows an epistle, if you dare venture on the length'. 1 *wit.* Creative intelligence. *presently.* immediately. 3 *that.* i.e. that it is true. 4–5 *provide . . . accidents.* Look after these incidental matters. 6 *benefit.* (i) kindness; (ii) good name. 8 *act.* i.e. approval of the play. 9 *professors.* practitioners.

10 *hear so ill.* Are so ill spoken of. *there . . . subject.* i.e. the work must be justifiable in itself. **11** *forehead.* confidence. **12** *mistress.* i.e. poetry. **14** *petulancy.* insolence. **20** *good man.* Strabo, *Geographica*, I. ii. 5. **20-7** Drawing on Horace, *Epist.* II. i. 126-31, and Minturno, *De Poeta* (1559), p. 8. **20** *inform.* Mould; instruct. **25** *manners.* Cf. *Disc.* 2417-19. **30** *abused name. Disc.* 284-5. **34** *abortive features.* i.e. botched plays. **37 ff.** Cf. Erasmus's defence of *The Praise of Folly* in his letter to Martin Dorp, 1515. **42** *youngest infant.* Probably *Sejanus* (1603), for which Jonson had been brought before the Privy Council. **43** *teeth.* Like the future Richard III: *3 Henry VI*, V. vi. 75. **44** *politics.* Worldly-wise schemers (F 'politiques', also recalling the name of the opportunist and moderate French political party of the 1570s). **46** *allowed.* By the Master of the Revels. **47** *entirely mine.* The co-authored plays *The Isle of Dogs*, *Eastward Ho!*, and *Sejanus* fared less happily. **48** *particular.* Cf. *Epig.* Dedn. 20. **48** *mimic.* Actor; malicious wit (*Epig.* 115. 28). **54** *obnoxious to construction.* Open to misinterpretation. **55** *Application.* Interpreting fiction as veiled fact; cf. *Alch.* Prologue, 19; *Epig.* Dedn. 4-6. **61** *raked up.* Raked over. **63** *styles.* pens. **64** *graved.* A pun: buried, engraved (cf. 'entrench'). **66** *providing.* foreseeing. **69** *exploded.* Hissed off the stage. **71** *Sibi . . . odit.* 'Whereupon everyone is afraid for himself, though untouched, and hates you', *Sat.* II. i. 23. **72-3** *And . . . sports.* i.e. the poetaster can justly be blamed for wantonly arousing such anger. **74** *misc'line interludes. Ludi miscelli*, variety entertainments. **75** *filth.* Q 'garbage'. **77** *prolepses.* anachronisms. **81** *name.* 'Poet'; remembering also Dekker's mockery of Jonson under the name of 'Horace' in *Satiromastix* (1601). **84** *vernaculous.* scurrilous. **88** *crown.* Recalling the coronation of poets; cf. *Epig.* 17. 4. **90** *reduce.* Bring back. **93** *comic law.* Possibly recalling Aristotle on comedy, *Poetics*, ch. 5. **94** *turning back to.* breaking. *promise.* i.e. to restore the ancient forms. **95-6** *of industry.* deliberately. **97** *faculty.* facility. **100** *goings-out.* conclusions. **102** *mulcted.* punished. **105** *elsewhere.* Perhaps in the commentary on Horace's *Ars Poetica*, lost in the fire of 1623 (*Und.* 43. 89-91); but cf. also *Disc.* 1039 ff. **106-7** *the understanding.* The discerning readers: cf. *Epig.* 1, etc. **114** *affected.* liked. **118** *genus irritabile.* Peevish lot: Horace, *Epist.* II. ii. 102. **122** *mankind.* Q continues: 'From my house in the Blackfriars this 11 of February 1607'.

The Persons of the Play *Volpone.* 'An old fox, and old reynard, an old crafty, sly, subtle companion; sneaking, lurking, wily deceiver' (John Florio, *A World of Words*, 1598). *Magnifico.* magnate.

Mosca. 'Any kind of fly' (Florio). *Parasite.* Flatterer and hanger-on; see Mosca's account, III. i. 7-33.

Voltore. 'A ravenous bird', 'a greedy cormorant' (Florio). The association with lawyers was traditional: cf. *Und.* 33. 9.

Corbaccio. 'A filthy great raven' (Florio).

Corvino. Crow; 'of a raven's nature or colour' (Florio, *Queen Anna's New World of Words*, 1611).

Politic Would-be. 'Politic' suggesting (i) Machiavellian scheming; (ii) temporizing and worldly wisdom (French *politiques*; see Epist. Ded. 44 n.); (iii) as 'Pol', a parrot-like loquacity.

Peregrine. (i) traveller; (ii) hunting falcon.

Bonario. 'Debonair, honest, good, uncorrupt' (Florio, 1598).
Celia. Cf. Lat. *caelum,* 'sky, heaven'.

The Argument The acrostic form is imitated from Plautus. **2** *state.* estate.
5 *told.* exposed. **7** *sold.* enslaved.

Prologue **1** *yet.* Q 'God'. **4** *reason.* Cf. *Und.* 29. 53. **6** *scope.* aim. **8** *To . . .*
pleasure. Horace, *Ars Poetica,* 333–46. **9** *some.* e.g. Marston, *The Dutch Courtesan,*
prologue. **12** *a year.* Dekker's gibe in *Satiromastix* (1601), v. ii. 217.
17–18 *coadjutor . . . tutor.* Summarizing the possible kinds of dramatic collaboration: a
'coadjutor' was an equal partner, a 'novice' an apprentice, a 'journeyman' a
literary hack, while a 'tutor' supervised and corrected another's work. **21** *custards.*
Mocking the opening of Marston's *Satire,* ii, 'Let custards quake, my rage must
freely run'; and recalling foolery with custards at Lord Mayors' feasts. **23** *gull.*
dupe. *old ends.* Tags; cf. *Epig.* 53. **26** *As . . . faction.* As if the inmates of the
madhouse had been recruited. **31** *laws.* That the represented action should occur
on the same day in the same place; that characters be not of high rank, and be
consistent to type. **33** *gall and copperas.* Both bitter, both used in ink-making, as
'salt' (l. 34; i.e. 'wit') is not.

I. i. **3** *world's soul.* In Platonic and Neoplatonic thought, the divine force
animating the universe. **5** *Ram.* Aries, which the sun enters on 21 March. **8** *flame*
by night. Pindar, *Olympian Ode,* I. i. 2. **10** *son of Sol.* Alchemists held gold to be a
child of the sun; 'sol' is also a coin (cf. IV. v. 97). **14–20** Jonson draws on Seneca,
Epist. cxv. 12–14. **15** *that age.* Yet the Golden Age, as described by Ovid (*Metam.* i.
89–122) and other 'wise poets', lacked gold. **22** *tongues.* Cf. *Timon of Athens,* IV. iii.
386. **23** *all things.* Cf. *UV* 3.5 ff. **24** *price.* Christians are 'bought with a price' (1
Cor. 6: 20; 7: 23), namely, the sacrifice of Christ, sold by Judas for thirty pieces of
silver. **25–8** Cf. Horace, *Sat.* II. iii. 94–8. **28–9** *Riches . . . nature.* Reversing Prov.
16: 16, 'How much better is it to get wisdom than gold!' (Creaser). **31** *purchase.*
acquisition. **37** *subtle.* Intricate. Venetian glass was famous. **39** *turn.* exchange.
43 *purge.* Require a laxative, i.e. suffer. **53–63** Cf. Horace, *Sat.* III. iii. 111–19.
58 *Romagnía.* Rumney, a sweet Greek wine. *Candian.* Malmsey from Candy (Crete).
66 *Hold thee.* Keep this for yourself. **71** *cocker up my genius.* Indulge my appetite
(Lat. *genio indulgere*). **76** *clients.* Dependants upon a patron. **88** *bearing them in*
hand. Leading them on. **89** *cherry.* As in the game of bob-cherry.

I. ii. **1** *gamesters.* Actors; playful people. **4** *false pace.* The old-fashioned four-
stress line of the morality plays. **6** *Pythagoras.* Who believed in the transmigration
of souls. The present humorous account of the transmigration of his own soul is
based on Diogenes Laertius's *Lives of Eminent Philosophers,* VIII. i. 4, 5, and
Lucian's dialogue *Gallus* (*The Cock*)—whose moral, that poverty is to be preferred
to riches, Mosca tactfully suppresses. **8** *fast and loose.* Slippery, shifty (from a
betting game played with a belt and dagger). **9** *Aethalides.* Herald of the
Argonauts; his father, Mercury, had bestowed upon him the gift of perfect
memory. **12** *Euphorbus.* The Trojan who first wounded Patroclus, *Iliad,* xvii.
13 *cuckold.* Menelaus. **14** *Hermotimus.* Greek prophet of Clazomenae, *fl. c.* 500 BC.
charta. Perhaps, Lucian. **16** *Pyrrhus.* 'A fisherman of Delos', according to

Diogenes Laertius, VIII. i. 5. **17** *Sophist.* Pythagoras. **19** *Aspasia.* Pericles' mistress. *meretrix.* courtesan. **21** *Crates.* Of Boeotia, fourth-century BC disciple of Diogenes the Cynic. *itself.* The 'charta' of l. 14; or the soul in Androgyno. **24** *cock.* The narrator in Lucian's *Gallus* (l. 6 n). **26** *one . . . quater.* Harmony for Pythagoras derived from numbers: 'quater' was an equilateral triangle (or 'trigon', l. 27) made up of ten dots, four to each side, and numerologically significant. **27** *golden thigh.* A legendary attribute. **30** *reformation.* Jonson was still a Catholic at this time. **33** *forbid' meats.* Which included fish and beans. **34** *Carthusian.* Members of this order ate mainly fish. **35** *silence.* Which Pythagoreans maintained for five years; cf. *Disc.* 389–90. **43** *precise . . . brother.* Puritan. **46** *nativity.* Puritan term for Christmas. **47** *nation.* group (cf. l. 66). **66–81** Cf. Erasmus, *The Praise of Folly*, 436 c. **72** *ladies' . . . pleasure.* Proverbial: Tilley, F528. **73** *Tongue.* Cf. *Disc.* 397–9 and n. *bauble.* (i) mace; (ii) phallus; (iii) talk, babble (Q, F 'bable'). **75** *slaughter.* retribution. **88–9** *vulture.* Voltore. *kite.* Lady Would-be. *Raven.* Corvino. *gor-crow.* Carrion crow, i.e. Corbaccio. **96** *gaping crow.* Horace, *Sat.* II. v. 55–7. **105** *foot-cloths.* horses' drapery. **126** *posture.* imposture.

I. iii. 'This and the following scenes are really a Roman *salutatio*, i.e. the morning visit of clients to their patron so often referred to and described by the satirists' (Rea). The 98-year-old Polystratus in the ninth of Lucian's *Dialogues of the Dead* reports how he controlled legacy-hunters in a similar fashion. **10** *St Mark.* i.e. a goldsmith's shop in St Mark's Square. **22** *Hath taste.* Can be sampled. **35** *write me.* Names of servants were written in a household book. **52–66** Partly prompted by Cornelius Agrippa's *De Incertitudine et Vanitate Scientiarum*, (1530; trs. 1569: *Of the Vanity and Uncertainty of Arts and Sciences*), ch. 93, and Horace, *Sat.* II. v. 33–4. **63** *perplexed.* intricate. **66** *cecchine.* Or sequin, a Venetian gold coin. **78** *business.* Cf. *Epig.* 28. 7.

I. iv. **11** *slumbers.* dozes. **20 ff.** Cf. Cornelius Agrippa, *De Incertitudine*, ch. 83; and Jonson, *Epig.* 13. **23–4** *physician . . . heir.* Proverbial wisdom: Tilley, F483. **28** *conceive.* understand. **47–8** Mosca describes what were popularly thought to be the terminal symptoms of a fatal illness. **49** *resolvèd.* slackened. **52** *scotomy.* Dizziness and dimness of sight. **68** *prevent him.* Beat him to it. **70** *weigh down.* outweigh. **73** *aurum . . . potabile.* Palpable, if not drinkable, gold. Gold was drunk medicinally. **80** *venture.* i.e. the gold. **96** *colour.* pretence. **124** *Rook go with you.* May you be rooked. **128** *blessing.* As Jacob did Esau, Gen. 27. **140** *give 'em words.* Spin them a tale (Lat. *dare verba*). **142** *punishment.* Seneca, *Epist.* 115. 16. **144–50** Cf. Pliny, *Nat. Hist.* vii. 167–8. **156** *Aeson.* Jason's father, restored by Medea, Ovid, *Metam.* vii. 162–293.

I. v. **9** *orient.* Eastern pearls were especially lustrous. **22–3** *weeping . . . visor.* A traditional sentiment: cf. Horace, *Sat.* II. v. 103 ('visor' = mask). **39–43** See Juvenal, *Sat.* x. 232–6. **46** *fable.* gossip. **48** *father of his family.* Possibly echoing Martial's irony about another paterfamilias, I. lxxxiv. **57–9** Juvenal, *Sat.* x. 191–5. **63–4** Ibid., 214–15. **63** *culverin.* hand-gun. **66** *draught.* privy. **101** *bold English.* The extreme restrictions placed upon the movements of Venetian wives were noted by Coryate and other English travellers. **104** *strange.* foreign. **105** *face.*

looks. **109** *O' the first year.* Unflawed (like a sacrificial lamb). **110–11** *skin. . . lilies.* Cf. *Und.* 2. iv. 21–30. **113** *blood.* passion. **126** *he.* Corvino. **129** *shape.* Physical appearance (*OED*, 6b); Volpone's disguise and role (*OED*, 7, 8) will vary.

II. i. **1** *wise. . . soil.* Tilley, M426. **4** *salt.* wanton. **10** *minds and manners. Odyssey,* i, opening; cf. Horace, *Epist.* i. 2; Jonson, *Epig.* 128. 2. **12** *height.* latitude. **13** *quote.* note. **14** *licence.* passport. **17** *lord ambassador.* Sir Henry Wotton, England's ambassador to Venice 1604–12. **18** *vents our climate.* Comes from our country. **22** *raven.* A bird of ill omen. *should build.* Is said to have built. **28** *tires.* Attires; head-dresses. **29** *courtesans.* Of interest to English visitors: cf. *UV* 10. 18–19 n. **30–1** *spider. . . flower.* Tilley, B208. **34** *whelping.* As a lioness in the Tower had done in August 1604 and February 1605. Cf. *Julius Caesar*, II. i. 17. **36** *fires.* Reported in January 1605. **37** *new star.* Discovered by Kepler, October 1604. **38** *meteors.* Commonly regarded as ill omens. **40, 46** *porpoises; whale.* On 19 January 1606 a porpoise was taken at West Ham, 1½ miles up river; a few days later, a whale was seen in the Thames 8 miles from London. Jonson may be indirectly satirizing John Stow, who records such 'monstrous observations' as these in his *Chronicle*: see *Conv. Dr.* 525. **49** *Stode fleet.* The English Merchant Adventurers' fleet at Stode (now Stade), north-west of Hamburg. **50** *Archdukes.* (Q 'Arch-duke') the Infanta Isabella and her husband Albert of Austria, rulers of the Spanish Netherlands. **51** *Spinola's whale.* Rumoured 'secret weapon' of the Spanish commander in the Netherlands; it would drown London 'by snuffing up the Thames and spouting it upon the City' (Herle, 1654). **53** *Stone.* His death-date is unknown; he was alive—and whipped—in March 1605. **70** *cabbages.* Then regularly imported from Holland. **73** *pome-citrons.* Citrons, lemons, and limes. **76** *ordinary.* inn. **77** *advertisement.* information. **78** *statesman.* agent. **82** *character.* cipher. **90** *Mamuluchi.* Mamelukes, Caucasian slaves who seized power in Egypt in 1254 and became the ruling class (they were not baboons, and not from China). **94** *advices.* dispatches. **95** *coat.* party. **113** *vulgar grammar.* There were several Italian grammars in English available; some contained tips for travellers. **114** *cried.* Chanted; i.e. taught. **118** *ingenuous race.* Noble descent.

II. ii. **2** *mount a bank.* Italian *monta in banco*; Venetian mountebanks touted their wares from a *banco* or platform. They are described in detail by Thomas Coryate, *Crudities* (1611). **3** *dear.* noble. **5** *quacksalvers.* quacks. **6** *venting.* vending. **14** *lewd.* ignorant. **17** *utter.* sell. **22** *Scoto of Mantua.* Leader of a troup of Mantuan actors; known in England as a 'juggler'. **28** *zany.* Mountebank's assistant. **36** *Procuratiá.* The Procuratie Vecchie on the north side of the Piazza di San Marco, with its arcade of fifty arches: residence of the Procurators of St Mark. **39–40** *cold on my feet.* Doing poorly and selling cheaply; cf. *UV* 34. 67. **42–3** *Buttone.* unidentified. **43** *'sforzato.* prisoner. **44** *Bembo's . . . .* Pietro Bembo (1470–1547), the humanist. The pause implies 'mistress'. **45** *attached.* Stuck to. **46** *ground ciarlitani.* Inferior charlatans operating without a platform. **48** *activity* (i) tumbling; (ii) sex. **49** *Tabarine.* A zany of this name (= 'short cloak') visited France in 1572. **55** *turdy . . . fartical.* An Aristophanic compound; 'facy' prob. = impudent. **57** *'scartoccios.* Apothecaries' wrappers. **59** *oppilations.* obstructions. **66** *canaglia.* rabble. **71** *Terra Firma.* Mainland Venice. **73** *splendidous.* Splendid (common variant). **74** *magazines.* storehouses. *moscadelli.* muscat. **76** *cocted.* boiled. **85** *humours.*

According to ancient physiological theory, the four humours—blood, phlegm, choler, black choler (melancholy)—corresponded to the four elements, air, water, fire, earth—themselves variously compounded of hot and cold, moist and dry. Health and temperament were determined by their balance. **88** *crude.* upset. **91** *fricace.* massage. *vertigine.* vertigo. **92** *mal caduco.* epilepsy. **94** *tremor cordia.* palpitations. *retired nerves.* Shrunken sinews. **95** *strangury.* Painful urination. *hernia ventosa.* hernia. **96** *iliaca passio.* 'Pain and wringing of the small guts' (Holland's *Pliny* (1601), ii. 39). **97** *hypocondriaca.* The hypochondria (spleen, liver, etc.) was seen as the source of melancholy. **101** *Aesculapian.* After Aesculapius, classical god of medicine. **102** *Zan Fritada.* A well-known zany; *fritate* = pancake. Volpone addresses Nano. **106** *Broughton's.* Hugh Broughton (1549–1612), Puritan divine and rabbinical scholar; see *Alch.* II. iii. 237–8. **107** *Hippocrates* (fifth century BC) and *Galen* (second century BC), the originator and exponent, respectively, of the theory of humours. **114** *Tobacco, sassafras.* Used medicinally. **115** *guacum.* Drug from the guaiacum tree. **116** *Lully.* Or Lull, *c.* 1235–1315, Catalan philosopher, linguist, mystic, missionary; but not (contrary to later popular belief) an alchemist. Cf. *Alch.* II. v. 8. **117** *Gonswart.* Unidentified; guesses include (i) Johan Wessel Gansfort, fifteenth-century Dutch theologian; (ii) Berthold Schwarz, fourteenth-century Franciscan friar of Fribourg, inventor of guns; (iii) Cornelius Hamsfort, sixteenth-century physician to Christian III of Denmark. **118** *Paracelsus.* Theophrastus of Hohenheim (1490–1541); said to have kept his medical secrets in the pommel of his sword. **125** *signiory . . . Sanità.* The 'health-masters' who licensed physicians and mountebanks. **136** *simples.* Separate herbs. **138** *decoction.* Boiling down to extract essence. **139** *in fumo.* In vapour; cf. *Alch.* IV. v. 58. **149** *balloo.* Or balloon, a Venetian ball-game. **158** *Montalto.* Felice Peretti became Cardinal di Montalto in 1570 and Pope Sixtus V in 1585. *Fernese.* Alessandro Fernese, Pope Paul III in 1534. **159** *Tuscany.* The dukedom was created in 1569 by Pope Pius V, and conferred upon Cosimo de' Medici. *gossip.* Godfather; intimate acquaintance. **167** *gazets.* Coin worth about 3s. 4d. **170** *coil.* fuss. **175** *Moist of hand.* Sign of sexual vitality; cf. *Venus and Adonis*, 143. **179** *aches.* Disyllabic ('aitches'); i.e. venereal disease. **185** *ducat.* Worth about 4s. 8d. **186** *moccenigo.* Worth about 9d. **187** *banner.* Advertising the mountebank's wares. **188** *bagatine.* Worth about one-third of a farthing. **190** *handkerchiefs.* With money knotted in a corner. **193** *pistolet.* Spanish gold coin worth about 17s. **195** *prevented you.* Beaten you to it. **212** *sophisticated.* adulterated. **215** *virginal jacks.* Wooden uprights at the back of a keyboard instrument, fitted with quills which pluck the strings when the keys are struck.

II. iii.   **1** *Spite.* Q 'Blood'. **2** *scene.* Corvino sees the incident in terms of a *commedia dell'arte* scene, which might similarly be set in a street overlooked by private houses, with characters appearing at windows. Flaminio was the stock *commedia* lover (Flaminio Scala being a leading *commedia* actor); Franciscina was the serving maid, and Pantalone di Besogniosi the aged, jealous, frequently cuckolded pantaloon.

II. iv.   **6** *ambitious.* rising. **9** *liver.* Seat of the passions. **22** *devotion.* disposal. **24** *crown.* Punning on the name of the coin. **34** *epilogue.* i.e. the beating; but also covertly hinting at Mosca's larger plans.

II. v. **4** *dole.* Repertoire (lit. 'share'). **10** *call* . . . *whistle.* For luring birds. **12** *toadstone.* Jewel supposedly taken from toad's head. **13** *cope-stitch.* Used for the edge of a cope. **14** *tilt-feather.* For tilting-helmet. **15** *starched beard.* A fashion censured in *Disc.* 1434. **21** *cithern.* Guitar-like instrument. *lady vanity.* Stock character in the morality plays. **22** *dealer.* i.e. sexually. *virtuous.* Ironically playing on 'virtuoso'. **24** *Dutchman.* Proverbially dull (Tilley, D654) and phlegmatic. **43** *point.* appoint. **44** *turn.* Cf. *Antony and Cleopatra*, II. v. 59, 'the best turn i' th' bed'. **56** *circle's safety.* Within which a conjuror prudently remained while raising supernatural spirits. For the innuendo, cf. II. vi. 65 and *Romeo and Juliet*, II. i. 24–6. **57** *lock.* chastity belt. **58** *backwards.* At the back of the house; with a double entendre at ll. 60–1. **70** *anatomy.* Topic of moral analysis; yet Corvino's threatened dissection may also be literal: cf. III. vii. 95–106.

II. vi. **14** *ostería.* inn. *tumbling.* In a double sense. **19** *sod.* boiled. **34** *young woman.* Recalling the story of David and Abishag, 1 Kings 1: 1–4. **42** *delate.* report. **49** *Prevent.* forestall. **59** *God's so.* God's soul; probably a polite variant of Italian *cazzo*, 'penis'. **64** *fever.* From Juvenal, *Sat.* x. 217–18. **71** *blood.* (i) passions; (ii) family: a crucial ambiguity. **84** *make your count.* Depend upon it.

II. vii. **3** *light.* Reviled as 'bawdy' by Corvino, II. v. 50.

III. i. **4** *whimsy.* whirling. **6** *subtle.* Delicate; supple; wily (Gen. 3: 1). **9** *clot-poles.* Thick heads. **10** *mystery.* craft. *science.* Academic discipline. **11** *liberally.* (i) widely; (ii) humanely. **13–22** Cf. *Disc.* 1601–50. **17** *bait.* (i) tempt; (ii) feed. **20** *fleer.* Smile obsequiously. **28** *humour.* whim. *occasion.* opportunity. **29** *visor.* Mask; i.e. personality.

III. ii. **2** *bound.* On my way. **6** *mate.* fellow (contemptuous). **14** *unequal.* unfair. **21** *careful.* hard-won. **22** *obsequy.* obsequiousness. **24.** *Out* . . . *observance.* Solely through service. **32** *Prove.* endure. **39** *main.* great. **45** *mere.* utter. **49** *for* . . . *respect.* For which reason alone. **65** *common* . . . *earth.* Of unknown parentage; a nobody.

III. iii. **4** *whether.* which. **5** *delicates.* Objects of pleasure. **15** *feat.* neat. **23** *return.* Playing on the commercial sense: 'profit'.

III. iv. Lady Would-be's speeches derive partly from Libanius of Antioch's *De Muliere Loquaci.* **2** *band.* collar, ruff. **7** *petulant.* insolent. **17** *tire.* head-dress. **20** *bird-eyed.* frightened. **32** *curious.* fastidious. **37** *fucus.* cosmetic. **38** *entertainément.* As at l. 90 ('Montaignié': Q), the added syllable indicates Lady Would-be's pronunciation. **47** *golden mediocrity.* Golden mean: a significant solecism. **51** *passion of the heart.* heartburn. **52–65** Popular remedies for diverse ailments, indiscriminately proposed. *Tincture of gold*: see I. iv. 73 n.; *elecampane*: a yellow-flowered perennial used as tonic; *Burnt silk* and *scarlet-cloth*: used against smallpox. **74** *concent.* harmony. **76** *poet.* Sophocles, *Ajax*, 293. **80** *Guerrini.* G. B. Guarini (1537–1612), author of *Il Pastor Fido* (1590). **81** *Cieco di Hadria.* Luigi Groto (1541–85), 'the blind man of Adria', poet, dramatist, and translator. **94** *trusted* . . . *much.* i.e. left much for English writers to borrow. **97** *pictures.* Marcantonio Raimondi's engravings (after Giulio Romano) for Pietro Aretino's *Sonnetti lussoriosi* (1523). **101–2** *passions* . . . *reason. Disc.* 31–3. **111** *Plato.* A perversion of his ideas. **125** *coaetanei.* Of the same age.

III. v. **7** *cockpit.* There were three in London, noisy with cries of wagerers. **9–10** Cf. Juvenal, *Sat.* vi. 338–42. **24** *lightly.* often. **36–8** *primero.* Popular card-game; *go*: wager; *draw*: take from pack; *encounter*: (i) winning card; (ii) sexual meeting.

III. vii. **32** *train.* trick. **35** *means.* (i) Financial resources; (ii) stratagem. **43–5** Cf. Juvenal, *Sat.* x. 228–32. **48** *jig.* trifle. **60** *prints.* III. iv. 97 n. **61** *quirk.* twist. **88–9** *fortune... reverence.* Cf. ll. 187–8 below; and *Und.* 26. 23–4. **95** *Eat... coals.* Like Portia, Brutus's wife. **99** *rochet.* red gurnard. **100–6** Varying and intensifying Tarquin's threat to Lucretia. **104** *aquafortis.* nitric acid. **105** *corsives.* corrosives. **118** *errant.* (i) wandering; (ii) arrant. **119** *Crocodile.* Popularly thought to lure its victims with tears. **126** *quit.* acquit. **127** *coming.* acquiescent. **137** *circumstance.* Trifle, non-essential. **144** *cope-man.* dealer. **153** *blue Proteus.* The sea-god (*caeruleus Proteus*, Virgil, *Georgics*, iv. 388) who could change shape at will. *hornèd flood.* The shape-changing river-god Achelous ('horned' as an ox in his fight with Hercules). **161** *Valois.* Henri, Duke of Anjou, King of Poland and later France; entertained by the Doge and senators of Venice, 1574. **162** *Antinous.* (i) Beautiful Bithynian youth, favourite of Emperor Hadrian; (ii) more probably, one of Penelope's suitors in the *Odyssey*. **165–83** Cf. *For.* 5; from Catullus, v, *Vivamus, mea Lesbia*: 'Let us live, my Lesbia, and love, and value at one farthing all the talk of crabbed old men. Suns may set and rise again. For us, when the short light has once set, remains to be slept the sleep of one unbroken night. Give me a thousand kisses, then a hundred, then another thousand, then a second hundred, then yet another thousand, then a hundred. Then, when we have made up many thousands, we will confuse our counting, that we may not know the reckoning, nor any malicious person blight them with evil eye, when he knows that our kisses are so many.' A musical setting was printed in Alphonso Ferrabosco's *Airs* (1609) (see *Epig.* 130). See F. W. Sternfeld in *Studies in the English Renaissance Drama*, ed. J. W. Bennett *et al.* (London, 1961), pp. 310–21; J. P. Cutts, *NQ* cciii (1958), 217–19; Mary Chan, *Music in the Theatre of Ben Jonson* (Oxford, 1980), pp. 89–98. **175** *toys.* trifles. **177** *household spies.* Cf. 'His Parting From Her', formerly attributed to Donne, l. 101; Yeats, 'Parting', l. 3. **184** *serene.* Noxious mist. **192** *Egyptian queen.* Cleopatra, who drank a dissolved pearl at a banquet; cf. *Alch.* II. ii. 76. **194** *St Mark.* Patron saint of Venice. A large carbuncle was kept in the Treasury of St Mark; another adorned the Doge's mitre. **195** *Lollia Paulina.* Caligula's wife, heiress of the plunder of provinces; Pliny describes her lavishly bejewelled, *Nat. Hist.* ix. 117. **213** *July-flowers.* gillyflowers. **215** *panther's breath.* Thought to entice victims. **220** *antic.* Grotesque dance. **223** *Erycine.* Venus. **229** *Sophy.* Shah. **236–9** Cf. Catullus, vii. 9–12 (see *For.* 6.12–22 n.). **239** *pined.* tormented. **262** *Nestor's hernia.* Juvenal, *Sat.* vi. 326.

III. viii **14** *like Romans.* i.e. by suicide. **15** *like Grecians.* dissolutely. **16** *Saffi.* sergeants.

III. ix. **22** *foists.* (i) tricks; (ii) stinks. **36** *stated.* instated. **55** *Scrutineo.* Court in Senate-house.

IV. i. **1** *a plot.* II. iii. 10. **2–3** *mentioned me* | *For.* Spoke of me as able to give. **4** *height.* latitude. **11** *slander.* accuse. **12** *garb.* behaviour. **15** *fable.* fiction. **17** *strangers.*

Foreigners; Sir Politic is frank with his fellow countryman. **19** *know.* acknowledge. **20** *be a saver.* Insure against loss. **25–7** Sir Politic misrepresents the views of Machiavelli, who valued the socially cohesive effects of religion, and of Jean Bodin (1530–96), who advocated religious toleration. **28** *fork.* Not yet commonly used in England. **29** *metal.* 'the material used for making glass, in a molten state' (*OED*, 9). **34** *Preposterous.* back-to-front. *has him straight.* Has his measure at once. **40** *Contarini.* Cardinal Gasparo Contarini's *De Magistratibus et Republica Venetorum* (1589) was translated into English in 1599. **41** *movables.* furnishings. **47** *discover.* reveal. **54** *States.* A member of the Dutch legislative assembly, the States-General. **56** *chandler.* The letter looks as if it had wrapped candles. **60** *hoy.* Small coastal vessel. **64** *defalk.* Reduce the amount. **69** *considerative.* speculative. **71** *goods.* benefits. **72** *cautions.* precautions. **74–5** *Great . . . Ten.* The administrative hierarchy of Venice. **79–80** *Sir . . . greater.* i.e. common sergeants may prompt senators just as much as greater men may do. **89** *Put case.* suppose. **91** *Arsenale.* Where Venice's ships and weapons were kept. **94** *Advértise.* warn. **98** *Sealed.* Registered under seal. **102** *Soría.* Syria. **106** *Lazaretto.* Quarantine station. **111** *livres.* French currency. **119** *perpetual motion.* A perpetual-motion machine existed at Eltham at the time: cf. *Epig.* 97. 2 and n. **136–8** Building upon Theophrastus' Character 16, of 'The Superstitious Man'. **141** *ragion del stato.* 'Reason of state'; statecraft. **142** *moccenigo.* II. ii. 185 n. **143** *piecing.* mending. **144** *cheapened.* Bargained for. **146** *quote.* note.

IV. ii. **1–2** *loose . . . fast.* I. ii. 8 n. **1** *housed.* With the supposed courtesan. **29** *knighthood.* Another hit at James's lavish bestowal of knighthoods. **31** *reach.* understand. **35** *The Courtier.* Castiglione's *Il Cortegiano* (1528; trs. Hoby, 1561), bk. iii. **43** *solecism.* Strictly, an error in grammar rather than conduct, hence itself a solecism here (cf. Mosca, v. ix. 4, and the general lament of Epist. Ded. 77). Yet Jonson himself elsewhere uses the word in a wider sense: *Epig.* 116. 16. **48** *Sporus.* Transvestite eunuch, favourite of Nero. **51** *Whitefriars.* A 'liberty' in the City of London and sanctuary for criminals. *nation.* 'lot'. **53** *forehead.* Modesty, ability to blush. **55** *fricatrice.* whore. **58** *liquid.* Transparent. Possibly Lady Would-be weeps. **60** *carnival.* Associated with sexual licence, transvestism, and disguise. **61** *liberty of conscience.* Lady Would-be's irony. Venice was known for its religious toleration. **62** *marshal.* Prison officer. **63** *disple.* Discipline: i.e. whip. **69** *nearer.* More direct. **73** *queen-apple.* A red apple; cf. III. iv. 16.

IV. iii. **4** *callet.* whore. **18** *see.* Q 'use', intensifying the innuendo (and giving rise to a prosecution for indecency in 1701: see H & S, ix. 198). **23** *salt-head.* Sir Politic's mind is seasoned, but also, Peregrine suspects, salacious.

IV. iv. **5** *burden.* refrain. **7** *formal.* elaborate. **14** *mummia.* Substance taken (genuinely or reputedly) from Egyptian mummies was used medicinally. **15–16** *buffalo . . . head.* i.e. relishes the story of his cuckolding. **21** *Mercury.* God of eloquence, as well as of thieves: *Disc.* 1800–2. **22** *French Hercules.* Symbol of eloquence (Hercules was thought to have fathered the Celts in Gaul). **26** *another witness.* Lady Would-be.

IV. v. **7** *monstrous.* Trisyllabic: 'monsterous'. **31** *frontless.* shameless. **36** *visor.*

Mask; i.e. air of innocence. **37** *close.* secret. **41** *timeless.* untimely. **45–7** From Tacitus, *Annals,* IV. xviii. 3. The 'gift' of l. 44 is pardon. **48** *extirp.* extirpate. **54** *fact.* crime. **61–2** Juvenal, *Sat.* xiv. 109. **79** *Mischief . . . begins.* i.e. keeps to the same path; varying Valerius Maximus, IX. i. 2. **85** *stale.* Prostitute used as decoy by thieves. *forged practice.* Fabricated plot. **87** *collections.* Summaries, conclusions. **92** *should owe.* Ought to pay. **97** *six sols.* About threepence. **102** *creature.* And answerable to the Creator; suicide is in her mind. Contrast Mosca's show of Roman confidence, III. viii. 14–15. **108** *mere portent.* utter freak. **118** *partridge.* Thought highly lustful: Pliny, *Nat. Hist.* x. 102. **119** *jennet.* Small Spanish horse, also associated with lust: cf. *Othello,* I. i. 114. **124** *well-timbered.* well-built. **125** *horn.* With a play on 'hornbook' = primer. **127** *shame.* Q 'harm'. **130** *Catholic.* Thus F, published when Jonson was Anglican; Q 'Christian' (published when Jonson was a Catholic). **139** *laid.* contrived. **146** *baited.* (i) enticed; (ii) harassed.

IV. vi.   **3** *hyena.* Symbol of treachery; but its semi-human voice, not its tears, were thought to delude. **7** *exorbitant.* excessive. **13** *pertinacy.* pertinacity. **15** *o'ercome.* i.e. have the last word. **21** *convince.* Prove guilty. **30** *proved.* tested. **32** *strappado.* Venetian torture instrument: victims were bound, swung aloft, and jerked. **33** *gout.* Proverbially said to be otherwise incurable (Tilly, G386). **34** *help.* relieve. **36** *left.* cured. **38** *equal.* just. **45** *face or colour.* appearance. **52** *constancy.* Juvenal, *Sat.* xiii. 237. **66** *want living.* Lack a livelihood. **81** *in.* i.e. in the inventory of Volpone's inheritance. **89–91** *What . . . age.* Juvenal, *Sat.* x. 254–5. **92** *take . . . notice.* As Lady Would-be approaches.

V. i.   **1** *brunt.* Shock, crisis. **3** *fled.* past. **4** *cavé.* Watch out. **16** *make me up.* Pull me together.

V. ii.   **7–8** *It . . . spirit.* Plautus, *Pseudolus,* 576. **15** *prize.* part. **23** *Too . . . 'em.* Proverbial; cf. *Disc.* 2263–4; Donne, *Sat.* iii. 68–9. **30–2** Plautus, *Epidicus,* 306–7. **40** *in a mist.* Lost, uncertain. **50** *heads.* Main points. *aggravate.* ?Lay charges. **52** *shift a shirt.* Indicating contorted gestures, or a sweaty performance. **54** *answer.* repay. **59** *jig.* Piece of sport. **62** *Sadly.* gravely. **70** *take . . . as.* Act as if. **81** *count-book.* Account book. **83** *parcels.* items. **88** *stark dull.* Utterly numbed (but Volpone plays on 'dull' = blunt). **90** *clarissimo.* Venetian grandee; Corbaccio is indicated. **91** *crump.* Curl up. **93** *rope . . . dagger.* Stock properties of the desperate or suicidal: e.g. Hieronomo, *The Spanish Tragedy,* III. xii. **97** *kissed.* Possibly (with greatest comic effect) at IV. vi. 28. **99** *medicine.* Playing on the fact that gold was indeed used medicinally. **102** *girdle.* 'Cestus' (F note); i.e. Venus' girdle, that bestowed beauty and amorous power on all wearers (*Iliad,* xiv. 214 ff.); Lucian, *Gallus,* 722, had made the comparison with gold. **104** *Acrisius'.* Danaë was shut in a tower of bronze by her father Acrisius; Jove visited her as a shower of gold. **107** *jealous of.* Lustful for. **111** *artificer.* (i) contriver; (ii) rogue.

V. iii.   **3** *tissue.* Rich cloth, often interwoven with gold or silver. **9** s.d. *traverse.* Low movable screen. **11** *thread.* Of life: spun, measured, and cut by the three Fates. **14** *diaper.* Woven linen fabric. **21** *i' their garters.* i.e. suicide: a proverbial formula (Tilley, G42). **22** *gasp.* Last gasp. **25** *glazen-eyes.* Corbaccio wears spectacles. **32** *salt.* Salt cellar. **40** *offered.* Possibly after IV. vi. 101. **51** *wittol.*

Conniving cuckold. **58** *extraordinary.* Supernumerary: Corvino is an honorary rather than an actual cuckold. **65** *Harlot.* rascal. **68** *three legs.* In the riddle of the Sphinx, man walks with four legs in the morning of life, two at noon, and three (i.e. with a stick) in the evening. **96** *Conceive me.* Don't mistake me. **102** *lettuce.* a laxative. **108** *feast.* Ironically recalling II. vii. 16. **114** *commendatori.* Officers of the court. **119** *cursed.* Because he escapes; Tilley, F632.

V. iv.   4 *Zant.* Zante, Ionian island then in Venetian possession. **5** *Book of Voyages.* Such as Hakluyt's. **6** *gulled story.* Story of his gulling. **9** *Know your approaches.* Be ready to enter. **14** *all female.* Sir Politic here imitates Venetian custom (Creaser, citing Fynes Moryson). **18** *exact him.* Require his appearance (legal). **23** *'tidings'.* Sir Politic speaks of 'intelligence', 'advertisement', 'advices', etc.: II. i. 68, 77, 94. **37** *plot.* IV. i. 130–1. **42** *better.* i.e. to convict him; Jonson perhaps remembers his own troubles with the authorities. **43** *essays.* Despised by Jonson: *Disc.* 731–41; *Epig.* 12. 15. **45** *frail.* Rush basket for figs, raisins, etc. **51** *engine.* device. **58** *tortoise.* Emblem of silence, policy, and self-containment. **60** *device.* Invention; and (less wittingly) emblem. **68** *go.* walk. **73** *God's so.* II. vi. 59 n. **77** *motion.* Puppet show (popular in Fleet St.). **78** *fair.* Bartholomew fair. **83** *freight . . . gazetti.* Theme (burden) of the news-sheets. **84** *ordinaries.* II. i. 76 n.

V. v.   s.d. *habit of a Commendatore*: 'a black stuff gown, and a red cap with two gilt buttons in front' (Gifford). **4–5** *hold . . . one.* Maintain my assumed role: a loaded utterance. **7** *hole.* Referring to the children's game of Fox-in-the-Hole. **8** *case.* dress.

V. vi.   5 *come.* Make a claim. **12** *varlet.* (i) sergeant of the court; (ii) rogue. **13** *change.* exchange. **17** *over-leavened.* Excessively puffed up; cf. *Epig.* 97. 20. **18** *wine-fat.* Wine vat. **20** *Avoid.* Out of the way! **25** *a'known.* = acknown, i.e. acknowledged.

V. vii.   2 *legs.* bows. **8** *reparations.* repair. **10** *Piscaria.* Fish market. **12** *customed.* Well patronized. **13** *(none dispraised)* .Without prejudice to the others. **18** *candle rents.* Rents from deteriorating property. **21** *Mistaking knave.* Jonson (or Volpone) parodies the comic malapropisms of a Dogberry; cf. *BF* Ind. 42–4.

V. viii.   2 *shoot.* Cf. Corvino's fantasy at II. v. 32–4. *gunstones.* Cannon-balls, bullets. **10** *traded.* experienced. **12** *moral emblems.* As in the contemporary emblem books, where symbolic illustrations were morally explained. **13–14** *Should . . . emptiness.* Recalling Aesop's fable of the crow that sings to the fox, and drops its cheese. **17** *jolt-head.* blockhead. *cecchines.* Coin-like buttons. **27** *basilisk.* Fabulous reptile whose breath and look were fatal.

V. ix.   1 *flesh-fly.* Blow-fly; the meaning of 'Mosca'. **4** *madam.* At IV. ii. 43. **5** *biggin.* Lawyer's skull-cap. **8** *familiar.* (i) Member of household; (ii) attendant devil. **9–11** *mule . . . advocate.* Mules were often ridden by advocates; Volpone's inversion recalls popular depictions of 'the world upside-down'. **10** *Justinian.* The Roman legal code, drawn up by the Emperor Justinian. **11** *quirk.* trick.

V. x.   4 *win upon.* Prevail over. **10** *possessed.* By a devil. **28** *gaped.* longed. **30** *The other.* Mosca. *somedeal.* somewhat. **33** *confer.* construe. **46** *forkèd.* Cf. I. iii. 58.

V. xi. 7 *sear up.* cauterize. 9 *kitlings.* kittens. 13 *conceits.* tricks. 15–16 *bear . . . soberly.* Ironically recalling III. vii. 88–9. 16. *crotchets.* Whimsical fancies. 17 *conundrums.* Whims, conceits.

V. xii. 9 *possession.* Entrance into the body of an evil spirit. 10 *obsession.* The working of an evil spirit from without. 12 *invent.* find. 19 *stood affected.* Were inclined. 23–32 The details of Voltore's pretended diabolical possession (the stopped breath, the crooked pins, the twisted and mobile mouth, the emergence of the devil as a small creature) can be paralleled in accounts of similar contemporary frauds: see H & S, ix. 731–2. 35 *dispossessed.* a pun. 42 *practice.* deceit. 50 *proper.* handsome. 54 *o' the hinge.* i.e. running nicely. 60 *quick.* alive. 61 *come about.* Turned around. 64 *voice.* Cf. Plautus, *Mostellaria,* 576. *Demand.* ask. 73–4 *I . . . enemies.* Plautus, *Mostellaria,* 562–3. 75 *pass.* Be passed. 85 *uncase.* disrobe. 91 *chimera.* A threefold monster, with lion's head, goat's body, and serpent's tail. 95 *knot.* Cf. I. iii. 57; but referring also to the play's denouement. 101–2 *These . . . them.* Cf. Seneca, *Epist.* cxix. 12. 108 *minister.* agent. 109 *lewd.* base. 114 *galleys.* Cf. Volpone as Scoto, II. ii. 44. 115 *thank you.* Gifford compares Mosca's response at l. 81. 120 *Incurabili.* The Incurables' hospital was founded in Venice in 1522 for the treatment of venereal disease (Brockbank). 125 *mortifying.* (i) killing; (ii) hanging (game) until tender; (iii) spiritual disciplining. 131 *San' Spirito.* On the Giudecca Canal. 137 *ass's ears.* Cf. I. ii. 111–12. 139 *berlino.* pillory. 140 *eyes.* For Corvino, a constant concern: II. v. 33–4, V. viii. 2, etc. 146–8 *Now . . . are.* Juvenal, *Sat.* xiii. 237–9.

[Epilogue] 1 *seasoning.* Plautus, *Poenulus,* 1370–1. 4 *fact.* crime. 6 *fare . . . hands.* The invitation to applaud is common at the end of Roman comedy; 'jovially' lightly bestows upon the audience a Jove-like power.

THE ALCHEMIST

The Alchemist was first performed by the King's Men in 1610, the year in which the action of the play is supposed to occur. This was a plague year in London. It is on account of the plague that Lovewit has left his house in Blackfriars to visit his hop-yards in the more salubrious air of Kent, thus enabling Face, Subtle, and Dol to take over the house for enterprises of their own. Mammon undertakes 'to fright the plague | Out o' the kingdom in three months' (II. i. 69–70), and Surly remarks that in that case actors will be grateful to him: for when plague cases reached a statutory level, the playhouses were compulsorily closed. The London playhouses were in fact closed from mid July to late November. In view of the fact that *The Alchemist* was performed in Oxford in September, it is likely that the original London performance took place before this July closure.

The events within the play are supposed to occur on 1 November 1610 (see III. ii. 131–2 n., V. v. 101–3). This creates a minor problem. Why should a play so full of contemporary references be seemingly set not in the present but several months in the future? Possibly in the original performances there was a closer match between the internal dating and the actual date of presentation, and the references to November were fixed when the play was being prepared for publication sometime after 3 October 1610, when it was entered on the Stationers' Register by Walter Burre. This is, however, a conjectural solution.

The King's Men played at the Globe and also at the Blackfriars theatre. Herford and Simpson assume that *The Alchemist* was first performed at the Globe, but F. H. Mares argues more plausibly for Blackfriars. It is in the Blackfriars area that Lovewit's house is located; once again, there may have been (though this is again conjectural) a satisfying match between the inner and outer worlds of the play. In all likelihood, Richard Burbage played the part of Face, John Heminges that of Subtle; John Lowin, Mammon; Henry Condell, Surly; and Robert Armin, Abel Drugger.

The play was initially successful, despite being unaccountably 'hissed', as Herrick (p. 150) records. It retained its popularity throughout the seventeenth century—even during the closure of the theatres, when strolling players presented drolls from the play—and in the eighteenth century, when David Garrick was a memorable Abel Drugger in his own streamlined version of the play. Notable productions in recent times include those at the Old Vic in 1947 (with Ralph Richardson as Face and Alec Guinness as Drugger) and 1962 (Tyrone Guthrie, director, Leo McKern as Subtle) and that of the Royal Shakespeare Company in 1978 (John Woodvine, Subtle; Ian McKellen, Face).

The plot of the play is almost wholly original, though there are incidental debts to Plautus' *Mostellaria* (for the opening quarrel between Face and Subtle, and the fifth-act negotiation between Face and Lovewit outside the house). Jonson was intimately acquainted with much alchemical literature, as E. H. Duncan has shown (*PQ* xxi (1942), 435–8; *PMLA* lxi (1946), 669–710), and with the exploits of contemporary dabblers in alchemy such as John Dee, Edward Kelley, and Simon Forman. The Queen of Faery episode (III. v) appears to be based upon an actual fraud practised upon one Thomas Rogers (C. J. Sisson, *Joseph Quincy Adams Memorial Studies*, ed. James G. McManaway (Washington, 1948), 739–41).

The Alchemist was published in Quarto in 1612 and in the Folios of 1616 and 1640. The 1616 Folio adds stage directions to the Quarto text, modifies its oaths and possible blasphemies, repunctuates, and makes other slight alterations. Points of major textual interest are indicated in the notes that follow.

[Dedication] *DESERVING HER NAME*: which was also spelled, and probably pronounced, 'Worth'. (Q reads: 'To the Lady most equal with virtue and her blood; the grace and glory of women'.) Mary, Lady Wroth, was born *c.*1586, and married in 1604 Sir Robert Wroth (see *For.* 3, and Jonson's comment on the marriage, *Conv. Dr.* 299–300). Her mother was Barbara, née Gamage; her father was Robert Sidney, first Earl of Leicester (see *For.* 2), brother of Sir Philip Sidney. Her romance, *Urania*, in the tradition of her uncle's *Arcadia*, was published in 1621 and addressed to the Countess of Montgomery (see *Epig.* 104). She is also addressed in *Epig.* 105 and *Und.* 28. 1 *age of sacrifices*. From Seneca, *On Benefits*, I. vi. 1; cf. the more solemn context of *Und.* I. i. 9–16. **3** *gums*. incense. *hecatomb*. Great public sacrifice. **3–5** *Or how . . . virtue?* The Q text addresses a problem implicit in the play itself: 'Or how yet might a grateful mind be furnished against the iniquity of fortune, except when she failed it, it had the power to

impart [i.e. distribute blessings] itself? A way found out to overcome even those whom fortune hath enabled to return most, since they yet leave themselves more. In this assurance am I planted; and stand with those affections at this altar, as shall no more avoid the light and witness than they do the conscience of your virtue.'
5 *love the light.* Contrast Subtle on Mammon, IV. v. 34. *conscience.* knowledge. **9** *assiduity.* Frequency (Q 'dailyness'). **10** *a Sidney's.* Cf. *Epig.* 103. 4, 10. **11** *faces.* Capitalized in F and Q, 'Faces'.

To the Reader　From Q; omitted in F. Jonson voices similar criticisms (drawn from Quintilian, *Inst. Orat.* II. xi and xii) in *Disc.* 645–54, 757–87. H & S wonder whether this preface contains an implied attack on Shakespeare (i) in ll. 4–6, which resemble the more open attacks on Shakespeare in *BF* Ind. 127–32, and (ii) in ll. 25–9, which distantly resemble Jonson's comments on Shakespeare in *Disc.* 658 ff. The evidence is not persuasive.
　1 *understander.* Cf. *Epig.* 1. 2. **2** *tak'st up.* Playing on the commercial sense (*OED*, 'take', 90d); cf. *Epig.* 12. **13** and n. *pretender.* To legal possession, as well as to knowledge. **5** *concupiscence of.* Passion for. *dances and antics.* Uncorrected Q 'jigs and dances'; *antics* = grotesque theatrical shows. **8** *professors.* practitioners. **9** *naturals.* Natural abilities. **12** *excellent.* Exceptional (bad sense: *OED*, 1 †b). **13** *judgement.* Censoriousness; cf. *Disc.* 769. **13–17** Cf. *Disc.* 645–50. **14** *robustiously.* boisterously. *put for it.* Push about. **15** *braver.* (i) More courageous; (ii) more showy. **16** *rudeness.* Lack of skill; uncouthness. **17** *foil.* defeat. **19** *good and great. Epig.* Dedn. 13 n. **24** *suffrages.* Votes of approval. **27** *copy.* copiousness. *election.* Judicious selection. **28** *mean.* moderation. **29** *scattered.* disorganized. *numerous.* (i) Abundant; (ii) harmonious. *composed.* Well put together.

The Persons of the Play　*Subtle.* The name implies (i) acumen; (ii) treachery; (iii) an association with chemistry ('subtle' = thin and penetrating: of gases): *OED*, 9, †10, 1.
　Face. Suggesting (i) confidence; (ii) effrontery; (iii) appearance as opposed to fact: cf. *Und.* 70. 23. *Housekeeper.* caretaker.
　Common. i.e. prostitute (*OED*, 6b; cf. *For.* 8. 41). *Colleague.* ally.
　Drugger. His first name, Abel (I. iii. 3), is associated with 'innocency' in *Disc.* 1114.
　Surly. His first name, Pertinax (II. i. 79), means 'obstinate' (cf. *Epig.* 69); it was also the name of a reforming Roman emperor, assassinated in AD 193, who 'failed to comprehend . . . that one cannot with safety reform everything at once' (Dio, *Roman History*, lxxiv. 10. 3). *Gamester.* (i) Gambler; (ii) 'one addicted to amorous sport' (*OED*, †5); cf. the innuendoes of III. iv. 49–51.
　Amsterdam. II. iv. 30 n.
　Ananias. II. v. 72–3 n.
　Kastril. i.e. Kestrel, a small hawk; one who 'strives to fill himself with wind, and flies against it' (Overbury, 1613). The word was confused with 'coistrel' = knave.
　Mutes. e.g. the Parson of V. v.

The Argument　The acrostic form is imitated from Plautus. **1** *sickness.* There had been a serious outbreak of plague in London throughout 1609, recurring in August 1610. **4** *punk.* whore. **5** *narrow.* (i) Restricted; (ii) unprofitable (*OED*, 3b).

10 *figures.* horoscopes. *news.* Newsmongering is a favourite Jonsonian target: cf. *Volp.* II. i. 18 ff., *Epig.* 107, 115, *S. of N.*, etc. 11 *flies.* Familiar spirits. *stone.* The elixir or philosopher's stone, thought to turn base metals into gold. 12 *fume.* Vapour, smoke (see IV. v. 58, IV. vi. 45).

Prologue 1 *Fortune . . . fools.* Proverbial: Tilley, F600. 4 *ourselves.* i.e. the actors, the King's Men. 8 *squire.* pimp. 9 *humours.* See *Volp.* II. ii. 85 n. Jonson castigates popular misuse of the term in *EMO* Ind. 110–17. 19 *apply.* See *Volp.* Epist. Ded. 55 n. 24 *own.* i.e. acknowledge as theirs; cf. *Epig.* 30. 2.

I. i. 3 *figs.* Piles; alluding also to an anecdote in Rabelais, *Pantagruel*, iv. 45. 7 *strong water.* acid. 10 *All . . . made.* Proverbial: 'the tailor makes the man' (Tilley, T17; *Und.* 2. ix. 37); pointed here by Face's constant dependence upon disguise. 16 *livery-three-pound-thrum.* Retainer in coarse livery, paid £3 p.a. 17 *the Friars.* Blackfriars, where Jonson lived about this time (*Volp.* Epist. Ded. 122 n.), and where, perhaps, the play was first presented; see headnote. 18 *vacations.* Between the legal terms. 19 *translated.* Transformed: i.e. bogus (cf. l. 127 below). *suburb-captain.* Cf. Doll Tearsheet's indignation with Pistol's appropriation of the title 'captain', 2 *Henry IV*, II. iv. 131–41; and *Epig.* 87. 22 *countenanced.* Favoured, patronized; with a play on Face's name. 23 *collect.* recollect. 24 *Not of this.* Playing on a second sense of 'hear well', to be well spoken of (Latin *bene audire*); cf. *Volp.* Epist. Ded. 10. 25 *Pie Corner.* The corner of Giltspur Street and Cook Lane in West Smithfield, so called from the cooks' shops which stood there. 27–37 Cf. Catullus, xxi; Martial, I. xcii. 7–10. 28 *costive.* constipated. *pinched-horn.* i.e. like a sharply-narrowing horn. 29 *Roman wash.* Liquid cosmetic. 30 *black . . . worms.* blackheads. 31 *powder-corns.* Grains of gunpowder. *Artillery Yard.* Or Artillery Garden, in Teasel Close (now Artillery Lane), Bishopsgate Street Without, where the City train-band exercised; cf. *Und.* 44. 23. 32 *advance.* raise. 35 *kibes.* chilblains. 36 *felt of rug.* Coarse woollen hat. 38 *algebra.* Often associated with alchemy. 39 *vegetals.* vegetables. 51 *Make . . . strange.* Don't pretend puzzlement. 52 *chippings.* Parings of the crusts of loaves: to be doled out to the needy, along with the beer. Face instead keeps the bread and sells the beer to the *aqua-vitae men* (l. 53), who distilled or sold spirits. 54 *vails.* gratuities. 55 *post and pair.* An obsolete card-game. *counters.* Gambling chips, given in return for a tip. 56 *marks.* A mark was worth 13s. 4d. 59 *scarab.* dung-beetle. 60 *thunder.* Which Paracelsus claimed alchemy could produce. 62 *hand.* i.e. Subtle's phial. 64–80 An extended analogy from alchemy. Subtle claims to have purified Face (*sublimed, exalted,* l. 68) as he might purify a base material while preparing the elixir; stabilized him (*fixed,* l. 68) in the highest state (*third region,* l. 69; as the air was divided into upper, middle, and lower regions). 74 *quarrelling dimensions.* Rules for quarrelling, here regarded as an exact study like algebra or geometry; cf. III. iv. 25–41. 76 *tincture.* Literally, colouring; an alchemical term. A touch of gallantry will transform Face as a touch of elixir transforms base metals. 79 *fly out.* explode. *projection.* 'The casting of the powder of the philosophers' stone . . . upon a metal in fusion to effect its transmutation into gold or silver' (*OED*, 2); the twelfth and final stage in the alchemical process. 83 *equi clibanum.* 'The heat of horse-dung': the lowest stage of alchemical heat. Cf. l. 64. 85 *deaf John's.* unknown. 90 *hang thyself.*

Ironically recalled at v. iv. 146. Hanging was traditionally associated with despair, as in *The Faerie Queene*, I. ix. *collier*. Alchemists worked with coal and, like colliers, were associated with sharp dealing, darkness, and the devil. Cf. v. v. 11. **91** *in picture*. By graphic report of his activities; cf. *Epig.* 115. 29. **93** *Paul's*. Notices were commonly displayed in St Paul's Cathedral. **94** *hollow coal*. In which gold or silver might be surreptitiously inserted, covered with 'dust' or 'scrapings', and then triumphantly revealed. Cf. Chaucer's *Canon's Yeoman's Tale*, G. 1159–64. **95** *sieve and shears*. A device to identify thieves and missing property. After the ritual preliminaries, the sieve was thought to turn towards the person or object sought. **96** *Erecting figures*. Making a diagram of planetary positions in order to cast a horoscope. *houses*. Zodiacal signs. **97** *glass*. Usually made of crystal or beryl; the *shadows* were thought to be angels, who answered questions put to them by a pure virgin (here, probably, Dol), who also interpreted the replies. **98** *red letters*. Used in contemporary typography to emphasize key passages. *face . . . thee*. i.e. an engraved representation. **99** *Gamaliel Ratsey*. A notorious highwayman who worked in a grotesque mask. *sound*. sane. **103** *trencher-rascal*. A 'trencher-friend' is a parasite; cf. *Und.* 37. 9; 45. 7–8. *dog-leech*. Dog doctor. **106** *For . . . basket*. i.e. for eating too much from the alms-basket of scraps sent from the sheriff's table to pensioners. Cf. *Songs and Poems*, 35. 22–30. **110** *republic*. i.e. the common cause; 'but Dol Common is also a "public thing", the literal meaning of the Latin *respublica*' (Mares). **111** *brach*. bitch. **112–13** *statute . . . Eight*. Of 1541, prohibiting sorcery. A statute of 1403 prohibited the 'multiplication' of gold and silver. Dapper has informed Face of the statute of the law: I. ii. 22. **114** *laundering*. Washing in acid. *barbing*. clipping. **115** *bring . . . cockscomb*. i.e. make a fool of yourself. **117** *menstrue*. solvent. **120** *marshal*. Prison officer. **121** *dog-bolt*. A term of insult; technically, a blunt-headed arrow, perhaps to be shot at dogs. **122** *cozened*. (i) Cheated; (ii) lived as equals (as sovereigns call each other 'cousin'). **127** *apocryphal*. bogus. **129** *feather*. Puritans handled the local feather trade. **133** *powder*. From the philosopher's stone, used in projection. **135** *tripartite*. i.e. agreed between three parties. **137** *couples*. Hunting dogs were joined in pairs. **139** *term*. There were four legal terms; probably the Michaelmas term, beginning in early November, is referred to here. **141** *part*. i.e. pecuniary share; but as in ll. 145 and 146, the theatrical sense is also lightly suggested. **142** *objects his pains*. Complains about his work. **151** *fermentation and cibation*. The sixth and seventh processes in the conversion of metals to gold. **152** *Sol and Luna*. Gold and silver. **160** *shark*. cheat. **164** *precise*. Puritanical. **165** *king*. James, in 1603: noted for his enmity to the Puritans. **167** *ride*. In a cart; the punishment for a whore. **168** *hole*. i.e. the stocks. **169** *pay ear-rent*. i.e. have your ears cropped. **170** *Don Provost*. The Provost-Marshal (see l. 120 n.), who will be bilked of the clothes of an expected judicial victim. **173** *crewel*. (i) Worsted; (ii) cruel. For the pun. cf. *King Lear*, II. iv. 7. **174** *worsted*. Playing on the sense 'cheated'. **175** *Claridiana*. Heroine of the popular Spanish romance *The Mirror of Knighthood*, by Diego Ortuñez de Calahorra. **177** *Common . . . Proper*. A multiple play on words, for the terms designate (i) two classifications of nouns; (ii) two methods of legal ownership; (iii) two types of ecclesiastical service; (iv) two kinds of sexual conduct. **178** *cut*. Straw; perhaps playing on a sexual sense (cf. *OED*, †29, †34; *Twelfth Night*, II. v. 80–4). **179** *Particular*. For the innuendo, cf. IV. i. 77–8. **189** *quodling*. Raw youth; from 'codling' = apple, and perhaps 'the *quods* and *quids* of legal phraseology' (Gifford). **191** *Dagger.* There were several inns of this name; see Chalfant, p. 65. **192** *familiar.* Attendant spirit, to offer tips. **193** *rifle.* gamble.

I. ii.   6 *watch.* An unusual possession for a clerk at this time; hence Dapper's added fuss. **8** *pass-time.* (i) Timepiece; (ii) source of amusement, pastime. **10** *broke.* Broached the matter. **11** *does . . . dainty.* Is so chary about it. **17** *Read's matter.* Dr Simon Read was pardoned in February 1608 for having invoked spirits the previous November in an attempt to discover who had stolen £37. 10s. from Toby Matthew (the *fool* of l. 19). The spirits successfully located and restored the money. **24** *court-hand.* The difficult handwriting used in the lawcourts. **25** *discover.* i.e. let on about it. **26** *chiaus.* Literally, messenger (Turkish *çavuş*). In 1607 a Turkish chiaus named Mustafa arrived in England claiming he was an ambassador from the Sultan. He was well entertained and paid by polite but suspicious Levant merchants. 'Chiaus' (or 'chouse') was subsequently used to denote either a swindler or his dupe. **37** *angels.* Gold coins worth nearly 10s., bearing the figure of the archangel Michael; Subtle sees them as *spirits,* l. 38. **43** *flies.* See Argument, 11 n. **46** *Clim-o' the-Cloughs.* Clim is an outlaw in the Ballad of Adam Bell ('clough' = steep-sided ravine). *Claribels.* 'Lewd' Claribel is a knight in *The Faerie Queene,* IV. ix. 20. **47** *five-and-fifty.* A complete (and unbeatable) sequence of cards in the same suit in the game of primero. **50** *vicar.* The vicar-general, acting for the bishop or archbishop in the ecclesiastical courts. **54** *six fair hands.* To wit: English secretary, French secretary, Italian, Roman, Chancellery, and court. **55** *ciphering.* Arithmetic, i.e. accounting. **56** *Xenophon.* Q 'Testament'. One of several small changes in the Folio text probably made to avoid the charge of profanity (prohibited on stage under the law of 1606). **58** *mistress.* But to no account: see III. v. 45. **61** *head.* i.e. cap; like the velvet on a stag's antlers. **63** *puck-fist.* puff-ball. **69** *assumpsit.* A voluntary verbal promise, usually sealed by cash. **78** *blow up.* Ruin; cf. *Epig.* 112. 6; *For.* 3. 79. **79** *crackers.* As fireworks are used in the puppet-play in *BF* v. iv. 23. **80** *familiar.* I. i. 192 n. **81** *set.* Gamble with. **99–101** i.e. every gambler will have to buy his tavern dinner on credit. **103** *set him.* Put before him as a stake. **109** *dead . . . Isaac.* The fifteenth-century Dutch alchemists John and John Isaac Holland, whose works had recently been published ('living' seems an error). **111–12** *put . . . cloak.* Cf. 'send them home in their shirts'. **119** *happy.* Fortunate, rich (Latin *beatus*). **128** *caul.* Membrane covering the foetus, sometimes enveloping a child's head at birth; superstitiously regarded as a charm against drowning. **130** *I' fac.* In faith. Dapper's oaths are governed by religious and legal caution. **157** *at any hand.* In any case. **173** *nobles.* Worth 6s. 8d. **174** *clean shirt.* The fairies were considered sticklers for cleanliness; cf. *Songs and Poems,* 12. 6–7.

I. iii.   5 *Free of the Grocers.* Admitted to the Grocers' Company. **9** *plot.* plan. **14** *wished.* recommended. **17** *If I do see 'em.* Subtle plays on the monetary sense of 'angel' (I. ii. 37 n.). The entry of Face (Dapper's good angel, or bad?) is nicely timed; cf. Dol's at II. iii. 210. **24** *Sophisticate.* Tobacco was often adulterated in order to remedy degeneration and raise profits. **25** *grains.* cardamom. **28** *lily-pots.* Ornamental jars, originally for flowers. **30–1** Tobacco was often publicly smoked in the shops in which it was sold. The *maple block* is for shredding the tobacco leaf;

the *tongs* for holding the coal of *juniper*, which retained its heat for a long time; *Winchester pipes* were famous throughout the seventeenth century. **32** *goldsmith.* Usurer (goldsmiths often served in this capacity). **36** *of the clothing.* Wear the livery. **37** *called to the scarlet.* Made sheriff. **40** *fine for't.* Pay the fine for refusing office. **43** *amused at.* Puzzled by. **44** *metoposcopy.* The art of reading character and fortune from the forehead and face. Subtle's interpretations tally with contemporary lore. **47** *long ear. Aures magnae* are a sign of intelligence according to Paracelsus, *De Signatura Rerum Naturalium,* but Subtle's phrase also suggests that Drugger is an ass. Cf. *Epig.* Dedn. 25. **55** *lord . . . horoscope.* 'The sign of the zodiac ascending on the eastern horizon at the time of one's birth governed the "first house" of the horoscope; the planet which ruled it was the lord of the horoscope. If Libra governed the house of life, Venus ruled Libra, and not Mercury' (H & S). Mercury is the god of thieves and of alchemists, who will indeed exert a dominant influence upon Drugger's fortunes. **57** *balance.* (i) Scales; (ii) balanced accounts. **59** *Ormus.* Modern Hormuz, in Iran, then a centre in the spice trade. **65–6** *Mathlai . . . Thiel.* These spirits will prevent Drugger's tobacco from becoming fly-blown. Their names are lifted from *Heptameron seu Elementa magica Pietri de Abano philosophi* appended to Cornelius Agrippa's *De Occulta Philosophia* (?Paris, 1567). **69** *lodestone.* magnet. **71** *seem.* Be seen (Latin *videri*). **72** *puppet . . . vice.* A doll moved by wires. **73** *court-fucus.* A cosmetic, as used at court. **76–7** *Vitriol.* Sulphuric acid; *sal-tartar:* potash; *argol:* crude cream of tartar; *alkali:* soda-ash; *Cinnabar:* the red or crystalline form of mercuric sulphide. **79** *give a say.* Make an attempt. **87** *portague.* Portuguese gold coin worth between £3. 5s. and £4. 10s. **95** *ill-days.* Unlucky days (today will be one such). **102** *beech-coal.* Beechwood made the best charcoal. *corsive.* corrosive. **103** *crosslets.* Melting pots. *cucurbits.* Retorts, originally gourd-shaped. **107** *intelligence.* information.

I. iv.   3 *Lambeth.* A disreputable area at the time; cf. *Epig.* 12. 2. **5** *trunk.* Speaking-tube. **9** *shift.* Change your clothes. **10** *make ready.* dress. **14** *magisterium.* Master-principle of nature: a substance that will transmute other substances. **16** *possessed.* A pun: (i) owner; (ii) crazed. **18 ff.** The elixir was also believed to cure diseases and prolong life indefinitely. **18** *ordinaries.* inns. **20** *Reaching.* offering. *Moorfields.* A stretch of reclaimed marshland north of the city that served as a public recreational area; Bedlam and the lazar-houses were near by, and mad folk and lepers begged here. **21** *pomander-bracelets.* Made of aromatic substances, thought to be a safeguard against infection. **23** *spital.* Hospital for the diseased. **24** *highways.* Cf. Matt. 22: 9–10. **26** *Nature . . . art.* Cf. the opening of *Merc. Vind.* **27** *step-dame.* Cf. IV. i. 76; *Merc. Vind.* 209. **29** *the age to gold.* In the classical golden age, gold was not yet discovered (*For.* 12. 25 and n.). Mammon's ambitions are as literal as Midas's.

II. i.   2 *novo orbe.* The new world, America. *Peru.* Conquered by Pizarro in 1532; tales of its vast resources of gold and silver attracted countless fortune-hunters. **4–5** *Great . . . months.* Solomon was thought to have possessed the philosopher's stone (see II. ii. 36–7) and to have made his gold in distant Ophir, fetching it by sea every three years (1 Kings 9: 28; 10: 22). Three years is thus seen as the necessary period for its manufacture. **8** *spectatissimi.* Specially looked up to. **9** *hollow die.*

Loaded dice. **10–14** The *livery-punk* is a prostitute hired specially to fleece the susceptible heir; to *seal* (l. 12) is (i) to have sexual intercourse and (ii) to execute a promissory note as recompense for this service (*OED*, †4). Forced by a beating to honour the note, the heir raises money through the device of *commodity* (l. 14), i.e. buying on credit a parcel of brown paper or other worthless goods from a usurer, and selling them at once (normally to the usurer) for ready cash at a lower price. Infuriated by the swindle and by his beatings, he beats in turn the deliverer of the commodity. **16** *entrails*. Lining. Cf. *Epig.* 97. 4. **17** *Madam Augusta's*. Probably a brothel. For the name, cf. Juvenal, *Sat.* vi. 118. **19–20** A confused allusion to the story of the golden calf, Exod. 32. Mammon at once denounces, and indulges in, the worship of gold. **23** *punketees*. Little punks (a nonce-word). **26** *fire-drake*. Fire dragon; i.e. assistant who tends the fire. **27** *lungs*. Assistant working the bellows (probably an established term). **28** *firk*. Stir; perhaps with a sexual innuendo: cf. III. iii. 69. **29** *faithful*. Ready to believe. **33** *Lothbury*. A street near Old Jewry inhabited by copper-founders. **35** *Devonshire and Cornwall*. With their tin and copper mines. **36** *perfect Indies*. i.e. they will produce gold. *admire*. Are amazed. **39** *Mercury*. Quicksilver; *Venus*: copper; *the Moon*: silver. **40** *the Sun*. gold. **47–68** Mammon's claims for the stone can be paralleled in the writings of Paracelsus, Arnold of Villa Nova, and Francis Anthony (H & S, x. 69–70). **48** *ruby*. The colour attained in perfect transmutation. **49–52** Cf. Volpone on the power of gold, *Volp.* I. i. 25–7; *Merc. Vind.* 86–104. **55** *eagle*. Ps. 103: 5. **56** *fifth age*. The years between 41 and 56. **57** *philosophers*. alchemists. **58** *patriarchs*. Who were said by the alchemists to have possessed the elixir; hence the potency of, e.g., Noah and Abraham in old age. **62** *vestals*. i.e. whores, who trafficked at *Pict-hatch*, near Goswell Road south of Old Street; their *fire* (l. 63) is venereal disease. **64** *nature naturized*. Alluding to the scholastic distinction between *natura naturata* (= created nature) and *natura naturans* (creative nature, i.e. God). Here the alchemist is the creative agent. **71** *the players*. London theatres were obliged to close when plague deaths rose to thirty or forty a week, as they had in 1609. **76** *waterwork*. Thames water was pumped into London houses via lead pipe systems laid down by Peter Moris in 1582 and Bevis Bulmer in 1594; work had commenced on Sir Hugh Myddelton's New River Scheme (see V. v. 77 n.; *Epig.* 133. 193–4 n.). **77** *humour*. Whim, disposition. **81** *a book*. For details of actual books containing such claims, see H & S, x. 71. **84** *High Dutch*. i.e. High German (*Hochdeutsch*). Goropius had argued as much in his *Origines Antuerpianae* (1569). **88** *Irish wood*. Which St Patrick was thought to protect against spiders and worms. **89–100** Aeetes, king of Colchis, promised Jason the golden fleece if he could tame fire-breathing bulls and use them to plough a field sacred to Mars, sowing it with dragons' teeth from which armed men would spring up. Jason succeeded with the help of charms provided by Medea, the king's daughter, who had fallen in love with him. Her arts, which could also restore lost youth, are here compared with those of the alchemists. Cornelius Agrippa had proposed a connection between the golden fleece and alchemical lore. **92** *Pythagoras' thigh*. Reputedly golden: Lucian, *A True Story*, ii. 21; *Volp.* I. ii. 27, etc. *Pandora's tub*. The beautiful box presented to Pandora by Jupiter; when it was opened by her husband, its harmful contents flew out. The connection of the box (and Pythagoras' thigh) with alchemy had been made by the contemporary writer Martin Delrio.

95 *argent-vive.* quicksilver. **98** *Jason's helm.* The cap at the top of the distilling retort through whose beak vapour was conveyed. **101** *Hesperian garden.* Where Hercules out-manœuvred the dragon to obtain three of the legendary golden apples. *Cadmus' story.* Also of sowing dragons' teeth from which armed men spring up. **102** *Jove's shower.* Jove transformed himself into a shower of gold in order to enjoy Danaë, confined in a brazen tower. *boon of Midas.* Granted him by Bacchus: that all he touched would turn to gold. *Argus' eyes.* One hundred in number: only two slept at a time. Juno set him to watch Io, whom Jupiter had changed into a heifer. Mercury at Jupiter's behest killed Argus after lulling all his eyes to sleep with the lyre. **103** *Demogorgon.* Seen by Boccaccio in *De Genealogia Deorum* as the primal god; hence the original mystery sought by the alchemists.

II. ii.   3 *colour.* (i) Reason; (ii) the red which signified the final stage in transmutation; cf. 'ruby' II. i. 48. **8** *Give . . . affront.* i.e. look them in the face. **9** *bolt's head.* Globular flask with long cylindrical neck. **14** *covering.* Of lead. **16** *thatch.* Probably cheaper than shingles, yet more susceptible to fire: see *Und.* 43. 138 and n. Mammon shares Face's apparent unconcern for the fate of churches. **19** *complexion.* Cf. Chaucer's Canon's Yeoman, G. 727–8. **23** *not beech.* Ibid., G. 928; cf. I. iii. 102 n. *just.* precisely. **24** *heat . . . even.* A crucial factor in the alchemical process. **25** *colours.* Indicating the various degrees of fermentation. **28** *sanguis agni.* Blood of the lamb; i.e. red, the final colour. **30** *devotions.* See ll. 97–9. **36** *Solomon.* II. i. 4–5 n. *stone.* Playing on a secondary meaning, 'testicle'. **39** *fifty.* The daughters of Thespius king of Thespis, all of whom were successfully impregnated. **40** *blood and spirit.* i.e. the right colour (red) and stage in the alchemical process; cf. I. i. 70. **41** *blown up.* From Lampridius, *Heliogabalus,* xxv. **43–4** Suetonius, *Tiberius,* xliii. **44** *Elephantis.* Erotic writer known only through references in Suetonius and Martial (XII. xliii. 4). *Aretine. Volp.* III. IV. 97 and n. **45** *glasses.* Perhaps remembering Seneca (*Natural Questions,* I. xvi) on Hostius Quadra, who observed his own sexual practices in mirrors. **48** *succubae.* i.e. whores (originally, demons in female form thought to have intercourse with sleeping men). *mists.* As Nero in his palace had perfumed mists sprinkled upon his guests: Suetonius, *Nero,* xxxi. **50** *lose.* F 'loose'. The spelling (and at times the sense) of the two words was interchangeable. **55** *sublimed.* Exaltedly; playing on the alchemical sense. **58** *fathers and mothers.* Juvenal, *Sat.* X. 304–6. **59–60** *flatterers . . . divines.* A common association for Jonson: cf. *Conv. Dr.* 317–19. **60** *pure and gravest.* = purest and gravest. **62** *burgesses.* Members of parliament. **63** *fart. Epig.* 133. 108 n. **64** *entertain.* employ. **74** *hyacinths.* i.e. jacinth: for the ancients, a blue gem (probably sapphire); later, a reddish-orange gem, a variety of zircon. **75** *tongues of carps.* Commended by Walton in *The Compleat Angler,* ch. ix. *dormice.* A Roman delicacy. **75–7** Apicius was said to have eaten camels' heels and nightingales' tongues to ward off the plague: Lampridius, *Heliogabalus,* xx. **76** *Sol.* i.e. gold. *dissolved pearl.* Like Cleopatra (and others), Pliny, *Nat. Hist.* ix. 121; *Volp.* III. vii. 193. **77** *Apicius.* Quintus(?) Gavius Apicius, Roman gourmand of the reign of Tiberius (often confused with Apicius Caelius, third-century AD author of a Roman cookery book). **80** *calvered.* Cut up while alive. **81** *Knots, godwits. Epig.* 101. 19, 20 n. *lampreys.* Eel-like fish. **82** *barbels.* Fish of the carp family, 'bearded'; eaten by Heliogabalus (Lampridius, xx). **83** *paps.* Pliny, *Nat. Hist.* xi. 210–11. **87** *a* *knight.* Another gibe at James's indiscriminate bestowal of knighthoods; cf. *Volp.* IV. ii. 29, *Epig.* 3. 10, etc. **89** *taffeta-sarsenet.* A very fine and soft silk. **91** *the Persian.* Sardanapalus, ninth-century BC king of Nineveh, notorious for his decadent living. **94** *gums.* Paradise was traditionally thought to have aromatic resins. **97** *homo frugi.* A temperate man.

II. iii. **4** *doubt.* suspect. **6** *prevent.* anticipate. **8** *importune.* untimely. **12** *watching.* wakefulness. **19** *prevaricate.* Deviate (literally, walk crookedly). **26** *costive.* Reluctant (literally, constipated). **29** *bright . . . robe.* i.e. the gold is prepared. **30** *triple soul.* Comprising the vital spirit (inhabiting the heart), the natural spirit (in the liver), and the animal spirit (in the brain). **32** *Ulenspiegel.* 'Owl-glass', knavish joker in the German jest-books. **33** *register.* Damper in chimney regulating draught. **35** *aludels.* Pear-shaped glass or earthenware pots open at both ends, used in sublimation. **40** *gripe's egg.* Vessel shaped like a vulture's egg. *Lute.* Seal in clay. **41** *balneo.* Sand- or water-bath (for gradual heat). **42** *canting.* Thieves' slang. **44** *philosopher's wheel.* Alchemical cycle. **45** *lent heat.* Slow fire. *Athanor.* Digesting furnace maintaining constant low heat. **46** *Sulphur o' nature.* Thought to form gold or silver combined with pure mercury. **48** *covetise.* Covetousness; a bar to success: II. ii. 97–9. **58** *sand-heat.* l. 41 n. **59** *imbibition.* soaking. *white.* i.e. mercury. **60** *red.* i.e. sulphur. **61** *St Mary's bath.* i.e. water-bath (l. 41 n.). **62** *lac virginis.* Mercury ('virgin's milk'). **63** *faeces.* sediment. **64** *calx.* Powder produced by burning (calcination). *salt.* oxide. **65** *rectified.* distilled. **66** *reverberating.* Placing in furnace where the flame is forced back upon the substance to be heated. **68** *crow's head.* II. ii. 26. **71** *The hay is a-pitching.* The snare is being set. The rabbit will be *bolted* (l. 88) or driven by the *ferret* (l. 80) into the net. **73** *nipped to digestion.* Sealed for gentle heating. **75** *liquor of Mars.* Molten iron. **78** *pelican.* Retort for distillation. The neck re-entered the body, allowing for circulation (l. 255 below). **79** *signed . . . seal.* Hermetically sealed. **80** *amalgama.* Mixture of metals with mercury. **83** *white shirt on.* i.e. has turned white. **84** *inceration.* Making waxy by slowly adding fluid. **97** *fixation.* Reducing a 'volatile spirit', e.g. mercury, to solid form. **98** *ascension.* distillation. **99** *oil of Luna.* White elixir. *kemia.* The cucurbit in which distillation occurred. **100** *philosopher's vinegar.* mercury. **101** *salad.* 'The compound of gold, salt, sulphur (= oil), and regenerate mercury (= vinegar) was seriously likened to a salad by some alchemists' (H & S). **102–14** Closely based on Arnold of Villa Nova's *Rosarium.* **103** *balneo vaporoso.* Vapour bath. **109** *loose.* solution. **116** *andirons.* Fire dogs: metal bars for fire. **128** *eggs.* In dunghills: Pliny, *Nat. Hist.* X. lxxv. **131–207** Jonson has borrowed extensively from Martin Delrio's *Disquisitiones Magicae* (1599–1600); see H & S, x. 81–2. **146** *concorporate.* united. **148** *propria materia.* i.e. its own substance. **157** *means.* Intermediate stages. **166** *extensive.* extensible. **171–4** The central claims of alchemy were commonly supported by appeal to the apparently analogous process of equivocal (or spontaneous) generation of insects from dead matter. It was not realized that eggs had previously been laid in such matter. **174** *herb.* Basil. Pliny, *Nat. Hist.* XX. xlviii. *ritely.* With all due rites (Delrio: *rite posita*). **178** *bray.* Pound; Prov. 27: 22–3. **185** *chrysosperm.* Seed of gold. **187** *oil of height.* See l. 99 n. *tree of life.* Probably, the stone. **188** *marcasite.* Iron pyrites. *tutty.* Crude zinc oxide. **189** *toad.* The black tincture appearing during the alchemical process; *crow:* the blue-black tincture;

dragon: mercury; *panther*: i.e. spotted. **190** *firmament*. The philosopher's stone. *adrop*. lead. **191** *lato*. Latten, a brass-like metal; *azoch*: mercury; *zarnich*: orpiment: trisulphide of arsenic; *chibrit*: sulphur; *heautarit*: mercury. **192** *red man*. sulphur. *white woman* mercury. **194** *eggshells*. According to Aubrey, a direct allusion to the practice of John Dee (*Brief Lives*, ed. O. L. Dick (1949), p. 181). See II. vi. 20 n. *terms*. menses. **200** *obscure*. A deliberate and serious aim of many hermetic writers wishing to protect their occult knowledge. **208** *cleared*. explained. *Sisyphus*. Who in hell was condemned perpetually to roll to the top of a hill a large stone, which rolled immediately again to the bottom; his punishment, like the alchemists' experiments with their stone, was therefore 'ceaseless'. **210** *common*. As Mares notes, a humorous cue for Dol's entry. **223** *warrant*. protect. **225** *Bradamante*. An Amazon in Ariosto's *Orlando Furioso*. **230** *Paracelsian*. A follower of Paracelsus, Theophrastus Bombastus von Hohenheim (?1490–1541), physician and alchemist, who was thought to have possessed the philosopher's stone. He laid stress on the necessary balance of mercury, sulphur, and salt in the human constitution, hence the prescription of *mineral physic* (l. 231). Cf. *Epig.* 133. 96. **233** *Galen*. With his traditional medicine (*Volp.* II. ii. 106 n.). **238** *Broughton. Volp.* II. ii. 105 n.; biblical *genealogies* (l. 241) were his forte: see IV. v. below. **255** *helm*. II. i. 98 n. *circulate*. l. 78 above, n. **256** *vegetal*. Cf. I. i. 39; also perhaps 'nimble worker': cf. Latin *vegetus* = active, healthy. **282** *And*. if. **283** *lapis mineralis*. The mineral stone 'perhaps . . . thought of as the *matrix* or mother of minerals' (Mares). *lunary*. (i) The fern moonwort; (ii) mercury. **284–5** *primero | Or gleek*. card-games. **285** *lutum sapientis*. Paste for sealing vessels. **286** *menstruum simplex*. Plain solvent. **287–8** *quicksilver . . . sulphur*. Standard cures for venereal and skin diseases. **289** *Temple church*. Off Fleet Street; a favourite meeting-place for lawyers and men of business. **295** *converse*. Moving about (*OED*, †1), with a sexual hint (*OED*, †2 †b). **303** *quainter*. A pun ('quaint' = cunt). **306** *fall*. The falling band: a collar lying flat. **307** *prove*. test. **310** *no philosopher*. i.e. no believer in the philosopher's stone; but like Diogenes the Cynic, laughing at the world's follies. **315** *parlous*. Dangerous, over-clever. **320** *Bantam*. In Java; its wealth was legendary. **325–6** *jack*. Device to turn spit; controlled by *weights*. **328** *weasel*. Because of (i) nimbleness; (ii) the future ermine coat. **331** *Count Palatine*. With jurisdiction over one of the Counties Palatine (Chester, Lancaster).

II. iv. **5** *firks*. II. i. 28 n. **7** *statelich*. In a stately manner (Dutch). **8** *race*. (i) Stock; (ii) sex; (iii) course of action (*OED*, *sb.*² 2, 8b; *sb.*¹ †8). **11** *Sanguine*. Ruddy; in humour theory, courageous, hopeful, amorous. **18** *gudgeons*. Small fry, ready to bite at anything. **20** *Anabaptist*. The Anabaptists first appeared in Germany in 1521, spreading to England a decade later; they refused civil oaths, and advocated adult baptism, common ownership, and a return to the spirit and forms of early Christianity. **21** *gold-end man*. One who bought and sold old gold. **30** *Amsterdam*. One of several Dutch towns in which the followers of John of Leyden had tried unsuccessfully to gain control in the 1530s. It continued to attract religious minorities.

II. v. **1** *recipient*. Receptacle for distillation. **2** *rectify*. purify. *phlegma*. 'Any watery inodorous tasteless substance obtained by distillation' (*OED*, 'phlegm', †2). **4** *macerate*. Soften by soaking. **5** *Terra damnata*. i.e. the dregs. **7** *Brother*. Subtle pretends that Ananias refers to an alchemical fraternity such as (Mares suggests) the tenth-century Arabian 'Faithful Brothers'. **8** *Lullianist.* Follower of Raymond Lully: see *Volp.* II. ii. 115 n. *Ripley.* Sir George Ripley, fifteenth-century Canon of Bridlington, alchemist and popularizer of the works of Lully. *Filius artis.* 'Son of art'; cf. *Merc. Vind.* 26. **9** *dulcify.* Wash out the soluble salts. **10** *sapor . . . stiptic.* The 'less sour' and 'yet less sour' of the various alchemical 'savours'. **11** *homogene.* Of the one kind; *heterogene:* of various kinds. **13** *Knipper-Doling.* Bernt Knipperdollink was a leader of the Anabaptist rising in Münster in 1534–6, under John of Leyden. **14** *chrysopoeia.* Making of gold. *spagyrica.* The science of alchemy (a Paracelsian word). **15** *pamphysic, or panarchic.* Pertaining to all nature and all power: probably nonce-formations. **17** *Hebrew.* Often venerated by Puritans as the language spoken in Paradise, and advocated as a universal language. Greek, the language of the New Testament, was less favourably regarded. **21** *putrefaction.* Decomposition by chemical action. **22** *Solution.* Changing a solid (or gas) to liquid form by use of a solvent. *ablution.* Washing off impurities. *sublimation.* I. i. 68. **23** *Cohobation.* redistillation. *calcination.* II. iii. 64 n. *ceration.* Making waxy (cf. II. iii. 84); also used of the *fixation* (l. 24) of mercury. **25** *vivification.* Restoration of a metal to its original state. *mortification.* Destruction or neutralization of the active qualities of a metal's chemical substance. **27** *aqua regis.* Mixture of nitric and hydrochloric acid; a solvent for gold. **28** *trine circle.* Planets in trine (one-third of a circle or 120° apart) were thought to be favourable in aspect; the *seven spheres* are the planets, including sun and moon. The alchemical process is to be thrice repeated. **29** *passion.* Manner in which they are affected (*OED*, 5 †b). *Malleation.* hammering. **30** *ultimum supplicium auri.* 'The final punishment of gold', to be made less malleable with antimony (native trisulphide). **32** *fugitive.* A recognized alchemical conceit: cf. *Merc. Vind.*, opening. **34** *oleosity.* oiliness. *suscitability.* excitability. **35** *calce.* calx. **36** *talc.* III. ii. 36 n. *magisterium.* I. iv. 14 n. **57** *Sincere professors.* i.e. true Anabaptists. **58** *deal justly.* Cf. Mic. 6: 8; but Ananias means business. **67** *instruments.* i.e. materials. **71** *pin-dust.* Metal dust from the manufacture of pins. **72–3** *Ananias* kept money back from the Apostles; he and his wife fell dead when accused by Peter: Acts 5: 1–11. **80** *Piger Henricus.* Lazy Henry, a composite furnace with one fire. **81** *sericon and bufo.* The red and black tinctures (cf. 'toad', II. iii. 189). **82** *bishops.* To whom the Puritans were hostile. **83** *antichristian.* i.e. ecclesiastical (authentic Puritan terminology). **84–6** i.e. the clarified mercury will be spoilt.

II. vi.   2 *mates.* riff-raff. *Bayards.* Wild horses; cf. the proverb (Tilley, B112), 'Who so bold as blind Bayard?' (Bayard was a magic horse given by Charlemagne to Rinaldo.) **11** *balance.* I. iii. 56–7. **17** *virtual.* powerful. **20** *Dee.* John Dee (1527–1608), mathematician, astrologer, alchemist, and sage; sometimes thought to be a model for Subtle. Cf. II. iii. 194 n.; IV. i. 90 n. **21** *rug.* Coarse wool. **24** *hieroglyphic.* Cf. *UV* 34. 43. **26** *legs.* bows. **30** *bona roba.* Well-dressed (or 'fancy') woman; Drugger misunderstands. **33** *hood.* A French hood, in contrast to the fashionable court hat. *a cop.* High on the head, not at the back as was customary. **34** *fucus.* cosmetic. **35** *deal.* Traffic in cosmetics and in love-philtres (l. 55); have sexual intercourse. **54** *dubbed.* II. ii. 87 n. **55** *water.* For a love-philtre. **61** *quarrel.* Cf. Touchstone on the dimensions of the art, *As You Like It*, V. iv. 85 ff. **64** *by line.*

accurately. **69** *instrument.* A formal document. The word is favoured: cf. II. v. 67. **86** *draw lots.* As for Dol, I. i. 178–9. **87** *in tail.* Legal entail (= limited ownership); with a sexual pun. **89** *grains.* i.e. of weight; Dame Pliant's financial rather than moral substance is the chief concern. 'Grains' are also 'legs': *OED, sb.*⁴ †I. **90** *whole.* More punning.

III. i.   **2** *Separation.* A community both exiled and elect. **6** *language of Canaan.* Isa. 19: 18. **8** *Beast.* Rev. 16: 2; 19: 20. **15–16** A confused memory of 1 Cor. 1: 27–8. **17** *give.* Concede; cf. l. 27. **18** ff. Cf. *Epig.* 133. 142–4. **28** *motives.* Moving causes. **32** *beauteous discipline.* A Puritan catch-phrase. **33** *menstruous cloth.* An ingenious allusion to the 'scarlet woman' of Rev. 17. **36** *Heidelberg.* II. v. 70. **38** *silenced Saints.* The Nonconformist clergy excommunicated after the Hampton Court Conference of 1604. **41** *aurum potabile.* Gold as a cordial; i.e. a bribe. **48** *motion.* impulse.

III. ii.   **2** *you see.* 'Possibly Subtle indicates an hour-glass' (Mares). **3** *Furnus acediae.* 'Furnace of sloth': see II. v. 80 n. *turris circulatorius.* Circulation tower; see II. iii. 78 n. **10** *qualify.* Mitigate; chemically, to dilute. **23** *Hollanders, your friends.* II. iv. 30 n. Subtle assumes implausibly that Dutch traders in the east were sympathetic to religious dissidents at home. **25** *make . . . faction.* Win you support; cf. *Volp.* Prol. 26. **33–4** *is past . . . mind.* (i) Feels younger than she looks (*feat* = featness, elegance); (ii) thinks about sex, but is not up to it (*feat* = act). **36** *oil of talc.* Used as a wash for the complexion (cf. *For.* 8. 33)—and also in alchemy. **38** *bone-ache.* syphilis. **40** *fricace.* rub. **41** *pregnant.* convincing. **43** *Christ-tide.* Common Puritan terminology, avoiding the Popish implications of '-mas'. **51** *oppone.* oppose. **53** *anything.* Cf. Mosca to Volpone, *Volp.* I. i. 28. **54** *exercises.* Religious ceremonies. **55** *'ha' and 'hum'.* A common feature of Puritan preaching; cf. *BF* I. iii. 97–8. **61** *Bells are profane.* Cf. Bunyan's guilty love of church bells, *Grace Abounding* (1666), § 33. **69–82** Cf. Dame Purecraft's confession in *BF* V. ii. 53 ff. **72** *start.* advantage. **77** *Abate the stiffness.* Beat down the obstinacy; with a *double entendre.* **78** *scrupulous bones.* Issues turning on fine distinctions. **79–82** Practices commonly denounced by such Puritans as Philip Stubbes. **87** *shorten . . . ears.* A punishment inflicted on various Puritans (e.g. William Prynne in 1634 and 1637). **88** *wire-drawn.* drawn-out. **89** *alderman.* The city magistrates often had Puritan sympathies. **90** *custard.* A feature at city feasts; cf. *Volp.* Prol. 21. **95** *wood.* Crowd (Latin *silva*). **99** *glorious.* Q 'holy'. **105** *From east to west.* The direction in which knowledge was thought to move; alchemy originating with the writings of Hermes Trismegistus in Egypt (Kernan). **113** *botcher.* A tailor who does repairs. **118** *orphan.* Mares emends to 'orphans' (F 'orphane'). **126** *expect.* wait. **128** *silver potate.* Liquefied silver. **129** *citronize.* Bring to the colour of citron: an advanced stage in the process. **131–2** i.e. 16 November 1610, *some fifteen days* hence; thus the action of the play occurs on 1 November. H & S, along with later editors, see an apparent discrepancy with the date of 23 October indicated by Ananias at V. v. 101–5. Ananias is there indicating, however, an earlier date at which the Brethrens' money was 'told out'; by the present date, they are impatient, and 'will not venture any more' (II. v. 65). **138–40** *ignis ardens* is the fourth and hottest grade of heat; the slower or *lenter heats* are *fimus equinus* (I. i. 83 n.), *balnei,* and *cineris* (II. iii. 41; 84). **144** *tincture.* To change the colour of pewter. **150** *no* *magistrate.* Such a claim was made by English Baptists in Amsterdam in 1611. Cf. *Disc.* 61–5. **151** *foreign coin.* Counterfeiting of foreign currency was also in fact a treasonable offence. **153** *Casting.* Satirizing Puritan hair-splitting.

III. iii. 1 *costive cheater.* Sceptical gambler; i.e. Surly (cf. II. iii. 26). **2** *came on.* Showed up. *walked the round.* A common phrase (cf. *For.* 3. 59), but the circular Temple church was also known as the Round. **4** *Quit him . . . quit him.* Let him go; requite him. **6** *grains.* Of flour, from the mill; of money (cf. II. vi. 89). **8** *mastery.* victory. *black boy.* Subtle, like Face, is blackened from the fire; cf. I. i. 90; IV. vi. 41; V. v. 11. **11** *compeer.* partner. *party-bawd.* Part-time bawd. **13** *munition.* Face pictures the Don as a Spanish invader. *slops.* Wide baggy breeches. **14** *hoys.* Small coastal vessels. *round trunks.* Trunk hose: knee breeches enormously puffed and stuffed. **15** *pistolets.* Spanish gold coins, worth about 17*s. pieces of eight.* Spanish dollars, worth about 4*s.* 6*d.* **16** *bath.* Cf. *Epig.* 7. 3 n. **17** *colour.* pretext. **18** *Cinque Port.* One of the group of defensive ports in south-east England, originally five in number; *Dover* (l. 19) was amongst them. **22** *epididymis.* Sperm duct leading from the testicles. **23** *doxy.* wench. **24** *John Leydens.* II. v. 13 n. **28** *portague.* I. iii. 87 n. **29** *reversions.* Future possessions. **30** *states.* estates. **33** *how . . . camp?* The opening line of Kyd's *The Spanish Tragedy.* **41** *Dousabel.* 'Sweet and beautiful'. **44** *drum.* i.e. sexual activity. **46** *great frost.* December 1607–February 1608; the Thames froze over. **47** *basin.* Banged to make a swarm settle: Virgil, *Georgics,* iv. 64. **49** *God's-gift.* The meaning of 'Dorothea' (Greek). **50** *Adelantado.* Provincial governor, grandee. **53** *a-furnishing.* Getting the necessities together. **54** *Would.* i.e. should. *festival days.* Cf. V. iii. 9. **64** *circle.* The Round, or Temple church, seen as a magician's circle. **65** *flies.* familiars. **67** *virginal.* Keyboard instrument; with a *double entendre.* **69** *Firk.* II. i. 28 n. **70** *mother-tongue.* Sexuality is seen as Dol's native language. **71** *Verdugoship. Verdugo* = hangman (Spanish); a mock title.

III. iv. 18 *carry a business.* Negotiate a duel. The niceties of duelling were much discussed; cf. *Und.* 59 and n. **28** *instrument.* Not a weapon, but a quasi-scientific treatise on the art of duelling. **39** *in diameter.* i.e. the direct lie. **40** *ordinarily.* A play on words, the eating-houses being known as ordinaries. **43** *reads.* understands. **52** *vented.* Got rid of. **61** *groom-porter's.* An officer of the Lord Chamberlain who supervised courtly games of cards, dice, and bowls, and adjudicated over disputes. **72** *buttered shrimps.* For Mammon, a sexually arousing dish: IV. i. 159–60. **73** *no mouth. Epig.* 28. 13–14. **76** *cast.* cashiered. **85** *vacation.* Between the legal terms (see I. i. 139 n.). **87** *perspective.* Either an anamorphic painting showing different scenes from different angles (cf. *UV* 2. 9–14), or a 'glass perspective' like that used in Greene's *Friar Bacon,* sc. vi. Cf. also I. i. 97 and n. **90** *commodity.* II. i. 10–14 n. **107** *melancholy.* Burton, *Anatomy of Melancholy,* pt. I, sec. 2, mem. 2, subsec. 1. **119** *Seacoal Lane.* It ran from Snow Hill to Fleet Lane. **120** *sodden.* boiled. *pellitory o' the wall.* Low bushy plant with medicinal properties. **123** *'sessed.* assessed. **124** *waterwork.* II. i. 76 and n.; with a secondary reference, perhaps, to venereal disease and water-casting (J.-M. Maguin, *NQ* NS xxix (1982), 141–2). **131** *pains.* efforts. **138–9** *do . . . worship.* Get you more renown. **143** *old Harry's sovereign.* = 10*s.* **144** *groat.* = 4*d.* **145** *just.* exact. **148** *best of all.* For no logical reason; Face is merely milking his victim.

III. v.   9–10 'Though nigh be my kirtel, yet nearer is my smock' (Heywood, Proverbs); playing on the notion of fortune as a whore (*Und.* 43. 153 and n.). **12** *to wrap him in.* Cf. the proverbial saying, 'To have been wrapped in fortune's smock': Tilley, M1203. **15** *eyes.* Fortune being blind: Tilley, F604. **16** *state.* fortune. **31** s.d. *cithern.* Guitar-like instrument. **33** *spur-rial.* Coin worth 15*s*. **40** *innocent.* (i) Guiltless person; (ii) fool. **55** *puffin.* Thought to be half fish, half bird; hence a person 'who is neither one thing or the other' (Mares). Aptly applied to Dapper in his petticoat. **56** *lay . . . back.* i.e. move to the back of the fire. **76** *crinkle.* shrink.

IV. i.   16 *state.* politics. **23** *modern.* Everyday, commonplace. **27** *Danaë.* II. i. 102 n. **30** *concumbere.* Copulate (Juvenal, *Sat.* vi. 191). **38** *Guinea bird.* prostitute. **39** *fierce idolatory. Epig.* 65. 3. **48–51** Cf. *Epig.* 109. 9–10. **56** *Austriac.* The large lower lip was characteristic of the Habsburgs. **75** *feature.* face. **78** *Particular.* Dol pretends he means 'sexually intimate'. **83** *mathematics.* The word could include geometry, astronomy, and optics. **84** *distillation.* Central to the business of alchemy. **90** *Kelley.* Edward Kelley, alias Talbot (1555–95), worked as medium with John Dee, claimed to possess the secret of the philosopher's stone, and was twice imprisoned by Rudolph II (the *emperor* of l. 89) in Prague; Gifford saw him as the original of Face. **92** *Aesculapius.* Classical god of medicine, able to restore the dead to life; Pluto, god of the underworld, complained to Jupiter, who killed Aesculapius with a thunderbolt. **101** *solecism. Volp.* IV. ii. 43 n. **118** *styles.* Ceremonial titles, including that of the sovereign himself; hence Dol's mock alarm. **119** *jealousy.* suspicion. **122** *mastery.* The magisterium (I. iv. 14). **126** *shower.* Still harping upon Danaë: II. i. 102; 27. **134** *hundred.* A subdivision of a county or shire. **136** *emp'rics.* Originally, a sect of ancient physicians who drew entirely upon practical observation and experience; but the word now meant 'quacks'. **137** *pearl.* II. ii. 76 n. **141–3** *Volp.* III. vii. 195 and n. **145** *Poppaea* Nero's second wife, who bathed in asses' milk, and died after a kick from Nero; S. Musgrove suggests she is 'named here because her name means "Dol": Jonson's joke, not Mammon's, since he apparently does not know her name'. **156** *mullets.* A luxury in ancient Rome. **159** *shrimps.* From Horace, *Sat.* II. viii. 42–3 (S. Pearl, *NQ* NS xxix (1982), 138–9). **174** *Rabbins.* II. iii. 238–9.

IV. ii.   5 *bonnibel.* Bonny lass. *draw lots.* II. vi. 86. **6** *suit.* His Captain's uniform; Face is still dressed as Lungs. **9** *hit . . . nostrils.* i.e. lead you by a ring through the nose. **13** *terrae fili.* 'Son of earth'. (i) In Latin, a person of obscure origin; Subtle pretends it designates a landowner. (ii) An alchemical term for 'geomantic spirits' (Greene, *Friar Bacon*, sc. viii). **21** *true grammar.* Vincentio Savioli's treatise on duelling and quarrelling (1595) stresses the importance of naming causes while giving the lie; otherwise one would lose the choice of weapons. Subtle employs the terminology of scholastic logic. **40** *subtlety.* Delicacy; also a sugary confection. **42** *myrobalan.* Plum-like fruit. **43** *rivo frontis.* The frontal vein. **45** *linea fortunae.* The line of fortune, running from beneath the little finger to the index or middle finger. **46** *stella . . . Veneris.* Star on the hill of Venus: at the base of the thumb; with a secondary sexual sense. **47** *junctura annularis.* The joint of the ring-finger. **59** *fustian.* bogus. *dark glass.* Crystal ball. **60** *dabchick.* The grebe, a dainty diving bird.

IV. iii. **3** *composition.* Financial settlement. **10** *serve.* i.e. sexually. **20** *Don John.* Like Diego (l. 37), a standard name for a Spaniard. **21** 'Gentlemen, I kiss your honours' hands.' **25** *trestles.* His legs. **27** *souse.* ear. *wriggled.* Cut in a wriggly pattern. **30** *D'Alva.* Fernando Alvarez, Duke of Alva (1508–82), Governor of the Netherlands 1567–73. *Egmont.* Flemish patriot, put to death by Alva in 1568. **33** *squibs.* Explosive devices. *sets.* Pleats of ruff, here compared with crenellations. **34** 'By God, gentlemen, a very fine house.' **40** *Donzel.* Little Don (or perhaps 'squire': cf. Italian *donzello*). *Entiendo.* 'I understand'—as indeed he does. **46** *See . . . monsters.* i.e. be taken for a ride. The lions in the Tower were a popular tourist attraction; 'to have seen the lions' was to have had experience of life. **47** 'If you please, may one see this lady?' **61–2** 'I understand the lady is so beautiful that I long to see her, as the great fortune of my life.' **74–5** *win . . . her.* A common phrase used of courting a wife; Face ironically varies Subtle's words of l. 15. **75** *work.* i.e. put her to work. **78** 'Gentlemen, why so great a delay?' **80** 'Perhaps you are mocking my love.' **91** 'By this honoured beard.' **92–3** 'Gentlemen, I fear you are practising deception upon me.' **98** *fubbed.* cheated. **100** *curried.* Soaked, scraped, and beaten, etc., like leather; *flawed*: flayed; *tawed*: made supple (of leather).

IV. iv. **2** *nick.* Critical moment. **9** *jennet.* Small Spanish horse. **10** *Stoop.* bow. *garb.* fashion. **13** *titillation.* scent. **14** *pike.* The Toledo. **29** *eighty-eight.* 1588, Armada year; Dame Pliant is thus 19 in 1610, the year of the play's action. **32** *rush.* Commonly strewn on floors; Face picks one up. **33** *strawberries.* As a street hawker; cf. *Epig.* 92. 1. **34** *shads.* Fish in the herring family. **41** *ruffled.* Because Surly wears a *ruff*: IV. iii. 24. **42** *state.* position. **44** *served.* IV. iii. 10 n. **49** *tires.* clothes. **50** *goose-turd.* Dark green. **53–4** 'Why does she not come, gentlemen? This delay is killing me.' **57–8** 'By all the gods, the most perfect beauty I have ever seen in my life!' **63–4** 'The sun has lost its light with the splendour that this lady brings, God bless me!' **69** 'Why does she not come?' **71** 'For the love of God, why is it she delays?' **76–7** 'My lady, my person is quite unworthy to approach so much beauty.' **80** 'Lady, if it is convenient, let us go in.' **83** *the word.* i.e. for her 'fit' to begin. **92** *erection . . . figure.* Casting her horoscope; cf. I. i. 96.

IV. v. **1–32** Dol's 'fit of talking' is a patchwork of quotations from *A Concent of Scripture* (1590), a study of biblical chronology by the Puritan writer Hugh Broughton (II. iii. 238; *Volp.* II. ii. 105 n.). Dol quotes principally from Broughton's commentary on Daniel's interpretation of Nebuchadnezzar's dream (Dan. 2), concerning the progressive degeneration of kingdoms. Broughton is led to think of the fate of the empire of Alexander the Great. *Perdiccas, Antigonus, Seleucas,* and *Ptolemy* (ll. 2–3) were Alexander's four generals who divided his empire after his death, and then fought amongst themselves. **10** *fourth chain.* i.e. the fourth stage of historical decline reviewed by Broughton. **16** *Eber and Javan.* i.e. Hebrew and Greek. **23** *All . . . letters.* From Broughton's preface; a comically apt cue for the babel that follows. **24** *lay.* The *double entendres* continue in ll. 26–7 (*stone* can also mean 'testicle'). **25** *Talmud.* The corpus of Jewish civil and canon law. **26** *fifth monarchy.* The last of the five great empires referred to in Dan. 2; in the seventeenth century identified with the millennium, the thousand-year reign of Christ predicted in Rev. 20. **28** *Thogarma.* Ezek. 38. *habergeons.* Sleeveless jackets of mail, 'dragged in here purely for the sound of the word' (H & S). **29** *Brimstony . . . fiery.* From Wyclif's version of Rev. 9: 17. **30** *King . . . Cittim.* The Pope. **31–2** Names of biblical scholars. **58** *in fumo.* Argument, 12 n. **70** *mine own man.* i.e. myself. **103** *case.* Costume: as Lungs. **107** *fetch him over.* Get the better of him.

IV. vi.   3 *clap.* Venereal disease. **5** *punctually forward.* Quick off the mark. **23** *upsee Dutch.* Dutch style (Dutch: *op zijn*). **29–30** *cart . . . whip.* Malefactors were commonly tied to a cart and whipped through the streets. **33** *parcel-broker.* Part-time go-between. **37** *boot.* Gold rubbed on a hard dark touchstone left an authenticating trace; on a boot treated with brimstone it did not. **45** *in fumo.* Argument, 12; IV. v. 58. **46** *Faustus.* Familiar on account of Marlowe's play. **48** *ephemerides.* Astronomical almanacs. **54** *ears.* I. i. 169 n.

IV. vii.   16 *foist.* rogue. **23** *mauther.* Awkward young girl. **25** *swabber.* Low fellow (deck-scrubber). **26** *out of company.* Because you have supporters. **33** *lotium.* Stale urine used as hair-dressing. **34** *Hydra. Epig.* 133. 83 n. **39** *trig.* coxcomb. **40** *Amadis . . . Quixote. Und.* 43. 29 ff. n. **41** *Knight . . . Coxcomb.* Referring to Surly's hat (see also l. 55) and indirectly to the title of Beaumont and Fletcher's play *The Coxcomb*, based on *The Curious Impertinent* from *Don Quixote.* **43** *Casting of dollars.* III. ii. 151–8. **45** *otter.* 'Neither fish nor flesh' (*1 Henry IV*, III. iii. 127); cf. Captain Otter in *SW. shad.* IV. iv. 34 n. *whit.* Particle, fragment. **46** *tim.* '?tiny particle (cf. Tim Item in *ML*)' (Wilkes). **53** *unclean birds.* Rev. 18: 2. *seventy-seven.* Perhaps a misdating of D'Alva's invasion of the Netherlands, 1567, or of the Armada of 1588, or a reference to strange birds with ruffs found in Lincolnshire and reported in a pamphlet of 1586 (M. A. Shaaber, *MLN* lxv (1950), 106–9), or to Catholic seminary priests (Malcolm H. South, *SEL* xiii (1973), 331–43). **57** *course.* turn. **63** *prevented.* forestalled. **66** *brokerly.* pimping. **69** *fool.* The part of Drugger was originally perhaps played by Robert Armin, famous for his comic roles with the King's Men. **71** *Hieronomo's.* From Kyd's *The Spanish Tragedy.* Jonson was paid for 'additions' to this play, and was alleged by Dekker in *Satiromastix* I. ii. to have played the part of Hieronimo wearing such a cloak. **81** *locked . . . tower.* As Lully was said to have been by Edward II, and Cornelius Lannoy by Elizabeth, for their failure to manufacture gold as promised. **110** *quiblins.* Word games. **116** *liberties.* The district outside the city walls, still subject to municipal authority. The point under dispute had not in fact been specified: see I. i. 182–3. **120** *shape.* role. **125** *Ratcliff.* In Stepney, down river. **130** *shave.* Playing on the sense 'to cheat'.

V. i.   6 *Pimlico.* A popular resort in the semi-rural village of Hoxton north of London, well known for its cakes, cream, and ale. **8** *calf.* Referred to again in *BF* III. vi. 7, V. iv. 84–5. **21** *ging.* crowd. **22** *motion.* Puppet show. **22–6** Popular curiosities, referred to in other writings of the period.

V. ii. This scene recalls the situation in Plautus' *Mostellaria*, 'The Haunted House'. **19** *threaves.* droves. *Hogsden.* Now Hoxton; see V. i. 6 n. **20** *Eye-bright.* Famous for its beer. **32** *black-pot.* Beer-mug. **44** *changelings.* (i) Idiots (changed in their cradles by fairies); (ii) waverers. **47** *Nothing . . . conscience.* 'Nothing's more wretched than a guilty conscience, and mine does bother me' (*Mostellaria*, 544–5).

V. iii. 2 *mere chancel.* No less than a chancel. 17 *lights.* The term for animals' lungs when sold as meat. 34 *cockatrice.* whore. 35 *marshal.* I. i. 120 n. 41 *fat . . . gentleman.* Mammon and Surly. 47 *unclean birds.* IV. vii. 53 n. 48 *scavenger.* Officer responsible for keeping the streets clean. 50 *Punk device.* Arrant whore. 55 *St Katherine's.* The old hospital (founded 1148) was removed from the building of St Katherine's docks on the north bank of the Thames, near the Tower. 62 *deceptio visus.* Optical illusion. 67 *sets out the throat.* Raises his voice. 89 *visited.* i.e. by the plague.

V. iv. 8 *down.* open. 11 *churl.* Countryman; referring to Lovewit's hop-yards. 14 *coil.* disturbance. 18 *presently.* At once. 34 *bird.* i.e. the *fly* (l. 35), or familiar. 41 *Woolsack.* An inn in Cheapside. 42 *Dagger.* I. i. 191 n. *frumenty.* What boiled in milk and seasoned with cinnamon and sugar. 43 *Heaven and Hell.* Two taverns near Westminster Hall. 44 *mumchance, tray-trip.* Dice games. 45 *God-make-you-rich.* A variety of backgammon. 47 *Gleek and primero.* II. iii. 284–5 n.; played for bigger stakes in more elevated circles. 72 *fit.* match. 82 *bird.* The word could also mean (i) young woman; (ii) bride. 88 *flitter-mouse.* bat. 89 *Pigeons.* 'The Three Pigeons' in Brentford market-place. 116 *and.* if. *Ward.* A well-known pirate. 126 *smock-rampant.* Playing on heraldic terminology, with reference both to Dol's promiscuity and to her anger. 128 *figures.* horoscopes. 131 *Determines.* ends. 141 *Mistress Amo.* Like *Madam Caesarean*, l. 142, a brothel-keeper. For the latter—called 'Madam Imperial' in Q—cf. II. i. 17, *Epig.* 133. 180.

V. v. 2 *Cheaters . . . conjurors.* I. i. 106–7. 5 *for failing.* To make sure. 9 *ding.* break. 11 *collier.* I. i. 90 n. 13 *Madam Suppository.* Referring (i) to Dol's occupation as whore; (ii) to her pretended study of medicine; (iii) to her supposititious or fraudulent way of life. 14 *Bel . . . Dragon.* Idols worshipped by the Babylonians, referred to in the Apocrypha. 20 *nun.* i.e. whore; cf. *Und.* 43. 148. 41 *of the candle.* Written with candle-smoke. 42 *dildo.* phallus. 48 *gone through.* married. 55 *putting forward.* Cf. IV. vi. 5. 56 *harquebusier.* Musketeer, armed with harquebus. 59 *choughs.* Of the crow family. 77 *ditch.* A super version of New Ditch, then under construction: see *UV* 35. 24 n. and II. i. 76 n. above. 79 *Moorfields,* I. iv. 20 n. 80 *tits and tomboys.* Young girls. 85 *hearken.* seek. 100 *seal.* Rev. 9:4. 101–3 See III. ii. 131–2 n. 103 *table dormant.* Permanent side-table (as distinct from removable board). 104 *The . . . Saints.* In reference to the millennium: IV. v. 26 n. 105 *Six . . . ten.* i.e. 1610. 111 *Gad in exile.* Gen. 49: 19. 117 *Harry Nicholas.* Henrick Niclaes, Anabaptist mystic and leader of the sect of the Family of Love. 121 *Westchester.* Chester. 126 *tupped.* The word was used of rams and ewes; cf. *Othello,* I. i. 90. 128 *mammet.* puppet. 131 *feize.* Do for. 134 *copy.* Pattern of behaviour. 135 *stoop.* Swoop, like a bird of prey; an apt challenge to Kastril (= kestrel). 144 *Jovy.* jovial. 152 *candour.* integrity. 154 *canon.* Rule of behaviour. 159 *decorum.* Behaviour appropriate to his type of character. 162–3 *put . . . country.* Appeal to you, my countrymen (as to a jury). 163 *pelf.* (i) Wealth; (ii) trash. 164 *quit.* acquit. 165 *guests.* Humorously identifying the audience with the play's gulls.

EPIGRAMS

Jonson's *Epigrams* were first published as a collection in the Folio edition of his *Works* in 1616. They had been written on various occasions, and a few (such as *Epig.* 110, 111, 130, 131, 132) had been published already. The earliest poems in the collection—*Epig.* 22, for example, 'On My First Daughter', and *Epig.* 40, 'On Margaret Radcliffe'—were probably written in the late 1590s; the majority date from the first decade of the new century. By 1612 Jonson was probably arranging the poems for publication. 'A Book Called Ben Jonson His Epigrams' was entered in the Stationers' Register on 15 May of that year by the publisher and bookseller John Stepneth. Stepneth died later in 1612, however, and the book seems never to have been published; no copies are known to exist. William Drummond of Hawthornden nevertheless recorded 'Ben Jonson's epigrams' amongst the 'books read by me anno 1612': had he seen a manuscript collection? Herford and Simpson date none of the epigrams in the 1616 Folio later than 1612. It now seems possible, however, that one or two of the epigrams were written after 1612, but the evidence is not conclusive (see *Epig.* 67 n.; 133. 193–4 n.).

In his dedication to William, Earl of Pembroke, Jonson describes the *Epigrams* as 'the ripest of my studies': a high valuation, when it is remembered that by 1616 Jonson had also written the dramatic works by which he is chiefly remembered today. The same high valuation is evident throughout the sequence itself. Jonson asserts that his *Epigrams* are neither aggressive nor obscene nor scandalous (*Epig.* 2, 49, 77); that to write and read them takes understanding, learning, subtlety (*Epig.* 1, 17, 112); that their qualities may be lost on the casual or careless reader, unacquainted with the best classical models (*Epig.* 28. 20; 58; 18). Martial is, for Jonson, the chief amongst these models: turns of phrase, entire poems, and certain arrangements within the sequence are borrowed from Martial, whose racier tendencies Jonson none the less strives to avoid (*Epig.* Dedn. 28 and n.). For the epigrams of his contemporaries, Jonson had no high regard. 'A great many epigrams were ill', he told William Drummond, 'because they expressed in the end what should have been understood by what was said: that of S[ir] John Davies' (*Conv. Dr.* 325–6). John Owen's epigrams were 'bare narrations'; those of Sir John Harington 'narrations, and not epigrams' (*Conv. Dr.* 152; 29). Jonson valued the witty turn or conceit to which, by tradition, the epigram laconically moves: the *point* for which Groom Idiot of *Epig.* 58 myopically and lucklessly gropes. Yet not all of the poems in this collection—least of all the last, 'On the Famous Voyage'—aim at a witty succinctness; their forms and moods, like their themes, are surprisingly various.

Certain preoccupations, however, are evident. 'In short and sweet poems framed to praise and dispraise, or some other sharp conceit, which are called epigrams, as our countrymen now surpass other nations, so in former times they were not inferior.' Thus wrote Jonson's old schoolteacher, William Camden, in his *Remains of a Greater Work Concerning Britain* in 1605. *Praise and dispraise* are the central activities of Jonson's *Epigrams*. Many of the poems celebrate 'good and great names'; others deride foolish and venal characters, whose names are strategically withheld. Throughout the collection these poems of praise and dispraise are carefully cut and mixed. Moral virtues are set off against, and in part defined by, their opposing vices. The 'fool or knave' of *Epig.* 61, lacking as he is in moral discrimination, lacks also that power to honour and to hurt which the poet himself exemplifies throughout the sequence as a whole:

> Thy praise or dispraise is to me alike;
> One doth not stroke me, nor the other strike.

The title-page in the 1616 Folio announces the *Epigrams* as a 'first book'. Evidently a second book was planned. Though Jonson continued to experiment with the form—more epigrams were to be published posthumously in 1640 both in *The Underwood* and in the pirated collection of John Benson—this second book of epigrams never materialized.

[Dedication] *William, Earl of Pembroke.* 1580–1630, nephew of Sir Philip Sidney, patron to Shakespeare, Jonson (*Conv. Dr.* 259–60), and others; also addressed in *Epig.* 102. On his moral character, see Clarendon, *History of the Rebellion*, i. § 123; Dick Taylor, Jun., in *Studies in the English Renaissance Drama*, ed. J. W. Bennett *et al.* (London, 1961), pp. 322–44; on his role as patron, see Margot Heinemann, *ELR* v (1975), 232–50. **4** *danger.* See *Epig.* 2. **6** *cipher.* Cf. the disclaimer in *Volp.* Epist. Ded., esp. 56–60. Jonson probably follows at a distance Martial's preface to Bk. I. **7** *facts.* crimes. *objected to.* charged against. **10** *make a party for.* Defend. For the sentiment, cf. *Alch.* Prol. 13–14; Seneca, *Epist.* lxxxix. 19. **13** *good and great.* A favourite collocation: cf. *For.* 14. 34–5; *Und.* 13. 2; 15. 187; 24. 5–6; 70. 105, etc. **14** *names.* On their significance in the *Epigrams*, see David Wykes, *RMS* xii (1969), 76–87, and E. Partridge, *SLI* vi (1973), 153–98; cf. *Disc.* 2326 ff. **15** *posterity.* Cf. *Epig.* 109. 15; 127. 4. *praised, unfortunately.* See *Epig.* 65; *Und.* 14. 19–22. **16** *numbers.* parts. **20** *avoided all particulars.* Cf. Martial, x. xxxiii. 10; Juvenal, *Sat.* i. 147 ff.; *Volp.* Epist. Ded. 48. **25** *trade.* way. *lend . . . against.* Listen with their long (asses') ears for scandal about. **27** *humanity.* The Latin sense is strong here ('learning or literature concerned with human culture'), but Jonson is also contrasting the human and the sub-human ('long ears'). **28** *Cato.* 95–46 BC, model of Roman virtue; when he visited the games of Flora in 55 BC, the usual dance of naked girls was not held, out of respect for his presence. Jonson significantly varies Martial, i, pref. [17–18]: 'let no Cato enter my theatre, or if he enters, let him look on'.

1. Jonson's first four epigrams are loosely modelled on Martial, i. i–iv. **2** *understand.* A characteristic stress: cf. *Epig.* 110. 16; *UV* 17. 2; *Alch.* 'To the Reader', 1, etc.

2. **3–4** *gall,* | *Wormwood.* i.e. bitterness. **4** *sulphur.* i.e. explosiveness. **5** *petulant.* insolent. **10** *another's shame.* Cf. Martial, VII. xii. 4, 'fame won from another's blush is not dear to me'. **12** *loose laughter.* Horace, *Sat.* I. iv. 82–3. **13** *departs.* parts. **13–14** Cf. Martial, i, pref. [6–7]: 'May my fame be bought at a lesser cost, and the last thing to be approved in me be cleverness.'

3. To the bookseller John Stepneth, 1612. **2** *Call'st . . . sell.* Cf. Martial, XIV. cxciv: 'some there are that say I am no poet; but the bookseller that sells me thinks

I am'. **7** *posts.* Hence modern 'poster'. Horace, *Sat.* I. iv. 71–2. **8** *cleft-sticks.* Holding the book open to display its title-page. *advancèd.* Propped up. **8–9** *make calls | For.* Attract the attention of. **9** *termers.* Visitors to London, for litigation or pleasure, during the legal term. **10** *knight.* A typical gibe at the ease with which knighthoods were granted under King James: cf. *Epig.* 19. 1; 46, etc. **12** *Bucklersbury.* A street near Cheapside inhabitated by grocers and apothecaries. The book can be used for wrapping paper. Cf. Catullus, xcv, Horace, *Epist.* II. i. 269–70, Martial, III. ii. 3–5, etc.; and *Und.* 43. 51 ff., *Disc.* 596–601.

4. **1** *best of kings.* Echoed by Denham (on Charles I—and on Waller, 'best of poets'), *Cooper's Hill,* 23–4, and by Dryden (on Charles II), 'To his Sacred Majesty', 54. **3** *two things rare.* From Florus, *On The Quality of Life,* ix: 'New consuls and proconsuls are made every year, only kings and poets are not born every year.' Cf. *Epig.* 79. 1; *Panegyre,* 163; *Disc.* 2456–7. **5** *green.* James was 18 when his *Essays of a Prentice in the Divine Art of Poesy* appeared in 1584, 25 at the appearance of *His Majesty's Poetical Exercises at Vacant Hours* in 1591 (poems composed 'in his very young and tender years'). Contrast Jonson's verdict in *Conv. Dr.* 488–90. **7** *such a prince.* Cf. Pliny on Trajan, 'such a prince as others can only promise to be', *Panegyricus,* 24.

5. Probably written in March 1604. 'What God hath conjoined let no man separate. I am the husband and all the whole isle is my lawful wife' (James to his first Parliament). See D. H. Willson, *King James VI and I* (London, 1956), pp. 249–54; *Hym.* 424–30.

7. **2** *purging bill.* Perhaps an edict against brothels. This one avoids the edict by a change of name. **3** *hot-house.* Bath-house; but also brothel: cf. *Measure for Measure,* II. i. 63–4. **4** *synonima.* synonyms.

8. **4** *Begged Ridway's pardon.* i.e. a pardon for Ridway.

9. **4** *no herald.* Cf. Sidney, *Arcadia,* Bk. I, ch. ii (*Complete Works,* ed. A. Feuillerat (Cambridge, 1939), i. 15); Webster, *The Duchess of Malfi,* III. ii. 259–60.

10. **1** *shame.* Cf. *Disc.* 284–5. **2** *revenge.* Perhaps pointing forward to *Epig.* II. 4–5 (cf. *Und.* 2. iii. 24 ff.).

11. **3** *statesman.* An observer (not necessarily a practitioner) of affairs of state. **5** *lord. Conv. Dr.* 282.

12. To 'shift' is to live by fraud or expediencies. Cf. Herrick, p. 144, 'Upon Shift'. **1** *squires.* pimps. **2** *Pickt-hatch . . . Whitefriars.* Disreputable parts of London at the time. On Whitefriars, see *Volp.* IV. ii. 51 n. **7** *quarter-day.* When rentals commonly fell due. **9** *'ssays.* Essays, tries on. **11** *ordinaries.* taverns. **13** *takes up . . . commodity.* Buys goods from a usurer on credit and resells cheaply for ready cash. **15** *essays.* Not esteemed by Jonson: see *Disc.* 731–41, *Volp.* V. iv. 43. **16** *papers.* Drug wrappings. **18** *stool.* Which cost an extra 6d. at Blackfriars at this time (*CR* Ind. 140–6). **21** *cockatrice.* whore. **23** *trim.* fashion.

13. **2** *Aesculape.* Aesculapius, classical god of medicine. The cock, symbol of vigilance, was sacred to him. **4** *From . . . thee.* Cf. *Volp.* I. iv. 20–2 and n.

14. *William Camden.* 1551–1623, celebrated antiquary; Jonson's master at Westminster School (*Conv. Dr.* 196–7). On Camden, and this poem, see Peterson, pp. 56–61. **4** *renown and name.* In 1604 James had styled himself, controversially, King of Britain (rather than of England) in his attempt to further the Union. Jonson suggests that the titles of Camden's *Britannia* (1586) and *Remains of a Greater Work Concerning Britain* (1605) had helped restore the popularity of the name 'Britain'. **5–6** Cf. Pliny, *Epist.* IV. xvii. 4. **7–9** Cf. Pliny on Titius Aristo, *Epist.* I. xxii: 'How consummate is his knowledge in both the political and civil laws of his country! How thoroughly conversant is he in history, precedents, antiquity! There is no article, in short, you would wish to be informed of, in which he cannot enlighten you.' **11** *free.* (i) Unchecked; (ii) generous. **11–12** Cf. Claudian, *On Stilicho's Consulship*, ii. 329: 'world-conqueror, conquer now thine own diffidence'. **13** *thine.* i.e. thy pupils. **14** *for.* In place of.

15. **1** *worms.* Job 25: 5–6, Ps. 22: 6. **4** *caterpillar.* Sometimes used of a rapacious person (*Richard II*, II. iii. 166, 'caterpillars of the commonwealth').

16. **8** *Make good.* prove. **10** *He . . . fight.* Cf. Plutarch, *Lysander*, viii. 4 ('he who overreaches his enemy by means of an oath, confesses that he fears that enemy, but despises God'); Sir John Davies, *Epig.* xxviii, *In Sillam.*

17. *Learned Critic.* Possibly William, Earl of Pembroke: see Dedn. n., and cf. Jonson's Dedn. to *Catiline.* **4** *Charge . . . hie.* Order them to hasten for commendation to thy sole judgement. 'Crown' (a favoured word: *Epig.* 94. 6, *Volp.* Epist. Ded. 88) is the laurel wreath. **6** *chaste tree.* The laurel, sacred to Apollo, god of poetry; 'chaste' because of the transformation of Daphne (*Epig.* 126. 3 n.).

18. *Mere English Censurer.* A critic knowing only the English writers. The poem recalls Martial, II. lxxvii and VI. lxv. **4** *Davies and Weever.* The *Epigrams* of Sir John Davies (1569–1626) appeared *c.*1590; *Epigrams in the Oldest Cut, and Newest Fashion* by John Weaver (1576–1632) were published in 1599 (cf. 'new'/'old', ll. 1–2). **6** *credit.* Glancing at the religious sense, 'credence' (cf. the religious overtones of 'the old way and the true', l. 2). **10** *faith.* Appropriate in spiritual matters but not in literary: contrast the learned critic's magistrate-like judgement, *Epig.* 17.

19. *Cod.* (i) Civet- or musk-bag; (ii) testicles. **1** *widow.* Cf. *Epig.* 46. 1 n. *knight.* See *Epig.* 3. 10 n. **2** *ill sprite.* (i) Evil genius; (ii) bad breath; (iii) poor sexual vigour.

20. Cf. Martial, II. xii.

21. **1** *close cut.* Frequently (though not invariably) a Puritan style. **4** *the word.* The common Puritan term for the Bible. **6** *bastinado* beating-stick.

22. The date of the poem is unknown, though it probably belongs early in Jonson's Catholic period, i.e. 1598–1610 (see esp. ll. 8–9). **3** *heaven's gifts. Epig.* 45. 3 and n. **10–11** *Where . . . birth.* While the soul remains in heaven, severed from the body, the grave retains ('takes a share in') the body for a while (i.e. until the resurrection). **12** *cover lightly.* A common classical formula (*sit tibi terra levis*): Martial on Erotion, V. xxxiv. 9–10 ('And let not hard clods cover her tender

bones, nor be thou heavy upon her, O earth; she was not so to thee'); IX. xxix. 11; XI. xiv, etc.

23. *John Donne.* 'The first poet in the world in some things' (*Conv. Dr.* 86). The friendship of the two poets was probably of long standing; see R. C. Bald, *John Donne: A Life* (Oxford, 1970), pp. 194–7. The poem was printed in Donne's *Poems* in 1650, 1654 and 1669. See also *Epig.* 94, 96. **1** *Phoebus.* God of poetry. **2** *Who . . . refuse.* Who, in favour of your brain, refuse to inspire others. **5** *Longer a-knowing.* Longer a skilled practitioner of your art. **7** *To it.* In addition to your wit. **8** *maintain a strife.* contend.

24. *Parliament.* Probably that of 1604. **2** *for your sake.* Probably, 'on account of enmity to you' (*OED*, 'sake', 5b).

25. **4** *Ganymede.* catamite. **5** *cuckquean.* Female cuckold. The wife is forced to impersonate other women to satisfy her husband's fantasies. Cf. *Volp.* III. vii. 221 ff. **6** *shapes.* Disguises; roles. **8** *change me.* (i) Provide variety for me; (ii) exchange me for another. *woman's haste.* i.e. to adultery; thus fulfilling traditional ideas about female changeability (Tilley, W673, W674).

26. **2** *adulters.* Matt. 5: 27–8; Seneca, *On Firmness*, vii. 4: 'If a man lies with his wife as if she were another man's wife, he will be an adulterer, though she will not be an adulteress.'

27. *Sir John Roe.* 1581–?1606, soldier, poet, and close friend of Jonson, in whose arms he died of the plague (*Conv. Dr.* 121–4, 148–50; see also *Epig.* 32, 33). See Alvaro Ribeiro, *RES* xxiv (1973), 153–64. **1** *scutcheons.* Tablets showing the armorial bearings of the deceased person. **2** *ornaments.* Commonly used in relation to poetry (e.g. Puttenham, *The Art of English Poesie* (1589), Bk. III, 'Of Ornament'). The poem is apparently a 'pillar poem', like Herbert's 'The Altar' (despite Jonson's apparent scorn for such 'finer flams', *Und.* 43. 36 ff.). **3** *sword.* *Epig.* 32. 1–2.

28. *Surly.* Cf. *Epig.* 82. Surly in *The Alchemist* is a different type. **1** *aspire.* attain. **3** *trade.* manners. **4** *rhinocerote's.* Rhinoceros's: recalling Martial's description of the superciliousness of Rome, where men and boys tilt their noses like rhinoceroses (*nasum rhinocerotis habent,* I. iii. 5–6). **7** *tympanies.* swellings. **13** *main.* mighty. *still.* silent. **15** *spice.* species.

29. *Sir Annual Tilter.* i.e. a once-yearly jouster, who had earned praise for an ingenious satirical representation, perhaps at a King's Day celebration (24 March, the anniversary of James's accession). Fleay (i. 317) guesses Sir Richard Preston. **5** *wine.* Which ran through London's water-conduits on great occasions (Sugden, p. 127).

30. *Person Guilty.* Cf. *Epig.* 38. **4** *name. Epig.* Dedn. 14 n.; *Disc.* 2347 ff.; *Epig.* 77.

31. **1** *gout.* Popularly associated with usurers (esp. 'hand-gout'): C. T. Wright, *SP* xxi (1934), 176–97; Horace, *Epist.* I. i. 31; Martial, I. xcviii: 'Diodorus goes to law, and suffers, Flaccus, from gout in the feet. But he offers his advocate no fee: this is gout in the hand.' **2** *travel.* F 'travail': a pun.

32. *Sir John Roe.* See *Epig.* 27 n. **1** *sword.* For Roe's duelling reputation, cf. *Epig.* 27. 3. **3** *self-divided Belgia.* After the Pacification of Ghent in 1576, hostility continued to exist between Protestants in the northern provinces of the Netherlands and Catholics in the south. **5–7** What the cold of Moscow and the moist Irish air . . . could not bring about (sc. his death). **6** *change . . . mind.* Horace, *Epist.* I. xi. 27: 'they change their clime, not their mind, who rush across the sea'. **7** *repair.* Usual place of dwelling. **10** *serenes.* 'A light fall of moisture or fine rain after sunset in hot countries, formerly regarded as a noxious dew or mist' (*OED, sb.*¹).

33. **1** *tear.* Also the term for a memorial verse (e.g. Spenser's *Tears of the Muses*; Milton, *Lycidas*, 14). **2–3** Seneca, *To Marcia on Consolation*, xix. 1 ('We have sent them on their way—nay, we have sent them ahead and shall soon follow'); *To Polybius on Consolation*, ix. 9 ('The way thither is the same for us all. Why do we bemoan his fate? He has not left us, but has gone before'); *Epist.* lxiii. 16.

35. Fleay (i. 317) dates the poem April 1604, noticing allusions in ll. 5–8 to the new laws of that year, in l. 9 to the treasons of Gowrie (1600) and Raleigh (1603), and in l. 10 to the plague of 1603. **2** *example . . . sway.* James's own ideal (see *Basilikon Doron*, ed. James Craigie (Edinburgh, 1944), i. 53), frequently repeated by Jonson; cf. Claudian, *Panegyric on the Fourth Consulship of the Emperor Honorius*, 299–300. **6** *laws.* The legislation of March and April 1604 reflected the uneasy relations between King and Commons over Goodwin's case and other matters.

36. **2** *Domitian.* Despotic and unpopular Roman emperor (AD 51–96, emperor from 81), finally murdered by conspirators; there is perhaps an implied contrast with James's preservation from plotting referred to in *Epig.* 35. **3** *royal subject.* An oxymoron, punningly reversing the roles of *Epig.* 35. 1. **4** *flattered.* Flattery is deplored by James in *Basilikon Doron*, i. 115, and by Jonson in *Epig.* 43. 10–12, *Conv. Dr.* 278, etc.

37. *Cheverel.* Cheverel- or kid-leather is pliant; so is the lawyer. He reappears in *Epig.* 54. See Tilley, C608. **1** *leese.* lose. **2** *both sides.* Cf. *Volp.* I. iii. 58–9. **3** *melts his grease.* Exerts himself.

38. **1** *late.* In *Epig.* 30. **8** *modesty.* Cf. *Epig.* 77. *name.* See *Epig.* Dedn. 14 n.

39. *Colt.* 'stud'.

40. *Margaret Radcliffe.* Or Ratcliffe, favourite maid of honour of Queen Elizabeth, died of grief on 10 November 1599 after the death of four of her brothers (William and Alexander, fighting in Ireland, 1598, 1599; Edmund and Thomas, of fever in French Flanders, 1599). A fifth brother is addressed in *Epig.* 93. The poem is an acrostic, a form which Jonson scorns in *Und.* 43. 39. **1** *weep.* As marble may seem to do. A common conceit; cf. Virgil, *Georgics*, i. 480, etc. **4** *remove her.* Suicides were not always accorded church burial; her status is otherwise. **17** *not such another.* As the line itself stands alone in the poem's verse pattern, 'another' rhyming internally (and aptly) with 'brother', l. 15.

41.   2 *College.* Of Physicians. 3 *quaint.* A sexual pun; cf. *Alch.* II. iii. 303.

42.   Cf. Martial, VIII. xxxv ('Seeing that you are like one another, and a pair in your habits, vilest of wives, vilest of husbands, I wonder you don't agree') and XII. lviii, and Herrick, p. 163, 'Jack and Jill'. T. K. Whipple, *Martial and the English Epigram*, (California, 1925), p. 398 n. 23, cites an epigram by Parkhurst as the 'immediate original' of the present poem. **16** *to will and nill.* To want and not to want. Cf. Sallust, *Catiline*, xx. 4: 'for agreement in likes and dislikes—this, and this only, is what constitutes true friendship'.

43.   *Robert, Earl of Salisbury.* Robert Cecil (1563–1612), Secretary of State under Elizabeth; created Earl of Salisbury 4 May 1605, when H & S believe the poem was written. Cf. *Epig.* 63 and 64. **3–4** Which, if not spoken of by thy country, out of love, would be made famous enough by her foes, out of hatred. **5** *'Tofore.* heretofore. **10–12** Cf. Pliny, *Panegyricus*, I. 6 ('and my vote of thanks be as far removed from a semblance of flattery as it is from constraint'); *Epig.* 36. 4 n.

44.   *Chuff.* (i) Churl, miser; (ii) chough (bird in crow family). Cf. Corvino in *Volp.*, a 'gaping crow' (I. ii. 96) awaiting a legacy. Bank appears in *Epig.* 31. **4** *blacker floods.* The Styx; i.e. death. **5–6** Perhaps: though Chuff had made Bank his executor, Chuff intended rather that he himself should be Bank's heir.

45.   *First Son.* Also called Benjamin Jonson; he died of the plague in 1603. For Jonson's premonition of his death see *Conv. Dr.* 214–24. Criticism: W. D. Kay, *SEL* xi (1971), 125–36. **1** *right hand, and joy.* In Hebrew, Benjamin means son of the right hand; dextrous; fortunate. In Gen. 35: 18 the name is implicitly contrasted with Ben-oni, 'son of my sorrow'. 'Right hand' suggests further (i) 'a favourite or darling' (Tilley, H73); (ii) indispensableness (*OED*, 'right hand', 1c); (iii) legitimacy (cf. *OED*, 'left hand', 2). **3** *lent.* A common classical notion: R. Lattimore, *Themes in Greek and Latin Epitaphs* (Urbana, 1962), pp. 170–1; cf. *Epig.* 22. 3; 109. 11; *For.* 3. 106; *Und.* 83. 80. **4** *just day.* Deut. 15: 1–2 (K. Walls, *NQ* NS 24 (1977), 136). **5** *lose all father.* Shake off all paternal feelings (F 'loose': the words were interchangeable). **10** *Ben . . . poetry.* The notion is that of the poet as maker: see *Disc.* 2369–70, 2432–3. **12** Martial, VI. xxix. 8: 'whatever you love, pray that it may not please you too much'. It was a common classical notion that excessive good fortune aroused the jealousy of the gods: Jonson subtly varies the emphasis. Cf. also Martial, XII. xxxiv. 8–11: 'If you wish to shun some bitternesses and to beware of sorrows that gnaw the heart, to no man make yourself too much a comrade: your joy will be less and less will be your grief.'

46.   **1** *waste wife.* Probably, a wealthy widow 'wasted' by age or illness: suitable prey for a fortune-hunter (R. Earley, *MLN* xii (1975), 265–8). **2** *knighthood bought.* On the abuses arising out of the sale of knighthoods in James's reign, see Lawrence Stone, *The Crisis of the Aristocracy* (Oxford, 1965), pp. 74–82. **3** *band.* bond. **5** *knight-wright.* Not in *OED*, but used also by Donne, *Paradoxes* (1652), p. 66 (Briggs, *Anglia*, xxxix (1916), 315).

48.   'The arms were usually portrayed upon the shield; so that on his entering into battle, he flung away his shield, that he might not be encumbered in his flight.'

This marks him for cowardice' (Whalley). **1** *bought arms.* Cf. Sogliardo in *EMO*
III. iv. 51 ff., who buys his arms for £30.

49. *Playwright.* This occurrence of the word predates *OED*'s first recorded
example (1687). Early usage is scornful: cf. 'Cygnus' on 'common playwrights'
(verses on *Sejanus*, 1605: H & S, xi. 314), and Henry Fitzjeffrey on Webster as
'playwright-cartwright' (*Notes from Blackfriars*, 1617). Jonson's fleer at 'stage-
wrights' (*Songs*, 35. 35) is similar in tone. He habitually referred to himself as a
'poet'. **2** *the tongue of epigrams.* Martial's *epigrammaton linguam*, 'the language of
the epigram', I, pref. [10–11]; Martial is justifying the freedom of his language.
3 *salt.* (i) Wit; (ii) salaciousness. **6** *chaste.* Probably varying Catullus, xvi: 'for the
sacred poet ought to be chaste himself, his verses need not be so'.

50. *Sir Cod.* See *Epig.* 19 and 20. **1** *tobacco-like, burnt gums.* The reference is to
gums as medicinal drugs. Tobacco, smoked or simply placed in the mouth, was
likewise thought to cure various ailments, including venereal disease. **2** *clysters.*
Normally, enema-pipes; here, tobacco-pipes. Cf. *Songs*, 32. 32. **3** *Arsenic.* A
common cure for venereal disease, but also a lethal poison; Jonson leaves the
choice open.

51. Actually 1606. The rumour that James had been stabbed while hunting
came not long after the Gunpowder Plot, causing widespread alarm. **3** *panic.*
groundless. **5** *doubt.* fear. **6** *gratulate.* Rejoice over. **8** *after-state.* future (probably a
nonce-formation).

52. *Courtling.* Addressed again in *Epig.* 72. **2** *frostily.* 'Faint praise is disparagement', Tilley, P538; cf. Pope's 'damn with faint praise', *Epistle to Dr Arbuthnot*,
l. 201.

53. *Old-End Gatherer.* i.e. plagiarist; literally, a collector of old ends of material
or candles; cf. *Volp.* Prol. 23–4. The poem may glance at Marston, who had
dedicated *The Scourge of Villainy* to himself in 1599 (yet Marston satirizes self-
commendation in *Satire* i. 7–10). **2** *pilled.* plundered. **3** *the author's name.* The
name of the original author and the plagiarist are both suppressed. **4** *the patron's.*
The plagiarist has dedicated the book to himself. **6** *both.* Author and dedicatee.
8 *witness.* Baptismal sponsor or godfather; a Puritan term (*BF* I. iii. 127–8).
9–10 For who but a fool—apart from thyself—could spare a line to dedicate to thee?

54. *Cheverel.* See *Epig.* 37 and n. **2** Cf. Horace, *Sat.* II. i. 47, 'Cervius, when
angry, threatens his foes with laws and the judge's urn'. **3** *petulant.* insolent.

55. *Francis Beaumont.* ?1548–1616, the dramatist. This is a reply to Beaumont's
well-known poem to Jonson from the country, written sometime between 1610
and 1613, and printed in H & S, xi. 374–6. For a cooler opinion of Beaumont, see
Conv. Dr. 120. **2** *religion.* Pious affection.

56. *Poet-Ape.* Not identified. **2** *frippery.* Old clothes shop. **3** *brokage.* Brokerage:
dealing in second-hand goods. **6** *reversion.* The right of succeeding to something
after another is done with it; also used of left-over food. **14** *the whole piece.* Cf. *UV*
42. 17.

57. The association of usury and sex (especially prostitution) was traditional: see Tilley, U28, U31; *S. of N.* II. v. 100; *Measure for Measure*, III. ii. 5–8; *The Merchant of Venice*, I. iii. 90–1; Herrick, p. 220, 'Upon Snare, an Usurer'. The Greek word τόκος means both 'interest' and 'offspring'. Bawds and usurers have commercial *ends* in common, but their *fruits* differ: for the bawds do not wish to multiply.

58. **6** *losing.* F 'loosing'; both senses are present. *points.* Punctuation; hence, meaning. Contrast *Disc.* 221–5.

59. Jonson may be thinking of the spies who visited him in prison in 1597: *Conv. Dr.* 212–13. Cf. *Und.* 43. 187–8.

60. *Lord Monteagle.* William Parker, 4th Baron Monteagle, a former Roman Catholic, received in 1605 the anonymous warning letter which led to the discovery of the Gunpowder Plot; he was rewarded, and hailed as the saviour of parliament. For the suggestion that he and Jonson possibly had prior knowledge of the Plot, see B. N. De Luna, *Jonson's Romish Plot* (Oxford, 1967), esp. ch. iv. **2** *obelisk or column.* Terms used of poetry by, e.g., Puttenham, *The Art of English Poesie*, Bk. II. x [xi]; cf. *Epig.* 93. 1. **4** *fact.* action. **5** *chance.* fortune.

61. **2** *stroke.* Flatter. The 'stroke'/'strike' contrast was proverbial: see *OED*, 'stroke', *v.*¹ 1c and e.

62. *Lady Would-Be.* Cf. the character of this name in *Volp.* The Collegiate ladies in *SW* hold similar views on child-bearing (IV. iii. 57–61); cf. also *Und.* 15. 95–6. **1–2** Why should you fear to bear a child when you so enjoy the act of making one? **4** *says no.* (i) Says you are not barren; (ii) says 'no' to your bearing a child, being abortifacient. **7** *feature.* figure.

63. *Robert, Earl of Salisbury.* see *Epig.* 43 n. **2–3** And how thy virtue has prevailed upon the times . . . Cf. Valerius Maximus on the elder Cato, VIII. xv. 2: he 'became great through his own personal merit rather than by favour of fortune'. Jonson's contrast between 'virtue' and 'fortune' is characteristic: cf. *Und.* 23. 16–18; *Sej.* III. 88–9; 321–5; IV. 68–9, etc. **5–6** Cf. Pliny, *Epist.* I. xxii. 5: '[Titius Aristo] cares nothing for show but refers everything to conscience, seeking reward for a good deed not in popular opinion but in performance' (*non ex populi sermone mercedem, sed ex facto petit*). **7** *declined.* Turned aside. **8** *equal.* just. **11** *his muse.* 'my voice' in the Cecil manuscript at Hatfield House; cf. *Epig.* 65 n.

64. *the Treasurership.* On 6 May 1608. **3–4** *golden age . . . age of gold.* A traditional contrast: see *Volp.* I. i. 15 n. **6** *thy father's rites.* Lord Burghley, Cecil's father, had been made Lord Treasurer in 1592; cf. *Und.* 30. **11–12** Cf. Pliny, *Epist.* V. xiv: 'I congratulate myself, therefore, no less than him, and as much upon public as private grounds, that virtue is now no longer, as formerly, the road to danger, but to office.'

65. The placing of this epigram suggests that Salisbury could be the 'worthless lord' (l. 2) in question (it also follows aptly the hypothetical curse of *Epig.* 63. 11–

12; cf. textual note there). Cf. *Conv. Dr.* 297–8; *For.* 2 n.; 2. 61 ff. n.; De Luna, *Jonson's Romish Plot*, p. 71. 3 *fierce idolatry*. *Alch.* IV. i. 39.

66.   *Sir Henry Cary*. ?1575–1633, created Viscount Falkland 1620; father of Sir Lucius Cary of *Und.* 70. 6 ff. In October 1605, 1,200 Dutch and English troops under the command of Maurice of Nassau fled before 400 Italians near the junction of the Ruhr and the Rhine; Cary was one of four men who stood their ground, and was subsequently captured. Jonson compares, and distinguishes, military capture and civil arrest. 8 *justify*. In the legal sense: 'to show or maintain sufficient reason in court for doing that which one is called upon to answer for' (*OED*, 7a). 11 *Love . . . loss*. 'In fact this unlucky capture was the beginning of the financial difficulties that dogged, and sometimes influenced, his steps, as payment of the ransom made crippling inroads into his patrimony', Sr. Veronica Delany, ed. *The Poems of Patrick Cary* (Oxford, 1978), p. xvi. 12 'The castle and river near where he was taken' (Jonson's note). 18 Cf. *Cat.* III. 480, and Juvenal, *Sat.* x. 141–2: 'For who would embrace virtue herself if you stripped her of her rewards?'

67.   *Thomas, Earl of Suffolk*. Thomas Howard (1561–1626), Lord Chamberlain 1603–14, Lord Treasurer 1614–19. In 1605 he rescued Jonson and Chapman from their imprisonment over *Eastward Ho!* H & S conjecture this may be the occasion of the poem. Whalley's suggestion that it was written on Suffolk's appointment as Lord Treasurer makes more sense of the concluding lines, but runs counter to H & S's general dating of the *Epigrams* (see headnote). 1 Cf. Pliny, *Epist.* III. xxi. 3. 5–6 Playing on the etymology of Howard: 'High Warden or Guardian' according to Camden, *Remains Concerning Britain* (London, 1870), pp. 148–9; cf. Pope, *Dunciad* (B), i. 297. 7–10 Cf. Claudian, *On Stilicho's Consulship*, i. 49–50: 'The silent suffrage of the people had already offered thee all the honours the court was soon to owe.' 12 Proverbial: *vox populi vox Dei*; Tilley, V95.

68.   *Playwright*. See *Epig.* 49 n.; 100. Jonson boasted of having beaten Marston: *Conv. Dr.* 235–6.

69.   *Pertinax*. Obstinate, stiff (Lat.). *Cob*. A lumpish person or thing. 2 *weapon . . . part*. For the *double entendres*, cf. Martial, IX. lxiii. 2; *Und.* 2. x. 8.

70.   *William Roe*. b. 1585, brother of Sir John Roe (see *Epig.* 27, 32, 33), and cousin of Sir Thomas Roe (*Epig.* 98 and 99). Jonson appeared on his behalf in a lawsuit (H & S, i. 223–30). He is also addressed in *Epig.* 128. 1–2 Seneca, *On the Shortness of Life*, iii. 5: 'How late is it to begin to live just when we must cease to live!' 2 *makes a state*. i.e. achieves an admirable state. 5 Seneca, op. cit. ix. 1: 'Yet postponement is the greatest waste of life . . . the greatest hindrance to living is expectancy, which depends upon the morrow and wastes today.' 6 Cf. Virgil, *Georgics*, iii. 66–7 ('Life's fairest days are ever the first to flee, for hapless mortals'), and Seneca's comment on those lines, *Epist.* cviii. 24 ff. For the general thought, cf. Horace, *Epist.* I. ii. 41 ff., Martial, I. xv; v. xx, etc.

71.   *Court-Parrot*. Mark Eccles suggests this may be Henry Parrot, a con-

temporary writer of epigrams, and sees a possible allusion to Parrot's *The Mousetrap, Epig.* xcvii, 1606 (*RES* xiii (1937), 388).

72. *Courtling.* Also addressed in *Epig.* 52. **2** *chamber-critic.* A critic who gives his opinions in private; the phrase also connotes 'effeminacy and wantonness' (*OED*). **6** *vice.* Cf. *Epig.* 115. 5 and n.

73. **5** *In primis.* first. **9** *Babylonian.* incomprehensible. **11** *belie.* As the posy (or motto) promises more than Grand intends to perform. **13** *partie-per-pale.* 'A term in heraldry denoting that the field, on which the figures making up a coat of arms are represented, is divided into two equal parts by a perpendicular line' (H & S). **14** *cypress.* Black crape. *cobweb-lawn.* White linen. **15** *impres'.* Impresa, device with motto, here probably on a shield. **20** *vain.* (i) Vanity; (ii) vein; (iii) weather-vane (cf. 'cock', l. 18).

74. *Thomas, Lord Chancellor* [*Egerton*]. ?1540–1617; created Baron Ellesmere and Lord Chancellor in 1603; addressed again in *Und.* 31 and 32. **2** *not of one year.* Imitating Horace's *consul non unius anni, Odes,* IV. ix. 39. **4** *affection.* animosity. **5** *present to.* Favourably attentive to. **7** While you remain true to your words, once spoken. **9** *The Virgin.* Astraea, goddess of justice, who dwelt on earth during the Golden Age, and later fled to heaven: Virgil, *Ecl.* iv. 6. Contrast *Und.* 15. 39.

75. *Lippe.* Suggesting both English 'lip' and Latin *lippus,* blear-eyed. Cf. Herrick, p. 325, 'Upon Trappe'. **2** *Puritans and players.* The Puritans, tradition- ally hostile to the theatre, were popularly known as 'hypocrites', a word deriving from the Greek for 'actors'. Cf. *BF* v. v. 50–1, *Disc.* 61–5.

76. *Lucy, Countess of Bedford.* ?1581–1627, celebrated patroness of poets; she befriended Jonson, Donne, Drayton, Daniel, and others. She danced in several of Jonson's masques, and is addressed again in *Epig.* 84 and 94. **1** *timely.* (i) Early; (ii) at an apt time (see ll. 7–8). **5** *free.* noble. **6** *more good than great. Epig.* Dedn. 13 n. **7** *day-star.* Morning star; see *Epig.* 94. 2 n. **8** *influence.* The power supposedly exerted by heavenly bodies. *lucent.* Playing on the derivation of Lucy's name, from *lux, lucis,* light ('a name given first to them that were born when daylight first appeared': Camden, *Remains*); cf. *Epig.* 94. 1; *For.* 12. 66; *Und.* 70. 97 ('Lucius'). **9** *facile.* Courteous, approachable. **10** Cf. Claudian, *On Stilicho's Consulship,* ii. 160–2: 'Nay, pride itself is far removed from thee, pride, a vice so familiar in success, ungracious attendant on the virtues.' **14** *even.* steady. **15** *rock ... spindle ... shears.* Emblems of the three Parcae or Fates: the distaff ('rock') of Clotho, who determines the moment of one's birth; the spindle of Lachesis, who spins our actions and fortunes; the shears of Atropos, who at last cuts life's thread. For a similar insistency upon the superiority of virtue to fate (and fortune), see *For.* 11. 1–2; *Epig.* 63. 2–3 n. **18** *that was she.* Cf. Donne, 'To the Countess of Bedford' ('Madam, | You have refined me', *Satires,* p. 92), ll. 11–12, 'there some must be | To usher virtue, and say *This is she*'.

77. Cf. *Epig.* Dedn. 20; *Epig.* 30 and 38.

78. *Hornet.* i.e. cuckold. Cf. Herrick, p. 253, 'Upon Slouch'. **1** *stall.* Market booth.

79. *Elizabeth, Countess of Rutland.* ?1584–1612, daughter of Sir Philip Sidney. Jonson reckoned her 'nothing inferior to her father' in poetry (*Conv. Dr.* 171–2); and addresses her again in *For.* 12 and *Und.* 50. 1 See *Epig.* 4. 3 n. 3–4 Jonson works up his hyperbole from Martial's more restrained figure: VIII. lxx. 3–4: 'Though he might have drained sacred Permessis in full draughts, he chose to slake his thirst with diffidence.' 6 *issue. The Arcadia.* 11 *absolute numbers.* Perfect verses.

80. 1 *ports.* gates. 6 *strifes.* strivings. 7 *front.* confront. 8 Matt. 16: 28.

81. *Prowl.* To 'prowl' was to pilfer. Cf. Martial, I. lxiii: 'You ask me to recite to you my epigrams: I decline. You don't wish to hear them, Celer, but to recite them.' 4 *wealthy witness.* 'This is a pure Latinism: *testis locuples* is the Roman phrase for a full and sufficient evidence' (Whalley). 8 *libel.* Probably, a defamatory epigram, naming the plagiarist.

82. 2 *cast.* Discarded (as Surly himself has been 'cast', i.e. cashiered).

83. 1 *put out.* delete.

84. *Lucy, Countess of Bedford.* See *Epig.* 76 n. The poem was a favourite of Jonson's: *Conv. Dr.* 68–9. 3 *prevented.* anticipated. 9 *transfer.* Transport; with a pun on the legal sense. 9, 10 *grant . . . gift.* Jonson distinguishes between the promise and its execution.

85. *Sir Henry Goodyere.* 1571–1628, of Polesworth in the Forest of Arden, Warwickshire; knighted 1599, Gentleman of the Privy Chamber 1605; close friend of Donne, who also speaks of his fondness for hawking (*Satires*, pp. 78–9). He took part in Jonson's *Hymenaei* in 1606. 4 *sacred to Apollo.* Apollo in his role as augur: the hawk was reckoned a bird of good omen (see Jonson's note to *Augurs*, 350). The bird's action was also likened to that of the intellect: see Ripa, *Iconologia* (Hertel edn.), ed. E. A. Maser (New York, 1971), no. 184. 6, 7 *tower . . . stoop.* Hawking terms: respectively, soar, swoop. 11–12 What would I have learnt from the serious actions of one whose pleasures have taught me this?

86. 7–8 Cf. *Und.* 70. 107–10.

87. *Captain. Alch.* I. i. 19 and n. *Hazard.* A dicing game. *Cheater.* Dishonest gambler. 6 *made.* Proceeds apace.

88. 6 *half-way tree.* Probably a landmark on the Dover Road. 10 *French disease.* The pox. 15 *motion.* puppet. 16 *Paul's.* The middle aisle of St Paul's Cathedral was a fashionable area to promenade (cf. *EMO* III. v).

89. *Edward Alleyn.* 1566–1625, the famous actor; he had taken leading roles in Marlowe's plays, and in 1608 acted in an entertainment by Jonson at Salisbury House (see Scott McMillan, *Renaissance Drama*, NS i (Evanston, 1968), 160). 3 *Roscius . . . Aesop.* Distinguished Roman actors in comedy and tragedy respectively. Jonson echoes Horace, *Epist.* II. i. 82, 'what stately Aesopus and learned Roscius once acted'. Several of Jonson's contemporaries compared Alleyn, and his great rival Burbage, to one or both of these actors. 6 *Cicero.* See *The Making of* *an Orator*, I. xxviii. 129–30; *In Defence of Sestius*, lvii. 121–2; lviii. 123. **12** Playing on the proverb, 'not words but deeds' (Tilley, W820).

90. 4 *wan.* won. **17** *Milo.* Famous athlete of Crotona, Italy, d. *c.*500 BC; said to have developed his strength by lifting a calf every day until it became a bull. *wull.* will. **18** A familiar proverb, 'applied unto those that, falling into small offences when they are young, commit great sins when they are of perfect age' (Baret, 1580; see Tilley, B711). Petronius applies the proverb in a sexual context, *Satyricon*, 25.

91. *Sir Horace Vere.* 1565–1635, distinguished soldier of distinguished family; exploits at Mulheim (1605), Mannheim (1625); created Baron Vere of Tilbury 1625. **3** *Illustrous.* illustrious. *Vere.* 'Truly' in Latin. Possibly Jonson is thinking also of Horace's friends Lucius Rufus Varius, the poet, or Quintilius Varus, the critic, both of whom are mentioned in *Ars Poetica* (Jonson's trs., ll. 79, 623). **4** *Horace.* Jonson perceived similarities between himself and Horace: see H&S, i. 418–22, 436–41. *free.* Noble, magnanimous. **8** *relish.* Musical embellishment. **9** *prosecute.* Treat in detail. **15** *Humanity.* Cf. *Epig.* Dedn. 27; *Epig.* 113. **8.** *piety.* In the Latin sense: loyalty, devotion, patriotism, affection. **16** Cf. Seneca, *On Mercy*, I. v. 4. **18** Cf. Pliny, *Panegyricus*, xlvi. 1.

92. 1 *Cherries ripe.* The common street cry; cf. Campion's and Herrick's poems, 'Cherry-ripe'. **3** *statesmen. Epig.* 11. 3 n. **4** *At six-and-twenty, ripe.* 'refers, I think, to the peerage bestowed on Carr 1611, Mar. 25' (Fleay, i. 319). **8** *states . . . places.* i.e. the politics of the countries, not the countries themselves. **10** *chapmen.* Salesmen; their knowledge is external. **12** *intelligence.* information. **15** *Tacitus.* Contrast *Epig.* 95. 3. **16** *Gazetti.* 'running reports, daily news, idle intelligences, or flim-flam tales that are daily written from Italy, namely Rome and Venice' (Florio, *Queen Anna's New World of Words*, 1616). *Gallo-Belgicus.* The famous register of news, *Mercurii Gallo-Belgici*, published at Cologne. **17** *talk reserved, locked up.* Cf. Sir Politic Would-be, (*Volp.* IV. i. 13), who also shows an interest in ciphers (II. i. 67–89; cf. ll. 25 ff. below). H & S (i. 254) wonder if there may be a covert allusion to Sir Thomas Monson, master of armoury at the Tower. **18** *in your ear.* Cf. Martial's repeated phrase, *in aurem*, I. lxxxix. **19** *Star-Chamber.* The court of (chiefly) criminal jurisdiction became unpopular under James I and Charles I, and was abolished in 1641. **23, 24** *Rimee's . . . Bill's.* James Rimee (or Rymer) and John Bill were London booksellers. **25** *Porta.* Giovanni Battista della Porta's book on ciphers, *De Furtivis Literarum Notis, vulgo de Ziferis Libri IV*, published in Naples in 1563. **28** *juice . . . piss.* Invisible ink. **30** *If the States make peace.* Complex peace negotiations between the States General of the United Provinces of the Low Countries and Spain began in 1604; a truce was achieved in 1609. **32** *Powder Plot.* Gunpowder Plot, November 1605. **33** *French king.* Henri IV was assassinated in 1610. **34** *the Pope and Spain.* Relations with the Papacy were particularly hostile after the introduction of the Oath of Allegiance in 1606. Though England and Spain made peace in 1604, the two countries remained on uneasy terms for some years. **35–8** John Whitgift, Archbishop of Canterbury from 1583 to 1604, had taken a severe line with the Puritans ('brethren'). This was maintained by his successor, Richard Bancroft. James I made his famous statement against the

Puritans and in favour of the bishops ('No bishop, no king') at the Hampton Court Conference of 1604.

93. *Sir John Radcliffe.* ?1580–1627, the remaining brother of Margaret Radcliffe, commemorated in *Epig.* 40 (see note to that poem). He was knighted by Essex in Ireland 24 September 1599. **5–6** 'In Ireland' (Jonson's note). **11** *a whiter soul.* Horace, *Sat.* I. v. 41–2. **14–16** Thy fortunes, which have offended against thy family, are willing to expiate that fault in thee.

94. Donne's *Satires* were first published in 1633, but were written considerably earlier. Jonson's poem was probably not written before 1607: see R. C. Bald, *John Donne: A Life* (Oxford, 1970), pp. 172–4; Donne, *Satires*, p. lix. It was printed in Donne's *Poems* in 1650, 1654, and 1669. For Lucy, Countess of Bedford, see *Epig.* 76 n. **1** *brightness of our sphere.* Playing on the meaning of the name Lucy, as in *Epig.* 76. 8 and *For.* 12. 66. **2** *morning-star.* So in *Epig.* 76. 7, 'day-star'. The planet Venus is called Lucifer ('light-bearing') when it appears in the morning before the sun, Hesperus when it appears after the setting of the sun (cf. l. 16). **3** *look.* Have regard to. **7–8** Cf. Horace, *Sat.* I. iv. 22 ff. **8** *unavoided.* inevitable.

95. *Sir Henry Savile.* 1549–1622, Fellow and later Warden of Merton College, Oxford; subsequently Provost of Eton. Translated Tacitus' *Histories* (1591), with an original section, *The End of Nero and the Beginning of Galba*; edited Chrysostom in eight volumes (1610–13). Jonson commends his learning and gravity in *Disc.* 921–2. **2** *doctrine of Pythagoras.* Transmigration of souls: cf. *Volp.* I. ii, *Conv. Dr.* 97 ff. **6** *numbers.* parts. **9** *proper.* Genius, personal gifts. **10** *gratulate.* Rejoice over. **14–15** 'It was then imagined, that Sir Henry Savile intended to have compiled a general history of England: but he gave over the design, and engaged in that excellent edition of Chrysostom, which he afterwards published' (Whalley). **16** *Minerva's loom.* Minerva was the goddess of weaving as well as of wisdom. But Jonson is probably also comparing the history which Savile might write with Minerva's great mantle (πέπλος), which was embroidered each year with the actions and figures of naval heroes and gods, and carried through the streets of Athens to her temple. See Briggs, *CP* xi (1916), 178. **23** *Sallust.* After serving in Africa with Julius Caesar, Sallust (86–35 BC) retired to his pleasure grounds to write his historical works, *Catiline, Jugurtha,* and the *Historiae* of the period 78–67 BC. Lines 17–26 of Jonson's poem contained several echoes of Sallust's *Catiline,* iii and iv. **25–6** Cf. Sallust, *Catiline,* iii. 1–2. **28** *apt.* Make fit. **29–30** Cf. Pliny on Pompeius Saturninus, the pleader: *Epist.* I. xvi. 4: 'His histories will please you even more by their conciseness and clarity, the charm and brilliance of their style, and their power of exposition.' **31–6** Cicero's essentials of history, *De Oratore,* II. xv. 62–3. **33** *censure.* Give an opinion of.

96. *John Donne.* Also addressed in *Epig.* 23. **1** *whe'er.* whether. **4** *censures.* judgements. **8** *the better stone.* The Roman manner of marking happy days; here compared with the sealing of a deed of title. See Persius, *Sat.* ii. 1, Martial, IX. lii. 5, and Jonson's note to *King's Ent.* 289. **10** *puisnes'.* novices'.

97. **1–2** *motion.* A piece of moving mechanism (*OED,* 14). But Jonson plays with several different senses of the word: a *fading* is an Irish dance (cf. 'motion', *OED,*

660

12a). *Captain Pod* was a master of puppets, commonly known as 'motions' (see *BF* v. i. 8; *Epig.* 129. 16). The *Eltham thing* was a perpetual-motion device: cf. *SW* v. iii. 63, and *England As Seen By Foreigners in the Days of Elizabeth and James I*, ed. W. B. Rye (London, 1865/NY, 1967), pp. 232–42. **3** *case.* i.e. clothing. **6** *parcel.* i.e. part of clothing. **10** *bawdy stock.* Prostitutes; the 'increase' being merely financial. Cf. *Epig.* 57 n. **12** *'bout the bears.* Cf. *Und.* 47. 50. *noise.* Band of musicians. **14** *need.* F 'neadd'. H & S, citing dubious precedents, take this as an abbreviated past participle, 'needed': 'Of any madam who has required pimps and must have them'. Whalley emends to 'need o''. *Must* is conceivably a noun = 'fermenting apple-juice'—with a play on *squires* = 'apple-squires' = 'pimps'. But the line remains obscure. **15–16** During 1606.

98. *Sir Thomas Roe.* 1581–1644, knighted 1603, later James I's ambassador to India and Constantinople. He was a cousin of William and Sir John Roe (see *Epig.* 70 n.), a friend of Donne and Jonson, and probably the lover of Cecilia Bulstrode (*Und.* 49, *UV* 9). **1** *stand well to.* Maintain. For Jonson, the verb has a special sense of moral endurance; cf. *Epig.* 93. 4; 106. 7; *Und.* 70. 45; Peterson, ch. 2. **3** *round within himself.* Self-knowing and self-contained. Jonson is imitating Horace, *Sat.* II. vii. 86–8: '[The wise man] in himself is a whole, smoothed and rounded, so that nothing from outside can rest on the polished surface, and against whom fortune in her onset is ever maimed.' Cf. 'But to live round and close and wisely true | To thine own self, and known to few', 'A Country Life', ll. 135–6, Herrick, p. 38. **4** *height.* Moral and strategic eminence. **11–12** These lines also form the conclusion of *Catiline* (1611).

99. **2** *that, thy skill.* i.e. thy trust to letters has in turn bettered thy skill in writing. **3–4** Cf. Pliny, *Epist.* VI. xvi. 3: 'The fortunate man, in my opinion, is he to whom the gods have granted the power either to do something which is worth recording or to write what is worth reading, and most fortunate of all is the man who can do both.' **6** If time would pay as much respect to noble deeds ('facts') as to persons. **7–9** Cf. Pliny, *Epist.* VI. xxiv. 1: 'How often we judge actions by the people who perform them! The selfsame deeds are lauded to the skies or allowed to sink into oblivion simply because the persons concerned are well known or not.'

100. *Playwright.* Cf. *Epig.* 49 and 68. **1** *toys.* trifles. **4** *passed him a play.* i.e. enabled him to make a passable play.

101. Three of Martial's poems of invitation lie behind this poem. XI. lii: 'You will dine nicely, Julius Cerialis, at my house; if you have no better engagement, come. You will be able to observe the eighth hour; we will bathe together: you know how near Stephanus' baths are to me. First, there will be given you lettuce useful for relaxing the bowels, and shoots cut from their parent leeks; then tunny salted and bigger than a small lizard-fish, and one too which eggs will garnish in leaves of rue. Other eggs will not be wanting, roasted in embers of moderate heat, and a lump of cheese ripened over a Velabran hearth, and olives that have felt the Picenian frost. These are enough to sharpen your appetite: do you want to know the rest? I will lie to make you come [*mentiar, ut venias*]: fish, mussels, sow's paps, and fat birds of the poultry-yard and the marsh, which even Stella is not used to serve except at a special dinner. More I promise you: I will recite nothing to you, even although you yourself read again your "Giants" straight through, or your "Pastorals" that rank next to immortal Virgil.' v. lxxviii: 'If you are troubled by the prospect of a cheerless dinner at home, Toranius, you may fare modestly with me. You will not lack, if you are accustomed to an appetizer, cheap Cappadocian lettuces and strong-smelling leeks; a piece of tunny will lie hid in sliced eggs. There will be served—to be handled with scorched fingers—on a black-ware dish light green broccoli, which has just left the cool garden, and a sausage lying on white pease-pudding, and pale beans with ruddy bacon. If you wish for what a dessert can give, grapes past their prime shall be offered you, and pears that bear the name of Syrian, and chestnuts which learned Neapolis has grown, roasted in a slow heat; the wine you will make good by drinking it. After all this spread, if—as may be—Bacchus rouses a usual appetite, choice olives which Picenian branches have but lately borne will assist you, and hot chick-peas and warm lupines. My poor dinner is a small one—who can deny it?—but you will say no word insincere nor hear one, and, wearing your natural face, will recline at ease; nor will your host read a bulky volume, nor will girls from wanton Gades with infinite indecency wiggle their bellies in skilful writhings; but the pipe of little Condylus shall play something not too solemn nor unlively. Such is your little dinner. You will follow Claudia. What girl do you desire to meet before me?' See also Martial, x. xlviii. The genre was a familiar one in classical poetry: cf. e.g., Catullus, xiii; Horace, *Epist.* I. v; *Odes,* I. xx; IV. xii. H & S suggest that the poem may be addressed to such a guest as William Camden (see *Epig.* 14 n.). **7–8** Cf. Martial, v. lxxviii. 16, 'the wine you will make good by drinking it': a common Roman formula; and 'Content, not cates', Herrick, p. 124. **9** *rectify.* Purify, set to rights: in preparation for the main dish. **16** Varying the proverb, 'If the sky falls, we shall have larks' (Tilley, S517). **19, 20** *godwit . . . Knat, rail and ruff.* Edible birds: the godwit is a marsh bird, like a curlew; the knat (or knot) and ruff are in the sandpiper family; the rail is otherwise known as the corncrake. Sir Epicure Mammon (*Alch.* II. ii. 80–1) reckons knat and godwit suitable only for his footboy. **20–4** It was a contemporary as well as a classical custom to listen to recitations at table. See Juvenal, *Sat.* xi. 179–82, and cf. Martial's assurances to his guests that he will not bore them by reading (v. lxxviii. 25) or by recitation (XI. lii. 16 ff.); and cf. *Leg. Conv.* 18, *Conv. Dr.* 394–6. Jonson's 'man' may be Richard Brome (see *BF* Ind. 8). **26** i.e. the cook may produce a pastry surprise (cf. *Nept. Tr.* 89 ff.) but Jonson will not produce a surprise reading. **30** *Mermaid's.* Famous tavern in Bread Street, Cheapside. **31** *Horace or Anacreon.* Both poets wrote in praise of wine; see especially Horace's ironical quotation of the sentiment, 'no poems can please long, nor live, which are written by water-drinkers', *Epist.* I. xix. 1–3. **33** *Tobacco.* Sometimes said to be 'drunk', rather than smoked; and thought by some to possess medicinal qualities. *Thespian spring.* At the foot of Mount Helicon, sacred to the Muses. **34** *Luther's beer.* Continental beer, made with hops, was thought inferior to the stronger old English ale, made with malt, yeast, and water. **36** *Poley or Parrot.* 'fool or parrot' in one manuscript. Robert Poley (or Pooly) was a government spy, who was present at the fatal stabbing of Marlowe at Deptford, 'after supper, as Jonson may have remembered' (Mark Eccles, *RES* xiii (1937), 386). Parrot was another informer; it is not known whether he is the Henry Parrot of *Epig.* 71: Franklin B. Williams, Jun., suggests not, *HSNPL* xx (1938), 19. Poley and Parrot may have been the spies who harassed Jonson in prison: see *Epig.* 59 n. **37–42** See Martial, x. xlviii. 21–4: 'To crown these there shall be jests without gall, and freedom [*libertas*] not to be dreaded the next morning, and no word you would wish unsaid; let my guest converse of the Green and the Blue [rival factions of charioteers]; my cups do not make any man a defendant.' Cf. *Leg. Conv.* 17, 24.

102. William, Earl of Pembroke. See *Epig.* Dedn. n. **3–4** Cf. Seneca, *On Tranquillity of Mind,* vii. **5**: 'For both classes were necessary in order that Cato might be understood—he needed to have good men that he might win their approval, and bad men that he might prove his strength.' **9–10** Cf. Seneca, *Epist.* cxv. **10**: 'We fulfil duties if it pays, or neglect them if it pays, and we follow an honourable course as long as it encourages our expectations, ready to veer across to the opposite course if wicked conduct shall promise more.' **12** *discerns.* distinguishes. **13** Cf. Seneca, *Epist.* lxxi. 8: 'virtue, however, cannot be increased or decreased; its stature is uniform'. **16** Cf. Seneca, *On Benefits,* IV. xvii. 2: 'and so attractive is virtue that even the wicked instinctively approve of the better course'. **17–18** Again recalling, and reversing, the sentiment of Martial's preface to his *Epigrams* ('let no Cato enter my theatre', etc.): see *Epig.* Dedn. 28 n. and Valerius Maximus, II. x. 8. **20** *study.* As E. B. Partridge points out (*SLI* vi (1973), 156), the word is significantly repeated throughout the *Epigrams,* with reference both to art and to persons: cf. *Epig.* 86; 122. 9. Cf. Valerius Maximus, III. ii. 17: 'let those who wish the republic to be secure, follow me'.

103. Mary, Lady Wroth. See *Alch.* Dedn. n. **5 ff.** Hunter notes that Camden in his *Remains* glosses 'Mary' as 'exalted'. But Jonson is clearly saying that 'Sidney' is the only name he intends to invoke, though others may find significance in 'every part' (l. 12) of Lady Mary's name. In the Dedication to *Alch.* she is addressed as 'the lady most deserving her name': 'Wroth' was alternatively spelt 'Worth'. **7** *imprese.* Emblems or devices with mottoes.

104. Susan, Countess of Montgomery. 1587–1629, daughter of Edward de Vere, Earl of Oxford, and granddaughter of Lord Burghley; in 1604 she married the Earl of Pembroke's brother, Philip Herbert, who became the Earl of Montgomery the following year. She danced in several of Jonson's masques. **2** *dew of grace.* i.e. baptism; 'dew' suggesting (i) baptismal water; (ii) the morning of life; (iii) 'due' (the spellings were interchangeable). **4** *Susanna.* The story of whose chastity is told in the Apocrypha. **6** *faithful.* believers. **10** *one.* F3 'own'. **15** *equally.* impartially.

105. Mary, Lady Wroth. See *Epig.* 103 n. Cf. the style of compliment paid in *Epig.* 122 and 125. **2** *crossed.* Struck out. **8** *Ceres.* Roman goddess of corn. **10** *Oenone.* Nymph of Mount Ida, and wife of Paris. *Flora.* Roman goddess of flowers. *May.* Or Maia, Roman goddess of growth and increase. A reference, perhaps, to Lady Mary's association with Jonson's lost pastoral, *The May Lord*: see *Conv. Dr.* 337–42. **11** *Idalian queen.* Venus. Lady Mary had danced in Jonson's *Masque of Blackness* in 1605. **16** *Pallas' plumèd casque.* Pallas Athene, classical goddess of war, wisdom, and all the liberal arts, was traditionally represented wearing a plumed helmet. **18** *peacock*. Sacred to Juno; here absent, for it is also an emblem of vanity. **19** *index*. Probably a pun: guiding principle (*OED*, 4), and list of names (*OED*, 5).

106. *Sir Edward Herbert.* 1583–1648, later Lord Herbert of Cherbury; courtier, soldier, diplomat, historian, poet, and philosopher, and brother of the poet George Herbert. **8** *piety*. *Epig.* 91. 15 n.

107. *Captain Hungry.* Newdigate suggests this may be Captain Thomas Gainford (or Gainsford), a veteran of the Irish wars, and later a prolific newsmonger; he is the Captain Pamphlet of *Und.* 43. 79–80. This poem is based on Martial, IX. xxxv; Martial's Philomusus is primarily an artful political gossip, rather than a braggadocio. **6** *two emperors*. Probably Charles V (1500–58), Holy Roman Emperor, and his son Philip II of Spain, to whom Charles resigned the Netherlands in 1555. **7** *their princes*. The stadtholders of the seven provinces of the Dutch republic, the most important of whom was Maurice, Prince of Orange (1567–1625), military leader in the war of independence against Spain. **8** *Moravian horse*. A famous breed. *Venetian bull*. The captain's confusion as to the city from which a bull (*OED*, *sb.*² 2) or papal edict, emanates, is itself a bull (*OED*, *sb.*⁴ 2), or ludicrous blunder. **18** *at twice*. twice. **21** *Villeroys*. Nicholas IV de Neufville (1543–1617), Seigneur, and later Marquis, de Villeroy, negotiator for Henry III during the Wars of Religion, and Secretary of State under Henry IV. *Silleries*. Nicholas Bruslaut (1544–1624), Marquis de Sillery, Chancellor of France under Henry IV and minister of Louis XIII. **22** *Janins*. Pierre Jeannin (?1541–1623), French statesman and diplomatic negotiator. *Tuileries*. Palace of the French sovereign in Paris. **23** *Beringhams*. Hunter suggests Pierre de Beringhen (d. 1619), Valet de Chambre and Commissaire des Guerres for Henry IV. **25–6** *Hannow* and *Rotteinberg* are probably the German cities Hanau and Rotenburg; the other names are probably invented: *Shieter-huissen* = shit-house; *Boutersheim* possibly alludes to the legendary fondness of the Dutch for butter. **29** tusk. Show the teeth.

108. Quoted in *Poet. Apol. Dial.* 131–40; both this and the preceding epigram were thus probably written in 1601 or shortly before. **6** See Jonson's brief account of his service in the Low Countries, *Conv. Dr.* 199 ff. **10** *such*. i.e. as he.

109. *Sir Henry Neville.* ?1564–1615, MP from 1584 to 1614, ambassador to France 1599–1600, had been imprisoned in the Tower and heavily fined for his involvement in Essex's plot; though released in 1603, he remained out of royal favour. **2** *titles*. Cf. *Epig.* 9; 116. 7. **4** *pedigree*. Neville's mother was the daughter of Sir John Gresham: the family had been influential in the sixteenth century. **6** *scope*. aim. **9–10** Cf. *Alch.* IV. i. 48–51. **11** *lent life*. See *Epig.* 45. 3 n. **13** Cf. Virgil, *Georgics*, ii. 290–2. **15** *posterity*. Cf. *Epig.* Dedn. 15; *Epig.* 110. 21; 127. 4. **17–18** *wombs ... tombs*. On the collocation of 'wounds' and 'tombs', see G. A. E. Parfitt, *RMS* xv (1971), 23–33; cf. *For.* 12. 45–7; *Und.* 70. 8. For the general sentiment, cf. *Und.* 84. viii.

110. *Clement Edmondes.* ?1564–1622, published his *Observations* on Caesar's *Gallic War* between 1600 and 1604; this and the following poem were prefixed to the 1609 edition. **6** *style.* With a pun on stylus. **13** *but one just age.* Cf. the tribute to Shakespeare, *UV* 26. 43. **14** *parts.* factions. **17** *Promethean.* Referring to the tradition that Prometheus created mankind from clay (Pausanius, X. iv. 4, etc.).

111. Edmondes had compared ancient and modern methods of warfare in his *Observations.* **4** *Beholding.* beholden (= 1609 reading). **7** *ignorant captains.* Perhaps recalling *Epig.* 107. **8** i.e. not to concede this knowledge to Caesar is to diminish the value of our own actions. **9** *grutch.* Complain, grudge. **11** *deprave.* disparage. **13** *help.* 1609: 'art'.

112. Cf. Martial, XII. xciv. Jonson introduces a new metaphor from the card-game primero. **4** *rank setting.* Excessive betting. **6** *blow me up.* Ruin; cf. *For.* 3. 79; *Alch.* I. ii. 78 ff. **7** *lay.* plan. **10** *epic poem.* Jonson mentions this intention to Drummond, *Conv. Dr.* 1. **18** *pluck.* Draw cards from a pack. **19** ff. *encountered . . . colour . . . rest . . . prime.* All terms from primero; 'colour' also perhaps picks up the sense of 'blush' (the gamester's brazenness contrasting with the author's modesty, l. 11.); 'rest' is a stake kept in reserve; 'prime' is a hand consisting of a card from each of the four suits, and the word also means in a more general sense 'first-rate'. **22** *vexation.* (i) Dissatisfaction; (ii) violent treatment.

113. *Sir Thomas Overbury.* 1581–1613, secretary and close adviser to James I's favourite, Robert Carr; poisoned at the instigation of Lady Essex, whose marriage with Carr he had opposed. Jonson's own relationship with Overbury underwent a reversal after Overbury had attempted to use him as a go-between in his suit to the Countess of Rutland: see *Conv. Dr.* 135, 172–6. Gifford conjectured that this poem was written *c.*1610, when Overbury had returned from his travels. **8** *humanity.* Cf. *Epig.* Dedn. 27 n.

114. *Mistress Philip Sidney.* 1594–1620, daughter of Sir Robert Sidney; she married Sir John Hobart. She was christened Philip, evidently after her famous uncle. For biographical details, see L. C. John, *JEGP* xlv (1946), 214–17. **3** *Cupid.* For the (non-classical) traditions concerning his blindness, see E. Panofsky, *Studies in Iconology* (1962 edn., New York and Evanston), ch. iv. **4** *out-forms.* External forms.

115. Probably aimed at the architect Inigo Jones (1573–1652), Jonson's collaborator in his court masques. Cf. *Disc.* 86–94, on specious honesty; and the gibe at Jones in *UV* 34. 104. **3** *Naming so many.* See *Epig.* Dedn. 13–14 and n. **5** Cf. Martial, XI. xcii: 'He lies who says you are vicious, Zoilus: you are not a vicious man, Zoilus, but vice.' Jonson alludes also to the character of the Vice or Iniquity (see l. 27, and cf. *UV* 34. 26–8) in the interludes. **7–8** Cf. *Und.* 47. 19–20. **10** *s[tr]ow out.* Intersperse. H & S's emendation of Folio 'sow': cf. *S of N.* III. ii. 183, *Und.* 47. 28. **11** *come from Tripoli.* 'To vault and tumble with activity. It was, I believe, first applied to the tricks of an ape or monkey, which might be supposed to come from that part of the world' (Robert Nares, *A Glossary*, rev. J. O. Halliwell and T. Wright (2 vols., London, 1859)). **12** *the anarchy of drink.* Cf. *Und.* 47. 10. **16** *lays on.* assails. **26** Probably referring to an Italian Zanni actor performing a quick change *lazzo*, or bobbing in briefly from behind a stage door; see also K. M. Lea, *Italian Popular Comedy* (Oxford, 1934), i. 246, 252. Whalley saw a possible allusion to Scoto of Mantua (*Volp.* II. ii. 22 n.). The Folio reading is 'dore': hence 'dor', meaning 'fool' or 'mockery', is a plausible alternative sense (cf. *CR* v. i. 19; v. ii. *passim*). **27** *old Iniquity.* See l. 5 n. **29** *in picture.* By his descriptions. *defect.* Probably, disparagement (cf. *OED*, *v.* 4). **30, 31** *architect . . . engineer.* Alluding to Jones's profession; but an 'engineer' is also a plotter or layer of snares: cf. *Sej.* I. 4.

116. *Sir William Jephson.* Of Froyle in Hampshire; knighted 1603; Privy Councillor, High Sheriff and MP for Hampshire from 1604 until his early death in 1611. See M. D. Jephson, *An Anglo-Irish Miscellany* (Dublin, 1964), pp. 17–18. **2** *flame.* Vigour, brightness: cf. *OED*, 6 †c, and *For.* 14. 56–60. **7** *title.* Cf. *Epig.* 9. **8** *My Lord.* See *Epig.* 11. 5; *Conv. Dr.* 282. **9–10** See Sallust, *Jugurtha*, lxxxv. 15: 'For my part, I believe that all men have one and the same nature, but that the bravest is the best born.' **16** *solecism.* Cf. *Volp.* IV. ii. 43 n.

117. *Groin.* Cf. *Disc.* 54–6. **2** *occupy.* The word also had a sexual sense: cf. *Disc.* 1560, and *2 Henry IV*, II. iv. 137–40.

118. *Gut.* Cf. *Disc.* 54–6; *Conv. Dr.* 68. **2** *meat.* Cf. the slang term 'mutton' = prostitute. *tasteth.* For the sexual sense of the word, cf. *Cymbeline*, II. iv. 57. **6** Cf. *Und.* 47. 13.

119. *Sir Ralph Sheldon*, Of Beoley in Worcester; a wealthy recusant, said to have been implicated in the plot to assassinate Queen Elizabeth in 1594; knighted 1607. **4** *press.* crowds. **8** *disease.* Annoyance; picking up the sense of 'illness' (cf. ll. 4, 9). **11–12** Cf. Seneca, *Epist.* v. 3: 'let us try to maintain a higher standard of life than that of the multitude, but not a contrary standard'. **14** Cf. Pliny, *Epist.* I. xxii. 5: '[Titius Aristo] places no part of his happiness in ostentation, but refers the whole of it to conscience.' **15–16** From Martial, VIII. lxxvii. 7–8. The context of Martial's sentiment is quite different: see Jonson's translation, *Und.* 89.

120. Headed in one manuscript: 'Upon Sal. Pavy, a boy of 13 years of age, and one of the company of the Revels to Queen Elizabeth' (for variants in this manuscript, see H & S, viii. 77). Pavy died in July 1602; he had acted in Jonson's *CR* in 1600 and *Poet.* in 1601. For an account of his brief career, see G. E. Bentley, *TLS* 30 May 1942, p. 276. **15–18** Cf. Martial's lines on the death of a young and successful charioteer: 'Me, snatched away in my ninth three-year span, jealous Lachesis, counting my victories, deemed old in years.' For Lachesis, one of the Parcae, see *Epig.* 76. 15 n. For the tradition of the *puer senex* glanced at here, see E. R. Curtius, *European Literature and the Latin Middle Ages*, tr. W. R. Trask (London, 1953), pp. 98 ff. **22** *baths.* As Jupiter restored to life the young Pelops, and as Medea rejuvenated the aged Aeson.

121. *Benjamin Rudyerd.* 1572–1658, knighted 1618; politician, poet, and friend of the Earl of Pembroke, whose poems were published with Rudyerd's in 1660.

122. This poem may be modelled in part on Martial, I. xxxix. **2** *Saturn's age.* On Jonson's fondness for this notion, see *Epig.* 64. 3–4 n. 'Show' in l. 1 may allude to the fact that Jonson used the theme in several court masques, e.g. *The Golden Age Restored* (1615).

123. 1 *writ.* writing. 2 *candour.* impartiality.

124. *Elizabeth, L.H.* Not firmly identified. Fleay and Newdigate guess that she may be Elizabeth, Lady Hatton, wife of Sir Edward Coke; but as this lady was still living in 1616, the identification seems unlikely. James McKenzie, *NQ* ix (1962), 210, argues for Elizabeth, Lady Hunsdon (formerly Lady Elizabeth Spencer of Althorpe), the date of whose death is unknown. John M. Major inconclusively surveys these and other candidates, *SP* lxxiii (1976), 62–86. S. E. Tabachnick speculates that 'Elizabeth died pregnant with an illegitimate child': this is guesswork (*Expl.* xxix (1971), item 77). See also O. B. Hardison, Jun., *The Enduring Monument* (Chapel Hill, 1962), pp. 124–6. The poem is variously titled in its various manuscripts: see H & S, viii. 79. 10 *sleep with death.* N. Strout sees an allusion to the etymology given in Camden's *Remains* for the name Elizabeth, 'peace of the Lord, or quiet rest of the Lord': *ELN* xvii (1979), 30–3. 11–12 Howard S. Babb paraphrases: 'It is a more appropriate thing to record this lady's death than her life, for she was much too good for this world' (*JEGP* lxii (1963), 741). But Jonson seems to be referring more specifically to the death of the lady's name; it is tempting to think that her husband may have suffered some disgrace. For Jonson's attitude to names throughout the *Epigrams*, see Dedn. 14 n.

125. *Sir William Uvedale.* Of Wickham, Hants; knighted 1613; later Treasurer of the Chamber and Treasurer-at-Arms of the army of the north; died 1652. On the poem, see Peterson, pp. 87–91. 1 *piece.* example. *first times.* The Golden Age. 9 *flattery.* Cf. *Epig.* 36. 4 n. 10 Cf. Jonson's praise of Shakespeare, *Disc.* 665–6.

126. *Mistress Cary.* Anne, daughter of Sir Edmond Cary of Devon: Uvedale's first wife. (His second wife, whom he married in 1640, was also a Cary: Victoria, daughter of Sir Henry Cary of *Epig.* 66 and sister of Lucius Cary of *Und.* 70.) 3 *plucked a branch.* Daphne, pursued by Phoebus Apollo, was turned into a laurel; the tree was thereafter sacred to Phoebus and associated with his art, poetry. 6 *prove.* experience.

127. *Esmé, Lord Aubigny.* Esmé Stuart, Seigneur d'Aubigny (1574–1624), with whom Jonson lodged for five years (*Conv. Dr.* 208–9), and to whom he dedicated *Sejanus.* 4 *posterity.* Cf. *Epig.* Dedn. 15, etc. 6 *swallowed up.* Cf. *Epig.* 64. 10. 12 *thank thy benefits.* A construction still current in the nineteenth century: *OED*, 'thank', †4b.

128. *William Roe.* See *Epig.* 70 n. Peterson, pp. 33–4, relates the poem to the classical *propempticon*, a poem on (or anticipating) the return of a friend; cf. Catullus, ix. 5–11; Horace, *Odes*, I. iii, Statius, *Silvae*, III. ii. 2 *manners and men.* Cf. Horace, *Epist.* I. ii. 20, quoting the opening lines of the *Odyssey*; and *Und.* 14. 33; 50. 22; 77. 18; *Volp.* II. i. 10, etc. 8 *circle.* The emblem of perfection. Cf. also *Epig.* 98. 3 n. 14 *travailed.* A pun. Cf. *Epig.* 31. 2.

129. *Mime.* Identified by H & S as Inigo Jones; they compare similar touches in *Epig.* 115. 25–9, and in the portrait of Lanthorn Leatherhead, *BF* III. iv. 123–9. 4 *Brentford.* A town in Middlesex on the junction of the Brent and the Thames, 8 miles west of London. *Hackney.* A village north of London, 2 miles from St Paul's.

Bow. Or Stratford-at-Bow, a suburb of London on the Lea, 4½ miles north-east of St Paul's. **7** *flag.* Flags were flown from theatres on days of performance. **9** *great.* Cf. *Epig.* 28. **12** *babion.* baboon. *brave.* bully. **13** (*mounted on a stool*). i.e. like a mountebank. Jones is called 'mountebank' in *UV* 34. **16**. The activities of Venetian mountebanks has been described in 1611 by Coryate (see l. **17** n.); and cf. *Volp.* II. ii. **14** *gesture.* Facial expression. **16** *Cokeley.* A jester who improvised at entertainments; cf. *BF* III. iv. 126, *D. is A.* I. i. 93. *Pod.* A puppet-master; see *Epig.* 97. **1–2** n. *Gue.* a showman. **17** *Coryate.* Thomas Coryate (?1577–1617) published in 1611 his *Crudities*, an account of his travels in France and Italy in 1608. See *UV* 10, 11, 12.

130. *Alphonso Ferrabosco.* ?1575–1628, composer, violist, lutanist, and musical instructor to Prince Henry. This poem was prefixed to the volume of Ferrabosco's *Airs* published in 1609, which included music for songs from *Volpone* and several of Jonson's masques. **2** Amphion, the legendary inventor of music, is said to have built the walls of Thebes by the sound of his lyre; Orpheus' music is reputed to have calmed wild beasts. See Horace, *Ars Poetica*, 391–5. **3** *known effects.* Discussed by John C. Meagher, *Method and Meaning in Jonson's Masques* (Notre Dame, 1966), pp. 69–80. **5** *Declineth.* Turns aside. *persuades.* Encourages the practice of. **12–14** In Ptolemaic astronomy, the earth was surrounded by seven spheres carrying the sun, moon, and five known planets, by an eighth sphere carrying the fixed stars, and a ninth, or crystalline, sphere; according to the Pythagoreans, the movement of the spheres created harmonious music. **18** *Shed.* imparted.

131. Printed with Ferrabosco's *Lessons* in 1609. **2** *our own right.* i.e. to be sole judge of the work. Cf. *Queens*, 679 f. (Q, Ff), *BF* Ind. 87, *Cat.* 'To the Reader', 3; Horace, *Epist.* I. xx, 6. **5–10** 'And even if we were able to hear all men and their criticisms, we ought not to give them any indication that we listened to them. For the capricious world may talk as much as they like, they can be fools to their own cost so far as I am concerned. Say they prefer this or that man to you; even those for whose sake they indulge in such praise know that they err . . .' **13** Cf. Persius, *Sat.* i. 7, 'look to no one outside yourself'. **14** *breath.* Fame being dependent upon popular talk. For the association of fame and flame, cf. the frontispiece to Raleigh's *History of the World* (p. 345).

132. *Joshua Sylvester.* 1563–1618, groom of Prince Henry's chamber. Jonson's poem was prefixed to Sylvester's translation of Guillaume Du Bartas's *Divine Weeks and Works* in 1605. **6** *confer.* Compare (languages). Later Jonson confessed to Drummond 'that Sylvester's translation of Du Bartas was not well done, and that he wrote his verses before it ere he understood to confer' (*Conv. Dr.* 21–2).

133. From the allusion in l. 108 to an unusual parliamentary utterance, H & S date this poem *c.* 1610. This was also a severe plague year: cf. ll. 17, 72, 173. For the possibility of a slightly later dating, see ll. 193–4 n. **2–4** *Theseus* and his friend Pirithous descended into hell to carry off Proserpine, and according to one tradition (*Aeneid*, vi. 617–18), remained there for ever. According to another tradition, *Hercules* rescued the two men when he visited hell for his twelfth labour,

the capture of Cerberus (see. l. 14 n.). *Orpheus* visited hell to recover his wife Eurydice; *Ulysses*, to consult Tiresias about regaining his country (*Odyssey*, xi). The *Latin muse*, Virgil, tells of *Troy's just knight*, Aeneas, visiting the underworld in the company of the Sibyl to learn his fate from the ghost of his father Anchises (*Aeneid*, vi). 5 *Sheldon*. Usually identified as Sir Ralph Sheldon of *Epig.* 119, but on grounds of age his grandson William (b. 1589) might seem a more likely candidate. Peter E. Medine, *SEL* xv (1975), 97-110, argues for Thomas Shelton, *fl.* 1610, poet and translator of *Don Quixote*. *Heydon*. Probably Sir Christopher Heydon, knighted 1596, d. 1623, a writer on astrology (see Whalley, and H & S index). 7-8 *Styx . . . Acheron . . . Cocytus, Phlegethon*. Four of the five rivers of Hades. 8 *our*. ours. *in one*. The Fleet Ditch, a stream rising in the Highgate and Hampstead hills, and flowing into the Thames at Blackfriars. Once easily navigable as far as Holborn Bridge, it had become a common sewer by the sixteenth century, and was now choked with refuse. See John Ashton, *The Fleet: Its Rivers, Prison, and Marriages* (London, 1888). 11 *wherry*. Light rowing boat: referring to the manner in which visitors were ferried into the classical underworld. Miller notes, however, that Ulysses 'journeyed to and from the land of the dead under sail and with fair winds', *Odyssey*, xi. 6-12, 639-40. 12 *Charon*. God of hell, who ferried the souls of the dead across the rivers Styx and Acheron. 13 *frogs*. Who form a croaking chorus in Aristophanes' comedy of that name, in which Charon ferries Dionysus to Hades. 14 *Cerberus*. Watch-dog of Hades; he had three (or, according to some, fifty) heads. 20 *adventer*. adventure. 28 *three for one*. A form of wagering on one's chances of successful completion of travel; a wagerer stood to treble, or forfeit, his stake. Such wagers, referred to again in ll. 31 ff., were common at the time; Jonson himself seems to have bet on his safe return from his foot-journey to Scotland: see *UV* 46. 6 and n. 29 *powerful moon*. i.e. a spring tide. 34 *without embassage*. Without being ambassadors. 35 *backward went to Berwick*. In 1589 Sir Robert Carey won £2,000 by walking from London to Berwick in twelve days (*Memoirs* (Edinburgh, 1808), p. 20). The unidentified 'backward' walker may have been attempting to outdo this feat. 36 *the famous morris*. Danced by the actor William Kemp in 1599. In 1600 he published *Kemp's Nine Day Wonder: Performed in a Dance From London to Norwich*. He and the Berwick walker are referred to by W. Rowley, *A Search for Money* (1609). 37 *Mermaid*. *Epig.* 101. 30 n. 39-40 Two of several daring small-boat enterprises of the time. The wherry journey to Bristol was undertaken by Richard Ferris and two companions in 1590. This journey and that to Antwerp are referred to in Samuel Rowland's verses prefixed to John Taylor's *The Sculler* (1612). 41 *Avernus*. Sulphurous lake in Campania, thought to be the entrance to hell (see *Aeneid*, vi. 126 ff.). 42 *Bridewell*. Bridewell dock, at the north end of what is now Blackfriars Bridge, was the outlet of the Fleet Ditch; Bridewell prison was situated here. 46 *bombard-style*. bombast. 48 *sibyl or a golden bough*. Which assisted Aeneas in the underworld (*Aeneid*, vi). 50 *Alcides*, Hercules. 'Hercules is not noteworthy as a patron of poets. Jonson perhaps alludes ironically to the story that Hercules was taught literature and music by Linus and, enraged at being corrected, killed him with his own lyre' (Miller). Cf. *For.* 10. 4-6. 55 *Club-fist*. Hercules inadvertently killed a man in Calydon with a blow of his fist. 57 *adventry*. Adventure (a nonce-formation). 60 *dock's no rose*. Punning on the name of the dock plant; a proverbial saying (*Oxford Dictionary of English Proverbs*: cf. Tilley, D420). **65** *merd-urinous.* Of dung and urine. **67** *scar.* scare. **68** *car-men.* Carriers, carters. **74** *ox in Livy.* See Livy, I. vii. 4–7, XXXV. xxi. 4–5. **75** *anenst.* beside. **77** *Castor brave and Pollux.* Who sailed with Jason in search of the golden fleece, and later cleared the Hellespont and neighbouring seas of pirates. **80** *Chimaera.* A monster which was lion in its foreparts, dragon aft, and goat amidships. **81** *Briareus.* A giant with 100 hands and fifty heads; encountered by Aeneas, *Aeneid,* vi. 287. **83** *Hydra.* A monster with 100 (or fifty, or nine) heads; when one was cut off, two more would grow in its place. **84** *the trull.* Scylla, daughter of Typhon, was changed by the jealous Circe into a monster with barking nether parts, twelve feet, and six heads; dismayed, she threw herself into the sea, and was changed again, into rocks. Jonson, like several classical authors, confuses her with the Scylla who cut off the hair of her father, Nisus, king of Megara. **85** *lighter.* Flat-bottomed barge. **86** *quite.* avoid. **89** *Cocytus.* The unsavoury river 'of lamentation' in the classical underworld. **95** *ab excelsis.* From on high. **96** *Paracelsus.* Theophrastus Bombastus von Hohenheim (?1490–1541), physician and alchemist, laid stress on the necessary balance of mercury, sulphur, and salt in the human constitution; he and his followers essayed 'strange cures with mineral physic' (*Alch.* II. iii. 231). Cf. the complaints of Mercury in *Merc. Vind.* **108** *the grave fart.* 'The peculiar manner in which Henry Ludlow said "no" to a message brought by the Serjeant from the Lords' in 1607 forms the subject of a poem written before 1610 and published in *Musarum Deliciae* in 1656. (Cf. *Alch.* II. ii. 63). **109** *in fume.* Cf. *Alch.* Argument 12; IV. v. 58. **112** *Polypheme. Odyssey,* ix. 431–4. **115** *sough.* Deep sigh. *lurdan.* Sluggard, i.e. the slow-moving boat. **116** *bottom.* The lower hull of a boat; a pun. **117** Butchers' offal was taken by boat to Paris Garden on the Bankside, immediately opposite the outlet of Fleet Ditch; bull- and bear-baiting were held here. For 'Bears' College' cf. *Songs,* 32. 30. **118** *Kate Arden.* Whose charms are also remembered in *Und.* 43. 148–9. **120** *foist.* (i) Barge; (ii) fart. **121** *Stygian pool.* Medine (p. 99) calculates this to be 'a point just south of Fleet Bridge'. **128** *Democrite.* Democritus, born *c.*460 BC, developed the theory of the atomic nature of the universe. *Hill Nicholas.* Nicholas Hill (?1570–1610), Fellow of St John's, Oxford, published in 1601 his *Philosophia, Epicurea, Democritiana, Theophrastica, proposita simpliciter, non edocta.* **133** *nare.* nostril. **139** *usurer's mass.* A common association: cf. *EMO* III. viii. 49. **143** *Fleet Lane.* Now Farringdon Street; then chiefly occupied by taverns and cookshops. **144** *hell.* The association of cooks with hell is traditional: cf. *Alch.* III. i. 17 ff., *BF* II. ii. 44–5. **145** *measled.* Spotty, infected. **152** *convince.* Convict, give away. **155** *Tiberts.* Cats; from the name of the cat in *Reynard the Fox* (trs. Caxton, 1481). **156** *Banks. fl.* 1588–1637, a showman, owner of the famous horse Morocco (or Marocco). The story of their both being burned by the Pope in Rome is probably untrue (see *DNB*). G. B. Johnston (*Ben Jonson: Poet* (New York, 1945), p. 26 n.) compares Banks's situation to that of Alessio Interminei in Dante's *Inferno* (xviii. 115–26). *Pythagoras.* See *Epig.* 95. 2 n. **162** *Thrice . . . thrice.* An expected number on epic (and mock-epic) occasions: cf. Virgil, *Aeneid,* ii. 792–4, vi. 700–2; Pope, *The Rape of the Lock,* iii. 137–8; *The Dunciad* (A), i. 203–4; etc. **166** *peason.* peas. **172** *the damnèd in the Fleet.* The prisoners in Fleet prison. New prisoners were taken by boat along Fleet Ditch, and entered the prison through a water-gate. **174** *Sepulchre's.* The bells of St Sepulchre's tolled for criminals proceeding to execution, and also, with great frequency, for the dead in time of plague. **175** *grisly Pluto's hall.* Probably Fleet prison. Pluto is king of the classical underworld. **176–7** The reference is obscure; H & S suggest it is to the three judges of the underworld (see 187–9 and n.). The 'sergeants' are sergeants-at-law in the nearby Inns of Court on Holborn Hill. **180** *Madam Caesar.* A brothel-keeper. Cf. *Alch.* v. iv. 142. **186** *a sop.* Aeneas pacified Cerberus with a drugged honey-cake, *Aeneid*, vi. 417–25. **187–9***Rhadamanthus. . .Aeacus. . .Minos.* The three judges of the classical underworld. Cf. *Poet.* III. i. 145 ff. **190** *fletcher.* arrow-maker. *high.* long. **193–4** Possibly referring to Sir Hugh Myddelton's New River Scheme, begun in 1609 and ceremoniously opened in 1613; the 'pyramid' may be the water-house and tower at New River Head, Clerkenwell (Dr Valerie Pearl, private communication). See illustration facing p. 58 in J. W. Gough, *Sir Hugh Myddelton, Entrepreneur and Engineer* (Oxford, 1964). The identification may require a slightly later dating for the poem than that proposed by H & S (see introductory note to this poem, and headnote to *Epigrams*). **193** *liquid.* (i) Watery (poetic: *OED*, 1b; cf. Latin *liquidus*, used to describe a journey, *Aeneid*, v. 217); (ii) manifest (*OED*, †4); (iii) bright, pure. **196** *A-jax.* Sir John Harington's punningly titled treatise on the jakes (1596), *A New Discourse of a Stale Subject, Called the Metamorphosis of Ajax.* But the reference is also, perhaps, to Homer, as G. B. Johnston suggests (*Ben Jonson: Poet*, p. 28). B. R. Smith (*SEL* xiv (1974), 109) sees a further gibe at Harington's long-windedness as an epigrammatist; cf. *Conv. Dr.* 26–9.

THE FOREST

The poems in *The Forest*, like those in *Epigrams*, were first published as a collection in the 1616 Folio edition of Jonson's *Works*. Some of the poems in *The Forest* had been published earlier, often in a somewhat different form: see *For.* 5, 6, 10, 11, and notes. The earliest poem in the collection is probably the Epistle to the Countess of Rutland (*For.* 12), composed as a gift for New Year's Day 1600. There is no evidence to suggest that any of the poems in *The Forest* were written later than 1612, but a number of them cannot be dated with any certainty.

The title is partly explained by Jonson's note 'To the Reader' prefixed to *The Underwood*. The Latin word silva (plural silvae, Greek ὕλη) means literally timber, raw material ready to be worked. The term was used by classical authors to describe improvised literary productions or rough drafts or to denote a literary miscellany: see Quintilian, x. iii. 17; *The Attic Nights of Aulus Gellius*, preface § 6; Suetonius, 'On Grammarians', x; Statius, *Silvae*; Alex Hardie, *Statius and the 'Silvae'* (Liverpool, 1983), p. 76. Jonson's use of the *silva* tradition and arrangement of poems in *The Forest* is examined by Alastair Fowler in *Poetic Traditions of the English Renaissance*, ed. Maynard Mack and George deForest Lord (New Haven and London, 1982), pp. 163–80.

1. **1–2** *bound . . . bind.* By poetic convention and poetic form, respectively. Alexander Leggatt observes that Sidney's *Astrophil and Stella* and Spenser's *The Shepherd's Calendar* open with similar complaints about the frustrations of love and art: *Ben Jonson: His Vision and His Art* (London and New York, 1981), pp. 219–20. **4–6** Vulcan caught his wife Venus and her lover Mars in a net, and exposed them to the ridicule of the gods. His informant was Apollo, god of poetry: Cupid therefore blames and suspects poets in general. **12** *old.* Jonson was not yet forty. Contrast *Und.* 2. i. 1–5.

2. *Penshurst.* Near Tonbridge, Kent; home of the Sidney family since 1552. The 'great lord' of l. 91 is Robert Sidney (1563–1626), second son of Sir Henry Sidney and younger brother of Sir Philip Sidney; knighted 1586; Baron Sidney of Penshurst 1603; Viscount Lisle 1605; Earl of Leicester 1618. The poem was written before the death of Prince Henry in November 1612: see l. 77. J. C. A. Rathmell, *ELR* i (1971), 250–60, suggests that Jonson had an intimate knowledge both of the estate and of Lord Lisle's difficult financial circumstances, and finds a further possible clue to dating in l. 45: walls were built at Penshurst in May 1612 with stone from a local quarry. G. R. Hibbard, *JWCI* xix (1956), 159–74, and W. A. McClung, *The Country House in English Renaissance Poetry* (Berkeley, etc., 1977) discuss the poem in relation to other 'country house' poems. Other important studies by P. M. Cubeta, *PQ* xlii (1963), 14–24, A. Fowler, *RES* xxiv (1973), 266–82 (revised and reprinted in *Conceitful Thought* (Edinburgh, 1975), pp. 114–34), and Raymond Williams, *The Country and the City* (London, 1973), pp. 27–34. **1–6** Jonson may be contrasting Penshurst with a particular, ostentatious, house such as nearby Knole, or—as John Carey suggests (Fowler, p. 268)—Theobalds, a house with which Jonson was familiar (see ll. 61 ff. n. below), and which boasted the architectural features mentioned here: see Daniel Lysons, *The Environs of London* (London, 1796), pp. 29–39. Salisbury's fondness for building—like that of his father, Lord Burghley—was notorious: see Jonson's *Ent. K. & Q. Theob.* 83, and P. M. Handover, *The Second Cecil* (London, 1959), p. 276. By this date, however, Theobalds was owned by King James, and too overt a reference would, in any case, have been indiscreet. G. E. Wilson, *SEL* viii (1968), 77–89, sees similarities with the description of Solomon's temple, 1 Kings 6–7. **2** *touch.* Black marble. **4** *lantern.* Glassed turret to admit light. **5** *ancient pile.* Penshurst was built about 1340, over 200 years before the Sidney family came to live there; a 'pile' may be a castle or stronghold (*OED*, *sb.*²) or a lofty mass of buildings (*OED*, *sb.*³ 4). **7** *marks.* Distinctive features. **10** *Mount.* A piece of high ground in the park, still called by this name. *dryads.* wood-nymphs. **10 ff.** Modelled on Martial's idealized description of a grove of trees planted by Julius Caesar on his estate at Tartessus, ix. lxi. **11–16:** 'Often drunken fauns played under this tree, and a late-blown pipe startled the still house; and, while over deserted fields the rustic dryad fled by night from Pan, she often hid under these leaves. And the dwelling has reeked when Lyaeus held revel, and the tree's shade has grown broader from spilt wine.' **13–14** An oak which still stands today at Penshurst is said to have grown from an acorn planted on the day of Sir Philip Sidney's birth, 30 November 1554. Cf. Suetonius on the poplar planted at Virgil's birth, *Vita Virgili,* 5. **16** *sylvan.* Inhabitant of the woods. *his flames.* 'Either "his passion" or "Sidney's passion: the same passion as Sidney's"' (Fowler). **18–19** 'There is an old tradition that a Lady Leicester (the wife undoubtedly of Sir Robert Sidney) was taken in travail under an oak in Penshurst Park, which was afterwards called *My Lady's Oak*' (Gifford). The same lady, Barbara Gamage, fed deer in a copse in the grounds, which became known as Lady Gamage's Bower.

(It cannot now be identified.) **20** *seasoned.* Of a suitable age. **25 ff.** As in many a 'pleasant place', Nature actively offers itself up to man: cf. stanza five of Marvell's 'The Garden', Dryden's description of Eden in *The State of Innocence*, III. i. 35–8, and Carew's 'To Saxham', 21–8. With Jonson's fish, compare those of Martial, x. xxx. 21–4 ('the fishpond feeds turbot and home-reared bass; to its master's call swims the dainty murry; the usher summons a favourite grey mullet, and, bidden to appear, aged surmullets put forth their heads'), and Juvenal, *Sat.* iv. 69: 'The fish himself wanted to be caught' (flatterer's hyperbole). For the fruit, see Virgil, *Georgics*, ii. 501–2: 'He plucks the fruits which his boughs, which his ready fields, of their own free will, have borne.' **25** *tops.* High ground. **26** *Ashour*'s Wood still exists at Penshurst on the east bank of the Medway; *Sidney's copse* was probably the north-east end of what is now Hawk's Wood, an extension of Ashour (Lord De L'Isle, personal communication). **29** *painted partridge.* Martial's *picta perdrix*, III. lviii. 15. **31** *Medway.* The nearby river was notoriously 'hard to be fished' (Rathmell, 255). **36** *Officiously.* obligingly. **40** *hours.* The Horae, the three female divinities which presided over the three seasons of the ancient year; hence, the seasons themselves. Cf. *UV* 44. 1. **45–7** Cf. 'A Panegyric to Sir Lewis Pemberton', 115 ff., Herrick, pp. 146–9. **48** *all come in.* As in Carew's 'To Saxham', 49–58, and Herrick's 'Panegyric', 12 ff. **49 ff.** Cf. Martial, III. lviii. 33–44: 'Nor does the country visitor come empty-handed: that one brings pale honey in its comb, and a pyramid of cheese from Sassina's woodland; that one offers sleepy dormice; this one the bleating offspring of a shaggy mother; another capons debarred from love. And the strapping daughters of honest farmers offer in a wicker basket their mothers' gifts. When work is done, a cheerful neighbour is asked to dine; no niggard table reserves a feast for the morrow: all take the meal, and the full-fed attendant need not envy the well-drunken guest.' **56** *emblem.* Of sexual maturity; cf. *Venus and Adonis*, 527–8, for the plum. The pear was sometimes associated with Venus (in place of the more usual apple), and thus with marriage; see Guy de Tervarent, *Attributs et symboles dans l'art profane 1450–1600* (Geneva, 1958–9), ii. 97–8. **58** *free provisions. For.* 3. 14 n. **60** *hospitality.* The tradition of keeping open house for neighbours and tenants: then in rapid decline. **61 ff.** Cf. Lucian, 'Laws for Banquets', *Saturnalia*, 17: 'All shall drink the same wine, and neither stomach trouble nor headache shall give the rich man an excuse for being the only one to drink the better quality. All shall have their meat on equal terms'; Juvenal, *Sat.* v. 24 ff., and Martial, III. lx. 1–2, 9: 'Since I am asked to dinner, no longer, as before, a purchased guest, why is not the same dinner served to me as to you? . . . why do I dine without you, although, Ponticus, I am dining with you?' Jonson reacted in a similar way to Salisbury's hospitality: ' "My Lord", said he, "You promised I should dine with you, but I do not" ', etc. (*Conv. Dr.* 265–6). G. E. Wilson (p. 85) sees similarities with the Lord's Supper. The ungrudging waiter is from Martial, III. lviii. 43–4 (see note to ll. 49 ff. above); cf. Carew, 'To Saxham', 47–8 and Herrick, 'Panegyric', 47 ff. **73** *livery.* Provisions; appointments. **82** *sudden.* prompt. **90** *fruitful.* Lady Lisle bore at least ten children. **95–6** Rathmell (p. 254) finds provision for these regular devotions in the Sidney papers. **98** *mysteries.* Skills; religious truths. **99** *proportion.* Compare or estimate proportionately. **100–2** Cf. Martial, XII. l. 8, on the builder of a great house: 'How well you are—not housed!' See also *For.* 3. 94.

3. *Sir Robert Wroth.* 1576–1614; knighted 1601; married Sir Robert Sidney's daughter, Lady Mary (see *Epig.* 103 n.; 105; *Und.* 28), 1604. Jonson later judged her to be 'unworthily married on a jealous husband' (*Conv. Dr.* 299–300). Durrants, in the parish of Enfield, was one of his estates. He was sheriff of Essex in 1613. An earlier draft of the poem, entitled 'To Sir Robert Wroth, in Praise of the Country Life', survives in two manuscripts: variants in H & S, viii. 96–100. **13** *at home* Cf. *For.* 4. 68; *Und.* 14. 30; 78. 8. **13 ff.** Cf. Virgil, *Georgics*, ii. 458–71: 'O happy husbandmen! too happy, should they come to know their blessings! for whom, far from the clash of arms, most righteous earth, unbidden, pours forth from her soil an easy sustenance. What though no stately mansion with proud portals disgorges at dawn from all its halls a tide of visitors, though they never gaze at doors inlaid with lovely tortoise-shell. . . . Yet theirs is repose without care, and a life that knows no fraud, but is rich in manifold treasures. Yes, the ease of broad domains, caverns, and living lakes, and cool vales, the lowing of the kine, and soft slumbers beneath the trees—all are theirs. They have woodland glades and the haunts of game . . .'. **14** *unbought provision.* Horace's *dapes inemptas*, *Epodes*, ii. 48 (see Jonson's translation, *Und.* 85. 48); cf. Martial, I. lv. 12; IV. lxvi. 5; Virgil, *Georgics*, iv. 133. **16** *lowing.* Playing, perhaps, on words (contrast 'proud', l. 15). **17** *Alongst.* Close by. **19** *courteous shade.* The force of the adjective lies in its derivation: manners appropriate to the court. Cf. the effect of Marvell's 'courteous briars', 'Upon Appleton House', 616. **23 ff.** Wroth was a keen sportsman, and King James occasionally visited Durrants for hunting. But the passage also contains memories of Horace, *Epodes*, ii and Martial, I. xlix. **25** *heart.* Middle; i.e. summer. Punning on 'hart'. **26** *lesser deer.* Smaller animals. **32** *full greatness of the cry.* Cf. Theseus on the harmony of his pack, *A Midsummer Night's Dream*, IV. i. 120–1. **34** *greedy.* 'Hungry' in early manuscripts. **37 ff.** Cf. the seasonal tasks and delights of Virgil, *Georgics*, ii. 516 ff. **40** *either shearers.* i.e. those who 'shear' the meadows or the sheep. **41** *yet . . . height.* 'Cut down in their most height' (early manuscripts). **44** *mast.* nuts. **45–6** Cf. Martial, I. xlix. 27: 'To your very hearth shall come down the neighbouring wood.' **47** *Pan and Silvane.* As in Virgil, *Georgics*, ii. 493–4. **48** *Comus.* 'The god of cheer or the belly', *Pleas. Rec.* 6. **50** *Saturn's reign.* The Golden Age: Virgil, *Georgics*, ii. 538. **53 ff.** Cf. Martial, I. xlix. 29–30. **54** *rudeness.* Want of refinement. **56 ff.** Cf. Statius, *Silvae*, I. vi. 43–5, 'One table serves every class alike, children, women, people, knights, and senators: freedom has loosed the bonds of awe.' **59** *wassail.* Spiced ale. *walks.* circulates. *often.* frequent. **60** *drowned.* Two manuscripts continue: 'The milk [n]or oil did ever flow so free | Nor yellow honey from the tree.' **61** *leese.* lose. **64** *head.* Fountain-head: i.e. the original kind of gold. But in the classical Golden Age metals were still hidden in the ground; the age was 'golden' in other ways. Cf. *For.* 12. 23–5. **67 ff.** Perhaps remembering several classical passages: Virgil, *Georgics*, ii. 503 ff.; Tibullus, I. x. 29–32; Martial, I. xlix. 37–40; Horace, *Epodes*, ii. 4–8 (see *Und.* 85. 4–8). **79** *blow up.* Ruin; cf. *Epig.* 112. 6; *Alch.* I. ii. 78 ff. **84** From Pithou, *Epigrammata* (1590): 'The miser does nothing aright, save when he dies.' **86** *organs.* instruments. **94** *dwell.* Cf. *For.* 2. 102. **95–106** Cf. Juvenal, *Sat.* x. 349–59: 'In place of what is pleasing, [the gods] will give us what is best. Man is dearer to them than he is to himself. . . . Still, that you may have something to pray for . . . you should pray for a sound mind in a sound body; ask for a stout heart that

has no fear of death, and judges length of days the least of nature's gifts.' **106** *lent.*
Cf. *Epig.* 45. 3 n.

4.   14 For the currency of this notion, see M. Macklem, *The Anatomy of the World*
(Minneapolis, 1958), V. Harris, *All Coherence Gone* (Chicago, 1949); Cf. *Disc.*
126–30, *Songs*, 26. 4. **18** Compare and contrast *Disc.* 304, 1451–8. **24** *gyves.*
fetters. **25** ff. Cf. Horace, *Sat.* II. vii. 68–71, on the habituating effect of adultery:
'Suppose you have escaped: then, I take it, you will be afraid and cautious after
your lesson. No, you will seek occasion so as again to be in terror, again to face
ruin. O you slave many times over! But what beast, having once burst its bonds
and escaped, perversely returns to them again?' **31** *wull.* will. **33** *sense.* Physical
senses. **36** *gins.* traps. **45** *soil.* Probably the court. **48** i.e. pride and ignorance are
the schools in which the 'envious arts' are practised. **56** *grutch.* complain. **68** *at
home. For.* 3. 13 n.

5.   Sung to Celia by Volpone (with a few small verbal differences), *Volp.* III. vii.
166–83: see notes there. **14** *our mile.* 'Many a mile' (two manuscripts).

6.   Lines 19–22 are sung by Volpone later in the same scene, *Volp.* III. vii. 236–9;
Catullus, v, is again the model. On the 'arithmetical' poem, see J. B. Leishman,
The Art of Marvell's Poetry (London, 1966), pp. 73 ff. **6–11** Cf. Catullus, v. 7–13
(see *Volp.* III. vii. 165–83 n.). **12–22** Cf. Catullus, vii: 'You ask how many kissings
of you, Lesbia, are enough for me and more than enough. As great as is the
number of the Libyan sand that lies on silphium-bearing Cyrene, between the
oracle of sultry Jove and the sacred tomb of old Battus; or as many as are the stars,
when night is silent, that see the stolen loves of men—to kiss you with so many
kisses, Lesbia, is enough and more than enough for your mad Catullus; kisses,
which neither curious eyes shall count up nor an evil tongue bewitch.' **13** *Romney.*
On the east coast of Kent, surrounded by marshy grazing land. **14** *Chelsea.* The
name is said to derive from OE *ceosel* = sand, pebbles. **22** *pined.* Pained, vexed.

7.   For the circumstances of composition of this poem, see *Conv. Dr.* 308–11. It
is based upon a Latin original by the sixteenth-century poet Bartholomaeus
Anulus (Barthelemi Aneau): see Oswald Wallace, *NQ*, 3rd series, viii (1865),
187. The thought is proverbial: 'Woman like a shadow flies one following and
pursues one fleeing', Tilley, L518; cf. *The Merry Wives of Windsor*, II. ii. 201–2.

8.   Subtitled 'Ode Anacreon' in two manuscripts. Cf. *Und.* 34, and *Conv. Dr.*
292–3, on Lady Sidney's smallpox. **9** *stalls.* Lodgings in almshouses. **10** *Spitals.*
lazar-houses. **18** *crown.* A pun: the coin (five shillings) and the pox (cf. *Measure for
Measure*, I. ii. 50); 'the truest trade', because one crown is given for another.
27 *price.* admirable. **29–30** Cf. *For.* 13. 73–4. **30** *decoctions.* Rendered-down herbs
and other substances, used medicinally or cosmetically. **31** *emp'rics.* Quacks; cf.
Alch. IV. i. 135–6. **32** *spirit of amber.* Succinic acid. **33** *oil of talc.* Used as a wash for
the complexion; recommended by Subtle for faces 'decayed | Beyond all cure of
paintings', *Alch.* III. ii. 34–6. **37** *water.* The popular brothel district was on the
south bank of the Thames. **39** *entail.* A pun. **41** *common game.* Promiscuous sex.
44 *starve.* die. **45** *prostitute.* Gathering in a secondary sense of the word (*OED*, 4),
'prostrate'.

9. As Richard Cumberland first pointed out in *The Observer* (1788), no. cix, p. 316, Jonson's lyric is based on a number of separate passages from the *Epistles* of Philostratus: (33) 'So set the cups down and leave them alone, especially for fear of their fragility; and drink to me only with your eyes; it was such a draught that Zeus too drank—and took to himself a lovely boy to bear his cup. And, if it please you, do not squander the wine, but pour in water only, and, bringing it to your lips, fill the cup with kisses and so pass it to the thirsty. Surely nobody is so ignorant of love as to yearn for the gift of Dionysus any longer after the vines of Aphrodite.' (32) 'I first and foremost, when I see you, feel thirst, and against my will stand still, and hold the cup back; and I do not bring it to my lips, but I know that I am drinking of you.' (60) 'And if ever you sip from the cup all that is left becomes warmer with your breath and sweeter than nectar. At all events it slips by a clear passage down to the throat, as if it were mingled not with wine but with kisses.' (2) 'I have sent you a garland of roses, not to honour you (though I would like to do that as well), but to do a favour to the roses themselves, so that they may not wither.' (46) 'If you wish to do a favour for a lover, send back what is left of [my roses], since they now breathe a fragrance, not of roses only, but also of you.' A. D. Fitton-Brown examines Jonson's revision of the poem and the debt to Philostratus in *MLR* liv (1959), 554–7, and compares also *Greek Anthology*, v. 91: 'I send thee sweet perfume, not so much honouring thee as it; for thou canst perfume the perfume.' Cf. also 'Upon a Virgin Kissing a Rose', Herrick, p. 51. **1** *only.* 'Celia', two manuscripts. **3** *or . . . in.* 'Leave but a kiss within', three manuscripts. **4** *not look for.* 'expect no', three manuscripts. **5** *doth rise.* 'Proceeds', three manuscripts. **7** *Jove's.* 'love's', one manuscript. **7–8** For the view held by Yvor Winters and others, that the speaker would prefer Jove's nectar to Celia's kisses, see M. van Deusen, *E. in C.* vii (1957), 95–103. This reading has little to commend it: see Fitton-Brown, loc. cit., p. 557, W. Empson, *Seven Types of Ambiguity* (London, 1953, 3rd edition revised), p. 242, J. G. Nichols, *The Poetry of Ben Jonson* (London, 1969), pp. 163–4; and A. D. Hope's witty 'reply' to the poem, *A Book of Answers* (Sydney, 1978), p. 6. **11** *giving . . . there.* 'Being well assured that there', three manuscripts. **15** *grows.* 'lives', three manuscripts.

10. This poem, along with *For.* 11, *UV* 4 and 5, Shakespeare's *The Phoenix and Turtle*, and poems by Marston, Chapman, and 'Ignoto', was first printed amongst the 'Diverse Poetical Essays' on the subject of *The Phoenix and Turtle* appended to Robert Chester's *Love's Martyr* in 1601. Carleton Brown argues that the turtle, a type of male devotion, and the phoenix, a type of female perfection, are intended to represent Sir John and Lady Salusbury, married in 1586; see his introduction to *Poems by Sir John Salusbury and Robert Chester*, EETS (Oxford and London, 1914). B. H. Newdigate, finding the inscription 'To L: C: off: B' in a manuscript version of *UV* 5, suggests that the phoenix is Lucy, Countess of Bedford: *TLS* 24 Oct. 1936, p. 862, and introduction to his edition of *The Phoenix and Turtle* (Oxford, 1937). The difficulties involved in accepting either of these theories are discussed by W. H. Matchett, *The Phoenix and Turtle* (The Hague, 1965). Matchett argues plausibly for a return to Grosart's identification of the phoenix and the turtle with Elizabeth and Essex. Reprinting the poem in *The Forest*, Jonson dropped its original title, 'Praeludium', changed almost all first person

plural pronouns to first person singular, and made a few more small verbal changes. **4** *his bones are yet sore.* Cf. *Epig.* 133. 55. **7** *cart.* The chariot of the sun. **9** *foundered.* lamed. **12** *green circle.* Bacchus' crown of leaves is likened to the magical circle of a necromancer. **13–15** Pallas Athene was born from Jupiter's head, cleft open by Vulcan. **13** *mankind.* masculine. **16** *cramp.* Narrowly confine: implying that Venus was responsible for her own and Mars' capture by her husband Vulcan (*For.* 1. 4–6 n.). **17** *tribade trine.* Lesbian trinity: the three Graces, often associated with Venus in the dance. **19** *old boy.* Cf. *Und.* 36. 16, 'The eldest god, yet still a child': a Platonic notion; cf. *Beauty*, 329–31. **21** *absence. For.* 1. **22** *Hermes, the cheater.* Mercury, god of thieves; at his birth he pilfered from many of the gods. **23** *sisters'.* The muses'. **24** *riffle.* Raffle, gamble away. *petasus.* Hermes' hat, broad-brimmed or winged. **25** *ladies of the Thespian lake.* The muses. **30** *epode.* A lyric poem, usually of grave character, alternating short and long lines; see Horace's *Odes*, Bk. V.

Proludium. An earlier version of the previous poem, sent to Sir John Salusbury but not printed in *Love's Martyr.* See Matchett's discussion of the two versions, *The Phoenix and Turtle*, pp. 95–6 n. 21. H & S translate the title as 'preliminary canter' (viii. 9). **1** *elegy.* i.e. a poem written in elegiac metre: in Greek and Latin, a dactylic hexameter and pentameter form the elegiac distich. **6** *chastity.* A typical claim by Jonson for his verse (cf. *Epig.* 17. 6; 49. 6), but here especially appropriated to the 'chaste love' about to be celebrated in *For.* 11. **13** *raps.* transports.

11. *Epode.* See *For.* 10. 30 n. Reprinting the poem in *The Forest*, Jonson reversed the procedure he had followed with *For.* 10, and changed almost all first person singular pronouns to first person plural. The discussion of the roles of reason and passion in the early part of the poem is similar to that of Thomas Wright, *The Passions of the Mind in General* (1601); Jonson was probably acquainted with Wright's ideas before 1601: see Theodore Stroud, *ELH* xiv (1947), 274–82. **1–4** Plato, *Gorgias*, 478E: 'Happiest therefore is he who has no vice in his soul. . . . Next after him, I take it, is he who is relieved of it'; and cf. Seneca, *Hercules Furens*, 1098–9, *Hippolytus*, 140–1. **1** *state. Epig.* 70. 2. **2** *virtue, and not fate.* See *Epig.* 63. 2–3 n.; 76. 15 n. **9** *ports.* gates. **13** ff. The extended figure is developed from classical commonplaces: cf. Plato, *Republic*, iv. 441–2, *Timaeus*, 69–70; Aristotle, *Politics*, i. v. **15** *taste.* detect. **15–16** *commit | Close . . . close.* Imprison securely . . . immediate. **18** *sense.* senses. **21** *affections do rebel. Disc.* 31–3; *Volp.* III. iv. 101 ff. **29** [*still*]. Not in Ff; H & S supply from *Love's Martyr* and manuscripts, though as Miller notes, the F reading is acceptable if 'passions' is read as a trisyllable. **36** *overblow.* Blow away. **37** ff. Cf. *In Praise of Demosthenes*, 13, attributed to Lucian: 'The two impulses of love that come upon men, the one that of a love like the sea, frenzied, savage, and raging like stormy waves in the soul, a veritable sea of earthly Aphrodite surging with the fevered passions of youth, the other the pull of a heavenly cord of gold that does not bring with fiery shafts afflicting wounds hard to cure, but impels men to the pure and unsullied form of absolute beauty, inspiring with a chaste madness.' **39** *sea.* From which Venus was born. **47** *golden chain.* Cf. *Hym.* 320, and Jonson's note on allegorical interpretations of Zeus' golden chain leading from heaven to earth, *Iliad*, viii. 19. **50** *soft.* softest. **56** *elixir.*

quintessence. **59** *time's virtue.* To reveal truth, proverbially the daughter of time. **63–5** Hunter suggests a memory of Satan's tempting of Christ, Luke 4, Matt. 4. **69** *luxury.* lust. **69–71** Cf. Montaigne, 'Of Judging of Others' Death', *Essays*, trs. John Florio, ed. J. I. M. Stewart (London, 1931), i. 694. **73** *sparrows' wings.* The sparrow is a symbol of lechery. **79** *doubt.* fear. **80** *for.* Because of. **87–90** Horace, *Epist.* I. xvi. 52–3 ('The good hate vice because they love virtue; you will commit no crime because you dread punishment'); Ovid, *Amores*, III. iv. 3–4 ('If she is pure when freed from every fear, then she is indeed pure; she who sins not simply because she may not—she in fact sins'). **88** *crown-worthy.* G. B. Johnston, *Ben Jonson: Poet*, p. 151, suggests a possible recall of Matt. 5: 28. (Manuscript: 'praiseworthy'). **91** *we propose.* 'I conceive' (manuscript). **101** *feature.* form. **115** *object.* Place before. **116** This line is attributed to Jonson in Robert Allot's *England's Parnassus*, published in 1600, the year before *Love's Martyr. securely.* Carelessly. Jonson's word-play is not original: see *OED*, 'secure', *a.* I. 1a, and examples. Possibly Jonson is remembering, and reversing, Seneca, *Hippolytus*, 163–4: 'Some women have sinned with safety, but none with peace of soul' (*scelus aliqua tutum, nulla securum tulit*). Leggatt argues that the poem concludes curiously by endorsing what had seemingly been rejected earlier: that fear is a good ground of virtue (*Ben Jonson: His Vision and His Art*, p. 138).

12. *Elizabeth, Countess of Rutland.* See *Epig.* 79 n. She had married early in 1599; this poem was sent to her on New Year's Day, 1600. It was a contemporary custom to send New Year poems (cf. *Und.* 79), but Jonson may have been specifically remembering Tibullus, III. i, and Horace, *Odes*, IV. iii. Jackson I. Cope, *Eng. Misc.* x (1959), 61–6, suggests the poem owes a general debt to Spenser's *Complaints*, but overlooks other sources and commonplaces. **2–4** Cf. *King's Ent.* 743, *Volp.* I. i. 24–5. **9** *ushers.* Servants; especially male attendants upon ladies. *serviceable.* In this derogatory sense, cf. Edgar on Oswald, 'a serviceable villain', *King Lear*, IV. vi. 254. **10** *apteth.* Makes fit. **22** Than this our age, which is not golden but merely gilded, can judge. The Folio spelling, 'guilt', enlarges the meaning. Cf. *For.* 3.64 n. **24** *Astraea.* See *Epig.* 74. 9 n. **25** *better placed.* Horace, *Odes*, III. iii. 49–52. **29** *quarter-face.* i.e. almost total disregard; cf. *Sej.* V. 389. **31** *great father's.* Sir Philip Sidney's. Jonson reckoned Elizabeth 'nothing inferior to her father' in poetry (*Conv. Dr.* 172–3). **32** *to think.* thinkable. **43 ff.** Cf. Seneca, *To Polybius, On Consolation*, xviii. 2: 'Among human achievements, this is the only work that no storm can harm, nor length of time destroy. All others, those that are formed by piling up stones and masses of marble, or rearing on high huge mounds of earth, do not secure a long remembrance, for they themselves will also perish; but the fame of genius is immortal.' Horace, *Odes*, IV. viii. 13–34: 'Not marble graven with public records [*non incisa notis marmora publicis*], whereby breath and life return to goodly heroes after death, nor the swift retreat of Hannibal and his threats recoiling on himself, nor the burning of wicked Carthage, declare more gloriously the fame of him who came back home, having won his name from Africa's subjection, than do the Muses of Calabria; nor would you reap your due reward, should the parchment leave your worthy deeds unheralded. What today were the child of Ilia and Mars, had jealous silence blocked the path of Romulus' deserts? The powers of gifted bards, their favour, and their voice rescue Aeacus from the Stygian waves and win for him a hallowed home in the Islands of the Blest. It is the Muse forbids the hero worthy of renown to perish. It is the Muse bestows the gift of heaven. It is thus that tireless Hercules shares Jove's hoped-for table. It is thus that Tyndareus' sons, gleaming fires, rescue storm-tossed ships from the sea's abyss, and Liber, his temples decked with verdant vine-sprays, brings vows to happy issue.' Horace, *Odes*, IV. ix. 13–28: 'Not Spartan Helen only became inflamed with love, marvelling at a lover's trim locks, his gold-bespangled raiment, his princely pomp and followers; nor was Teucer first to speed the shaft from Cretan bow. Not once alone has an Ilium been beset; nor has great Idomeneus or Sthenelus alone fought battles worthy to be sung by the Muses. Nor were doughty Hector and keen Deiphobus the first to encounter heavy blows for chaste wife and children. Many heroes lived before Agamemnon; but all are overwhelmed in unending night, unwept, unknown, because they lack a sacred bard.' **43** *glorious*. Vainglorious, boastful. *notes*. Horace's *notae publicae*, public records: *Odes*, IV. viii. 13. **44** *touch*. Black marble. **45–6** *tombs . . . wombs*. *Epig*. 109. 17–18 n. **49** *the Argive Queen*. Helen. **52** *in an army's head*. At the head of an army. *locked in brass*. Vulcan fashioned for Achilles an impenetrable suit of armour (*Iliad*, xviii), in which Achilles subsequently killed many Trojans. **54** *Idomen*. Idomeneus, King of Crete, who accompanied the Greeks to Troy with ninety ships. **57 ff**. After his death, *Hercules* was immortalized in the heavens as the sun, his twelve labours being represented in the twelve signs of the zodiac (Ovid, *Metam*. ix. 239–72). The *Tyndarides* are Castor and Pollux, twin sons of Tyndareus; Jupiter made them into the constellation Gemini. *Argo*, the famous ship in which Jason recovered the golden fleece, was sent by Minerva (Hyginus, *Fab*. xiv. 13) to the sky, and is the southern constellation the Ship. *Ariadne's crown* of seven stars, given to her after she had been forsaken by Theseus, was similarly dispatched by Bacchus after her death (Ovid, *Metam*. viii. 177–82). *Berenice's hair*, donated to Venus and subsequently lost, was changed by Venus (or by Jupiter) into the constellation Coma Berenices (Catullus, lxvi. 59–68). *Cassiopeia*, mother of Andromeda, was made into a northern constellation of thirteen stars (Hyginus, *Fab*. lxiv). **63** *only poets*. A reminder not only that poets are powerful, but that the pagan gods are not: for the legends are feigned. **66** *Lucina . . . Lucy the bright*. Queen Elizabeth, and Lucy, Countess of Bedford, respectively; playing in each case simply on etymology; *lux, lucis* = light. Cf. *Epig*. 76. 8 n.; 94. 1 n. **68–9** *verser . . . 'poet'*. Cf. *Disc*. 2469–72. *CR* II. i. 48–9. The distinction is an ancient one. The reference is almost certainly to Daniel, 'no poet' (*Conv. Dr*. 17); confirmed by Drummond's annotation of his copy of Jonson's 1616 Folio (J. R. Barker, *RES* NS xvi (1965), 287). **72** *less sanguine*. Less bloody: than, e.g., Daniel's *Civil Wars*. **75** *which*. The fruits of the hours: the poems to Lucy. **75–6** *bring | To curious light*. Jonson had planned to write an account of the worthy ladies of the kingdom, hoping it would be 'helped to light' by the favour of the queen (*Queens*, 666–9). It did not appear. **79 ff**. Cf. the emphasis of *Epig*. Dedn. 12–18. **81** *strange*. Probably in the sense of un-English, based on classical models; cf. *Epig*. 18. **83–5** Cf. the descriptions of the House of Fame in *Queens*, 360–3, 683–8. **87** *tickling rhymes*. 'Tinkling rhymes' in one manuscript (cf. *Disc*. 286; *Fort. Is*. 291). With the animus against rhyme expressed here, cf. *Und*. 29. **88** *commonplaces*. For a different attitude towards their use in poetry, see *Disc.* 2303. **92** *brave friend.* Her husband Roger Manners, 5th Earl of Rutland (1576–1612), a follower of Essex. He had been travelling extensively for some years; in 1599 he had been in Ireland, and at about this time was on service with the Dutch. **93 ff.** This part of the poem was not lost, but cancelled after it was revealed that the Earl was impotent, and the poem's final wish consequently unrealizable. Cf. *Conv. Dr.* 179 n. **98** *ominous.* auspicious.

13. *Katherine, Lady Aubigny.* Daughter of Sir Gervase Clifton (later Baron Clifton) of Nottinghamshire; married Esmé Stuart, Seigneur d'Aubigny (*Epig.* 127 n.), 1609; d. 1627. For the poem's approximate date, see note to ll. 94 ff. below. **11** *dangerous.* Cf. *Epig.* Dedn. 4. **16** *fortune.* Alluding perhaps to his deteriorating relationships at court (e.g. with Salisbury and Inigo Jones) and the failure of *Catiline* on the public stage (1611). **25** *slightly.* With slight attention. **27–8** 'The glass he presents (i.e. his poem) is as *much remov'd* from *giving* a flattering and false likeness, as the *lady* from *wanting* any such assistance' (Whalley). **33** *taken up o'.* Acquired from. **35** *censured.* judged. **39** *farmer of the customs.* tax-collector. **52** *good . . . great. Epig.* Dedn. 13 n. **57** *single paths.* Seneca, *Epist.* xxiii. 7. **59** *decline.* Turn aside. **63** *seem.* Come into view. **64** the turning world. Jonas A. Barish detects an allusion to the *machina versatilis* of the masques; 'Jonson and the Loathèd Stage', in *A Celebration of Ben Jonson*, ed. W. Blissett *et al.* (Toronto, 1974), p. 39. **72** *liegers.* agents. *wires.* Frames to support hair. **73–4** Cf. *For.* 8. 29–30. On New Year gifts, cf. *For.* 12. 1–19. **78** *bawds.* henchmen. **84** *gone wrong to man.* Cf. the idiom of *Epig.* 90. 3. **85–6** Cf. Seneca, *Epist.* cxxii. 18: 'They are unwilling to be wicked in the conventional way, because notoriety is the reward of their sort of wickedness.' **93** *charge.* burden. **94 ff.** Lady Aubigny eventually bore her husband nine children: Jonson's poem is written before the birth of the first of her six sons, James, in April 1612. Herrick speaks again of this 'noble stem' in 'To the Right Gracious Prince, Lodowick, Duke of Richmond and Lennox', 1–4 (Herrick, p. 170). **101** *their priest.* Horace, *Odes*, III. i. 3, *musarum sacerdos*: cf. *Und.* 25. 11; 70. 82. **102** *triple trine.* i.e. nine months. **124** This poetic portrait will remain constant; so too will Lady Aubigny's mind.

14. *Sir William Sidney.* 1590–1612, eldest son of Robert Sidney, Lord Lisle. The poem was evidently written in November 1611, for his twenty-first birthday. His career so far had been unpromising: see L. C. John, *MLR* lii (1957), 168–76. **11** *Thespian well.* Of poetic inspiration; cf. *For.* 10. 25. **18** *forced.* (i) Forceful; (ii) communal: celebrated in force. **20** *best genius.* Native talents, figured as a guiding spirit. **21** *number.* Twenty-one; a fact appropriately introduced at this line of the poem. **30** *run wrong.* At the age of 15, Sidney had stabbed a schoolmaster, with near-fatal consequences (L. C. John, p. 169). *stand still.* Fowler notes that these words occur punningly at the poem's centre ('The Silva Tradition', p. 172). **34–5** *good | And great.* See *Epig.* Dedn. 13 n. **40** *dust of ancestors. Und.* 84. viii. **41** *exacted.* demanded. **42** *Whose nephew, whose grandchild.* Sir Philip Sidney's and Sir Henry Sidney's, respectively. **49–50** Proverbial: 'One today is worth two tomorrows', Tilley, T370.

15. **1 ff.** '. . . the meaning is not—"Can I not think of God without its making me melancholy?" but "Can I not think of God without its being imputed or set down by others to a fit of dejection?"' (A. C. Swinburne, *A Study of Ben Jonson* (London, 1889), p. 103). It was thought that melancholy gave rise to specious piety: see Burton, *The Anatomy of Melancholy*, III. iv. and L. Babb, *The Elizabethan Malady* (East Lansing, 1951), pp. 47–54, 177–8. As W. Kerrigan argues, however, Jonson's primary concern throughout the poem is with the judgement not of his fellows but of God: *SLI* vi (1973), 199–217. **5–6** *reins . . . hearts*. Ps. 7: 9: 'the righteous God trieth the hearts and reins'; cf. Jer. 17: 10. **10** *converted*. Perhaps in the sense of a mathematical conversion, in which different numbers may be taken as equivalents. **11** *My faith, my hope, my love*. 1 Cor. 13: 13. **12** *judge . . . witness . . . advocate*. Respectively: Acts 10: 42, Rev. 1: 5, 1 John 2: 1; and elsewhere. **14** *And . . . me?* Edgar F. Daniels, *Explic.* xxxvi, 3 (1978), 12–13, suggests 'the sense is "Why has the speaker been so long alienated from God, that only now God condescends to him?"'; and compares *Comus*, 1021–2. **17** *scorn*. Matter for scorn (*OED*, 3 †a: cf. Milton, *Samson Agonistes*, 34). **18** *Conceived . . . born*. Cf. Ps. 51: 5; Gen. 3: 19 (Miller). **21–2** Adapted from a very different context, exiled Ovid complaining that the gods are conspiring to destroy him: '. . . so am I wounded by the steady blows of fate until now I have scarce space upon me for a new wound', *Epist. Ex Ponto*, II. vii. 41–2. **21** *ground*. A pun (also present in Ovid's Latin): (i) space; (ii) cause. **24** *holy Paul*. 'O wretched man that I am! who shall deliver me from the body of this death?', Rom. 7: 24; cf. Phil. 1: 23, 2 Cor. 5: 1. Kerrigan (pp. 210–12) pertinently compares Calvin's commentary on these passages.

THE UNDERWOOD

In the early 1630s Jonson seems to have begun to prepare for publication a second major collection of his writings, designed to complement the Folio of 1616. By the time of his death in 1637, this collection had still not appeared. Jonson's papers passed after his death into the hand of his friend and literary executor Sir Kenelm Digby, who was responsible for the publication in 1640 of Jonson's second Folio, in which the poems known as *The Underwood* first appeared as a group. (Some had already been published earlier in 1640 in John Benson's pirated Quarto and Duodecimo editions.) Most of the poems in *The Underwood* are to be dated post-1616, though the gathering includes one or two earlier pieces such as the Ode to the Earl of Desmond, 'Writ in Queen Elizabeth's Time, Since Lost, and Recovered' (*Und.* 25).

The final choice and arrangement of poems within *The Underwood* must have been Digby's own. It is tempting, however, to see the organization of the early part of the collection, in particular, as revealing Jonson's own design. *The Forest* had ended with a poem addressed to heaven; *The Underwood* aptly opens with a trio of devotional poems to the holy trinity, to God the Father, and upon Christ's nativity. *The Forest* had opened with a short poem on the elusiveness of love and the advent of age. After its devout opening, *The Underwood* moves to a sequence of 'ten lyric pieces' dealing in a more extended way with a similar theme; these are followed in turn by a group of songs with a related subject-matter. Towards the end of *The Underwood* comes another (but this time imperfect) sequence of 'ten pieces' celebrating Sir Kenelm Digby's wife, Lady Venetia, who had died in

1633; Digby himself was presumably responsible for placing them at this point in
the collection, and it is possible that he saw them as gravely balancing the earlier
sequence of poems on Charis. At the very end of *The Underwood* comes a group of
classical translations, which again refer, in a refracted way, to the poet's age and to
the continuing provocations of love.

The Underwood is Jonson's most varied collection of poems, and also his richest.
It contains epistles, epitaphs, epigrams, elegies, odes, sonnets, songs, an epithalamion, and an 'execration'. Towards the end of the collection are a number of
occasional verses written during the last years of his life, in a period of deepening
political and personal insecurity. They commemorate royal birthdays and register
loyal sentiment and puzzlement over the growing troubles in the land. They
record, too—often in an ingenious and moving way—Jonson's various personal
debts, receipts, disabilities, and material needs.

The title-page and some of the headlines in the 1640 Folio record the plural
form 'Underwoods'; this is probably a misprint (see B. H. Newdigate, *TLS* 7 Feb.
1935, p. 76; W. W. Greg, *RES* xviii (1942), 159–60 and n.). The title-page
includes a tag from Martial (I. xxv): *cineri gloria sera venit*. Martial is urging his
friend Faustinus to publish before he dies: 'To the ashes of the dead, glory comes
too late.' Whether Jonson or Digby selected this motto, it bears in the circumstances a certain irony.

To the Reader   Partly a translation of Caspar Gavartius' Latin note in his
edition of Statius' *Silvae* in 1616; the Latin note itself is prefixed to *Disc.* See
headnotes to *For.*, *Disc.*

1. *Poems of Devotion.* Examined by P. M. Cubeta, *JEGP* lxii (1963), 96–110.
H & S suggest the poems are the work of Jonson's closing years; for a further clue
to dating, see *Und.* 1. ii n., below.

1. i.   9–16 Cf. *Alch.* Dedn. 2 n. 10 Ps. 51: 16–17: 'For thou desirest not
sacrifice; else would I give it; thou delightest not in burnt offering. The sacrifices
of God are a broken spirit: a broken and a contrite heart, O God, thou wilt not
despise.' Cf. Herbert, 'The Altar'. 11 1 Sam. 15: 22: 'Behold, to obey is better
than sacrifice, and to hearken than the fat of rams.' 19 *with state.* Meet, ready.
24 *All's done.* 'It is finished', John 19: 30. 32 *seeing your face.* Rev. 22: 4. 34 *union.*
Gifford's emendation of F 'unitie'. 35 *dark.* 1 Cor. 13: 12. 42 *meditate.* Thus 1640
Folio; H & S (following Gifford), 'mediate'. But the sense is, 'sweeten my desire
to hear and to meditate'; see Cubeta, pp. 105–6.

1. ii   John Reichert, *NQ* NS xxx (1983), 147–8, gives an early text of this hymn
from Thomas Myriell's collection *Tristitiae Remedium* (1616), where it appears as
an anthem for five voices set by Ferrabosco; the stanzas are differently ordered.
See also Macdonald Emslie, *NQ* cxcviii (1953), 466–8; Daniel O'Connor, *NQ* NS
xii (1965), 379–80; and Herrick's imitation (p. 363), 'An Ode, or Psalm, to God'.
2 *broken heart. Und.* 1. i. 10 n. 14 *Rarely.* 'Cannot' in two manuscripts. 22 *With all.*
'From death' in Myriell text. 22 *since.* 'Sins' in one manuscript. 28 *come in.* submit.

1. iii.   10 *take.* Contain, a Latinism.

2.   *A Celebration of Charis.* Charis is the name of one of Vulcan's wives (see note to *Und.* 2. v. 37–8, below), and also the singular form of *Charites*, the graces; an ironical touch, as the lady's favours here are strictly limited. Fleay (i. 324–5) believed that Charis was Elizabeth, Lady Hatton, and guessed that she was also addressed in *Epig.* 124 and *Und.* 19, and took the part of Venus in *Haddington*—a role which would in fact have been played by a boy actor—being also the model for Mrs Fitzdottrell in *D. is A.* (1616). Parallel passages are noted below; in themselves, they hardly add up to evidence of a long-continued real-life love-affair. H & S consider the first poem of the sequence was written in 1622 or 1623 (a literal reading of 'fifty years', 2. i. 3), subsequent poems between 1612 and 1616. For further clues to dating, see notes to *Und.* 2. vi. 28 and 2. vii, below. The sequence is discussed by P. M. Cubeta, *ELH* xxv (1958), 163–80, by Trimpi, pp. 209–28, and by R. S. Peterson, *SLI* vi (1973), 219–68.

2. i.   3 *fifty years.* Perhaps remembering Horace's appeal to Venus not to trouble him 'at his fiftieth year', *Odes*, IV. i: see Jonson's translation, *Und.* 86. Cf. Jonson's references to his age in *For.* 1. 10–12; *Und.* 9. 15; 20. 5. 4 *my peers.* e.g. Horace, Anacreon, Ronsard. 9 *feature.* Proportions, shape of body. 19 *it was sung.* Not identified. H & S compare *Gyp. Met.* 484–5: a long shot. Cf. *Volp.* Epist. Ded. 20–3, on the power of poetry and the poet. 22 *high.* In both temporal and qualitative senses: well advanced, exalted (*OED*, 6). 23–4 Cubeta (p. 166) suspects burlesque; but these lines are also addressed, without apparent mockery, to Lady Purbeck, *Gyp. Met.* 540–1. Trimpi (pp. 215–16) compares *NI* III. ii. 96–8, 105, and Ficino, *Commentary on Plato's 'Symposium'*, II. viii.

2. ii.   4 *fields.* Ironically reversing Matth. 6: 28–9. 12 *cloud.* Clout, cloth. 22 *with.* Gifford's emendation of F 'which'. 32 *Hercules's shape.* Cf. Odysseus' sight of Hercules in Hades, *Odyssey*, ii. 606–8: 'like dark night, with bow bare and with arrow on the string, he glared about him terribly, like one ready to shoot'. But the reference may be to Hercules during his period of infatuation with Omphale, Queen of Lydia.

2. iii.   11 *scope.* target. *draught.* Shot (literally, drawing of the bowstring). 18 *repented.* Cf. Marlowe, *Hero and Leander*, ii. 209–12. 21 *Loser-like.* Proverbial: 'Give losers leave to speak', Tilley, L458. *wreak.* revenge. 26 *make example.* Take example; learn from this.

2. iv.   *Triumph.* i.e., victory procession, as well as victory; ironically following on the promise of 'revenge', *Und.* 2. iii. 24 (S. P. Zitner, in *The Elizabethan Theatre*, iv, ed. G. Hibbard (London and Basingstoke, 1974), pp. 127–42). 3 *a swan or a dove.* Birds sacred to Venus; in *Haddington*, 44, they draw her chariot, in which the *Charites* or graces are seated. Cf. Ovid, *Amores*, 1. ii. 23 ff. 10 Trimpi (p. 219) compares Spenser, 'An Hymn in Honour of Love', 228, where lovers follow Cupid 'Through seas, through flames, through thousand swords and spears', and sees a source in Plato, *Symposium*, 178–80; cf. Castiglione, *The Book of the Courtier*, trs. Sir. T. Hoby (London, 1928), p. 234. *whither.* wherever. 11–30 Wittipol woos Mrs Fitzdottrell with these lines, *D. is A.* II. vi. 94–113. On the musical setting (by Robert Joiner?) see Mary Chan, *Music in the Theatre of Ben*

Jonson (Oxford, 1980), pp. 105–9. These lines were parodied by Suckling (*Non-Dramatic Works*, ed. T. Clayton (Oxford, 1971), pp. 29–30), imitated by Shirley and ascribed to Carew (*Poems*, ed. Rhodes Dunlop (Oxford, 1949), p. 197), and sung in Garrick's operatic *Tempest* (*Plays*, ed. H. W. Pedicord and F. L. Bergmann (Carbondale and Edwardsville, 1981), iii. 294). H & S (viii. 135–6) also print an alternative version of ll. 21–30, and two additional stanzas, from a seventeenth-century manuscript. **14** *Love's star.* Venus. In *Haddington*, 46, Venus sits in her chariot 'crowned with her star'. **17** *grace.* Playing on the meaning of 'Charis': cf. 2. i. 8; 2. v. 51; 2. vi. 20. **17–18** Trimpi (pp. 219–20) and Peterson (*SLI* p. 227) refer to the Neoplatonic association of the light which emanates from God and from a lady's eyes. **21–4** Cf. Martial, v. xxxvii. 4–6, on Erotion ('before whom you would not choose Eastern pearls, nor the tusk new polished of India's beast, and snows untrodden, and the untouched lily'); and Ovid, *Metam.* xiii. 789 ff. **24** *smutched.* Blackened, smudged. **28** *nard.* An aromatic balsam.

2. v. **4** *various.* variable. **10 ff.** Cf. Cupid's confusion in *Songs*, 5. 10–11, and in Marlowe's *Hero and Leander*, i. 39–40. **13** *Homer.* See *Iliad*, xvii. 51. **14** *Anacreon.* See the advice to a painter concerning a lady, *Anacreontea*, xvi. **16** *above.* H & S's emendation of F 'about'. **17** *like my bow.* Cf. *Chall. Tilt*, 45 ff., Sidney, *Astrophil and Stella*, xvii. 10. **21–6** Cf. *Und.* 19. 7–10: Cubeta (pp. 171–2) thinks Jonson is allowing Cupid to make fun of this poem; but cf. the version of these lines addressed to Lady Purbeck in *Gyp. Met.* 534 ff. See also *CR* v. iv. 439–40, and Wittipol to Mrs Fitzdottrell, *D. is A.* II. vi. 82–7. **31–2** The chain of lovers' hearts is usually associated with Cupid himself: see E. Panofsky, *Studies in Iconology* (New York, 1972), pp. 115 ff. **35** *proyne.* preen. **37–8** A double confusion of identities: for one of Vulcan's wives, in Lemnos, is also called Charis, while the other, in heaven, is Venus: *Iliad*, xviii. 382; *Odyssey*, viii. 266–366. The Charites were furthermore the daughters of Venus. **40** *the glass hangs by her side.* A contemporary fashion; but a large looking-glass was also associated with Venus, as an emblem of pride, in Renaissance art: see Peterson, p. 237. **41** *girdle.* Which aroused desire; Venus lent it to Hera for her seduction of Zeus, *Iliad*, xiv. 214. Cf. *Chall. Tilt*, 50–2, and Jonson's note to *Hym.* 407. **47** *the apple.* Thrown down by the goddess of discord, it led to the dispute between Venus, Juno, and Minerva, concerning their relative beauty; Paris judged in favour of Venus. **51** Cf. *Und.* 2. i. 7 ff., above. **52 ff.** From Angerianus, 'Erotopaegnion'; for Juno's stately walk, cf. *The Tempest*, IV. i. 102: from Virgil, *Aeneid*, i. 46 (and see T. W. Baldwin, *Shakespere's Small Latine* (Urbana, 1944), ii. 481). 'But' (l. 53) appears to come too early for the contrast proposed.

2. vi. **6** *lost, or won.* A central notion in the sequence; cf. 2. iii. 21, etc. **10** *her hair.* A bride traditionally wore her hair loose: cf. *Und.* 75. 45, *Hym.* 57. **26** *all the graces lead.* As Venus does in the dance. **28** *the queen.* Queen Anne of Denmark was famed for her dancing, and had performed in Jonson's masques. She died on 2 March 1619.

2. vii. Amongst 'the most commonplace of his repetition' when Jonson visited Drummond in 1618–19; see *Conv. Dr.* 66–75. **16** [*the*]. Inserted by Gifford. Two manuscripts: 'out'. **17** *perplexèd.* intertwined. **18** *our death.* Cubeta compares 2. i. 24.

2. viii. **17** *emissary eye.* Spying eye; from Plautus, *Aulularia*, 41. A new word in English; see *S. of N.* i. ii. 47 ff. **18** i.e., assess the passing men. **19** *band.* Collar or ruff. **23** *say over.* Try on. *purl.* Lace, frill. **25** *secretary.* Confidante. The original name of Prue, the chambermaid in *NI*, was Secretary Cis. **26** *fucus.* cosmetic.

2. ix. *Dictamen.* Pronouncement. Peterson (*SLI*, pp. 362–3) detects a play on 'dictamen'/'dictamnum'/'dittany', a herb eaten—according to Pliny—by wounded deer to make their arrows drop out; Renaissance commentators contrasted the plight of lovers irretrievably wounded by Cupid. Hence 'cure for love' is possibly an ironical secondary meaning. **7–8** See Jonson's attack on French fashions in *Epig.* 88. **9** ff. Cf. the advice to a painter on painting a boy, *Anacreontea*, xvii. **13** *slack.* Pale, dull. **23** *cherished.* cultivated. *beard.* Unlike the poet: 2. ii. 30. **37–8** Playing on the proverb, 'the tailor makes the man', Tilley, T17. **39** Proverbial: Tilley, S810. **40** *brake.* A framework to hold something steady, e.g., a horse's foot while being shod. **42** *danger.* power. **50** Cf. Mosca's praise of the lawyer Voltore's ability to 'make knots, and undo them', *Volp.* i. iii. 57.

2. x. **8** *part.* Cf. *Epig.* 69. 2.

3. A version of this poem existed before 1618; Jonson quoted it to Drummond (*Conv. Dr.* 66–7). The poem originally had six stanzas, and was a musical duet between two women; for details, see H & S, viii. 11, 143. The present version is examined by John Hollander in *The Untuning of the Sky* (Princeton, 1961), pp. 338–40. **5** ff. Alluding to the legendary effects of Orpheus' music; see *Epig.* 130. **24** Echoed by Dryden, *A Song for St Cecilia's Day*, 53–4; cf. *Alexander's Feast*, 161–70. See also *Und.* 67. 20–1.

4. **8** *spill.* kill. **11** *spread.* Open wide.

5. **11** *parcels.* i.e. the various bits. **13–16** Seneca, *Epist.* ix. 7; cf. *Disc.* 1735–7, and *Dubia*, 1. 57–8. **14** *curious.* Carefully wrought.

6. **1** *Hang up.* ignore. **4** *proper virtue.* A doubly playful phrase, for 'virtue' hints at a moral duty, and etymologically means conduct appropriate to men. **18** *vexed.* Severely tested. **19** *store.* abundance.

7. For Coleridge's reworking of this poem, see his *Complete Poetical Works*, ed. E. H. Coleridge (Oxford, 1912), ii. 1118–19. **24** *torches.* Tibullus, iii. viii; *Und.* 19. 2.

8. Borrowed from the Italian poet Girolamo Amaltei's *Horologium Pulverum*. The conceit is varied by Herrick (p. 44), 'The Hour-glass', and the poem is reworked by Coleridge: *Complete Poetical Works*, ed. E. H. Coleridge, ii. 1119–20. Ferrabosco's musical setting of the poem is discussed by E. Doughtie, *RQ* xxii (1969), 148–50. The poem exists in several manuscripts; for variants, see H & S, viii. 148–9. A version was sent to Drummond: *Conv. Dr.* 572–84. **1** *small.* fine.

9. This poem, 'which is (as he said) a picture of himself', was sent to William Drummond in a slightly different form: for variants, see *Conv. Dr.* 585–603. The present version dates from 1619. **7** *close.* The conclusion of a musical phrase or theme. **8** *sentence.* thought. **11** *conscious.* guilty. **14** *hundred.* Thus H & S, from Drummond; F 'hundreds'. For the singular form, cf. *Volp.* I. ii. 120. **16** *waste.* A pun. **17** *mountain belly.* Echoed ironically by Dryden, of Shadwell: *Mac Flecknoe,* 193–4.

10. **16** *health . . . disease.* Seneca, *On Anger,* I. xii. 6: 'A method of cure that makes good health dependent upon disease must be regarded with detestation.'

12. *Vincent Corbett.* Father of Richard Corbett, Bishop of Oxford and Norwich, and Caroline poet, whose elegy to his father is referred to in ll. 3–4 below; see *Poems,* ed. J. A. W. Bennett and H. R. Trevor-Roper (Oxford, 1955), pp. 67–9. (The identity of the 'friend' of l. 4 is not known.) The father, a nurseryman of Whitton in the parish of Twickenham, died on 29 April 1619. **1** *piety. Epig.* 91. **15** n. **6** *Of.* in. **11** *canon.* A pun. **14** *disposure.* Methodical arrangement. **17** *uncleanness.* 'Maliciousness', one manuscript. **20** *specious.* lovely. **28** Martial, x. xxxiii. 10. **37 ff.** Richard Corbett also concludes his elegy with a four-line address to the reader. **37** *whose.* He whose. **40** *first.* Perhaps 'first-rate' (Hunter).

13. *Sir Edward Sackville.* 1591–1652; succeeded his brother Richard as Earl of Dorset 1624; Lord Chamberlain 1628; Commissioner for Planting Virginia 1631, 1634; Lord Privy Seal 1644. See *Und.* 26 and n. Jonson's extensive borrowings in this poem from Seneca's *On Benefits* are traced by W. D. Briggs, *MP* x (1913), 573–85. **1–4** Seneca, *On Benefits,* I. i. 1, 1–2. **2** *Great and good.* See l. 124 below, and *Epig.* Dedn. 13 n. **5–6** *On Benefits,* I. i. 3, 8; cf. Tilley, G97: 'A gift is valued by the mind of the giver.' **5** *owed.* acknowledged. **9–12** *On Benefits,* II. i. 3. **11** *prevent.* Come before. **16–17** *On Benefits,* II. xviii. 2. **18–22** *On Benefits,* I. xv. 4. **24** *On Benefits,* I. i. 7. **25–8, 30–2** *On Benefits,* I. i. 6. **33** *corrupts the thanks.* Seneca's phrase, *gratiam omnem corrupimus*: *On Benefits,* I. i. 4. **34** *On Benefits,* I. ii. 3. **37–8** *On Benefits,* II. xiii. 1. **40** Cf. Tilley, G125: 'He that gives quickly gives twice.' **45** *air or print.* i.e. spoken or written thanks. **46** *conscience.* consciousness. **47–9** *On Benefits,* II. xxiii. 1–2. **57** *On Benefits,* II. xxiv. 1. *too is.* H & S's emendation, 'to, as', is unnecessary. **64** *commission of the blade.* Knighthood. Cf. *Epig.* 19. 1 n. **67–72** From a fable of Phaedrus, *Fab.* II. iii. **77–8** Seneca, *On Benefits,* I. ii. 1 ff., justifies generosity even to the ungrateful. **78** *p[l]ace.* Thus Whalley, H & S; F 'pace'. **82** *Bermudas . . . straits.* A notorious maze of lanes and alleyways north of the Strand, near Covent Garden. **83** *shift. Epig.* 12 n. **101** *Reresuppers.* Lavish late-night suppers. **105–8** Cf. Lovel's speech on true valour, *NI* IV. iv. 40 ff.; from Seneca, *Epist.* lxxxv. 28. **114–15** Seneca, *On the Happy Life,* xviii. 3: 'It is enough for me if every day I reduce the number of my vices, and blame my mistakes.' **117** *tarries . . . beast.* Remains in a bestial state. **118–23** Cf. Plutarch, *How a Man May Become Aware of His Progress in Virtue,* iii. **124–30** Plutarch, ibid. i. **128** *Coryate.* Thomas Coryate, the traveller: see *UV* 10 n. **135 ff.** Seneca, *Epist.* cxviii. 16. **143** *notes.* i.e. noteworthy objects. **145–6** Seneca, *Epist.* cxi. 3, on the true philosopher's not needing to walk on tiptoe. **149–54** Plutarch, op. cit. iv. **156** *indice.* indicator.

14. *John Selden.* 1584–1654, the jurist: 'the law-book of the judges of England, the bravest man in all languages' (*Conv. Dr.* 530–1). This poem is prefixed to Selden's *Titles of Honour* (1614); in his preface, Selden testifies to Jonson's learning and friendship. **1–2** Horace warns that brevity can lead to obscurity, *Ars Poetica*, 25–6; Jonson suggests that his own brevity cannot be misunderstood by such a friend as Selden. **4** *naked.* On the graces, see E. Wind, *Pagan Mysteries in the Renaissance* (London, 1958), ch. 2; on naked truth, E. Panofsky, *Studies in Iconology* (New York, 1939), ch. 5. **7** ff. i.e. with most works given for an opinion, one is not performing a service so much as a penance; a man may not be free when he must temper his criticism out of friendship. **19–22** For Jonson's awareness of particular instances of over-praise, see *Epig.* 65 and 132. 6 n.; *UV* 26. 5–14; *Disc.* 175–6. **21** *terms.* Limits, capacities. **24** Horace, *Epist.* I. xviii. 68, 76. **25** *vex.* Test, sift. **30** *at home. For.* 4. 68; *Und.* 78. 8. **31–2** Cf. *Und.* 47. 60, and Donne, 'A Valediction: Forbidding Mourning', 25–35. **33** *men, manners.* See *Epig.* 128.2 n. **36** *things. Epig.* 14. 7. **39** *vexed.* See note to l. 25 above. **47** *nominal mark, or real rite.* Title of address or royal ceremony: Selden's own terms in *Titles of Honour.* **48** *art.* F 'act'. **54** Ovid, *Metam.* ii. 5.: 'the workmanship was more beautiful than the material'. **56** *manly. Disc.* 809; *Und.* 46. 13. **56–60** '. . . a masterly summary of the intellectual qualities Jonson most admired. The newness of sense is the Baconian insistence upon the observation of particulars and all that this implies in the investigation of the real world; antiquity of voice is the use of recorded history which gives chronological and ethical coherence to the fragments of individual experience' (Trimpi, p. 146). **58** *colours.* Of rhetoric. **72** *chamber-fellow.* Edward Hayward (d. 1658), of the Inner Temple. **74** *approve.* Attest to. **76** *same.* 'Rich' in Selden. **80** *comings-in.* Gains, income. **83** *take up.* borrow.

15.   The friend is named as Colby in l. 176; Newdigate conjectures he may be Sir Huntingdon Colby of Suffolk, or another member of that family. Judith K. Gardiner (*NQ* xxii, July 1975) identifies him with 'Colbie XXV yeres' who went with Suckling to join the English volunteers serving under the Earl of Wimbledon in the Dutch Wars in October 1629 (PRO, E. 157/14, f. 40: see Herbert Berry, *Sir John Suckling's Poems and Letters from Manuscript* (London, Ontario, 1960), pp. 49–50). But the poem was probably written, as H & S suggest, near the beginning of the Thirty Years War, e.g. in 1620, when English volunteers were recruited to aid Frederick of the Palatinate. **1** *from . . . lethargy.* 'And find thyself; awake', one manuscript. **10** *end.* ended. *spoil.* destruction **16** *proves.* tries. **26** Cf. Seneca on flatterers, *On Benefits,* I. ix. 2. **34** *sects.* A pun: religious factions; cuttings from plants. **37** *capital.* fatal. **43** *clownage.* rudeness. **46** *groin. Epig.* 117; *Disc.* 56. **51** *lord.* See *Epig.* 11. 5 and n. **55** ff. Cf. *Und.* 42. 25 ff. **55** *blood.* Good stock; also hinting at a secondary sense, sexual appetite. **56** *The bravery makes.* The show suffices. *leese.* lose. **57–8** Cf. Juvenal, *Sat.* xi. 176–8: 'In men of moderate position, gaming and adultery are shameful; but when those others do these same things, they are called gay fellows and fine gentlemen.' **57** *stuffs.* Woven fabrics; with a sexual innuendo (cf. Nick and Pinnacia Stuff in *NI*). **58** *spirit.* Style; but also sexual energy: cf. l. 82 below, and Shakespeare's Sonnet 129. **61–2** Cf. Juvenal, *Sat.* i. 79: 'Though nature deny me, indignation will prompt my verse.' **65** *purls.* Laces, frills. **67** *pound a prick.* For the *double entendre,*

cf. Middleton, *The Changeling*, III. iii. 9–10. **69** *cast.* vomit. *band.* Collar or ruff.
70 *piccadill.* Frame to hold band upright. **72** *firk.* Move brisky. **76** *salt.* On heat.
77–8 He who pays may feel her, or do what he will. **78** *steel.* i.e. in her moral
insensibility, not (like Milton's Lady, *Comus*, l. 421) in moral invincibility.
80 *Pitts, or Wright, or Modet.* Notorious women of the time. *venter.* venture. **85 ff.** Cf.
Seneca on adultery, *On Benefits*, I. ix. 3–4; I. x. 2–3. **86** *commodity. Epig.* 12. 13 n.
90 *Nature.* character. **92** *in his eyes.* 'Before his face' (Hunter); or, in his esteem.
94 *to the lady's end.* To seduce his lady. **96** *like her embryons. Epig.* 62 and n.
97 ff. For he who has not yet been made infamous by a great mistress is scornfully
named a fellow of coarse lechery, the servant of the serving woman, one who has
never tasted the plenteous delights of marriage. (The *marriage-horn* is at once the
cornucopia of marriage and the cuckold's emblem; *plenteous* refers ironically to
lovers rather than offspring.) **104** *his back.* i.e. in clothing. **105** *Counters.* The city
prisons for debtors. *Fleet.* The prison for Star Chamber and Chancery Court
offenders. **107** *on foot-cloth.* On a richly caparisoned horse. **110** *cast.* abandon.
113 *[God].* The Folio leaves a blank; 'friend' in one manuscript. **116** *voids.* Abstains
from. **119–20** Cf. Herbert, 'The Church Porch', 25 ff. **121** *soft peace.* Cf. *UV* 3,
'Peace'. **128** *fell.* hard. **135–9** Horace, *Sat.* II. vii. 15–18 ('Volanerius, the jester,
when the gout he had earned crippled his finger-joints, kept a man, hired a daily
wage, to pick up the dice for him and put them in a box'); Seneca, *Epist.* cxiv. 24–5;
Disc. 1482–93. **136** *bones.* 'Bales', one manuscript. **141** *this worm. Epig.* 15. 1.
143–4 Seneca, *On Tranquillity of Mind*, ii. 11–12. **147** *cry.* 'Try' in one
manuscript. *bowl.* Cf. Marston, *Certain Satires* (1598), ii. 94. **153** *buttered beer.* 'A
beverage composed of sugar, cinnamon, butter, and beer brewed without hops'
(*OED*, 'ale', †4). **160** *boot.* 'Both' in one manuscript. **161** *O times!* Cicero, *Against
Catiline*, I. i. 2: *O tempora!* Cf. *Und.* 64. 17. **165** *slanderers.* 'standers', one
manuscript. **165–6** *let blood | The life and fame-veins.* Bleed the lives and
reputations of others. **181** *commanding first thyself. Disc.* 1007–8. **183–4** *Disc.* 1–7.
187 *great . . . good. Epig.* Dedn. 13 n.

16.   *Philip Gray.* Perhaps the eldest son of Sir Edward Gray of Morpeth Castle;
d. *c.*1625/6.

17.   **5** *there.* In friendship. **7** *protested.* Declared bankrupt. **9** *where.* whereas.
band. bond.

18.   **4** *amaze.* bewilder. **7–8** Cf. Seneca, *Epist.* lxxi. 24. **8** *so that doth my conceit.*
i.e. so fear acts on my imagination. **10** Ovid, *Ars Amatoria*, i. 608: 'Fortune and
Venus help the brave'; cf. Tilley, F601, H302. **13** *error.* winding. **16** *wink.* Close
their eyes. **21** *come love, and fortune go.* Parallel constructions; both are summoned.

19.   **1–10** For parallels, see *Und.* 2. v. 21–6 n.; *CR* v. iv. 439–42; *D. is A.* II. vi.
78–87; and, for the *torches* of l. 2, *Und.* 7. 24 and n. **3** *stand.* Place from which to
shoot. **17–18** Cf. Donne, 'The Canonization'. **22–3** Cf. Wittipol's plea to Mrs
Fitzdottrell, *D. is A.* II. vi. 64–6. **25** *That . . . can.* i.e. a cuckold.

20.   *Shrub.* Playing on the title of the collection, *The Underwood*; and in *Und.* 21
picking up a secondary sense, a mean or insignificant person. Neither victim in

these two poems has been identified. Probably written in 1621 or 1622 ('fifty years, almost', l. 5). Cf. 'A Rodomontade on his Cruel Mistress', once attributed to Rochester: *Complete Poems* ed. Vieth, p. 159. 5 *fifty years, almost. Und.* 2. i. 3.

21. See *Und.* 20 and n. Jonson's reluctance to name his victim is characteristic: see *Epig.* Dedn. 14 n.; *Epig.* 30. 4; 38. 8; 77. 8 *lay-stall.* Dung heap. 10 Proverbial: 'The more you stir the more you stink' (Tilley, S862).

22. 5 *alloy.* i.e. a tempering (rather than a devaluing) additive. 6 *that.* beauty. 8 *This.* virtue. 23 *acquit.* requite. 23–4 From this hint Fleay deduces (i. 326) that the elegy is addressed to Lady Covell, of *Und.* 56. 29 *offering.* Thus Whalley; F 'off-spring'.

23. Cf. *Songs*, 35, on the failure of *The New Inn.* The occasion of the present poem is not known. 1–2 Cf. Ovid, *Amores*, I. xv. 1–2, translated by Jonson in *Poet.* I. i. 43–4: 'Envy, why twit'st thou me, my time's spent ill? | And call'st my verse fruits of an idle quill?' 4 *security.* carelessness. One manuscript: 'obscurity'. 6 [*oft*]. Supplied by H & S. 7 *Aonian springs.* Sacred to the muses. 8 *Thespia.* Town at the foot of Mt. Helicon, also sacred to the muses. 9 *Clarius'.* Apollo's (worshipped in Claros, in Ionia). 12 *chattering pies.* Cf. Pindar, *Olymp.* ii. 87; Jonson's birds are not only noisy but dirty (Carol Maddison, *Apollo and the Nine* (London, 1960), p. 298). *defaced.* 'Displaced', one manuscript. 16 *great.* 'Quick', one manuscript. 17–18 For the contrast of fortune and virtue, see *Epig.* 63. 2–3 and n. 18 A commonplace; see, e.g., Seneca, *On the Happy Life*, xi. 4, *On Mercy*, i. 1. 21 *worded balladry.* Fleay (i. 327) suspects a gibe at Daniel—'no poet' (*Conv. Dr.* 17). 23 *die.* 'Drink', one manuscript. 27 *Japhet's line.* Prometheus; see Horace, *Odes*, I. iii. 25–8; cf. *Epig.* 110. 17. *aspire.* mount. 30 *issue of Jove's brain.* Minerva; see *For.* 10. 13–15 n. 35–6 These lines are also spoken by the Author in *Poet.* Apol. Dial. 238–9; 'dull ass's hoof' is echoed by W. B. Yeats, *Collected Poems* (London, 1963), p. 143.

24. *a Book.* Sir Walter Raleigh's *History of the World* (1614). Jonson's poem describes its frontispiece (see p. 345); A. H. Gilbert suspects Jonson may have helped with its design (*The Symbolic Persons in the Masques of Ben Jonson* (Durham, N. Carolina, 1948), pp. 121–2). Jonson had helped in other ways with Raleigh's work: see *Conv. Dr.* 159–62. With 'The Mind', cf. the body/soul distinction of Jonson's masques: see *UV* 34. 50 n. See further M. Corbett and R. Lightbown, *The Comely Frontispiece* (London, 1969), pp. 132–3. 3 *Raising.* 'Razing' in Raleigh. 5 *Wise.* 'High' in Raleigh. 8 In Raleigh: 'And the reward and punishment assured.' *dured.* lasted. 17–18 Cicero's definition of history, which 'bears witness to the passing of the ages, sheds light upon reality, gives life to recollection and guidance to human existence, and brings tidings of ancient days': *De Oratore*, II. ix. 36.

25. *James, Earl of Desmond.* James Fitzgerald (?1570–1601), son of the attainted 'Rebel Earl', Gerald Fitzgerald. Imprisoned in Dublin Castle and the Tower of London from 1579 to 1600; restored as Earl of Desmond, 1 October 1600, to defeat the pretensions of a cousin. The poem was probably written shortly before this date. 4 *tower.* A play on words. 8 *Cinthius.* Apollo, born on Mt. Cinthus.

('Pythius', manuscript). **9** *bolder.* 'Flowing', one manuscript. **19** *her stony arms.*
The Tower. **20** *hold*[s]. 'Curbs', manuscript. **26** *Palm.* An emblem of patience
and fortitude; said to flourish even when beaten: see Alciati, *Emblemata* (Paris,
1602), pp. 231–4. **29** *wries.* Distorts, convulses. **37** *her dead.* 'Thy white',
manuscript. **38** *Surgeons' Hall.* Or Barber-Surgeons' Hall, in Monkswell Street,
near Cripplegate; here criminals' bodies ('anatomies') were dissected. **39** *statist's.*
politician's. *phlebotomy.* Blood-letting. **40–2** *Brontes . . . Steropes . . . Pyracmon.*
The three Cyclopes who assisted Vulcan at his forge on Mt. Aetna; they make the
shield of Aeneas, *Aeneid*, viii. 424 ff. **42** 'An hour will come they must effect their
ease', manuscript. **45** Proverbial, of stoical sufferers: see Tilley, G284; cf. *Und.*
47. 3–4. **48–50** Seneca, *On Firmness*, iii. 3: 'The invulnerable thing is not that
which is not struck, but that which is not hurt'; cf. *Poet.* Apol. Dial. 38–9, *NI* IV. iv.
204–5. **58** *fair Phoebe's.* Queen Elizabeth's ('dread Cynthia's', manuscript).

26. Trimpi (pp. 197–8, 278–9) and Alvaro Ribeiro (*RES* xxiv (1973), 164 n. 1)
suspect that this poem is addressed to Sir John Roe; see *Epig.* 27 and n., and the
duels referred to in *Epig.* 32. But the 'high-spirited friend' might equally be Sir
Edward Sackville (see *Und.* 13 and n.), who killed Lord Bruce, and was himself
seriously wounded, in a duel in 1613; Sidney Lee (*DNB*) guessed that Venetia
Stanley (see *Und.* 78 and n.) was the cause of the quarrel. On the duel and on
Sackville's qualities, see Clarendon, *History of the Rebellion*, i. 129–30. Sackville
had married in 1612; the reference in ll. 3–4 may be to his wife. Sara van den
Berg, *Explic.* xxxv. 2 (1976), 24–6, thinks the wound may be Cupid's. **2** *corsives.*
Corrosives, sharp medicines. Cf. Plutarch, *How to Tell a Flatterer*, xi. **10** *this paper.*
i.e. the poem itself; playing on the fact that drugs were wrapped in paper.
18 *husband.* Perhaps a play on words. **20** *fame.* Newdigate's emendation of F 'same'.
23 From Ausonius, *Epig.* ii. 7–8; cf. *Volp.* III. vii. 88–9.

27. **5** *Phao*[n]. Handsome boatman of Mitylene; for love of him, Sappho is said
to have thrown herself into the sea. *the boy.* Named Bathyllus; see *Anacreontea*,
xvii. Horace speaks of this boy living on in Anacreon's verse, *Odes*, IV. ix. 9–12.
8 *he whom Maro did rehearse.* The child Virgil prophesies in *Eclogue* iv. **11** *Propertius'
song.* Propertius himself, in celebrating his Cinthia, names—as Jonson does—
other women celebrated by other poets: *Elegies*, ii. 85–94. **12** *she.* The moon.
15 *Lycoris.* Also called Cytheris and Volumnia; a freedwoman, loved by Gallus. See
Virgil, *Eclogue* x. **17–20** Jonson's Ovid in *Poet.* I. iii. 37 'veils' Caesar's daughter,
Julia, under the name of Corinna; cf. Ovid. *Tristia*, ii. 339–40. **23** *new Cassandra
. . . old.* Cassandra Salviati, to whom Ronsard addressed his sonnet cycle, *Amours*,
in 1552; Cassandra the Greek prophetess, daughter of Priam. **25** *Stella.* Lady
Rich (née Penelope Devereux), of *Astrophil and Stella*. **27** *Constable's ambrosiac
muse.* Henry Constable, 1562–1613, author of *Diana* (1592). **30** *The swan.* Hugh
Holland; see Jonson's poem on his *Pancharis* (1603), *UV* 6. **31** *my Celia.*
Suggesting a real identity for the girl addressed in *For.* 5, 6, and 9?

28. *Lady Mary Worth.* Or Wroth; see *Alch.* Dedn. n. **3** *exscribe.* Copy out. *your
sonnets.* 'Pamphilia to Amphilanthus', appended to Lady Mary Wroth's *Urania*
(London, 1621). **6** *numerous.* Poetic, musical. **11** *yours.* Your poetic, but also your
personal, properties. The remaining lines turn on a similar ambiguity. **14** *Venus'*

ceston. The girdle which conferred beauty on the wearer and excited love in the beholder; see *Und.* 2. v. 41.

29. In 1602 Campion published his *Observations in the Art of English Poesy*, attacking the 'childish titillation' of rhyme; in 1603 Daniel replied with *A Defence of Rhyme*. Jonson told Drummond that 'he had written a discourse of poesy both against Campion and Daniel, especially this last, where he proves couplets to be the bravest sort of verses': 'he detesteth all other rhymes' (*Conv. Dr.* 3–8). G. B. Johnston, *Ben Jonson: Poet*, p. 7, points out that every poem in the Folio is rhymed. Cf. Dryden's 'To the Earl of Roscommon, on his Excellent Essay on Translated Verse', esp. ll. 11–12. **2** *fits.* A pun: spasms, sections of poems. **5** *measure.* A pun. **10** *Jointing syllabes.* i.e. breaking a word on a syllabic unit to achieve a rhyme, as in *Und.* 70. 92–3; on the practice, see K. A. McEuen, *Classical Influence on the Tribe of Ben*, pp. 166, 277. 'Syllabe' is Jonson's usual spelling, e.g. in *Eng. Gram.* and *Und.* 70. 63. **17** *Parnassus.* The mountain of the muses. **19** *Pegasus.* The muses' winged horse. **20** *well.* (F 'wells'); Hippocrene, sacred to the muses: it was produced by Pegasus striking the ground with his hoof. **25** *Starveling rhymes did fill the stage.* Cf. Marlowe's gibe in the prologue to *Tamburlaine the Great*, Part 1. **27** *a-crowning.* H & S; F 'crowning'. **34–5** Contemporary Latin verse was sometimes rhymed. **48** *caesure.* Caesura, metrical pause. **56** *feet.* A pun: poetic feet.

30. 'Presented upon a plate of gold to his son, Robert, Earl of Salisbury, when he was also Treasurer' (Jonson's note). William Cecil, Lord Burghley (1521–98), was Elizabeth's senior minister; Baron of Burghley 1571, Knight of the Garter and Lord High Treasurer 1572. For Robert Cecil, Earl of Salisbury, see *Epig.* 43 n. A version of ll. 1–10 is inscribed on the underside of a silver-gilt paten (hallmark 1609) in the chapel of Burghley House, with the concluding lines: 'Whose worthy sonne besides his owne high graces | Inheritts all his vertues, all his places. | —To the memorye of W. Lo: Burleigh, | late high Treasurer of Englande.' C. C. Oman, who describes the paten, doubts if a 'plate of gold' ever existed: *English Church Plate, 597–1830* (London, 1957), pp. 233–4. The poem may be a delayed tribute to father and son after the latter's preferment to the Treasurership in May 1608: see *Epig.* 64. **8** *poor's full.* 'Poor man's', Burghley House plate. **16–19** Five of Burghley's seven children actually predeceased him. Several of his children and grandchildren married into noble families.

31. 'For a poor man' (Jonson's note). Jonson's intercession may be related to a suit in a letter to Ellesmere's secretary, printed in H & S, i. 201. For Ellesmere, see *Epig.* 74 n. Hilary term 1617 was his last as Chancellor.

32. 'For the same' (Jonson's note).

33. *the Counsellor.* The rhyme-word in l. 6 is missing in Folio; Whalley conjectured 'Benn', i.e. Sir Anthony Benn, Recorder of London, d. 1618. **2** *more . . . war.* Lucan, *Pharsalia,* i. i. **9** *gownèd vultures.* Cf. the lawyer Voltore (= vulture) in *Volp.* The association is traditional. **12** *dog's eloquence.* From Quintilian, XII. ix. 9: 'For it is a dog's eloquence, as Appius says, to undertake the task of abusing one's opponent.' **19** *vex.* try. **21** *the scar fair.* Cf. *Und.* 38. 49–52 and n. **23** *touch.*

test. **30** *at all pieces.* At all points. **31** *style.* Stylus, pen; for the play, cf. *Epig.* 110. 6; Horace, *Sat.* II. i. 39–41; Quintilian, X. i. 29–30.

34. Cf. *For.* 8, 'To Sickness', and *Conv. Dr.* 292–4, on Sir Philip Sidney's mother's smallpox. **7** *Sir Hugh Platt.* Or Plat (1552–1608); his *Jewell House of Art and Nature* (1594) and *Delights for Ladies* (1602) include advice on cosmetics. **10** *Madam Bawd-be's bath.* Probably a sweating-bath to improve the complexion (recommended by Platt). Bath-houses enjoyed a doubtful reputation: see *Epig.* 7 and n. **11** *Turner's oil of talc.* See *For.* 8. 33 n. H & S take 'Turner' to be Anne Turner, the poisoner of Overbury. Her husband, George, had been a doctor of physic. **12** Several popular dentifrices of the time had this calamitous effect.

35. *Elizabeth Chute.* d. 18 May 1627, aged 3½ years. The epitaph is inscribed on her memorial tablet in Sonning Church, near Reading. (The present text is from the Folio.) **3–6** *filed,* | *Upon record . . . the roll.* Cf. *Und.* 70. 126; 75. 155–6.

36. **16** *For.* 10. 19 and n.

37. **9** *friendship of the spit.* As in *Und.* 45. 8; cf. *Disc.* 1103, and the proverbial 'trencher-friendship', Tilley, F762. **12** *mix spirits.* Cf. Donne's 'To Sir Henry Wotton', l. 2: 'Sir, more than kisses, letters mingle souls' (*Satires*, p. 71). **19–33** These lines are repeated in *UV* 49. 12–26. **20** *scant.* Restrict, do small justice to. **27** As it is an act of flattery always to fall in with a friend's whims.

38. The authorship of this poem and of *Und.* 39, 40, and 41 has been the subject of doubt. *Und.* 39 was printed with Donne's *Poems* in 1633, and all four poems have from time to time been thought to be Donne's. Evelyn Simpson, *RES* xv (1939), 274–82, argues persuasively for the ascription of *Und.* 38, 40, and 41 to Jonson. Helen Gardner, agreeing with Mrs Simpson that *Und.* 39 is not Jonson's, suspects it may have been written not by Donne but by Sir Thomas Roe: see *Elegies*, pp. xxxv–xxxviii, 224–5. D. Heywood Brock confirms Mrs Simpson's ascriptions on stylistic grounds, but does not consider alternative authorship: *PBSA* 72 (1978), 519–27. **5** *blocked up.* Cf. *Und.* 71. 10. **17** *goodness . . . great.* See *Epig.* Dedn. 13 n. **27** *cast.* Found guilty. **30** *Seneca, On Mercy*, I. xxi. 2. **40–50** Ibid. I. xiv. 1–3: 'What, then, is his duty? It is that of a good parent who is wont to reprove his children sometimes gently, sometimes with threats, who at times admonishes them even with stripes. Does any father in his senses disinherit a son for his first offence? Only when great and repeated wrongdoing has overcome his patience, only when what he fears outweighs what he reprimands, does he resort to the final pen [= disinheritance]; but first he makes many an effort to reclaim a character that is still unformed, though inclined now to the more evil side; when the case is hopeless, he tries extreme measures. No one resorts to the exaction of punishment until he has exhausted all the means of correction. . . . Slow would a father be to sever his own flesh and blood; indeed, after severing he would yearn to restore them, and while severing he would groan aloud, hesitating often and long; for he comes near to condemning gladly who condemns swiftly, and to punishing unjustly who punishes unduly.' **49–52** Ibid., I. xvii. 2: 'It is a poor physician that despairs of his ability to cure . . . the aim of the prince should be not merely to restore the health, but also to leave no shameful scar'; cf. *Und.* 33. 21.

67 ff. *On Mercy*, I. vii. 1–3. **69** *goes by.* Lets pass. **95–6** Cf. *BF* I. i. 33–41. **96** *pump.* work. **98** *wall.* Cf. *UV* 36. 11. **99** *chore.* Band, company. **101** *of the race.* Of that kind. **102** *danger.* Perhaps, disdain (cf. *OED*, †2). **114–15** Possibly a masquing expedition out of London, as H & S suggest, though the lines seem to hint at a weightier mission.

40. See *Und.* 38 n. **13** *blazon.* Show (literally, of heraldic arms); i.e. divulging of identity. **21** *Not . . . Shut up in himself.* Cf. Truewit's advice in *SW* IV. i. 55–66. **29–30** Cf. *Disc.* 728–30. **34–7** Compare and contrast *Und.* 14. 30–3.

41. See *Und.* 38 n. Cf. 'His Parting From Her', formerly attributed to Donne: 'Since she must go, and I must mourn, come night.'

42. Written about 1624. For criticism, see Barbara Hutchison, *ELN* ii. (1965), 185–90. **1–2** See Suetonius' *Life of Virgil*, 10–11, and *Life of Horace*, and for the parallel between Jonson and Horace, *Epig.* 91. 4 n. Lucian, *Octogenarian*, reports that Anacreon lived to 85. Cf. Pope's 'I cough like Horace', etc., *An Epistle to Dr Arbuthnot*, ll. 116–18. **3–4** A classical commonplace; e.g. Cicero, *The Orator*, II. xlv. **7** *endorse.* Put on the back of his writings; with an equestrian pun: cf. *Und.* 53. 11 n. **8** *horse.* Pegasus. **9** *ivy garland.* Of Bacchus, seen as god of inspiration. **11–12** Distantly following Ovid, *Amores*, II. iv. **12–13** *take . . . fair.* i.e. it is easier not to look at what is beautiful than to look and remain unmoved. **16** *purl.* Lace, frill. **19** *consent.* Thus H & S; F 'Content'. **29 ff.** Jonson alludes to his involvement with masquing at court. **31** *whale-bone.* For farthingales, to hold out skirts of kirtles. **32** *span.* Measure with outstretched hand. **39–42** An idea more fully developed in *NI* IV. iii. 63–73. **42** *preoccupy.* Have first use of; the word also has a bawdy sense. Cf. *NI* IV. iii. 79–80. **43** *tissue.* Rich cloth often interwoven with gold or silver. **46** *caparison.* Ornamental saddle-cloth. **50** *brave.* Finely dressed. **63** *withers.* Hutchison (p. 189) sees a secondary reference to George Wither. ('Withers' was in fact an alternative form of the poet's name; he was attacked by Jonson in *Time Vind.* in 1623.) **67** *spent.* With a play on the sexual sense. **69** *French hood.* With a round front, framing the face; out of date with all but citizens' wives by the early seventeenth century. **71** *Spittle sermon.* Preached in Easter week near St Mary Spittle of Bishopsgate Without, and attended by civic dignitaries. **72** *Exchange.* The new Exchange on the south side of the Strand; occupied by milliners' shops; a fashionable resort for ladies. **73** *Moorfields.* Flat marshy ground just north of the city; laundresses dried their clothes here. **75** *l'envoy.* Afterthought; literally, a concluding stanza. **76** *Cheapside.* At the east end of which were mercers' shops. **82** *block.* Wooden dummy for hat; blockhead. **85** *scabbard.* i.e. dress. **87** *case.* Clothing; with a sexual innuendo.

43. On the fire of November 1623, which destroyed Jonson's library and many of his unpublished writings. Chapman's 'Invective written against Mr Ben Jonson' (*Poems*, ed. P. B. Bartlett, pp. 374–8) was evidently prompted by this poem; see R. B. Sharpe, *SP* xlii (1945), 555–63, and H & S, x. 692–7. **1** *lame.* See note to ll. 111–17 below. **6** *wife.* Venus; alluding to her affair with Mars. **8** *in horn.* In a lantern. Lanterns were made of horn; hence, by popular etymology, the spelling 'lanthorn': in l. 10, a punning allusion to Vulcan's cuckolding. **11–12** Jove agreed that Vulcan might marry Minerva, but privately persuaded Minerva to refuse him. **14** *issue of the brain.* Minerva sprang from Jove's head, cleft open by Vulcan (see *For.* 10. 13–15). Jonson wryly contrasts the fate of his own brain-children. **20** *s[c]urrile.* scurrilous. **22** *vote.* (i) Verdict; (ii) votive offering (Miller). **29 ff.** *Amadis de Gaul.* Early sixteenth-century romance by Garcia de Montalvo, from older originals. Its fifth book concerns Esplandian, son of Amadis; separate continuations of his adventures were also published. *Palmerin d'Oliva* and *Palmerin of England,* romances translated into English by Antony Munday (ridiculed in *C. is A.*). *The Adventures of Splandian* and *Palmerin d'Oliva* join the bonfire of romances from Don Quixote's library made by Cervantes's curate and barber, who nevertheless spare *Amadis de Gaul* and *Palmerin of England* (*Don Quixote,* I. vi). **34 ff.** Some of these 'courtly trifles' are described by Thomas Puttenham in *The Art of English Poesie* (1589), ed. G. D. Willcock and A. Walker (Cambridge, 1936), Bk. II, ch. xi. **34** *logogriphs.* 'A kind of enigma, in which a certain word, and other words that can be formed out of all or any of its letters, are to be guessed from synonyms of them introduced into a set of verses' (*OED*). *palindromes.* Words, phrases, or verses that read the same backwards as forwards. **35** *pumped.* laboured (F 'pomped'). *anagrams.* See Puttenham, ed. cit., pp. 108 ff. Jonson expresses his contempt for anagrams again in *Conv. Dr.* 375, but employs them in *Hym.* 232–3 ('Iuno'/'Unio'), *UV* 40. 23–4 ('Celia'/'Alice'), and elsewhere. **36** *eteostics.* Or chronograms, in which certain letters indicate a date or a numerical value: e.g. 'LorD haVe MerCIe Vpon Vs', for a day of national humiliation in 1666 (the date being also the sum of the capitalized letters) (*OED*). *flams.* Fanciful compositions, conceits. **37–8** See Puttenham, ed. cit., pp. 91 ff. for illustrations of verses in similarly fanciful shapes. **39** *Acrostics.* A form Jonson occasionally in fact used, e.g. *Epig.* 40. *telestichs.* A kind of acrostic, in which the final (rather than the initial) letters of each line of verse spell a word or phrase. *jump.* Coinciding, exactly equivalent (manuscripts: 'fine'). **40** *colour.* warrant. **43** *parcels.* Parts; probably of *The Staple of News:* see G. B. Johnston, *MLN* xlvi (1931), 150–3. **45** *Adulterate.* counterfeit. *go.* Pass as current. **50** 'More change, and taste of tyranny', manuscripts. **52** *light tobacco. Conv. Dr.* 406–8; a stock joke. **53** 'Cloathe spices, or guard sweetmeats from the flies', manuscripts. **54** *with the pies.* Cf. Dryden, *Mac Flecknoe,* l. 101 ('Martyrs of pies, and relics of the bum'); another traditional joke. **55** *a whole age.* The pies being continually rejected, and continually warmed up for resale: cf. *Epig.* 133. 149 ff. **65** *Talmud.* The corpus of Jewish law. *Alcoran.* Koran. **66** *the Legend.* Or *Golden Legend,* a medieval manual of ecclesiastical lore. **67** *errant.* A pun: the wanderings are both geographical and moral. **68** *charmèd boats.* Such as Guingelot, the magic boat of Wade. **69** *Tristrams, Lancelots.* Cf. Arthurian legend. *Turpins.* Turpin, eighth-century AD archbishop of Rheims; thought to have been at Roncesvalles, and to have chronicled the deeds of Charlemagne. **69–70** *Peers.* Or Paladins, who accompanied Charlemagne. *Roland,* the most famous of the Peers, is celebrated by Boiardo and (mad) by Ariosto; *Oliver* is his companion. **71** *his cabal's loss.* The loss of Merlin's secret art after his infatuation with Niviene; see *The Works of Sir Thomas Malory,* ed. E. Vinaver (Oxford, 1967), i. 125–32. **72 ff.** *chimera of the Rosy Cross.* Rosicrucianism, first heard of in England around 1614, though allegedly founded much earlier by (the probably mythical) Christian Rosenkreuz (1378–1484). In

1652 Thomas Vaughan was to defend 'that admirable chimera' of Rosicrucianism, and to describe some of its mysteries (e.g. the properties of the 'bright stone' of l. 74): *Works*, ed. A. E. Waite (London, 1919), pp. 343–76. Members of the fraternity were bound by seals of secrecy, and devised a magic writing, based on divine 'characters' which they found in nature and the Bible. **76** *True Coal.* See *Alch.* I. iii. 102 n. *Lungs.* One who blows an alchemist's fire. **77** Probably a lost pamphlet by Nicholas Breton (? 1545–?1626), who is addressed in *UV* 2. The title is proverbial: Tilley, M747. **78** *strong lines.* For the term, see George Williamson, *Seventeenth-Century Contexts* (London, 1960), pp. 120–31. **79–80** The 'Letters of News' of Captain Thomas Gainford (see *Epig.* 107 n.), ostensibly written from foreign parts but in fact from Pope's Head Alley, home of printers and booksellers. **81** *weekly Courants.* The news-sheets of the printer and journalist Nathaniel Butter, published from St Paul's Churchyard. **82** *prophet Ball.* A mad tailor who prophesied that King James would become Pope. **84** *Vulcan to lick up.* Cf. Pope, *Dunciad* (A), iii. 73: 'From shelves to shelves see greedy Vulcan roll.' **85** *accite.* Arouse, excite. **88** *of search.* Of an introspective and reflective nature. *mastery in the arts.* A reference to Jonson's Oxford MA of 1619? See the marginal note to the manuscript of Chapman's 'Invective', *Poems*, ed. Bartlett, p. 478. **89–91** Horace's *Ars Poetica*, translated and commented upon in the light of the *Poetics*, from which it was thought to derive. (Venusia was Horace's birthplace, Stagira Aristotle's.) The commentary was read to Drummond in 1619: *Conv. Dr.* 61–2. Two versions of Jonson's translation of *Ars Poetica* were published in 1640. **91** *a Grammar.* Later rewritten, though not finished. **94** *journey into Scotland.* By foot, 1618–19. Drummond speaks of Jonson's intention of writing this account, *Conv. Dr.* 347–9. **96** *the Sicilian maid.* John Barclay's *Argenis* (1621), a Latin romance which alluded to recent political events in Europe; James invited Jonson to translate it in 1622. **99–100** Manuscripts, with minor variants: 'Wherein, besides the noble aids were lent, | By Carew, Cotton, Selden, oil was spent.' Richard Carew (1555–1620) and Sir Robert Cotton (1571–1631), the antiquaries, and Sir John Selden (1584–1654), the jurist (see *Und.* 14 n.). Some books about Henry V, borrowed from Cotton's library, are known to have perished in Jonson's fire. **101** *stored-up humanity.* Probably a commonplace book along the lines of *Discoveries.* **102** *gleanings in divinity.* Probably written after 1610, when Jonson abandoned Catholicism. **103** *wiser guides.* i.e. pre-Reformation. **109** *wit.* Minerva being goddess of wisdom. **111–17** For the tradition that Vulcan had no father, see Apollodorus, *Bibliotheca*, I. iii. 5, Hyginus, *Fabulae*, preface; Juno's impregnation by the wind is Jonson's invention. Frightened by Vulcan's appearance, Juno is said to have thrown the child from heaven (*Iliad*, xviii. 394–8). According to other traditions, Jove rejected Vulcan as his cup-bearer ('his cup', l. 115), and threw him from heaven when he tried to intervene in a dispute on behalf of his mother. He landed on Lemnos, was lamed by his fall, and was cared for by peasants. **119** *Squire of the squibs.* John Squire, deviser of the Lord Mayor's show of 30 October 1620 (Fleay, i. 329; J. Nichols, *Progresses . . . of King James I* (London, 1828), iv. 619–27). **120** *Vulcanale.* Hymn to Vulcan. **123** *Bankside.* On the south bank of the Thames, between St Saviour's Church and the modern Blackfriars Bridge. **126** *a Vulcan of a sheaf of reeds.* i.e. a torch or beacon, made from the reeds which then grew plentifully along the Thames. Boats were sometimes adorned in this way on festive occasions, e.g. for the Lord Mayor's procession. **132** *the Globe.* The famous theatre was burnt to the ground on 29 June 1613, during a performance of *Henry VIII.* It was rebuilt the following year. **134** The land on which the Globe stood was formerly a marsh; surrounding ditches were for drainage and sewerage. See J. C. Adams, *The Globe Playhouse* (London, 1961), p. 13. **135** *chambers.* Pieces of ordnance, which caused the fire. *taken in.* conquered. **137** *the world's ruins.* Playing on the theatre's name. **138** *tiles.* Instead of the original thatch ('those reeds!', l. 129), in which the fire began. **139** *The brethren.* Puritans, who saw the burning of the Globe as a divine judgement: see E. N. S. Thompson, *The Controversy Between the Puritans and the Stage* (New York, 1903), p. 151. **142** *Winchestrian goose.* Venereal disease (the brothels of the Bankside were within the liberty of the Bishop of Winchester). **144** *mystery.* trade. **145** *fell with that conceit by the ears.* Quarrelled with that idea. **147** *Parish Garden.* Or Paris Garden, the centre for bull- and bear-baiting; the place had a bad reputation. Cf. *Epig.* 133. 117. **148** *the nun, Kate Arden.* The unsavoury lady of *Epig.* 133. 118. Three manuscripts read 'Venus' nun'; evidently Jonson is remembering Marlowe's phrase in *Hero and Leander,* i. 45, 'So lovely fair was Hero, Venus' nun'. **153** *Fortune, for being a whore.* The Fortune Theatre burnt to the ground on 9 December 1621. The phrase was proverbial: cf. Webster, *The White Devil,* I. i. 4. **156** The Banqueting House at Whitehall burnt down on 12 January 1618. **160** *Venus' care.* As evidenced in the *Aeneid.* **169** *the Rolls.* The Six Clerks' Office in Chancery Lane was burnt on 20 December 1621. **183–5** *or . . . about.* Manuscripts: 'some four miles hence, and have him there disgorge | Or else in penny faggots blaze about'. **187** *bellman's lanthorn.* The bellman was a night-watchman, who called the hours; he commonly carried a lantern, staff, and bell. **187–8** *like . . . die.* Cf. *Epig.* 59. **193** *Paul's steeple.* Struck by lightning and burnt, 4 June 1561; it was not re-erected. **194** *Ephesus.* Where Herostratus burnt down the Temple of Diana in 356 BC. **195** *Alexandria.* In AD 640, after Arabian conquest, it is said that books from the great library of Alexandria were used for six months to feed the furnaces of the public baths. **198** *glaives.* Swords, bills, or lances. **199–200** *Bilbo . . . Milan.* Bilbao and Milan were famous for their swords. **201** *the friar.* Roger Bacon, who was (erroneously) thought to have invented gunpowder (H & S); or —more probably—Konstantin Anklitzen, a Franciscan friar and chemist otherwise known as Berthold Schwarz, who was accredited with the invention of the gun *c.*1320 (Newdigate). **202** *Devil's Arse.* A cavern near Castleton, in the Peak District of Derbyshire. **204** *both sides.* The Dutch and the Spanish. **206** *petards.* Small explosive devices used to breach walls, etc. *granats.* grenades. **213** *Pandora's pox.* Pandora and her box of evils were created by Vulcan at Jove's command, to punish mankind for Prometheus' theft of divine fire. Jonson insinuates that Pandora suffered from one of her own evils, the pox. **216** *B[ess] B[roughton]'s.* A famous courtesan, who died of the pox; her career is described by John Aubrey, *Brief Lives,* ed. O. L. Dick (London, 1949), pp. 40–1. F 'B.B.'

44. *A Speech according to Horace.* 'Speech' is Jonson's rendering of Horace's *sermo*; as H & S point out, the poem also recalls Horace's attacks on national degeneracy in *Odes,* I. xxxv. 33–40, III. i–vi, xxxiv. 54–8, etc. Jonson's main target is the growing indifference of the nobility to military service: see Lawrence

Stone's *The Crisis of the Aristocracy* (Oxford, 1965), ch. v, esp. p. 239, for background. Amateur military bodies such as the Artillery Company revived considerably after 1610, and especially after 1613, with increased fears of a Spanish invasion; see Lindsay Boynton, *The Elizabethan Militia 1558–1638* (London and Toronto, 1967), chs. vii and viii. Dekker, amongst others, celebrated this activity, in *The Artillery Garden* (1616, rediscovered 1936; facsimile ed. F. P. Wilson, Oxford, 1952). Jonson's poem was probably written *c.*1626; see ll. 27, 40–2, and notes. George Parfitt analyses tensions in the poem, *SEL* xix (1979), 85–92. See also Richard C. Newton, *SEL* xvi (1976), 105–16. **2** *King's Day.* The anniversary of James's accession, 24 March; it had last been celebrated in 1624 (Fleay, i. 330): hence 'we have powder still'. **5** *Aesop Gondomar.* Diego Sarmiento d'Acuña, Count of Gondomar, Spanish ambassador in England 1613–18, 1620–2; highly skilful, highly unpopular. 'Aesop', in reference to his habit of telling animal fables: see e.g. Bacon, *Works*, ed. J. Spedding *et al.*, vii. 170, for a parable about rats (Keith Thomas, pers. comm.). **9** *feathers.* The Gentlemen of the Artillery wore a scarlet ostrich feather. **10** *Saint George's Day.* On 23 April, when the annual procession of the Feast of the Garter takes place. **15** *dirty.* despicable. **16** *pride.* display. **20** *Swinnerton.* Captain John Swinnerton, enrolled in the Artillery Company in 1614 (Lt.-Col. G. A. Raikes, *The Ancient Vellum Book of the Hon. Artillery Company* (London, 1890), p. 21). **21** *Pimlico.* The fort was used by the train-bands. **23** *Artillery Yard.* Or Artillery Garden (hence 'seed-plot', l. 24), where the train-bands exercised. **25–6** *to bring up . . . truth.* Echoing *D. is A.* III. ii. 45–6. **27** *ten years' day.* i.e. the period since 1616, when special *Orders* were drawn up for training in the Artillery Garden. **28** *posture-book.* The standard, but not the only, work was Jacob de Gheyn's *The Exercise of Arms* (1607). Cf. *D. is A.* III. ii. 38. **29** *curious.* Careful, painstaking. **30** *Flushing or the Brill.* Towns in the Netherlands handed over to Elizabeth in August 1585, in return for an English military presence; Leicester had a costly and disastrous period of service there until recalled in November 1586. **33–6** Sir Hugh Hammersley (d. 1636) was President of the Artillery Company 1619–33; Captain Edward Panton had command of the Company 1612–18, when he was suspended for neglect of duty. Panton's immediate successor, as Newdigate points out, was not Hammersley but Sir John Bingham, translator of Aelian's *Tactics* (1616) and advocate of the revival of ancient methods of warfare. Jonson confuses Hammersley and Bingham. **40** *in.* of. **40–2** Ambrosio Spinola (1569–1630), general-in-chief of the Spanish army in the Netherlands, failed to take the town of Bergen-op-Zoom in 1622; after a long siege (28 August 1624 to 5 June 1625) he successfully took Breda. Maurice of Nassau, Prince of Orange (1567–1625), commander of the armed forces of the Netherlands, was especially famed for his knowledge of siege warfare. **46** *aldermanity.* Body of aldermen: Jonson probably coined the word. Many aldermen and several Lord Mayors of London were members of the Artillery Company. **48** *surfeits.* For which blood-letting might be prescribed. **51–2** *bold* | *Beauchamps.* 'A stock epithet of the family' (H & S). **53–4** Names of captains in the Artillery Company (identifiable from its *Ancient Vellum Book*, ed. Raikes): John Hodges, Thomas Styles, both enrolled 1614; Richard Dyke, Edward Ditchfield, enrolled 1624; Nicholas Crips (or Crispe), enrolled 1621; Sir Richard Fenn, enrolled 1614, sheriff 1626, President 1632–4,

Lord Mayor 1637. 'Millar' may be Edward Mullar, enrolled 1625. In the margin Jonson adds (evidently as an afterthought) the name 'Waller', captain and Treasurer of the Company in 1621. **58** *the use of guns.* Which the nobility regarded with suspicion and distaste. **60** *militar.* military. **63** *hear.* Gifford, H & S: 'not hear'. **70–3** Cf. *Disc.* 2696–9. **77** *turns us.* Keeps in circulation for us; cf. *Volp.* I. i. 39. **81** *Guy, or Bevis.* Guy of Warwick, Bevis of Hampton, heroes of romance. **89** *Academy.* Cf. *D. is A.* II. viii. 19–22: it taught 'postures' of a quite unmilitary kind. **98** *these pictures.* Cf. Justice Clement's dismissal of Bobadill—'this picture'—*EMI* v. ii. 27; and *UV* 34. 25 ff. **99** *tailors' blocks. Und.* 42. 82 n. **100** *tissue. Und.* 42. 43 n. **102** *moulds.* Tailors' dummies or frames.

45. *Arth[ur] Squib.* A teller in the Exchequer; addressed again in *Und.* 54. **6** *jack's pulse.* A jack or jack-of-the-clock is a metal figure which strikes the hours; hence, a would-be friend, chiming in mechanically with one's mood. **8** *the spit.* See *Und.* 37. 9 n., and cf. Martial, IX. xiv. **10** *purse.* Cf. Tilley, P667. **12** *virtue.* Tilley V84: 'Virtue is the only ground for friendship to be built upon.' **13–16** Plutarch advises that friends, like coins, must be well examined before acceptance: *How to Tell a Flatterer.* ii; *Of Having Many Friends,* iii. **17** *slips.* Counterfeit coins; playing on a secondary sense, twigs or shoots for grafting ('fruitful', l. 18). **20** *No lie grew ever old.* A classical commonplace, but Jonson may be remembering Seneca, *Epist.* lxxix. 18. Cf. *Disc.* 552. **22** *Friend to himself.* Proverbial: 'Be a friend to thyself and others will be so too' (Tilley, F684); and cf. Seneca, *Epist.* vi. 7. **26** *richer purchase.* Proverbial: 'A true friend is better than a rich farm', James Howell, 1659 (see Tilley, F719).

46. *Sir Edward Coke.* 1552–1634; judge and jurist. Solicitor-General 1592, Speaker of the House of Commons 1593, Attorney-General 1594; Chief Justice of Common Pleas 1606, and of King's Bench 1613; dismissed from the Chief Justiceship in 1616. **4** *fortune . . . virtue.* A favourite antithesis for Jonson: see *Epig.* 63. 2–3 n. **9** *process.* Progress; with a legal hint. **13** *manly eloquence.* Cf. *Und.* 14. 56, *Disc.* 809. **14–15** *Stood up . . . | stand.* A favourite Jonsonian idea: cf. *Und.* 70. 44–5, etc. **17** *Solon's self.* The Athenian statesman and lawgiver, born *c.*638 BC. *explait'st.* Unravellest (literally, take out the plaits or pleats: *OED*'s only example of this word). **24** *her eyes.* Fortune is traditionally represented as blind.

47. *Tribe of Ben.* Jonson's followers or 'sons'; glancing at Rev. 7, where the four angels at the earth's corners undertake to seal 'the servants of our God in their foreheads' (verse 3); 'Of the tribe of Benjamin were sealed twelve thousand' (verse 8). Written in 1623. For criticism, see Hugh Maclean in *Essays in English Literature . . .*, ed. M. MacLure and F. W. Watt (Toronto, 1964), pp. 47–51; Peterson, ch. 3. **3–4** Cf. *Und.* 25. 45 and n. **5–6** *fly | To speak.* i.e. hate to speak. **9** *merely talk.* Cf. *Disc.* 343–6. **10** *anarchy of drink. Epig.* 115. 12. **13** *glutted in and lechered out.* Cf. *Epig.* 118. **16** *on their borders.* Like them. **17** *absent.* Cf. *Epig.* 115. 16. **19–20** Cf. *Epig.* 115. 7–8. **26** *issue rhymes.* Cf. *Und.* 70. 103. **28** *strew out the long meal.* Cf. *Epig.* 115. 10. **29** *one.* i.e. constant. **32** *Valtelline.* Or Valtellina, the upper valley of the Adda in Lombardy; of critical strategic importance, it was held by the Spanish from 1621 to 1623, by the French from 1624 to 1627, and changed hands frequently thereafter. **33–4** Frequent skirmishing between Dutch and Spanish shipping occurred after the resumption of hostilities between the two countries in 1621. The Spanish Mexico fleet was overtaken by storm and badly damaged before it left the West Indies in 1622. **35** *the dispensation.* The papal dispensation to allow Prince Charles to marry the Infanta finally arrived in Madrid at the end of April 1623. There were deep misgivings about the match in both Spain and England. **40** *that which will not be restored.* The Palatinate, invaded by Spain in 1620. Popular sympathy for the defeated Frederick, James's son-in-law, was strong in England. **44** *Brunsfield.* Hunter suggests the reference may be to Christian of Brunswick (1599–1626), who raised an army in aid of Frederick in 1621, and conducted several unsuccessful battles in subsequent years. *Mansfeld.* Ernst, Graf von Mansfeld (1580–1626), commander of Frederick's army. **48** *late mystery of reception.* Elaborate preparations for the reception of the Infanta at Southampton, and subsequently in London, were in train during the summer of 1623. Jonson's collaborator and rival Inigo Jones, who is sniped at in the following lines, had been busy in both places. Other 'mysteries' of Jones are referred to in *UV* 34. 46. **49** *to his not under-hears.* Is not inferior to his. Probably a coinage: cf. *OED*, 'hear', 12: 'to be reported or spoken (well or ill) of'. **50** Cf. the gibes in *Epig.* 97. *Motions* = puppets. **52 ff.** *Christmas clay . . . animated porcelain . . . earthen jars . . . frail pitcher.* 'The danger of supersession at Court has made Jonson unusually modest' (H & S); but the first three of these references are not only to Jonson's masques but (less modestly) to those who watch and take part in them. Peterson, ch. 3, finds sources for the imagery here in Cicero, Seneca, Horace, Plutarch, and Aesop. **60** *dwell as in my centre.* Cf. *Und.* 14. 30–3. **62** *reverence. Und.* 26. 23 n. **64** *well-tagged.* Well-fastened. **69** *reason's flame.* Cf. the lamp carried by the figure of Reason in *Hym.* 134. **74** *stairs.* 'Undoubtedly those leading to the Apollo Room itself', Peterson, p. 156.

48. *The King's New Cellar.* At Whitehall; built under Inigo Jones's direction. **10** *races.* varieties. **18** *Lyaeus.* Bacchus. **28** *Hippocrene's liquor.* From the fountain of the muses, on Mt. Helicon. **29** *make many a poet.* Including, no doubt, Jonson himself: 'drink . . . is one of the elements in which he liveth', *Conv. Dr.* 607–8; cf. *Und.* 57. 24–5. **44** *Saint George's union.* The Feast of the Garter on St George's Day, 23 April. **54** *Charles brings home the lady.* The Infanta; their arrival from Spain was expected in July 1623. Charles finally arrived without her on 15 October 1623, and was greeted with jubilation. **55** Horace, *Sat.* II. i. 25: 'The heat has mounted to his head, and the lamps are double.'

49. *Court Pucelle.* i.e. whore. Two passages in *Conv. Dr.* (76–7, 569–71) identify her as Lady Bedford's friend Cecilia Bulstrode (1584–1609), of Buckinghamshire. Jonson's epitaph of this lady gives quite another picture of her qualities: see *UV* 9 and n.; and cf. Donne, 'Death, I recant', *Epithalamions*, pp. 59–61. For biographical details, see Percy Simpson, *TLS* 6 Mar. 1930, p. 187. James E. Savage in his introduction to a facsimile reprint of Overbury's *Conceited Newes* (1616; Gainesville, Florida, 1968) suggests that the 'news' of ll. 8–9 is a courtly game played in Cecilia Bulstrode's chamber; and that 'cocks' in l. 4 alludes to the name of one of the players, John Cocke or Cooke. **7** *tribade.* lesbian. **11** *can at once.* Whalley's emendation; Folio (and H & S): 'cannot once'. **18** *endued.* clothed. **25** *statesman. Epig.* II. 3 n. **28** *stuffs. Und.* 15.57 n. **32** *by candle-light.* By which light

all women are said to be attractive: cf. Tilley, W682. **33** *case. Und.* 42. 87 n.
36 *day.* power. **39** *sermoneers.* A coinage. **40** *mother.* Hysteria; a pun. **42** *Darrel's deed.*
John Darrel (*fl.* 1562–1602), Puritan preacher; practised exorcism until
imprisoned for imposture in 1599. **44** *babes of grace.* Probably children allegedly
born by parthenogenesis. Newdigate compares Jonson's story of the lady who lay
with a Puritan preacher hoping to conceive an angel or saint: 'which having
ob ained, it was but an ordinary birth' (*Conv. Dr.* 446–7).

50. [*Elizabeth,*] *Countess of* [*Rutland*]. The name is not found in the poem's title
in Folio; the identification is Cunningham's. *Epig.* 79 and *For.* 12. are also
addressed to her: see notes to those poems. **2** *widowed wife.* The Countess's
husband was impotent: see *For.* 12. 93 ff. n., *Conv. Dr.* 179 n., and Beaumont's
elegy, *The Works of Beaumont and Fletcher*, ed. A. Dyce (1846), xi. 508. It is a sign
of Jonson's tact that the phrase might be taken as referring simply to the Earl's
absence: see ll. 20 ff. (Homer likewise speaks of Penelope's 'wisdom' during
Ulysses' absence.) **6** *the suspicion too. Disc.* 1337–9. **22** *manners and men.* Cf. *Epig.*
128. 2, *Und.* 14. 33. Rutland travelled extensively in Europe. In 1603 he was
engaged upon a mission to Christian IV of Denmark. **27–8** Cf. *Epig.* 102. 20 n.

51. *Lord Bacon's Birthday.* Francis Bacon (1561–1626), the essayist: Attorney-
General 1613; Privy Councillor 1616; Lord Keeper 1617; Lord Chancellor and
first Baron Verulam 1618; Viscount St Albans 1621. Bacon's sixtieth birthday fell
on 26 January 1621. Later in the same year he was found guilty of corruption, and
deprived of the Great Seal. Jonson praises him highly in *Disc.* 894–907. **1** *ancient
pile.* York House, Bacon's residence on the Embankment. **2–3** Cf. *For.* 14. 1, 60.
4 *mystery.* J. O. Fuller sees an allusion to masonic ritual: *Francis Bacon: A Biography*
(London and The Hague, 1981), pp. 279–80. **8** *thy.* Manuscript: 'my'. **9** *grave
wise Keeper of the Seal.* Sir Nicholas Bacon (1509–79); he held this office from
1558. **19** *deep-crowned.* Deep and brimming.

52. *Sir William Burlase.* Of Little Marlow, sheriff of Buckinghamshire 1601, d.
1629.
　　My Answer. 1 *prodigious waist.* Jonson weighed nearly twenty stone: see
Und. 54. 12; 56. 11. **3** *lines.* Playing on the sense of poetic lines, as in *Und.* 84. iv.
22. **5** *lump.* 'Part', manuscripts. **6** *tun at Heidelberg.* Of great size, it was bound by
twenty-six hoops; see Thomas Coryate's description in *Crudities* (London, 1611),
pp. 486–92, and the illustration facing p. 486. **8** *square my circle.* Attempt the
impossible; with a play on words. **11** *describèd by.* H & S: 'described [but] by'.
monogram. A picture without shading or colour, a sketch; 'here the letter O, in
allusion to Ben's girth' (Newdigate). **12** *blot. Disc.* 604. **17** *sprite.* Manuscripts:
'slight', 'light'. **21** *colours.* Figures of rhetoric. **24** *posterity. Epig.* Dedn. 12–15.

53. *William, Earl of Newcastle.* William Cavendish (1592–1676), Viscount
Mansfield 1620; Earl (1628) and later Duke (1665) of Newcastle. He published
two works on horsemanship (1657, 1667) and instructed the future Charles II in
the art. The poem was written between 1620 and 1628 ('Viscount Mansfield' in
one manuscript). Newcastle is addressed again in *Und.* 59. **1** *back.* Ride, break in.
5–6 Cf. Sidney, *Arcadia* (1590), II. v, ed. A. Feuillerat (Cambridge, 1912), p. 178;

Hamlet, IV. iii. 85–8. **7** *Perseus upon Pegasus.* Pegasus is actually Bellerophon's horse, but the misattribution is traditional: see T. W. Baldwin, *PQ* xx (1941), 361–70; G. B. Johnston, *RES* vi (1955), 65–7; J. D. Reeves, ibid. 397–9. **8** *Castor . . . Cyllarus.* Castor was especially skilled in horsemanship; Cyllarus was his (or his brother Pollux's) horse. **10** *Sir Bevis . . . Arundel.* Bevis of Hampton, romance hero; his horse's name means 'swift as a swallow' (French *hirondelle*). **11** *endorse.* Confirm; with a pun on the literal sense: to put on the back of, to ride. **12** *wish myself a horse.* Cf. Sidney's remark about his Italian riding-master: 'I think he would have persuaded me to have wished myself a horse', *An Apology for Poetry*, ed. G. Shepherd (London, 1965), p. 95; Shepherd compares a similar wish expressed by one of Crato's pupils in *De disciplina scholarium*, once attributed to Boethius. A traditional reversal (the horse being customarily instanced in the logic-books as a non-rational creature): cf. Gulliver amongst the Houyhnhnms, and Rochester's 'Tunbridge Wells', 166–75. **18** *Hercules.* Who cleansed the Augean stables. **19–20** Alluding to a story that the young Virgil worked in the imperial stables, displaying such skill that he was rewarded with a double ration of bread: see A. C. Taylor, *TLS* 28 August 1937, p. 624.

54. *Arthur Squib.* See *Und.* 45. 'The wager, it seems, was that the poet weighed full twenty stone, but he found that he wanted two pounds of that weight. This he artfully turns to a reason for borrowing five pounds in money of his friend Mr. Squib, which added to the pound he had of his own, would make up the deficiency in his weight. Six pounds in silver, he says, will weigh two pounds in weight: it may be so; we will take his word' (Whalley). R. L. Wadsworth computes the matter more exactly, *Explic.* xxxiii (1975), item 42. **6** *ill commodity.* Bad bargain. **7** *corporal.* A play on words: his fear is substantial; so is his body. **13** *socket.* The image is of a candle burning low. **18** *or protestation.* Thus Folio; H & S 'on protestation'. A protestation was a formal written declaration of non-acceptance or non-payment of a bill.

55. *John Burgess.* A clerk in the Exchequer; addressed again in *Und.* 57.

56. *Lady Covell.* See *Und.* 22. 23–4 and n.; she is otherwise unknown. **3** *a few lines.* Perhaps *Und.* 22. **11** *twenty stone, within two pound.* See *Und.* 54 n. **16** *rounds.* Possibly playing on a secondary sense of the word, 'whispers'. **24** *Joan.* Maid (Manuscript: 'Cary').

57. *John Burgess.* See *Und.* 55 and n. Jonson had been granted an annual pension by James in 1616; in 1630 Charles agreed to an increase: see *Und.* 68 and 76 and notes. Payment was evidently tardy. Jonson uses the Skeltonic verse-form again in the speeches of the Patrico in *Gyp. Met.* and of Skelton himself in *Fort. Is.* **4** *Sir Robert Pye.* 1585–1662, Remembrancer of the Exchequer from 1618; ironically, an ancestor of the poet laureate Henry James Pye, himself destined to run into acute financial difficulties. **6** *debenture.* Voucher for payment from the Exchequer. **15–21** 'Jonson has to prepare sport for the Court, viz. *Callipolis* and *Chloridia*': Fleay, who dates the poem December 1630 (i. 331). **24–5** Cf. *Und.* 48. 29. **27** *warming-pan.* Perhaps in the slang sense (cf. *NI* I. iii. 13), a bed-companion.

NOTES TO PAGES 386–390

58. *My Bookseller.* Probably Thomas Alchorne, who published *NI* in 1631 (Fleay, i. 331); possibly Robert Allot, who published *BF*, *D. is A.*, and *S. of N.* earlier the same year. Cf. *Epig.* 3, to John Stepneth. **1** *censures.* Judgements (good or bad). **2** *stomachs.* dispositions. **4** *coat.* sort. **8** *cramp-ring.* A ring formerly hallowed by royalty on Good Friday, and thought to be efficacious against cramp, falling sickness, etc. Jonson implies that thoughtless laughter is a similar disease, which might be more appropriately warded off if the ring were worn not on the finger but through the nose. Cf. *Epig.* 2. 12 and n. **12** ——. A word, probably obscene, has been omitted from the Folio. **13** *alife.* dearly.

59. *William, Earl of Newcastle.* See *Und.* 53. Written after 1628, when the earldom was conferred. Newcastle wrote, but did not publish, a treatise on fencing. **1–6** Jonson may be glancing at a work such as *Vincentio Saviolo his Practice* (London, 1595), which makes much of the importance of 'time' and 'measure' in fencing. **9** *dazzling.* 'darling', manuscripts. **14 ff.** Cf. Lovel on true valour, *NI* IV. iv; and Seneca, *On Benefits*, II. xxxiv. 3: 'Bravery is the virtue that scorns legitimate dangers, knowing how to ward off, to meet, and to court dangers.'

60. *Henry, L[ord] La Warr.* Henry West, 13th Baron De La Warr (1603–1 June 1628); MP 1621; son of Francis West (1586–?1633), the American colonist, after whom the state of Delaware is named. **5** *What could their care do . . .* Cf. *Lycidas*, 57–8: 'Had ye been there—for what could that have done? What could the muse herself, that Orpheus bore . . .' **10** *virtue . . . name.* A favourite Jonsonian theme: cf. *Und.* 84, viii, etc. **13–14** *war . . . star.* Cf. *Und.* 15. 195–6.

61. Gifford deduced that this poem is addressed to John Williams (1582–1650), Dean of Westminster 1620, Bishop of Lincoln 1621; Lord Keeper of the Privy Seal (in succession to Bacon) 1621, and removed from that office by Charles, 25 October 1628: Jonson's poem may relate to this last event. A Star Chamber prosecution was brought against Williams in the same year; he was imprisoned 1637–40.

62. *My Sickness.* Jonson suffered a paralytic stroke in 1628. He spoke of his sickness and poverty in the epilogue to *NI* in January 1629, obliquely soliciting royal assistance. Charles responded with the gift referred to here. **4** *king's evil.* Scrofula, thought to be curable by royal touch; the parliamentarians soon attempted to discredit this practice. **10** *ten score.* Those touched for the king's evil were given an angel: Jonson reckons Charles's gift to be worth 200 angels. **12** *difference.* differentiate. **14** *people's evil.* Referring to the differences between king and parliament, which led to Charles's dissolution of parliament in March 1629.

63. *First-Born.* A son, Charles James, who was born prematurely on 13 May 1629, and lived only a few hours. **1–4** See Exod. 22: 29 on the need to offer God first-fruits and first-born sons; and Exod. 34: 20 on the redemption of the first-born. **7** *grutch.* Grudge, complain. **9** *his greatness, and his goodness.* Cf. *For.* 15. 1: 'Good and great God'.

64. **1–2** Possibly a memory of Virgil, *Georgics*, ii. 458–9: 'O happy husbandmen! too happy, should they come to know their blessings!'; but Jonson also alludes to the rising trouble in the land; cf. *Und.* 82. 5. **5** *turns our joyful year about.* Charles's Anniversary Day fell on 27 March; the calendar year began on 25 March. **17** *O times! O manners!* Cicero, *Against Catiline*, I. i. 2; cf. *Und.* 15. 161. **18** *epidemical disease. Disc.* 296.

65.   The future Charles II was born on 29 May 1630. Poems of celebration were also written by Corbett, Herrick, Hoskyns, King, Randolph, Shirley, and others. See also *Dubia* 5, and 'A Parallel of the Prince to the King', H & S, viii. 429. **3** *lily . . . rose.* The flowers of France and of England; Henrietta Maria and Charles. Cf. *UV* 33. 8. **7** *nephews.* i.e. grandchildren, posterity; cf. Latin *nepotes.* **8** *eye.* Brightest spot. **9–12** An eclipse of the sun occurred two days after Charles's birth. **12** *son.* A pun. **13–14** 'He deserves not to displease you, Caesar, who hastes to please you' (Martial, *On the Spectacles*, xxxi).

66.   The lying-in at St James's was elaborate, and attended with some apprehension; the queen wore a trinket around her neck, to avert miscarriage. **1** *Hail Mary.* Luke 1: 28. **14** *safety . . . realm.* Manuscripts: 'health, both to our land'.

67.   **4–12** The silence of the bells and of the Tower guns probably reflects Henrietta Maria's unpopularity; Davenant likewise refers to the Londoners' reluctance to ring church bells and light bonfires on her behalf: 'The Queen, returning to London after a long absence', *Shorter Poems*, ed. A. M. Gibbs (Oxford, 1972), p. 47. **17** *theorbo.* A large kind of lute, with a double neck. **20–1** Cf. *Und.* 3. 21–4 and n. **22–3** An *intelligence*, in the old cosmology, was thought to control each of the heavenly spheres; *a sense* = one equipped with human faculties of perception. **26** *Harry.* Henri IV. **27** *Louis.* Louis XIII. **36** *ceston.* Venus' girdle, which made the wearer irresistible: cf. *Und.* 2. v. 41 and n., *Und.* 28. 14. **38** *taken twice the ring.* i.e. twice speared a suspended ring while riding at full gallop: a courtly pastime. **46** *the play.* Randolph's *Amyntas* (H & S). **54** *a Caroline.* (i) a little Charles; (ii) one loyal to Charles: predating the *OED*'s first recorded usage of 1652.

68.   Increasing Jonson's pension from 100 marks (£66. 13s. 4d.) to £100 p.a. in March 1630, Charles added the grant of an annual tierce (42 gallons) of Canary wine from the royal cellars at Whitehall. **8** *Greencloth.* The Board which controlled expenditure of the royal household. **12** *spill.* Spoil; playing on words.

69.   Fleay (i. 332) suggest this may be addressed to Sir Lucius Cary (see *Und.* 70 and n.). **3** *Profit, or chance. Und.* 70. 99–101. **9–13** Plutarch, *How to Tell a Flatterer*, xxiv: 'Whenever, then, the flatterer, who is but a light and deceptive plated-ware, is examined and closely compared with genuine and solid-wrought friendship, he does not stand the test, but he is exposed, and so he does the same thing as the man who had painted a wretched picture of some cocks. For the painter bade his servant scare all real cocks as far away as possible from the canvas; and so the flatterer scares all real friends away, and does not allow them to come near.' **15** *circling.* devious.

70.   Sir Lucius Cary (?1610–43), second Viscount Falkland, of Great Tew,

Oxfordshire; son of Sir Henry Cary of *Epig.* 66; Secretary of State 1642. He behaved generously towards Jonson in the latter's last years, and wrote an elegy on Jonson's death (printed in H & S, xi. 430–7). For biographical details, see K. B. Murdock, *The Sun at Noon* (New York, 1939); Kurt Weber, *Lucius Cary, Second Viscount Falkland* (New York, 1940). Sir Henry Morison, son of Sir Richard Morison and nephew of Fynes Morison, the traveller, died at Carmarthen, probably of smallpox, in late July or August 1629, on or near his twenty-first birthday: see Cary's elegy on Morison, ll. 181, 317–20: printed by K. B. Murdock, *HSNPL* xx (1938), 29–42. Jonson's poem is the first sustained attempt in English to imitate the Pindaric ode; see Robert Shafer, *The English Ode to 1660* (New York, 1966), pp. 106 ff.; Paul H. Fry, *The Poet's Calling in the English Ode* (New Haven and London, 1980), ch. i. 'Turn', 'counter-turn', and 'stand' are Jonson's renderings of Scaliger's *volta, rivolta,* and *stanza,* which in turn represent Greek 'strophe', 'antistrophe', and 'epode', the three sections of the choral ode. For criticism, see Ian Donaldson, *SLI* vi (1973), 139–52; John Lemly, *ELH* xliv (1977), 258–63; Susanne Woods, *SEL* xviii (1978), 57–74; Mary I. Oates, *SEL* xix (1979), 387–406; Peterson, ch. 5. **1** *Saguntum.* Hannibal captured and destroyed this town in Spain in 219 BC, thus breaking the truce between the Romans and the Carthaginians and beginning the second Punic war. The story of the infant is from Pliny, *Nat. Hist.* VII. iii. 40–2: 'an infant at Saguntum . . . at once went back into the womb in the year in which that city was destroyed by Hannibal'. *clear.* Noble, shining (Latin *clarus*). Peterson and Oates read as a verb: 'clarify, explain'. **3** *prodigious Hannibal.* Horace's *Hannibal dirus, Odes,* III. vi. 36. **8** *womb thine urn.* For the collocation, see *Epig.* 109. 17–18 n. **9** *summed.* complete. *circle.* The emblem of perfection: 'the perfectest figure is the round', *Hym.* 404; cf. *Epig.* 128. 8. **12** *sack.* Devastation, plunder. **19** *life's miseries.* Cf. *Epig.* 45. 5–8. **20** *thee.* F 'thee?' **21–2** Seneca, *Epist.* xciii. 4: 'Let us measure [our lives] by their performance, not by their duration.' **23** *face.* Cf. the character of that name in *Alch.* **24** *fact.* deeds. **25–32** Seneca, *Epist.* xciii. 3: 'What benefit does this older man derive from the eighty years he has spent in idleness? A person like him has not lived; he has merely tarried a while in life. Nor has he died late in life; he has simply been a long time dying. He has lived eighty years, has he? That depends upon the date from which you reckon his death.' 'The only well-known statesman who was approaching four-score years old in 1629 was Sir Edward Coke' (Newdigate). Is his name glanced at in l. 42? *Und.* 46 was written before Coke's fall. **30** *stirrer.* agitator. **31** *twenty.* Probably the age at which Morison died. **38** *stooped.* Predating *OED*'s first recorded usage in this (moral) sense, 1743; evidently by analogy with the stooping (plummeting) of a bird. **40** *dead sea.* Seneca's *mare mortuum, Epist.* lxvii. 4 (of 'an easy existence, untroubled by the attacks of fortune'). **43 ff.** Seneca, *Epist.* xciii. 4: 'Your other friend, however, departed in the bloom of his manhood. But he fulfilled all the duties of a good citizen, a good friend, a good son; in no respect had he fallen short. His age may have been incomplete, but his life was complete [*licet aetas eius inperfecta sit, vita perfecta est*]. The other man has lived eighty years, has he? No, he has existed eighty years, unless perhaps you mean by "he has lived" what we mean when we say that a tree "lives".' **43–4** *fell . . . fall'st.* Playing on the physical and moral senses of the verb. Cf. Seneca's *in nulla parte cessavit*: 'in no respect had he fallen short'. **45** *stood.* Remained steadfast: cf. *Epig.* 98. 1. **49** *round.* complete. **50** Cf. Wisd. 11: 21: 'But by measure and number and weight thou didst order all things'; *UV* 31. 23–4. **52** *humanity. Epig.* Dedn. 27, *Epig.* 113. 8. *the sphere.* 'The perfectest form', *Haddington* 276–80; cf. l. 9 above. **53–9** These lines are probably self-referring; cf. the self-pitying epilogue to *NI.* The present passage is in the spirit of 'Come, leave the loathèd stage', *Songs*, 35. **53** *summed up.* Filled out; cf. l. 9 above. **57** *Repeat of.* Reiterate; celebrate. **58–9** *been . . . lived.* Seneca, *Epist.* xciii. 4 (see n. to ll. 43 ff. above); and cf. *Und.* 75. 153–4. **59** *spell.* Discover, or denote. **61–2** *brought | To light.* Jonson uses the phrase elsewhere with reference both to childbirth (*Und.* 75. 144) and to publication (*Epig.* 131. 1–2). **62** *measures.* Criteria; but the musical and poetic senses are also hinted at. **63** *syllabe.* Jonson's usual form of this word, e.g. in *Eng. Gram.* **64** *lines.* Lineaments; playing on the sense of lines of verse. 'Lines of life' also suggests the threads spun by the fates: *OED* 'line', *sb.*² 1 †g; for a similar word-play, cf. Hugh Holland's verses on Shakespeare's 1st Folio: 'Though his line of life went soon about | The life yet of his lines shall never out'; and Shakespeare, Sonnet 16. 9. *air.* Manner, melody. **65** *a tree.* The hint is from Seneca, *Epist.* xciii. 4 (see n. to ll. 43 ff. above). **72** *flower of light.* Cf. *UV* 26. 29 and n. **73–4** Seneca, *Epist.* xciii.: 'Just as one of small stature can be a perfect man, so in a life of small compass can be a perfect life.' Cary himself was a small man: see *The Life of Edward Earl of Clarendon, written by himself* (Oxford, 1857), i. 36. **77** *garland.* The poem itself; perhaps suggested by the 'plant' of l. 72. **78–84** Seneca, *Epist.* xciii. 5: 'We should therefore praise, and number in the company of the blest, that man who has invested well the portion of time, however little, that has been allotted to him; for such a one has seen the true light. He has not been one of the common herd. He has not only lived, but flourished. Sometimes he enjoyed fair skies; sometimes, as often happens, it was only through the clouds that there flashed to him the radiance of the mighty star [the sun]. Why do you ask, "How long did he live?" He still lives! At one bound he has passed over into posterity and has consigned himself to the guardianship of memory.' A common turn; cf. *Und.* 84. ix. 45 ('Indeed, she is not dead'); Milton, *Lycidas*, 165–7 ('For Lycidas your sorrow is not dead', etc.); Shelley, *Adonais*, xxxix ('he is not dead', etc.). **81** *bright eternal day.* Cf. *Und.* 84. ix. 121. **92–3** *twi- | Lights, the Dioscuri.* Twin-lights; Castor and Pollux. After Castor's death, Jupiter allowed him to share his brother Pollux's immortality: while one brother was on earth, the other was in the infernal regions; they changed places at regular intervals. They became the constellation Gemini, the twin stars which were (erroneously) thought never to appear simultaneously in the heavens. On the enjambment, see *Und.* 29. 10 n., and John Hollander, ed., *Ben Jonson* (New York, 1961), Introduction, pp. 19–20. **95** *alternate.* reverse. **98** *star.* Horace, *Odes*, II. xvii. 17–22; Persius, *Sat.* vi. 45–51; *Disc.* 112; *Epig.* 94; *Und.* 15. 196; *UV* 26. 77. **99–101** Cf. *Und.* 69. 2–3. **103** *rhymes. Und.* 47. 26. **105** *of greatness, and of good. Epig.* Dedn. 13 n. **107–10** Cf. *Epig.* 86. 7–8. **112** *copy.* Peterson suggests several senses, including 'duplicate' (playing on the legal sense; cf. 'indentured', l. 100), and 'exemplary pattern'. **114** *titles.* Both legal and nominal (Peterson). **125** *so early men.* Clarendon speaks of Cary's remarkable intellectual attainments at an early age: *Life*, i. 35, 40–1. Cary testifies to Morison's similar attainments in 'An Anniversary': see W. D. Briggs, *Anglia*, xxxvii (1938), 476. Cf. the phrase 'thy most early wit' (of Donne), *Epig*. 23. 3; and *UV* 18. 7. **126** *lines*. Two manuscripts: 'lives'. *rolls . . . records*. Cf. *Und*. 35. 3–6; 75. 155–6.

71. *Lord High Treasurer*. Richard Weston, 1st Earl of Portland (1577–1635); he held this office 1628–33. See *Und*. 73 and n.; 75. 97 ff.; 77; 78. 27–8. **5** *Want*. G. B. Johnston (*NQ* cxcix (1954), 471) suggests a play on 'want' (*OED*, *sb.*¹) = 'mole', comparing Jonson's letter to Newcastle (H & S, i. 213–14). His suggested emendation, 'wants', seems unnecessary. **6** *five years*. An approximate figure: Jonson suffered a paralytic stroke in 1628. Possibly he had an earlier attack (see *DNB*). **7** *faussebraies*. Artificial mounds or walls thrown up in front of a main rampart. **8** *Redoubts*. Small fortifications within a larger bastion; *half-moons*: or demilunes, crescent-shaped fortifications; *horn-works*: single-fronted outworks with two connected half-bastions.

72. **1–4** Cf. *Hamlet*, v. ii. 267–9. **9** *can*. i.e. can speak (see l. 1); 'speak' is again understood after 'bells' in l. 10, and 'All noises else', in l. 12. **11** *man*. Man-of-war? **12** *wind*. Thus manuscripts; H & S follow F 'wine'. **18** Cf. *Panegyre*, 162 (of James): 'Still to have such a king, and this king long' (from Martial, xii. vi. 5–6, on the accession of Nerva); varied here by way of allusion to the young Prince Charles, now two years old.

73. *To the Envious*. When Weston first took office as Lord Treasurer in 1628, 'the extreme visible poverty of the exchequer sheltered that province from the envy it had frequently created' (Clarendon, *History of the Rebellion*, i. 39). But not for long: Weston quickly became unpopular through his ambition, his timorousness, his apparent Catholic sympathies, his meanness with public funds and ostentatious spending with his own. See *Und*. 71 and n. **2** *faint and narrow eyes*. Envy is traditionally pictured as blind or narrow-eyed: see Ovid, *Metam*. ii. 760–805, Dante, *Purgatorio*, xiii. **4** *port . . . land*. Punning on Weston's new title; 'port' = tribute, income, payment (*OED*, †*sb.*⁵). **5** *That waking man, that eye of state*. Cf. *Und*. 75. 109–11. Weston's coat of arms displayed an eagle, traditionally famed for its powers of sight (*Gentleman's Magazine* (1823), i. 413; Pliny, *Nat. Hist*. x. iii. 10); the contrast is with imperfect sight of the envious. Peterson (p. 100) points out that Weston was an art connoisseur as well as being Charles's principal source of intelligence.

74. *Jerome, L[ord] Weston*. 1605–63, 2nd Earl of Portland, son of Richard Weston of *Und*. 71 and 73; styled Lord Weston from 1633; succeeded to the earldom 1635. He returned in March 1633 from a mission to Paris (1632) and Turin. See also *Und*. 75. **26** *travail*. Manuscripts: 'travel', a play on words. **28** *an olive*. Perhaps referring to Weston's role as a peace-negotiator. **29** *shadow*. Companion, Latin *umbra* (Newdigate). *to his heir*. Manuscripts: 'of the air'.

75. For Jerome Weston, see *Und*. 74 and n.; for his father, *Und*. 71 and 73 and n. Frances Stuart (1617–94) was the daughter of Jonson's former patron Esmé Stuart (see *Epig*. 127 and n.); he died shortly after inheriting the dukedom in 1624, and was succeeded by his son James (1612–55). The marriage took place at Roehampton Chapel on 25 June 1632. Davenant also wrote an epithalamion for the occasion: *Shorter Poems*, ed. Gibbs, pp. 45–6. Shirley's 'Epithalamion: to his noble friend I.W.' perhaps celebrates the same event: *Works*, ed. W. Gifford and A. Dyce (London, 1833), vi. 438–9. **1** *summer standing*. Solstice. Spenser's *Epithalamion*, written for his own wedding on the year's longest day (St Barnabas: 11 June, old calendar), also has an invocation to the sun. **11** *caroches*. Stately coaches. *all the way*. A distance of about ten miles. **16** *consent*. With a play on 'concent' = harmony. **17–18** *at charge | Of*. Probably, expensively decked out in. **25** *kindly*. (i) Natural; (ii) benign. **28** *perfection*. The word is commonly used of marriage; e.g. Donne, 'Epithalamion Made at Lincoln's Inn': 'Today put on perfection, and a woman's name'; Marlowe, *Hero and Leander*, i. 268; *Hym*. 197, 295, 404, 559; Tilley, W718. **30–1** *Hym*. 455–8. **40** *hair*. Cf. Spenser, *Epith*. 154–5. **41** *virgin white*. Ibid. 151: 'Clad all in white, that seems a virgin best.' **44** *simplesse*. i.e. simplicity of dress. **45** *tresses*. Cf. *Und*. 2. vi. 10 n. **51** *Porting the ensigns*. Carrying the heraldic arms or badges. **54** *clear*. illustrious. **57–8** The roses and lilies, as the flowers of England and France, represent the union of Charles and Henrietta Maria, who were present at the marriage; cf. *Und*. 65. 3 and n. But they are also flowers traditionally associated with marriage: see *Hym*. 219–20 and Jonson's note, and cf. Spenser, *Epith*. 43, Statius, *Silvae*, I. ii. 22, etc. **59** *thine*. i.e. the sun's. **60** *intertex*. Weave together. **73** *grandees*. James Stuart, the bride's brother, had been made a grandee of Spain in January 1632. **75** *journals*. Days' travels. **80** *exampled*. exemplary. **81–2** The phoenix is traditionally sexless; ever since Petrarch had compared Laura to that bird, however, it had been common for poets to refer to it as though it were feminine: see W. H. Matchett, *The Phoenix and Turtle* (The Hague, 1965), Introduction. Jonson's specific allusion may be to King James's *Phoenix*, in which Esmé Stuart (James's cousin, and the bride's grandfather) is represented as a female phoenix: *Poems*, ed. James Craigie (Scottish Text Society, Edinburgh and London, 1955), i. 39–59. **88** *go less*. Are abated or diminished. **99** *say-master*. Assay-master. **109–11** Cf. *Und*. 73. 5. **112** *Barbican*. Watch-tower. **113–20** Repeated in prose in *Disc*. 1306–11; from Sidonius, *Letters*, I. iv. 1, to Gaudentius (Peterson): ' "O three and four times happy thou" [*Aeneid*, i. 94] by whose elevation joy is brought to your friends, punishment to your detractors and distinction to your posterity; an example, moreover, to the energetic and zealous and a spur to the idle and lazy.' **119** *envious*. *Und*. 73 and n. **121 ff.** Cf. Spenser, *Epith*. 204–41. **124** *Charles*. After Esmé Stuart's death in 1624, his children had passed into royal guardianship. The wedding had been arranged by Charles. **129** *bands*. (i) Bonds; (ii) companies. **132** *bishop*. Laud, then Bishop of London. **141** *behind*. i.e. ahead. **145** Cf. Spenser, *Epith*. 282 ff.: 'Haste thee, O fairest planet, to thy home', etc. **153–4** *Und*. 70. 58–9; *Pleas. Rec*. 102–3; *Love's Tr*. 92–6. **155–6** *recorded on the file | Of life*. Cf. *Und*. 35. 3–6; 70. 126. **160** *fescennine*. Bawdy, obscene: as in many Roman weddings. **161** *will*. i.e. will ask. **165–8** Cf. *UV* 18. 23–4 and n. **170–2** Richard and Jerome, after the groom's father and the groom himself; Thomas, after the groom's brother, and Francis, perhaps, after his great-grandfather, or the bride herself (one manuscript for 'Francis' reads 'sister'); Kate, after the bride's mother, formerly Katherine Clifton; Frank, the groom's mother, Frances née Waldegrave. One son, Charles, was born in 1639. **178** *watchful servant*. Recalling the terms in which the groom's father had been praised: ll. 109–10 above, and *Und*. 73. 5. **180** *reaching*. Far-reaching. **184** Recalling Lucan's comparison of the aged Pompey to an old oak, *De Bello Civili*, i. 135–43; prompted, no doubt, by the idea of the genealogical tree. *now . . . the*. One manuscript: 'then, not boughs, project his'. **187–8** The notion is a common one (cf., e.g., Donne's 'Epithalamion . . . on the Lady Elizabeth and Count Palatine', 87–96), but is sharpened by the fact that Weston's father's 'office' was that of Lord Treasurer. **192** *elder lovers*. Cf. Marlowe, *Hero and Leander*, ii. 69: 'Which taught him all that elder lovers know.'

76. Jonson's petition met with success: see *Und.* 57 and 68 and notes. The warrant for the new pension (printed in H & S, i. 245–8) is dated 26 March 1630. Jonson's poem is based on Martial, IV. xxvii: 'Oft are you wont to praise my poems, Augustus. See, a jealous fellow denies it: are you wont to praise them the less for that? Have you not besides given me, honoured not in words alone, gifts that none other could give? See, the jealous fellow again gnaws his filthy nails! Give me, Caesar, all the more, that he may writhe!' **2** *Monarchs, Masters, Men*. Cf. *Und.* 79. 7. **23** *decayed*. Owen Felltham had referred to Jonson's 'declining wit' in a poem replying to 'Come leave the loathèd stage' (printed in H & S, xi. 339–40). In the same year (1629) Jonson had admitted in the epilogue to *NI* that his strength was waning. **24** *unlaid*. '?laid out (as a corpse); laid in the grave' (*OED*, 1b, citing this example only). **31–2** Referring to Aesop's story of the compassionate farm-hand who puts a frozen snake to his bosom, and is eventually bitten for his pains. Charles is evidently being warned that it is dangerous to tolerate one of Jonson's rivals, though the point is clumsily made: Jonson forgets that he has already rendered Martial's *invidus* (= jealous man) by a plural (l. 20, etc.). In the margin of his own copy of Martial Jonson wrote 'Inigo'.

77. *Lord Treasurer*. Weston: see *Und.* 71 n. The poem is an adaptation of Horace's address to Censorinus, *Odes*, IV. viii. **1** i.e. if my circumstances were as fine as my wishes. **3** *Nuremburg*. A famous centre for silversmiths. **4** *Arras . . . Persian*. 'Arras' had by now become a generic term for any hanging; Persian carpets were naturally esteemed. **6** *Romano*. Giulio Romano, 1492–1546. **12** Cf. *Hym.* 1–6. **18** *men and manners*. *Epig.* 128. 2 and n. **19** *murmuring subjects*. Manuscripts: 'froward citizens'. **22** *sweets and safety*. Manuscripts: 'fame and honour'. **25** *Which*. Referring to 'the arts of life' (l. 17), just listed. *as an architect*. 'Another expression of Jonson's perennial antagonism to Inigo Jones' (Newdigate). **26** *piles or pyramids*. Cf. *Epig.* 60. 1–5.

78. Sir Kenelm Digby (1603–65), naval commander, adventurer, diplomatist, scientist, scholar; he married Venetia Stanley (see *Und.* 84 and n.) in 1625 after a period of enforced separation during which she believed him to be dead. He was later to act as Jonson's literary executor. For biographical details, R. T. Peterson, *Sir Kenelm Digby* (London, 1956). **1** *muse*. See *Und.* 84. iv. 21; *Und.* 84. ix, title. **8** *at home*. A favourite thought: *For.* 4. 68; *Und.* 14. 30. **13** *Scanderoon*. In Turkey; defeating the French and Venetian fleet, 1628. **14** *my birthday*. Sometimes emended to 'his' (the reading of Quarto and Duodecimo editions), on the strength of Richard Ferrar's *Epitaph* on Digby (1665); in defence of 'my' see W. D. Briggs, *MLN* xxxiii (1918), 137–45. **15** *Barnaby the bright*. St Barnabas's Day, the longest day under the old calendar. The phrase occurs in Spenser's *Epithalamion*, but is also traditional. **17–18** Variant: 'That day which I

predestined am to sing, | For Britain's honour, and to Charles my king.'
18 *posterity*. Cf. *Epig*. Dedn. 15. **19** ff. Cf. Martial, VII. xcvii: 'if you knew well, little
book, Caesius Sabinus, the pride of hilly Umbria, fellow townsman of my Aulus
Pudens, you will give him these, though he be engaged. Though a thousand
duties press on and distract him, yet he will be at leisure for my poems. For he
loves me, and next to Turnus' famous satires, reads me. Oh, what a reputation is
being stored up for you! Oh, what glory! How many an admirer! With you
banquets, with you the forum will echo, houses, by-ways, colonnades, bookshops!
You are being sent to one; by all you will be read.' **24** *Spenser's noble book.* Digby
wrote some *Observations* upon *The Faerie Queene*, a work for which he had a
particular affection. **28** *Weston*. For further evidence of Weston's interest in
Jonson's verse, see Cary's poem in *Jonsonus Virbius* (H & S, xi. 434), l. 168.

79.   Gifts were customarily given at New Year rather than at Christmas; on the
practice of New Year poems, see *For.* 12 n. The present poem is a reworking of
material from *Pan's Anniversary* (1620): there James, in the figure of Pan, was
praised for his policy of peace; there Charles, in the figure of Pan, is praised in
the same terms: but from l. 54 the identification of Charles with Pan breaks down.
See E. Simpson, *RES* xiv (1938), 175–8. Another version of the last stanzas turns
up in a separate manuscript, with a setting by Nicholas Lanier. **2** *theorbo. Und.* 67.
17 n. *called.* Called for. **3** *mean.* 'Applied to the tenor and alto parts and the tenor
clef, as intermediate between the bass and treble' (*OED, a.*² A †b). **5** *warp.* Woven
garment. **7** *monarchs, masters, men.* Cf. *Und.* 76. 2. **9** *Rector chori.* Leader of the
chorus. **18** *Mira.* Henrietta Maria; here figured as Pan's sister (l. 25) rather than
wife for decorous reasons: Pan is traditionally ruttish. Newdigate, taking 'sister'
literally, argues that Pan must represent Henrietta Maria's brother, Louis XIII,
but it is difficult to imagine that Jonson would address Louis in such extravagant
terms (see, e.g. ll. 42–3). **22** *Silvanus.* A rural god, half goat, half man. **30** *great
Pales.* The Italian country goddess (Virgil's *magna Pales, Georgics,* iii. 1). **34** *were
she lost. Epig.* 105.

82.   The future James II was born 14 October 1633, and christened by Laud
24 November 1633. **5** *Would they would understand it!* Alluding to the rising
discontent in the land; cf. *Und.* 64. 1–2. **8** *first seisin. Primer seisin* was an ancient
feudal right by which the Crown exacted from the heir of a deceased tenant his
first year's profits. **12** *grandsire's.* James I's. **15** *triple shade.* The three (living)
children born to Charles and Henrietta Maria at this stage: Charles, Mary, and
James. **16** *rose and lily.* See *Und.* 65. 3 n. **17** 'Secure in my sea, secured more in the
(triple) shades': not a classical quotation, but probably a tag of Jonson's own
composition.

83.   *Lady Jane Paulet.* b. 1607, daughter of Thomas, Viscount Savage, of Rock
Savage in Cheshire; married in 1622 John Paulet, 5th Marquis of Winchester,
loyal friend of Henrietta Maria and Charles. She died 'big with child' on 15 April
1631. Milton and other Cambridge poets also wrote tributes to her. Jonson's
poem is discussed by O. B. Hardison, *The Enduring Monument* (Chapel Hill,
1962), pp. 142–5, 149, 166. **1–3** Echoed by Pope, *Elegy to the Memory of an
Unfortunate Lady,* 1–2: 'What beck'ning ghost, along the moonlight shade |

Invites my step, and points to yonder glade?' Cf. the beckoning ghost of *Hamlet*, I.
iv. 58. 3 *fatal tree*. Various superstitions concerning death are associated with the
yew, primarily because it is commonly found in churchyards, and its leaves are
poisonous. 16 *disposure*. Arrangement, disposition. 20 *heralds*. Cf. *Epig*. 9. 4 and n.
21 *Earl Rivers'*. Thomas Darcy, her mother's father. *forms, good*. 'titles,' (variant).
23–4 A common classical formula; cf. Homer, *Iliad*, ii. 489; Virgil, *Georgics*, ii.
42–4, *Aeneid*, vi. 625, etc. 25 *dotes*. Endowments, natural qualities. 29 *heaven*.
'God' (variant). 34 *enlive*. Impart spiritual life to. 45 *institution*. education. *fact*.
Noble deeds. 47 ff. Cf. Pliny, *Epist*. v. xvi. 3–4: 'She bore her last illness with
patient resignation and, indeed, with courage; she obeyed her doctors' orders,
cheered her sister and her father, and by sheer force of will carried on after her
physical strength had failed her.' 49 *affection*. passion. 50 *assure*. Encourage, give
confidence to. 53 *cupping-glasses*. For bleeding. 54 An abscess on the cheek had to
be lanced. 57 *son*. Charles Paulet, b. *c.*1625, 6th Marquis of Winchester 1674;
Duke of Bolton 1689. 58 *sisters*. Elizabeth and Dorothy Savage, who had danced
in *Chloridia*. 61–2 The Christian art of dying is implicitly compared with the art of
the tragic actor, who merely feigns death: cf. Marvell, *An Horatian Ode*, 53–8.
66 *complement*. i.e. the body. 68 *birthday*. Cf. Donne's *Second Anniversary*, 214.
69 ff. Cf. Seneca, *To Marcia, On Consolation*, xxv. 2. 76 *they . . . crown*. Jas. 1: 12,
Rev. 2: 10; 'the elect of God' (variant). 80 *but lent*. See *Epig*. 45. 3 n. 85 ff. Cf.
Donne's *Anniversaries*. 94 Proverbial: Tilley, M73. 95–7 1 Cor. 15: 19: 'If in this life
only we have hope in Christ, we are of all men most miserable.' 98–9 Gen. 3: 15.

84. *Eupheme*. The word is Jonson's coinage, and 'fair fame' his translation of it.
For Sir Kenelm and Lady Venetia Digby, see *Und*. 78 and n. Jonson evidently
sent this (now imperfect) sequence of poems to Sir Kenelm on his wife's death in
1633; some of the poems appear, however, to have been written during Venetia's
lifetime. *Absolute in All Numbers* (= perfect in all ways) is a rendering of Pliny's
omnibus numeris absolutum (*Epist*. IX. xxxviii: of Rufus's book). The motto is from
Silvae, v, preface: 'to love [a wife] is a joy, while she is alive, and a religion, when
she is departed'; Statius is writing to console Abascantus, Secretary of State to
Domitian, on the loss of his wife, Priscilla.

84. i. 1–5 The contrast between 'fair fame' and 'envy' is reminiscent of that
between *fama bona* and *fama mala* in Jonson's poem on Raleigh's frontispiece,
Und. 24, and may owe something to C. Ripa, *Iconologia* (Padua, 1611), pp. 154–5.
13 *posterity*. *Epig*. Dedn. 13. 14 *crepundia*. Childish toy, rattle. 16 *rattling rhyme*.
Playing on 'crepundia'. For the animus against rhyme, see *Und*. 29 and n.
17 *timbrels*. Tambourine-like instruments. 17–28 Cf. *Disc*. 1451 ff. 21 *prime coats*.
i.e. children's first skirt-like garments. 26 *cobweb cauls*. Gauze caps for women.
31 *tent*. care. 36 *gree*. Degree, descent. 38 *Jacob's ladder*. Gen. 28: 12.

84. ii. *Her Descent*. Jonson has versified a manuscript account of Venetia's
family tree. 1 *uncontrolled*. Unchallenged, unreproved. 5–6 *Northumberland | And
Stanley*. On her father's and mother's sides, respectively; relating her to the Percy
family, and the Earls of Derby. 13 *Alderley*. Adam de Alderley (the name is
variously spelt) was the father of the first Stanley: Camden, *Remains Concerning
Britain* (London, 1870), p. 116. 16–18 Hugh de Avranches (d. 1101), nicknamed

lupus (the wolf), and his grandson Ranulf or Randulf (d. *c.*1129), nicknamed *le meschin* (the mean), were Earls of Chester ('Cestrian'). There were later two other famous Randulfs in the family.

84. iii. Jonson may be remembering the opening of Statius' *Silvae*, v. i. from which he twice draws mottoes for this sequence: Abascantus, trying to recall the memory of the dead Priscilla, commissions craftsmen to model her likeness in metal and wax; Statius at first laments his lack of skill in these crafts, then asserts that his way of celebrating her is more lasting. This poem and the next also echo Lucian's *Essays in Portraiture*, in which Lycinus models a statue of a girl's body, and Polystratus attempts a portrait of her soul. Van Dyck painted Venetia on several occasions; a death-bed portrait of her is in the Dulwich Portrait Gallery. **13–14** Cf. *Beauty*, 181–2: 'She was drawn in a circle of clouds, her face and body breaking through.' **15** *her face.* Variants: 'a face', 'a fire', 'the sun'. **16** *all light rose there.* Cf. *Und.* 2. iv. **17–18** and n. **22** *youth or it.* Variants: 'it and youth'; 'art and youth'; 'youth and wit'; 'youth and art'; 'youth and love'. **23** *Four rivers.* As in Eden, Gen. 2: 10–14. **24** *confining.* Bordering upon. **28** *beauty's world.* Cf. *Und.* 2. iv. 12, 'Love's world'.

84. iv. This poem has many manuscript and textual variants; for details, see H & S, viii. 277–81. **6** *colours.* Playing on the sense of rhetorical colours. **9–12** Ripa associates the mind with the eye, *Iconologia* (Padua, 1611), p. 157, and takes the towering eagle as an emblem of noble thought, p. 415 (*Pensiero*). The sun (associated with Apollo, and hence with intellection) is an emblem of wisdom: see Guy de Tervarent, *Attributs et symboles dans l'art profane 1450–1600* (Geneva, 2 vols., 1958, 1959), ii. 355. **21** *muse.* Cf. the titles of *Und.* 78 and 84. ix. **22** *line.* Playing on the poetic and artistic senses of the word, as in *Und.* 52. 3 ('My Answer'). **32** The circle was an emblem of perfection and of infinity. **72** *God thy guest.* Seneca, *Epist.* xxxi. 11: 'What else could you call such a soul than a god dwelling as a guest in a human body?'; cf. *Disc.* 1225–6; and Digby himself on Venetia: 'Her soul was a fit guest for her lovely body: both together made her the most admired woman of her time' (letter of 17 July 1633, in V. Gabrieli, *Sir Kenelm Digby* (Rome, 1957), p. 262).

84. viii. *quaternion.* A quire of four sheets folded in two. **1** *growing gentlemen.* 'In the contrast between the frail reeds and these sturdy aspiring trees lies the point of the poem' (Peterson, p. 109). **8** Kenelm, 1625–48; John, b. 1627; George, b. 1632, died during the Civil War. Another son, Everard, was born in 1629 and died in infancy. There was also a daughter. **10** *none of yours.* Cf. Ulysses in Ovid's *Metam.* xiii. 140–1: 'For as to race and ancestry and the deeds that others than ourselves have done, I call those in no true sense our own.' **15–17** Juvenal, *Sat.* viii. 76–7: 'It is a poor thing to lean upon the fame of others, lest the pillars give way and the house fall down in ruin'; cf. Tilley, R61. **19–20** Juvenal, *Sat.* viii 19–20: 'Though you deck your hall from end to end with ancient waxen images, virtue is the one and only true nobility'; cf. Tilley, V85.

84. ix. *Muse.* As om *Und.* 78, title, 84. IV. 21. Ἀποθέωσις. in apotheosis. *Sera quidem . . . dolori.* 'Late indeed is the balm composed for so great a sorrow'; Statius,

Silvae, v. i. 16; see note to motto at head of this sequence. **6** *the old nine.* The muses; cf. the dismissiveness of *For.* 10. **12–13** *remorse* | *On.* Pity for. **18** *clees.* claws. **32** *blaspheme in fashion.* Like Donne, perhaps, in the *Anniversaries*, regarding one woman's death as the end of everything: see *Conv. Dr.* 32–5 (A. Leggatt, *Ben Jonson: His Vision and His Art*, p. 221). **37** *crown.* Jas. 1: 12; Rev. 2: 10. **40** *greet.* Weep for. *euthanasy.* Euthanasia, gentle and easy death. **40–4** Cf. Digby's own account of Venetia's peaceful death, V. Gabrieli, *Sir Kenelm Digby*, p. 247. **46–7** Matt. 25: 33. **51–5** Cf. Aquinas's discussion of the relationship of soul and body, *Summa Theologiae*, I. lxxv; and Donne's 'Letter to the Countess of Bedford' ('T'have written then . . .'), ll. 57 ff., *Satires*, p. 97. **65** *full sight.* Rev. 22: 4; 1 Cor. 13: 12. **70** *interpel.* Break in on, disturb. **78–80** Cf. Exod. 33: 20–3; Luke 8: 10. **87** *virtues.* Manuscript: 'victors'. **90** *new song.* Rev. 5: 9. *I am.* Exod. 3: 14. **95–6** Rev. 7: 9. **96** *victrix.* Female victor. **101** *oil of gladness.* Ps. 45: 7. **102** *heaven's empyrean.* H & S's emendation of corr. F 'heaven's empire and'. **120** *all in all.* 1 Cor. 15: 28. **121** Cf. *Und.* 70. 81, 'that bright eternal day'. **140** *heirs.* Rom. 8: 17. **141–2** Like the prodigal son, Luke 15; *possessèd* = owing to God. **146** *Equal with angels.* Luke 20: 36. **150** *knows the hearts.* Rev. 2: 23. **152** *a span.* i.e. its full extent. **153** *creeks.* Nooks, secret places. **157** *two such veins.* The Northumberlands and the Stanleys. **163–8** Cf. Statius, *Silvae*, v. i. 117–18 and 150–3 (Peterson). **164** *lady-air.* Airs thought befitting to a lady. **167** *manage.* command. **173** i.e. she combined, in the one personality, many roles in life. **177** *petty.* small. **183** *rod.* Ps. 23: 4. **187** *the incense.* Ps. 141: 2; Rev. 8: 3–4. **226** *intelligence.* Conveyance of news; information. **229–33** 'In memory of the devotion which you show to your most illustrious Venetia, I offer to you and to yours, worthy husband Digby, this apotheosis.'

85.   Robert Shafer points out that in this translation and in *Und.* 86 and 87 Jonson is trying to represent the form as well as the content of his originals, by using couplets and the same number of lines as Horace: *The English Ode to 1660* (New York, 1966) p. 100. Drummond says that Jonson read the translation to him, 'and admired it' (*Conv. Dr.* 57–8). **9–10** Vines were trained to grow on black poplars and elms; the 'marriage' analogy was traditional (cf. *Paradise Lost*, v. 215–17). Manuscripts: 'There, on the tall witch-hazel he doth twine | With sprouting tendrils.' **13–14** In the original, these lines precede ll. 11–12, but were sometimes editorially rearranged. *bending vale* is Jonson's rendering of *reducta valle*, 'in a remote valley'. **21** *Priapus.* God of generation, and of gardens and orchards. *thank.* Manuscripts: 'greet'. **22** *Silvane.* Silvanus, who presided over gardens and boundaries. **24** *rooted.* Latin *tenaci*, firmly rooted. **26** *quarrel.* Translating Latin *queruntur.* **35** *crane.* Which visited Italy in the summer. **41** *Sabines'.* From the central Apennines; the women had the reputation of being excellent farmers' wives. *blowze.* Red-faced woman. **42** *Apulian's.* From Apulia (now Puglia), between Daunia and Calabria; the inhabitants were known for their industry. **51** *bright floods.* 'East floods' in manuscripts, translating Horace's *Eois fluctibus.* The scar-fish ('golden-eyes') was common in the eastern Mediterranean; it was believed that storms in the east would drive the fish westward. **53** *godwit.* A marsh bird like the curlew; for Horace's *attagen*, a kind of grouse, which came to Italy from the east. *Guinea-hen.* A new delicacy in Italy. **59** *feast of bounds.* In honour of

Terminus, Roman god of bounds and limits: a chance to eat fresh meat. **60** *the wolf.* Customarily said to kill the best young animal of the flock. **66** *steaming.* Manuscripts: 'shining'. **67** *thoughts.* Manuscripts: 'things'. **69–70** *ides . . . calends.* Roman days for settling debts and making new financial arrangements. Despite his praise of the country life, Alfius will stay where he is.

86.   6 *fiftieth year.* Cf. *Und.* 2. i. 3. **10** *bright swans.* Sacred to Venus; cf. *Und.* 2. iv. 3. *Paulus Maximus.* Probably Ovid's patron, and friend of Augustus. **12** *liver.* The seat of love. **14** *files his tongue.* Makes smooth his speech. **27** *Salian manner.* The Salii, priests of Mars, danced and postured through the streets beating their shields. **31** *propound.* propose. **39** *Mars's field.* Campus Martius, the large plain outside Rome.

87.   Also translated by Herrick (p. 70), and others. **6** *sound.* celebrate. **8** *Ilia.* Mother of Romulus and Remus. **14** *Thurine.* From Thuriae (the name is variously spelt), a town in southern Italy. **23** *Adria.* The Adriatic.

88.   Not in fact by Petronius, but printed in the edition of his works published in Paris in 1585. Read to Drummond: *Conv. Dr.* 58–60. **9** *long.* Omitted in one manuscript.

89.   7–8 Cf. *Epig.* 119. 15–16.

90.   Also translated by Surrey, *Poems*, ed. Emrys Jones (Oxford, 1964), pp. 34–5, and by Randolph, *Poems*, ed. G. Thorn-Drury (London, 1929), p. 88. See also *Conv. Dr.* 11–12, 79–80. **5** *in office gowned.* A mistranslation; Jonson mistakes the kind of toga to which Martial refers. **6** *free powers.* Martial's *vires ingenuae*, 'i.e., the natural strength of a gentleman, not the coarse strength of a labourer', W. C. A. Ker, *Martial's Epigrams* (London and Cambridge, Mass., 1968), ii. 189. **7** *alike-stated.* Similarly placed. **9** *laid waste.* Jonson evidently means 'set free' (Martial: *soluta curis*, freed from cares). **11** *swift-paced.* H & S punctuate here with a semicolon, a misreading of the Dulwich College MS, as A. Miller shows; 'Will' is thus a verb, not a noun.

UNGATHERED VERSE

The title and (roughly chronological) sequence of poems in this group are taken from H & S. The contents differ slightly: three short Latin pieces printed by H & S (*UV* 13, 14, 15) are not reproduced here, and one poem that now seems unlikely to have been written by Jonson (*UV* 27) is relegated to *Dubia*, where it appears as no. 4. Whether Jonson wrote *UV* 41 is not entirely certain, but as the case against his authorship is less persuasive, the poem is retained in this section. H & S's numbering of the poems throughout this section have been preserved, in order to simplify cross-reference.

The poems in this group were not collected by Jonson, nor were they found amongst the papers that passed to Sir Kenelm Digby after his death. Many of them are commendatory poems which had appeared at the head of various books published by Jonson's friends and acquaintances; a few are poems which, for various reasons, he chose not to publish with his collected work.

1. Thomas Palmer was Principal of Gloucester Hall, Oxford, 1563–4, and Fellow and Lecturer in Rhetoric at St John's College, Oxford, until 1566; deprived of these posts because of his Catholicism, he retired to Exeter, where persecution continued. *The Sprite of Trees and Herbs*, a botanical emblem book, was composed 1598–9 but never published (BM Additional MS 18040). *7 storms and thunder.* Alluding to the persecution which Palmer suffered. *8 Unseasoned.* unseasonable. *envious weather.* Cf. *Love's Labour's Lost*, I. i. 100–1: 'envious-sneaping frost'. *14 carbuncle.* Exod. 28: 17; 39: 10. *15 seven-fold flower of art.* The seven liberal arts. *23 circumvol[v]ed.* Turned around. *30 travails.* With a pun on 'travels': a palmer being a religious traveller. *32* ' 'Tis the muse forbids the hero worthy of renown to perish', Horace, *Odes*, IV. viii. 28.

2. Nicholas Breton, ?1545–?1626, is dismissively referred to in *Und.* 43. 77. *1 habit.* A pun. *3 modes.* 'Moodes' in the original spelling: playing again on words. *5 master print.* From which a print (of a book, a picture, or a fabric) is taken: the phrase unites the poem's various metaphors. *7 look asquint.* Cf. Ovid, *Metam.* ii. 787, where envy looks *obliquo*, askance; and see *Und.* 73. 2 n. *10 perspective.* H & S compare Chapman and Shirley, *The Tragedy of Chabot*, I. i. For a partial explanation of the phenomenon Jonson describes, see E. H. Gombrich, *Art and Illusion* (London and New York, 1960), pp. 254–5. *11 censure.* judgement. *14 this line.* The line of the poem, and the line of vision.

3. Three of the fourteen quotations from Jonson's work in *England's Parnassus*, ed. Robert Allot: the others are from *EMO*, *EMI*, *For.* 11, and *Und.* 25. *1–2 Juvenal, Sat.* x. 112–13: 'Few indeed are the kings who go down to Ceres' son-in-law [Pluto] save by sword and slaughter—few the tyrants that perish by a bloodless death.' *3–4* Cf. *Und.* 15. 121. *5 ff.* Cf. *Volp.* I. i. 22–7. *6 palm.* Honour, glory (a Latinism). *10 Aetna gates.* By which Jupiter secured the giants imprisoned under this mountain.

4. On *Love's Martyr*, See *For.* 10 and n. *4 a woman.* See *Und.* 75. 81–2 and n.

5. ἐνθουσιαστική. Inspired. Newdigate discovered a manuscript copy of this poem addressed to Lucy, Countess of Bedford: see notes to *For.* 10. W. H. Matchett considers that the poem was originally written for the Countess of Bedford, and then used again in the quite different context of *Love's Martyr* as a final compliment to the 'Phoenix', whom he believes to be Queen Elizabeth: see his *The Phoenix and Turtle* (The Hague, 1965), pp. 100–1. *3 illustrate.* Resplendent, illustrious.

6. Like Jonson, Hugh Holland, the author of *Pancharis*, had been at Westminster School, and had been subsequently converted to Catholicism. He died in 1633. Camden, whose life Holland wrote, ranked him among the 'most pregnant wits of these our times, whom succeeding ages may justly admire', *Remains Concerning Britain* (London, 1870), p. 344. For biographical details, see L. I. Guiney, *Recusant Poets* (London and New York, 1938), pp. 361 ff. In his prefatory verses to *Pancharis* and in the poem itself, Holland represents himself as a swarthy and unattractive lover, and an incompetent and inexperienced poet. Jonson neatly turns these disclaimers by figuring Holland as a swan, a bird associated with

Venus (and hence with love) and also with Apollo (and hence with poetry; according to one Greek legend, Apollo had been turned into a swan). The swan's, and Holland's, blackness is taken as a sign that he is more than ordinarily dear to Apollo, god not only of poetry but of the sun (see ll. 16 ff.). The existence of real black swans was not known in Europe at this time; 'a black swan' (l. 2) meant a person of mythical rarity (for Juvenal, a chaste wife: *Sat.* vi. 165); cf. ll. 32–3, below. ἀλληγορικὴ = allegorical. 5 *other swans'*. Andrew Downes, Nicholas Hill, and E.B. (probably Edmund Bolton), who had also written commendatory verses. 17 *hoof-cleft spring*. Hippocrene, the fountain of the Muses, produced by a blow from Pegasus' hoof. Contrast Holland himself: 'My lips I never yet have soused | In Hippocrene ... | The climate where I was begotten | Of father Phoebus is forgotten', etc. (sig. A11). 18 *Thespiades*. The nine muses. 19 *Dircaean fount*. At Thebes, the birthplace of Pindar, whom Horace calls 'the Dircaean swan', *Odes*, IV. ii. 25. 21 *pale Pyrene*. An inspiring spring near Corinth; 'pale', because poets were supposed to look wan after their exertions: cf. Persius, *Sat.* prologue, 4. *the forkèd mount*. Parnassus; cf. Persius, *Sat.* prologue, 2. 24 *close*. Cover, protect. 25 *his down*. In *Pancharis* (sig. A10ᵛ) Holland describes the 'black down' of his beard. 35 *one river*. Holland briefly celebrates the Thames in *Pancharis*, sig. B7ᵛ–B8. 38 *Mon*. The Welsh name for Anglesey. 39 *Clwyd*. The valley in Denbighshire, Holland's home. 42 *Iërna main*. The Irish Sea. 43 *Eugenian dale*. Munster, Ireland. 44–54 Referring to the rebellion of Hugh O'Neill, 2nd Earl of Tyrone. Charles, Lord Mountjoy, defeated Irish and Spanish forces at Kinsale in Munster in 1601, and thereafter negotiated with Tyrone, who submitted formally in 1603. 53 *kerne*. Light-armed Irish foot-soldiers; peasantry, 'rabble'. 56 Proverbial: cf. Tilley, T326. 57 *sipped at Baphyre river*. Tried to write poetry (the Baphyrus in Macedonia was thought to be the same river as Helicon). Mountjoy was praised by John Davies of Hereford in *Microcosmus* (1603); by Sylvester in three sonnets prefixed to the second *Week* of de Bartas (*c.*1598; published 1641); by Daniel in his *Funeral Poem on the ... Earl of Devonshire* (1606); and by Ford in *Fame's Memorial* (1606). 58 *spite*. Which might have been aroused by Mountjoy's association with Essex and the rebellion of 1600–1; by his methods of government in Ireland (from which he was recalled on 26 May 1603); or by his liaison with Penelope, Lady Rich, whom he eventually married on 26 December 1605. 61 *entheate*. inspired. *tracts*. Course, career. 67 *Orcades*. Orkneys. 69 *Thule*. Traditionally, an island in the extreme north, of uncertain location; here perhaps the Shetland Islands. 69–70 *backs the seas | To Caledon*. Goes back across the sea to Scotland. 71 *Grampius*. Grampians. 72 *Tweed's black-springing fountain*. Tweeds Well, near Moffat in Peeblesshire. 78 *reeking fumes*. Probably from the pottery kilns, already in operation in this area by the end of the sixteenth century. 84 *nimble French*. Perhaps a reference to the visit of the Duke of Biron and a large party of French noblemen on 5 September 1601; they arrived at Tower Wharf: see J. Nichols, *Progresses ... Of Queen Elizabeth* (London, 1823), iii. 565. 85 *The Dutch*. See *Epig.* 32. 3 n. The division in fact reflected religious hostility. 86–7 Cf. Hamlet on the Danes' heavy drinking, which 'makes us traduced and taxed of other nations': *Hamlet*, I. iii. 18. 88 *slower Spain*. 'The Spartans and Spaniards have been noted to be of small dispatch', Bacon, 'Of Dispatch'. 99 *Cygnus*. Son of Neptune; after his death, Apollo changed him into a swan, and placed him in the heavens as a constellation. **100–1** At the beginning of *Pancharis*, Holland asks Cupid for a pinion from his wing to assist him in writing; throughout the poem he mentions the fact that he is in love. **104** *Leda's white adulterer's place.* Jupiter, who changed into a swan in order to rape Leda. **109** *Eridanus.* A constellation; also the river Po. **114–17** European rivers: the *Iberus* is in Spain; the *Tagus* in Spain and Portugal; the *Scheldt* in France, Belgium, and Holland; the *Maas* in Holland; the *Arar* is the Saône, in France.

7. Thomas Wright was a Yorkshireman and Jesuit who had taught in several Jesuit colleges in Europe; he was perhaps the priest who converted Jonson to Catholicism in 1598: see L. I. Guiney, *Recusant Poets* (New York and London, 1938), p. 335. An account of his career is given by Theodore A. Stroud, *ELH* xiv (1947), 274–82. *The Passions of the Mind in General* was first published in an unauthorized edition in 1601; Jonson's verses are in the second edition of 1604, along with others by H.H. (probably Hugh Holland). Wright's work may have influenced Jonson's notions about dramatic character: see Robert E. Knoll, *Ben Jonson's Plays: An Introduction* (Nebraska, 1964), *passim.* For the analogy with painting, cf. *Disc.* 1555, 1563 ff., and ll. 15–23 of Chapman's address to Royden prefixed to *The Banquet of Sense*, in *Poems*, ed. P. B. Bartlett (New York and London, 1941), p. 19. **1** *truly understand.* See *Epig.* 1. 2 and n. **5** *throughly.* thoroughly. **6** *limiting.* outlining. **12** *sense.* Sensory perception. Wright's view of the relationship between reason, passion, and sense is set out in pt. I. ch. ii of his work.

8. *The Faithful Shepherdess* was in print by 1610. Jonson in *Conv. Dr.* 184–5 referred to it as 'a tragicomedy well done'. **1** *many-headed.* Horace, *Epist.* 1. i. 76. *bench.* Cf. *BF* Ind. 104. **4** *pucelle.* whore. **5** *cap.* See *Und.* 42. 28. **7** *his sixpence.* The lowest price of admission mentioned in *BF* Ind. 88. **7–8** *before | They saw it half.* Jonson speaks with feeling: *Sejanus* had been hissed off the stage in 1603. **14** *crown.* Punning on a now obsolete sense of the verb, to hold a coroner's inquest on (*OED, v.*²); cf. *Epig.* 17. 4. **15–16** *fire | Or moths.* Matt. 6: 19–20, Luke 12: 33.

9. For Cecilia Bulstrode, see *Und.* 49 and n. She died at Lady Bedford's house in Twickenham on 4 August 1609, evidently in physical and spiritual distress: see Lord Herbert of Cherbury's epitaph, *Poems*, ed. G. C. Moore Smith (Oxford, 1923), pp. 20–1. Jonson's epitaph is quite at odds with his attack in *Und.* 49, for which he may have wished to make amends. Jonson sent the epitaph to his friend George Garrard with a note explaining that he wrote at speed and in sorrow. **2** *a little . . . much.* Cf. *Epig.* 124. 2. **6** *four.* Manuscript: 'poor'. **9** *eye.* Bright spot, centre of intelligence: cf. *Und.* 65. 8, *Conv. Dr.* 349. **14** *fable of good women.* Chaucer's *Legend of Good Women.*

10. Thomas Coryate (?1577–1617) of Odcombe in Somerset, traveller and buffoon, journeyed nearly 2,000 miles across Europe, mainly on foot, between 14 May and 3 October 1608. Failing at first to find a publisher for his account of his travels, *Crudities*, he appealed to people of eminence to write commendatory verses upon himself and his undertaking. The response was enthusiastic, if largely facetious. There is no evidence to support the notion that Jonson edited this volume: see Michael Strachan, *The Life and Adventures of Thomas Coryate* (London, etc., 1962), p. 125. Jonson refers scornfully to Coryate in *Epig.* 129. 17 and *Und.* 13. 128. **2** *carnosities.* Morbid fleshy growths. The reference is to William Hole's title-page illustrations: see p. 443. **3** *front.* Forehead; frontispiece. **5** *Crudities.* In the old physiology, the word meant imperfectly 'concocted' humours. **5–6** *heads . . . pricked . . . pointed.* Playing on words. **10–11** Coryate explains that his sea-sickness on the crossing to France came from a wish 'to satiate the gormandizing paunches of the hungry haddocks', *Crudities* (1611), p. 1. Arion, about to be pushed overboard during a sea voyage to Italy, played melodiously to a dolphin, who carried him ashore on its back. **12–13** See *Crudities*, p. 9. Holborn Hill leads to Tyburn. **14–15** Probably referring to a misadventure outside Lyons, p. 55. **16–17** Coryate paid 18*d.* to be carried the last, steep, half-mile over the Alps (pp. 69–70). 'As plain as Dunstable highway' is proverbial: Tilley, D646. **18–19** Coryate took a scholarly interest in the courtesans of Venice; he visited one in order to 'view her own amorous person, hear her talk, observe her fashion of life'; but no more (p. 271). **21–3** Coryate visited the Jewish ghetto in Venice, and was rescued by Sir Henry Wotton from an angry debate with a rabbi (pp. 230–7). **24–5** A 'German boor' seized Coryate's hat after Coryate had taken some grapes from a vineyard (pp. 524–6). **26–7** Coryate hung up in Odcombe church the clothes (*case*) he had worn on his travels; his shoes remained there until the eighteenth century. **29** 'Not meaning by F and K as the vulgar may peevishly and unwittingly mistake: but that he was then coming from his courtesan, a Freshman, and now, having seen their fashions and written a description of them, he will shortly be reputed a Knowing, proper, and well-travelled scholar, as by his starched beard and printed ruff may be as properly insinuated' (Jonson's note). **31** *horns.* Of plenty, but also of the cuckold: the ambiguity is apparent in the illustration itself. Hence perhaps the gibe of l. 29, at Coryate's inadequacy with (past) whore and (future) wife. *Germany.* Coryate discusses German drinking habits on pp. 438–9. **32–3** At Bergamo (p. 350). **34–5** Fearing he was to be robbed by two 'ragged boors' outside Baden, Coryate pretended he was a beggar; they gave him 4½*d.* (p. 465).

11.   This 'Characterism Acrostic' (acrostic character-sketch) follows a prose 'Character' of Coryate, probably also by Jonson: it is printed by H & S, whose subsequent line-numbers are given here. *Travails . . . Travel.* The usual play on words; cf. l. 89 below. **[80]** *Try and trust Roger:* a proverbial saying: 'trust the plain man'. **[83]** *at his own charge.* Coryate seems to have published *Crudities* at his own expense. **[85]** *Paul's Churchyard.* Home of publishers. **[91]** Bacchus was born from Jupiter's thigh, Pallas Athene from his head.

12.   Coryate's *Crambe* was one of two appendices to *Crudities* published in 1611. *Polytopian.* A nonce-word: one who visits many places. **4–5** Horace, *Epist.* I. vii. 98. **5** *philosophers.* i.e. of the Peripatetic school. **14** *self-same spirit.* i.e. pedestrian. **15 ff.** At the end of *Crudities*, Coryate gives the statistics of his travels: 1,975 miles and 45 cities (etc.) in 5 months. **22** *Pize.* pox. **29–31** Travellers were proverbially said to be liars: Tilley, T476. **34** *pediculous.* lousy. **36** *grapes.* See *UV.* 10. 24–5 and n. **37** *tergum o!* O my back! **38** *Bergamo. UV* 10. 32–3. **40** *suspended.* See *UV* 10. 26–7 and n. **43–6** In his 'Epistle to the reader', Coryate names twelve learned men he has met and conversed with during his travels. **48** *black taffeta.* Admired by Coryate in Venice, *Crudities*, pp. 248, 259. **53** *cart. UV* 10. 12–13 and n. **54–5** Perhaps referring to Coryate's visit to Sir William Browne of the English garrison at Flushing, *Crudities*, p. 653.

16.   Sir Robert Rich, 2nd Earl of Warwick (1587–1658), and Sir Henry Rich, 1st Baron Kensington and 1st Earl of Holland (1590–1649) were sons of Robert Rich, 1st Earl of Warwick, and Penelope, née Devereux, Sidney's Stella. The tilting took place on 24 March 1613. **12** *prospective.* magnifying.

17.   *Cynthia's Revenge* was published anonymously, the Dedication being signed I.S.: identifiable from certain title-pages as John Stephens of Lincoln's Inn. **2** *understand.* Cf. *Epig.* 1. 2 and n. **5** *rove.* A term from archery: to shoot arrows at random; hence guess, conjecture.

18.   King James's favourite, Robert Carr, Earl of Somerset, married the divorced Countess of Essex (formerly Frances Howard) on 26 December 1613. Carr's friend Sir Thomas Overbury, who opposed the marriage, had been sent to the Tower (by Carr's contrivance) in April of that year, and poisoned (by the Countess's) in September. Jonson also wrote *A Challenge at Tilt* and *The Irish Masque* for this occasion. **6** *ends.* Ulterior motives. **7** *early.* Cf. *Epig.* 23. 3, *Und.* 70. 125. **12** *that wife.* Sir Thomas Overbury's poem, *The Wife*, which was published in 1614; Jonson knew it in manuscript (*Conv. Dr.* 173–5). **13–14** i.e. do better than Essex: the bride's first marriage had been annulled because of Essex's alleged physical incapacity (the 'fault' of l. 14). **23–4** Cf. Martial, IV. xiii. 9–10; as H & S observe, it is disconcerting to notice that Jonson had expressed much the same wish at the bride's first wedding, *Hym.* 561–4. Cf. *Und.* 75. 165–8.

19.   The author of *The Ghost of Richard the Third* was Christopher Brooke (d. 1628) of Lincoln's Inn, Donne's friend, and witness at his wedding. Brooke was associated with the pastoral revival of 1613–16. **1** *such.* Chapman, Browne, Wither, and others. **3** *broad seals.* Warrants, authorities (after the Broad or Great Seal of England).

20.   The authorship of *The Husband* is unknown. The work followed Sir Thomas Overbury's *The Wife* (*UV* 18. 12 n). **6** *uttering.* Offering for sale.

21.   The first book of William Browne's *Britannia's Pastorals* was published in 1613; the second, dedicated to William, Earl of Pembroke, in 1616: Jonson's *Epigrams* were dedicated to Pembroke the same year. The volume carried other commendatory verses. Browne praises Jonson's talents in his second song. **2** *hurt them.* Cf. *UV* 26. 14.

22.   Sir Charles Cavendish, of Welbeck, Notts., was the husband of Lady Katherine Ogle of *UV* 31, and the father of Jonson's patron, William Cavendish, of *Und.* 53 and 59. He died 4 April 1619; Jonson's lines are on his monument in the Cavendish chantry at Bolsover, and are followed by a prose inscription (printed in H & S, viii. 388). **4** *turn.* 'Be', on monument. **8** *To which.* Compared with which. **10** *nephews.* Descendants (Latin *nepotes*).

23. 3 *rich Homer's mine.* Chapman had published a specimen of his *Iliad* in 1598, the whole *Iliad* in 1611, and his *Odyssey* in 1614. 11 *trade.* Peterson (p. 14) sees a play on 'Chapman'.

24. *The Rogue* was a translation (1622) of Matheo Aleman's *Guzmán de Alfarache* (pt. I 1599; pt. II 1604) by James Mabbe (1572–?1642), Spanish scholar and Fellow of Magdalen College, Oxford. Jonson's tribute implies that he had a reasonable familiarity with Spanish. On the poem, see Isaac d'Israeli, 'Ben Jonson on Translation', in *Curiosities of Literature.* 5 *Spanish Proteus.* Like some of Jonson's own comic heroes, Guzmán assumes many roles. 7 *good book.* Aleman's story is interspersed with moral digressions, and ends with Guzmán's conversion. 10 *true glass.* Cf. *For.* 13. 26 ff.

25. Printed with the Droeshout portrait in the First Folio. 3 *graver.* engraver. *strife.* Cf. 'To the Painter to Draw Him a Picture', 3–4, Herrick, p. 38; *Venus and Adonis*, 291–2, etc. 5–8 Cf. Martial, x. xxxii. 5–6: 'Would that art could limn his character and mind! More beautiful in all the world would no painting be' (on Marcus Antonius Primus). Cf. *UV* 26. 22 n.

26. *My Beloved.* 'For I loved the man, and do honour his memory, on this side idolatry, as much as any', *Disc.* 665–6. For criticism, see T. J. B. Spencer in *Elizabethan Theatre*, IV, ed. G. Hibbard (London and Basingstoke, 1974), pp. 22–40; Peterson, ch. 4; Lawrence Lipking, *The Life of the Poet* (Chicago, 1981), ch. 3. 1 *envy.* A constant preoccupation for Jonson: cf. *Epig.* 102. 16; 111. 14; *Und.* 73; 76. 17 ff.; 84. i. 3, etc. Dryden nevertheless characterized the poem as 'an insolent, sparing, and invidious panegyric': 'A Discourse Concerning the Original and Progress of Satire', in *Of Dramatic Poesy and Other Critical Essays*, ed. G. Watson, 2 vols. (London and New York, 1962), ii. 75; cf. Trimpi, p. 149. 2 *ample.* '. . . means, not "adequate", but "copious". In Cicero an *amplus orator* was one who orates richly and with dignity' (Spencer). 3 *confess.* Make known (Spencer). 14 *what could hurt her more?* Cf. *UV* 21. 2. 18 Cf. Martial, IX. xxviii. 1–2: 'The darling pride of the stage, the glory of the games . . . the favourite of your applause.' 19–21 Tilting at the opening of William Basse's *Elegy on Shakespeare*: 'Renownèd Spenser, lie a thought more nigh │ To learnèd Chaucer; and rare Beaumont lie │ A little nearer Spenser, to make room │ For Shakespeare in your threefold, fourfold tomb.' 22 *a monument without a tomb.* Cf. Horace, *Odes*, III. xxx. 1–2: 'I have finished a monument more lasting than bronze and loftier than the pyramids' royal pile': localized by a further allusion to Shakespeare's Stratford monument (cf. Leonard Digges's poem in the First Folio, declaring that Shakespeare's work will outlive his monument). The line is echoed by William Cavendish and varied by John Taylor in their poems on Jonson's death in 1637 (H & S, xi. 489, 426), and remembered in Milton's 'On Shakespeare', l. 8: 'hast built thyself a livelong monument'. 27 *of years.* Mature. Trimpi (p. 150) finds this modesty uncharacteristic. Spencer (p. 33) suggests that the phrase means 'temporary'. 28 *commit.* In the sense of Latin *committo*, match, bring together for comparison. 29 *our Lyly outshine.* Cf. the lily as the 'flower of light' in *Und.* 70. 72, and Virgil, *Aeneid* vi. 708–9, Matth. 6: 28–9. 30 *sporting Kyd.* Playing on the dramatist's name. 31 *small Latin, and less Greek.* A charge massively refuted by

T. W. Baldwin in *William Shakespere's Small Latine and Lesse Greeke* (Urbana, 1944), 2 vols.; interpreted by Peterson as 'a paradox, rather than a slight' (p. 179). J. E. Spingarn finds a source for the phrase in A. S. Minturno, *L'Arte Poetica* (Venice, 1564), p. 158: *A History of Literary Criticism in the Renaissance* (New York, 1908), p. 89 n. **35** *Pacuvius, Accius.* Roman tragedians; their names had been linked by Horace, *Epist.* ii. ii. 55–6, and by Quintilian, x. i. 97. *him of Cordova dead.* Seneca. **36** *buskin.* The high thick-soled boot worn by Athenian tragic actors. **37** *socks.* Light shoes worn by comic actors on the Greek and Roman stage. **39** *insolent Greece or haughty Rome.* Cf. *Disc.* 926–8, on Bacon's having 'performed that in our tongue which may be compared or preferred either to insolent Greece or haughty Rome'; recalling Seneca the elder, *Controversiarum*, i, preface, 6: 'all that Roman eloquence could put beside or above that of insolent Greece flourished about the time of Cicero'. **45–6** *Apollo . . . Mercury.* Gods of poetry and eloquence, respectively. Spencer sees a memory of Virgil, *Eclogues*, vi. 3–4 (plucking the ear), combined with the idea of the sun-god rising and warming us. **49** *spun and woven.* Perhaps remembering the literal and figurative senses of Greek ῥάπτω: to sew together, to plot or contrive. Cf. Pindar, *Nemean Odes*, ii. 2; and Jonson, *UV* 42. 14–18; *ML* Chor. before Act I, 133–41; before Act V, 1–9. **51** *merry Greek.* Playing on words: a 'Greek' was a merry fellow (*OED*, 5: cf. the related phrase 'merry as a grig'). **51–4** Trimpi, p. 151, thinks these lines can with 'improvement' be transferred to follow l. 40, but ignores the developing argument concerning art and nature. **52** *Neat.* Elegant, pithy. **55 ff.** Contrast *Conv. Dr.* 37, 'That Shakespeare wanted art'. See also *Disc.* 2528–9. For the background to this opposition of art and nature, see T. W. Baldwin, *William Shakespere's Small Latine*, i. 13 ff., 41; and for the place of these terms in the developing debate about the nature of Shakespeare's genius, see E. N. Hooker (ed.), *The Critical Works of John Dennis* (Baltimore, 1943), ii. 428–31. **58** *fashion.* i.e. fashioning; uniting the imagery of dress and smithing. **59** *casts.* Intends (*OED*, †44); and plans, shapes, disposes: of material things and artistic works (*OED*, †45). *living line.* As in ll. 48–9 and 67–8, Shakespeare's lines are seen as being at once artificial and organic. **60–2** Cf. *Disc.* 2466, 'bring all to the forge, and file again; turn it anew'. Briggs, *MP* xv (1917), 279–80, compares Horace's assertion that the poet who wishes to write a 'legitimate poem' must turn and twist himself like a mime: *Epist.* ii. ii. 124–5. **63** *for.* Instead of. **65** Cf. *EMI* v. v. 38–40. **66** *race.* Combining several senses: (i) offspring, posterity (*OED*, *sb.*² 1), i.e. his writings; (ii) liveliness, piquancy, raciness (*OED*, *sb.*² 10b: of writing); (iii) onward movement, rush (*OED*, *sb.*¹ 5). **69** *shake a lance.* Playing on the poet's name, as in l. 37. **71** *Sweet swan of Avon.* As Homer had been known as the swan of Meander, Virgil as the swan of Mantua, and Pindar as the Dircaean swan. On the association of the swan with poetry, see *UV* 6 and n., and cf. Horace, *Odes*, ii. xx. Spencer notes that Shakespeare's company, the Lord Chamberlain's Men, wore an insignia of a flying silver swan. **76** *a constellation.* The stellification of the dead person is a common theme in classical epitaphs: see Richmond Lattimore, *Themes in Greek and Latin Epitaphs* (Urbana, 1962), pp. 311–13; and cf. *Und.* 70. 89 ff.; *UV* 6. 97–112. **80** Cf. *Cat.* iv. 761.

28. Lady Jane Ogle, Countess of Shrewsbury, was the eldest daughter of

Cuthbert, Lord Ogle, and sister of Lady Katherine Ogle of *UV* 31; Jonson's patron William Cavendish, Earl (later Duke) of Newcastle, was her nephew (see *Und.* 53 and 59). She died 7 January 1625, and was buried in St Edmund's Chapel, Westminster Abbey, next to her husband. Jonson's lines are not on the monument. **1** *grave.* A pun. **12** *a herald's wit.* Cf. *Epig.* 9. 4 and n. **18** *inmate.* Lodger; cf. *UV* 31. 26 and Donne, 'The Anniversary', l. 18. **23** *Importune.* importunate.

29.   Thomas May (1595–1650) also translated Martial and Virgil's *Georgics.* Marvell later satirized him in *Tom May's Death.* **1** *mighty pair.* Caesar and Pompey. **7** *peised.* balanced. **11** *start.* swerve. **18** Cf. *Disc.* 1900–2. **24** *sun.* Phoebus Apollo. *son of May.* Mercury (Hermes) was the son of Maia; a strained pun on the translator's name.

30.   Jonson told Drummond in 1618–19 that 'Drayton feared him, and he esteemed not of him' (*Conv. Dr.* 119). Jonson's poem, a late insertion in Drayton's volume, was perhaps written in response to Drayton's own praise of him later in the same volume (see note to l. 91 below). J. W. Hebel considers Jonson's poem 'sly satire rather than compliment' (*PMLA* xxxix (1924), 830–2); B. H. Newdigate sees it as 'too fulsome to be taken seriously . . . a bit of good-tempered leg-pulling' (*Michael Drayton and His Circle* (Oxford, 1941, 1961), p. 136). The extravagance of the poem may perhaps merely reflect Jonson's anxiety to make lavish amends to an unexpected admirer. **8** *rhyming club.* Cf. the 'play club' of *Songs,* 35. 26. **10** *conferring symbols.* Contributing shares, as in an eating club: Plautus' *symbolarum collatores,* in *Curculio,* IV. i (474). **11, 13** *dream . . . vision.* Jonson distinguishes between a fantasy and a revelation. **20** *regions seven.* The seven poems (or groups of poems) set out on the title-page of Drayton's *Poems* (1619). **23** *Ideas.* Drayton's *Idea, The Shepherd's Garland* (1593). **25** *Legends three.* There were actually four: *Pierce Gaveston* (1593/4); *Matilda* (1594); *Robert, Duke of Normandy* (1596); *Great Cromwell* (1607). **29** *epistolar Heroic songs. England's Heroical Epistles* (1597). **32** *Naso.* Ovid. **34** *Owl.* Drayton's *The Owl* (1604). **42** *Barons' Wars.* 1603; a rewriting of *Mortimeriados* (1596). **43** *these times.* Referring to the rising political trouble between Charles and his parliament. **46** *authorized.* i.e. permitted when it should not be permitted: cf. a similar sense in 'licensed'. **47** *Lucan.* Who, in *Pharsalia,* had written about the Roman civil wars. **50–1** *periegesis . . . circumduction.* Both words mean 'leading around'; the first recalls the title of a versified geography of the world written *c.*AD 300 by Dionysius of Alexandria. **52** *Poly-Olbion.* 1612 and 1622. Contrast the opinion expressed in *Conv. Dr.* 18–20. **55 ff.** Referring to the contents of Drayton's *Battle of Agincourt* volume: first, to the title poem; to *The Miseries of Margaret the Queen* (75); *Nymphidia, The Court of Fairy* (79); *The Quest of Cynthia* and *The Shepherd's Sirena* (80), and *The Mooncalf* (84); *Ends* (89) refers to the *Elegies Upon Sundry Occasions.* **61** *catalogue of ships.* In *Agincourt,* 361 ff.; in Homer's *Iliad,* ii. 484 ff. **68** *Tyrtaeus.* Greek lyric poet, who roused the Spartans just as they wished to raise the siege of Ithome, and helped them to defeat the Messenians. **86** *Lapland.* Traditionally the home of witches and wizards. *Cobalus.* Demon of the mines. **87** *Empusa.* A spectre who had power to change her shape: see Aristophanes, *Frogs,* 293. *Lamia.* In classical mythology, a female demon who devoured children; sometimes identified with Empusa.

91 *not there.* Jonson is in fact praised in 'To My Most Dearly-Loved Friend, Henry Reynolds, Esq', *Works*, ed. J. W. Hebel (Oxford, 1961), iii. 229; what he regrets is that he is not a recipient of a verse letter.

31. Katherine, Lady Ogle (Baroness Ogle, 1628) was the widow of Sir Charles Cavendish (*UV* 22); the mother of William Cavendish, Earl (and later Duke) of Newcastle (*Und.* 53 and 59); and the younger sister of Lady Jane Ogle, Countess of Shrewsbury (*UV* 28). She died 18 April 1629, and was buried at Bolsover. The Greek motto is a proverb: 'In the fullness of time Zeus observes the records.' **3** *nephews.* Descendants (Latin *nepotes*). **8** *digests, pandects.* Collections of Roman civil laws made under Justinian. *Dip[h]thera Jovis.* i.e. Jove's record; διφθέρα being prepared hide used for writing upon. **9** *reflex.* reflection. **14–16** The circle was regarded as the perfect figure: cf. *Und.* 84. iv. 32 n. **23–4** See *Und.* 70. 50 and n. **26** *inmate.* Temporary lodger; cf. *UV* 28. 18.

32. Sir John Beaumont (1583–1627), brother of the dramatist Francis Beaumont. Jonson is perhaps punning on his name: *beau mont.* **1** *a genius.* 'A book, to live, must have a genius', Martial, VI. lxi. 10. **4** *ravelins.* Outworks with double face outside main ditch before curtain. **9** *muniments.* (i) Documents; (ii) fortifications. **10** *engine.* Wit; with a play on military engine. **22** *ethnicism.* paganism.

33. Filmer (d. 1669) translated the songs in this volume from the French of Pierre Guedron and Antoine Boesset. This poem appeared in the second Folio as *Epigram* 129. **8 ff.** The marriage of French music and English verse is likened to the marriage of the French Henrietta Maria and the English Charles; for the lily and the rose, see *Und.* 65. 3 and n. **14** *sweet upon her tongue.* Cf. Chaucer's Friar, Prologue to *The Canterbury Tales*, 264–5: 'Somewhat he lipsed, for his wantownesse, | To make his Englissh sweete upon his tonge'; echoed again in *NI* 1. iii. 68–9.

34. The quarrel between Jonson and his collaborator in his court masques, Inigo Jones (1573–1652), flared up again in 1631 when Jones took objection to his name appearing second to Jonson's on the title-page of *Love's Triumph Through Callipolis* ('The Inventors, Ben Jonson, Inigo Jones'). Jonson responded by omitting Jones's name altogether from the title-page of the Quarto of *Chloridia*, and by writing this poem and *UV* 35 and 36. As presented in the *Expostulation*, the quarrel was a fundamental one concerning the relative places of visual and verbal elements in the court masque: its intellectual background is analysed by D. J. Gordon, *JWCI* xii (1949), 152–78. Yet Jones's and Jonson's theories about the masque were in fact surprisingly similar, and their partnership more deeply harmonious than Jonson's satire allows: see Stephen Orgel's Introduction to *The Complete Masques of Ben Jonson* (New Haven, 1969), and Stephen Orgel and Roy Strong, *Inigo Jones: the Theatre of the Stuart Court* (London, Berkeley, and Los Angeles, 1973), *passim.* The *Expostulation* must have been written in or after July 1631, not immediately after Shrovetide, as H & S suggest: see note to l. 104 below. **1** *M[aste]r Survey[o]r.* Jones had been appointed Surveyor of the King's Works in 1615. **2** *thirty pound in pipkins.* Pipkins are pots and pans; H & S take this as a reference to 'commodity', a species of usury: see

Epig. 12. 13 and n. Little is known about Jones's early life: his father was a cloth-worker of humble means. Jonson's taunts about social origins are reminiscent of those in the comedies: cf. the quarrels of Face, Subtle, and the Otters. **5** *Archytas.* Pythagorean philosopher and mathematician, *c.*430–390 BC. **7** *Ctesibius.* Alexandrian engineer of the third century BC. **8** *Vitruvius.* Jones probably could not read Vitruvius' *De architectura* in Latin; his copy of the Italian translation of 1567 survives. Jonson had read (and annotated) at least the first chapter of the Latin text. **10** *architectonike.* The term used by Aristotle (ἀρχιτεκτονικὴ τέχνη, *Nicomachean Ethics*, 1. i) to denote the ultimate end to which all knowledge is directed and subordinated, viz., virtuous action. To illustrate his notion of a hierarchy of kinds of knowledge, Aristotle takes over an analogy used by Plato (*Politics*, 259E): 'The architect conceives the design, the labourers carry out the details.' Jonson implies that Jones has literally set up architecture as the highest kind of knowledge, yet has trivialized the art. Cf. also Sidney's *Apology for Poetry*, ed. G. Shepherd (London, 1964), p. 104. **14** *your sirship.* i.e. your reverence; perhaps a coinage (*OED*'s first usage 1873). **16** *Tire-man.* Man in charge of costumes. *Mountebank.* Cf. *Epig.* 129. 13 n. *Justice.* Jones was a JP for Westminster. **18** *wit.* Cf. the gibes at Jones's 'wit' in *Epig.* 115. 28; 129. 14. **20** *asinigo.* Spanish *asnico*, little ass; glancing at Inigo's name and his social ambitions (see *UV* 35). **22** *Langley.* Francis Langley, owner of the Paris Garden and builder of the Swan Theatre. *Inigo.* Punning on Italian *iniquo*, 'impious, wicked, unrighteous' (Florio, *Queen Anna's New World of Words*, 1616); cf. *Conv. Dr.* 402–3. **26** *velvet sheath.* The fashionable velvet scabbard. **27** *wooden dagger.* Traditionally carried by the Vice in the interludes: cf. *Epig.* 115. 5; 27. **33–4** Juno and Iris appear in *Chlor.* 248 ff. **34** *shrouds.* fly-ropes. **35–9** Cf. *Chlor.* 306–15, where Fame ascends to the heavens: '*Poesy*: We that sustain thee, learnèd Poesy, | *History*: And I, her sister, severe History, | *Architecture*: With Architecture, who will raise thee high, | *Sculpture*: And Sculpture, that can keep thee from to die, | *Chorus*: All help to lift thee to eternity.' Jonson implies that Jones's own fame is being hoisted aloft. **36** *sided.* flanked. **41** *sense.* Cf. the key definition in *Disc.* 1903–4. **42** *spectacles of state.* (i) Spectacular entertainments of the state; (ii) (ironically) models or patterns of behaviour of the state (*OED*, 5 b). **43** *hieroglyphics.* The word was used in relation to symbolic figures in the court masque: see *Blackness*, 269, and Daniel's Address to Lucy, Countess of Bedford (l. 33), prefixed to *The Vision of Twelve Goddesses*. But Jonson also implies that the shallowness of the masque illusion is a hieroglyph or symbol of the shallowness of the court itself. See Don Cameron Allen, *PQ* xviii (1939), 290–300. **46** *mysteries.* Secrets; playing on the technical, theological, and political senses of the word (for the latter, see *OED*, 'mystery', *sb.*¹ 5c, and cf. the French *mystère d'état*). The colours of masque costumes frequently had symbolic significance: in ll. 54–5 Jonson suggests that Jones had carried such symbolism to the point of obscurity. **50** *soul.* A bitter reversal of the distinction made in *Hym.* 1–10, where the spectacular side of the masque is compared to the human body, which must perish, while the words of the masque are compared to the soul, which will endure. Cf. *Blackness*, 8. **56** *design.* Cf. *Disc.* 1148; and see D. J. Gordon (pp. 169–70) and Lucy Gent, *Picture and Poetry 1560–1620* (Leamington Spa, 1981), pp. 8–9, for contemporary usages of the term. Jonson hints at the theological sense of the word, as in l. 96; hence the contrast with 'destruction', l. 57.

60 Σκευοποίος. Maker of masks and other stage properties. Perhaps recalling Aristotle, *Poetics*. vi. 28. **63** *music-master*. According to Cicero, *De Oratore*, iii. 174, the same artist was originally responsible for both music and poetry. There is no record of Jones's attempting to write music for a masque. *fabler*. On the importance of the fable as 'the form and soul of any poetical work or poem', see *Disc.* 2376–7. Jonson had in fact praised a scene which Jones had written for *Queens*, 680–709. In 1632 Jones wrote the fable for *Tempe Restored*. **64–5** *Dominus Do- | All*. Jones had to do almost everything in the way of preparing the masques for performance, including direction. In-and-In Medlay—a character modelled on Jones—also wants to 'do all' in *T. of T.* v. ii. 35–40; v. vii. 13–14. **66** *whistle*. The one who gives the orders; but the word is contemptuous ('mouthpiece'). **67** *warm on his feet*. Doing nicely: cf. *Volp.* II. ii. 39–40 n. **68** *Swim without cork*. Get on without the assistance of others; cf. the proverbial 'swim without bladders'. *Queen Anne*. Referring not merely to her central role in many of the court masques, but to her architectural commissions for Jones: e.g. the Queen's House at Greenwich, commissioned in 1617 (two years before her death) but not finally completed until 1635. Her brother, the King of Denmark, was possibly Jones's earliest patron. **69** *fat . . . lean*. The figure of Envy is traditionally represented as lean: cf. Macilente, 'a lean mongrel', in *EMO* I. ii. 212, and Marlowe's Envy in *Dr Faustus* (B), II. ii. 699. **72** *lantern-lurry*. An effect of moving lights ('lurry' = a confused mass), e.g. Jones's region of fire in *Hym.* 223–4, which 'with a continual motion was seen to whirl circularly', and for which Jonson once professed admiration (*Hym.* 668–9). W. A. Armstrong notices that Jonson's characteristic attack is 'against scenes, lights and machines which *moved* before the spectators' eyes; i.e. against those most likely to distract attention from the spoken word', *Jacobean Theatre*, Stratford-upon-Avon Studies, 1, ed. J. R. Brown and B. Harris (London, 1960), p. 51. *fuliginous*. Sooty; but the word was also used of thick noxious vapours that trouble the head: hence it refers to Jones himself, as well as his invention. **76** *puppet-play*. Cf.*Epig.* 97. 1–2 n.; 129. 16; and the indirect satire on Jones in the puppet-plays of *BF* and *T. of T.* **78** *toy*. (i) Amusement, entertainment (*OED*, 2); (ii) foolish or idle fancy, whim, caprice (*OED*, †4). Cf. Bacon, 'Of Masques and Triumphs': 'These things are but toys, to come amongst such serious observations.' **79** *firk*. Move briskly. **79 ff.** In 1630 Jones and other JPs for Westminster carried out inspections of houses suspected of being infected by the plague: see J. A. Gotch, *Inigo Jones* (London, 1928), pp. 147–8. Jonson likens this to the officiousness of Justice Overdo in *BF*: see esp. II. i. for the cellar-diving and quest for enormities (alluding in turn to the activities of a former Lord Mayor of London, Sir Thomas Hayes). **83** *Under the moral*. i.e. as one commissioned by, or representing, the king; see *OED*, 'moral', *sb.* †3, and examples, and cf. *BF* II. i. 1. **84** *stroked up*. Playing on a secondary sense, 'flattered'. *survey*. Referring primarily to Jones's position as Surveyor of the King's Works, but implying also that he is setting himself up as a surveyor of state morality. **89** *dead standards*. Literally, faded posts, properties in the masques; metaphorically, dead moral standards. **90** Jones had re-used material from *Nept. Tr.* in *Fort. Is.* in 1625, but so too had Jonson himself. *Imagery* refers primarily to masquing properties but has religious overtones ('Thou shalt not make unto thee any graven image', Exod. 20: 4) which are developed in the lines which follow.

92 *Almighty architecture.* God is sometimes referred to as 'the great architect' (e.g. by Raphael in *Paradise Lost*, vii. 72); now architecture itself has been deified. 94 *cinnabar.* crimson. 97 *On a wall.* i.e. graffiti; cf. *Alch.* v. v. 41–2. 101 *the Feasting Room.* The Banqueting House at Whitehall, burnt down on 12 January 1618, was rebuilt on grander lines by Jones (completed 31 March 1622). The bottom of the vault of the new building was paved with Purbeck stone, from Dorset. 104 *remonstrance.* In June 1631 Jones—acting on the authority of the Commissioners for Pious Uses—stopped the parishioners of St Gregory's Church from digging a vault which he judged to be a threat to the foundations of St Paul's. The parishioners petitioned the Privy Council to overthrow this order; the Privy Council turned down the petition in July, but the affair was to drag on for many years. See Gotch, *Inigo Jones*, ch. xi. The word here also refers to the poem as a whole: the 'expostulation'. *honest man.* Cf. *Epig.* 115, title; *Disc.* 86–90.

35. For background, see *UV* 34 n. 1–2 In 1626 Philip IV of Spain had rewarded his architect Giovanni Baptista Crescentzi for his work on the Escorial by creating him Marquis della Torre. 6 *honest.* *UV* 34. 104 and n. 8 *a cave for wine.* See *Und.* 48 and n. 9–10 *a shop . . . a-top.* H & S suspect the allusion is to Jones's plans for the new Whitehall; W. A. Armstrong (*Jacobean Theatre*, ed. Brown and Harris, p. 51) suggests it may rather be to Jones's *machina ductilis* in *Oberon* (esp. 139–40, 420–2). Both identifications have their difficulties. But an extant drawing by Jones in the library of Worcester College, Oxford (i. 53 B, HT 80; drawn to my attention by John Harris and Stephen Orgel) shows a four-storey arcade of shops which appears closely to match Jonson's description. Mr Harris dates the drawing pre-1630. 11 *quadrivial.* Leading in four directions. 12 *Thumb.* Tom Thumb, who appeared in an antimasque in *Fort. Is.* 423. *pygmy.* Jeffrey Hudson, Henrietta Maria's dwarf; he appeared, with other dwarfs, in a masque concerned with Gargantua (who is perhaps the 'canvas giant' of l. 15) performed at Somerset House on 24 November 1626 (Orgel and Strong, *Inigo Jones*, i. 389–92); and—again, with other dwarfs—in *Chlor.* in 1631. 15 *channel.* Gutter, artificial watercourse. 16 *Dowgate torrent.* Which flowed after heavy rain down the steep Dowgate Hill into the Thames west of London Bridge. Jonson is satirizing Jones's seascapes (in *Blackness*, *Fort. Is.*, and *Love's Tr.*, etc.); for Jones's wave-machines, see A. Nicoll, *Stuart Masques and the Renaissance Stage* (London, etc., 1937), pp. 59–60. 17 *fleet.* Such as that in *Fort Is.* 619 ff. (see Nicoll, *Stuart Masques*, p. 79), and perhaps in *Love's Tr.* (see Orgel and Strong, *Inigo Jones*, i. 407–8). 20 *Pancridge earl.* One of the mock-titles used amongst the Finsbury archers, who had an annual procession. 23 *pitch.* Plan, lay out. 24 *New Ditch.* Not an (unknown) city ditch, as H & S and others have suspected, but New River, Sir Hugh Myddelton's forty-mile-long artificial river which supplied water to Londoners; it was opened in 1613 (see *Epig.* 133. 193–4 n.). Jonson is referring to Jones's similar interest in artificial waterways. (For the name, cf. the variants Fleet Ditch/Fleet River.)

36. From Martial, XII. lxi: 'You are afraid, Ligurra, I should write verses on you, and some short and lively poem, and you long to be thought a man that justifies such fear. But your fear is vain, and your longing is vain. Libyan lions rage against bulls; they are not hostile to butterflies. Look out, I advise you, if you are anxious

to be read of, for some dark cellar's sottish poet, one who with coarse charcoal or crumbling chalk scrawls poems which people read in the jakes. Your brow is not one to be marked by my brand.' For the background, see *UV* 34 n. **12** *design.* Cf. *UV* 34. 56 and n. **13** *draught.* privy. *strand.* Sewer, gutter.

37. *Detractor.* I.E. (probably John Eliot), who had written these lines on *Und.* 77 (addressed to Lord Weston): 'Your verses were commended, as 'tis true | That they were very good—I mean to you: | For they returned you, Ben, I have been told, | The seld seen sum of forty pound in gold. | These verses then being rightly understood, | His Lordship, not Ben Jonson, made them good.' Jonson's poem dates from 1631 or 1632. **9** *blatant beast.* From Spenser, *The Faerie Queene*, v. xii. 37, 41, etc. **19** *the pest.* Dogs were popularly thought to be carriers of the plague. **20** *dog-days.* In July or August, when dogs were thought liable to run mad; so called from the heliacal rising of the dog-star.

38. **1** *servant.* Cf. *BF* Ind. 8. R. J. Kaufmann, *Richard Brome, Caroline Dramatist* (New York and London, 1961), pp. 20 ff., thinks the term implies that 'Brome's initial status was a menial one'. **10** *'prenticeship.* Fleay (i. 37) assumes that Jonson refers to a formal seven-year apprenticeship, 1623–9: this is a guess. **12–16** Horace, *Epist.* II. i. 114–17 'A man who knows nothing of a ship fears to handle one; no one dares to give southernwood to the sick unless he has learnt its use; doctors undertake a doctor's work, carpenters handle carpenters' tools, but, skilled or unskilled, we scribble poetry, all alike.' **15** *Bilbo smith.* In Bilbao, Spain, where fine blades were made. **18** Persius, *Sat.* v. 102–4.

39. Milton's friend Alexander Gill the younger was son of the headmaster of St Paul's School, whom Jonson had attacked in 1623 in *Time Vind.* (171–88). In 1628 the Star Chamber found the son guilty of speaking disrespectfully of James, Charles, and the recently murdered Duke of Buckingham: he was degraded from the ministry and from his degree in divinity, fined £2,000, and condemned to lose both his ears: after interventions on his behalf, the penalties were remitted. Jonson himself had at one time been suspected of writing libellous verses about Buckingham's murder; D. L. Clark suggests that he 'had to detest Gil[l] very hard indeed to avoid being blamed along with him': *John Milton at St. Paul's School* (New York, 1948), p. 96. But Jonson had sufficient cause to attack Gill for his satirical lines on *ML* in 1631 (printed by H & S, xi. 346–8), inviting Jonson to abandon the theatre and resume his old trade of bricklaying. **7** *Denis.* Tyrant: after Dionysius the younger, tyrant of Syracuse, who kept a school after being deposed (H & S). Gill had been formally dismissed from his post as usher at St Paul's School in 1628, but evidently lingered on. **11** *blatant.* Noisy, clamorous; cf. *UV* 37. 9 and n. **12** *ballads of thy father.* Satirical songs about him: see Clark, op. cit., pp. 79–83, 91–3.

40. Alice Sutcliffe (née Woodhouse) was the wife of John Sutcliffe of Yorkshire, Esquire of King James and later Groom of the Privy Chamber of King Charles. Jonson may not have known her personally. The first edition of her work appeared probably in 1633; the dedicatory verses of Jonson and others were prefixed to the second edition of 1634: see Ruth Hughey, *RES* x (1934), 156–64.

Jonson's poem alludes to the headings in the book's table of contents. **23** *Celia.* i.e. heavenly; Latin *caelum*, sky, heaven.

41. The author of *The Female Glory* was Anthony Stafford (1587–?1645), who wrote a number of books on religious and philosophical subjects. Jonson's authorship of these verses (signed B.I.) is not certain. It is usually assumed that Jonson wrote them during his Catholic period, i.e. between 1598 and 1610, but the evidence is not particularly convincing. (Stafford himself was not a Catholic, though he was attacked for his apparent Catholic leanings.) The 'garland' is the poem itself (cf. *Und.* 70. 77), which in turn may be, as Newdigate suggests, 'the interpretation of some emblematic picture of the Holy Child and His Mother, crowned with a garland'. Paul Cubeta suggests the emblem may be a pendant on the Bridgettine rosary: *JEGP* lxii (1963), 98–101. **3–4** Cubeta (p. 99) takes the myrtle as the symbol of joyous love, the almond, the rose (and the lily) as symbols of hope, the ivy as the symbol of friendship in adversity, and the eglantine of poetry. **7** *implexèd.* entwined. **9–10** Cf. Spenser, *The Faerie Queene*, I. vii. 32: 'Like to an almond tree ymounted high | On top of green Selinus all alone'; echoed by Marlowe, *Tamburlaine the Great*, pt. II, IV. iii. 119–21. Selinus is in Sicily. **14** *eye.* Choicest; cf. *Und.* 65. 8. **17** *intersert.* Inserted, interpolated. **20** *flat.* Plain, absolute. **24** *Moses' bush.* Exod. 3: 2 ff. **38–40** These attributes of the Virgin, as Newdigate points out, are to be found in the Litany of Loretto, translated into English in 1620 as *The Paradise of Delights.* **47** *in thy reflex.* In thy reflection; i.e. vicariously. **52** *two-fold point of noon.* When the two hands of the clock point upright.

42. Rutter was one of the 'sons of Ben'; he later wrote an elegy on Jonson's death (H & S, xi. 459–60). Jonson's verdict on Rutter's play is examined by Freda L. Townsend, *MP* xliv (1947), 238–47. **6** *How well I loved truth.* Perhaps referring to *BF* Ind. 127–32; cf. *Sej.* 'To the Readers', 18–19. **7** *deep-grounded, understanding.* Cf. the word-play of *BF* Ind. 49–50 ('the understanding gentlemen o' the ground') and 76 ('the grounded judgements and understandings'). **14–15** For the metaphor, see *UV* 26. 49 n. **17** *the whole piece.* Cf. *Epig.* 56. 14. **19** *censure.* judgement. **19 ff.** Cf. the 'rhyming club' of *UV* 30. 8 and the 'play club' of *Songs*, 35. 26; its members cannot now be identified. **25** *pyx.* The box at the Royal Mint in which specimen gold and silver coins are formally tested for purity and weight. **26** *say-master.* assay-master. **27** *fineness.* Comparative freedom from alloy. **28** *wit's new mint.* Cf. *Love's Labour's Lost*, I. i. 164.

43. Captain Robert Dover (?1575–1641) was the reviver (*c.*1612) of the Cotswold Olympic Games, which took place annually at Whitsun on Dover's Hill, near Chipping Campden and the Vale of Evesham in Gloucestershire. The Games were discontinued during the Commonwealth but resumed at the Restoration, and were an annual event until the middle of the nineteenth century. Over thirty writers contributed to *Annalia Dubrensia*, including Drayton, Randolph, Davenant, and T. Heywood; some of the verses had been written considerably earlier. See Christopher Whitfield's edition, *Robert Dover and the Cotswold Games* (London and New York, 1962). **1** *drop [her] vies.* i.e. refrain from comparing; a 'vie' is a challenge or sum ventured in card-playing. **9** *hypocrites.*

Puritans. Dover's Games, performed with royal licence, 'were a protest against the rising puritanical prejudices' (*DNB*; cf. Whitfield, op. cit., pp. 15 ff.). James had defended holiday games against Puritan attack in his *Declaration of Sports* in 1617/18.

44. An untitled fragment from a lost entertainment: H & S suggest that it belongs to the early years of Charles's reign. Yet ll. 7–8 refer to the fact that Charles's Anniversary Day fell on 27 March, the beginning of the new year, and also of spring; it may or may not have been the beginning of Charles's reign. Cf. Dryden, 'To his Sacred Majesty', ll. 26–32. 1 Cf. *For.* 2. 40.

45. From a lost entertainment, which apparently took place near the Peak in Derbyshire. The title is Gifford's. 1 *wonders of the Peak.* Enumerated in *Ent. Welb.* 92 ff. **3–4** *break | My mind.* Then a well-established phrase (see *OED*, 22); 'as some would say' probably hints not at its newness but its possible ambiguity (see *OED*, 12 †b). **13–15** Cf. the saying ' ''Tis merry in hall when beards wag all', *T. of T.* v. ix. 12; *Christmas*, 10–11; etc. **15** *Morts.* Girls of easy virtue; gypsy girls. *merkins.* Artificial pubic hair; female private parts. **26** *heads.* Gives horns to, cuckolds. **27** *standard.* Standard-bearer. **30** *circle.* For the sexual sense, cf. *Romeo and Juliet*, II. i. 24. **34** *For the breeches.* i.e. who rules the household: cf. Tilley, B645. **39** *Pem Waker's.* Cf. the alewife Pem in *Ent. Welb.* 122 ff.

46. Referring to Jonson's journey on foot to Scotland, 1618–19. The author of the original lines may be Sir William Craven (?1548–1618), Yorkshireman, philanthropist, and Lord Mayor of London 1610–11. Jonson may have wagered on his ability to walk to Scotland and back: see H & S, i. 76, and, on this general practice, *Epig.* 133. 28, 35, 36, and notes. Do these verses commemorate a wager with Craven himself (who was to die before Jonson's return)? **7** *gate.* Going, journey.

47. H & S date this poem shortly after 1617, when Buckingham obtained his earldom. The second version, perhaps delivered at Lady Bedford's table, is dated in the margin '1613': but Villiers did not come to court until the following year. 1 *Our . . . bless.* One manuscript: 'Our royal king and queen, God bless.' 2 *Palsgrave . . . Lady Bess.* Frederick V, Elector Palatine, married Princess Elizabeth in 1613. **5** *the Council of Estate.* i.e. the Council of State. One manuscript: 'God bless Pembroke, and the state.' **6** *Buckingham the fortunate.* George Villiers (1592–1628), court favourite: Viscount Villiers 1616; Earl of Buckingham 1617; Marquis of Buckingham 1618; Duke of Buckingham 1623; murdered 1628. **8** *Ralph.* 'The king was mighty inquisitive to know who this Ralph was: Ben told him 'twas the drawer of the Swan tavern by Charing Cross, who drew him good Canary. For this drollery his majesty gave him an hundred pounds': John Aubrey, *Brief Lives*, ed. O. L. Dick (London, 1949), p. 179.

Another Version 7 *Bedford.* 'Countess of Bedford' (manuscript marginal note). **8** *Ralph.* 'The Countess's man who won the race' (manuscript marginal note); H & S compare 'light-foot Ralph' of *S. of N.* II. iii. 11.

48. Established as Jonson's on internal evidence by W. D. Briggs, *The Athenaeum*, 13 June 1914. **2** *face.* Condition, appearance. **16–17** He dies with a bad smell that is perceptible to everyone, and to the scorn of those who saw (etc.). Cf. *Epig.* 59. **19–21** Cf. *Poet.* Apol. Dial. 209–11. **22** *Thy.* This edition; conj. emendation of 'Their'. **24–7** Cf. *Poet.* Apol. Dial. 233–6. **32–6** Ibid. 228–32. **34** *ground.* A play on words: earth, melody. **38** *crystal shield.* Minerva's mirror-shield, which she lent to Perseus to enable him to kill the gorgon. **39** *charm the round.* i.e. those who fall within the circle of Minerva's power; playing on the musical and dancing senses of the words (cf. *Macbeth*, IV. i. 129–30: 'I'll charm the air to give a sound, | While you perform your antic round').

49. **12–26** Repeated from *Und.* 37. 19–33: see notes there.

50. A translation of the eunuch Photinus' speech to Ptolemy, urging the murder of Pompey: Lucan's *Pharsalia*, viii. 484–95. Cf. 'Shame, no statist', Herrick, p. 182, and Massinger's *The False One*, i. i. 302–12. **9–16** Cf. *Sej.* II. 180–7. **19–20** Cf. *Sej.* II. 178–9.

SONGS AND POEMS

On the music of Jonson's songs, see W. McC. Evans, *Ben Jonson and Elizabethan Music* (New York, 1965); H & S, xi. 605–9; E. and L. Pissarro, *Songs by Ben Jonson* (London, 1906); Mary Chan, *Music in the Theatre of Ben Jonson* (Oxford, 1980).

1. For Lucy, Countess of Bedford, see *Epig.* 76 and n. Though it falls outside the category of dramatic lyrics and poetic excerpts that make up this section, this inscription may nevertheless be appropriately placed before the songs from *Cynthia's Revels.*

2. For a musical setting of this song (perhaps that used in the first performance) see Henry Youll's *Canzonets To Three Voices* (1608), no. viii. The song is discussed by W. McC. Evans, pp. 48–51, by M. Chan, pp. 49–54, and by Catherine Ing, *Elizabethan Lyrics* (London, 1951), pp. 118–24; and is remembered by Marianne Moore, *Complete Poems* (New York, 1967), p. 189. **1** *keep . . . tears.* Cf. *Lucrece*, 1127. **4** *division.* '. . . A rapid melodic passage, originally conceived as the dividing of each of a succession of long notes into several short ones . . .' (*OED*, †7).

3. **5** *blacking-men.* Who sold blacking. **6** *Corn-cutters.* chiropodists. *car-men.* Carriers, carters. **7** *marking-stones.* For marking cattle. **8** *marrow-bones.* Used, with cleavers, for 'rough music'. **14** *fadingers.* Those who danced the fading, an Irish dance. **15** *Thomalins.* 'Beggarly itinerants' (H & S). **16** *skinkers.* tapsters. **17** *There goes the hare away!* A proverbial saying: Tilley, H157. **20** *Paritors.* Apparitors, summoning officers of the ecclesiastical courts. **21** *cuttlebungs.* cutpurses. **22** *Hookers.* Thieves, pilferers, who used hooks. *horn-thumbs.* Cutpurses (who used horn thimbles). **23** *cast.* cashiered. **24** *post-knights.* Men who lived by giving false evidence in the courts. **26** *testers.* sixpences. **29** *jags.* Rags, tatters. **30** *muscle-bags.* thighs.

4. This song (like the next) is gently parodic: l. 5 glances at Ford and Dekker's *The Sun's Darling*, II. i. 139–40, and the final 'die' of l. 12 (as subsequent dialogue reveals) was elaborately drawn out in the singing. See A. J. Sabol in *NQ* NS v (1958), 384, and *RN* xiii (1960), 222, and Mary Chan, *SR* xviii (1971), 134–69, and *Music in the Theatre of Ben Jonson*, pp. 57–61.

5.   The song is probably an ironical imitation of Dorus's song on Pamela's glove in Sidney's *The Countess of Pembroke's Arcadia*, Bk. III; see his *Poems*, ed. W. A. Ringler (Oxford, 1962), p. 70. **10–11** Cf. Cupid's confusion in *Und.* 2. v. 10 ff.

6.   Cynthia (Diana), goddess of the moon, of chastity, and of hunting; the name, and hence the song itself, also refer to Queen Elizabeth. **5** *Hesperus*. The name given to Venus when it appears after sunset. **7** *envious*. Cf. *Und.* 65. 9. **17** *day of night*. Earl Miner (*The Cavalier Mode: From Jonson to Cotton* (Princeton, 1971), pp. 197–8) compares Isa. 9: 2.

7.   On the original setting, see M. Chan, *Music in the Theatre of Ben Jonson*, pp. 64–7; for Henry Lawes's later setting, see W. McC. Evans, op. cit., p. 9. From Martial, 1. lvii: 'Do you ask, Flaccus, what sort of girl I like or dislike? I dislike one too yielding, and one too coy. That middle type between the two I approve: I like not that which racks me, nor that which cloys.' **19** *delicates*. delights.

8.   Jonson quoted these lines to Drummond, *Conv. Dr.* 70. **2** *Lyaeus*. Bacchus.

9.   **9** *Cypris*. Venus.

10.   **12** *division*. See *Songs*, 2. 4 n. **13** *feast of sense*. Cf. Chapman's poem, *Ovid's Banquet of Sense* (1595); ll. 15–20 reverse the Ficinian hierarchy of the senses, which begins with the most physical sense, touch, and proceeds to the most spiritual, sight. See J. F. Kermode, *BJRL* xliv (1961), 68–99.

11.   **5** *apes . . . scarlet*. Cf. *Volp.* 1. ii. 111–13.

12.   Much of Jonson's fairy-lore may be paralleled in Corbett's 'The Fairies' Farewell', *Poems*, ed. Bennett and Trevor-Roper, pp. 49–52, and in Herrick's 'The Fairies', p. 201. **10–11** *feast her. . . tester*. On the rhyme, see *Songs*, 19. 1–2 n. A tester is sixpence. **20** *franklins'*. Landowners not of noble birth. **22** *St Anne's night*. i.e. St Agnes' eve, 20 January: Keats's poem remembers the same tradition. H & S suggest that the form 'Anne's' here may have been by way of compliment to Queen Anne, in whose honour the entertainment was given. ('Agnes' was then pronounced 'an-yas'.) **25** *empty*. i.e. fasting; but the primary sense, 'worthless', is also present. **28** *Lady Summer*. 'For she was expected there on Midsummer Day at night, but came not till the day following' (Jonson's note). **38** *cock-shut light*. twilight.

13.   **12** *follow . . . flee*. Cf. *For.* 7 and n.

15.   For Ferrabosco's setting, see Chan, pp. 159–63. **6** *elder. For.* 10. 19 and n.

16.   For Ferrabosco's setting, see Chan, pp. 178–82. **2** *no soul*. 'There hath been such a profane paradox published' (Jonson's note); cf. Donne's verse letter 'To the Countess of Huntington', *Satires*, p. 85. **6** *world's soul*. 'The Platonics'

opinion. See also Mac[robius], lib. I. [6. 43] and II. [2. 1 and 19], *Som[nium]
Scip[ionis]*' (Jonson's note). Cf. *Volp.* I. i. 3.

17.   On the marriage of John Ramsey, Viscount Haddington, and Elizabeth
Radcliffe, 9 February 1608. On the music, see Chan, pp. 193–5. **9** *perfection. Und.*
75. 28 and n. **11** *Hesperus. Songs* 6. 5 n. **25** *behind.* Still to come. **26** *kind.* nature.
50 *mother.* 'A Wife or matron, which is a name of more dignity than virgin': Jonson's
note, referring to Daniel Heinsius, *In Nuptias Othonis Heurnii,* 'Tomorrow you
will return like your mother'.

18.   **2** *cat-o'-mountain.* Leopard or wild cat. **6** *spindle.* 'All this is but a periphrasis
of the night in their charm, and their applying themselves to it with their
instruments, whereof the spindle in antiquity was the chief, and . . . of special act
to the troubling of the moon . . .' (Jonson's note). **9** *ditch.* 'This rite also of making
a ditch with their nails is frequent with our witches . . .' (Jonson's note).
14 *Martin.* 'Their little Martin is he that calls them to their conventicles, which is
done in a human voice; but coming forth, they find him in the shape of a great
buck-goat, upon whom they ride to their meetings . . .' (Jonson's note).

19.   Modelled on a poem in the *Anthologia Latina,* and imitated by Herrick,
'Delight in Disorder', p. 28. There are two extant seventeenth-century settings of
the song, one by John Playford; both seem to be later than the first performance of
The Silent Woman. **1–2** *dressed . . . feast.* Contemporary pronunciation made the
rhyme possible. **10** *sweet neglect.* Cf. *Disc.* 2285–7.

20.   For Edmund Nelham's later setting, see Chan, pp. 238–9.

23.   **6** *greater powers.* The ladies in the audience (cf. *brighter planets,* l. 8), who will
join in the dancing.

24.   **8** *true.* Proverbial: Tilley, D591; cf. Horace, *Sat.* I. x. 33.

25.   Sung to the tune of Packington's Pound: see William Chappell, *Old English
Popular Music,* revised H. Ellis Wooldridge (London and New York, 1893), i.
259. During the course of the song, Bartholomew Cokes (a rapt listener) is
robbed of his purse. **9** *for and.* And moreover. **22** *known well.* The incident is now
unknown. **26–8** Sir Thomas More, with the help of a professional cutpurse, had
played this trick on a judge who had rebuked others for their simplicity in allowing
themselves to be robbed. **38** *At court.* The offence was committed by John
Selman, executed 7 January 1612. **42** *nation.* tribe.

26.   **4** *old.* Cf. *Disc.* 126–30, *For.* 4. 14.

27.   Stephen Dedalus murmurs these lines by the Liffey in Joyce's *A Portrait of
the Artist as a Young Man.* The musical setting of the song is ascribed to Nicholas
Lanier; see J. P. Cutts, *NQ* NS iii (1956), 64; McD. Emslie, *NQ* cxcviii (1953),
466; Chan, pp. 276–7. **2** *Tithon.* Tithonus, Aurora's husband, to whom Aurora
had granted eternal life, but not eternal youth and vigour.

28.   On Comus ('the god of cheer, or the belly') and on this song, see Stephen

Orgel, *The Jonsonian Masque* (Cambridge, Mass., 1965), pp. 152–9. **3** *Prime master of arts*. Persius, Prol. *Sat.* 8–11. **5** *hopper*. Funnel for grain mill. **6** *hutch*. bin. *bolter*. Cloth for sifting. **7** *bavin*. Brushwood bundle used to light fires, especially for bakers' ovens. *mawkin*. A mop for cleaning bakers' ovens. *peel*. Baker's shovel. **8** *the dog and the wheel*. To operate the spit. **10** *gimlet and vice*. To tap the cask. **11** *hippocras bag*. Conical strainer for wine. **12** *cries swag*. Proclaims himself a pot-belly. **14** *weezle*. Weasand, windpipe. **19** *sod*. boiled. **22** *pudding . . . laced*. A double play on words: for a 'pudding' is also, in nautical terminology, a thick rope or tow binding; and 'laced' means both 'strapped up' and 'fortified' (of food or drink). **24** *break'st forth*. With a scatological *double entendre*.

29. **7–8** Hercules in early manhood is said to have met two women, Virtue and Vice (alias Happiness); Vice showed him an easy road to travel, Virtue a difficult one: Hercules chose the latter. See Xenophon, *Memorabilia*, II. i. 21–34. **10** *labyrinth*. Daedalus had constructed a labyrinth in Crete. **13** *numerous*. rhythmical.

30. *Jackman*. A learned beggar. A musical setting for this song is attributed to Robert Johnson: Chan, pp. 284–5. **2** *Devil's Arse*. A cavern near Castleton; see *Und.* 43. 202. **16** *cut your laces*. The standard way of reviving fainting ladies. **23** *Burley*. Burley-on-the-Hill, the Marquis of Buckingham's estate.

31. *Patrico*. A beggars' priest. **5** *firedrake*. Meteor, will-o'-the-wisp, or fiery dragon.

32. **6** *common*. Promiscuous; cf. Dol Common in *Alch*. **7** *smock rampant*. Shrew; the same phrase is used of Dol Common, *Alch.* V. iv. 126. **15** *without a file*. i.e. rough. **18** *cuckoo*. Cf. Tilley, A309: 'In April the cuckoo can sing her song by rote; in June, out of tune, she cannot sing a note.' **19** *Lothbury*. Street in London where candlesticks were made: a noisy trade. **20** *Banbury*. A Puritan centre. **30** *Bears' College*. Paris Garden, on the Bankside, where bear-baiting was held: the 'students' are the bears. Cf. *Epig.* 133. 117. **32** *clyster-pipe*. See *Epig.* 50. 2 n. James's *Counterblast To Tobacco* was published in 1604. Tobacco, pig, and ling were his special aversions: hence the benedictions in this and the following stanza. **49** *St Anthony's old fire*. erysipelas. **52** *grutching*. complaint. **57** *fall*. James had twice fallen while riding.

33. For the music, see Chan, pp. 300–1. **7** *Pallas' and Arachne's arts*. Of weaving.

34. Discussed by Barbara Everett, *Crit. Q.* i (1959), 238–44. **6** *skein of silk*. Disc. 2016.

35. Jonson's ode on the failure of *The New Inn* in 1629 provoked a number of immediate replies (see H & S, xi. 333–40) and subsequent imitations, e.g. Rochester's 'Leave this gawdy, gilded stage' (see J. Treglown, *RES* xxiv (1973), 43). On Jonson's hostility to the stage, see Jonas Barish in *A Celebration of Ben Jonson*, ed. W. Blissett *et al.* (Toronto, 1973), pp. 27–53. **5** *Indicting and arraigning*. Cf. *BF* Ind. 105. **7** *fastidious*. Proud, scornful. **22** *Pericles*: printed in 1609; additionally 'mouldy', no doubt, because of its use of older romance elements.

25 *common tub.* Left-overs from city and court feasts were collected in a tub for the poor. **26** *play club.* Cf. *UV* 30. 8; 42. 19 ff. **27** *There sweepings.* Replacing an earlier reading, 'Brome's sweepings': i.e. Richard Brome's. **30** *alms-basket of wit.* Cf. *Love's Labour's Lost,* v. i. 35–6, 'the alms-basket of words'. **33** *orts.* scraps. *stage-clothes.* Cf. Fitzdottrell's theatre-going finery in *D. is A.*; and *Und.* 15. 108–10. **35** *stagers.* stage-players. *stage-wrights. OED*'s only example: probably a coinage; cf. 'playwright' in *Epig.* 49. **40** *gamesters.* players. **42** *Alcaic.* After Alcaeus of Lesbos (seventh–sixth century BC), imitated by Horace; Alcaic metre is named after him. **45** *nerves.* Sinews; referring to Jonson's paralytic stroke. **58** *hit the stars.* Horace, *Odes,* I. i. 35–6. **60** *wain.* Charles's Wain, the Great Bear.

36.   For Nicholas Lanier's and John Wilson's settings, see Chan, pp. 358–65. On the association of the figures of Cupid and Death, see E. Panofsky, *Studies in Iconology* (New York, etc., 1972), pp. 124–5, and B. A. Harris's introduction to Shirley's *Cupid and Death* in *A Book of Masques* (Cambridge, 1967), pp. 373–7; and cf. 'To Cupid', Herrick, p. 333. **5–6** Cf. Donne, 'The Paradox', 7–8, *Elegies,* p. 38.

Martial. 'We may enjoy now full draughts of Helicon': XII. vi. 2, on Nerva's becoming emperor, AD 96. **6** *realm.* Pronounced 'ream': a true rhyme. **20** *Themis.* Wife of Jupiter, and mother of *Dice, Eunomia,* and *Irene* (ll. 24, 27), who represented justice, order, and peace, respectively. The comments on Irene refer to James's policy of peace. **21** *chain. For.* 11. 47 and n. **40** *red.* i.e. with excitement. **47** *four short days.* James had progressed through the streets of London on 15 March. **53** *this town.* Westminster; London is *her great sister,* l. 55. **57–68** Jonson borrows details from Pliny's *Panegyricus,* xxii, and that of Claudian, 543–9. **102** *bury churches.* Jonson was at this stage a Catholic. **115–20** *Disc.* 1199–1200. **125** *example . . . sway. Epig.* 35. 2 and n. **143–7** Borrowed from Pliny, *Panegyricus,* xix. **161–2** Martial, XII. vi. 5–6; cf. *Und.* 72. 18. **163** See *Epig.* 4. 3 n.

The *Leges Conviviales* are a set of rules for tavern behaviour drawn up by Jonson for the benefit of the intimate circle of friends over which he presided in the Apollo Room of the Devil and St Dunstan Tavern, near Temple Bar. They were engraved in gold letters on a marble tablet over the mantelpiece. See Percy Simpson's full account in *MLR* xxiv (1939), 367–73 (largely repeated in H & S, xi. 294–300). John Buxton (*MLR* xlviii (1953), 52–4) has shown that John Chamberlain's statement in 1624 that the Apollo Room was 'lately built' is unreliable; it is therefore probable that Drayton's ode of 1619, 'The Sacrifice To Apollo', *Works,* ed. J. W. Hebel (Oxford, 1961), ii. 357–8, derives from the *Leges Conviviales,* rather than the other way about. The *Leges* owe something to Horace, *Epist.* I. v, and Martial, x. xlviii.

Leges Convivales   *Rule* I *umbra.* 'The Roman term for a guest not invited by the host, but brought by a guest whom he had invited' (Simpson, p. 369, comparing Horace, *Epist.* I. v. 28). **5** Cf. Horace, ibid., 23. **17, 24** Cf. Martial, x. xlviii. 21, 24; Jonson, *Epig.* 101. 39–41. **18** Cf. *Epig.* 101. 24. **22** Cf. Horace, *Odes*, I. xviii. 7–9; I. xxvii. 1–4. The Lapithae were a tribe of mountaineers in Thessaly; they disturbed the wedding of their king by fighting with the Centaurs (cf. *SW* IV. v. 45–7). **23** Cf. Horace, *Epist.* I. v. 24–5. *Focus perennis esto.* Martial, x. xlvii. 4 (trs. Jonson, *Und.* 90).

[Brome's translation] Alexander Brome (1620–66), poet and attorney. **16** *chirping.* cheering.

[Over the Door] The verses were painted on a panel still preserved in the dining-room of Williams & Glyn's Bank, Ltd., 1 Fleet Street; a bust of Apollo also surmounted the door. See K. A. Esdaile, *E. & S.* xxix (1943), 93–100. **2** *oracle of Apollo.* H & S compare Rabelais's 'Oracle of the bottle', *Pantagruel*, v. 34, and *S. of N.* IV. ii. 8. **3** *pottle.* Two-quart tankard. **4** *tripos.* drinking-bowl. *tower.* i.e. tower-shaped. **6** *Truth itself. In vino veritas.* **8** *Sim.* Simon Wadloe, keeper of the inn; cf. the drinking song, 'Old Sir Simon the King'. *skinkers.* tapsters. **13** *poets' horse.* Pegasus. **15** *Phoebeian.* Of Pheobus Apollo.

DUBIA

The poems in this section fall into two categories: (i) Poems which were printed in the 1640 Folio, or in H & S's *Ungathered Verse*, and which now appear to be probably not by Jonson. (ii) Other poems for which a plausible but inconclusive case for Jonsonian authorship may be made out. Several of the poems printed in H & S's Appendix XVI, 'Poems Ascribed to Jonson' (viii. 424–52), fall into a third category of implausibly or incorrectly attributed miscellaneous pieces, and are not reprinted here.

1. Printed as an elegy, 'The Expostulation', in Donne's *Poems* of 1633, and subsequently in Jonson's 1640 Folio (*Und.* 39 in H & S). These texts vary considerably: see collations in H & S, viii. 194–7; Donne, *Elegies*, pp. 94–6. On the question of authorship, see *Und.* 38 n. **4** *false, because she's fair.* Cf. Tilley, F3. **10–11** Cf. Catullus, *Carm.* lxx. 3–4; Tilley, W698. **19** *break.* Go bankrupt. **19–22** Cf. 'Woman's Constancy', Donne, *Elegies*, pp. 42–3. **27–32** Cf. Ovid, *Tristia*, I. viii. 1–10. **36** *cast.* condemn. **39** ff. Cf. Catullus, *Carm.* cviii; Donne, 'The Curse' and 'The Bracelet', 91–110 (*Elegies*, pp. 40–1, 4). **57–8** Cf. *Und.* 5. 13–16 and n. **59–64** Perhaps recalling Ovid, *Amores*, III. ii. 1–7. **64** *officious.* obliging. **68–70** Cf. Ovid, *Ars Amatoria*, ii. 13–14.

2. Printed in the 1640 Folio (*Und.* 80 in H & S), but attributed to Sidney Godolphin in one manuscript. W. D. Briggs wavers over the attribution to Godolphin (*Anglia*, xxxix (1915), 41–4), which is nevertheless accepted by William Dighton in his edition of Godolphin's *Poems* (Oxford, 1931), pp. 60–1, and by H & S. F. R. Leavis—perhaps unaware of its disputed authorship—finds the poem 'characteristic Jonson', *Revaluation* (London, 1953), pp. 22–4; the verdict is echoed by F. W. Bradbrook ('typical of the Jonsonian lyric'), *From*

Donne to Marvell, ed. Boris Ford (Harmondsworth, 1956), p. 138. The stylistic evidence in fact favours Godolphin: cf. 'Or love me less, or love me more', and 'No more unto my thoughts appear', *Poems*, pp. 8–9, 22–4.

3. Printed in the 1640 Folio (*Und.* 81 in H & S), but attributed to Sir Henry Wotton in two manuscripts and in *Reliquiae Wottonianae* (London, 1651), p. 521, where it is said to have been written on the king's return from his coronation in Scotland (in 1633). H & S consider it to be by Wotton, and quote from a letter of Wotton's of 1628 which parallels the expression in l. 2 of the poem. But Briggs (*Anglia*, xxxix (1915), pp. 213–15) draws attention to other Jonsonian parallels, noted at ll. 18 and 21. **7** *best of crowns*. Cf. *Und.* 76. 2; 79. 7. **18** *example... dread*. See *Epig.* 35. 2 n. **21** *His roses and his lilies*. See *Und.* 65. 3 n.

4. These verses, signed B.I., appeared in the second edition of *The Touchstone of Truth*—a Puritan compilation—in 1624. H & S, with considerable misgiving, print them as *UV* 27. Jonson's authorship seems improbable both on grounds of style (especially the concluding lines) and of Puritan context; 'warrant of the word' (l. 9) was a Puritan catch-phrase which Jonson had ridiculed in *BF* IV. i. 109. **17** *Warre*. The Dedication of the work is signed 'James Warre'.

5. On the birth of the future Charles II, 29 May 1630; cf. *Und.* 65 and n. The poem appears in the 1640 Quarto and Duodecimo, but not in the Folio or Newcastle MS. G. B. Johnston (*Poems*, p. 344), like the present editor, is inclined to accept the poem as Jonson's; Briggs (*Anglia*, xxxviii (1914), 119) and H & S suspend judgement. **1** *the first is dead*. Charles's and Henrietta Maria's first son died on 13 May 1629; see *Und.* 63. **14** *sun*. Cf. the pun of *Und.* 65. 12. **16** *wink*. An eclipse of the sun occurred two days after Charles's birth; cf. *Und.* 65. 9–12. **17–20** G. B. Johnston detects an allusion to the language of alchemy, in which gold (called 'sol') and silver ('luna') were spoken of as father and mother of the elixir or philosopher's stone. **19** *envy*. Cf. *Und.* 65. 9. **21** *a star*. At Charles's birth, the planet Venus was visible in the heavens throughout the day; Herrick (pp. 85–7) and other poets commented upon this phenomenon. **24–5** *On earth... In heaven*. Cf. *Und.* 70. 96. **24–5** *great Charles... little Charles*. Cf. *Und.* 67. 54. **26** *great... good*. A favourite Jonsonian conjunction: see *Epig.* Dedn. 13 n.

6. Ascribed to Jonson in one manuscript. Briggs (*Anglia*, xxxix (1915), 244) is inclined to accept the attribution, H & S to reject it, chiefly because it 'is unlike any work of Jonson's at that date [after the birth of Charles, 29 May 1630], when his powers showed symptoms of decline'. This test does not seem decisive. The identity of the 'rocker' and the nature of her offence are not known. **5** *Though an infant*. Playing on the etymology of the word, 'unable to speak'.

7. The tone and style of assertion seem characteristically Jonsonian; Briggs (like the present editor) thinks Jonson's authorship 'quite probable' (*Anglia*, xxxix (1915), 250). **4** *courtlings*. A favourite word of Jonson's: cf. *Epig.* 52 and 72; *OED* credits him with the first usage, in *CR* v. iv. 33. For 'pied', cf. *UV* 2. 4. *secure*. smug. **5–7** Cf. *Epig.* 11. 5. **10** *faces*. Cf. *Epig.* 11. 4, 'It made me a great face', etc.; *Und.* 70. 23. **14** *surquedry*. pride. **16–17** Cf. *Und.* 84. viii. 19–20 and n.

8.   Printed in John Ashmore's *Certain Selected Odes of Horace, Englished* (1621—
i.e. during Jonson's lifetime), with a note by Ashmore that the translation 'came
unto my hands under the name of Mr. Ben Jonson . . .'. H & S consider the
freedom of the translation uncharacteristic of Jonson; G. B. Johnston (*Poems*,
p. 341) argues that 'it is no more free than several of his adaptations of classical
poems'.

DISCOVERIES

The *Discoveries* were first published several years after Jonson's death in the
1640–1 two-volume Folio edition of his works. They are Jonson's commonplace
book, containing miscellaneous thoughts 'made upon men and matter'. Some of
these thoughts are original, but many are gathered from classical and Renaissance sources. Some of the problems occasioned by the high proportion of
borrowed work in the *Discoveries* are touched on in the Introduction to this
edition. In his 'Execration upon Vulcan' (*Und.* 43. 101), Jonson laments the loss
of what appear to be similar commonplace books—'twice twelve years' stored-up
humanity'—in the fire that destroyed his books and papers in November 1623.
The present collection presumably consists in the main of writings made after
that date, though it is possible that certain papers escaped the fire, or that certain
notes were rewritten from memory. C. J. Sisson, noting the apparently pedagogi-
cal turn of phrase in some sections of the *Discoveries*, has suggested that these
writings may have been notes for lectures which Jonson delivered at Gresham
College, London—where we know he was resident in 1623—while deputizing
for a Professor of Rhetoric: Henry Croke, perhaps, who held that office from
1619 to 1627 (*TLS* 21 September 1951; H & S, xi. 582–5). Sisson's hypothesis
could at best apply only to certain parts of *Discoveries*; others seem improbable
lecture material even for a deputy Professor of Rhetoric, while others again can
be dated later than 1627 (see, for example, ll. 325 ff., which refer to an incident
occurring in 1630, and ll. 2490–503, which draw upon a book published in 1633).
     The side-notes are probably the work of Jonson himself, but we cannot be sure
whether Jonson or (say) his executor Sir Kenelm Digby is responsible for the
overall arrangement of the collection, beginning as it does with a succession of
short, miscellaneous items, and concluding with more extended essays on style
and poetics. Herford and Simpson believed that this arrangement, together with
the wording of the title-page, suggested that Jonson must have hoped to publish
the *Discoveries* in some form or another, but this evidence does not seem
conclusive.
     The notion of *discovery* recurs throughout these writings (see, for example,
ll. 231, 239, 1122, 2143). We may guess, however, that the following passage from
Seneca (*Epist.* xxx. 11) may have made a particular impression upon Jonson, for it
helps in turn to shape a passage of crucial importance to the collection as a whole
(ll. 131 ff.):

> However, the truth will never be discovered if we rest contented with
> discoveries already made [*Numquam autem invenietur si contenti fuerimus
> inventis*]. Besides, he who follows another not only discovers nothing, but is not

even investigating. What then? Shall I not follow in the footsteps of my predecessors? I shall indeed use the old road, but if I find one that makes a shorter cut and is smoother to travel, I shall open the new road. Men who have made these discoveries before us are not our masters, but our guides. Truth lies open for all; it has not yet been monopolized. And there is plenty of it left even for posterity to discover.

[*Motto*] *Tecum* . . . *supellex*. Persius, *Sat.* iv. 52: 'live in your own house, and recognize how poorly it is furnished'.

Silva. 'Silva, or the rough timber (ὕλη) of facts and thoughts, so called from the multiplicity and variety of their contents. For just as we are wont commonly to call a great mass of trees growing indiscriminately a *wood*, so the ancients called those of their books in which varied and diverse materials were randomly crowded together *woods*: timber trees.' From Caspar Gavartius' edition of Statius' *Silvae* (1616); partly translated in Jonson's note 'To the Reader' prefixed to *The Underwood*. See also *For.*, headnote.

1 (margin) *Fortuna.* 'fortune'. **1–13** From Seneca, *To Helvia, On Consolation*, v. 4; *On Providence*, iii. 3; iv. 5–6. Cf. *Und.* 15. 183–4. **11–12** *Yet . . . every man.* Seneca, *To Marcia, On Consolation*, ix. 5; *On Tranquillity of Mind*, xi. 8, quoting Publilius Syrus (a familiar adage). **12–13** *But . . . make it.* Plutarch, *On Tranquillity of Mind*, 475, quoting Menander.

14 (margin) *Casus.* 'Change' (lit. 'fall').

18 (margin) *Consilia.* 'counsel'. **22** (margin) Αὐτοδίδακτος. self-taught. **23** *fool to his master.* Repeated at ll. 2929–32. Proverbial: Tilley, F490.

24 (margin) *Fama.* 'fame'. **28** *he is . . . emergent.* 'He will not easily extricate himself'; a Latinism (Juvenal, *Sat.* iii. 164).

29 (margin) *Negotia.* 'business'. **31–2** *passions . . . rebels.* Cf. *For.* 11. 21; *Volp.* III. iv. 101 ff.

34 (margin) *Amor patriae.* 'Love of country'. **34–6** *There is . . . there.* Euripides, *Phoenissae*, 358–61.

37 (margin) *Ingenia.* 'Innate dispositions.' **37–8** *sooner break.* Quintilian, I. iii. 12. **39** *attempting.* influencing.

40 (margin) *Applausus.* 'praise'. **40–3** *We praise . . . the other.* Velleius Paterculus, *Historia Romana*, ii. 92. **43** *overlaid.* smothered.

44 (margin) *Opinio.* 'opinion'. **46–8** *We labour . . . presseth us.* Seneca, *Epist.* xiii. 4.

51 (margin) *Impostura.* 'imposture'. **56** *gut . . . groin.* Cf. *Epig.* 117 and 118.

57 (margin) *Jactura vitae.* 'The throwing away of life.'

61 (margin) *Hypocrita.* 'A hypocrite.' **61–5** *Puritanus . . . Deo.* 'A Puritan is a heretical hypocrite whom conceit in his own perspicacity has disturbed in the

balance of his mind; so that it seems to him that he, along with a few others, has discovered certain errors in the dogmas of the Church; hence, stirred up by a sacred fury, he fights madly against civil authority, convinced that he is thus showing his obedience to God.' No source has been found for the passage; the Latin may be Jonson's own. Cf. *Epig.* 75, and, on the Puritan hostility to the magistracy, *Alch.* III. ii. 150.

66 (margin) *Mutua auxilia.* 'Mutual aids.' **66–176** Jonson borrows extensively here from the Spanish humanist Juan Luis Vives (1492–1540), friend of Erasmus. **66–74** *Learning . . . faithful.* Vives, *Epistola Nuncupatoria* (*Opera* (Basel, 1555), i. 322–3). **68** *consociation.* Intimate association.

75 (margin) *Cognit[io] universi.* 'The knowledge of all nature.' **75 ff.** Vives, *De Consultatione* (*Opera*, i. 169 ff.).

86 (margin) *Consiliarii . . . sapientia.* 'Joint counsellors: honesty, wisdom.'

91 *honesty.* Cf. *Conv. Dr.* 555–6; *Epig.* 98. 10–12; *Epig.* 115, title; *UV* 34. 104. *mere craft.* Cf. the character Merecraft in *D. is A.* **93** (margin) *Vita recta.* 'A good life.'

95 ff. (margin) *Obsequentia, humanitas, sollicitudo.* 'Complaisance, courtesy, solicitude.' **102** *Dat nox consilium.* 'Night gives counsel'; proverbial: Tilley, N174. **106** *spice.* kind.

110–11 (margin) *Modestia, parrhesia.* 'Modesty, openness.' **111** *empire.* Absolute control. *precept.* command. **116–17** *Absit . . . ego.* The tactful riposte of a harp-player when Alexander's father, Philip (not Alexander himself—the mistake is in Vives), disputed with him about the technique of his instrument: 'Heaven forbid, O king, that you should ever [fall so low as to] know more about these things than I do.' Plutarch, *On the Fortune or the Virtue of Alexander*, ii. 1; *Moralia*, 334.

118–19 (margin) *Perspicuitas, elegantia.* 'Clarity, elegance.' **118–61** Vives, *In Libros de Disciplinis Praefatio* (*Opera*, i. 324–5). **123** *braky.* bushy.

126–7 (margin) *Natura non effeta.* 'Nature not spent.' Cf. l. 304 below, and contrast *For.* 4. 14.

131–3 (margin) *Non . . . antiquitati.* 'Do not rely too much on the ancients.' **135** *precipitation.* precipitateness; over-hasty judgements. **141** *non domini . . . fuere.* 'They were not our lords but our leaders'; from Vives, quoting Seneca, *Epist.* xxxiii. 11 ('sunt' for 'fuere'). **142** *several.* private possession. **142–4** *Patet . . . relictum est.* 'Truth lies open for all; it has not yet been monopolized. And there is plenty of it left even for posterity to discover'; Seneca, *Epist.* xxxiii. 11, quoted by Vives. F 'relicta'.

145, 149 (margin) *Dissentire . . . cum ratione.* 'Dissent if you will, but with reason.'

152, 160 (margin) *Non mihi . . . veritati.* 'Submission is not owed to me, but to truth.' **152** *nulla ars . . . absoluta.* 'No art is discovered and completed at the same moment.' **155** *evict.* Establish, evince. **156** *fautor.* Adherent, patron. **157** *addict.* devote.

162, 170 (margin) *Scientiae liberales . . . sunt.* 'Liberal studies are not for the vulgar.' **162–9** *Arts that . . . pascitur.* From Vives, *De Causis Corruptarum Artium* (*Opera*, i. 326). **167** *generous.* noble. **168** *acquiesce.* Remain intellectually satisfied. **169** *opere pascitur.* 'It is fed with labour' (from Vives). **173** *carat.* Worth (a confusion with 'caract'). **175–6** *It is as . . . nature.* Cf. *UV* 26. 13–14.

177–8 (margin) *Honesta ambitio.* 'Honourable ambition.' **177–80** *If divers . . . of praise.* From Pliny, *Epist.* IX. xix. **179** *leave.* permission. Whalley and others emend to 'love'.

181–2 (margin) *Maritus improbus.* 'A shameless husband.'

184–5 (margin) *Afflictio pia magistra.* 'Affliction the teacher of piety.'

186–8 (margin) *Deploratis . . . Averni.* 'To the lost, easy is the descent into hell.' Virgil, *Aeneid*, vi. 126. **188–9** '*The devil . . . all!*' Proverbial: Tilley, D267. H & S compare the fool's song in William Wager's *The Longer Thou Livest* (1569).

190–1 (margin) *Aegidius . . . superat.* 'Aegidius ["Giles", i.e. a cripple] wins the race.' **190** *in the way.* Heading in the right direction. *footman.* i.e. a servant who ran before his master's carriage.

192–3 (margin) *Prodigo . . . nauci.* 'To a spendthrift, money is worthless.'

194–5 (margin) *Munda et sordida.* 'Neat and filthy.' Cf. Tilley, D594.

196–7 (margin) *Debitum deploratum.* 'A hopeless debt.' Cf. Tilley, M939. **196** *little.* Castelain and others: 'a little'.

198–9 (margin) *Latro sesquipedalis.* 'With the sesquipedalian ["foot and a half long"] belly.' **199** *gallows.* Fielding's Jonathan Wild similarly robs his own hangman at Tyburn. A traditional story?

202 *arms set up.* A custom of grand people while travelling. **203** *harborough.* inn.

208–9 (margin) *Calumniae fructus.* 'The fruits of calumny.'

212 (margin) *Impertinens.* impertinent. **215–16** *touched . . . discourse.* Cf. Petronius, *Satyricon*, 44. **220** *same destiny.* Tilley, W232.

221–2 (margin) *Bellum scribentium.* 'The writers' war.' **221** *committed together.* Hostilely engaged. **222** *points.* Contrast *Epig.* 58. **223–4** *fires . . . altars.* Latin *pro aris et focis.*

227 *these quarries.* Possibly referring back to the squabbles of authors; but this may be, as H & S believe, 'a loose note, not worked out'. **227–8** *Sed . . . usus.* 'But I enjoy the possession of a wit and mind better in all ways than my fortune.' **229** *Pingue . . . labor.* 'A fat soil wearies, but the very labour delights', Martial, I. cvii. 8.

230–2 (margin) *Differentia . . . sciolos.* 'The difference between scholars and smatterers.' **232** *disquisition.* Systematic investigation. **237** *welt.* border.

238–9 (margin) *Impostorum fucus.* 'Imposture is a deceit.'

242–3 (margin) *Icuncularum motio*. 'Puppet-play.' **243** *et sordet gesticulatio*. 'And the gestures become nasty.'

244–5 (margin) *Principes et administri*. 'Princes and ministers.' **251–2** *Finis . . . promptissimo*. 'The end of every man's life should be awaited, since a man is most likely to change'; from Vives, *Libri de Disciplinis* (*Opera*, i. 525): see P. J. McGinnis, *NQ* ccii (1957), 162–3.

253–4 (margin) *Scitum Hispanicum*. 'A Spanish maxim.' **253** *quick*. acute. **253–4** *artes . . . dividi*. 'A person's skills cannot be divided amongst his heirs.' **258** *frontless*. shameless.

260–1 (margin) *Non . . . livor*. Translated in the text. **260–308** *Envy . . . frenzy*. From J. J. Scaliger, *Confutatio Stultissimae Burdonum Fabulae*, in *Opuscula* (Frankfort, 1612), pp. 419–22. The passages are marked in Jonson's own copy. **262–3** *quorum . . . placet*. 'To whom hatred is a pleasure, virtue being forsaken' (a slight mistaking of Scaliger's text).

276–7 (margin) *Nil . . . lib[ro]*. 'Nothing is more welcome than a shameless book.' **277** *petulant*. insolent. **277–8** *convenient*. appropriate.

283 *had in price*. esteemed. **283–4** (margin) *Jam litterae sordent*. 'Now literature is nasty.' **284** *upbraidingly . . . poet*. Cf. *Epig*. 10. 1; *Volp*. Epist. Ded. 30. **285** *professors*. i.e. those who profess poetry. **290** (margin) *Pastus . . . ingen[ii]*. 'The diet of the times.' **293** *clearest*. purest. **296** *epidemical*. Cf. *Und*. 64. 18.

303–4 (margin) *Sed . . . morbus*. 'But it is the disease of the age.' **304** *growing old*. Cf. *For*. 4. 14; contrast ll. 126–7 above.

309–10 (margin) *Alastoris malitia*. 'The malice of Alastor' (spirit of revenge).

317–18 (margin) *Mali . . . fuere*. 'They were bad *choragi*' (who trained and dressed the chorus in Athens). **321** *meritorious*. Meretricious, whorish.

325 *630*. i.e. 1630. H & S note that an elephant was sent to King James in 1623 by the King of Spain, with instructions that it be given wine regularly to drink. **327** *cast*. batch. **331** *practise*. plot. *Archy*. Archibald Armstrong, the court fool.

334–8 (margin) *Lingua . . . optanda*. 'The wise person's tongue is preferable to that of the talkative person.' **334–92** *A wise tongue . . . labellum*. This section, with its various classical commonplaces, is drawn largely from Aulus Gellius, *Attic Nights*, 1. xv, and Claude Mignault's edition of Alciati's *Emblems* (1573, revised 1577): eleventh emblem, 'Silentium'. **337** *that philosopher*. Plutarch, *Concerning Talkativeness*, 3, *Moralia*, 503 (gathering up older classical ideas). **339** *petulancy*. Wantonness, insolence. **344** *security*. carelessness.

348 *downright*. Cf. George Downright in *EMI*. **349–50** *Bedlam-like*. The Hospital of St Mary of Bethlehem catered for the insane.

358 *Homer's Thersites*. The epithets (translated by Jonson in the text) are applied to Thersites in *Iliad*, ii. 212, 246. **359–60** *Loquax . . . facundus*. 'Loquacious rather than eloquent', Quintilian, IV. ii. 2. **360** *Satis . . . parum.* 'Eloquence enough, but little discretion'; Sallust on Catiline, *Catiline*, v. 5. **361–4** 'The greatest treasure is a tongue that measures each thing by sparing words': Hesiod, *Works and Days*, 719–20; approximately translated in the Latin.

365 *Ulysses. Iliad*, iii. 216–24. **367** *Pindar.* Not in fact Pindar (Jonson inherits the mistake from Mignault) but Spintharus of Tarentum, reported by Plutarch, *On the Sign of Socrates*, 23, *Moralia*, 592–3: 'nowhere in his generation has he met a man of greater knowledge and fewer words'. **368** *Demaratus.* King of Sparta. Plutarch, *Sayings of the Spartans*, 4, *Moralia*, 220. Solon is credited with a similar riposte (seemingly a classical commonplace). **372** *indice.* Sign (*OED*'s first example of the word; but cf. *Und.* 13. 156). Cf. l. 2449 below, and n. **373–4** *Dum . . . tegit.* 'While the fool is silent, he may be thought wise, for he covers the diseases of his mind with his silence.' (margin) *Vid[e] . . . Megabizum.* When Megabyzus in Zeuxis' studio talked ignorantly of art, Zeuxis asked him to be silent, as the colour-grinders were laughing at him: Aelian, *Vera Historia*, ii (H & S).

375–85 The story of Zeno (fifth century BC founder of the Stoics) is in Plutarch, *Concerning Talkativeness*, 4, *Moralia*, 504.

386 (margin) *Argute dictum.* 'A witty saying.' **389–90** Ἐχεμυθία . . . *laudabilis!* 'How praiseworthy is the silence enjoined by Pythagoras!' See Athenaeus, *Deipnosophistae*, vii. 308, c. **390–2** γλώσσῆς . . . *exemplum.* 'Above all things, control your tongue, following the example of the gods.' The Latin translates the Greek: a maxim of Pythagoras, recorded by Iamblichus, *Pythagorae Fragmenta*, ed. Lipsius (1603), p. 24. **391** (margin) *Vide Apuleium.* 'See Apuleius': *Metamorphoses*, I. viii. **392** *Digito . . . labellum.* 'Press back your lips with your finger': Juvenal, *Sat.* i. 160.

393–5 (margin) *Acutius . . . virtutes.* 'Vices more sharply discerned than virtues.' **393–4** *There is . . . virtues.* Cicero, *De Oratore*, i. 116. **398** *comic poet.* Plautus, *Poenulus*, 625. Cf. *Volp.* I. ii. 73: 'tongue and bauble are his treasure'. **399** *nation.* Group: cf. *Volp.* I. ii. 66. **402** (margin) *Trin[ummus].* Jonson has misunderstood the context of Plautus' play (ll. 520 ff.): the slave Stasimus is in fact trying to prevent the sale of his master's farm. **409** *Hospitium . . . calamitatis.* 'It was the lodging of calamity.' **409–10** (margin) *Sim[iliter] . . .* Martial's epigram concerns an auctioneer who discloses too freely an owner's reasons for attempting to sell his land.

411–1 (margin) *Vulgi expectatio.* 'Expectation of the vulgar.' **411–19** *Expectation . . . a feast.* From M. Seneca, *Controversiae*, iv, preface, 1. **414** *naught.* corrupt. **419** *a feast.* Gollancz: 'at a feast'.

420 (margin) *Claritas patria.* 'Fatherly fame.' Thus F3, H & S; F *'patriae'*, Gifford: *'patris'*.

426–44 *Eloquence . . . in a pond.* From M. Seneca, *Controversiae*, iii, preface, 11–14. **433** *mooting.* Conducting mock cases. **437** *umbratical.* i.e. sitting in the shade (cf. Petronius, *Satyricon*, 2). **438** *sub dio.* 'In the open.' **441** *they that.* Thus H & S; F 'that they'.

445 (margin) *Amor et odium.* 'Love and hate.' **445–53** *Love . . . mischief.* From Seneca, *On Benefits*, VI. xxv. **451** *courtesy.* F 'countrey'; Swinburne's emendation.

454 (margin) *Injuriae.* 'injuries'. **454–79** *Injuries . . . Smithfield.* From Seneca, *On Benefits*, VI. v. 1; vi. 3; vii; viii; xii.

459 (margin) *Beneficia.* 'benefits'. **468–9** *I myself . . . water.* John Aubrey tells of the Cambridge doctor William Butler (1535–1618) curing a patient of the ague by having him thrown unexpectedly into the Thames: *Brief Lives*, ed. O. L. Dick (London, 1949), p. 149. **479** *Smithfield.* The main London market for horses and cattle.

480 (margin) *Valor rerum.* 'The price of things.' **480–6** *The price . . . labours.* From Seneca, *On Benefits*, VI. xv. 2. **486** *serve.* Thus H & S; F 'serv'd'. *gratify.* reward.

487 (margin) *Memoria.* 'memory'. **487–516** *Memory . . . vexation.* Closely modelled on M. Seneca, *Controversiae*, i. preface, 2–5. **491 ff.** *I myself . . .* During his stay with William Drummond at Hawthornden in 1618–19, Jonson—then in his late forties—recited a number of poems written by himself and his friends. **505, 510** *presently.* immediately.

517 (margin) *Comit[iorum] suffragia.* 'Popular votes.' **517–21** *Suffrages . . . same.* From Pliny, *Epist.* II. xii.

522–3 (margin) *Stare a partibus.* 'To stand by one's party.'

531–2 (margin) *Deus in creaturis.* 'God in his creatures.' **532** *creature of glory.* The phrase is Tertullian's: *De Anima*, i. **534–6** *For to . . . knowing.* Justus Lipsius, *Politica*, I. ii. (drawing on Cyprian and Augustine).

540–2 (margin) *Veritas . . . hominis.* Translated in the words opposite. **540–5** *Truth . . . wisdom.* Lipsius, *Politica*, I. i (drawing on Tacitus, iv. 17; Seneca, *Epist.* xcviii. 9). **545** Homer. *Iliad*, ix. 312–13. **550–2** *Beside . . . grows old.* Hippolytus à Collibus, *Palatinus* (1595), p. 31. **551** *Euripides.* Actually from a fragment of Sophocles' *Acrisius.* Cf. *Und.* 45. 20.

553–4 (margin) *Nullum . . . patrocinio.* 'No vice without its patronage.' **553–78** *It is strange . . . together.* Gathered from Seneca, *Epist.* cxvi. 2; cxxii. 2; cxii. 3, 4. **561** *antipodes.* antipodeans.

579 (margin) *De vere argutis.* 'Of the truly witty.' **585–95** *But now . . . curious.* Quintilian, II. v. 11. **588** *baudekin.* Rich material. **592–5** *All must . . . curious.* Cf. *Und.* 15. 106–13; 44. 88–97. **593** *sweet bags.* Scented bags used for perfuming clothes, etc. **594** *night-dressings.* Night clothes were still regarded as a novelty and luxury at this time. **595** *curious.* fastidious.

596–7 (margin) *Censura de poetis.* 'Judgements on poets.' **596–7** *preposterous.* topsy-turvy. **600** *wrap . . . drug.* Cf. *Epig.* 3. 12. **601** *light . . . tobacco.* Cf. *Und.* 43. 52.

604 *one blot.* Cf. *Und.* 52, 'My Answer', 12. **608–9** *comitetur . . . spongea.* 'Let a Punic sponge attend the book.' **610** *Et paulo post.* 'And a little further on.' **611** *Non . . . potest.* 'Many [corrections] cannot [emend my jokes]; one wiping-out can.' **615** *Cestius.* L. Cestius Pius, rhetorician of Smyrna, who declaimed against Cicero. From M. Seneca, *Controversiae*, iii, preface, 15. **620–1** *The puppets . . . players.* A taste ironically celebrated in the puppet show of *BF.* **621** *Heath's epigrams.* John Heath's *Epigrams* were published in 1610. **622** *the Sculler.* John Taylor, 1580–1653, the 'Water Poet'; cf. *Conv. Dr.* 316, 533. **626** *non illi . . . judicant.* Translated in the preceding phrase. **628** *Spenser's.* Testimony of Jonson's high valuation of Spenser, despite apparently limiting judgements elsewhere (*Conv. Dr.* 15–16; *Disc.* 1823–5). **632–3** *a mean mistress.* This passage is laced with personal feeling; cf. *Conv. Dr.* 493. **635** *saluted . . . the by.* i.e. been part-time writers. **638** *law . . . gospel.* Perhaps referring to such writers as Sir John Davies, Hall, and Donne. **645–54** *Indeed . . . than composed.* Quintilian, II. xii. 1–3; cf. *Alch.* 'To the Reader', 13–29. **647** *put for it.* Push about. **653–4** *scattered . . . composed.* 'Loose writing more harmonious than careful and well-arranged writing' (H & S).

658–60 (margin) *De Shakespeare nostrat[i].* 'Concerning our Shakespeare'; 'ours' as both colleague and fellow-countryman. Cf. the view of Shakespeare expressed in *UV* 26 and in *Conv. Dr.* 37. **660** *blotted out line.* F3 (followed by Gollancz and Schelling) 'blotted out a line'. Cf. the testimony of Heminges and Condell, in their address to readers prefixed to the First Folio, concerning the easy rapidity of Shakespeare's writing and the cleanness of his manuscripts: 'we have scarce received from him a blot in his papers'. **665** *candour.* Partiality; well-disposedness. **667** *honest.* For the force of this praise, see ll. 86–90 above. **669 ff.** *wherein he flowed . . .* Modelled on M. Seneca's comments on Quintus Haterius, a senator and rhetorician whose words sometimes ran away with him: *Controversiae*, iv, preface, 7–11. **670–1** *Sufflaminandus erat.* 'Sometimes he needed the brake': Augustus' comment on Haterius, as reported by M. Seneca (and others). **676** *'Caesar . . . just cause'.* Caesar's words are in fact: 'Know, Caesar doth not wrong, nor without cause | Will he be satisfied' (*Julius Caesar*, III. i. 47–8). Was the passage altered, or did Jonson carelessly misquote? H & S (xi. 231–3) sift the possibilities, noting that the version Jonson quotes is in any case elliptical rather than nonsensical. Jonson mocks these lines again in *S. of N.* Ind. 35–7 (in 1626, three years after the publication of Shakespeare's First Folio).

680 (margin) *Ingeniorum discrimina.* 'The difference of wits': i.e. the diversity of kinds of intelligence. **680–92** *In the difference . . . spur.* From Quintilian, II. viii.

681 *notes.* Characteristic features. **693–702** *There be . . . no higher.* Quintilian, I. iii. 3–5. **698** *presently.* immediately. **701** *ingeni-stitium.* Explained in the marginal note: an intellectual standstill. 'Formed on the analogy of *iustitium* from "ius" and "sisto" ' (H & S). **704** *colours and surface.* H & S see an allusion to the Euphuists. **707–17** *Others . . . looked on.* Seneca, *Epist.* cxiv. 15, 21. **708** *Quae per . . . cadunt.* 'That fall over rough places and high cliffs.' Cf. ll. 2839–43 below and n. **709** *trouble . . . purpose.* Swinburne thinks Donne is aimed at: *A Study of Ben Jonson* (London, 1889), pp. 141–2. **710** *rubs.* Uneven places on a bowling green.

722–3 *Others . . . write.* Seneca, *Epist.* cxiv. 15. **724** *Women's poets.* H & S believe Daniel, and possibly Campion and Middleton, are glanced at here. **726–7** *They write . . . stream.* Unidentified; perhaps invented. **729–30** *cream-bowl . . . puddle-deep. Und.* 40. 29–30. **736** *all the essayists.* e.g. Bacon (*Essays*, 1597), who is praised nevertheless in more general terms below, ll. 894 ff., 924 ff.; Cornwallis (*Essays*, 1610). **739** *undigested.* Cf. ll. 2895–8 below. **742–6** *Some again . . . curious.* Quintilian, I. viii. 21. **748** *venditation.* Favourable display, as for sale. *naturals.* Intellectual abilities. **749** *sagacity.* Used of the tracking power of fox-hounds; hence the following metaphor. **757–71** *But the wretcheder . . . loose.* Quintilian, II. xi. 1–3. **768–9** *excellent . . . judgement. Alch.* 'To the Reader', 12, 13, and nn. **772–92** *It cannot but . . . gapers.* Quintilian, II. xi. 5–7. **782** *copy.* Abundance (Latin *copia*). **782–3** *election and a mean.* Selection and moderation. **784–5** *true artificer. Alch.* 'To the Reader', 5–6. **789–90** *Tamerlanes.* Marlowe's *Tamburlaine the Great*, Pt. I (*c.* 1587), Pt. II (*c.* 1588). *Tamer-chams.* A lost play, probably modelled on Marlowe's; acted by Henslowe's company in 1592 and 1596. **791** *strutting.* Alleyn's acting in Marlowe's plays is thus described by other contemporaries, e.g. Joseph Hall, 1597. **792–813** *He knows . . . naught.* Quintilian, II. xii. 11, 12; v. 8–10. **798** *gratulates them.* Wishes them joy. **799** *Another age.* A characteristic Jonsonian appeal to the verdict of posterity. **800** *dividing.* i.e. in the disposition or structure of his writing. **808** *translated.* Expressed metaphorically or in a transferred sense.

814 (margin) *Ignorantia animae.* 'Ignorance of the soul.' **822** *Think . . . contrary.* Seneca, *Epist.* xxxi. 6.

823 (margin) *Scientia.* 'knowledge'. **826** *agent.* Active power. **828** *like a silkworm.* Cf. Montaigne, *Essais*, iii. 13. **829** *indagations.* investigations. **830** *put her by.* Put her out.

832–3 (margin) *Otium studiorum.* Scholarly relaxation. **834** *temper.* balance. **835** *favour.* Treat gently. **835–55** *I have known . . . be right.* Cf. M. Seneca's account of the rhetorician M. Porcius Latro, *Controversiae*, i, preface, 13–15 and (less closely) 21–4. **848** *absolute.* consummate. **853** *figures.* Cf. ll. 1913 ff. below.

856–7 (margin) *Et stili eminentia.* 'And greatness of style.' **856–71** *It is no wonder . . . panniers.* M. Seneca, *Controversiae*, iii. preface, 8, 9, quoting Cassius Severus the rhetorician. **857–8** *Virgil's . . . verse.* Suetonius mentions Virgil's weakness as a pleader in the courts; fragments of a correspondence with Augustus are all that remain of his prose (Macrobius, *Saturnalia*, I. xxiv. 11). Juvenal refers to Cicero's poetic inabilities, *Sat.* x. 124. **858** *Sallust's orations.* Sallust invented speeches for Caesar and Cato in his history of Catiline, although the original speeches, taken down by shorthand writers, were extant. **859** *Plato's speech. The Apology of Socrates.* **861** *patron.* advocate. **864** *fit.* Do the job (Castelain emends to 'fill').

872–3 (margin) *De claris oratoribus.* 'Of famous orators.' **872–93** *I have known . . . chosen.* M. Seneca, *Controversiae*, iii, preface, 1; i, preface, 6. **873** *suddenly.* i.e. off the cuff. *admiration.* astonishment. **877–8** *Their fortune . . . care.* i.e. they were more fortunate than their preparation strictly deserved. **879** *present spirits.* With their wits about them. **894–5** (margin) *Dominus Verulamius.* Lord Bacon. (Thus

F3; F, H & S: 'Veralanus'.) Cf. *Und.* 51 and n.; *Conv. Dr.* 279 ff. **894-907** *One . . . an end.* M. Seneca, *Controversiae*, i, preface, 6; iii, preface, 4, on Cassius Severus. **899** *pass by a jest.* Cf. M. Seneca on Cassius Severus: 'so long as he steered clear of jokes, his oratory was worthy of a censor' (*censoria oratio erat*). **900** *pressly.* Concisely; precisely (*OED*'s first recorded occurrence of the word). **902** *member.* part. **902-3** *the own graces.* i.e. his own graces (and so emended, F3). **905** *devotion.* Power to command.

908-9 (margin) *Scriptorum catalogus.* 'List of writers.' **908** *Cicero.* M. Seneca, *Controversiae*, i, preface, 11; '*ingenium par imperio*' (translated in the text) is Seneca's phrase. **911** *the former seculum.* The last age. *Sir Thomas More.* 1478–1535, the great Lord Chancellor; author of *Utopia* (in Latin, two books, 1515, 1516), the *Life of John Picus, Earl of Mirandula* (1510), the *Dialogue* (against Tyndale, 1528), and *The History of King Richard III* (published 1543, 1557). **911-12** *the elder Wyatt.* Thomas Wyatt, the poet, ?1503–42; *Certain Psalms* had been published in 1549, and other poems in Tottel's *Miscellany* (1557). **912** *Surrey.* Henry Howard, Earl of Surrey, ?1517–47, the poet; poems in Tottel's *Miscellany* (1557). *Chaloner.* Sir Thomas Chaloner, 1521–65, diplomatist, poet, and translator of *An Homily of St John Chrysostome* (1544) and Erasmus's *Praise of Folly* (1549); his Latin verses were published in 1579. *Smith.* Sir Thomas Smith, 1513–77, Secretary of State, Greek scholar and English grammarian, author of *De Republica Anglorum* (1583), on the Tudor constitution. *Elyot.* Sir Thomas Elyot, ?1490–1546, diplomatist and author of *The Book Named the Governor* (1531) and other works. **913** *B[ishop] Gardiner.* Stephen Gardiner, ?1483–1555, Bishop of Winchester 1531, imprisoned under Edward VI, Lord Chancellor under Mary; scholar, patron of learning, and author of Catholic tracts. **914-15** *Sir Nicho[las] Bacon.* 1509–79, Lord Keeper (= 'L.K.', margin) from 1558; famed for his oratory. **916** *Sir Philip Sidney.* 1554–86, poet, soldier, statesman; cf. *For.* 2. 13–14, *Conv. Dr.* 187–9. **917** *Mr Hooker.* Richard Hooker, 1533–1600, author of *Of the Laws of Ecclesiastical Polity*; see *Conv. Dr.* 108–9 and n. **919** *Earl of Essex.* Robert Devereux, 1566–1601, the second earl, Elizabeth's favourite; patron of letters, and himself a minor sonneteer and writer; cf. *Conv. Dr.* 312–14 and n. **920** *Sir Walter Raleigh.* ?1552–1618; see *Und.* 24 and n.; *Conv. Dr.* 159 ff. **921** *Sir Henry Savile.* See *Epig.* 95 and n. **922** *Sir Edwin Sandys.* 1561–1629, author of *Europae Speculum* (1629) (the authorized reissue of *A Relation of the State of Religion* (1605)). **923** *Egerton.* See *Epig.* 74 and n. ('L.C.' in margin = Lord Chancellor.) **925** *successor.* Lord Bacon. **925-6** *filled up all numbers.* Excelled in every respect (Latin, *omnes numeros explevit*). **926-8** *and performed . . . Rome.* Cf. the tribute to Shakespeare, *UV* 24. 39; from M. Seneca, *Controversiae*, i, preface, 6. Seneca believed that Roman oratory had reached its peak in Cicero's day, and that standards had since then steadily declined. **932** ἀκμή. acme.

934-5 (margin) *De augmentis scientiarum.* The title of Bacon's work (1623): the Latin translation and completion of *The Advancement of Learning* (1605). **941** *books of Analogy. De Analogia* (or *De Ratione Latine Loquendi*), now lost; partly written while Caesar was crossing the Alps, and dedicated to Cicero. See Suetonius, *The Deified Julius*, lvi. 5; Cicero, *Brutus*, lxxii. 253. **942-3** *Novum Organum.* Published in Latin in 1620. **944** *nominals.* 'As opposed to "reals", things existing in name only' (H & S). **947** *Qui . . . aevum.* Horac *The Art of Poetry*, 346 ('*Et longum noto scriptori prorogat aevum*'), 'with honour make the far-known author live' (Jonson's trs.). **948–57** Jonson has here transcribed almost word for word a letter by Fr. Fulgenzio Micanza to the first Earl of Devonshire, sent from Venice on 14 May 1621; Thomas Hobbes may have shown it to Jonson. See A. T. Shillinglaw, *TLS* 18 April 1936. **948** *conceit.* estimation. **950** *that . . . himself.* That related simply to his personal qualities.

958–9 (margin) *De corruptela morum.* 'On the corruption of manners.' **958–68** *There cannot . . . sick mind.* Seneca, *Epist.* cxiv.

969–70 (margin) *De rebus mundanis.* 'Of worldly affairs.' **969–76** From Seneca, *Epist.* cx. 3. **970** *belong.* Surround, lie next to; a nonce-usage, translating Seneca's *contingere* (P. J. McGinnis, *NQ* ccii (1957), 163). **974** *gratulation.* pleasure.

980 *venery.* sex.

983 (margin) *Vulgi mores.* 'The manners of the mob.' **986** *Hercules . . . bull.* The seventh (or eighth) labour of Hercules was to capture the mad bull sent by Neptune to devastate Crete. **991–2** (margin) *Morbus comitialis.* 'The disease of parliament.' In classical Latin the phrase referred more literally to epilepsy: meetings to elect magistrates (*comitia*) were postponed if an attack of epilepsy inauspiciously occurred. The political conservatism of this passage is character-istic of Jonson: cf., for example, *Und.* 64 for similar sentiments. **991–2** *Then . . . events.* Cf. Montaigne, *Essais*, iii. 7.

997 (margin) *Princeps.* 'The prince.' **1000** *put off man.* Forsake humanity. **1003** (margin) *De eodem.* 'On the same.' **1005** *to correct . . . destroy.* Cf. *BF* v. vi. 112. **1006–7** *prayers . . . Jupiter.* See *Argonautica*, 128–9. **1010–11** (margin) *De opt[imo] rege Jacobo.* 'Concerning James, the best of kings.' Cf. *Epig.* 4. 1. **1010–13** *It was a great . . . condemned.* The reference may be to the Visitors (or 'Ordinaries') of Newgate, chaplains responsible for the spiritual welfare of the prisoners. **1014–17** (margin) *De princ[ipum] . . . bonus.* 'On the attributes of princes.—But truly a prince could scarcely be thought of as wise unless at the same time he was good.' The sentiment is from Erasmus, *The Education of a Christian Prince*, i. **1014 ff.** Drawing upon Franciscus Patricius, *De Regno et Regis Institutione* (1567), and H. Farnese, *Diphthera Jovis* (1607). **1018** *Lycurgus.* Legendary Spartan legis-lator, seventh century BC. *Sulla.* Lucius Cornelius Sulla, 'Felix', *c.* 138–78 BC, a vigorous legislator with a poor reputation for personal conduct. **1019** *Lysander.* Died 395 BC, Spartan general and statesman. **1027** *Cyrus . . . bitch.* Lucian, *On Sacrifices*; Herodotus, i. 110 (rationalizing: his mother's name was also the word for 'dog'). **1028** *ill.* F 'it'.

1031–2 (margin) *De malign[itate] studentium.* 'On the malignity of the learned.' **1032** *habent . . . deliciis.* 'They have poison for their food, even for their delicacies.' **1039–43** *But if . . . worse study?* Cf. *Volp.* Epist. Ded. 102–4. **1044** *piety.* Gifford's emendation of F 'poetry'. **1045–56** *But that he . . . best things.* Quintilian, i, preface, 9–14. **1046** *govern.* Whalley's emendation of F 'gowne'; translating Quintilian's *regere*. **1052** *proper embattling them.* Cf. *Epig.* 102. 5–8. To 'embattle' is to array troops for combat. **1053** *challenge.* claim.

1057–73 From Erasmus, *De Libero Arbitrio*, preface (W. David Kay, *ELN*, xvii (1979), 108–12). **1057–8** (margin) *Controvers[iales] scriptores.* 'Controversial writers.' **1060** (margin) *More . . . pugnant.* 'In the manner of the *andabatae*, who fight with closed eyes.' (The *andabatae* were gladiators who wore helmets with no eye openings.) **1060–1** *The one milks . . . a sieve.* Proverbial expressions for hopeless tasks; cf. Tilley, R27, Lucian, *Demonax*, 28. **1062** *fluxive.* Fluid, fluctuating.

1069 (margin) *Morbi.* 'diseases'. **1069–73** *The body . . . discovered.* From Erasmus, *Hyperaspistes diatribae adversus servum arbitrium Martini Lutheri.* **1070–2** *As if . . . murdered child.* It was a medieval (and post-medieval) belief that a cure could be thus effected. **1072** *dissimuled.* overlooked.

1074–5 (margin) *Jactantia intempestiva.* 'Untimely boasting.'

1081–1127 *I have seen . . . food to him.* From John of Salisbury's *Policratus*, Bk. III: see Margaret Clayton, *RES* NS xxx (1979), 397–408. **1084–5** *That hour . . . rich.* Seneca, *Natural Questions*, iv a, preface, 7. **1087** (margin) *Adulatio.* 'flattery'. **1091** *springes.* snares. **1095–7** *But now . . . malign them.* Seneca, *Natural Questions*, iv a, preface, 9. **1099–1100** *When . . . for praise.* Seneca, *Epist.* lix. 11. **1103** *friends . . . spit. Und.* 37. 9; 45. 8.

1105 (margin) *De vita humana.* 'Of human life.' *life . . . play.* A classical and contemporary commonplace; cf., for example, Petronius Arbiter, *Fragmenta*, 10.

1112 (margin) *De . . . probis.* 'Of the virtuous and good.' *stars.* Cf. *Epig.* 94; *Und.* 70. 98; 15. 196; *UV* 26. 77. **1113** *illustrate.* illuminate. **1114–16** *Abel . . . rest.* See Hebrews 11: 4–8. **1118–20** *But . . . fortune.* Cf. Lucretius, *De Rerum Natura*, ii. 7–11.

1122 (margin) *Mores aulici.* 'Courtly manners.'

1128–9 (margin) *Impiorum querela.* 'Complaint of the wicked.' **1128–34** *The complaint . . . affairs.* See Suetonius, *Caligula*, 31. **1131** *defeat of Varus.* In the Teutoburgerwald in the summer of 9 BC. **1132** *theatre at Fidenae.* (F 'Iidenae'.) In AD 27; fifty thousand people were said to be killed or injured. See Tacitus, *Annals*, iv. 62–3. **1136** *but one neck.* Suetonius, *Caligula*, 30; Dio Cassius, *Roman History*, lix. 30. **1137–9** *A tyrant . . . animal.* Darius' comments on Alexander before the battle at Granicus, recorded by Curtius Rufus (Quintus) in his history of Alexander, IV. xiv. 18.

1140–1 (margin) *Nobilium ingenia.* 'Characteristics of the nobility.' **1140–51** From Machiavelli, *The Prince*, ch. ix. 4. Daniel Boughner traces the extent of Jonson's debt to Machiavelli in this section and following sections in *The Devil's Disciple* (New York, 1968), ch. vii. **1148** *design.* See *UV* 34. 55 and n. **1152–3** (margin) *Principum varia[tio].* 'The difference in princes.' **1154–7** (margin) *Firmissima . . . principis.* 'Certainly the firmest basis of all is the hereditary right of the prince.' See Machiavelli, *The Prince*, ch. ii, 1. **1154–70** *The first . . . faithful. The Prince*, ch. ix. 2–7. **1162–3** *common proverb.* Tilley, P225. **1171** (margin) *Clementia.* 'mercy'. **1171–4** *A prince . . . Machiavel.* Machiavelli, *The Prince*, ch. vii, refers to Caesar Borgia's tactical execution of his own minister Ramiro de Lorgua on discovering that the minister's severity had made him unpopular. **1174–5** *puts off man.* See l. 1000 above, n. **1178–83** *Many . . . number.* Seneca, *On Mercy*, I. xxiv. 1, 3; iii. 3; viii. 6; x. 4. **1181–5** (margin) *Haud . . . callere.* 'It is not the least art in a prince to judge where levity, where severity may best prevail for the common good.' **1189–90** (margin) *Clementia . . . optima.* 'Mercy the best safeguard.' F 'tutelat opima'. **1190** *factors.* deputies. **1191–5** *He that . . . the thanks.* Machiavelli, *The Prince*, ch. viii. 8. **1191** *to halves.* By halves. *St Nicholas.* i.e. Niccolò Machiavelli, ironically conflated with St Nicholas of Bari, forerunner of Santa Claus. **1197** *obnoxious.* (i) vulnerable; (ii) submissive. **1199–1209** *they must go on . . . benefits.* Seneca, *On Mercy*, I. xiii. 2–5. **1205** *entrap true subjects.* Cf. James VI and I on the need for moderation in a ruler when interpreting the laws, which are 'not to be snares to trap your good subjects': *Basilikon Doron*, ed. J. Craigie (2 vols., Edinburgh and London, 1944, 1950), i. 141. Jonson also perhaps remembers his own experiences with spies: see *Epig.* 59 and *Conv. Dr.* 212–13. **1211** *Palladium.* An image of Pallas Athene said to have been sent by Zeus to Dardanus, founder of Troy; the city was safe until it was carried off by Diomede and Ulysses. See Virgil, *Aeneid*, ii. 162–79; and cf. H. Farnese, *Diphthera Jovis* (1607), p. 105. **1214** *they.* i.e. mercy and justice. **1215–17** *Justice . . . mercy.* Seneca, *On Mercy*, I. i. 9. **1219** *capital.* Fatal; punishable by death. **1224–6** *God . . . body.* Cf. *Und.* 84. iv. 72; Seneca, *Epist.* xxxi. 11. **1227** (margin) *Tyranni.* 'tyrants'. **1229** *Terminus.* Roman god of boundaries, often represented by a stone. **1230** *fable.* Of Reynard the fox; see, e.g., Caxton's version of 1481. **1239** *Sejanus.* The notion sketched here is developed in Jonson's tragedy *Sejanus.* **1239–40** *about them . . . above them.* F 'about him', 'above him'; H & S 'about 'hem', 'above 'hem'. **1240** *affect.* aspire. **1242–3** *For no . . . such.* Pliny, *Panegyricus*, xliv. **1248** (margin) *Illiteratus princeps.* 'An unlettered prince.' **1249–53** *In sovereignty . . . from us?* Justus Lipsius, *Politica*, preface; *Opera*, vii (1623), p. 6. **1255–8** *They say . . . groom.* Plutarch, *How to Tell a Flatterer From a Friend*, xvi, quoting a saying of Carneades. **1264** (margin) *Character principis.* 'The characteristics of a prince.' **1268–85** The adages here are gathered from Justus Lipsius, *Politica.* **1269** *shear, no[t] to fly.* Suetonius, *Tiberius*, 32; Herrick, 'Moderation', p. 261. **1273** *Alexander the Great.* The saying is recorded by Erasmus, *Adagia*, III. vii: in reply to a suggestion that Alexander increases taxes. **1275–7** *A man . . . followeth.* Prov. 30: 33. **1277–9** *He is . . . grow again.* Cicero, *Epistle to Atticus*, IV. ii. 5. **1281** *affect.* Aspire to. **1283** *surnames.* e.g. 'Africanus', 'Asiaticus', applied to various Scipios. **1283–4** *seek . . . war.* Contrast *Und.* 15. 195, 'go seek thy peace in war'. **1290** *price.* reputation. *disquisition.* Diligent search. **1291** *suffrages.* opinions. **1291–4** *Sell no . . . mend it.* Schelling notes that this ideal contrasts sharply with James I's indiscriminate bestowal of knighthoods, satirized elsewhere by Jonson. **1304** *Delphic sword.* Proverbial, for a thing serving two purposes.

1306 (margin) *De gratiosis.* 'Of the favoured.' **1306–11** *When a . . . punishment.* Cf. *Und.* 75. 113–20 and n.

1312 (margin) *Divites.* 'The rich.' **1315–16** (margin) *Heredes ex asse.* 'Sole heirs.'

1320 (margin) *Fures publici.* 'Thieves of the public estate'; remembering Aulus Gellius, *Attic Nights*, XI. xviii. 18, quoting Cato the Censor. **1320 ff.** *The great* *thieves* . . . Schelling notes that Sir George Carey, Lord Bacon, Lionel Cranfield, and Sir Thomas Gresham were amongst those who misappropriated public funds during this period. **1320** *lightly.* often. **1325** *Dat . . . columbas.* Juvenal, *Sat.* ii. 63: 'Our censor absolves the crow and passes judgement on the dove.' **1326** *Non . . . miluo.* Not from Plautus but Terence, *Phormio*, iii. 331: 'a net is not spread for a hawk or kite'. **1328–9** *They can . . . looks.* i.e. their masters can reduce their huffing and puffing. **1330** *counter.* A token coin, variable in value. **1332** *clerk.* unidentified.

1337–8 (margin) *De bonis et malis.* 'Of the good and the bad.' **1337–63** *A good man . . . prove of them.* Apuleius, *Apologia sive de magia*, i, iii. **1337–8** *The very aspersion.* Cf. *Und.* 50. 6. **1344** (margin) *De innocentia.* 'Of the innocent.' **1346** *precipices.* Playing on the legal term *praecipes* = 'writs'. **1347–8** *I have been accused.* In relation to *The Isle of Dogs* (1597); *Poet.* (1601); *Sej.* (1603); *Eastward Ho!* (1605); *D. is A.* (1616); verses on Buckingham's death (1628); *ML* (1632). **1352** *starting-holes.* Hiding-places; loop-holes. **1372–86** *At last . . . to riches.* Apuleius, *De Magia*, xviii. **1373** *my domestic.* Member of my household. **1376** *delicate impertinences.* Sensuous follies. **1379–80** *wealthy . . . hunters.* Schelling sees a possible allusion to the murder of Overbury: *Epig.* 113 and n. **1382** *the ancient poverty.* Cf. Theocritus, *Idyll*, 21. **1387** (margin) *Amor nummi.* 'Love of money.' **1387–1428** *Money . . . ends famine.* Seneca, *Epist.* cxix. 9–11; cx. 9–12; cxix. 13–14, 6; CX. 14–19. **1396** *search and dig. For.* 12. 25 and n. **1403** ff. *What need . . .* Cf. *King Lear*, II. iv. 267 ff. **1407** *praemunire.* A writ involving forfeiture of land and goods to the Crown, and imprisonment. **1408** *proscribed.* banished. **1411** *stews.* fishponds. **1412** *tissues.* Rich cloth, often interwoven with gold or silver. **1419** *foreign king.* Christian IV of Denmark, who visited James in July 1606; Jonson's *Ent. K. & Q. Theob.* was written for this occasion. *hither also.* Schelling's emendment of F 'hither. Also'.

1429–30 (margin) *De mollibus et effeminatis.* 'Of the soft and effeminate.' **1429–81** *There is nothing . . . but glory.* Seneca, *Epist.* cxv. 2, 6–18; cf. *Songs*, 19. **1430** *kempt.* combed. **1431** *curious.* pernickety. **1433** *morphew.* Leprous or scurfy eruption. **1434** *gumming.* Stiffening with gum. *bridling.* Drawing in, arranging in a dignified manner. **1436** *pickedness.* spruceness. **1437** *Nor.* Castelain's emendment of F 'Not'.

1451 (margin) *De stultitia.* 'Of folly.' **1451** ff. *What petty things . . .* Cf. *Und.* 84. i. 17–28. **1452** *fairing.* Purchase at a fair. **1458** *lime . . . loam.* Used respectively for mortar and for bricks and plaster.

1469 (margin) *De sibi molestis.* 'Of those who are a trouble to themselves.' **1473** *others' envy.* i.e. the envy they bear to others. **1473–7** *A man . . . others.* Cf. *Und.* 47. 59–60. **1480** *his virtue published.* Cf. ll. 1074–80 above.

1482–3 (margin) *Periculosa melancholia.* 'A dangerous melancholy.' **1482–93** *It is a dangerous thing . . . vicious enough.* From Seneca, *Epist.* cxiv. 25. Cf. *Und.* 15. 135–40, and Rochester's 'The Disabled Debauchee', *Complete Poems*, ed. D. Vieth (New Haven and London, 1968), pp. 116–17. **1489** *drabbing.* whoring.

1494–5 (margin) *Falsae . . . fugiendae.* '[Even] the appearance of evil to be avoided.' **1494–9** *I am glad . . . place.* Adapting a remark made by Diogenes to a man fleeing back into a tavern; reported by Plutarch, *How a Man May Become Aware of his Progress in Virtue*, xi, *Moralia*, 82. **1497** *Black Lucy.* A well-known prostitute of the day.

1503–4 (margin) *Decipimur specie.* 'We are deceived by the appearance [of truth]'; from Horace, *The Art of Poetry*, 25 *(decipimur specie recti).* **1505** *under our sense.* Within our perception. **1512** *endenizen.* Make a citizen of.

1516–17 (margin) *Dejectio aulic[orum].* 'The despondency of courtiers.'

1523 (margin) *Poesis et pictura.* 'Poetry and painting.' **1525** *Plutarch.* Quoting Simonides, in *On the Fame of the Athenians*, 3 *Moralia*, 346 F. **1528** *more noble.* Cf. *Und.* 52, 'My Answer', 19–21; *Und.* 84. iv. **1530–1** *pleasure and profit.* Horace, *The Art of Poetry*, 333–4. **1532** *err.* stray. **1534** *born . . . made.* Contrast *UV* 27. 64. **1536** (margin) *De pictura.* 'On painting.' *Whosoever . . . truth.* Philostratus, *Imagines*, opening bk. i. **1538–42** *It is itself . . . oratory.* Quintilian, XI. iii. 67 (J. K. Houck, *NQ* NS xv (1968), 367–8). **1542–54** *There are divers . . . the lines.* Modelled on Quintilian, XII. x. 6–9, 4. **1544** *in reason.* i.e. in working out optical laws and artistic technique (Quintilian: *ratione*); see ll. 1552, 1571 below. **1551** *Zeuxis.* Greek painter of Heraclea in southern Italy, *fl.* late fifth century BC; renowned for his depictions of women, and his illusionist technique. *Parrhasius.* Greek painter of Ephesus, *fl. c.* 400 BC; surpassed Zeuxis himself in a famous contest in painterly illusion. **1553** *lights and shadows.* 'Pliny often uses *umbra* and *lumen* to denote background and foreground' (H & S). **1555–7** *In picture . . . humble.* Cf. *UV* 7. 1–4; and Pliny, *Epist.* III. xiii. 4. **1556** (margin) *De stilo.* 'On style.' **1557–8** *Regulus' writings.* Pliny (*Epist.* IV. vii. 7) is commenting on the inept eulogy which Regulus—informer, orator, lawyer—had written on his dead son. **1560** *'occupy'.* See *Epig.* 117. 2 n. *'nature'.* The word could mean semen, menses, or the female pudendum (*OED*, †7 a and b; †8). **1561** *curious.* painstaking. **1561–2** *of having . . . good.* i.e. of thinking any kind of word suitable for any occasion. Jonson is defending plain terms, but also the notion of stylistic decorum. **1563–5** (margin) *De progress[ione] picturae.* 'Of the progress of painting.' **1563–81** *Picture took . . . breaking.* From the Jesuit writer Antonio Possevino's *Bibliotheca selecta qua agitur de ratione studiorum* (1593), bk. XVII. xxiii; which in turn derives from Pliny, *Nat. Hist.* XXXV. x. 67 and xi. 126–7. **1569** *outer lines.* outlines. *Eupompus.* Greek painter contemporary with Zeuxis and Parrhasius; of Sicyon; founder of the Sicyonic school. **1570** *numbers.* ?Rules of mathematical proportion. **1574** *recessor.* Background (Lat. recessus = 'going back'). Schelling emends to 'recession'. **1581** *all solids . . . breaking.* i.e. all solid objects on a broken (uneven) ground. **1581** (margin) *Vitruv[ius].* Jonson's note refers incorrectly to bk. 8 (rather than bk. 3) of *De Architectura.* The passage on architectural 'chimaeras' or 'grotesques' is in bk. 7. Jonson is drawing on Possevino's account (XVII. xxiv) of Johannes Andreas Lilius's *Dialogus Alexandro Farnesio.* **1585** *Horace.* See *The Art of Poetry*, ll. 9–14. **1589–91** *Socrates . . . imagery.* Xenophon, *Memorabilia*, III. x. 1–8. **1589** *Clito.* Nothing more is known about him. **1591** *Polygnotus.* Of Thasos; active in Athens after the Persian wars (fifth century BC); praised by Aristotle (*Poetics*, 6) for his delineation of character. *Aglaophon.* Father and teacher of Polygnotus.

1592 *lawgiver.* Cf. Quintilian on Parrhasius, XII. x. 5. **1594** *about Philip's time.* In fact, earlier; Jonson has misread Quintilian. **1596** *six famous painters.* Seven names in fact follow. Jonson is borrowing wholesale from Possevino, who is in turn quoting Giovanni Battista Armenini's *De' veri precetti della pittura* (1587). **1599** *Sebastian of Venice.* Sebastione del Piombe, *c.*1458–1547. *Giulio Romano.* 1492–1546; cf. *Und.* 77. 6. **1600** *Andrea Sartorio.* Andrea del Sarto, 1486–1530.

1601 *There are.* F 'These are'. **1601** (margin) *Parasiti ad mensam.* 'Parasites at the table.' **1602** *oraculous.* oracular. **1610–11** *compound.* Do deals. **1611** *delate.* Report, offer up. **1629** *simulties.* quarrels. **1632** *pies.* magpies.

1635 (margin) *Immo serviles.* 'Indeed, slaves.' **1643** *disquisitions.* See l. 1290 above, n. **1645** *undertaken.* Taken in hand. **1645–6** *thriftily.* thoroughly. **1649** *vice in praising.* A constant concern: cf. *Volp.* III. ii. 28; *UV* 26. 14, etc.

1651–2 (margin) [*De liberis educandis*]. 'On the education of children.' **1651** *your lordship.* Schelling (dubiously) and H & S (confidently) believe this may be William Cavendish, Earl (later Duke) of Newcastle: see *Und.* 53 n. **1658** *venture.* Dare to express. **1659–68** *I confess . . . their natures.* Quintilian, I. i. 21. **1665** *apting.* fitting. **1672–3** *school itself . . . game.* As in Latin *ludus.* **1675–9** *A youth . . . deserves it not.* Quintilian, I. i. 20. **1679–1712** *For which . . . servile.* From Quintilian, I. ii. 1, 17–21; iii. 7–11, 13. **1694** *age.* maturity. **1699** *singulars.* individuals. **1704** *wit.* intelligence. **1712** *deformed.* Disgraceful; following Quintilian's *deforme atque servile est.*

1713–15 (margin) *De stilo . . . genere.* 'Concerning style, and the best kind of writing.' **1713–51** *For a man . . . his mettle.* From Quintilian, X. iii. 4–10. **1723** *forward conceits.* First notions. **1726–7** *the consequence.* i.e. what follows in the writing. **1731** *fetch . . . largest.* Have the longest run-up. **1733** *Loose.* throw. **1734** *steering out of our sail.* Running before the wind without use of tiller; i.e. being carried along freely by inspiration. **1736** *please us.* *Und.* 5. 13–16; *Dubia,* I. 57–8. **1755–71** *Besides . . . parts.* Quintilian, II. vii. 2–5; viii. 12–15. **1771** *concent.* Accord, harmony (Lat. *concentus*).

1772–3 (margin) *Praecipiendi modi.* 'Methods of teaching.' **1781** *election.* choice. **1784–7** *But arts . . . barren soil.* Quintilian, I, preface, 26. **1789–1837** *As we should . . . jests.* Quintilian, II. iv. 3–6, 14, 10–11; I. i. 5; ii. 27–8; II. v. 19–23; I. viii. 5–9. **1815** *Donne.* Cf. *Conv. Dr.* 158. **1816** *Chaucer.* Cf. ll. 1964–5 below. **1822** *squalor.* Aridity, roughness (*OED*'s only example). **1824** *writ no language.* Cf. Sidney's criticism of Spenser's *The Shepherd's Calendar*: 'That same framing of his style to an old rustic language I dare not allow', etc., *An Apology for Poetry*, ed. Geoffrey Shepherd (London, 1965), p. 133. **1825** *his matter.* Contrast *Conv. Dr.* 15–16. **1826** *Quintilian.* I. viii. 5. **1835** *the later.* i.e. Greek New Comedy. **1836** *sentences.* Moral sentiments.

1838–40 (margin) *Fals[a] querel[a] fugiend[a]* 'False quarrels to be avoided.' **1838–74** *We should not . . . thing long.* Quintilian, I. xii. 16; i. 1–2; xii. 10–11; 15; 2–7. **1838** *patronage.* defence. **1850–1** (margin) *Platonis . . . Italiam.* 'Plato's travel to

Italy.' This was after the death of Socrates in 399 BC. **1853** *Egypt.* Cicero, *De Finibus*, v. xxix. **1868** *lose.* F 'loose'; both senses are present.

1875–6 (margin) *Praecept*[a] *element*[aria]. 'Elementary precepts.' **1879–80** *elementarii senes.* 'Old men still learning the rudiments'; cf. Seneca, *Epist.* xxxvi. 4. **1880** *bank.* A money-dealer's shop; hence the following metaphor (the modern sense of the word was still emerging). **1882** *talking and eloquence.* Quintilian, VIII, preface, 13. **1887–8** *Pure . . . customary.* Quintilian, VIII, preface, 23, 25. **1891** *all knowledges.* Quintilian, II. xxi. 14, quoting Cicero, *De Oratore*, I. vi. 20. **1896–7** *If a man . . . no end.* Quintilian, I, preface, 25.

1898–9 (margin) *De orationis dignitate.* 'On the dignity of speech.' **1898–1933** *Speech . . . the bowline.* From Vives, *De Ratione Dicendi*, i (*Opera* (1555), i. 85). **1901–2** *deorum hominumque interpres.* 'The interpreter of gods and men'; cf. Virgil, *Aeneid*, iv. 356, '*interpres divum*'. **1903** *soul.* Cf. *UV* 34. 50 and n. **1907** *Ἐγκύκλο παιδείαν.* 'General education'; see Quintilian, I. x. I. **1908–9** *verborum . . . eloquentiae.* 'The choice of words is the beginning of eloquence'; from Julius Caesar's lost work *De Analogia*, quoted by Cicero, *Brutus*, 253. **1915** *translation.* Figurative language; in Greek, 'metaphor' (Quintilian, VIII. vi. 4). **1917** *nam . . . prudenti.* 'For the wise man uses no metaphor thoughtlessly': from Vives, loc. cit. above (ll. 1898–1933 n.). **1917–18** *commodity.* Convenience; appropriateness (Vives: *commoditas*). **1922** *obsceneness.* Stylistic offensiveness (cf. l. 2044). *property.* propriety. **1923** *far-fet.* far-fetched. *to be understood.* understanding. **1934–6** *castratam . . . Alpes.* From Quintilian, VIII. vi. 15, 17 (quoted in part by Vives), giving examples of metaphors which are unseemly (*deformis*): 'The state was gelded by the death of Africanus'; 'Glaucia, the excrement of the senate-house' (both examples from Cicero, *De Oratore*, III. xli. 164); '[Jupiter] bespewed the Alps with white snow' (from Furius, second-century epic poet; cf. Horace, *Sat.* II. v. 11). **1936–8** *All attempts . . . use.* Cf. Horace, *The Art of Poetry*, 46 ff. **1937** *hard.* Cf. l. 1941. Latin *durus*, used by Quintilian for harsh or far-fetched metaphors, VIII. vi. 17–18, etc. **1942–3** *It is an honest . . . chiefs.* Quintilian, I. vi. 2. **1944** ff. (margin) *Consuetudo; Perspicuitas; Venustas; Auctoritas.* 'Custom'; 'perspicuity'; 'grace'; 'authority'. **1944–62** *Custom . . . consent of the good.* Quintilian, I. vi. 3; v. 39–41, 43–5. **1952** *intermission.* i.e. temporary disuse. **1962–3** *Virgil . . . pictai!* Quintilian, I. vii. 18. *Pictai* and *aquai* are archaic genitive spellings (for *pictae, aquae*), used by Virgil, *Aeneid*, ix. 26; vii. 464. **1963** *scabrous.* harsh. **1964** *Chaucerisms.* i.e. archaisms. Cf. l. 1816 above. **1969–70** *mere . . . greenness.* i.e. grass and greenness alone. **1972** *paronomasies.* Word-play; puns. **1973–4** *quae per . . . cadunt.* See l. 708 above and n.; cf. ll. 2839–43 below. **1975** *grateful.* pleasing. **1976–2048** *Our composition . . . figured language.* From Vives, *De Ratione Dicendi*, i (*Opera* (1555), i. 93–101). **1983** *veer out.* Let out. **1986** *profits by.* Is of value on account of. **1988** (margin) *De stilo.* 'Of style.' **1989** (margin) *Tacitus.* An instance of the 'strict and succinct' style; Jonson substitutes him for Vives' example, Lysias. **1993–4** (margin) *Seneca et Fabianus.* Vives is referring to M. Seneca's criticism of the obscure style of Papirius Fabianus, a Greek rhetorician of the first century AD: see *Controversiae*, ii, preface, 1–5. **1999** (margin) *Periodi.* 'sentences'. **2008–9** *Rectitudo . . . offuscat.* 'Directness gives light; ambiguity and circumlocution darken.' From Vives.

2013–15 (margin) *Obscuritas . . . tenebras.* 'Obscurity spreads darkness.' **2015** *the fable.* Of the cock on the dunghill; Phaedrus, III. xii; Aesop's first fable in Caxton's version. **2016** *skein of silk.* Cf. *Songs*, 34. 6; *ML* Ind. 136–40. *found.* H & S suggest 'wound' as a possible emendment. **2019** (margin) *Superlatio.* 'Exaggeration; hyperbole'. **2021–8** *It was ridiculous . . . spoken.* Jonson takes these examples from M. Seneca, *Suasoriae*, i. 11–12. Cestius: 'The ocean roars, as though angry that you are leaving the land behind.' Virgil: 'You might suppose there floated the Cyclades uptorn', *Aeneid*, viii. 691; Quintilian, VIII. vi. 68. **2029–30** *eos . . . perrumpere.* 'Those armies of the Roman people which might break through the heavens'; from Vives, slightly misquoting Caesar's *The Spanish War*, 42. **2044** *obsceneness.* See l. 1922 n. **2046** *commodity.* convenience.

2049–50 (margin) *Oratio . . . animi.* 'Speech, the image of the mind.' **2049–2108** *Language . . . et nervos.* From Vives, *De Ratione Dicendi*, ii (*Opera* (1555), pp. 103–5). **2049** *Language . . . see thee.* Proverbial: see Tilley, S735, 'Speech is the picture (index) of the mind', and examples. **2053–4** *feature and composition.* Physical and mental make-up. **2055 ff.** (margin) *Structura . . . pumila.* 'Structure and stature: sublime, low, dwarfish.' **2058** *the absolution plenteous.* i.e. the sentences sonorously rounded off. **2061** *members and periods.* Clauses and sentences. **2062** *knitting or number.* Ciceronian sentences were especially admired (i) for the integration of their component parts—the sentences could not be rearranged, abbreviated, or prematurely terminated without loss; and (ii) for their rhythmical qualities. **2062–3** (margin) *Mediocris . . . placida.* 'The middle [style]: clear and easy.' **2064–5** *well-turned.* Cf. the tribute to Shakespeare, *UV* 26. 68. **2065–9** (margin) *Vitiosa . . . abjecta.* 'Faulty speech: harsh, swelling, irregular, affected, mean.' **2072** *tumorous.* Swelling, turgid. **2076** *flat cap.* At this time worn only by working townsfolk, though originally introduced at court by Henry VIII. *trunk-hose.* Baggy breeches, sometimes stuffed with wool, covering the hips and upper thighs; fashionable a century earlier, now worn by pages. *hobby-horse cloak.* A long cloak, worn e.g. by servants and soldiers. **2077** *gloves . . . girdle.* Probably the style of coachmen, grooms, post-boys, etc. **2080** (margin) *Figura.* 'form'. **2082** *numerous.* rhythmical. **2085** (margin) *Cutis sive cortex.* 'Skin or rind.' **2086** *coagmentation.* Fitting together. (margin) *Compositio.* 'composition'. **2088–9** *run your finger . . . joint.* Cf. Horace, *The Art of Poetry*, ll. 292–4. **2089** *horrid.* rough. **2091** (margin) *Carnosa.* 'fleshy'. **2092** *circuit.* circumlocution. **2093** *arvina orationis.* 'The lard of speech.' (margin) *Adipata.* 'fat'. **2096** *picked.* Refined; carefully chosen. *oratio . . . pasta.* 'Speech rich ["oily"] and well fed.' **2097** (margin) *Redundans.* 'redundant'. **2098–9** *redundat . . . est.* 'It abounds in blood, by which much more is said than is necessary.' **2102–4** (margin) *Jejuna . . . strigosa.* 'Thin, lean, scraggy.' **2107** (margin) *Ossea et nervosa.* 'Bony and sinewy.' **2109–13** (margin) *Notae . . . intemper*[*antia*]. 'Viscount St Albans's observations on the excesses of learning.' **2109–44** *It was well noted . . . level.* Jonson is here summarizing passages from bk. i of Bacon's *The Advancement of Learning* (Everyman edn., ed. G. W. Kitchin (London and New York, 1915), pp. 24–33). **2126** *affectations of.* Strivings for. **2127** *separation.* divergence. **2130** *undertakers.* Committed students. **2133** *digladiations.* Crossing of words. *facility of credit.* Easy credulity. **2136** *convenience.* Agreement, accord. **2142** *monte potiri.* Translated in the text. Cf. Ovid, *Metam.* v. 254; Bacon, ed. cit. above (ll. 2109–44 n.), p. 33.

2145–6 (margin) *De optimo scriptore.* 'Of the best writer.' **2148–311** *The conceits . . . serve you.* Taken from John Hoskyns's *Directions for Speech and Style* (composed *c.*1599), preserved in three manuscripts in the British Library; Harley MS 850 helps to correct Jonson's printed text. See Louise B. Osborne,*TLS* 1 May 1930, p. 370. From l. 2182 Hoskyns is in turn following Lipsius, *Epistolica Institutio, Opera* (1623), iii, pp. 3–18. **2149** *tongue . . . interpreter.* Horace, *The Art of Poetry*, 111. **2154** *Cicero.* 'For no one can be a correct speaker who is not a sound thinker': *Brutus*, vi. 23 (*recte* for Cicero's *bene*, following Hoskyns). **2164** *frame.* order. **2165** *preposterous.* Back to front. **2179** *wit.* sense.

2183 (margin) *De stilo epistolari.* 'Of the epistolary style.' *Inventio.* 'Invention': i.e. selection of topics to be treated. **2184** *business.* F 'baseness' (correction from Hoskyns, Harley MS). **2205–6** [*you are*]. From Harley MS. **2208** [*most*]. Harley MS. **2209** *brief.* Harley MS; F 'beliefe'. **2211** *consequence.* sequence.

2214 (margin) *Modus.* 'Fashion'—i.e. the process of making. **2215** (margin) *Brevitas.* 'brevity'. **2227** *cense.* Endowments (Latin *census*). **2234** *submiss.* submissive. **2238** *discharges.* Performance of duties. **2241** *breviates.* summaries. **2243** *circuit.* See l. 2092 n. **2249** *baits.* Stops for refreshment. **2257–8** *my reading . . . accuse him not.* Jonson is still quoting Hoskyns throughout this long passage. **2259** (margin) *Perspicu[i]tas.* 'perspicuity'. **2260** [*endangered . . . often-times*]. From Harley MS. **2262** *terms of art.* Technical terms. **2264** *too much light.* See *Volp.* v. ii. 23 and n. **2269** *conceiving.* Harley MS; F 'concerning'. **2272** *censure.* judgement. **2282** *curious.* fancy. **2285** [*and words*]. Harley MS. **2296–7** *cast a ring for.* Strive after. **2297–8** '*accommodation*'. See *2 Henry IV*, III. ii. 66–79. **2298** '*compliment*'. Both the (comparatively recent) word and the activity it denoted were suspect: cf. *Twelfth Night*, III. i. 96. '*spirit*'. Cf. *EMI* I. iii. 112; *Epig.* 19. 2 and n. **2301** *pithy.* Harley MS; F 'pretty'. **2303–4** *The Courtier.* Castiglione's *Il Cortegiano* (1528; trs. Hoby, 1561). **2305** (margin) *Discretio.* 'discrimination'.

2313 *in the primogeniture.* Poetry is here regarded as the 'first born' of the literary kinds. *peccant humours.* Unhealthy characteristics. Cf. Bacon, *The Advancement of Learning*, ed. cit. above (ll. 2109–44 n.), pp. 31, 35. (margin) *De Poetica.* 'Of poetry.' **2317** *charact.* Stamp, mark. **2320** *professors*'. practitioners'. **2324** *Placentia.* Complaisance. **2326–56** *Whilst I name . . . be such.* From Erasmus's letter to Martin Dorp, 1515, *Collected Works*, 3, *Correspondence 1514–1516* (Toronto and Buffalo, 1976), pp. 117–21. **2328–9** *Ubi . . . injuriam?* 'Where discussion of faults is general, no individual is hurt'; cf. Jerome, *Epist.* cxxv. 5. **2334** *Auriculas . . . vero?* 'Gnaw tender ears with biting truth': Persius, *Sat.* i. 107–8 (Jonson reads *rodere*, 'gnaw', for *radere*, 'rasp'). **2335** *Remedii . . . spes.* 'Our vows for a remedy were always more genuine than our hopes.' Source untraced; despite Jonson's sidenote, not in Livy (nor in Livius Andronicus). **2337–8** *sharp . . . corrosives.* Cf. *Und.* 26. 2 and n. **2343** (margin) *Sexus femin[arum].* 'The female sex.' **2345** *the contumely . . . particular.* The reproach concerned them personally. **2347–56** *If I* *see* . . . *be such.* Cf. *Epig.* 30 and 38. **2351** *on the mending hand.* Bent on mending matters. **2352** *ingenuously.* F 'ingeniously' (the words were commonly confused). **2359** *several.* Private possession. **2366–7** *concomitancy.* accompaniment.

2369–70 κατ' ἐξοχὴν. 'The maker *par excellence.*' **2372** Aristotle, *Poetics*, i. 2–4. **2374–5** *not he* . . . *only.* Cf. Sidney, *An Apology for Poetry*, ed. Shepherd, p. 103. **2376** *like the truth.* Cf. *SW*, second prologue, 9–10: 'For he knows, poet never credit gained | By writing truths, but things like truth, well feigned.'

2380 *alone.* single. **2385** *Aeneas* . . . *arma.* 'These arms Aeneas from victorious Greeks': *Aeneid*, iii. 288. **2387** *Omnia* . . . *vendas.* 'You buy everything, Castor; so the result will be that you sell everything'; a one-line epigram of Martial, VII. xcviii. **2389** *Pauper* . . . *pauper.* 'Cinna wishes to appear poor, and he is poor': another one-line epigram, Martial, VIII. xix. **2391** *designs.* designates. **2392** *Quod* . . . *claret.* 'Which is also made clear in my first book' (*carmen*, 'poem'): Lucretius, *De Rerum Natura*, vi. 937. **2394** *sentence.* sentiment. **2395–6** *dramatic* . . . *poem.* Cf. Jonson's own terminology, e.g. his address 'To the Readers', *Sej.*, l. 14.

2398–2404 *A poem* . . . *the poet.* From Joannes Buchler, *Reformata Poeseos Institutio* (1633), vol. vi, p. 414, drawing in turn upon Pontanus, *Poeticae Institutiones* (1594), ch. vii (H & S, xi. 282). **2404** *habit.* practice. **2405** (margin) *Artium regina.* 'The queen of arts.' **2409** *Aristotle.* Perhaps a remote memory of *Poetics*, VIII. ix. 3 and *Politics*, VII. xv. 5. Cf. *Volp.* Epist. Ded. 17 ff. **2411** *Tully.* Cicero, *Pro Archia Poeta*, vii. 16. **2414** *travels.* F 'travails'; both senses are present. **2415** *earnest.* seriousness. **2416** *recesses.* retreats. **2419–23** *And whereas* . . . *sweetness.* Cf. Sidney, *An Apology for Poetry*, ed. Shepherd, pp. 112–13. **2420–1** *poesy* . . . *philosophy.* Strabo, *Geography*, I. ii. 3. **2426–7** (margin) *Poet[ae] differentiae.* 'The distinguishing marks of the poet.' **2434** (margin) *Ingenium.* 'Talent': Jonson's 'natural wit'. Cf. Hobbes, *Leviathan*, I. viii. **2434–6** *For whereas* . . . *mind.* Cicero, *Pro Archia Poeta*, viii. 18. **2437–46** *as Seneca* . . . *ascend.* See Seneca, *On Tranquillity of Mind*, xvii. 10–11. **2437–8** *aliquando* . . . *esse.* 'Sometimes it is a pleasure to Anacreon to rave.' **2439–40** *frustra* . . . *pulsavit.* 'The sane mind knocks in vain at the door of poetry': Plato, *Phaedrus*, 245 A (Jonson's *pulsavit* replaces *pepulit* in Seneca's quotation of this passage). **2440–2** *nullum* . . . *mens.* 'No great genius has ever existed without some touch of madness' (Aristotle, *Problems*, xxx. i). 'The lofty utterance that rises above itself is impossible unless the mind is excited' (Seneca, loc. cit.). **2449–50** *Est deus* . . . *venit.* 'There is a god within us. It is when he stirs us that our bosom warms; from celestial places comes our inspiration.' Merging two passages from Ovid: *Fasti*, vi. 5; *The Art of Love*, iii. 549–50. **2451–2** *scio* . . . *aurae.* 'I know there has never been an outstanding poet without a richer than usual share of divine inspiration'; Lispius, *Electa*, II. xvii: *Opera* (1623), p. 427. **2454** *mediocres, or imos.* The ordinary or inferior. **2456–7** *solus rex* . . . *nascitur.* See *Epig.* 4. 3 n.; and cf. *Epig.* 79. 1; *Panegyre*, 163. (The passage is from Florus, not Petronius.) **2459** (margin) *Exercitatio.* 'exercise'. **2459–66** *If his wit* . . . *anew.* Cf. Horace, *Sat.* II. iii, opening; Persius, *Sat.* i. 106; Quintilian, X. iii. 21. **2466** *forge* . . . *anew.* Horace, *The Art of Poetry*, 439–41; cf. *UV* 26. 59–62. **2468** *the first quarter.* i.e. in the first three months of trying. **2471** *sense.* 'A passage, context, or set of sentences, expressed in bare prose, used as material for the composition of Latin or Greek verses': *OED* 'sense', 26 (first example, 1693). *rhymer . . . poet.* Cf. *For.* 12. 68–9 and n.; *Conv. Dr.* 17 (etc.); Sidney, *An Apology for Poetry*, ed. Shepherd, p. 121. **2472** *Virgil.* From Donatus's *Life*, ll. 78–82. **2474** *Scaliger the father.* J. C. Scaliger (1484–1558), father of J. J. Scaliger (1540–1609). **2477** *Valerius Maximus. De Dictis et Factis Memorabilibus*, III. vii. 11. **2487** *rattles.* Cf. *Und.* 84. i. 16–20. **2490–503** *The third requisite . . . follow them.* From Buchler, *Institutio Poetica* (1633), xi, p. 421. **2497** *concoct.* digest. **2498** *Horace. The Art of Poetry*, 133. **2500** *with the bee.* Seneca, *Epist.* lxxxiv. **2504** *Archilochus.* Iambic and elegiac poet, of Paros; eighth–seventh century BC. **2505** *Alcaeus.* Lyric poet of Lesbos, born *c.* 620 BC. *lyrics.* Lyric poets. **2507** (margin) *Lectio.* 'reading'. **2507–8** *reading . . . full man.* Tilley, R39; Bacon, 'Of Studies'. **2512–14** *And not . . . Helicon.* Persius, *Sat.*, prologue. **2516** (margin) *Ars coron*[*at*]. 'Art crowns.' **2518** *it is art only.* Cf. *UV* 26. 55–8. **2520** *Tully.* Cicero, *Pro Archia Poeta*, vii. 15. **2521** *conformation.* Formative influence (Cicero's *conformatio*). **2523** *Simylus.* Athenian comic writer, *fl.* 354 BC. *Stobaeus.* Compiler of an anthology of miscellaneous writings, early fifth century AD. Jonson has picked up the quotation from Pontanus, *Poeticae Institutiones* (1594), p. 2. **2525–6** οὔτε . . . κεκτημένη. 'Neither is nature sufficient without art, nor art in any way without nature.' **2530–1** *fool . . . master.* Cf. l. 23 above and n. **2535–51** *Aristotle . . . school of men.* From Daniel Heinsius, *De Tragoediae Constitutione* (Leyden, 1611), ch. 1. **2540** *offices.* tasks. **2549** *shadow.* Cf. l. 1689 above. **2550–1** (margin) *Virorum . . . respub*[*lica*]. 'The state, the school of men.' **2551–2** *the poet . . . the orator.* Cicero, *De Oratore*, I. xvi. 70. **2553** *numbers.* See l. 2062 n. **2556** *stirring of affections.* Cf. *Volp.* Epist. Ded. 104. **2558–9** *Lysippus . . . Apelles.* Alexander the Great is said to have forbidden any sculptor other than Lysippus (of Sicyon, active from 370 BC) to model him in bronze, and any painter other than Apelles (of Ionia; famed for his realism) to paint him: Horace, *Epist.* II. i. 239–41. **2559** *graver.* Engraving tool. **2561** *insulting.* exulting. **2568** *comic poet.* Gnaeus Naevius, *c.* 270–*c.* 199 BC, outspoken Roman poet and dramatist. The epitaph, said to have been composed by Naevius himself, is quoted (in a slightly different form) by Aulus Gellius, *Attic Nights*, I. xxiv: 'If immortals could weep for mortals, then the divine Camanae [the muses] would weep for Naevius; for after he was consigned as treasure to Orcus, the Romans immediately forgot how to speak Latin.' **2574–5** *Musas . . . locuturas.* 'If the muses wished to speak Latin, they would speak in the style of Plautus': the opinion of Stilo (Roman grammarian and teacher of Varro and Cicero) as quoted by Varro (116–27 BC, scholar and poet), as quoted in turn by Quintilian, X. i. 99. **2577** *prince . . . elegancy.* Aulus Gellius, *Attic Nights*, VI. xvii. 4. **2579–602** *I am not . . . absolute.* From Heinsius, *De Tragoediae Constitutione*, i. **2579** *conclude.* confine. **2582** *those laws.* Cf. *EMO* Ind. 247 ff. **2585–6** *Demosthenes.* The great Athenian statesman and orator, *c.* 500–429 BC. Plutarch (*Demosthenes*, iv) suggests his welfare and tuition were neglected in his youth; hence the notion that he was entirely self-taught. **2587** *'heavenly' . . . lighten.* Aristophanes, *Acharnians*, 530–1; cf. Cicero, *Letters to Atticus*, I a. **2589** *Alcibiades.* Born shortly before 450 BC; Demosthenes (*Against Meidias*, 145) testifies that he was regarded as the best general and ablest speaker of his day. **2598–9** *Aristophanes wittily reprehended.* See *Acharnians*, 407–79; and *Thesmophoriazusae, passim.* **2603–4** *To judge . . . best.* A common Renaissance notion, but Jonson is drawing (as his side-note indicates) upon J. J. Scaliger, *Confutatio Fabulae Burdonum*, in *Opuscula* (1612), p. 85; who cites Giraldi of Ferrara, 1479–1552 (Lilius Gregorius Gyraldus). **2604–5** *Nemo . . . scripsit.* 'No one has judged of poets so unhappily as he who wrote about poets.' **2606** *tinkers.* Tilley, T347: 'A tinker stops one hole and makes two.' Jonson's side-notes refer to Seneca's strictures on the triviality of much literary and seemingly humanistic study. **2609–14** *But the office . . . a man.* From Heinsius, *Ad Horatii de Plauto et Terentio Judicium, Dissertatio*, prefixed to his edition of Terence (1618). **2610** *throw by.* Reject, put aside. **2611** *syllabe.* Jonson's usual spelling: cf., for example, *Und.* 70. 63. **2615** *civility.* cultivation. **2625** *Cato, the Grammarian.* Publius Valerius Cato, poet and rhetorician, born *c.*100–90 BC. *Lucilius.* 180–102 BC, founder of Roman satire. Horace deplores the 'muddy stream' of his verse, *Sat.* I. iv. 11. **2621–2** *Cato . . . poetas.* 'Cato the grammarian, the Latin siren; he alone reads and makes poets.' Suetonius, *On Grammarians*, xi (Jonson reads *et* for *ac*). **2623** *Quintilian . . . same heresy.* i.e. in defending Lucilius against Horace's criticism; but Quintilian also thought that Lucilius had been generally over-praised: x. i. 94. *but rejected.* By Heinsius. **2624** *Choerilus.* A poet who followed Alexander the Great and wrote epic verses on his victories. For Horace's scorn, see *The Art of Poetry*, 357–8; *Epist.* II. i. 232–4. **2625** *Laberius.* Politically outspoken Roman knight and writer of mimes (*c.*105–43 BC). Julius Caesar forced him to appear in one of his own mimes in competition with Publilius Syrus. Horace refers disdainfully to him, *Sat.* I. x. 6. *Julius.* Julius Caesar Scaliger, father of Joseph. **2625–47** *But chiefly . . . condemn Plautus.* From Heinsius, op. cit. See Horace, *Epist.* II. i. 170 ff. **2629** *censor.* critic. **2637** *gracious.* favoured. **2638** *Augustus . . . manling.* See Suetonius' *Life of Horace.* **2641** *p[a]lace.* F 'place'. **2642** *esteem Terence.* Horace, *Epist.* II. i. 59. **2644** *joins him with Menander.* Not so; Jonson has misread.

2648–700 *The parts of a comedy . . . original dung-cart.* From Heinsius, op. cit. **2650** διδάσκαλοι. 'Teachers'; but this was actually because they trained the chorus. **2653** *fowling.* i.e. hunting. F3 'fooling'. **2654** *Aristotle.* Heinsius has misunderstood Aristotle, who in fact says (*Poetics*, v. 1–2) that comedy 'is a representation of inferior people, not indeed in the full sense of the word bad, but the laughable is a species of the base or ugly. It consists in some blunder or ugliness that does not cause pain or disaster, an obvious example being the comic mask which is ugly and distorted but not painful'. Cf. *Epig.* 2. 12; and Sidney, *Apology*, ed. Shepherd, pp. 136–7. **2661** *Plato. Republic*, iii. 388–9, referring to laughter in heaven at the lame Hephaestus, *Iliad*, i. 599. **2662** *he presented.* F 'the presented'. **2664** *Aristotle.* See note to l. 2654. **2671** *sinister.* malicious. **2686** *Socrates.* In Aristophanes' *The Clouds*, 218 ff. **2689–90** *measure . . . scale. The Clouds*, 144 ff. **2690** *the engine.* The Greek stage machinery that could hoist an actor aloft. **2694** *tasten.* pleased. **2697** *a horse-race or a hunting-match. Und.* 44. 70–3; *SW* I. i. 34–6. **2699** *tumbril.* The cart in which tragedy was once acted: Horace, *The Art of Poetry*, 275.

2701–end. From Heinsius, *De Tragoediae Constitutione*, ch. iv, drawing in turn upon Aristotle, *Poetics*, vii and viii. **2702–3** (margin) *fable or plot.* Jonson's use of 'fable' in this sense predates the *OED*'s first example (of Rymer, 1678). **2732** *convenient.* fitting. **2734–5** [*an elephant . . . less than*]. Castelain conjecturally supplies these words, from Heinsius's Latin. **2736** *rhinocerote.* Rhinoceros (cf. *Epig.* 28. 4). **2737** *absolute.* perfect. **2744** *Tityus.* A famous giant, son of Terra (or Elara and Jupiter); said to cover nine acres when outstretched; consigned to hell by Latona. **2752** *pismire.* ant. **2759** *produce and determine it.* Extend it, and round it off. **2768** *one day.* Jonson's own characteristic practice; though Aristotle (*Poetics*, v. 4) is actually more approximate in his prescription. **2773–4** *considerable.* To be considered. **2795** *pretermitted.* omitted. **2797** *fought with Achilles. Iliad,* xx. 156–352. **2798** *by Venus. Iliad,* v. 311–18. **2799** *prosecutes.* follows. **2800** *error.* wandering. **2802** *laid by.* Set aside. **2805** *the philosopher.* Aristotle, *Poetics,* viii. 2. **2807** *Juvenal. Sat.* i. 1–2 (the name is 'Cordus'; though 'Codrus' appears in *Sat.* iii). **2835** *of which hereafter.* Jonson seems to have intended to translate Heinsius's eleventh chapter. **2837** *in Homer. Iliad,* vii. 181–312.

2841–3 *Et quae . . . frugiferai.* Three altered and rearranged lines from Martial, xi. 90 (not 91, as Jonson's note says): 'And those who fall over rough places and high cliffs'; 'And whatever Accius and Pacuvius [Roman tragedians] spew'; 'And in amazed wonder you read of the "frugiferous terrene"'. This detached segment perhaps belongs near ll. 707 ff., where this epigram is quoted again. Cf. also ll. 1973–4.

CONVERSATIONS WITH DRUMMOND

In the summer of 1618 Ben Jonson (a very large man, even before his final illness) journeyed by foot from London to Scotland, arriving in Edinburgh in early August. The precise reasons for his journey are unknown. As a former pupil of the author of *Britannia,* Jonson must have been curious to see something of the northern parts of the kingdom, and especially to glimpse the country from which his own family had come. He planned to commemorate his journey in verse, and also to write 'a fisher or pastoral play' set on Loch Lomond, and accordingly scouted for historical and geographical materials as he travelled. The journey aroused the solicitous interest of King James, the affectionate amusement of Lord Bacon, and the skittish emulation of John Taylor, the 'Water Poet'. Possibly Jonson wagered on his chances of successfully completing this athletic undertaking (see *UV* 46 and n.).

Some time late in 1618 and early in 1619 (before 17 January) Jonson stayed with William Drummond (1585–1649), laird of Hawthornden, which lies seven miles south of Edinburgh. Drummond, a bachelor thirteen years Jonson's junior, had originally trained in the law; he was a scholarly poet with old-fashioned tastes, well read in several languages, and methodical in his ways. He and Jonson shared a passion for poetry and scholarship, but in other ways were temperamentally opposed, as Drummond's notes frequently reveal (see, e.g., 81–5, 512–13, 605–12). Drawn by his host's questioning and his drink, reassured (or perhaps bored) by the isolation of Hawthornden and its distance from London, Jonson spoke freely about himself and his great contemporaries. The 'conversations' which Drummond records are entirely one-sided: they are in fact the 'informations' and opinions of Jonson himself. Only in the final postscript, evidently written after his outspoken guest had departed, do Drummond's own views of the meeting finally emerge.

The *Conversations* are a unique and tantalizing source of contemporary gossip and information: tantalizing, because they present so many textual and interpretative difficulties. They were first published in an abridged form in the Folio edition of Drummond's prose and verse writings that appeared in 1711. The original manuscript has vanished, but in the early 1830s David Laing discovered a seemingly reliable transcription of the *Conversations* that had been made sometime before 1710 by Sir Robert Sibbald, an Edinburgh antiquary and physician who was probably a friend of Drummond's son (who died in 1713). The present text, based on H & S, is taken from Sibbald (= MS), corrected occasionally from the 1711 Folio of Drummond's *Works*. Drummond's notes—at least in Sibbald's transcription—are syntactically compressed, often to the point of ambiguity. They contain occasional obvious errors of nomenclature and fact. To present them in a modernized edition is inevitably to close off certain possibilities of meaning; the editorial notes attempt to indicate the more crucial of these regularizings.

Drummond is sometimes accused of having recorded certain of Jonson's jocular or ironical comments as though they were solemn facts. Yet one cannot fairly deduce humourlessness from these jottings alone, which were intended not for publication but as shorthand reminders of the views and opinions of his famous guest.

1. 1 *Heroologia*. Cf. the similarly titled *Heroologia Anglica* (1620), by Jonson's friend Henry Holland (*UV* 6 n.); and Jonson's celebration of English worthies in *P.H. Barr.* and *Queens*. **2** *his country*. Thus 1711; MS: 'this country'. **4** *Campion and Daniel*. See *Und.* 29 n. Daniel had found 'those continual cadences of couplets used in long and continued poems . . . very tiresome and unpleasing', *Poems and A Defence of Rhyme*, ed. A. C. Sprague (Chicago and London, 1965), p. 155. Jonson's preference is expressed again at l. 327 below. **6** *broken*. i.e. with a caesura. **6–7** *cross-rhymes*. i.e. non-couplet rhymes.

2. 11–12 *Martial . . . translated. Und.* 90.

3. 14 *a decorum*. Cf. the criticism made of Guarini, Lucan, and (again) of Sidney, ll. 47–8, 537–8 below. **16** *papers . . . Raleigh*. Spenser's letter to Raleigh was appended to the 1590 edition of bks. i–iii of *The Faerie Queene*; Jonson seems to refer here to a fuller document. **17** *no poet*. Cf. *For.* 12. 69 n. **18** *Poly-O[l]bion*. For a different opinion, see *UV* 30. 48 ff. **20** *long verses*. The twelve-syllable lines of *Poly-Olbion*, rhyming in couplets. **22** *his verses*. See *Epig.* 132 and n. **23** *Fairfax*. Edwar[d] Fairfax (d. 1635) published in 1600 his *Godfrey of Bulloigne*, the first complete translation of Tasso's *Gerusalemme liberate*. **24** *Homer and Virgil*. Arthur Hall's and George Chapman's translations of the *Iliad* (1581, 1598) were both in fourteeners, as was Thomas Phaer's translation of the *Aeneid* (1558, 1562; completed by Thomas Twyne, 1584). **26** *Harington's Ariosto*. Sir John Harington's translation of *Orlando Furioso* was published in 1591. **28** *epigrams*. Harington's epigrams were published after his death (in 1612): collections in 1613, 1615, 1618. Cf. the judgement on Owen, ll. 181–2 below. **30** *Warner*. William Warner, ?1588–1609. *Albion's England* is a metrical history of England from the time of Noah; the section to which Jonson objects, dealing with events since 1603, was published posthumously in 1612. **32** *Donne's Anniversary.* The First and Second *Anniversaries: An Anatomy of the World* and *Of the Progress of the Soul.* The implications of Jonson's comment and Donne's reply are examined by W. Milgate in his general introduction to Donne's *Epithalamions,* pp. xl ff. **36** *accent.* See Helen Gardner's comments on Donne's versification in her edition of *Divine Poems,* pp. 54–5, and of *Elegies,* pp. 109–10. **37** *Shakespeare wanted art.* See *UV* 26. 55 ff. and n. **38** *Sharpham.* Edward Sharpham of the Middle Temple published two plays in 1607, *The Fleire* and *Cupid's Whirligig. Day.* John Day, dramatist, author of *The Isle of Gulls* (1606), *Law Tricks* (1608), and *Humour out of Breath* (1608). Cf. l. 133 below. *Dekker.* Thomas Dekker had collaborated with Day and also with Jonson himself, for Henslowe; Jonson ridiculed him in *Poetaster* in 1601 (as 'Demetrius'); Dekker retorted in *Satiromastix* (1602). *Minsheu.* John Minsheu, lexicographer and linguist, author of Spanish dictionaries, a grammar, and a *Guide to Tongues* (1617). **40** *Abraham Fraunce. fl.* 1587–1633; published in English hexameters *The Countess of Pembroke's Ivychurch* in three parts (1591, 1592) and *The Countess of Pembroke's Emmanuel* (1591). **41** *Fletcher.* No masques by Fletcher are known; possibly a slip for 'Beaumont' (*Masque of the Inner Temple and Gray's Inn,* 1613). *Chapman.* George Chapman's *Memorable Masque of . . . the Middle Temple and Lincoln's Inn* (1613).

4.   **42** *stranger.* i.e. foreign. **43** *poet . . . verser.* Cf. the judgements at ll. 17, 50; a familiar classical distinction. *wrote not fiction.* Cf. 'For he knows poet never credit gained | By writing truths, but things like truths, well feigned': *SW,* second prologue, 9–10. **45** *tyrant's bed.* Procrustes of Attica tied travellers to a bed; if they exceeded its length, they were trimmed; if shorter, they were stretched to equal it. Stefano Guazzo had used the same figure in criticizing the sonnet in *Dialoghi Piaceuoli* (1587); as had Thomas Campion, of the tyranny of rhyme, in *Observations in the Art of English Poesy* (1602) (*Elizabethan Critical Essays,* ed. G. Gregory Smith (Oxford, 1904), ii. 331). **47** *Guarini.* See *Volp.* III. iv. 80 n., and the judgements at ll. 13–14 above and 537–8 below. **49** *Lucan.* Cf. l. 539 below. For Jonson's translation of a speech from Lucan, see *UV* 50. **51** *Bonefonius.* Jean Bonnefons of Clermont, author of *Pancharis* (1587). **52** *de Perron.* Cardinal Duperron (1556–1618), son of a Huguenot refugee, had converted Henri IV to Catholicism, and was a powerful figure in his day. For details of the encounter (in 1613) and of Jonson's criticism of Duperron's free translation of parts of *Aeneid* bks. i and iv, see H & S, i. 67–9. **54** *Ronsard.* Duperron had delivered his funeral *éloge* in 1585; hence, perhaps, the conversational transition here from the subject of Duperron to that of Ronsard. Ronsard's odes, in imitation of Horace, were published in five books (1550, 1553). Jonson refers to his sonnets in *Und.* 27. 22–4. **55–6** *French nor Italian.* Drummond's statement is almost certainly an exaggeration; Jonson had some competence in French (though see ll. 21–2 above) and in Italian (see Daniel C. Boughner, *The Devil's Disciple: Ben Jonson's Debt to Machiavelli* (New York, 1968)).

5.   **57** *Beatus ille. Epode,* ii; translated as *Und.* 85. **58** *Petronius.* See *Und.* 88 and n. The first line of the original should read 'Foeda est in coitu et brevis voluptas.' **60** *pant.* The word is not clear in MS. **61** *preface.* Destroyed in the fire of 1623; see *Und.* 43. 89–91 and n. It is referred to in the Q dedication to *Sej.* in 1605, and must have been rewritten after the performance of *BF* in 1614. It was apparently in dialogue form: see ll. 356–7 below. For a guess at its possible argument, see Freda L. Townsend, *Apologie for Bartholomew Fayre* (New York and London, 1947). **63–4** *Sir Edward Herbert's*. Praising Jonson, whose 'glory is | To be the Horace of our times and his'; see *The Poems . . . of Edward, Lord Herbert of Cherbury*, ed. G. C. Moore Smith (Oxford, 1923), pp. 19–20. **64–5** *Lord Aubigny's*. See *Epig.* 127 and n. **65** *ten years since*. i.e. ten years before *BF* (acted 1614). **66** *dialogue pastoral*. *Und.* 3. **68** *Parabostes' Parian*. A debated phrase; Patterson emends to 'Ferrabosco's pavan', guessing that Jonson may have written words to a dance tune of Alfonso Ferrabosco (*Epig.* 130 n.). The reference may rather be to one of Girolamo Parabosco's *Lettere Amorose* (third book, Venice, 1553), written in honour of various Venetian ladies. *Parian* = belonging to the island of Paros; hence, perhaps, pertaining to Venus; amorous. **68** *'Of Gut'*. *Epig.* 118. **68–9** *Lady Bedford's buck. Epig.* 84. **69** *'Drink. . . eyes'. For.* 9. **70** *'Swell. . . bowl'. Songs*, 8. **71–5** *'But kiss . . . long'. Und.* 2. vii, imperfectly remembered. **76** *lady . . . bath*. Now lost. **77** *Mistress Bulstrode. Und.* 49 and n.; see also ll. 569–71 below. **77–8** *satire . . . satire of*. Now lost. **79** *insisted in*. Dwelt upon. **80** *'Vitam . . . beatiorem'. Und.* 90; see ll. 11–12 above.

6.   81 *censure*. judgement. **82** *epitaph . . . prince*. Tears on the Death of Moeliades (1613), on the death of Prince Henry (d. November 1612): Drummond's first published work. See *William Drummond of Hawthornden: Poems and Prose*, ed. Robert H. MacDonald (Edinburgh and London, 1976), pp. 3–7. **84** *in running*. ?Effortlessly, with a flowing pen: cf. Latin *currente calamus*. Trimpi (pp. 124–5) thinks the reference is to run-over lines, as in l. 327 below. **85** *'Forth Feasting'*. Subtitled 'A Panegyric to his King's Most Excellent Majesty'; written to celebrate King James's return to Scotland in May 1617. See *Poems and Prose*, ed. MacDonald, pp. 83–7.

7.   87 *lost chain*. Donne's elegy 'The Bracelet'. Helen Gardner dates it 'not much after 1593', Donne, *Elegies*, p. 112. **88** *dust and feathers*. 'No use of lanterns; and in one place lay | Feathers and dust, today and yesterday', 'The Calm', ll. 17–18, Donne, *Satires*, p. 58. **89** *ere . . . old*. Cf. *Epig.* 23. 3–4, on Donne's 'most early wit'. **90** *Sir Edward Wotton*. A mistake for Sir Henry Wotton, his half-brother (1568–1639): poet, diplomatist, ambassador to Venice. For 'The Character of a Happy Life' see Helen Gardner's *New Oxford Book of English Verse*, no. 181. A slightly different text survives in Jonson's hand. **91** *Chapman's translation*. See l. 24 above, n. **93–4** *'Look to me, faith'*. Donne, *Epithalamions*, pp. 63–6; first published in *Lachrymae Lachrymarum* (3rd edn., 1613). For Herbert's elegy, see *Poems*, ed. Moore Smith, pp. 22–4. **95** *Spenser's Calendar*. From the October Eclogue of *The Shepherd's Calendar*, ll. 104–8, commending wine as an inspirer of poetry; a passage likely to appeal to Jonson. **96** *Colin*. A slip for 'Cuddy'.

8.   97 *'Transformation'*. Donne's *Metempsychosis* or *The Progress of the Soul*: *Satires*, pp. 25–6; see Milgate's general introduction, p. xxvi, on the puzzling aspects of this description. Jonson had explored this theme in *Volp.* I. ii: on the link between Donne's treatment and Jonson's, see Harry Levin, *PQ* xxii (1943), 231–9.

102 *doctor.* In March 1615. Walton in his *Life of Dr John Donne* gives partial confirmation of this story.

9. **105** *Quintilian.* See l. 9 above. **107** *Pindar.* Imitated by Jonson, e.g. in the opening of *Volp.*; *Und.* 70; *Und.* 23. 12. *Hippocrates.* Still seriously esteemed at this time; cf. *Volp.* II. ii. 106 and n. **108** *Hooker's Ecclesiastical History.* See *Disc.* 917–19. Bks. i–iv of *The Laws of Ecclesiastical Polity* were published in 1594, bk. v in 1597; after Hooker's death in 1600, three further books were published. **108–9** *children . . . beggars.* Hooker left £100 to each of his four daughters at his death (see Walton's *Appendix to the Life of Mr Richard Hooker*). **109** *Titles of Honour. Und.* 14 n.; ll. 530–2 below. **110** *Gods of the Gentiles. De Diis Syris Syntagmata Duo* (1617).

10. **114–15** *King Arthur's fiction.* Touched on by Jonson himself in *P.H. Barr.*

11. **118** *Daniel.* See l. 17 above. **119** *Drayton.* See *UV* 30 and n.; and l. 127 below. He and Drummond were on good terms. **120** *Beaumont.* Contrast *Epig.* 55. The criticism recalls Quintilian on Ovid, x. i. 88. **121** *S[i]r John Roe. Epig.* 27 and n.; 32; 33; and ll. 148–50 below. **122** *Suffolk. Epig.* 67 and n. *masque.* Probably Daniel's *Vision of the Twelve Goddesses,* 8 January 1603. **123–4** *'That . . . do us'.* 'The state and men's affairs are the best plays | Next yours . . . God threatens kings, kings lords, as lords do us': see Grierson's edition of *The Poems of John Donne,* i. 414. (The epistle first appeared in the 1635 edition of Donne.) **125** *beat.* This is written over another word in MS. *Marston.* Cf. *Epig.* 68 n., and ll. 235–7 below. The relationship of the two men was generally stormy. **126** *Alexander.* Sir William Alexander of Menstrie (?1567–1640), author of four *Monarchic Tragedies,* and other poems; tutor to Prince Henry and then to Prince Charles; Earl of Stirling, 1633. He had been a friend of Drummond since *c.*1613, and had brought him into correspondence with Drayton. **128** *Ayton.* Sir Robert Ayton or Aytoun (1570–1638) of Fife, minor poet, and secretary to Queen Anne. **129** *Field.* Nathaniel Field (1587–1633), actor and dramatist. **131** *Markham.* Gervase Markham (?1568–1637), author of *The English Arcadia, Alluding his beginning from Sir Philip Sidney's Ending* (1607, completed 1613). He passed other writers' work off as his own, and republished his own old work under new titles. **132** *faithful.* Patterson compares Catullus, xiv. 7. **133** *Day.* See l. 38 above, n. *Middleton.* Thomas Middleton, the dramatist, ?1570–1627. **134** *Chapman.* The two men were good friends, despite Chapman's 'Invective' against Jonson, written after 1623: *Poems,* ed. P. B. Bartlett, pp. 374–8. *Fletcher.* Cf. ll. 184–5 below. **135** *Overbury. Epig.* 113 and n., and ll. 173–8 below.

12. **137–4** Spenser fled with his wife and four children to Cork after their castle at Kilcolman was burnt in an O'Neill uprising in October 1598. (The 'little child' mentioned here need not have been Spenser's own.) He died a month later in King Street, Westminster, in distress, but probably not in such extreme poverty as this account suggests. **142** *paper.* See l. 16 above, n. **143** *Blating Beast.* The Blatant Beast of *The Faerie Queene,* v. xii. 37, 41, etc. (Cf. *UV* 37.9.) **144** *Duessa.* Who sometimes represents Catholic falsehood, sometimes (e.g. *FQ* v. ix. 38–50) Mary, Queen of Scots. The identification was evident to Mary's son, James VI of

Scotland (later James I of England), who wanted Spenser punished for slander.
145 *Southwell.* Robert Southwell (?1561–95), Jesuit and poet; after prolonged
imprisonment and torture, he was convicted of high treason and hanged, drawn,
and quartered at Tyburn. For 'The Burning Babe' see his *Poems*, ed. James H.
McDonald and N. P. Brown (Oxford, 1967), pp. 15–16. **147** *thirty years.*
Beaumont actually lived slightly longer: 1584–1616. **148** *Roe.* See l. 121 above
and n. He sold the family manor to his stepfather in June 1603 to raise ready
money. **151** *Mortimeriados.* Published 1596; rewritten and republished as *The
Barons' Wars* (1603). The earlier title had been criticized ('challenged') on
grammatical grounds. **152** *epigram on Drayton.* 'In Decium', *Poems of Sir John
Davies*, ed. Robert Krueger (Oxford, 1975), pp. 139–40: 'Methinks that gull did
use his terms as fit, | Which termed his love a giant for his wit.' **153** *ninth.* Actually
the tenth. See *Idea*, 18, in *Works of Michael Drayton*, ed. J. W. Hebel (Oxford,
1961), ii. 319. **156** *Heywood.* John Heywood, ?1497–?1580, author of *The Four P's*
and *The Play of the Wether*. **159** *fame . . . conscience.* Cf. *Epig.* 98. 10. **160** *best wits of
England.* These included Robert Burhill, John Hoskyns, and Jonson himself; Sir
Robert Cotton lent books from his library. *The History of the World* (1614; see *Und.*
24 and n.) was nevertheless principally researched and written by Raleigh
himself. **161** *Punic War.* Treated in bk. v of Raleigh's *History*. **162** *life of Queen
Elizabeth.* Now lost. **164** *psalms.* Mary, Countess of Pembroke, probably got
possession of her brother Sir Philip Sidney's unfinished translations of the
Psalms after his death in 1586, and revised and completed them. They circulated
in manuscript but were not published until the nineteenth century. **166–7** *Marston . . .
comedies.* Marston's father-in-law was the Revd William Wilkes, chaplain
to James I. **168–70** *Shakespeare . . . miles.* The eccentric geography of *The
Winter's Tale* is inherited from the play's principal source, Greene's *Pandosto*.
171 *Civil Wars.* Published in eight books between 1595 and 1609, but never
completed. **172** *Countess of Rutland.* See *Epig.* 79 and n. **173** *Overbury.* *Epig.* 113
and n.; *UV* 18 and n.; and l. 135 above. **174** *'Wife'.* Published 1614, and then
entitled *A Wife, Now the Widow, of Sir T. Overbury*—the author having been
poisoned in the Tower the preceding year. Ironically, the poem counsels chastity:
'in part to blame is she | Which hath without consent been only tried; | He comes
too near, that comes to be denied.' The Countess evidently took its message
literally. **176** *intend.* Maintain, prosecute (a Scotticism; *OED*, †23). **178** *that elegy.*
See Dyce's edition of *Beaumont and Fletcher*, xi. 508. The elegy alludes to the Earl
of Rutland's impotence: see *For.* 12. 93 ff. and n.; and cf. ll. 301–4 below. **179** *half
of his.* A full stop follows this phrase in MS, probably indicating a word or words
suppressed. **180** *Owen.* John Owen, ?1560–1622, headmaster of King Henry
VIII's School, Warwick; published eleven books of epigrams, highly popular in
his day. *pure.* Thus MS; 1711: 'poor'. **183** *Musaeus.* Probably translated before
1598, but published 1616; see E. S. Donno (ed.), *Elizabethan Minor Epics*
(London, 1963), pp. 16, 70–84. *verses.* i.e. heroic couplets (as in Chapman's
Odyssey, but not his *Iliad*). **184–5** *The Faithful Shepherdess.* See *UV* 8 and n. The
play was probably written by Fletcher alone, and acted 1609–10. **186** *Dyer.* Sir
Edward Dyer, d. 1607, poet and courtier; author of 'My mind to me a kingdom
is.' **187** *S[i]r P. Sidney.* Who had died in October 1586, when Jonson was only 13;
this is therefore probably second-hand evidence. **189** *Worcester.* A mistake for

'Leicester': Robert Sidney, Lord Lisle, had become 1st Earl of Leicester in 1618 (see *For.* 2 n.). His eldest son was William (*For.* 14 and n.), who had died in 1612; it is the second son, Robert Sidney (1595–1677), who is referred to here. He became 2nd Earl of Leicester in 1626.

13. **191** *Annandale.* See l. 514 below and n. **192–3** *His father . . . minister.* 'It is hardly doubtful that the father adopted the Reform doctrines under Edward, suffered for them under Mary, and took orders, finally, under Elizabeth' (H & S, i. 2). **196** *Camden.* See *Epig.* 14 and n. Camden was appointed second master at Westminster School in 1575 and headmaster in 1593. It is not necessary to assume that Camden himself was the 'friend' referred to here. **197** *wright.* Artificer, workman. *bricklayer.* Confirmed by the accounts of Aubrey and Fuller and numerous contemporary gibes. **198** *Low Countries.* Jonson refers to this period of service in *Epig.* 108. **200** *opima spolia.* The arms taken on the field of battle by the victorious from the vanquished. **201** *appealed . . . fields.* i.e. challenged to a duel. It took place in Hoxton Fields, north of the city, on 22 September 1598. **202** *his adversary.* Gabriel Spencer, an actor in Henslowe's company. **203–4** *almost at the gallows.* Jonson escaped by claiming benefit of clergy; his goods were confiscated, and he was branded on the thumb. **204** *a priest.* Possibly Thomas Wright: see *UV* 7 and n. **205** *twelve years.* 1598–1610. **206–7** i.e. these were honorary degrees. Jonson was formally inducted into the Oxford degree on 19 July 1619, after his return from Edinburgh; the degree had been conferred considerably earlier. **208** *married a wife.* On 14 November 1594 (M. Eccles, *RES* xii (1936), 257–72). **209** *Aubigny.* *Epig.* 127 and n.; ll. 64–5 above. **210** *close imprisonment.* The nature of Jonson's offence is not clear. H & S (i. 19) suspect it was connected with his recent conversion to Catholicism; Mark Eccles, *RES* xiii (1937), 385–97, thinks rather it was trouble over *The Isle of Dogs.* **213** *epigram.* *Epig.* 59 and n. **214** *When . . . England.* 1603. **215** *S[i]r Robert Cotton.* 1571–1631, the antiquary; he had been with Jonson at Westminster School; both Jonson and Camden (Cotton's former teacher and fellow antiquary) used his library in his country house at Conington in Huntingdonshire. **216** *eldest son.* Benjamin; see *Epig.* 45 and n. **220** *apprehension.* figment. **221** *disjected.* dejected. **225** *delated.* impeached. *S[i]r James Murray.* Knighted 1603; gentleman of the Privy Chamber to Prince Henry 1610. **226** *Eastward Ho.* First performed in 1606. James's lavish bestowal of knighthoods and (possibly) his Scottish accent were mocked. For circumstances and documents of the resulting troubles, see C. G. Petter's edition of the play (London, 1973), and H & S, i. 190–200. *voluntarily.* Yet in letters written at this time Jonson complains of being committed to prison without a hearing: see H & S, i. 191. **228** *had.* = Have had. **235** *Marston.* See l. 125 above. **236** *Poetaster.* In which Marston is depicted as Crispinus. **237–8** MS reads 'represented him in the stage in his youth given to venery'; the emendation is J. H. Penniman's. Marston had attempted well-meaningly but gauchely in 1599 to depict Jonson as the pedant Chrisoganus in *Histriomastix.* **240** *accidents.* occurrences. **245** *his son.* Walter Raleigh, b. 1593; at Oxford (according to his tutor) addicted to 'strange company and violent exercises'; killed during his father's expedition to Guiana, 1618. **247** *favours.* Ribbons, gloves, etc. bestowed by ladies to their lovers. **249** *pioneers.* workmen. **252** *his father.* Who had been accused of 'atheism' in his younger days. **254** *horoscopes*. Like Subtle, *Alch*. I. i. 96, etc. **260** *Pembroke*. See *Epig*. Dedn. n. **261** *reconciled . . . church*. In 1610. **264***Salisbury*. See *Epig*. 43, 63, 64; *For*. 2 n. **266** *dine with you*. Cf. *For*. 2. 61 ff. and n; and ll. 371–2, 548–9 below. **271** *Northampton*. Henry Howard, 1st Earl of Northampton (1540–1614), second son of the Earl of Surrey, the poet; a learned and unprincipled man, he changed his religion on four occasions. *brawling.* reviling. **273** *Sejanus*. Acted 1603, published 1605. The accusation of popery and treason need not have been related to this play or made on the same occasion. **278** *flatter*. A constant concern: cf. *Epig*. 36. 4, and l. 318 below. James was in fact frequently criticized from the pulpit. **279** *Bacon. Und.* 51 and n.

14. **282** *a lord*. Cf. *Epig*. 11; and the comment on Bacon, *Disc*. 948–9. **283–4** *Queen Elizabeth . . . nose*. H & S corroborate from Chettle's similar account in *England's Mourning Garment* (1603). **287** *membrana*. A 'quite irresponsible' story (J. E. Neale, *Queen Elizabeth I* (London, 1934), p. 220), but in popular currency. **289** *Monsieur*. The Duke d'Alençon, brother of Henri III, came to woo Elizabeth in August 1579 and October 1581. **290** *King Philip*. Philip II of Spain married four times; his second wife was Queen Mary of England. **292** *Sir P. Sidney's mother*. Lady Sidney (born Mary Dudley) contracted smallpox, after nursing Queen Elizabeth through the disease, in October 1562. She died in 1586. Jonson (born ?1572) would not have known her, but his story is confirmed in Fulke Greville's *Life of Sidney* (1652). Cf. *For*. 8; *Und*. 34. **294** *Earl of Leicester*. Robert Dudley, Queen Elizabeth's favourite, died allegedly of a fever in 1588. He had been suspected of poisoning his first wife in 1560 so that he might marry Elizabeth. According to a contemporary account (see Bliss's note to Antony a'Wood's *Athenae Oxonienses*, ii. 74–5), Leicester tried later to poison Christopher Blount, with whom his second wife had fallen in love; suspecting a plot, she allegedly poisoned Leicester himself instead. **297** *Salisbury*. See l. 264 above and n. **299** *Lady Wroth*. See *Alch*. Dedn. n. Sir Robert Wroth (*For*. 3 and n.) had in fact died in 1614. **301** *my lady Rutland*. See l. 172 above and n. **304** *challenged him*. i.e. took him up on the matter (cf. l. 151 above; duelling is not necessarily at issue). **305** *Lord Chancellor*. Francis Bacon, Lord Chancellor 1617–21. See *Disc*. 894–907; *Und*. 51; l. 279 above. **309** *maintained th[e]m*. i.e. argued in support of women. **310** *it*. i.e. Pembroke's proposition. **311** *epigram*. See *For*. 7 and n. **312** *Essex*. The third edition (1604) of Sir Henry Savile's translation of the first four books of Tacitus' *Histories* (first published 1591; see *Epig*. 95 and n.) is prefaced by an address by 'A.B. To the Reader'. Richard Greenway's translation of Tacitus' *Annals* and *Description of Germany* (1598) had been dedicated to Essex. On Essex, see *Disc*. 919. **314** *Jews*. Tacitus displays strong anti-Jewish prejudice in the fifth book of the *Histories*. **315** *The king*. For a higher estimation of the poetic judgement of King James (who had in fact written a sonnet on the death of Sidney), see *Epig*. 4. **316** *the Sculler's*. John Taylor, 1580–1653, the 'Water Poet'; see l. 533 below, and *Disc*. 622. **318** *flatter*. Cf. l. 278 above.

15. **323** *colours*. Stylistic ornament. **325–6** *A great many . . . S[ir] John Davies*. Cf. the comments at ll. 27–9 and 181–2 above. H & S take the last phrase to be a misplaced line which should precede ll. 331–4. **327** *running verses*. i.e. with run-over syntax. Contrast the examples of, e.g., *Und*. 70. 84–5. *plus mihi com[m]a* *placet.* From an anonymous epitaph on Lucan: 'the short phrase pleases me more'. See Trimpi, pp. 124–5. **328** *Bonefonius.* l. 51 above. The poem has not survived. **330** *transponed.* transposed. **331–4** *Where . . . hear?* Playing with the first two lines of Sir John Davies's *Orchestra* (1596) ('fair' should read 'chaste').

16. **336** *half of his comedies.* Including *C. is A., BF, D. is A.,* and the lost play *Hot Anger Soon Cold.* **337** *The May Lord.* Now lost. It must have been performed before August 1612, when the Countess of Rutland died. Though there are some similarities between this pastoral and the fragment *The Sad Shepherd,* it is unlikely they were the same work: see H & S, ii. 216–17. Raymond Urban, *HLB* xxiii (1975), 295–323, straining syntax and chronology, suspects the earlier piece contained topical satire, traces of which survive in *Sad Shep. Alken.* The name occurs in *Sad Shep.* **338** *Ethra.* Cf. Greek αἴθριος = clear, bright (of weather); playing on Lucy's name, as in *Epig.* 94. **338–9** *old Countess of Suffolk.* Catherine, née Knevet, wife of Lord Thomas Howard, 1st Earl of Suffolk; an influential lady. **342** *clowns making mirth.* Cf. *Sad Shep.* prologue, 31–2. **344** *Lomond Lake.* Later in 1619 Jonson and Drummond corresponded about this project. **345** *epithalamium. Hym.* 445–564. The occasion of the masque is specified in Q but not in F: the marriage had ended scandalously (see *UV* 18 n.). **347** *A Discovery.* This perished in the fire of 1623: see *Und.* 43. 94–5. **348** *a poem.* The poem is lost; it may be the account of his Scottish travels. *heart.* MS: 'part'. **349** *eye.* Bright spot, centre of intelligence; cf. *Und.* 65. 8; *UV* 9. 9. **350** *upon which . . . accused.* Nothing is known about this accusation. Fitzdottrel in *D. is A.* is given the title 'the Duke of Drowned Land' (II. iv. 22); a particular target must have been seen. **351** *comedia vetus.* The old English comedy (not the Greek). **352** *vice.* MS: 'voice'; Laing's emendation. Jonson oversimplifies the vice's role. **354** Πάρεργως. i.e. as an incidental theme. **356–7** *Horace . . . Donne.* See ll. 61–5 above and n. **358** *The Art of English Poesy.* Actually published anonymously thirty years previously, in 1589. Jonson possessed a copy.

17. **363** *jests and apothegms.* Drummond made a separate collection of some of these, which is preserved in the Hawthornden MSS. **364** *Henry the fourth.* Brought up as a Protestant, he forsook his religion in July 1593. *Pasquil.* A mutilated statue disinterred in Rome in 1501; satirical verses (pasquinades) were affixed to it on St Mark's Day. Replies were attached to the Marfario (Drummond's *Morphorius*), an ancient statue of a river-god. Hence the two are imagined to be in dialogue. **369** *Rex Catholicus.* Ferdinand of Aragon (1452–1516) unified Spain by his marriage to Isabella of Castile; together, they were known as the *Reyes Católicos,* the Catholic kings. **370** *Christianissimus.* A title bestowed upon the kings of France in 1469. **372** *ad . . . notam.* 'To a meal, not to a punishment or branding'; varying Pliny, *Letters,* II. vi. 3 ('I serve the same to everyone, for when I invite guests it is to a dinner, not to a branding [*sc.* to make class distinctions]'). Cf. ll. 264–7 above, 548–9 below, and *For.* 2. 65–6. **373** *that panegyrist.* Unidentified. Cf. *Und.* 43. 36–40. **374** *homo miserrimae patientiae.* 'A man of most wretched submissiveness'. **375** *scorned anagrams. Und.* 43. 35 and n. Drummond's *Moeliades* (see l. 82 and n.) was an anagram of *miles a deo,* 'soldier from God'. **376–7** 'It is degrading to undertake difficult trifles; and foolish is the labour spent on puerilities', Martial, II. lxxxvi. 9–10. **378–80** Cf. *Epig.* 133. 143–4. **382** *chase.*

'Applied to the second impact on the floor (or in a gallery) of a ball which the opponent has failed or declined to return; the value of which is determined by the nearness of the spot of impact to the end wall. If the opponent, on sides being changed, . . . can "better" this stroke (i.e. cause his ball to rebound nearer the wall) he wins and scores it; if not, it is scored by the first player; until it is so decided, the "chase" is a stroke in abeyance' (*OED*, *sb.*¹ 7). *brother . . . Northumberland.* H & S guess Sir Josceline Percy (l. 480 below). 386–7 *Another . . . gallery.* The ambiguous punctuation leaves it uncertain whether the face was the cause of the lord's loss or simply the subsequent target of his wrath. 388 *An Englishman.* Nicholas Hill; see *Epig.* 133. 128 n., and the preface to Hill's *Philosophia.* 393 *Lucifer.* i.e. light-bearing. 394 *Butler.* Probably William Butler, 1535–1618, physician and eccentric; with his table rules, cf. *Leg. Conv.*; *Epig.* 101. 24. 396 *mistered.* needed. 403 *Inigo. UV* 34. 22 and n. 406 *tobacco pipe.* Cf. *Und.* 43. 52; *Disc.* 600–1. 408 *a ballad maker.* A characteristic gibe: cf., e.g., *Und.* 23. 21–2. 412–13 *'And wilt . . . house?'* Esther 7: 8. 418–20 Cf. *S. of N.* III. ii. 190–1. 421–3 Cf. *S. of N.* IV. ii. 90; *Sad Shep.* prologue, 61–2. 426 *Sir Henry Wotton.* In 1602 Wotton was dispatched by Ferdinand, Duke of Florence, to warn King James of a plot against his life; he disguised himself as an Italian, Octavio Baldi (see Walton's *Life*). 428 *occupation.* Sexual intercourse. 444 *Mr Dod.* John Dod, ?1549–1645, Fellow of Jesus College, Cambridge, and University Preacher. 448 *Scaliger.* Joseph Scaliger, *Epistles*, IV. 362; to Stephanus Ubertus, not Casaubon. 450–6 See ll. 331–4 above and n. 457 *cockered.* coaxed. *muscadel and eggs.* A well-known aphrodisiac. 462–5 Actaeon, turned into a stag and pursued by his own hounds, 'longs to cry out: "I am Actaeon! Recognise your own master!" [*Actaeon ego sum: dominum cognoscite vestrum!*] But words fail his desire': Ovid, *Metam.* iii. 230. 'Actaeon' was the popular name for a cuckold (on account of the horns). 469 *Cardan.* Geronimo (or Girolamo) Cardano, 1501–76, Italian physician, mathematician, and astrologer; he had visited London and Edinburgh in 1552, but nothing more is known of this incident. 473 *make the danger of it.* i.e. try it; *periculum* meaning both 'danger' and 'trial'. 475 *Emperors' Lives.* H & S identify as Lord Berners's *Golden Book of Marcus Aurelius* (1535). 477 *'harlot'.* This fanciful etymology was first advanced by William Lambarde in the 1570s, and repeated later by other writers. 'Harlot' in fact derives from OF *herlot, harlot, arlot*, and is originally used not of women but men. *'Arlott'.* William's mother was Arlette or Herleva. 478 *'rogue'.* Another fanciful (or jocular) etymology. 480 *S[i]r Josceline Percy.* Seventh son of Henry, 8th Earl of Northumberland; involved in Essex's rebellion; died 1631. 484 *he struck.* Another version of this story in the Hawthornden MS reveals that the 'he' is Percy, not Jonson. *S[i]r Jerome Bowes'.* Ambassador to Russia 1583, died 1616; a man of fiery temperament. The knocking joke is repeated in *D. is A.* I. v. 2. 486 *An epitaph.* The complete form is given in the Hawthornden MSS: 'At a beard's end, here lies a man, | The odds between them was scarce a span; | Living, with his womb it did meet, | And now dead, it covers his feet.' 488 *M[r] G. Buchanan.* George Buchanan, 1506–82, was tutor to James from age four to twelve (1570–8). 491 *S[i]r Francis Walsingham.* Queen Elizabeth sent her secretary to Edinburgh in 1583 to dissuade James from negotiating with Spain on his mother's (Mary, Queen of Scots') behalf. James protested that he was an absolute king; Walsingham responded forcibly. The tag recalls Luke 19: 14, *Nolumus hunc regnare super nos*, 'We will not have this man to reign over us'. **495–6** *So long. . . death.* Unidentified. **497** *Mr Gryse.* MS originally 'Guyse'. H & S suggest Robert Gryse, knighted 1628, translator of *Argenis*. *consumed.* Presumably with venereal disease. *occupied.* Had intercourse with. **498** *sleepery.* sleepy. **499** *left his.* The sense is abbreviated, as at l. 179. **500** *Heywood.* See l. 156 above and n. **505** *impresa.* emblem. In July 1619 Drummond sent Jonson detailed information about other imprese. **506** *deest . . . orbem.* 'That which might draw the circle [*or* lead the world] is missing.' Cf. Ovid, *Metam.* viii. 249; *Und.* 14. 30–3; and *Beauty*, 221–2, where the figure of Perfection has 'in her hand a compass of gold, drawing a circle', her familiar emblem. **507** *Mr Devereux.* Walter Devereux, Robert's younger brother, born 1569, killed at Rouen 1591. **508** *par. . . dolori.* 'A figure of grief equal to none'. Mentioned by Camden in his chapter on imprese in *Remains* (London, 1870), p. 375, and illustrated by Henry Peacham, *Minerva Britannia* (London, 1612), p. 114. **509** *ashes.* i.e. dust. **510** *dum formas minuis.* 'While you fashion it, you diminish it.' See Camden, *Remains*, pp. 384–5. **511** *fax. . . honestae.* 'Fame is the incitement to honest minds', from Silius Italicus, vi. 332–3. The motto was inscribed on Prince Henry's armorial bearings in Westminster Abbey, and adopted for the Nova Scotia baronets created by Charles in 1625. Cf. Milton, *Lycidas*, 70. **514** *His arms.* J. A. Symonds, *Ben Jonson* (London, 1886), pp. 2–3, has connected these arms with those of the Johnstones of Annandale: see l. 191 above. *spindles or rhombi.* In heraldry, elongated lozenge shapes. **515** *percontabor.* 'I shall enquire.' (MS, H & S: 'percunctabor'; Patterson: 'percunctator'.) *perscrutator.* 'enquirer'. **523** *not a beard.* Tucca in Dekker's *Satiromastix*, i. ii, calls Horace (= Jonson) a 'thin-bearded hermaphrodite'. Contrast the epitaph above, ll. 486–7.

18. 525 *John Stow.* The antiquary (?1525–1605); he continued also to practise as a tailor until late in life. Here, and perhaps in *Volp.* (ii. i. 40, 46 nn.), Jonson mocks Stow's credulous interest in apparently portentous events. Stow lived in continual poverty, and always travelled on foot. **528** *Sejanus.* Cremutius Cordus's speech, iii. 407–60, from Tacitus, *Annals*, iv. 34–5. **528–9** *first four books.* The translation of Richard Grenewey, 1598. Cf. *Sej.* 'To the Readers', 37–8. **530** *J. Selden. Und.* 14 and n. **532** *Hayward. Und.* 14. 72 and n. **533** *Taylor.* John Taylor, the 'Water Poet' (see l. 316 above), undertook to walk from London to Edinburgh and back without begging and without money; he left in July 1618, got as far as Braemar, saw Jonson in September, and was back in London in October. In *The Penniless Pilgrimage* (1618) he denied any attempt to mock Jonson. **534** *Remains of Britain.* First published anonymously in 1605. Drummond probably possessed a copy: see Robert H. MacDonald, *The Library of Drummond of Hawthornden*, p. 50. **535** *Joseph Hall.* 1574–1656, had been appointed rector of All Saints, Hawstead, in 1601 at Lady Drury's instigation, and had known the young Elizabeth Drury, whose death in 1610 was the occasion of Donne's *First Anniversary* and *Second Anniversary*. Hall is thought to have written the prefatory verses to both poems; those to *The Second Anniversary* are entitled 'The Harbinger to the Progress'. See Milgate's introduction to Donne's *Epithalamions*, pp. xxx–xxxi. **536** *In verpum.* Martial's epigram xi. xciv on a circumcised man (*verpus*) who criticizes and plagiarizes his poems and seduces his boy. Jonson's friend Selden and others had wrestled with the famous crux in its final line. MS: 'Vin verpum'; Patterson conjectures 'XI in verpum'. *vaunts to expone.* Boasts to expound. **537** *Lucan, Sidney, Guarini.* Cf. ll. 13–14 and 47–8 above. **538** *Dametas.* The 'doltish clown' of *The Arcadia;* see l. 154 above. **539** *Lucan.* See ll. 49–50 above. **540** *beggared him.* Cf. l. 493 above, and *Disc.* 632–44. **545** *'Floods', 'hills'.* Remembering Latin *fluvius, mons,* etc. In *Eng. Gram.* ch. x Jonson declares that English nouns have six genders. **547** *quintessence[th].* Extracts the most perfect quality from. **549** *Messalinus.* Pliny, *Letters,* IV. xxii. At a dinner party given by the Emperor Nerva, discussion turns to Domitian's agent, the blind and unscrupulous Catullus Messalinus. 'The Emperor said: "I wonder what would have happened to him if he were alive today." "He would be dining with us", said Mauricus.' The remark is aimed at one of the present guests. **550** *gross turbot.* Juvenal, *Sat.* iv. **551** *an epigram . . . father.* A muddled memory of Campion's epigram on Barnaby Barnes, *Epigrammatum,* ii. 80, *Works,* ed. Percival Vivian (Oxford, 1909), p. 284. **554** *S[ir] J. Davies' epigram.* 'In Katam. 8', *Poems,* ed. Krueger, p. 132. *cowl.* Cloak or frock. In Davies's poem, a buff-jerkin. **558–9** *Thy flattering . . . be.* Donne's epigram 'Phryne', *Satires,* ed. Milgate, p. 53. **561** *25 of January.* Drummond wrote to Jonson on 17 January, so he had left Hawthornden before that date. **562** *Darnton.* Darlington in Co. Durham. **563** *Coryate's.* See *UV* 10. 26–7 n., and the frontispiece to *Crudities* (p. 443 above). **564** *excoriate.* i.e. with the skin rubbed off his feet; a pun. **567** *borough-laws.* Drummond and Jonson corresponded on this matter later in 1619. **568** *Lomond.* See l. 344 above and n. **569** *the pucelle.* See *Und.* 49 and n.

19. **573–603** Variant texts of *Und.* 8 and 9; printed from Jonson's autograph in Drummond's 1711 Folio. **606** *rather to lose . . . jest.* Cf. the description of 'Horace' (= Jonson) in *Poet.* IV. iii. 110–11. **612** *vindicative.* Probably in the older Latin sense: asserting claims or opinions, seeking judgement. **613** *versed in both.* See ll. 204–5 above. **614** *fantasy.* (i) Delusive imagination; (ii) perhaps: changeableness (*OED,* 3 and 6). **615** *inventions.* i.e. original poems. **617** *first acted.* December 1609 or January 1610 at Whitefriars theatre. **619** *plaudite.* Applaud!

FURTHER READING

For editions of Jonson's works, see section (iv) of Abbreviations, pp. 615–16 above.

The most comprehensive studies of Jonson's poetry are those of Richard S. Peterson and Wesley Trimpi, listed on p. 616.

Two Macmillan Casebooks contain useful collections of essays on *Volpone* and *The Alchemist*: *Jonson: 'Volpone'*, edited by Jonas A. Barish (London and Basingstoke, 1972), and *Jonson: 'Every Man in his Humour' and 'The Alchemist'*, edited by R. V. Holdsworth.

Further guidance can be found in J. B. Bamborough's 'Jonson and Chapman', in *English Drama (Excluding Shakespeare): Select Bibliographical Guides*, edited by Stanley Wells (Oxford, 1975), and *The Plays of Ben Jonson: A Reference Guide*, edited by Walter D. Lehrman, Dolores J. Sarafinski, and Elizabeth Savage, SSJ (Boston, 1980).

INDEX OF TITLES AND FIRST LINES

(Titles are indicated in italic, first lines in roman.)